Forbidden History

Forbidden History

The State, Society, and the Regulation
of Sexuality in Modern Europe

Essays from the
Journal of the History of Sexuality

Edited by John C. Fout

The University of Chicago Press
Chicago and London

The essays in this volume originally appeared in various issues of the
Journal of the History of Sexuality. Acknowledgment of the original publication date
may be found on the first page of each essay.

The University of Chicago Press, Chicago, 60637
The University of Chicago Press, Ltd., London
© 1990, 1991 by the University of Chicago
© 1992 by The University of Chicago
All rights reserved. Published 1992
Printed in the United States of America
ISBN (cl.) 0-226-25782-7
ISBN (pa.) 0-226-25783-5

96 95 94 93 92   5 4 3 2 1

Library of Congress Cataloging-in-Publication Data

Forbidden history : the state, society, and the regulation of
    sexuality in modern Europe / edited by John C. Fout ; essays from
    the Journal of the history of sexuality.
        p.   cm.
    Includes bibliographical references and index.
    ISBN 0-226-25782-7 (cloth) : $39.95 (est.). — ISBN 0-226-25783-5
    (paper) : $17.95 (est.)
    1. Sex customs—Europe—History. 2. Sex crimes—Europe—History.
    3. Sex and law—Europe—History. I. Fout, John C., 1937–   .
    II. Journal of the history of sexuality.
    HQ18.E8F67   1992
    306.7'094—dc20   92-4423
                                                                    CIP

The paper used in this publication meets the minimum requirements of
American National Standard for Information Sciences—Permanence of Paper
for Printed Library Materials, ANSI Z39.48-1984. ⊗

3

Contents

Acknowledgments

An anthology of this caliber was only possible through the dedication of the many people involved with the *Journal of the History of Sexuality*. I wish I could acknowledge individually the specialists who have read manuscripts for us, along with our associate editors and the members of our editorial board who have offered such invaluable advice to us and our authors. Of course, it is the staff who have played such an essential role in the success of *JHS:* Maura D. Shaw Tantillo, managing editor, Susan F. Rogers, assistant editor, and Professor Michèle D. Dominy, review editor and my colleague at Bard College. I thank as well our former editorial assistant Elizabeth F. Cornell and our many student assistants, especially Mary Carol DeZutter and Ephen Glenn Colter. I also thank the faculty and staff at Bard who have aided us, along with the many people at the journals division of the University of Chicago Press. I salute all for their contributions and commitment to this enterprise.

John C. Fout
Annandale-on-Hudson, New York

Introduction

THERE HAVE BEEN two great debates in modern western culture over sexuality. In the hundred-year period from the 1860s through the 1960s much of what was published on sexuality was authored by "medical authorities," who wrote from the perspective of a biological and gender imperative. It was widely theorized and generally accepted throughout western culture that what made women or men uniquely feminine or masculine were the physical attributes of their bodies. In turn, what society generally assumed and the medical authorities sought to "prove" was that growing out of this biological imperative were innately acquired gender characteristics that determined and presumed certain forms of sexual behavior inherently molded by gender roles, that is, dominant males and passive females. These roles naturally shaped "normal" sexual behavior, it was believed, within a framework of either nature-mandated or divinely ordained heterosexual marriage and family life; the ultimate rationale for the sex act was procreation. Governments, often with the support of the churches, passed legislation criminalizing most other forms of sexual behavior that did not conform with such values and at the same time legislated a variety of statutes that protected the family as it was then defined.

These medical authorities who theorized about sex increasingly came to be known as sexologists; one of the most prominent was Professor Richard Freiherr von Krafft-Ebing at the University of Vienna, who wrote about sexuality in order to establish a standard of behavior for heterosexuality within this family context. Krafft-Ebing and others also sought to confirm the perversity or the danger of all other sexual acts, especially sexual intercourse outside marriage, prostitution, masturbation, and homosexuality, since they violated acceptable principles of gender behavior and bourgeois standards of morality. Abnormal development of sexual organs or even dysfunctional ones were described as additional signposts of abnormal sexuality, indicating the tendency of those individuals with such bodies to

1

engage in perverse sexual behavior. Surprisingly, many of the sexologists actually argued in favor of the decriminalization of certain sexual acts, including homosexuality, since they believed that they were innately acquired. Sexual reformers, including birth control advocates, homosexual rights activists, feminists, free love champions, and others promoted new standards of sexual behavior, very often different from those of the medical authorities; many of the former sought to legalize all forms of sexual behavior between consenting adults while preventing only violent or coercive sex and prostitution.

Conversely, moral purity movements emerged and mounted antivice campaigns, which sought to prevent changes in attitudes toward sexual behavior and gender roles condoned by the reformers; these morality movements had already made brief appearances in the seventeenth and eighteenth centuries as well, often responding similarly to changes in the organization of the family and gender roles that were occurring in those centuries, primarily in large urban areas such as London. Vice, as defined by the moral purity advocates, was any form of sexual behavior that did not conform with "Christian family values," or sexual acts outside the framework of obligatory marital heterosexuality and procreative sex. Furthermore, vice was in reality sexual behavior that violated gender standards within this limited framework. All in all, then, the medical discourse created the parameters in which others spoke about issues related to gender and sexuality from a nonmedical perspective.

Over the past ten or fifteen years literally hundreds of scholarly articles and books have been published on the history of sexuality, but most of these studies have not been written by medical authorities. Rather, scholars in history, other social sciences, literature, and the humanistic disciplines have begun to study sex and gender from radically different viewpoints, and new theoretical perspectives have been developed by such individual theorists as Michel Foucault, by feminist thinkers, and by gay studies specialists; the study of sexuality will never be the same. The second western debate over sexuality, like the first that began a century earlier, has been highly politicized by feminists and gay rights advocates, and these new ideas have spawned counterreform endeavors spearheaded by the churches, including efforts to reverse the legalization of homosexuality and abortion and to restrain further changes in the parameters of gender roles.

The essays in this volume are representative of the new approach to the history of sexuality and reflect the dramatic change in perspectives of contemporary scholarship. The entire volume is concerned with issues around the regulation of sexuality, among other crucial issues, but on that central question alone, a comparative perspective is provided because there are a number of essays on the early modern period, on the changes in ideas about sexuality in the latter part of the eighteenth century, and on the crucial developments in the nineteenth and twentieth centuries, especially the emergence of modern sexual politics. Many of the essays in fact suggest that further periodization of the history of sexuality from the fifteenth century to the present is an absolute necessity. While prominent specialists such as Lawrence Stone and Randolph Trumbach have posited that major alterations in the organization of gender, sexuality, and the family were instituted in the latter half of the eighteenth century in western culture, other scholars now argue that significant developments were taking place in the past hundred years; these changes have brought further portentous changes in the organization of family life and in cultural assumptions about gender and gender relations, factors that are inherently linked to suppositions about appropriate sexual behavior. Thus it is probably not possible to argue that the structures that evolved in the late eighteenth century remained unchanged or unchallenged right up to our own time.

The authors not only address issues in male and female heterosexuality as a whole, especially within the context of women in the family, but many speak concretely to the attempt to control women's bodies at specific moments in time, the desire to dominate reproduction, the debate over male homosexuality and lesbianism, and even male heterosexual and homosexual anxieties about appropriate male behavior and the regulation of masculinity. Thus this anthology is meant to engage scholars interested in complex gender issues and their relationship to the control of certain forms of sexual behavior, especially those that were perceived at various moments in time as deviant. Perceptions of deviancy, of course, as this anthology demonstrates, were constantly undergoing revision in the past five centuries, just as judgments about appropriate gender behavior were being modified as well.

The essays in this anthology, all published in the first two volumes of the *Journal of the History of Sexuality* between 1990 and 1992, also illustrate the broad array of cross-disciplinary and interdisciplinary approaches that now dominate research and writing on the new history of sexuality; scholars from a variety of fields are represented in this collection, and their work reflects varying disciplinary and methodological approaches and thereby provides a rich collage of contrasting ideas. All the articles in this anthology were based on extensive archival research or the examination of important published sources, or both. Many of the essays are written from the perspective of social-constructionist theory, but as is generally the case with theory, new archival research often subverts earlier findings; many interpretations of the 1980s have been challenged with this innovative research and the so-called essentialist/social-constructionist debate is perhaps already passé.

With this general overview in mind, it would be appropriate to very briefly introduce the essays themselves in *Forbidden History*. Three of the essays focus on central issues in the regulation of sexuality in the early modern period—syphilis, infanticide, and bestiality—and they are set within the context of the age of scientific revolution, a period of rapid secularization of society, and ongoing economic and social changes in an era of preindustrial capitalism. An additional six essays examine critical revisions in attitudes toward gender and sexuality in the latter half of the eighteenth century. Issues of expressed concern in the eighteenth century included maternity, incest, male homosexuality and lesbianism, prostitution, and libertinism, as well as the interrelationship between the private world of family and sexual life and the very public world of politics. Western society was increasingly obsessed with divisions between the two spheres, as it was also concerned about the gender-specific roles of males and females in those spheres.

Bruce Thomas Boehrer analyzes the medical discussion of early modern syphilis from the perspective of the history of science but also from the standpoint of the specialist in literature. He scrutinizes a number of early modern treatises on syphilis written by medical authorities from across Europe, and he examines how the discussion of this disease inaugurated a new medical literature that moved away from dependence on the ancient and medieval texts. Moreover, he discusses how the new disease was seen as a social problem that needed an explanatory popular discourse for society at large and a private but more scientific discourse for the medical experts, differentiating between the disease as a just punishment of God and as a medical problem that demanded careful scrutiny and study. Thus from the beginning of the early modern world in the fifteenth and early sixteenth centuries to the present, the cultural response to such diseases has been polarized and politicized, as Boehrer and other essayists in the anthology demonstrate.

René Leboutte, a specialist in historical demography, traces modifications in the criminalization of infanticide in the early modern and modern eras in Belgium, ideas that were surely widespread in western Europe as a whole. Leboutte's analysis is based on more than one hundred cases in the judicial archives and on accounts in newspapers, dating from the end of the fifteenth through the early twentieth centuries. He shows how society understood infanticide and how, in turn, standards for criminalization changed, as public opinion shifted, often because of changing attitudes toward women, and these transformations were reflected in statements by religious, medical, and government authorities, which Leboutte discusses at some length. As one might suspect, issues concerned with reproduction and population control are included in Leboutte's discussion.

Jonas Liliequist, a Swedish historian, contributes a study of perceptions about bestiality in early modern Sweden, drawing on an array of fascinating court records from provincial archives. He seeks to understand why early modern society was so anxious about the boundaries between man and animal, and he contrasts traditional folklore with popular and learned opinion. Bestiality was primarily understood as a male sex crime, and Liliequist examines in detail the gender-specific connections between male and female occupations and activities where humankind, especially men, came into contact with animals, a daily occurrence in preindustrial rural society. He also examines the criminalization of sex acts between men and animals and demonstrates how long the death penalty was used to penalize this activity. He contextualizes this form of criminalization with other sex crimes elsewhere in Europe, asking, for example, what was the relationship between bestiality and the sodomy and witchcraft trials that dominated the regulation of sexuality in early modern Europe, and what shaped the regional or national differences in such issues?

The six essays that discuss the significant reorganization of the family, sexuality, and gender relations in the latter half of the eighteenth century suggest a major shift in western values in that period. Randolph Trumbach, a historian with a specific interest in early modern Britain, argues that female prostitutes and male sodomites, a small minority in society, were given the same public status in eighteenth-century London and asks what such status suggests about cultural assumptions regarding sexuality for the rest of society. Trumbach maintains that modern society arrived in the latter part of the eighteenth century, in London at least, and with it came alterations in sex and gender relations, as well as in the character of the modern family where companionate marriage was now the accepted standard. He makes the case that a modern gender role for heterosexual men was shaped in these decades (and has survived until the present), which mandated that the vast majority of men only desired women and that masculine behavior was thus patterned upon this form of desire. His study, which grows out of a comprehensive project on the sexual life of eighteenth-century London, is based on extensive archival sources, including court, hospital, and asylum records and even those from houses of correction, magistrates' books, and other rare published materials.

Ruth Perry's essay, in contrast to Trumbach's focus on men's issues, examines transformations in attitudes about women's bodies and women's sexuality in the eighteenth century, but from quite a different perspective. She looks at these issues from the vantage point of literary sources, since she is a specialist in early modern British literature; in addition, her essay makes a major contribution to feminist theory by rethinking how that society understood women's roles. She examines a developing social phenomenon that, she posits, established not only a cultural identity but also a new sexual identity for women, namely, bourgeois motherhood, a motherhood that was production-geared. These major alterations in attitudes toward women's roles suggest that motherhood has a history that is ever undergoing transformation. She argues that this new definition of motherhood was a form of colonialism, a domestic counterpart, which in a real sense mirrored British imperialism abroad and the establishment of the nation state and the industrialization of manufacturing at home. Thus she discusses the colonization of the breast for population needs, how society deeroticized the breast on the one hand and domesticated it on the other for the purpose of reproduction, making women's bodies serve the needs of the new motherhood, rather than for any form of sexual enjoyment or sexual independence for women. Perry also demonstrates how these nurturing features of motherhood came to be associated with gender imperatives for women, which influenced opinions about women well into the Victorian era.

Polly Morris, a social historian, looks at the intersection of class, sexuality, and family in eighteenth-century Britain, focusing on plebeian marriage. Drawing upon church court records in Somerset and the diary of a local parson, she examines how the plebs understood marriage and kinship and how these values shaped the marriage choices they made; this essay, therefore, is an important addition to our limited knowledge of working-class sexual and family life. It also examines the complex problem of incest—complex because it was not treated as a criminal offense in Great Britain until 1908, but the church subsumed it under canon law and treated it as a part of the regulation of marriage. The church forbade marriage with all relatives by marriage or blood and punished such unions, as it also punished various forms of illicit sex, including adultery and fornication. Morris discusses many of the cases involving marital incest and she culls from these cases attitudes toward sexuality. The church's responses to issues of this kind reflect how the church's role in the regulation of sexuality changed over time, actually decreasing substantially by the early nineteenth century.

Jeffrey Merrick, a specialist in early modern French history, scrutinizes sexual politics in the last decades of the ancien régime through an examination of opinions about family, marriage, sexuality, sexual scandals, and public order at the court and in high society, basing his research on two popular publications, the *Mémoires secrets* and the *Correspondance secrète,* which offered gossip and news from Paris and Versailles. Merrick demonstrates that, through such a remarkably large body of source material, scholars can discern a range of opinion on what late eighteenth-century society perceived was the relationship between appropriate or inappropriate gender roles and socially acceptable sexuality or illicit sexual acts. He also discusses how such perceptions of behavior affected and shaped attitudes toward the royal family. Merrick offers fascinating insights on the close relationship between assumptions about the private lives of sovereigns and public response to their governmental policies. As was the case in London, with the emergence of modern political society, sexual politics became a part of modern political life.

Theo van der Meer, a Dutch social historian, while completing extensive archival research on male sodomy in the Netherlands in the early modern period, discovered a number of remarkable court cases regarding same-sex behavior between women—relatively marginal women, as society perceived them, some earning their livelihood through prostitution. These cases, which include detailed testimony about the sex acts in which these women engaged, shed remarkable new light on the history of lesbianism and the emergence of the modern lesbian role in the eighteenth century, rather than in the nineteenth, as was earlier presumed. While a host of male sodomy trials were held in the Netherlands starting in 1730—others followed in the 1760s and 1770s—involving somewhere between six and eight hundred people, it was not until 1792 that the first case involving women was taken up by the courts, with the last case considered in 1798. Van der Meer's material challenges the notion that the modern lesbian identity only developed with the medicalization of lesbianism in the late nineteenth century; rather, this evidence suggests that the real origins of the modern lesbian role might be associated with prostitutes and other lower-class women, who engaged in what society assumed was illicit sexual behavior with members of their own sex, and that they were perhaps prosecuted for it because of their class.

Robyn Cooper, an Australian scholar who is a specialist in British women's history, evaluates the writings of the Scottish author and self-styled physiologist Alexander Walker, well-known and widely published in the 1830s and 1840s in both Great Britain and America, but largely ignored since then. She analyzes his views on women within the context of the ongoing social and economic transformation brought about by the introduction of industrial capitalism and the male fascination with understanding female behavior, evident since the latter part of the eighteenth century. Walker's commentaries on women were influential in his own time and important because he conducted such a comprehensive investigation with the aim in mind, Cooper argues, of definition and control. Cooper also examines his ideas from the perspective of Walker as a man of science, the kind of "scientific thinking" that informed his work, and the influence of the Scottish Enlightenment, with its confidence in the possibility of formulating a science of "man." Walker's ideas, along with many other theorists writing in his time, shaped the dominant male ideology about women in the Victorian era.

Three of the essays in the anthology address issues in men's sexuality in the latter part of the nineteenth and the early part of the twentieth centuries, a crucial period for the conditioning of modern masculinity. Gert Hekma, a Dutch social historian and historical sociologist, writes about the prosecution of sex crimes in the Dutch army during the period. He is specifically interested in a number of important issues concerned with the regulation of homosexuality, including homosexual behavior within what Hekma calls homosocial arrangements, that is, an all-male institution such as the army. This essay is based on an analysis of sex crimes of all types brought before the military court in Haarlem. By including all the sexual crimes that soldiers were accused of committing in the period under study, Hekma is able to demonstrate how perceptions about homosexuality fit into the larger picture. In turn, this material makes it possible for Hekma to question other developments in the history of homosexuality, especially the impact of medicalization, assumptions about gender roles for men, and the scholarly debate about the evolution of new forms of homosexuality. Hekma's piece makes an important contribution to the ongoing debate over the modern homosexual role in the way that this newly discovered evidence supports or challenges existing interpretations of homosexuality elsewhere in western culture since the eighteenth century.

My own essay focuses on the moral purity movement in Wilhelmine Germany and its attacks on the homosexual rights movement, which was emerging at the very same time. It is part of a larger research project on sexual politics and the antivice campaign in the decades before World War I. There was an intense public debate about sexual politics in Germany on a range of issues from abortion to prostitution, from pornography to state regulation of sexuality; this essay specifically focuses on the fierce debate over the decriminalization of homosexuality. Many of my findings about homosexuality suggest similarities to the circumstances and assumptions that Gert Hekma discovered in the Netherlands, which suggests that the shift in attitudes Randolph Trumbach charted in eighteenth-century London may only be occurring elsewhere in Europe in the late nineteenth century. Hence this material may of necessity force the reevaluation of the periodization of the history of sexuality in general and the emergence of the modern homosexual role specifically. My essay contrasts moral purity ideology with demands of the homosexual rights movement, drawing upon extensive archival materials, especially in church archives, and relatively rare published sources.

Lesley A. Hall is an archivist who studies the history of medicine, and her essay is part of a larger project on male sexuality in nineteenth- and twentieth-century Britain. She examines commonly held ideas about male masturbation from the middle of the nineteenth century through the middle of the twentieth century, which makes it possible for her to challenge assumptions about sexuality in the Victorian period and the shift away from those values in the period after World War I. Her research sources on male attitudes and anxieties toward their own sexuality provide her with the opportunity to evaluate those views as separate from women's notions about men and men's sexuality. At the same time, she is interested in the crucial question of the regulation of male sexuality by men and male concern about the solitary sexuality represented by masturbation. In addition to using a variety of published sources from the latter half of the nineteenth century, especially moral purity writings, she was able to draw upon thousands of letters from men written in the interwar period to the most famous "authority" on sexuality in those years, Marie Stopes, whose books on marriage, family, and sexuality were best-sellers.

John Macnicol, a specialist in social policy, examines the campaign for voluntary sterilization in Great Britain in the interwar years. Britain—unlike Germany, certain Scandinavian countries, and some states in the United States—never adopted a forced sterilization law. Macnicol in fact discusses how the excesses in Nazi Germany undermined efforts in Britain to adopt even voluntary sterilization laws. He contextualizes his discussion within what he characterizes as two contradictory demographic trends that were enormously politicized in the twentieth century, namely, the increased use of birth control to limit family size and a steady increase in the proportion of older people in the population. The adoption of birth control, Macnicol believes, gave people greater freedom of choice, but it also made possible a new role for the authoritarian state, the possibility of social engineering on eugenic grounds. Since, however, Britain epitomized the modern liberal state that had witnessed the dramatic expansion of various democratic rights for the individual, eugenic social engineering would naturally have to violate such rights for the larger social good of society.

Robin Ann Sheets, a literary scholar and feminist, looks at the debate over pornography in relation to the British writer Angela Carter, whose writings on this issue have been controversial and extremely complex, thus defying easy categorization; Carter herself has even been accused of writing pornography. Sheets believes that it is essential to include works of fiction in the examination of the contemporary discourse on sexuality, just as it is also critical to approach this subject from an interdisciplinary perspective. Sheets sets Carter's views within the controversy over pornography in general since the mid-1970s, a vituperative debate that has so often polarized British and American feminists, as Sheets points out; she contrasts the views of a number of important Anglo-American theorists with those of Carter. Sheets also provides a detailed analysis of Carter's own counterviews, especially Carter's concerns about freedom of artistic expression, especially for women, fear of the repression of women's sexuality, and her desire to offer a feminist political critique of the pornography debate. This essay suggests how an antipornography stance might further inhibit women's desire to control their own bodies and how, therefore, Carter sought a new perspective through a female discourse on violent sexuality.

James W. Jones, a specialist in German literature in the twentieth century, also takes up a controversial issue in contemporary sexual politics, namely, the debate over AIDS; he views this complex problem from the vantage point of the discourse in West Germany, drawing upon two mainstream magazines, *Der Spiegel* and *Stern,* for one discourse and publications from the gay community for the other, thus contrasting two radically different perspectives. Such an approach allows Jones to examine how the discussion on AIDS converges on various outsiders in German society, including women, gays, drug addicts, blacks, hemophiliacs, and even prostitutes, the very groups around which the AIDS debate has revolved there, as elsewhere in western culture. Jones also stresses that these same groups have often come together in earlier discourses on sexuality, going back into the medieval period. Most important, he chose *Der Spiegel* and *Stern,* since these mass-circulation magazines have a readership of educated middle-class and upper-middle-class people, to establish if possible what is the liberal opinion on AIDS. Moreover, he argues that the attitudes represented in articles on AIDS in these publications have largely shaped the response to AIDS in Germany. He then discusses how much of the gay community's response has focused on criticizing this mainstream reporting, but also how the gay community has sought to create its own discourse on AIDS.

I hope that the methodologies and interpretations represented in this collection will serve to introduce most of the major issues in the regulation of sexuality in early modern and modern European history, and that the anthology will become a valuable resource for those scholars interested in undertaking further research on these issues or in the presentation of this complex material in the college and university classroom, at both the undergraduate and graduate levels. These essays will surely stimulate discussion and debate by students and provide them with the analytical tools to comprehend this complex but fascinating body of material on the history of the regulation of European sexuality.

Early Modern Syphilis

BRUCE THOMAS BOEHRER
Department of English
Florida State University

I N 1579 THE SURGEON William Clowes the Elder published his first book, a little English-language pamphlet entitled *A Short and Profitable Treatise Touching the Cure of the Disease Called (Morbus Gallicus)*. At that time Clowes had been on the medical staff of Saint Bartholomew's Hospital in London for about five years, and he still stood at the beginning of a long and illustrious medical career. Thus his choice of subject matter and form in his first publication becomes especially interesting, for not only does Clowes's *De Morbo Gallico* discuss a newfangled disease—syphilis— but it does so in a newfangled way, in English, with a prefatory address to the general reader, and without most of the cumbersome textual apparatus of medieval scholastic medicine. From the very outset, that is, Clowes allies himself with the progressive elements in a profession that had been revolutionized by the discovery/invention of syphilis not quite a century earlier; he is a young turk in a rigid and venerable business.[1]

A shorter version of this essay was originally presented at the 1989 convention of the Modern Language Association of America. I am grateful to Anne Hudson Jones for organizing the session and to my copanelists for their participation. I would also like to thank John Fout, Eric Mallin, and the journal's two anonymous readers for their help in revising this work.

[1]Indeed, the very act of *publishing* a medical treatise serves to ally Clowes with the radical elements in his profession; for, as Robert G. Frank has recently observed in a study of the Royal College of Physicians, "Status in the College [in the sixteenth century] bore no real relationship to literary activity, much less to the prosecution of original research. Almost the reverse was true. Of books published by College members from 1590 to 1620, most were written by men of lower or marginal status in the College. Conversely, many important men in the College's hierarchy had no publications at all" ("The Physician as Virtuoso in Seventeenth-

This essay originally appeared in the *Journal of the History of Sexuality* 1990, vol. 1, no. 2.

For Clowes, the treatment of syphilis is an ideal subject of inquiry, not only because it is still a new and controversial problem in Elizabethan England, but also because it engages practical issues at the very heart of progressive Renaissance medicine. For instance, the *De Morbo Gallico* almost advertises itself as a universal self-help book; Clowes writes, he says, "partly to helpe those good poore people that be infected by unwary eating, or drinking, or keeping company" with syphilitics, and who "either for shame, dare not bewray [their infection], or for lack of good Chyrurgions, know not how to remedye it."[2] And yet, having thus offered his treatment to all "good poore people" afflicted with the disease, and having written his book in English so that it might reach the general reading public, Clowes immediately restricts himself to fit audience though few; the *De Morbo Gallico* is not meant for the "great number of rogues, and vagabondes: The . . . lewd and idell persons, both men and women, about the citye of *London,* and the great number of lewd alehowses, which are the very nests and harbourers of such filthy creatures: By meanes of which disordered persons, some other of better disposition are many tymes infected" (sigs. B1v–B2r). Indeed, Clowes continues, if the wrong people use his book for the wrong reasons, the result will be disaster, for "the Lord god in iust wrath [may] one day make ye disease to be incurable, eyther by the order of this booke, eyther by all the Chyrurgions art in the world" (sig. B3r). Clowes's work thus moves in two different directions at once; it eschews elitism and addresses a kind of common reader, good and poor; yet at the same time it insists that—even though the "good poore" reader is its chosen audience—some readers are simply too common and too poor to deserve the treatment it offers. Apparently all readers are equal, but some are more equal than others; syphilis should be cured, but only a little.

In this way Clowes's treatise embodies contradictory propositions both about the function of medicine (medicine aims to heal people; medicine aims to ensure that certain people *do not get* healed) and about the nature of disease (disease is an unfair and unnecessary evil; disease is a just punishment from God). And thus the language of the *De Morbo Gallico* is forced to do two fundamentally incompatible things more or less at once, and with-

---

Century England," in Barbara Shapiro and Robert G. Frank, Jr., *English Scientific Virtuosi in the 16th and 17th Centuries* [Los Angeles, 1979], p. 65). Further, of course, Clowes is technically not a physician at all, but a surgeon; and he thus represents an entire body of upwardly mobile yet marginal professionals who achieve increasing recognition in the sixteenth and seventeenth centuries.

    [2]William Clowes, *A Short and Profitable Treatise Touching the Cure of the Disease Called (Morbus Gallicus)* (1579; Amsterdam, 1972), sig. B3r. Further citations will be to this edition and will be made in the text. In quoting from early texts I have expanded nasal superscripts and ligatures wherever they have occurred.

out acknowledging the fact: to make itself available to the general public while actively excluding the *wrong sort* of reader. Given this difficulty, we may expect Clowes to be evasive about just what constitutes the wrong sort of reader, and indeed the external indices of wrongness never emerge in any systematic way in the pages of Clowes's book. Nonetheless, it becomes gradually clear that Clowes demands certain qualities of his readers other than an internal sense of repentance; for instance, they are not to frequent "lewd alehowses" (sig. B2r)—or, presumably, similar establishments of entertainment. They are not to be "rogues [or] vagabondes," nor are they to be "lewd and idell," whether "men or women" (sig. B1v). Instead, they are to be honest, educated, gainfully employed, and well established in a single locale (one can imagine here a barely suppressed preference for homeowners). And in a later remark, Clowes's studied avoidance of gender bias suddenly and revealingly breaks down; "both men and women" may help spread the disease, he notes, but "such as are great eaters and drinkers and inordinate users of women are unfit to be cured: and their health almost is not to be looked for" (sig. C5v). This language, so effortless in its choice of the euphemism for fornication, helps reveal what we may already have suspected; in addition to being industrious, employed, educated, stable, and opposed to pastime, Clowes's ideal patient is also male.

In other words, Clowes's *De Morbo Gallico* justifies its existence on the ground that it is a liberating book—that it frees or relieves poor, good, and honest people who have been unjustly oppressed by disease and ignorance; and thus Clowes himself emerges from Elizabethan medical history as a progressive, even revolutionary figure, whose biographer in the *Dictionary of National Biography* waxes rhapsodic over his enlightened procedures and attitudes.[3] Yet as soon as the *De Morbo Gallico* has made its claim to progressivism, it hedges and equivocates in ways that make the claim itself virtually meaningless. For the oppressed masses whom Clowes is liberating in fact turn out to be the very people who need his help least—not prostitutes, not women, not vagabonds, not the unemployed, not the poor in any material sense of the word, but instead something like a coalition between the (male) upper and emergent middle classes. The present essay regards this gesture as typical of how progressive medical practice develops in the Renaissance and will use the early treatment of syphilis—instanced in the works of Clowes, Joseph Grünpeck, and Girolamo Fracastoro—as a

[3]Thus, for instance, the *Dictionary of National Biography* remarks that Clowes "trusted much to his own observation, and a modern spirit of inquiry pervades his pages which makes them altogether different from the complications from authorities which are to be found in the surgical works of his contemporaries Baker and Banester." And although "he cared little for critics, favourable or unfavourable," he nonetheless "always [spoke] with generosity of his contemporaries Goodrouse, Banester, Bedon, and Baker, the surgeons; . . . he never made bargains for cures, and never touted for patients as some surgeons did at the time."

case in point. In brief, this study will argue that Renaissance progressive medicine develops not out of liberating impulses at all but, rather, to protect an aristocratic social order that feels itself threatened from without; the claims to liberation and revolution merely supply a necessary justifying rhetoric. In effect, we may see the Renaissance medical profession radicalized in service of the ruling classes; syphilis is invented as a new medical category and various treatments are explored when the illness becomes a recognized challenge to the power elite: hence the *real* audience for which William Clowes writes, and hence also Clowes's new medical language, new medical procedures, and (apparently) new notion of medical professionalism itself.

I

Syphilis is the ideal focus for any analysis of early modern medicine's social dimension, for at least two reasons. First, syphilis is itself a social disease—one communicated by intimate personal contact, and thus one on which matters like class stratification and demographic movement will have a particularly clear bearing;[4] indeed, it threatens the integrity of social boundaries in a world that—as Steven Mullaney notes—relies upon those very boundaries to reaffirm "the coherence of its own authority."[5] And further, syphilis is probably the quintessential disease of Renaissance Europe, more so even than plague. It comes into being, as a distinct medical entity, in the last decade of the fifteenth century, and indeed it helps to occasion a whole new mode of medical discourse, as Karl Sudhoff has remarked: "All the early Syphilis tracts . . . were handed over direct from author to publisher or printer for immediate reproduction and distribution to the public. This is the method of book production to which we are nowadays accustomed, but it was not current in the fifteenth century. . . . The custom of using the printed page to record one's own views or experience seems perfectly obvious to us now, yet it crept but slowly into practice. [In the first literature on syphilis] we see the new system in its earliest developed form."[6] Thus the

---

⁴Thus, as part of his demographic study *Epidemic Disease in Fifteenth-Century England* (New Brunswick, NJ, 1978), Robert Gottfried discusses the outbreak in 1475 of the "Frenchpox"—apparently a venereal malady, possibly even syphilis itself. Examining wills probated by "the very wealthiest segment of the . . . population" (p. 106), Gottfried concludes that "wealth and mobility were important . . . in providing some degree of immunity from crisis-level mortality, usually induced by epidemic plague, in fifteenth-century England" (p. 117). However, Gottfried notes, "the graphed testamentary data" for his privileged population "show . . . that the peak period of mortality came between the spring of 1474 and the spring of 1476" (p. 106)—a potentially significant exception to the rule of class-specific immunity.

⁵Steven Mullaney, *The Place of the Stage: License, Play and Power in Renaissance England* (Chicago, 1988), p. 10.

⁶Karl Sudhoff, ed., *The Earliest Printed Literature on Syphilis, Being Ten Tractates from the Years 1495–1498* (Florence, 1925), p. xi.

advent of syphilis marks the beginning of a new approach to disease itself, leading physicians out of their traditional dependence upon medieval and classical texts and instead forcing them to interact with each other, and with their patients and patrons, to an unprecedented degree. One result is the publication of a treatise on syphilis in the vernacular—German, in this case—as early as 1496. This work, Joseph Grünpeck's *Ein Hübscher Tractat von dem Ursprung des Bösen Franzos,* becomes the most popular fifteenth-century discussion of the disease,[7] and in it already we may encounter the very same practical difficulties that inform Clowes's *De Morbo Gallico* nearly a century later.

Grünpeck's general sense of the nature of syphilis is indeed remarkably close to Clowes's; the two authors differ only in that Clowes repeatedly advocates the use of mercurial ointments, whereas Grünpeck spends vast amounts of time ascribing the origin of syphilis to a grand astrological conjunction that occurred in the year 1484. Otherwise, both men generally agree as to what causes the disease and how it should be avoided and/or treated. Grünpeck is specific and detailed on this latter point, advising a strict regimen of personal hygiene and social segregation:

> Darum Natürlich zereden Sind drey ergney Die erst die flucht der ein yegklicher fliehe von den selbigen menschen die dise kranckeyt haben. wann sy einen von dem andern an kumbt. und sich behaltet an einer güten frischen stat do die selbigen menschen nit gewesen sind oder gewonet haben. Auch vermeyde ire kleyder. und schlechtigklich alle ding die sy in irem brauch gehabt haben. Es sollt sich auch ein yegklicher enthalten von grosser gesellschafft.[8]

> (Therefore there are naturally three remedies to be urged: the first being to flee or shun each several person who suffers from this disease, whenever one encounters them, and to keep oneself in a good clean condition, such as these same people are not accustomed to. Also avoid their clothing, and all other unclean things that they habitually use. One should also hold oneself away from general company.)

This advice, standard for the first century of research on syphilis, emphasizes proper personal cleanliness—or, "rechte reynigung," as Grünpeck himself calls it (sig. C4r). However, Grünpeck's notion of cleanliness extends well beyond the specifics of washing and diet to involve a more general notion of spiritual purity, to be reflected (of course) in the way one comports oneself and in the company one keeps: "Wan die ergney uber die natur die von oben herab kommet. ist. das der mensch sey in der genad

---

[7] Ibid., p. xxvii.

[8] Joseph Grünpeck von Burkhausen, *Ein Hübscher Tractat von dem Ursprung des Bösen Franzos* (Augsburg, 1496), sig. C3v; reprinted in Sudhoff, ed., pp. 69–111. Further citations will be to this edition in the text; translations of Grünpeck are my own.

gottes. und sich reynige durch beycht und büss" (sig. C3v) (In order for a remedy over nature to descend from above, one must be in God's grace and cleanse oneself through confession and penance). Thus one avoids syphilis, according to Grünpeck, by avoiding *people;* and this avoidance is an accurate marker of spiritual regeneration.

In short, Grünpeck—like Clowes—bases his work upon two premises that are always threatening to erupt into open contradiction, and whose contradictory nature becomes progressively clearer in the transition from medieval to early modern medicine. On one hand, the immediate sources and treatments for syphilis are to be found in nature; one contracts the disease by mingling with the wrong sort of people, and one avoids it by carefully monitoring one's food, drink, and personal and social habits. (Indeed, even one's thoughts are to be carefully censored in this regard: "[Man] sol . . . frölich sein unnd nit an die kranckeyt gedenken" [sig. C5r].) Yet on the other hand the illness derives from a force *beyond* nature, coextensive with God; and thus the real remedies for the disease are not corporal but spiritual:

> Und vor allen dingen des rats pflegen des aller höchsten arztes Jhesu Christi. der uns von allen kranckheyten mag erledigenn. Bitten darauff dye Junckfrawen müter Mariam. das sy unser fürsprecherin gegen dem Selben irem lieben kynnde sye. [sig. C5r]

> (And above all things seek the care of the greatest of all physicians, Jesus Christ, who will heal us of all sickness. Pray also to the Virgin Mother Mary, that she may be our advocate to her dear child.)

But if the ultimate source and remedy for the disease is to be found in God, what good is any regimen of corporal treatment? And similarly, if one's faith needs to be supplemented by a course of bodily physic, how pure can it actually be? Indeed, Grünpeck himself insists that disease is in fact a punishment for sinful behavior:

> Drey haubtsünd sind darauss all ander sünde entspringen. Also auch sind drey geyseln domit die menschen gestrafft werden. Die drey sünde sind. die Hoffart. Geyttigkeit. unkeusche. Aber die straffen sind. Pestilenz. Blütvergiessen. und hunger. [sig. A7v]

> (There are three cardinal sins from which all others are derived. Thus also there are three scourges with which people are punished. The three sins are pride, avarice, and unchastity. But the three punishments are pestilence, bloodshed, and hunger.)

And if syphilis is thus a just punishment sent from heaven, why should one interfere with it at all? The notion of spiritual causality threatens to short-circuit the project of physical medicine at all points—to render the very idea of medical treatment itself morally reprehensible.

William Clowes was clearly more or less aware of this threat, as his various disclaimers and attempts at self-justification amply attest. Grünpeck, on the other hand, seems more or less oblivious to the tension between spiritual and corporal physic (arguably because social conditions have not yet rendered it consciously available to physicians in the fifteenth century). And yet the retributive God is not present in his work by accident. In fact Grünpeck's spiritualism parallels that of the very earliest vernacular text on syphilis—an edict issued by the Holy Roman Emperor Maximilian on August 7, 1495. The immediate subject of this document is not disease at all but foul language; and yet it construes syphilis as "a punishment sent by God *for blasphemy*,"[9] and thus it promotes a moralized view of the illness that will prevail for the next century and more. Indeed, Maximilian's edict so firmly associates him with the new disease that the frontispiece of Grünpeck's work (see fig. 1) presents the emperor as a kneeling crusader, receiving a crown from the Virgin Mary while others less fortunate perish from the new illness. And not only does the document of 1495 specify the relationship between syphilis and divine retribution, it does so in language that generally prefigures Grünpeck's:

> Auch vormals aus solichem Hunger/ Erdpiden/ Pestilenntz/ und annder plagen auf erden kumen und gefallen sein/ und netzoben unsern zeitten als offenbar ist dergleich vil und menigerlen plagen und straffen gevolgt haben und sunderlich in disen tagen swer kranckheiten und plagen der menschen genant die pösen plattern die vormals bey menschen gedechtnüss nye gewesen noch gehört sein Aus dem wir die straffe gottes billich gedenncken.[10]

> (Also in earlier times, hunger, earthquakes, pestilence, and other plagues came and fell upon the earth. And now in our time as is apparent many severe plagues and punishments have followed—and particularly in these days serious illnesses and plagues of people named the *pösen plattern*, which have never before been seen or heard within memory, and because of which we are mindful of the just punishment of God.)

Yet being simply *mindful* of the just punishment of God is not sufficient for the Emperor Maximilian, who has far other matters in mind. Thus the busi-

---

[9] Theodor Rosebury, *Microbes and Morals: The Strange Story of Venereal Disease* (New York, 1971), p. 24.

[10] Das Gotteslästerer-Edikt Maximilians vom 7, August 1495, in Karl Sudhoff, *Graphische und Typographische Erstlinge der Syphilisliteratur aus den Jahren 1495 und 1496* (Munich, 1912), Tafel 1. Further references will be to this edition in the text.

¶ Tractatus de pestilentiali Scorra siue mala de Franzos.
Originem.Remediaq; eiusdem continens.cōpilatus a vene
rabili viro Magistro Joseph Grunpeck de Burckhausen.
sup Carmina quedam Sebastiani Brant vtriusq; iuris pro
fessoris.

FIG. 1   Frontispiece to Joseph Grünpeck, *Tractatus de pestilentiali scorra sive mala de Franzos* and *Ein Hübscher Tractat von dem Ursprung des Bösen Franzos* (Augsburg, 1496). (Courtesy of the Historical Collections of the Library, College of Physicians of Philadelphia.)

ness end of his edict consists of a series of penalties for cursing; any person caught swearing "bey gott seiner heilgsten marter/ wunden oder glidern/ der Jungfrawen Maria/ und seinin heiligen tüt" could be subject to the penalty of death if the infraction were determined to be premeditated and deliberate. On the other hand, if one sins out of "bewegter hitz des zorns/ aus trunckenheit oder der gleichen zufall" (the heat of anger, drunkenness, or a similar accident), the punishment is reduced to a fine and/or imprisonment (in the case of nobles committing a first offense, the penalty may be made lighter). Thus Maximilian's "Gotteslästerer-Edikt"—as it has come to be known—depends upon an almost miraculous logical circularity; syphilis appears as a punishment from heaven, and those who suffer from it, being clearly guilty of blasphemy, ought therefore to be punished again by imperial decree. The edict significantly ignores any notion of natural medical causality. Syphilis emerges here as purely and simply a judgment from God, and as such it supplies the perfect excuse to institute close censorship and surveillance of speech—which is, after all, the edict's declared purpose.

To put it simply, such early texts on syphilis presume divine causality because divine causality is of practical value as a political instrument. In this way the exigencies of politics actually interfere with the project of healing the sick. Moreover, there is an indisputable (and highly conventional) connection between the apparatus of government and the earliest publications on syphilis; the very first medical treatise on the disease, for instance, is written at the request of Philip, Elector Palatine, by his personal physician, Konrad Schellig;[11] and the byzantine processes of literary patronage inform virtually every other work published on syphilis for the first century of its recognized existence. (The first Latin edition of Grünpeck's work, for instance, not only exhibits the flattering portrait of Maximilian, but it is openly indebted to Sebastian Brandt and dedicated to one "Bernard de Walikirch. Liberalium studiorum Magistro. litterarie sodalitatis Danubiane lumini et ornamento. Ac Canonico kathedralis Ecclesie Augustensis." The first German edition, on the other hand, is addressed to the "fürsichtigen Ersamen und Weysen Burgermeistern unnd Rate Loblicher Stat Augsburg" [sig. A2r]. Grünpeck clearly wished to get as much mileage as possible out of his book.) It is thus hard to avoid viewing these early texts as to some degree government documents, responsive to the needs and expectations of an aristocracy that claims its authority as God-given and immutable. In effect, when we read early texts like Grünpeck's, with their careful appeals to patronage and their oblique echoes of theological and imperial authority, we witness the elaborate mutual fondling whereby political orthodoxies are established and maintained. The remarkable thing, given this arrangement, is that any sort of effective medical study could proceed at all.

II

Yet effective medical study *did* proceed, at least in a manner of speaking; and one must therefore consider the conditions that made it possible. For if, on one hand, conservative political interests actually impede the work of

---

[11]Schellig thus ends his work, a brief treatise entitled *In Pustulas malas consilium* (Heidelberg, 1495), by crediting the "Illustrissimi pricipis & domini domini Philippi Comitis Palatini" with its inspiration (sig. B4v—reprinted in Sudhoff, ed., p. 22).

medicine, on the other hand, they vigorously demand it—again at least partly within the context of the patronage relationship. Caspare Torrella's early *Tractatus cum consiliis contra pudendragum seu morbum gallicum* (1497) supplies probably the most incisive case from the standpoint of sheer statistics.[12] This early treatise on syphilis is distinguished both by its close, useful observation of the disease and by the patron to whom it is dedicated: Cesare Borgia, cardinal and archbishop of Valencia. Indeed, subject and patron are inextricably connected, for Torrella's medical clarity derives in part from Borgia's own excesses; by 1497, Torrella had treated the young cardinal (then twenty-one) for syphilis, together with at least seventeen other patients drawn from the Borgia family and the papal court *within a single two-month period*. In at least this early and important instance, thus, the physician's duties can only be served by a potentially self-destructive double discourse. The authority of the cardinalate forces one to view disease as the just, ineluctable *flagellum dei;* and yet the body of the stricken cardinal himself demands that one somehow find a way to avoid the whip—preferably without registering any nervousness or ambivalence in the process.

Insofar as Renaissance medical authors deal with this contradiction, they often do so within the context of what now seems decidedly literary—even ornamental—language. Hence the tendency to oscillate between pious sermonizing on one hand and formative medical observation on the other; and hence too the occasional tendency for Renaissance physicians—when they are not writing practical medical treatises—to deal with syphilis in elaborate fictional narrative. Rabelais provides a noteworthy instance of such work;[13] but for present purposes Girolamo Fracastoro's *Syphilis sive morbus gallicus* (1530) is more useful. For not only does Fracastoro's work perfectly illustrate the interdependence of medical and literary idioms by bequeathing medicine the very name that would ultimately stick to the new disease, but his poem also clearly demonstrates how new medical discourses can be shaped in response to the expectations and needs of a governing few.

Dedicated in whole to the future Cardinal Pietro Bembo—and in part to Pope Leo X—Fracastoro's *Syphilis* openly solicits the attention and approval of a powerful and wealthy readership. Moreover, it brilliantly attracts the very audience it seeks; Bembo was not merely pleased with the

---

[12]These figures are drawn from Torrella's treatise itself (*Tractatus cum consiliis contra pudendragum seu morbum gallicum* [Rome, 1497], sig. C4r; reprinted in Sudhoff, ed., p. 207). Yet Torrella clearly refers only to cases *cured;* it is at least possible that his less successful treatments within this two-month period have gone unlisted.

[13]William H. Myer ("Syphilis and the Poetic Imagination: Jean Lemaire de Belges and Girolamo Fracastoro," *Renaissance Papers* [1955], p. 76) makes this observation while discussing the larger literary ramifications of syphilis in the Renaissance.

poem but made it a sort of personal cause, offering over a hundred precise suggestions on the revision of various passages;[14] and Fracastoro's poem eventually earned him a statue in Verona's Piazza dei Signori, beside one of Dante himself. Yet the dedication to the *Syphilis* begins on, if anything, a note of grave diffidence: "Bembo, Italy's fame and glory, if it happens that Leo allows you to be free for just a little while from great matters of state and from that lofty political structure by which he sustains the whole globe: and if you find pleasure in retreating for a while to be with the sweet Muses: do not disdain my undertaking, this labour of medicine, such as it is. The god Apollo once dignified these matters: small things, also, often have within them their own peculiar delights."[15] Fracastoro describes his poem as a sort of distraction from the "great matters" of politics—as a retreat from loftier affairs; and while this description may simply express the typical humility of a poet seeking patronage, it is unnecessary to characterize the poem's subject itself as a "small thing." And indeed Fracastoro himself retracts this assertion as soon as it is made, assuring Bembo that "beneath the slender appearance of this topic there lies concealed a vast work of Nature and of fate and a grand origin" (1.22–23).

Again, in the dedication to Pope Leo X that begins book 2 of the *Syphilis,* Fracastoro maps his poem onto a space of retreat and seclusion, apart from the Edenic political order that the pope has generated—and that stands in noteworthy contrast to the dire vision of political entropy promoted by Maximilian's 1495 blasphemy edict:

> We must never fail to mention, among the gifts given us by the gods, great-hearted Leo, under whom Latium, under whom the mighty Rome lift high their head and Father Tiber rises from his banks and roars congratulations to triumphant Rome. Under his auspices the evil stars have now at last retreated from the world, and now Jupiter in his benign sphere reigns and pours pure rays through heavens freed from tempests. . . . Therefore, while others sing of these great events and make poetry from his famous deeds . . . , let us, whom the fates call to tasks which are not so great, continue with this amusement we have begun, so far as our slender Muse allows. [2.46–65]

Fracastoro's self-abasement is programmatic and largely conventional: his muse is slender, his verse simply an amusement, and his subject inferior to the qualities and accomplishments of his audience. Meanwhile, Leo emerges from these lines as something close to an overwhelming natural force, restoring the golden age, returning the stars to their proper spheres of influence, and commencing an era of peace and prosperity that—one would

---

[14]Geoffrey Eatough, ed., *Fracastoro's Syphilis* (Liverpool, 1984), p. 4.
[15]Ibid., bk. 1, lines 15–21. Further citations in the text will be to this edition.

assume—has little place for a disease as novel and odious as syphilis itself. Given these premises, one would indeed hope to make the illness disappear, for its presence challenges the pope's own virtue as ruler; and thus one of the functions of Fracastoro's poem is in effect to make syphilis go away: to claim that it is not only curable but *already cured,* thereby reconciling the poem's awkward subject with the political vision of its dedicatory remarks.

Yet elsewhere the poem betrays its own deep concern over the ravages of the new disease; and interestingly enough the victims Fracastoro describes are invariably distinguished in birth, appearance, and station. Thus, for instance, the following miniature elegy laments a youth of outstanding "wealth and ancestry," destroyed by the malign influence of the planets:

> I myself remember having seen one of the Cenomani from where the River Oglio with waters from Sebinus flows with its abundance past rich meadow-lands, a conspicuous youth, more brilliant and more gifted than any in Italy. Scarce adolescent he was in the flowering springtime of his youth, a man of parts through his wealth and ancestry, with a handsome frame as well. . . . Gradually that glistening springtime, that flower of his youth perished utterly, that vigor of mind: then the wasting sickness with its filthy scabs (sheer horror) covered his sorry limbs, and, deep within, his bones began to swell large with hideous abscesses. [1.382–403]

Taken in aggregate, these passages (and there are others) suggest that Fracastoro's medical concern is inseparable from his social situation, while being bound in an elaborately tense and ambivalent relationship to it. He praises his patrons in ways incompatible with the novelty and gravity of the disease he is describing, and thus at those moments in the poem he has no choice but to regard his own subject matter as a trifle; then, when he needs to emphasize the illness's importance, he does so by embodying it in a wealthy and privileged man—one "more brilliant and more gifted than any in Italy."

Perhaps the final irony of this rhetorical strategy is that it works so well. For it not only earns Fracastoro a place of honor among his contemporaries, both as physician and as poet; it also seems to have somehow coexisted with traditions that Fracastoro was a selfless healer who devoted himself to the poor.[16] And yet records suggest that practical medicine was, if anything, a relatively minor commitment for the poet, who seems to have practiced it only when financial need arose. And for Bembo, too, the *Syphilis* is not a purely disinterested contribution to literary history; the cardinal, a notorious womanizer who dallied with Lucrezia Borgia and kept a mistress after entering holy orders, would certainly have had a more than intellectual in-

---

[16]Ibid., p. 3.

terest in the new disease.[17] Thus an exercise in coterie back-patting contributes to the reputations of two prominent Renaissance humanists, while also supplying the necessary conditions for the development of an apparently new medical discourse—a discourse whose principal enabling premise is that only the wealthy and privileged count: these are, roughly speaking, the same "good poore" people whom William Clowes will endeavor to heal fifty years later.

III

Michel Foucault has argued that in early modern medicine,

> disease has, as a birthright, forms and seasons that are alien to the space of societies. . . . The more complex the social space in which it is situated becomes, the more *denatured* it becomes. Before the advent of civilization, people had only the simplest, most necessary diseases. . . . [Yet] as one improves one's conditions of life, and as the social network tightens its grip around individuals, "health seems to diminish by degrees"; diseases become diversified, and combine with one another; "their number is already great in the superior order of the bourgeois; . . . it is as great as possible in people of quality."[18]

We may see the earliest medical texts on syphilis conforming to this model almost deliberately; for syphilis in fact comes into being *as a treatable ailment* only when it is associated with those figures at the heart of the political and social order—with cardinals, popes, electors, and later with "the superior order of the bourgeois." When identified with the poor and socially undistinguished, the disease almost ceases to be a disease at all; instead, it emerges in its concomitant character as an instrument of discipline and punishment—that is, as an appendage of government itself. This essay has argued that works like Fracastoro's (and Grünpeck's and Clowes's) become possible only because of a manifest need both to consolidate and to justify such class-specific notions of medical practice; and these works typically perform their job by constructing themselves within a traditional patronage relationship while at the same time largely rejecting the conventional language and authorities and practices of medical scholarship. Such texts are indeed iconoclastic, even revolutionary, but only within carefully prescribed limits; and thus one may reasonably ask just how far their commitment to liberating change really extends.

[17]Alessandro Perosa and John Sparrow, eds., *Renaissance Latin Verse: An Anthology* (London, 1979), p. 166.

[18]Michel Foucault, *The Birth of the Clinic: An Archaeology of Medical Perception*, trans. A. M. Sheridan Smith (New York, 1973), pp. 16–17.

One obvious answer to this question may simply be that the commit-ment to change extends only so far as it is compatible with the author's own immediate interests: readership, patronage, advancement, remuneration. This formula, at least, helps to explain the readiness with which a physician like Fracastoro seeks to retail syphilis on the literary market; and it helps also to explain the progressive glamorizing of the disease that occurs in the sixteenth and seventeenth centuries.[19] At the very least, Fracastoro's de-scription of King Alcithous and his servant, the shepherd Syphilus—the putative first sufferers of the ailment—manages to repackage venereal dis-ease in an attractively consumable form: "Syphilus, a shepherd by this very river, so the story goes, used to pasture a thousand oxen and a thousand snow-white sheep over these pastures for king Alcithous: the time was at the summer solstice; Sirius was scorching the thirsty fields. . . . He pitied his flock, and provoked by the fierce heat lifted up his eyes and face to the Sun in its eminence. 'Why, Sun, do we call you Father and God of all things? . . . What a fool I am, that I don't rather perform divine rights for the king'" (3.288–305). And notably enough King Alcithous, although "delighted by the honour due to Gods being shown to him" (3.317), sur-vives the plague while his servant Syphilus is chosen as a human sacrifice to restore order; Fracastoro, like Grünpeck, preserves both the notion of ve-nereal disease as divine punishment and the narrowness of vision that exempts rulers from the judgments inflicted upon their people. It is almost as if there were *two* diseases in Fracastoro's account: one for figures like his patrons and another for the rest of humanity; one regrettable, unmerited, and ultimately curable, the other hideous, just, and irresistible. When, in the mid-seventeenth century, Sir William Davenant has himself painted at an angle that proudly displays both his poet's laurels and his decayed, syph-ilitic nose (fig. 2),[20] it is clear that he has claimed the former version of the disease as his own. And the frontispiece of Grünpeck's *Hübscher Tractat*—with its pious, crusading emperor and its naked, beggarly corpse covered by syphilis sores—just as clearly invokes the latter version.[21]

In effect, texts of the sort we have surveyed work in aggregate not to

[19]In this regard it is useful to compare Susan Sontag's well-documented claim (*AIDS and Its Metaphors* [New York, 1988], pp. 22–23) that by the nineteenth century syphilis had ac-quired "a darkly positive association" with intellectual activity and personal achievement.

[20]Sir William Davenant's original portrait, by John Greenhill, is lost; however, it supplied the model for William Faithorne's frontispiece engraving to Davenant's 1673 *Works*. This is the illustration reproduced here.

[21]Grünpeck's frontispiece is itself in fact a reworking of the woodcut that accompanies Sebastian Brandt's verse broadsheet *De pestilentiali scorra sive mala de Franzos, Eulogium* (Strassburg, 1496). This earlier version of the illustration more clearly presents the syphilis as emanating from the infant Christ, while similarly segregating the emperor and his followers from the infected multitude.

Fig. 2 Frontispiece to Sir William Davenant, *Works* (1673). (Courtesy of the Robert Manning Strozier Library, Special Collections, Florida State University, Tallahassee.)

make syphilis generally understood but, rather, to make it selectively acceptable; and this tendency is perhaps at its strongest when it is least openly apparent—for instance, in the work of Clowes. For Clowes, whose choice of patronage is both more diffuse and less conventional than either Fracastoro's or Grünpeck's (he addresses his work to the "Maisters and Governors of the Barbars and Chirurgions" of London), nonetheless threatens ultimately to be the greatest prig of the lot. Thus his work oscillates between a kind of fraternal egalitarianism and an arch, repent-ye-sinners piety. Offering his book on one hand as testimony of his "*harty good will and faythfull zeale to* [his] *country, and countrymen*" (A5v), he nonetheless betrays an ill-concealed loathing of the very people he seeks to cure: "The worshipfull masters of the hospitall can witnes that I speake the truth: as also, I w^t my brethren can testifie with them, with what griefe of minde they are dayly enforced to take in a number of vyle creatures that otherwise would infect many, seeking with like care, to restrayne this greevous sinne" (sig. B2v). Can it be purely accidental that in this context syphilis is not a disease but a "sinne"? And can the author have been totally unaware of the vast tonal gulf separating a phrase like "worshipfull masters of the hospitall" from one like "vyle creatures"? It is as if Clowes's work were in fact consciously formulated to widen the gap between surgeon and patient, learned and ignorant, worshipful and vile, in the very process of offering aid to the afflicted; and we may explain this reinforcement of professional and class distinctions by noting that the author's own success and reputation depend upon them.

In this sense Clowes tentatively voices what Foucault has called "a *collective consciousness* of pathological phenomena, a consciousness that operate[s] at both the level of experience and the level of knowledge, in the international as well as the national space."[22] And we may see this consciousness emerging specifically from the encounter with a *social* disease— an ailment that, simply by existing, attests to the porosity and provisionality of the very class distinctions we have discussed. In this sense syphilis is very much what Steven Mullaney has called "an incontinent disorder": one that "exceed[s] the bounds of community and classifications."[23] Hence the unavoidable vagueness of terms like "power elite" and "ruling class" as they occur in the present analysis: for the new discourse of early modern medicine arises precisely to bring governor and governed closer together at the same time that it distinguishes more fully between them. Operating through a "medicalization of the effects of confession,"[24] Clowes's lan-

---

[22]Foucault, *The Birth of the Clinic,* p. 28.

[23]Mullaney (n. 5 above), p. 37.

[24]Michel Foucault, *The History of Sexuality: An Introduction,* vol. 1 of *The History of Sexuality,* trans. Robert Hurley (New York, 1978), p. 67.

guage seeks to erase the physical barriers between classes even as it extends the domain of traditional authority: that of ruler over subject, of doctor over patient. As a result, works like the *De Morbo Gallico* complexly resist any *formal* distinction between classes even as they make the *practical* distinction more unavoidable. The apparent egalitarianism of a work that—unlike its forebears—seeks no aristocratic or clerical protection collapses only when applied to the specific site of medical practice—where the hegemony of doctor over patient is more manifest than ever. One may recall George Orwell's remark that "it is curious how people take it for granted that they have a right to preach at you and pray over you as soon as your income falls below a certain level." For that assumption subtends the entire discourse of early modern syphilis.[25]

IV

The social and professional discrimination thus built into Renaissance responses to syphilis is by no means unique or peculiar. On the contrary, the literature of early modern syphilis clearly prefigures contemporary thinking about AIDS, as Susan Sontag has persuasively argued. Yet where Sontag has claimed that AIDS paranoia reinscribes "a premodern experience of illness,"[26] this study would prefer to view the sixteenth-century experience of syphilis as itself an innovation of sorts. And we may perhaps best explain the connection between syphilis and AIDS by considering who most benefits—and has benefited—from official efforts to deal with both these ailments.

In the case of syphilis, as we have seen, the benefits are distributed among a fairly select assortment of interrelated groups: medical professionals, who gain wealth, publicity, and the recognition of major political figures; the political figures themselves, who gain a method for coping with the disease that both reinforces their authority and privileges them as patients; and, to a lesser extent, the larger body of "good poor" bourgeois, whose declared morals and mercantile success are ratified by books like Clowes's *De Morbo Gallico*, and who in turn contribute to Clowes's success by buying his work. The language of this distribution, in effect, turns syphilis into a managed political event—rather like the staged executions so

[25]Quoted in Sontag, p. 34.

[26]Thus, interestingly, Doreen Nagy refers to Clowes's later treatise on the struma to illustrate the class-specificity of Renaissance medical practice: "Clowes accepted the fact that if you were poor and could not pay for a cure, or could not avail yourself of the 'royal touch,' your fate was sealed: to perish 'miserably.' There is no suggestion that the young surgeon, to whom Clowes specifically addressed his tract, should consider a non-paying client deserving of his healing skills" (Doreen Nagy, *Popular Medicine in Seventeenth-Century England* [Bowling Green, OH, 1988], p. 25).

typical of Renaissance judicial procedure. And this sort of management helps intensify the medical profession's *social* dimension, placing physicians and patients equally under a series of potentially distorting economic pressures. In short, through its responses to syphilis, medical practice begins to relocate itself *"within* the social body, rather than . . . *above* it."[27]

Similarly, much of the current response to AIDS in the United States has involved a contest over how the ailment is to be represented in literature and film and television, and who is to be the prime beneficiary of that representation. And while the most obvious instances of such struggle are those residual members of the Christian Right—like Jerry Falwell—who subscribe to the Emperor Maximilian's retributive logic, other political groups, too, have scrambled for control of AIDS signification. Indeed, Randy Shilts has rightly described the 1987 agreement between Ronald Reagan and Jacques Chirac designating Robert Gallo and Luc Montagnier as codiscoverers of the HIV virus to be "one of the first times in history that heads of state [have been] called upon to resolve a dispute over a viral discovery."[28] And arguably thus with AIDS—as with early syphilis—we are in social fact confronting two separate and exclusive ailments: one that afflicts needy and/or oppressed populations like the Third World poor, gay men, drug users, and prostitutes; and one associated with researchers, government spokespeople, and the occasional movie star.

For these latter figures and their associates, AIDS clearly has its benefits—as well as its unique and intense social pressures. Similarly, Joseph Grünpeck, Girolamo Fracastoro, and William Clowes reap the rewards of professional success at least as much for the political convenience of their attitudes and observations as for the therapeutic value of their work. And for each of these authors, the rewards of orthodoxy are substantial. Grünpeck, although merely a layman in physic, has the distinction of seeing his work on syphilis run through five Latin and two German editions in less than five years. Fracastoro, favored by popes and cardinals, is eventually appointed honorary physician to the Council of Trent;[29] and in this century he is praised as the author of "perhaps the most famous Renaissance Latin poem."[30] And William Clowes proceeds in 1595 to a coat of arms—while in his later years holding the office of personal surgeon to Queen Elizabeth I.

[27]Michel Foucault, *Power/Knowledge: Selected Interviews and Other Writings, 1972–1977*, ed. Colin Gordon (New York, 1980), p. 39.

[28]Randy Shilts, *And the Band Played On: Politics, People, and the AIDS Epidemic* (New York, 1988), p. 593.

[29]Perosa and Sparrow, eds. (n. 17 above), p. 233.

[30]Eatough, ed. (n. 14 above), p. 1.

Offense against Family Order:
Infanticide in Belgium from the Fifteenth through the Early Twentieth Centuries

RENÉ LEBOUTTE
Department of History and Civilization
European University Institute, Florence

INFANTICIDE TODAY is regarded as an archaic crime but not at all unusual.[1] The press regularly reports new cases, with headlines such as "Horrible—Dead Body of Newborn Discovered in Garbage Bag Thrown in Refuse Dump at Marchin."[2] Although infanticide has drawn the attention of anthropologists working on non-European countries[3] and its legal aspects have been studied by historians,[4] scholars have only recently begun

I would like to acknowledge my indebtedness to George Alter (Indiana University, Bloomington) and Etienne Hélin (University of Liège, Belgium) for their comments and criticisms. Moreover, I express my gratitude to Monsieur le Procureur général près la Cour d'appel de Liège, who permitted me to use the archives of the Court of Assizes.

[1] See, for instance, "Recherches sur l'infanticide, 1955–1965," *Annales de la Faculté de Droit et des Sciences politiques et économiques de Strasbourg,* vol. 17, Travaux de l'Institut des Sciences criminelles et pénitentiaires (Paris, 1968), pp. 42, 73–75, 91.

[2] *La Meuse,* August 14, 1989. Unless otherwise specified, all newspapers cited below were published in Liège. In the present article I am developing a research topic begun in an earlier essay: René Leboutte, "L'infanticide dans l'Est de la Belgique aux XVIIIe–XIXe siècles: Une réalité," in *Annales de Démographie historique,* ed. Société de Demographie historique (Paris, 1983), pp. 163–92.

[3] Mildred Dickemann, "Concepts and Classification in the Study of Human Infanticide: Sectional Introduction and Some Cautionary Notes," in *Infanticide: Comparative and Evolutionary Perspectives,* ed. Glenn Hausfater and Sarah Blaffer Hardy (New York, 1984), pp. 427–37; Susan C. M. Scrimshaw, "Infanticide in Human Populations: Societal and Individual Concerns," in ibid., pp. 439–62, and "Infant Mortality and Behavior in the Regulation of Family Size," *Population and Development Review* 4 (1978): 383–403; William Petersen, *Population,* 2d ed. (London, 1969), pp. 186–87; Mildred Dickemann, "Demographic Consequences of Infanticide in Man," *Annual Review of Ecology and Systematics* 6 (1975): 100–37.

[4] Peter C. Hoffer and N.E.H. Hull, *Murdering Mothers: Infanticide in England and New England, 1558–1803,* vol. 2, New York University School of Law Series in Legal History (New York, 1981); Richard Lalou, "L'infanticide devant les tribunaux français (1825–1910)," *Communications* ("Dénatalité: L'antériorité française, 1800–1914") 44 (1986): 175–200;

This essay originally appeared in the *Journal of the History of Sexuality* 1991, vol. 2, no. 2.

to examine the practice of infanticide as a means to understand the physical environment and the psychological milieu in which poor women experienced unwanted pregnancy.[5]

In antiquity and until the past century in the great agrarian civilizations of the Far East (such as Japan), infanticide was accepted as a means of family planning. In western Europe, on the contrary, the constant pressure of the Catholic church from the end of the fourth century supported societal disapproval. The destruction of a fetus or a newborn baby was punished by ignominious execution of the culprit.[6] In spite of stern deterrents, infanticide is widely observed in early modern and modern Europe, and it is associated with the breaking of the natural link between mother and child in other forms: abortion, abandonment, exposure, and trade of children.[7] Until the end of the nineteenth century such attacks on the family are not exceptional, even after contraceptive methods became more accessible.[8]

Dominique Vallaud, "Le crime d'infanticide et l'indulgence des cours d'assises en France au XIXe siècle," *Social Science Information* 21 (1982): 475–98; Keith Wrightson, "Infanticide in European History," *Criminal Justice History* 8 (1982): 1–20.

[5]R. W. Malcolmson, "Infanticide in the Eighteenth Century," in *Crime in England,* ed. J. S. Cockburn (Princeton, NJ, 1978), pp. 187–209; Jacques Gélis, *L'arbre et le fruit: La naissance dans l'Occident moderne, XVIe–XIXe siècle* (Paris, 1984), pp. 415–24, 481–85. For medieval times, see Yves-B. Brissaud, "L'infanticide à la fin du Moyen Age, ses motivations psychologiques et sa répression," *Revue historique de droit français et étranger* 50 (1972): 229–56; Emily R. Coleman, "L'infanticide dans le haut Moyen Age," *Annales: Economies, sociétés, civilisations* 29 (1974): 315–35; William L. Langer, "Infanticide: A Historical Survey," *History of Childhood Quarterly* 1 (1974): 353–65; Lionel Rose, *Massacre of the Innocents: Infanticide in Britain, 1800–1939* (London, 1986). For Japan, see Osamu Saito, "Infanticide and Japan's Pre-transition Demographic Regime," in *Historiens et population: Liber amicorum Étienne Hélin,* ed. Société Belge de Démographie (Louvain-la-Neuve, 1991), in press. For Italy, see Giovanna Da Molin and Pietro Stella, "Famiglia e infanticidi nell'Europa preindustriale" (report of the International Congress, "Structure e rapporti familiari in epoca moderna: Esperienze italiane e riferimenti europei," University degli studi di Trieste and Società Italiana di demografia storica, Trieste, September 5–7, 1983).

[6]Petersen, pp. 186–87; Marcel Reinhard, André Armengaud, and Jacques Dupaquier, *Histoire générale de la population mondiale* (Paris, 1968), pp. 137–38; Scrimshaw, "Infant Mortality," pp. 386–87; Susan B. Hanley, "The Influence of Economic and Social Variables on Marriage and Fertility in Eighteenth- and Nineteenth-Century Japanese Villages," in *Population Patterns in the Past,* ed. Ronald D. Lee (New York, 1977), pp. 176–83.

[7]Langer, p. 355; on abortion in Belgium, see Raoul van der Made, "Histoire de la répression de l'avortement," in *Revue de droit pénal et de criminologie* (Louvain, 1948), pp. 1–19.

[8]Jean-Louis Flandrin, "L'attitude à l'égard du petit enfant et les conduites sexuelles dans la civilisation occidentale," *Annales de Démographie historique,* ed. Société de Demographie historique (Paris, 1973), pp. 143–210; François Lebrun, *La vie conjugale sous l'Ancien Régime* (Paris, 1975), pp. 147–53; Keith Wrightson, "Infanticide in Earlier Seventeenth-Century England," *Local Population Studies* 15 (1975): 10–22; Peter E. H. Hair, "Homicide, Infanticide, and Child Assault in Late Tudor Middlesex," *Local Population Studies* 9 (1972): 43–45. For the nineteenth century, see Regina Schulte, "Infanticide in Rural Bavaria in the Nine-

Most of the source material used in this essay concerns Belgium between the end of the fifteenth century and the early twentieth century. More than one hundred cases have been collected from judicial archives of the ancien régime and the nineteenth century and from contemporary newspapers to describe the attitudes both of the guilty women and of society toward unwanted pregnancy and its outrage to the social meaning of family and motherhood. In general, historians have observed the court slowly shifting from rigid adherence to the law to a more comprehensive (and compassionate) understanding of the distress of the culprit.[9] But here we will be less concerned with the legal aspect of infanticide, which has already been studied, than with the social pressures that these unfortunate women confronted.[10]

WHAT IS INFANTICIDE?

According to the Napoléonic Penal Code of 1810, infanticide is the willful destruction (murder or premeditated assassination) of a baby at the moment of delivery or immediately afterward through starvation, strangulation, smothering, poisoning, or other violence. The culprit theoretically was invariably sentenced to death. But more and more in the first half of the nineteenth century, the jury of assizes preferred to recognize extenuating circumstances, taking into account the passion, the shame, and the psychological suffering that might have led the mother astray. For this reason, in 1867, the legislature assimilated infanticide to murder or to assassination (in cases of premeditated action) but did not consider infanticide as a crime inevitably punished by death. If the child was a bastard, the Penal Code of 1867 imposed a rather lenient penalty—ten to fifteen years' imprisonment for murder and fifteen to twenty years' imprisonment for assassination. In other cases the murderer was condemned to hard labor for life and to have the right arm branded with the letters "TP" (*travaux forcés à perpétuité*,

---

teenth Century," in *Interest and Emotion: Essays on the Study of Family and Kinship*, ed. Hans Medick and David W. Sabean (Cambridge, 1984), pp. 77–102; Peter E. H. Hair, "Deaths from Violence in Britain: A Tentative Secular Survey," *Population Studies* 1 (1971): 18; George K. Behlmer, "Deadly Motherhood: Infanticide and Medical Opinion in Mid-Victorian England," *Journal of the History of Medicine and Allied Sciences* 34 (1979): 403–27; R. Sauer, "Infanticide and Abortion in Nineteenth-Century Britain," *Population Studies* (1978): 81–93.

[9]On the psychological aspect of infanticide, also see Louis-Vincent Thomas, *Anthropologie de la mort* (Paris, 1976), pp. 121–23.

[10]Wilhem Wächtershäuser, *Das Verbrechen des Kindesmordes im Zeitalter der Aufklärung: Eine Rechtsgeschichtliche Untersuchung der dogmatischen, prozessualen, und rechtssoziologischen Aspekte*, vol. 3, Quellen und Forschungen zur Strafrechtsgeschichte (Berlin, 1973).

indicating hard labor), to the *carcan* (an iron collar or shackle)—or to death.[11]

Abandonment or exposure of a child is not considered infanticide except when the baby intentionally is left in a dangerous place, such as on the railroad tracks. Infanticide involves three prerequisites: (1) the mother willfully has killed the newborn child; (2) the baby has been killed during the delivery or just after it; and (3) the baby was born alive.

In other circumstances and if the murderer is not the mother, the crime is not infanticide but common murder. The requirement of being "born alive" does not mean that the baby is actually viable but only that he shows some signs of life. "It is not even necessary that he spends an extrauterine life, in other words that he breathes. A motion, a wail is enough to attest his life. Such a clue can be regarded as a flickering glimmer ready to go off but enough to place the baby under the protection of the law."[12] In this essay, however, I use a broader definition of infanticide: the killing of an infant less than one year old.

In the early nineteenth century, forensic pathologists distinguished between "infanticide by oversight," an infant who died from voluntary lack of care, and "infanticide by commission," a newborn child who perished from external violence conducted against him in order to extinguish life.[13] We can divide incidents involving the death of a newborn into groups, according to the typology proposed by Susan Scrimshaw.[14]

Deliberate killing.—The first group covers the victims of intentional acts. In 1857, for instance, the organs of a baby "after having been violently dismembered from the trunk with an incredible violence [were] thrown into the river." In 1860 some workers in Braine-le-Comte discovered a small corpse wrapped in a piece of rough blue cloth—the skull was smashed. In the same year a child bound in a scarf, with a stone attached to the body, was found in Bruges. In 1864 a miller retrieved from the Légia brook near Liège a newborn baby with a string around his neck, attached to a heavy stone.[15]

Placing the child in a dangerous situation.—The second group is made up

[11] For instance, Marie Elisabeth, twenty-eight years old, condemned to the *carcan,* to be branded, and to hard labor for the murder of her twelve-day-old child (Cour d'assises de Liège, B.75, February 22, 1848, Archives de l'Etat à Liège [hereafter AEL]); Marie Claudine, condemned to the same penalty (Cour d'assises de Liège, B.76, November 23, 1849, AEL).

[12] "Infanticide," in Edmond Picard, Nicolas d'Hoffschmidt, and Jules de le Court, *Pandectes belges: Encyclopédie de législation, de doctrine, et de jurisprudence belges* (Brussels, 1895), 52:989–97; Code pénal: Promulgué le 8 juin 1867, publié le 9 juin 1867, mis à exécution le 15 octobre 1867, bk. 2, sec. 8, chap. 1, art. 393, 394, 396. See Langer, p. 353.

[13] J. B. Montfalcon, "Infanticide," in *Dictionnaire des sciences médicales par une société de médecins et de chirurgiens* (Paris, 1818), pp. 408–40.

[14] Scrimshaw, "Infanticide in human populations" (n. 3 above), pp. 442–44.

[15] *La Meuse,* May 18, 1857; June 6, 1860; October 23, 1860; March 2, 1864.

of children who were exposed to mortal dangers, by being left in the woods, near a pigsty, in a deserted spot, and so on.

Abandonment.—Abandoning (also termed "exposing") a child was a way to leave his life to fate. If found alive, perhaps the infant would survive. If he died, it could be attributed to the will of God. In 1817, for instance, the police in Bois-de-Breux (Liège) found the corpse of a baby who had died during exposure; in 1861, the body of a newborn baby exposed on Cockerill's wharf in Liège was carried to the mortuary; in January 1864 a man found a newborn child who had died from the cold in Andrimont.[16]

Leaving a newborn baby in a deserted spot (where he was not likely to be discovered) was viewed as a delayed infanticide, but the judge generally sentenced the accused for homicide through carelessness. In 1857 a thirty-seven-year-old factory worker of Hodimont was condemned to five years' imprisonment: she had hidden her baby in the woods under a pile of leaves, but the child was fortunate enough to survive. The question remains, How should we interpret the actions of the mother—as homicide through neglect or as intentional abandonment to the perils of cold and wild animals? Let us consider another story. In 1862 a seventeen-year-old mother from Liège left her newborn baby "on a pile of ashes in the cellar"; drawn by the crying of the baby, "a woman rushed into the cellar and gave the child first aid; the baby was still breathing but was already injured by the cold, and he died a few hours later." The jury passed sentence of only three months' imprisonment on the mother "for unintentional homicide through carelessness and neglect."[17]

"Accidental" death.—Unmarried mothers were not the only ones suspected of infanticide. Some couples were also troubled by suspicious and even malevolent neighbors, as in a case in Sprimont in 1649 where women charged a couple with smothering their baby in the conjugal bed, a frequent and perhaps voluntary negligence.[18] In nineteenth-century Europe, babies placed in bed with their parents frequently were found smothered to death in the morning. It was often a covert form of infanticide.[19]

Excessive physical punishment and/or lowered biological support.—In 1863, in Verviers, an organ-grinder and his wife left their newborn child without nourishment until he starved. The woman was sentenced to death by the jury of assizes.[20] But it was not always easy to decide whether the baby had been the victim of injuries or not. Most of the bodies betrayed no special evidence of criminal acts, and many of them were in fact stillborn or victims

[16]Fond hollandais, Police, no. 805, April 3, 1817, AEL; *La Meuse,* March 25, 1861; and January 19, 1864.

[17]Cour d'assises de Liège, B.81, June 9, 1857, AEL; *La Meuse,* January 4, 1862.

[18]Cour de justice, Sprimont, no. 60, fol. 36v, 1649, AEL; Langer (n. 5 above), p. 356.

[19]Langer, p. 356.

[20]Cour d'assises de Liège, B.83, August 8, 1860, AEL; *La Meuse,* August 9, 1860.

of a natural accident at delivery. The mother may have feared being wrongly charged or simply may have wished to avoid the costs of a burial by hiding the corpse. Sometimes there is no question of infanticide, but these affairs provide an interesting insight into the circumstances of unmarried motherhood.

In January 1733 the priest of the church of Sainte-Véronique in Liège received people carrying the corpse of a baby, "making me believe he was born from parents recently moved into Saint-Nicolas-en-Glain, and after their departure I was informed that it was a child who had burned himself and that the parents had sent him here in order to escape or avoid justice."[21] In 1768, the following note was found on the corpse of a child in the church of Notre-Dame-aux-Fonts in Liège: "Baptized. I have no [financial] means to have him buried."[22] Such discoveries at the front doors of churches were frequent. Some of the babies were set down alive but died before discovery: for example, in December 1810 two inhabitants of Theux early in the morning found "a dead child hidden under a box on the stairs of the main entrance of the parish church." The baby had been registered the day before in the civil register and was abandoned at night by his mother, an unmarried spinner.[23]

If we look at parish and civil registers, especially for communities located along a river, we can read numerous entries relating the discovery of a fetus or newborn child retrieved from the water. Most of the perpetrators remained unknown.[24] Between 1861 and 1875, 127 women were accused of having committed infanticide, but in the same period 397 perpetrators escaped pursuit.[25]

As shown below, a large majority of those who committed infanticide were young servants of rural origin.[26]

SOME STATISTICAL EVIDENCE

One must not forget that records—judicial archives or newspapers—capture only a portion of all the infanticides perpetrated. We observe only the tip of the iceberg. For this reason a statistical approach seems to me hazardous. However, in order to appreciate the extent of infanticide, this section furnishes some figures for nineteenth-century Belgium.[27]

---

[21]Parochial registers, Liège Sainte-Véronique, no. 314, January 26, 1733, AEL.

[22]Parochial registers, Liège Notre-Dame-aux-Fonts, no. 26, April 22, 1768, AEL.

[23]Civil registers, Theux, no. 26, p. 75, December 15, 1810, AEL.

[24]Many examples can be found in Leboutte (n. 2 above), pp. 189–91.

[25]*Exposé de la situation du royaume de 1861 à 1875* (Brussels, 1885), 1:805–7.

[26]Leboutte, pp. 180–81; Schulte (n. 8 above), pp. 70–80.

[27]For information on infanticide in France, see Lalou, pp. 175–200; Alain Vlamynck, "La délinquence au féminin: Crime et répression dans le Nord (1880–1913)," *Revue du Nord* 63 (1981): 675–702.

TABLE 1   Proportion of Infanticides among All Murders in Belgium, 1796–1830

| | Persons Condemned | | |
Period	Infanticide (N)	All Murders (N)	Infanticides (%)
1796–1815	11	445	2.5
1816–30	24	144	16.7

Source.—*Exposé de la situation du Royaume: Période décennale de 1851 à 1860* (Brussels, 1865), 2:134–35.

From 1816 until 1850, infanticides represent 15 to 18 percent of all murders committed (see tables 1 and 2).

During the decade 1831–40, 20 percent of those found guilty of infanticide were sentenced to death. In the next decade, the proportion was 26.5 percent, and after 1850 it continued to rise, to 34.1 percent in 1851–60 and 40.8 percent in 1861–70; but between 1871 and 1875, the figure was reduced to 37.9 percent.

After an increase in the proportion of infanticides during the decade 1851–60 (to 24 percent of all murders), the rate regularly decreased from 1861 to 1870 and from 1896 to 1900 (see tables 3, 4, and 5).

A DIABOLIC CRIME

Until the mid-seventeenth century, those women convicted of infanticide were condemned to death not only for murder but for the practice of witchcraft. At the end of the fourteenth century in Namur, they were burned on the hillside of the city.[28] Before being executed the culprits were also tortured, forced to confess to having hidden their pregnancy and to having destroyed their fruit.[29] In the Duchy of Luxembourg they were buried alive near the gallows or strangled or killed by sword.[30] In the principality of Liège, infanticide was punished by death—women were "thrown and suffocated in the river."[31] In 1679 a woman of Tilff was drowned in the Ourthe River, and in 1718 a woman of Soiron was executed in the same

[28]Charles Lamsoul, *La peine de mort à Namur aux XIVe et XVe siècles* (Namur, 1934), p. 6. The writer also relates the sentence in August 1393 of a woman "who had dismantled her baby."

[29]Haute Cour de justice, register 45, fol. 193v, September 23, 1529; register 51, fols. 97–98, February 1542; register 51, fols. 191r, 204v–205r, January 1544; register 58, fol. 125v, February 20, 1557; register 62, fols. 29v, 30r, 31v, 32, September 1562; all found in Archives de l'Etat à Namur (hereafter AEN).

[30]Marie-Sylvie Dupont-Bouchat, Willem Frijhoff, and Robert Muchembled, *Prophètes et sorciers dans les Pays-Bas, XVIe–XVIIIe siècle* (Paris, 1978), pp. 54–55, 69.

[31]D. F. de Sohet, *Instituts de droit, ou sommaire de jurisprudence canonique, civile, féodale, et criminelle pour le pays de Liège, de Luxembourg, Namur, et autres* (Brussels and Namur, 1781), 3:18. Sohet quoted the *Nemesis Carolina*.

TABLE 2   Proportion of Infanticides among All Murders in Belgium, 1831–60

| | Persons Accused | | |
Period	Infanticide (N)	All Murders (N)	Infanticides (%)
1831–40	100	550	18.2
1841–50	83	545	15.2
1851–60	123	517	23.8

| | Persons Condemned to Death | | |
Period	Infanticide (N)	All Murders (N)	Infanticides* (%)
1831–40	20	86	23.3
1841–50	22	161	13.7
1851–60	42	162	25.9

Source.—See table 1.
*Among those persons accused of infanticide, the percentage of those condemned to death in the period 1831–40 is 20 percent; 1841–50, 26.5 percent; and 1851–60, 34.1 percent.

TABLE 3   Proportion of Infanticides among All Murders in Belgium, 1861–75

| | Persons Condemned | | |
Period	Infanticide (N)	All Murders (N)	Infanticides (%)
1861–70	98	757	12.9
1871–75	29	397	7.3

Source.—*Exposé de la situation du Royaume: Période dècennale de 1861 à 1875* (Brussels, 1885), 1:742–45.

TABLE 4   Proportion of Women Condemned for Infanticide among All Culprits, 1861–75

| | Accused Women | | |
Period	Acquitted (N)	Condemned (N)	Condemned (%)
1861–70	58	40	40.8
1871–75	11	18	37.9

Source.—See table 3.

TABLE 5   Proportion of Infanticides among All Murders in Belgium, 1876–1900

| | *Persons Condemned* | | |
Period	Infanticide (N)	All Murders (N)	Infanticides (%)
1876–80	24	231	10.4
1881–85	31	245	12.7
1886–90	14	239	5.9
1891–95	23	318	7.2
1896–1900	23	276	8.3

Source.—*Exposé de la situation du Royaume: Période décennale de 1876 à 1900* (Brussels, 1912), 2:223.

way.[32] But if the infanticides were too numerous, the accused "must be sentenced to be impaled and after to be buried alive. Or if they are thrown in the river, they must first be condemned to be tormented."[33]

In October 1553 a woman of Theux confessed, after twenty years of marriage, to having killed two bastards she bore before her wedding. This belated confession was strongly sentenced: she was "first buried alive, then dug up and hung on a pitchfork, where the corpse did not hang for long, however, thanks to her friends and because of the good repentance that she had expressed."[34]

The penalty was symbolic—it was the sentence reserved for witches. Sometimes the particular portion of the woman's body through which the offense happened was targeted. In 1613 Girt Kreins, a woman of Bütgenbach, was first designated to undergo a special torment: to have the lower part of her abdomen pierced by a post. Then she was "simply" strangled.[35] The horror of such a crime against family and descendants was thought to require an exemplary sentence, as observed in the city of Liège in 1663. The wife of a butcher had severed the neck of her three-year-old child with her husband's cleaver. Condemned to be strangled, she first was made to walk in the marketplace with the knife tied to her neck and then had her hand cut off.[36]

Mothers who killed their children were regarded as witches acting under

[32]Pierre Baar, "Un manuscrit de la Compagnie de la Charité pour le secours des pauvres prisonniers à Liège," *Bulletin de l'Institut archéologique liégeois* 89 (1977): 146, 151.

[33]Sohet, p. 18.

[34]The court was at first so astonished by this belated repentance that the judges thought the woman was "mad and caught by some hot fever or other illness" (*Chroniques liégeoises,* ed. Sylvin Balau and Emile Fairon [Brussels, 1931], 2:429).

[35]Dr. Bernhard Willems, "Aus der Geschichte des Hofes und der Herrschaft Bütgenbach," *Ostbelgische Chronik* 1 (1948): 67, and "La cour de justice du Bütgenbach," *Folklore Stavelot-Malmédy* 10 (1946): 57–59.

[36]Jules Freson, *La justice criminelle dans l'ancien pays de Liège* (Liège, 1889), p. 75.

the control of the devil.[37] The child was deprived not only of earthly life but above all of eternal life, as he died without baptism. In France, the famous decree of Henry II in 1556 can be seen as a desperate effort to curb the increasing number of infanticides and to discourage motherhood outside marriage: it obligated the unmarried mother to declare her pregnancy and come under the watchfulness of the clergy.[38] In 1562 Marguerite Oudenne of Wangenies (in the county of Namur) was sentenced to death as a witch. She had tried to murder her husband and one of her young children by giving them a powder she had received from a devil called Houzeau.[39] In 1610 Damide Fardeau of Moxhe was prosecuted because all of her children, except one, had died unbaptized. She was said to have bewitched them, as well as her sister's baby who suddenly died before baptism.[40] Infanticides were regarded as crimes against God and the sacred nature of the family; in fact, the victims of infanticide were usually the fruit of an impossible love, and the culprits were left alone to be charged (and not their lovers).[41]

ABANDONMENT OF CHILDREN

Abandonment in an isolated place was considered postponed infanticide. In 1568 a woman of Huy who had left her unbaptized daughter in a deserted spot was condemned to spend one hour in the *carcan* and to attend church on the first Sunday of Advent barefoot, holding a burning candle. Abandonment of a child was a practice severely censured not only by the authorities but also by public opinion.[42] This opinion often was the expression not of compassion but of self-interest. In May 1789 a baby was discovered in front of a chapel in Limbourg, and an anonymous letter immediately arrived for the priest: "The scoundrel who left here the unhappy

[37]In Friuli (Italy) in the sixteenth century, the *benandanti* fought witches who attacked babies and ate them (Carlo Ginzburg, *Les batailles nocturnes: Sorcellerie et rituels agraires aux XVIe et XVIIe siècles* [Paris, 1984], p. 106). Also see Dupont-Bouchat et al., pp. 54–55.

[38]Gélis (n. 5 above), pp. 416–17.

[39]Emile Brouette, "Exécution d'une sorcière à Wangenies en 1562," *Bulletin de la Société royale paléontologique et archéologique de l'arrondissement judiciaire de Charleroi* 18 (June 1949): 25–26.

[40]Emile Brouette, "La sorcellerie dans le Comté de Namur au début de l'époque moderne (1509–1646)," *Annales de la Société archéologique de Namur* 67 (1954): 376–77. In seventeenth-century Châtillonnais (France), the witches were sentenced to death not only because they had had sexual intercourse with the devil but also because they killed newborn babies to make ointment from their fat (Yvonne Verdier, *Façons de dire, façons de faire: La laveuse, la couturière, la cuisinière* [Paris, 1979], p. 342).

[41]Gélis, p. 417.

[42]Cour de Huy, Oeuvres, register 23, fol. 387, Archives de l'Etat à Huy (hereafter AEH), quoted by Nadia Vilenne in "Matrones, accoucheuses, sages-femmes: L'assistance aux accouchements du XVIe au XVIIIe siècle" (Lic. dissertation, University of Liège, 1983), p. 77.

fruit of her criminal debauchery could be one of your parishioners. If it is the case, I hope you will contribute to heighten our charge and to give back a poor little orphan to those who gave him the life." The reproachful language can hardly mask the actual motive—fear that the child would become the charge of the community.[43]

Another practice was also frequent in the ancien régime, that of carrying orphans or abandoned babies to the hospital of a distant city, such as Paris.[44] It was common knowledge that most of these innocents died during a very uncomfortable journey. From a record of the Council of Namur, we know the cost of this questionable business. In 1779 the father of a bastard entrusted the care of his baby to a poor old couple assisted by the *manse des pauvres* (the relief committee) of Presle. The charge was twelve escalins per month, but the father did not pay the foster parents and finally decided to send the child away. He went to Fosses-la-Ville "to seek some people accustomed to carrying children to Paris" and agreed to pay ten écus for the trip. Just before starting out, however, the *hauliers* changed their minds, because they heard of the enquiry of the court of justice. Finally the authorities retrieved the baby and gave him back to his mother.[45]

Hauliers were not always trustworthy people. In 1797 a young mother of Vaux-sous-Chèvremont entrusted her bastard to a woman who was supposed to carry him to his father. But "the *haulier,* instead of fulfilling her duty, had not only unclothed the baby and stolen the napkin and the rags with which the child was covered, in particular a skirt estimated at eight francs, but had also suppressed and murdered him by leaving the baby in a deserted spot where he died from hunger and destitution." In spite of the criminal act, the prosecution of murder was rejected by the jury, who passed sentence of one year's imprisonment on the culprit.[46]

In 1819 a servant gave birth at the civil maternity hospital of Liège. The baby promptly was baptized and entrusted to Thérèse, a forty-five-year-old day laborer accustomed to delivering children to the orphans' hospital in Namur, where a baby could be left without the mother revealing her identity. A week later the mother went to the hospital in Namur, but no child corresponded to the particulars of her baby. Back in Liège she heard that Thérèse had changed her mind and carried the newborn to the hospital in Maastricht. The mother went there but could not find her baby. Desperate,

[43]Commune de Limbourg, no. 906, May 14, 1789, AEL.

[44]Etienne Hélin, "Une sollicitude ambiguë: L'évacuation des enfants abandonnés," *Annales de Démographie historique* 9 (1973): 225–29, and "Le sort des enfants trouvés au XVIIIe siècle," *Bulletin de la Société royale Le Vieux-Liège* 100 (January–March 1953): 203–6; Nicole Haesenne-Peremans, *La pauvreté dans la région liégeoise à l'aube de la révolution industrielle: Un siècle de tension sociale (1730–1830)* (Paris, 1981), pp. 416–17.

[45]Informations judiciaires du Conseil de Namur, no. 783, AEN.

[46]Cour d'assises de Liège, B.3, 15 nivôse an 6 (January 4, 1798), AEL.

she informed the police, and Thérèse finally confessed to having gotten rid of the burden, "estimating that she was ill-paid for the job." The court passed sentence of five years' imprisonment on Thérèse.[47]

NEW PERCEPTION OF A TRADITIONAL CRIME

In the sixteenth and seventeenth centuries, an ignominious penalty was reserved for women who killed their babies. But even in the sixteenth-century trials we perceive some discomfort on the part of the judges. They felt the ambiguity of such a crime: was it truly a deliberate act—thus an infanticide—or was it a natural misfortune or an accident provoked by panic and destitution? In 1529, when a servant gave birth to a child who resembled her "from mouth and face," she pushed him under the bed. She endlessly repeated that "she did not want to kill him." The Court of Justice of Namur, convinced by the argument, decided not to torment her.[48]

According to Jacques Gélis, the local courts of justice usually imposed heavier penalties than the superior courts, which were more inclined to leniency by taking into account all the circumstances in which infanticide had taken place.[49]

In the beginning of the eighteenth century, the magistrates did their best to consider the circumstances and the psychological suffering of the accused. When a corpse was discovered, the court requested an enquiry, a "visitation of a dead body" conducted by a surgeon in the ancien régime and by a local policeman later. After having retrieved a baby's corpse from the Vesdre river at Olne, the bailiff asked for a surgeon, who testified "to having examined on the 6th of February 1778 at the request of Mr. J. Lemoine, officer, the body of a newborn baby found in the water. After a careful inspection I certified that I have not found on the surface of the corpse, which seemed well formed, any trace of wound but on the contrary that the umbilical cord was cut off at eight or ten *travers de doigt* [width of a finger, more or less] from the stomach without any trace of binding and after having opened the chest I have found healthy lungs. I have thrown two pieces of them in the water and they have floated: it is the ordinary sign that the child had breathed before his death."[50] The *docimacie pulmonaire* (lung test) regularly was used to reveal whether the baby had been born alive: "A body thrown alive into water has the lung bloated; if on the contrary it has been thrown dead, the lung is flat. Man can also cut off a portion of the lung and throw it into water: if it floats, it is the clue that it contains

[47]Cour d'assises de Liège, B.33, February 2, 1820, AEL.

[48]Haute Cour de justice, cour de Flavion, register 45, fol. 193v, September 23, 1529, AEN.

[49]Gélis, pp. 420–21.

[50]Cour de justice, Olne, no. 133, 1778, AEL.

air and that the body was fallen alive in the water; if it sinks, it is proof that it was fallen dead."[51]

Infanticide came to be seen less as witchcraft than as an accident involving two victims—the baby and the mother. A more deliberate and circumspect view was behind the enquiry pursued in 1702 by the local court of justice of Sprimont. Marie Hanotte, a seventeen-year-old servant, was pregnant, and her masters were on the point of expelling her from the farm. Just before leaving Hanotte was overcome with labor pains. Alone and panic-stricken in the darkness of a barn, she gave birth to a child who seemed dead to her. She quickly carried him to a nearby fountain, where she buried the corpse. Unfortunately it was immediately discovered, and a lawyer took the matter in hand, determined to see her sentenced to death. But the court was more cautious and asked for an enquiry. Surgeons were requested to perform an autopsy. Their report was extremely precise, and the question of the viability of the baby was broadly discussed with references and quotations from Pierre Bayle, the famous physician who had written the *History of the Human Fetus* (Leiden, 1688). Circumstances of the drama, especially the young woman's psychological torment, were seriously taken into account. There was no question of putting Marie Hanotte to torture or of bringing a degrading interrogatory proceeding against her. The servant clearly appeared to be the victim of loneliness, hostile opinion, and social ostracism because of her pregnancy. Left alone in her destitution, she had wrapped the stillborn child in an old cloth and, before burying him, had taken care to baptize him with saliva, saying: "If you are alive and if it is good for you, I baptize you in the name of the Father, of the Son, and of the Holy Spirit." When she had laid the body in the improvised grave she again had thrown some water on the head, to be sure he was actually dead. Marie Hanotte was promptly discharged but the court could not refrain from reprimanding the public prosecutor: "Man is not allowed to presume a mother and moreover a Christian mother to be so unnatural as to attempt to try to destroy her fruit."[52]

Enlightened social reformers paid more and more attention to questions of abandonment, exposure, and infanticide. In Liège, Charles de Velbrück (prince-bishop of the principality from 1771 to 1784) strongly supported the founding of a general hospital to fight pauperism (but without success). Too often, he said, babies were thrown in the river or into the coalpits around Liège or even buried in dung heaps.[53]

At the end of the eighteenth century, infanticide was still equated with

[51]J. Lamborelle, *Style et manière de procéder en matière criminelle au Pays de Liège* (Herve, 1779), p. 15. On the lung test, see also Montfalcon (n. 14 above), p. 417.

[52]Cour de justice, Sprimont, no. 92, January 3 and March 9, 1702, AEL.

[53]Hélin, "Le sort des enfants trouvés au XVIIIe siècle," pp. 203–6.

parricide, that is, the most unnatural crime. In 1804 the *Gazette de Liège*, describing an infanticide, commented: "You must have seen the mother laying a parricidal hand on her fruit" to understand the real horror of such an unnatural gesture.[54] But authorities and social reformers were increasingly convinced that the roots of infanticides and of abandonments were to be found in poverty and loneliness. The provision of maternity hospitals was designed as a solution: in 1811 Napoléon Bonaparte signed a decree that required every department of the Empire to have a hospital specially equipped with a *tour* (turntable), "so that the mother or agent could place the child on one side, ring a bell, and have a nurse take the child by turning the table, the mother remaining unseen and unquestioned."[55] Later, questions arose about the efficacy of the turntable: Was the *tour* encouraging abandonments? No *tour* existed in the province of Liège, but some were maintained in the neighboring provinces of Namur and Hainaut. Edmont Ducpétiaux observed in 1843, however, that abandonments were less frequent in Liège than in the latter. M. Hennau, who thought that *tours* encouraged parents to be irresponsible, also explained the relative scarcity of abandonments and infanticides in the province of Liège by an attitude common in the countryside: the unmarried mother was not ostracized because, people assumed, sooner or later she would be married by the father of her bastard.[56]

In the beginning of the nineteenth century, two very different aspects of infanticide were recognized. In the first, the act occurred because of anguish of the soul: "If a young unfortunate girl, victim of a seducer more condemnable than she was, becomes pregnant without knowing her condition, and, suddenly caught by the pains of labor far from any help, she gives birth to the fruit of her weakness, panic-stricken by the fear of her dishonor and unaware of the needs of the soul she has just conceived, she can, in a wild moment of the senses and in a situation as oppressive as strange, leave her baby to perish by the lack of care of which nothing had taught her the necessity. By deploring her offense the moralist cannot refuse her his compassion." In the second, infanticide was the ultimate step of a deviation that began with sexual intercourse outside marriage. Killing the fruit of such

[54]*La Gazette de Liège,* 17 nivôse an 12 (January 8, 1804).

[55]Langer (n. 5 above), p. 358; Napoléon's decree of January 19, 1811, concerning abandoned children and poor orphans (*Pasinomie ou collection complète des lois, décrets, arrêtés en réglements généraux qui peuvent être invoqués en Belgique, de 1788 à 1832 inclusivement* [Brussels, 1837], pp. 271–73).

[56]Edmont Ducpétiaux, "Du sort des enfants trouvés et abandonnés en Belgique," *Bulletin de la Commission centrale de statistique,* vol. 1, Mémoires (Brussels, 1843), pp. 207–72; M. Hennau, "Recherches sur les causes de la criminalité dans la province de Liège," *Bulletin de la Commission centrale de statistique,* vol. 3, Mémoires (Brussels, 1847), pp. 183–208; see also Faider, "Rapport sur les causes de la criminalité en Belgique," *Bulletin de la Commission centrale de statistique,* vol. 4, Procès-verbaux (Brussels, 1851), p. 126.

intercourse was viewed by the guilty party as a means of erasing the offense and coming back to society. "General execration must join human justice to punish those miserable women who, fearing infamy, have premeditated in cold blood the murders of their children and have attempted to destroy in secret the fruit of their crimes by such a crime a hundred times more horrible."[57] In such cases, the jury of assizes was generally severe and sentenced the culprits to death. In the first instance, the jury was disposed to admit the innocence of the girl and to accept the repentance of a woman who recognized, through her fault, the grandeur of marriage, legitimate motherhood, and the family order.[58]

The absence of preparations to receive the child was the crucial clue of premeditated crime. In 1865, for instance, a twenty-one-year-old woman baptized her newborn baby, slit his throat, and hid the body under her pillow until the next morning. She was sentenced to death "because she had made no preparations for the delivery." In 1885 another young woman, "dressed as were the poor servants in the countryside," was condemned to five years' imprisonment not only because she had left her baby in a pigsty (thus exposed to being devoured by pigs) but above all because she had made no preparations for the delivery.[59]

The severity of the jury toward women who tried to escape justice and were sentenced for contumacy was proof of this attitude: lenience for the repentant women, severity for the women who refused to accept the social norm. In 1828 a servant of Jupille was condemned to death for contumacy: she killed her nine-month-old daughter "by throwing her into brambles in a deserted spot and by putting on her stomach a five- or six-pound stone."[60]

THE ELIMINATION OF CUMBERSOME BURDENS

Privies were frequently used for disposal of the victims of infanticide. Some guilty women refused to have any contact with the baby, who was regarded as merely something unclean: "The unborn child produced no picture, no projection, no fantasy about its existence after its birth or its presence in the life of its mother or in the future of a family. It remained in an ambiguous indeterminateness, a marginal state, whose dissolution in birth apparently aroused anxiety in many women confronting the reality of a child."[61] In 1857 a nineteen-year-old woman was sentenced to death for assassination. She confessed that, in agreement with her lover, she had

[57]Montfalcon (n. 14 above), p. 409.
[58]Schulte (n. 8 above), pp. 85–91; Lalou (n. 4 above), pp. 194–96.
[59]*La Meuse,* May 11, 1865; December 14, 1885.
[60]Cour d'assises de Liège, B.48, July 5, 1828, AEL.
[61]Schulte, p. 89; a case is given in Leboutte (n. 2 above), p. 174. On the frequency of those crimes see Montfalcon, p. 422.

strangled the child and had entrusted her young brother to throw the corpse in the privy.[62]

In the countryside, domestic animals such as dogs or pigs were often the executors of the crime. In 1863 a young woman of Orgeo rumored to have killed her child confessed "that she gave the baby to pigs, which devoured him." In 1885 a servant came back from the field with pigs: "She had difficulties with the male pig, which did not want to go into its cell. She followed the animal through the pigsty and suddenly heard the wails of a child hidden in the swill." Fending off the nervous pig with one hand, with the other she lifted the baby out of the garbage. It was clear enough that "everything was arranged to have the child devoured by leaving him to such a ferocious and ravenous beast coming back from the field starving." At this time the mother rushed into the pigsty and cried that the child "was just a small pig." She grabbed and threw him once again into the garbage, picked up a stone, and threatened to smash the servant "if she continued to pretend it was a baby and not a pig." Horrified, the servant ran out of the pigsty to find help. In the meantime the mother smashed the baby's head. Despite such a horrible crime, she was condemned to only five years' imprisonment. The next year a similar story took place at Nîmes in France. A woman put her bastard "into the pigs' trough of her neighbor, and this shrew had the evil courage to wait until the foul beast devoured the child."[63]

Just after delivery, some women simply drowned their babies in a bucket of water or in a cesspool, without according any consideration to the victim, who appeared to be just excrement.[64]

Professional training was sometimes very useful in executing a child with all possible efficiency. In 1859 a twenty-one-year-old servant was sentenced to death because she had smashed the skull of her child with a clog, in just the same way a man knocked out a rabbit. Another one severed the neck of her baby in the same way a professional cook decapitated a goose. In 1909 a twenty-one-year-old scullery maid of Liège let the blood from her baby just as if he were a chicken: "The depraved mother introduced a knife into the mouth of the child and cut off the tongue and the lower jaw exactly as a housewife does to slaughter the poultry."[65]

Less frequently, poison was used to eliminate the baby. In 1817 a twenty-six-year-old servant of Jauche was accused of killing her nine-month-old child. The baby was fostered by a widow in Lincent. One day the mother

[62]Cour d'assises de Liège, B.81, June 11, 1857, AEL; *La Meuse,* May 25 and June 12, 1857.

[63]*La Meuse,* July 27, 1863, and December 14, 1885; *Echo de Namur* (Nîmes), September 18, 1886.

[64]*La Meuse,* January 20, 1863; *La Gazette de Liège,* January 18, 1877.

[65]*La Meuse,* November 17, 1859, and May 11, 1865; *L'Express,* May 28, 1909.

visited them and told the widow that "for many days she had dreamed that her child was dead and that she deliberately went to Lincent in order to see how the baby was." The mother insisted on feeding the child herself and then left. Later the child began to vomit and finally died during the night. The mother was acquitted, however.[66]

PSYCHOLOGICAL SUFFERING

As historians have often observed about witches' trials, avowals made under torture cast light less on a presumed unnatural action than on the social perception—on the actual norm and on the perception of what must be regarded as a psychological drama. Poor women were caught in the cogs of a society that repressed sexuality outside marriage. The assaults of that society and its justice were so strong that it was impossible to escape from recognition of guilt. In 1544 a young servant, who was seriously ill after a painful clandestine delivery, vigorously denied having been pregnant and refused to give the name of the father of the baby she was supposed to have killed. The court waited until she recovered her health so that she could be subjected to repeated episodes of torture. Half dead, she admitted that she had suffocated the child and had intended to leave the body to the voracity of a dog.[67]

When the accused arrived at court with the expectation of torment, she had already endured months of endless stress and fear. Moreover, she was confronted—young, poor, and illiterate—with the pomp of the court and the higher classes of society, the establishment. We should not forget what had happened prior to her arrest. Since the discovery of her pregnancy, the young woman was watched with obsessive suspicion by her neighbors, excluded from the community, often jobless. In the closed little world of the village, the farm, or the master's house, how difficult it was to keep anything hidden. Everyone moved under the inquisitorial gaze of everyone else. Servants usually shared the same room, even the same bed. In 1670 an enquiry of the court of Namur underlined the obsessive watching of the neighborhood. A woman reported that Jacqueline Dinon "has hidden her pregnancy as much as she could" until "the woman her neighbor" told her she must make an official declaration of pregnancy. Another witness heard that Dinon "has made herself bleed from the foot in the water"—in other words, she was bled by a surgeon. During her delivery Dinon "would not allow the midwife to approach." According to the matron, Dinon was "a poor girl of a miller," forced, after the death of her father, to go to work as a

---

[66]Cour d'assises de Liège, B.26, February 4, 1817, AEL.

[67]Haute Cour de justice, Cour de Waret-la-Chaussée, register 51, fol. 191r (January 2, 1544), fols. 204v–205r (January 31, 1544), AEN. She was sentenced to be burned.

families.

humble servant. Dinon had told the midwife that "a physician had given her some drugs during her pregnancy and had thrown blood from her foot in the water." People also told the midwife that Dinon had met a domestic servant of the Augustine convent at Bouvignes in order to "receive consecrated charcoal, being true that Jacqueline had always hidden her stomach until one month or so before her delivery." Dinon had asked for charcoal, explained another witness, to cure "a rib pain." The social pressure became so strong that Dinon's stepmother was no longer able to refrain from saying "that her girl was wrongly charged and, the evil tongues notwithstanding, that it was clear enough that Jacqueline was really pregnant."[68]

In 1687 the janitor and the servants of the abbey of Malonne in Namur suspected Martine Gillain of hiding her pregnancy. One morning, a young woman who shared a bed with Gillain found the corpse of a newborn baby under the straw mattress. "He was born like this," said Gillain, but everyone thought that "she could well have suffocated her child in her filth." Fortunately the surgeon agreed with Gillain's version. We do not know the verdict of the court. But, as we can see, the argument of having given birth to a stillborn child ultimately was the one adopted to escape the sentence of death.[69]

THE BURDEN OF RUMOR

Most cases of infanticide came to light because of rumor. A majority of the records begin with the words, "It was rumored that . . ." Statements such as "The clamor did not take long to point out Marie-Louis to be the unnatural and barbarous mother of the newborn baby" or "The police squad of Fraiture heard rumors that Marie-Catherine was recently delivered and that her baby vanished" are extracts from only two of a dozen similar reports that can be given.[70] Rumors were the mainstream of information in the world of the village; the following story of a servant of Lierneux in 1858 is the archetype of infanticide in rural areas. "She took the greatest care to conceal her pregnancy and denied the fact with the strongest insistence in front of people who murmured about her condition. The rumor quickly accused her of having been secretly in labor and having slaughtered the child. The justice got wind of it and ordered an enquiry." The young woman, "whose garment pointed her out as a peasant," admitted at court that "she went to her room and without any help gave birth to a baby who

[68]Enquêtes judiciaires du Conseil de Namur, no. 6479, September 30, 1670, AEN.

[69]Jean Hockay, *Vivre à Malonne (1680–1706)* (Namur, 1990), pp. 104–5. Another example from France appears in Guy Citerne, "Un procès d'infanticide au XVIIIe siècle: Justice et vie quotidienne à la veille de la Révolution," *Revue B.T. 2* 181 (December 1985): 1–10.

[70]Cour d'assises de Liège, B.36, December 1, 1821, AEL; *La Meuse,* April 10 and May 13, 1889.

seemed to her not to be able to breathe; she put him under her mattress." According to the autopsy, however, the child actually died by suffocation. Moreover, "the midwife of the village explained that, confessing her fault [her pregnancy], the young woman had offered her one hundred francs for an abortifacient drug." The jury passed sentence of six months' imprisonment on the culprit.[71]

In 1804, a twenty-four-year-old spinner, married to a day laborer, was charged by her neighbor. This suspicious man had found a trail of blood from the woman's door to a pool. Puzzled, he rushed into the woman's house and found her "sitting round the fire with her naked bloodstained legs" while her mother was cleaning the room. Surprised by such a visit, the woman explained that "her blood pouring out might be due to another reason," in other words, from abundant menstruation and not from delivery. But the busy neighbor ran to the police, who requested that the young woman come to the courthouse. Accompanied by her father, she brought "in her petticoat" the corpse of her baby, covered with scratches and dust. The lung test revealed that the baby had been born alive. At the court, the girl explained that the baby died just after delivery, "the scratches observed on the back of the corpse could have been made by pins in her mother's apron or shawl" in which the body was wrapped, and "the dust that covered the corpse could have been blown into the house by the wind, because she lives in a thatched cottage made with turf in which the dust flies as on the fields." And to prove her maternal feeling, she "introduced to the court her eldest child, who, as reported by witnesses, she brought up with motherly love." She was discharged by the court.[72]

Infanticide followed an interminable psychological trial imposed by society, which could not admit motherhood outside marriage. Rumor played the role of public prosecutor in such a way that sometimes the rumor itself was the actual instigator of the crime—to silence the talk, the accused tried to eliminate her child.

Nothing escaped the inquisitorial glance of the community. In 1810 a forty-one-year-old widow named Anscelot was suspected by her neighbors of being pregnant once again as a result of "her licentious life." Alerted by the rumor, the mayor and the priest seriously reproached her, but she replied that she led her life as she pleased, and if she prostituted herself it was because she "had no other means of subsistence for her and her children. Her attitude offered offense to nobody and if she was pregnant—of which she absolutely was not convinced—she would make the best use of her fruit." Her way of life, however, stirred the inquisitiveness of the neighbors. One of them "noted that, not long before her stoutness vanished, she

[71]*La Meuse,* November 1, 1858.

[72]Cour d'assises de Liège, B.6, 15 nivôse an 12 (January 4, 1804), AEL; *Gazette de Liège,* 17 nivôse an 12 (January 6, 1804), no. 107.

went out less frequently. On one occasion, having scrutinized her, it seemed to the witness that without any doubt she was actually pregnant." A few days after Easter, "the rumor broadly diffused in the community reported that the accused had been delivered. In fact at this time one of her neighbors going to work in the field observed that the Anscelot widow had some spots of blood on her skirts and that her stomach did not at all present the same size as before." Interrogated once again, Anscelot said that she had not been pregnant for five years and that her stoutness might only be the result of a retention of menstruation for six or seven months. The affair progressed no further until July, when children playing near an old limekiln found the corpse of a baby. The rumor revived but the widow, who was confronted with the corpse, continued to deny it. Finally she was acquitted.[73]

Maternal feeling was often present even in such a horrible crime as infanticide. It was expressed by the care of the mother who baptized the child before killing him. In 1884 a twenty-four-year-old servant, "destitute and left alone by her lover," drowned her twenty-one-day-old baby in the canal, "thinking [to herself] that he might be an angel in Paradise." The jury of assizes, however, passed sentence of ten years' imprisonment on her.[74] Psychological suffering at the time of delivery was more and more taken into account by juries, who acquitted or sentenced the culprits to a rather lenient penalty for "unplanned homicide through lack of foresight or caution."[75]

ESCAPE FROM SOCIETAL CONDEMNATION

Retention of menstruation and sudden abundant flow of blood or diarrhea were frequently cited as the reasons for what seemed to be a delivery. In 1819 a woman persecuted by her neighbors replied that "they believed her to be pregnant, but that she suffered only from a retention of menstruation. One would sooner or later see that she had been troubled without any reason." Another day when she was at the house of Pantij, a widow, she spoke about taking a certain drug:

> "You do not need any medicine, do you?" replied the widow. "You cannot ignore in which situation you are?"
> "I am not pregnant! And even if I had all the straw of the community, I could not close all the mouths!"

A few days later the woman gave birth in the barn of the farm. Her mistress "saw some blood falling drop by drop through the ceiling to the kitchen

[73]Tribunal, cour criminelle, no. 18, October 26, 1810, AEN.
[74]*La Meuse,* June 10, 1885.
[75]Cour d'assises de Liège, B.86, November 14, 1866, AEL; *La Meuse,* August 9, 1866; November 9 and 14, 1866.

floor." The mistress rushed up into the barn and found the servant, who answered "by guffawing that she was very happy because she had recovered her menstruation." The next morning she went away from the farm, "declaring her usual happiness." She was condemned to death for contumacy.[76]

The fear of being dismissed because of pregnancy was often the origin of the crime, as in the case of a servant of Henri-Chapelle, who three times had been dismissed because of motherhood and who had smashed her last newborn in order not to be expelled once again.[77] To avoid any suspicion a woman had to perform her job regularly and with as much zeal as possible. In 1863 a farmer could hardly believe that her servant had been pregnant—she was "so hardworking and so devoted."[78] In 1866 another servant suspected by her mother and her brother of being pregnant found in her master a strong support, in that she had done her job "in a way absolutely usual." When she delivered during the night, she simply invoked abundant menstruation and nasal hemorrhage to explain the fact that the bed and the floor were stained with blood.[79]

In 1885 Joséphine, a twenty-two-year-old housemaid of Aywaille, was finally acquitted. For six months she had complained of bowel pains. The doctors she had visited did not notice she was pregnant, and she continued to ignore her condition until delivery, when the child died of hemorrhage.[80]

To be forced to conceal pregnancy could be so disturbing that some women went so far as even denying prior motherhood. In 1882 a woman, who was already the mother of a bastard, was selling milk in a street of Jupille when the pedestrians "saw something slipping out and falling down on the paving stone, a thing the woman had tried to retain. They heard the cry of a baby. The woman picked him up and packed him in her smock. Although everybody rushed for help, she went away, leaving after her a trail of blood on the road." A few minutes later a strangled body was found in the bushes, but "the woman did not stop denying having killed her child, and she always pretended she could not at all remember any details of the story or even having been pregnant."[81]

Psychological distress was frequently mentioned at the court: "I was totally beside myself," said a twenty-four-year-old servant who had strangled her newborn baby. She was condemned to two years' imprisonment for

---

[76]Cour d'assises, arrêts, March 20, 1819, AEN.

[77]Cour d'assises de Liège, B.84, March 17, 1863, AEL; *La Meuse,* March 18, 1863.

[78]Cour d'assises de Liège, B.84, August 17, 1863, AEL; *La Meuse,* August 18, 1863.

[79]Cour d'assises de Liège, B.86, November 14, 1866, AEL; *La Meuse,* September 8, 1866; November 9 and 14, 1866.

[80]*La Meuse,* January 12, 1885.

[81]*La Meuse,* July 5 and 27, 1882.

homicide through neglect. Another young woman confessed in 1884 "that she was panic-stricken, beside herself, when she went out at night to the garden where the delivery took place. She had prepared nothing because, she thought, it was not yet the moment." In 1860 a nineteen-year-old woman, accused by rumor of having hidden her pregnancy and slaughtering the baby, admitted to cutting off the baby's head with "a slender knife," being under the power of "a bout of hot fever." She was acquitted.[82]

AMBIGUOUS SOLICITUDE

As we have already seen, society was busier spying on and denouncing these impoverished mothers than assisting them. Hypocrisy was patent and sometimes verged on inhumanity. In 1803 a spinner gave birth to a still-born child: "After having desperately asked for help, she went out and buried the body in the churchyard of the village." In November 1859 a servant of Battice was expelled just at the time of her delivery. All day long she roamed from one place to another, "but everywhere she was pushed away." At night she arrived at a farm where she had formerly worked. She cried and asked for assistance, but no one took care of her. "The unfortunate young woman huddled in the hedge of the garden to spend the night, despite the cold. A few hours later the inhabitants heard some moans. They went out and found the poor woman half dead from cold and holding in her arms a newborn baby."[83]

The story of Elisabeth, a dressmaker in Verviers, was even more pathetic. In February 1813 Elisabeth went to a midwife who had helped her with a delivery six years earlier. But the matron refused to welcome Elisabeth, arguing that at seventy-nine she was too old. Elisabeth asked to be allowed to stay in the attic, but the midwife refused her. She went to the midwife's daughter, who also refused to help her. She knocked at the next door "to ask to be allowed to be in labor in the stable," but the woman wanted to hear nothing of it because she was afraid "of being scolded by her husband." Elisabeth wandered through the streets, where someone saw her entering a cul-de-sac "strongly biting her lips" from suffering, but he did nothing to assist the poor woman. Two hours later two women saw Elisabeth going away with her bloodstained coat. Finally she was put up by a widow, who gave her coffee and allowed her to sit down in front of the stove. Exhausted, Elisabeth said that she had very abundant menstruation. In the meantime the police heard the rumor and rushed into the room. Elisabeth was forced

[82]*La Meuse,* August 17 and 18, 1863, and July 26, 1884; Cour d'assises de Liège, B.83, August 7, 1860, AEL; *La Meuse,* August 8, 1860.

[83]Cour d'assises de Liège, B.7, 19 thermidor an 13 (August 7, 1805), AEL; *La Meuse,* November 23, 1859.

to confess to giving birth to a child who seemed to her to be stillborn. The baby immediately was found alive on a pile of bricks in the cul-de-sac, although he died soon after. Elisabeth, who already had three children, eventually was acquitted.[84]

Neighbors spent their time spying, trying to catch a woman getting rid of suspect things or behaving unusually. In 1819 a servant of Cornesse "was seen emptying a bucket into a drain near the house and immediately afterward an afterbirth was found." The baby was found in the woods. The woman argued that he was stillborn, and she was acquitted.[85] A similar case occurred in Seraing in 1883, where the mother of an accused woman went out into the garden carrying a bucket and a spade. Later the young woman herself was seen carrying a bloodstained bucket. The neighbor was so inquisitive as to go secretly at night to the garden and dig out the dead body of a child.[86]

Such a "solicitude" sometimes created a criminal panic when a woman was caught giving birth clandestinely. For example, in 1861 a servant was in labor in a ditch. Hearing her moans, people rushed out but the woman escaped: "The witnesses saw the mother throwing the body over the hedge beside the path." She was sentenced for homicide through exposure of a child in a deserted spot.[87]

Women's Solidarity

If the neighborhood created rumors, the female network also mobilized itself to sustain women incriminated by rumor. In 1884 Marie Jeanne gave birth in Vottem to a bastard, who immediately died. The midwife, who arrived too late at the delivery, thought she detected evidence of strangulation on the corpse. Marie Jeanne at first was acquitted after having received strong support from the women in Vottem. "One could not do better than she did, declared one of them. She went in rags to leave to her son decent garments." When Marie Jeanne left the court free of charges, the audience, "nearly exclusively composed of women from Vottem," met her with prolonged applause and "the women escorted the encaged coach up to the prison, where Marie Jeanne had to sign the prison register, and they gave her a clamorous ovation at the exit and offered her a bunch of flowers." A few months later, however, Marie Jeanne was condemned to six months' imprisonment: "This young woman, who already was a mother, did not make any preparations to receive her newborn child; hence, she could not

[84]Cour d'assises de Liège, B.18, December 11, 1813, AEL.

[85]Cour d'assises de Liège, B.33, February 10, 1820, AEL; Fonds hollandais, Police, no. 808, September 23, 1819, AEL.

[86]*La Meuse,* November 9, 1883.

[87]Cour d'assises de Liège, B.83, December 6, 1861, AEL; *La Meuse,* June 6, 1861.

invoke her lack of skill. There was thus an offense on her part and she must be punished," concluded the judge.[88]

In 1883, in Mirwart, a twenty-year-old dressmaker was accused of strangling her newborn child with the complicity of a twenty-five-year-old woman. Both were finally acquitted after the authorities of Mirwart insisted upon the "impeccable behavior" of the dressmaker. "The judgment was welcomed by an ovation from the audience."[89]

THE FAMILY

Some crimes were perpetrated by parents or relatives, and young women found assistance among their kin. In 1542 the court of Brogne condemned Jehenne to be strangled and burned after the death of her child. But Jehenne's mother too was tortured because she knew that Jehenne was pregnant and also had intended to eliminate the baby. She was suspected of having hidden the corpse under her straw mattress, where it stayed for a week. Just before being executed Jehenne exonerated her mother, but the latter was nevertheless sentenced to be thrashed by birch, to have her cheeks branded, and to be banished from the land of Brogne.[90]

A few more examples may suffice. In 1859 an honorable bourgeois family of Indre-et-Loire (France) was pursued because the wife had burned the newborn child of her daughter, "in order that there was no improper alliance." A father suffocated in cold blood the child he had conceived with his daughter and burned the corpse in the bread oven.[91] Lovers also intervened to kill their offspring, but here we can no longer speak about infanticide but rather about murder or assassination of babies.[92]

But the fear of parental sanction was enough to breed morbid behavior reflecting psychological distress rather than some kind of depravity. In 1884, a young woman had been held in high regard by society because she perfectly took the place of her deceased mother in household activities. When the doctor informed her that she was pregnant, "she seemed in dismay, wept for a long time, and was particularly affected by the shame that she might cause to the family. Nevertheless she made some of the preparations required in such circumstances." Alone at home on a Sunday morning, she gave birth to a child after having vainly asked for help. "Being afraid of her father's arrival she hastened to hide the baby under the mattress of her bed. The day after she hid the corpse in the cellar." In 1863 a

[88]*Gazette de Liège,* November 2 and 7, 1884; January 9, 1885.

[89]*La Gazette de Liège,* February 20 and March 16, 1883.

[90]Haute Cour de justice de Namur, register 51, fols. 97r–v, 98, AEN.

[91]*La Meuse,* December 10, 1859; *La Meuse,* April 10 and May 13, 1889.

[92]Cour d'assises de Liège, B.83, August 8, 1860, AEL; *La Meuse,* August 9, 1860, and March 14, 1861.

twenty-three-year-old servant of Dison drowned her three-day-old child after having given it first aid: "I had wanted to protect my honor and that of the family. But now I was deeply repentant of my crime." Just before throwing the child in the river she baptized him. She was sentenced to two years' imprisonment for homicide through neglect.[93]

For the family, a baby was not always regarded as a person. A pig or a cow sometimes was seen as more valuable than a human life. In 1889, the jury of assizes of Rambouillet (France) condemned Pauline, who had left her newborn to die without any care. Her family, well-off farmers, had at first assisted at the delivery but quickly left their daughter alone. The head of the family justified his attitude by saying, "We had too many other troubles to spend very much time helping Pauline; at the same time, our cow calved."[94]

POSTNATAL FAMILY PLANNING

The infanticides mentioned above underline the ambiguity of the crime. Except for women condemned to death for contumacy, most of the culprits were acquitted or sentenced to a relatively lenient penalty because circumstances weighed in their favor.

Some cases allow us to see infanticide as a primitive kind of "postnatal family planning."[95] Some women were recidivists, such as Jeanne, a forty-year-old day laborer guillotined on the marketplace in Namur in 1822. She had given birth to twins at the maternity hospital of Liège. On the road to Jemeppe with her two babies, she visited a woman named Douha and told her: "It is peculiar. There is a proverb saying that 'a boy and a girl born together do not stay alive.' Would it be true? I was asked to place my boy to be fostered but I did not want to give him." On the road again the babies began to cry so loudly that some women told her to nurse them, but Jeanne refused and replied "that she had only one baby, that the other died at the hospital." One of the women opened the bundles and saw the twin: "You want thus to kill him, you scoundrel! since he is alive in your arms!" The matter did not go further and Jeanne went away. At eight o'clock in the evening, a coal miner passing by Kinon's coal shaft heard a child crying and saw Jeanne leaning over the hole. She said to him: "I shall take you into my confidence. I have just thrown a stone into the shaft to see whether it is deep enough to throw myself and my child in it." The miner took the woman back to the road and saw that at this moment she carried only one child. Arriving at her brother's house, she broke down and confessed to having

---

[93]*Gazette de Liège,* December 1, 1884; Cour d'assises, B.84, June 4, 1863, AEL; *La Meuse,* March 13 and June 5, 1863.

[94]*La Meuse,* August 2, 1889.

[95]Schulte (n. 8 above), p. 91.

killed one of the twins. The corpse was found later at the bottom of the shaft; an old handkerchief was tied tightly around the neck of the fifteen-day-old child. Testimony at the trial described another bastard born to Jeanne a few years earlier, who also had died in mysterious circumstances.[96]

In 1819 a thirty-six-year-old woman was guillotined because she had killed her three newborn children, one after another, at birth.[97] In 1848 a forty-three-year-old widow, denounced by rumors, admitted three infanticides. The corpse of the last child was dug up from the floor of the cellar and beside it the police found "the bones of another baby," while the corpse of the eldest one could not be found "because after having kept the body in her bedroom for three weeks it went rotten, and she had thrown the remnants into the manure where the bones were dissolved." The woman was nevertheless acquitted.[98] In 1889 a widow, who already had six legitimate children, and her lover were accused of having killed their four successive bastards in order to conceal their sexual intercourse. She was condemned to seven years' imprisonment and her accomplice to twenty.[99]

CONCLUSION

The study of infanticide casts light on the social and psychological milieu in which illicit motherhood took place. Until the early eighteenth century, infanticide was viewed as an unnatural crime, in conflict with the family and its reproductive role, which required an exemplary sentence: torture and death. Infanticide (along with parricide) was regarded as the most horrible of crimes against God and the holiness of family and motherhood. But beginning in sixteenth-century trials, we see some discomfort on the part of the judges, who recognized the ambiguity of such a crime and how difficult it was to distinguish between a natural misfortune and accident provoked by fear and destitution on the one hand and a deliberate act on the other. At the beginning of the eighteenth century, the magistrates did their best to take into account the circumstances and the psychological suffering of the accused. We have seen that this attitude encouraged the development of forensic medicine, through the use of the lung test to determine whether the baby had been born alive.

The Penal Code of 1810 and the studies of moralists and forensic pathologists indicate increasing awareness of both aspects of infanticide—the anguished response to psychological torment and the ultimate step in a deviation that began with sexual intercourse outside marriage—which led to consequent adjustment in the penalties imposed on the culprits. More

---

[96]Cour d'assises, arrêts, September 28, 1822, AEN.
[97]Cour d'assises de Liège, B.31, February 17, 1819, AEL.
[98]*L'Eclaireur: Journal de la province de Namur* (Namur), May 29, 1848.
[99]*La Meuse*, January 16, 1889.

lenient penalties or outright acquittal became more common in the former cases, whereas the death penalty was reserved for the latter, treated as premeditated murder.

As we have seen, society was busier spying on and denouncing destitute mothers than assisting them. The psychological effects of trying to conceal or deny a pregnancy, to avoid loss of job and criminal charge, must have been horrific. Combined with the "ambiguous solicitude" of neighbors and the power of rumor, these poor women were put under enormous strain. However, we have also seen a female network mobilize itself to sustain incriminated women.

Infanticide was a crime typical of rural areas in Belgium. As the cases above demonstrate, the accused generally were servants on farms, and they were poor, illiterate, and often abandoned or ostracized by society. Our analysis agrees with the study by Regina Schulte on infanticide in rural Bavaria in the nineteenth century in all points except one. In Bavaria, apparently, the problem of disgrace and loss of honor did not arise for women of the servant class, many of whom already had illegitimate children. In Belgium, it appears that the fear of losing honor was stronger and the social pressure also more unbearable.[100]

[100]Schulte, pp. 77–96.

Peasants against Nature: Crossing the Boundaries between Man and Animal in Seventeenth- and Eighteenth-Century Sweden

JONAS LILIEQUIST

Department of History
University of Umeå

IN THE HISTORY of human culture animals have been exploited and used in many ways for various purposes. Animals have been "good for eating" and "good for thinking," providing an endless resource for nourishment as well as for symbolic thinking and metaphor. In the course of their connection with human society, animals have been subjected to all kinds of treatment arising out of such human attributes as cruelty and compassion, aversion and affection—and, occasionally, human sexual needs and desires. Today little attention is paid to this latter phenomenon, but throughout history human-animal sexual relations have formed a recurrent theme in mythological and religious contexts, often of a sacral character such as in the rock carvings depicted in figures 1A and 1B.[1] In practice, however, the act of what is now called bestiality has often been the subject of intense taboo and prohibition.

In western Christian tradition, bestiality—together with homosexual relations, coitus interruptus, and various other sexual acts or positions—was labeled as "unnatural" and "a sin against nature." Nature referred to the hierarchical order of God's creation, where every living thing had its determined and appropriate position. Crossing the boundaries of creation, or using a member not intended for procreative purposes, was a direct injury to God. This concept of unnatural sex was incorporated into the medieval canon law and also gradually made its way into the secular legisla-

---

[1]Figures 1A and 1B are described in Ove Bruun Jørgensen, *Billeder og Myter fra Bronzealderen,* Jutland Archaeological Society Publications, vol. 20 (Aarhus, 1987), pp. 38, 25. Jørgensen argues that these motifs have a direct connection with the Baal myth of the Near East.

This essay originally appeared in the *Journal of the History of Sexuality* 1991, vol. 1, no. 3.

A   B

FIG. 1   Motifs of rock carvings from the Scandinavian Bronze Age (second millennium B.C.), Bohuslän, southwestern Sweden. A, Tanum parish, Hoghem. B, Tanum parish, Vitlycke. Fig. 1A is reprinted from Peter Gelling and Hilda Ellis Davidsson, *The Chariot of the Sun* (London, 1969), p. 66, by permission of the publisher, J. M. Dent & Sons. Fig. 1B is reprinted from Ove Bruun Jørgensen, *Billeder og Myter fra Bronzealderen,* Jutland Archaeological Society Publications, vol. 20 (Aarhus, 1987), by permission of the author and the publisher, Jysk Arkaeologisk Selskab.

tion in western Europe.[2] In Sweden bestiality first was made a capital crime in the provincial laws of the late thirteenth and fourteenth centuries and later in the National Law Codex of 1442.[3] But it was not until the beginning of the seventeenth century that trials for bestiality occurred frequently, and the peak of the prosecutions was not reached until the eighteenth century.

From the third decade of the seventeenth century through 1778, when the last person convicted of bestiality was beheaded and burned at the stake in Sweden, approximately six hundred to seven hundred persons, mostly male adolescents and young men, were executed, together with hundreds of cows and mares and a smaller number of sows, ewes, and bitches. An

[2]Vern L. Bullough and Bonnie Bullough, *Sin, Sickness and Sanity: A History of Sexual Attitudes* (New York, 1977), has a short but comprehensive survey of the history of this concept in chap. 3, "Unnatural Sex." A more inquiring discussion and analysis of the tradition from Aristotle to Aquinas from the more specific point of homosexual acts has been undertaken by John Boswell in his *Christianity, Social Tolerance, and Homosexuality* (Chicago, 1980). The early history of ecclesiastical and secular legislation is treated in Michael Goodich, *The Unmentionable Vice* (Oxford, 1979). Mosaic regulations against bestiality are found in Exod. 22:19, Lev. 18:23 and 20:15–16, and Deut. 27:21.

[3]Jan-Eric Almquist, *Tidelagsbrottet, en straffrätts-historisk studie* (Lund, 1939). This regulation was reinforced in the printed edition of 1608, by an appendix to the law containing direct quotations of the Mosaic regulations in the Bible. Until 1734 persons charged with bestiality were sentenced according to "the Law of God and Sweden."

TABLE 1   Prosecutions for Bestiality (B) and Homosexual Acts (H) Reported to the Royal Superior Courts in Sweden (not including Finland), 1635–1754

Period	Court	Trials* (B/H)	Charged/ Reputed Persons† (B/H)	Death Penalty (B/H)	Corporal Penalties/ Forced Labor (B/H)	Acquittals‡ (B/H)	Sentence Not Preserved (B/H)
1635–74	S	107/0	108	38	28	36	6
	G	64/0	64	24	4	24	12
1675–1714	S	256/1	267/2	100	65/2	96	6
	G	119/1	119/2	45/1	27/1	41	6
1715–54	S	523/3	527/5	112	214	122/4	79/1
	G	431/3	435/5	152/4	141	136/1	6
1635–1754	S+G	1,500/8	1,520/14	471/5	479/3	455/5	115/1

Sources.—(S) Executorial letters from the Royal Superior Court in Stockholm, Svea Hovrätt, to the county governors in the north and middle of Sweden, deposited in the Swedish Provincial Archives. Figures from three counties and the town of Stockholm are missing for the period. Major gaps: the county of Stockholm, 1665–84, 1715–37; the county of Uppsala, 1665–84. Total population in the jurisdictional area, 1749 (counties missing in the statistics not included): 492,000. (G) Resolutions in criminal cases by the Royal Superior Court in Jönköping, Göta Hovrätt, the Archive of the Superior Court, Jönköping. Major gap: 1676–80, 1682–92. Total population in the jurisdictional area (the south of Sweden), 1749: 1,041,000.

*Including defamation cases reported to the Superior Courts (less than 4 percent of the trials).

†The actual number of persons charged with and suspected of bestiality is 1,500 (1,486 males and 14 females), of which 20 males appeared a second time before the court as suspected recidivists or to make entirely new confessions.

‡Including conditional acquittals "absolutio ab instantia" and exemptions from punishment due to insanity or physical weakness.

even greater number of males were sentenced to flogging, church penalties, and public forced labor in chains. The rate of indictments per 100,000 of the population rose to a maximum of five or six in some provinces in the middle of the eighteenth century, and at the same time executions for bestiality accounted for 25–35 percent of all capital punishment.[4] Bestiality,

[4]Statistics based on resolutions from the Royal Superior Courts and executorial letters to the county governors, 1635–1754 (for exact figures, see table 1). The number of executions between 1755 and 1778 is based on compilations from population tables in the Archive of the Swedish Commission of Tables, published in Almquist. Some reservations must be made concerning the actual number of executions in table 1, as these figures are not based on confirmations of the executions. Some convicts could have escaped or died in jail before the day of execution. On the other hand, there is no reason to believe that any person convicted of bestiality received royal pardon without the passing of a resolution by the superior court. Personal appeals to the supreme justice of the king were not allowed in capital cases during the period, and any request for mitigation had to be initiated by the superior court, usually on strictly judicial grounds. The figures from the first period in the table instead may underestimate the actual frequency of executions. Although all charges of capital crimes brought before

together with infanticide, was ranked as a most serious problem by the authorities, in contrast to an almost total silence (and very few indictments) regarding homosexual acts. This intensive attention to and persecution of bestiality seems to have had few if any counterparts in early modern Europe.[5] How could this happen?

---

the local courts had to be reported to the superior court for a final resolution (which enables the historian to compile national statistics for the prosecutions of capital crimes), there were some exemptions made for bestiality and other crimes labeled as heinous. During most of the seventeenth century the county governors had the permission to arrange an immediate execution before reporting the case to the superior court when the perpetrator was caught in the act and there was full proof. It is probable that these executions were not always appropriately reported or approved of in a formal resolution afterward. A more detailed presentation of statistics and a discussion of the rather profound regional differences in the distribution of bestiality trials will appear in my forthcoming dissertation, entitled "'Den onda andans ingivelse': En historisk-antroplogisk studie av tidelagsbrottet i 1600 och 1700-talets Sverige" ("At the devil's instigation": The historical anthropology of bestiality in seventeenth- and eighteenth-century Sweden). In general, the rates of indictments per 100,000 of the population were higher in the north and the middle of Sweden than in the southern parts, as can be concluded from the table.

[5]So far there are few comparable studies. In his pioneering study "La sodomie à l'époque moderne en Suisse Romande" (*Annales* 29, no. 4 [1974]: 1023–33), William Monter found thirty-two trials for bestiality in the agrarian and Catholic canton of Fribourg during the period 1599–1648, and after that—none. Bestiality trials still occurred from time to time in other parts of Switzerland during the eighteenth century, but with nothing like the frequency found in the first half of the seventeenth century. No population figures are given, but it appears from the article that the population at least exceeded 25,000, indicating a maximum rate of 3.2 indictments per 100,000 of population, which is probably much too high. The impression of an earlier culmination and lower rates of indictments on the European continent is further strengthened by a French study of bestiality trials under the jurisdiction of the Parlement of Paris, including the northern two-thirds of France, except Brittany, Normandy, and Burgundy. In this region, containing a population of eight to ten million people, the number of trials culminated in the period 1600–1629, never exceeding a maximum of two or three per year (Alfred Soman, *Pathologie historique: Le témoignage des procès de bestialité aux XVIe–XVIIe siècles,* in *107e Congres national des Sociétés savants: Philologie et histoire jusq'ua 1614* [Paris, 1982], 1:149–61). These figures, however, only reflect the number of convictions, but they would still be very low if supplemented with the acquittals from lower courts. According to Alfred Soman, executions for bestiality never accounted for more than 1 percent of all executions in France (personal communication, February 1989). As for Denmark and the Netherlands, the pattern of prosecution seems to be the same with very few known cases (Denmark: only seventeen cases, 1619–1756, in the Provincial Court of Viborg; the Netherlands: ten cases, 1630–1805, in the provinces of Holland, Zeeland, and Brabant [personal communication with Dutch historian Florike Egmond, September 1988]). In England the Assize records show low frequencies in general for bestiality trials during the seventeenth century (Keith Thomas, *Man and the Natural World* [London, 1983], p. 119; see also James Sharpe's study of the county of Essex in his *Crime in Seventeenth-Century England* [Cambridge, 1983]). A study of eighteenth-century Somerset still shows very low frequencies (Polly Morris, "Defamation and Sexual Reputation in Somerset, 1733–1850" [Ph.D. diss., University of Warwick, 1985]). So far I have no figures from the German countries, but it seems that we

The symbiosis in the seventeenth century of an increasing state power and the church representing a religious orthodoxy based on the Mosaic law of the Old Testament forms a necessary condition but does not provide a satisfactory explanation. While several crimes labeled in the Bible as capital crimes were reduced in severity and later excepted from the Mosaic rule, legal praxis in cases of bestiality was still very harsh. Moreover, the remarkably high frequency of charges can only be attributable in part to more efficient law enforcement and policing of village life. Without the active cooperation of the local village population there would not have been many prosecutions. Bestiality seems not to have been tolerated, except perhaps among groups of very young boys, and there was no double standard protecting males from this kind of charge. On the contrary, the trial records reveal a strong watchfulness and suspicion of male activities in cowsheds and pastures. What, then, contributed to making bestiality such a sensitive matter in early modern Sweden?

I shall argue that part of the explanation can be found in the underlying cultural meaning of bestiality as a transgressional act—transgression of the culturally constructed boundaries between man and animal, between male and female, between men and boys. According to a number of cultural anthropologists, a concern for boundaries and ambiguous marginal situations is universal to human culture, serving as the basis for moral order and for structuring and perception of social reality. Obvious transgressions and composite phenomena are causes for anxiety and repulsion, or possibly could be assigned (or be signs of) sacral power, but they would hardly be met with indifference.[6] It is the aim of this article to reveal some of these aspects of bestiality underlying the harsh penalties and high frequency of charges.

First I shall deal very briefly with an example of changing symbolic meaning at the level of myth and folklore. I shall continue with the consequences of ambiguity in crossing the boundaries between man and animal, and finally I shall discuss male ambivalence and the threat to masculinity. The source material consists mainly of about seven hundred trial records concerning bestiality from the whole of Sweden during the period from 1630 to 1760. Throughout the text, I use the term "buggery" as synonymous with bestiality.

---

must turn to the Mediterranean area and the Spanish Inquisition before we can count bestiality trials in hundreds and thousands again; however, they are exceeded in numbers by trials for homosexual acts. See n. 102 below.

[6]The most well known and debated contributions to this approach have been made by Mary Douglas, *Purity and Danger: An Analysis of the Concepts of Pollution and Taboo* (London, 1966); and Edmund Leach, "Anthropological Aspects of Language: Animal Categories and Verbal Abuse," in *New Directions in the Study of Language*, ed. E. H. Leenberg (Cambridge, 1964).

CHANGING SYMBOLIC MEANINGS IN MYTH AND FOLKLORE

In the seventeenth century, the rock carvings from the Bronze Age would probably have been interpreted as nothing other than the devil's work. In the concept of nature as reflecting God's order of creation, every action or phenomenon implying a transformation or mixing of categories was against nature and thus potentially evil. But in the sixteenth century it was still possible for learned members of the elite culture to retell old folkloristic and mythical themes of animal descent and mixed marriages between humans and animals with respect for their original meaning. The Swedish Catholic priest Olaus Magnus, in his extensive work on the history of the Scandinavian people (published in Italy in 1555), wrote about a connection between a Swedish farmer's daughter and a bear. The young virgin was abducted by the bear when she was out playing, but the cruelty and hunger of the wild abductor was overcome by the prisoner's beauty and, instead of eating her, the bear fell in love with her. After some time the bear was killed by hunters, and the girl gave birth to a son with human appearance and the fierceness of a bear. The son took revenge on the hunters and later became the progenitor of a Danish royal family.[7]

This story was first told by Saxo Grammaticus in his *Gesta Danorum,* dating back to the late twelfth century. But the motif is much older than that, appearing, for example, in English historical sources of the early Middle Ages, which mentioned Sivard the Strong as being descended from a bear (Sivard's father has bear ears on account of his origin).[8] In the sixteenth century, Olaus Magnus told the story with a certain ambivalence. In the margin he noted, "Nature's work, to be admired rather than despised." And a picture showed the bear and the girl facing each other at some distance, decorously holding hands. This contrasted with a more erotic contemporary illustration of the Saxo motif, made on a German backgammon board as a wooden relief of a bear embracing a nude girl.[9] But later in the seventeenth century, the unnatural was emphasized at the expense of the mythological meaning, and in 1730 the story of the bear-wife ended up as an example under the heading "De coitu sodomitico" in a historical-medical treatise.[10]

---

[7] Olaus Magnus, *De nordiska folkens historia,* trans. John Granlund (Stockholm, 1976), bk. 18, chap. 30.

[8] C. M. Edsman, "The Story of the Bear Wife," *Ethnos,* nos. 1–2 (1956), pp. 36–56. Saxo tells the story in chap. 15 of the tenth book in his *Gesta Danorum,* translated into Danish by Jørgen Olrik, *Sakses Danesaga* (Copenhagen, 1908–12).

[9] N. L. Rasmusson, "En Saxoillustratin från 1537," *Nordisk numismatisk unions medlemsblad* (January 1949), pp. 1–4.

[10] Martin Shurig, *Gynaecologia historico-medica, congressus muliebris consideratio physico-medico-forensis qua utriusque sexus, salacitas et casitas deinde coitus ipse ejusque voluptas* (Dresden,

The fate of the early Saxo motif reflects the growing influence and dominance of Christian and theological distinctions between natural and unnatural. The old themes were not only deprived of their original meanings but were also, under the influence of the same theological doctrines, replaced by a new kind of mythical theme in which transformations and interminglings between humans and animals acquired an extremely and unambiguously negative meaning; the chapter on sodomy was followed by one entitled "De coitu cum Daemone." In learned demonology, the devil could have "carnal knowledge" of humans, appearing as a beautiful woman (succubus) or an attractive man (incubus), but also appearing in the shape of an animal. The latter was most frequently found in the stereotype of the witches' sabbath. In the great witch trials of 1668–76 in the central and northern parts of Sweden, the devil often appeared as a black dog, sitting under a table, and the witches were said to go under the same table to copulate with him, sometimes after fighting each other over who should be first. One twenty-nine-year-old man witnessed that after the frequently arranged weddings, the bride lay down upon a black goat who was lying on his back and had sexual intercourse with him. The children attending the witches' sabbath also got married—the boys to cats, bitches, heifers, and sows, and the girls to dogs, oxen, and boars, with resulting short-term conceptions and offspring. Often these animals appeared as humans in the beginning.[11]

There is a fundamental difference between human relations with bears, representing wild, untamed, and distant nature, and human relations with cows, mares, goats, and dogs, belonging to nature but at the same time remaining part of human culture. As social categories, farm and domestic animals are closer to humans—and hence the human-animal boundaries are more fragile and easier to cross.[12] In this respect both the repertoire of the witches' sabbath and its list of participants reflected the more ambiguous human-animal relations of ordinary life in early modern agrarian society where humans and animals lived close to each other and farm and domestic animals outnumbered humans. But in this black drama, consist-

---

1730). In fact Saxo already uses the story of animal descent to discredit Ulf Jarl, the father of the Danish king Sven Estridsson. Ulf Jarl once betrayed the Danes by deceiving the king's sister into marriage with him instead of organizing the attack and defense against the Swedes. In this respect he was taking after his animal great-grandfather, the lecherous bear, according to Saxo. Olaus Magnus naturally leaves out "this passage" and, paradoxically, restores some of the mythical meaning in his nationalistic interpretation.

[11]Records of the Commission of Witchcraft 1668 (Orsa), 1674 (Nora, Torsåker), 1675 (Boteå, Nordingrå), in transcription, in the Collected Papers of Emanuel Linderholm, University Library of Uppsala.

[12]This is Leach's basic point in his "Animal Categories and Verbal Abuse," asserting a correspondence between the degrees of taboo or sacredness in our relations to animals and the relative social distance of animals from a postulated Self.

ing of an amalgamation of learned doctrines and popular notions, sexual transgressions of human-animal boundaries were subordinated to a third, demonic, element. The act of bestiality was either the devil's work or the illusory appearance of an intimate relation with the devil himself. This was as far as possible from the stories of prestigious animal descent.

AMBIGUITY: POPULAR ATTITUDES AND LEARNED DOCTRINES

The trials for bestiality were contemporary with the witch trials, but not as dramatic and concentrated in time, reaching their culmination nearly a hundred years later. Far more people were executed for bestiality in Sweden than for witchcraft. At the witches' sabbath, children and ordinary farm and domestic animals were the passive victims of the devil's manipulations and illusions. In reality farm and domestic animals could be the passive victims of human, primarily male, sexuality.

Popular attitudes toward bestiality can be studied in the reactions of witnesses and the treatment of a suspected and disreputable person. The spontaneous reactions as reported in the trial records were, first of all, those of astonishment and horror. Many witnesses were so shocked and frightened at the sudden and unexpected sight of a bugger in action that they experienced a temporary loss of speech and mobility, preventing them from making any immediate attempt to interrupt the act. Complaining about her unfortunate confrontation, one woman told the court that she had fainted three times before she could even get away.[13] Fainting was not the only physical sign of great emotional stress; one maid, surprising her male colleague in action, moaned and cried bitterly the whole day and night. During the night she fell ill, and the next morning she screamed out her anxiety.[14] Such strong and long-lasting emotional reactions were not an exclusively female matter. One master found his male servant in front of the cowshed, trembling like a leaf, sighing and groaning for a long while before he could mention what he had witnessed.[15] A soldier reported that none of his horrible experiences in the battlefield had caused him such heartache and remorse as the sight of this act being committed before his eyes.[16]

The sudden unexpectedness intensified the reactions of the witnesses, and a too close and immediate confrontation with the perpetrator could also contribute to the fear, especially if the witness was alone and female or very young and the bugger was a strong adult male. In such situations some

[13]Court record, Uppsala län; Lagunda 22/10, Uppsala Provincial Archives (hereafter ULA).

[14]Court record, Jönköpings län; Tveta 13/2 1739, Vadstena Provincial Archives (hereafter VLA).

[15]Court record, Västmanlands län; Sala rådstuga 20/1 1733, ULA.

[16]Court record, Kopparberg; Stora Tuna 14/5 1720, ULA.

witnesses did not even dare to reveal their presence for fear of the perpetrator resorting to desperate violence. But irrespective of whether the witness was seen or not, there was one further fear that originated not so much from the specific character of bestiality as from the situation of the witness, especially the solitary witness. If not revealed, the mere viewing of an act of deadly sin such as bestiality implicated the witness morally and made him or her subject to God's condemnation. In a way the act can be said to have been contagious; the bugger not only endangered his own soul but also, through exposure to his action, violated and injured the soul of any eyewitness. This was even more true for witnesses who were alone. Without the accused's confession, a solitary witness's testimony before the court was not sufficient for conviction, and things could turn the other way around, putting the witness into the dock on charges of false testimony. Therefore, witnesses often talked about their unexpected encounter as an unfortunate moment and a personal misfortune.

Surprise, fear of a violent confrontation, and fear of God's wrath were all general ingredients in the spontaneous reactions of astonished horror. A more specific source of the faintings and tremblings was the powerful association with the devil. Bestiality officially was called deviltry and a devil's deed, and a feeling of satanic presence is obvious in many of the witnesses' immediate comments: "Watch out for the devil"; "The devil has taken you"; "You are doing like a hell's fire." When a young maid caught a herdsboy red-handed behind a cow, she lifted up her hand, made the sign of the cross with her fingers, and exclaimed: "God help you, you have let the devil betray you."[17]

Sometimes the devil in human or animal shape showed himself to the witness, and there were stories about the devil appearing to young boys and men, tempting them and forcing them to commit bestiality. But there seems not to have been any connection between the commitment of bestiality and becoming a witch, such as has been documented from the legal records on the European continent.[18] On the other hand, crossing the boundaries between man and animal was something characteristic and in-

[17]Court record, Västernorrlands län; Ångermanland, Nordingrå 13/11 1727, Härnösand Provincial Archives (hereafter HLA).

[18]Monter (n. 5 above) has found a strong association between witchcraft and bestiality in early modern Switzerland. According to a recurrent theme in the confessions made by male defendants, the devil had taken advantage of a committed act of bestiality to persuade the perpetrator to do homage and thus recruit him as a witch. The confessed act of bestiality confirmed the alleged witch status of the charged person and vice versa. This was never the case in Sweden. In contrast, the physical appearance of the devil in connection with bestiality was most often introduced by the defendants in direct confrontation with the aim and interest of the often skeptical judges and authorities. This popular use of the devil, which I have called "demonization from below," and its connections with popular notions of sin and sexuality will be discussed in detail in my dissertation (forthcoming).

herent in the devil's nature, and in this sense the bugger could be equated with or sometimes even mistaken for the devil. A young woman testified that she had unexpectedly seen "an evil one" behind a cow and became very frightened, not knowing if it was a human being or not.[19] While such confusions could be experienced in daily life, there is no hint of any inverse correspondence to the witches' sabbath, in the sense that the devil would partake in the act as the female animal partner.

Far more frequent, and perhaps also more significant, was the likening of the bugger to a brute beast. In itself the position of coitus degraded the perpetrator to a bestial level: "he moved his rump like a dog on a bitch," "he was hanging on the back of the mare, copulating like a dog and a brute beast."[20] One witness claimed that he had heard the bugger neighing like a horse while penetrating the mare.[21]

In popular expressions, the bugger was said to have taken over the duties of a goat or the office of a bull, and it was said about one suspected bugger that "he had no need of any billy goats, he could make kids himself."[22] In addition the physical appearance of the bugger would sometimes be described as dehumanized: "eyes wide open with the whites turned up, an awful and horrible look, the face flushed and sweaty, the lips all red."[23]

This aspect of brutalization and human degradation was of central importance in the reactions of the authorities. In accordance with the learned concept of God's order of creation as reflected in nature and spelled out in the Bible, the court remonstrated with and reproached the bugger convicted of this unchristian and unnatural behavior. Reason and soul distinguished man from the brute animals, but in sexual functions and other basic needs and instincts, where similarities were great, the boundary was fragile and easily transgressed in practice. Although reason and natural law invoked aversion to and horror of such mixing of categories as happened in bestiality, this taboo was not a sufficient barrier.[24] "Left to themselves," wrote one Swedish bishop and poet, "humans live like animals and brute beasts."[25] Christian morality was necessary to curb the human will in accordance with reason and human nature. The Swedish translator of Erasmus's moral textbook, *De civitate morum puerilium*, wrote

[19]Court record, Värmlands län; Philipstads rådstuga 22/10 1663, Archive of the Superior Court Göta Hovrätt, Jönköping (hereafter GHA), Criminalia EVAA, 42.

[20]Court records, Uppsala län, Trögd 30/6 1686, ULA; Elfsborgs län, Väne 22/11 1723, Gothenburg Provincial Archives (hereafter GLA).

[21]Resolution of the Superior Court Göta Hovrätt 20/11 1706, GHA BIIA, 16.

[22]Court records, Kopparbergs län, Vika 1/10 1729, Västmanlands län, Åkerbo 1/8 1711, ULA, Jönköpings län, Norra Vedbo 26/9 1682.

[23]Court record, Elfsborgs län; Väne 22/11 1723, GLA.

[24]For example, the comments by the court in Hallands län, Wilske 14/7 1724, Lund Provincial Archives (hereafter LLA); Västmanlands län, Torstuna 29/10 1735, ULA.

[25]Haquin Spegel, quoted in Bernt Olsson, *Spegels Guds Werk och hwila* (Stockholm, 1963), p. 242.

in a foreword in 1620 that persons without interest in acquiring knowledge of virtue, wisdom, and good manners could not be considered human
beings, or at least could not claim human dignity, "but are even cruder and
more despicable than the animals which showed no other interest than in
food and carnal lust."[26] This pessimistic view of man and the fragile boundaries between mankind and beast was a recurrent theme in theological and
moralistic writings of the seventeenth century, as well as in the measures
taken by the Swedish authorities against the spreading of the "abominable
sin and crime of bestiality."

Defilement and Mixing of Categories

The mixing of categories and the comparison of the bugger with a brute
animal connoted a deeper cultural meaning, reflecting both popular attitudes and learned doctrines. First of all, if reason distinguished man from
animal in God's order of creation, then bestiality was an act against reason.
In the trial records bestiality was occasionally referred to as "foolishness,"
and the bugger could sometimes be reproached for showing less reason in
his actions than the reluctant beast.[27] In legal doctrine reason meant responsibility. Plain ignorance of God's commandments and Christian
morality made little difference to the court unless it was caused by insanity.
Insane or temporarily confused persons could not be held fully responsible,
and one primary task of the court was to determine whether the act had
been committed against reason or out of a temporary or constant loss of
reason.

Central to the investigation of the charged person's mental health and
capacity were the testimonies of witnesses, neighbors, relatives, and the
parish priest—but also, of course, was the person's behavior and answers
before the court. Talking to fools and confused persons sometimes spurred
the court to be more explicit and to try to spell out the meaning of the act.
The confused look and ignorant answers of a thirty-year-old male servant,
already considered a fool, provoked the court to bring the question to a
head: was he really unable to understand the meaning of his act? "*Q:* Does
the accused know any difference between human beings and animals? *A:* I
don't know. *Q:* Is he himself a human being, a horse, or a fish? *A:* I'm not
feeling well . . . *Q:* Does he know any difference between a human being
and a fish? *A:* No. *Q:* Does he eat fish? *A:* Yes. *Q:* Does he eat human
beings? *A:* No. *Q:* Why doesn't he eat human beings? . . . No answer."[28]
The poor servant was probably not considered much more reasonable

[26]Jonas Hambraeus, "Foreword," in *En gyldenne book* (Stockholm, 1620), reprinted in
Årsböcker i svensk undervisningshistoria, 1926 (Stockholm, 1926).
[27]See, for example, court record, Uppsala län; Åsunda 21/10 1693, ULA.
[28]Court record, Västernorrlands län; Hälsningland, Hanebo 1763, HLA.

(and human) than the cow he had buggered, and that saved him from the ax and the stake. But in the formulation of the questions, an implicit analogy was set up between bestiality and cannibalism: making love to a beast is like eating human flesh. This correspondence reveals an essential meaning of bestiality, as it implies not only moral corruption and foolishness but a defilement in the most physical sense. This is also the connotation of the word *abominable* used in the Pentateuch and in legal texts.

This sense of physical defilement is obvious in some of the reactions and utterances expressing disgust and contempt: witnesses spitting at the bugger; a male servant throwing to the watchdogs the bun he had just received from a runaway suspected bugger; a son refusing to sleep in the same bedroom as his father, who was suspected of bestiality; a wife not permitting her husband to touch her after catching him red-handed.[29] In this regard the suspected or reputed bugger could be met with the same reactions and sanctions as the members of the most infamous professional groups in Sweden—the executioner and the skinner.[30]

Infamy and Dishonesty

Avoidance of touch and personal relations, especially refusal to eat and drink together, were the hallmarks of discrimination against the executioner and the skinner and obviously could also be applied to the bugger. One witness testified that the accused had such an evil reputation for bestiality that all the other servants at the manor refused to eat and drink together with him.[31] Another person of ill repute was exhorted to clear himself of his bad name, otherwise no honest man would ever drink with him out of the tankard.[32] Personal relations with a bugger could be considered just as disgraceful; one witness, a servant girl, feared the condemnation of others because of her keeping company with such a person.[33] The brother of an accused bugger deprecated his ties of kinship.[34] Alleged

[29]Court records: Hallands län; Viske 14/7 1724, Malmö län; Skytt 18/4 1724, LLA, Skaraborgs län; Vassbo 2/11 1669, GHA Criminalia EVAA:51, Kopparbergs län; Söderbärke 12/8 1748, ULA, Värmlands län; Gillberg 2/9 1731, GLA.

[30]This correspondence was even spelled out explicitly by a reputed bugger asking a man who refused to drink with him if the man considered him to be an executioner or a skinner (court record, Örebro län; Örebro rådstuga 13/4 1708, ULA). There were more associations between buggers and skinners in particular: in popular language there existed certain nicknames with a double connotation of skinner and bugger. See Brita Egardt, *Hästslakt och rackarskam* (Lund, 1962).

[31]Resolution of the Superior Court Göta Hovrätt 20/11 1706, GHA BIIA.

[32]Court record, Jönköpings län; Norra Vedbo 26/9 1682, VLA.

[33]Court record, Västernorrlands län; Skog 16/10 1677, HLA.

[34]Court record, Värmlands län; Näs 3/9 1739, GLA.

kinship could be the subject of insulting jokes and libels—a cavalry captain sued his sergeant major over a written pasquinade about a certain bugger sentenced to the stake, who was said to have called the captain a brother and brother-in-law.[35]

Thus the sense of uncleanliness was closely connected to infamy, as was the case with the executioner and the skinner. But some reservations must be made to avoid an excessive and generalizing comparison. The social stigmatization of the executioner and the skinner was institutionalized not by the authorities but by the local community. The executioner and the skinner were well known, and although their work was considered infamous it was performed in public and was accepted. Their infamy was reproduced continuously in daily life. The secret bugger, however, could be anyone. When the offense was revealed, usually there was no time for any of the more sophisticated mechanisms of social stigmatization to work. A quick imprisonment, subsequent trial, and execution at the stake was the fate of many buggers. On the other hand, there were more persons who were sentenced to public forced labor and corporal punishment for attempted bestiality than were executed. But their life and treatment after punishment could not be studied in the court records, except by chance. Often these persons were forbidden to return to the district where the crime had been committed to prevent "further annoyance." In these cases the conditions for a more firmly developed and lasting tradition of discrimination were weaker and also were counteracted by the authorities and perhaps by the knowledge of the harsh penal consequences. The public display of defamatory symbolic acts of discrimination would sooner or later be equated with a denunciation and brought before the court by local officials.

Bearing in mind these reservations, it could be said that insofar as the reputed or convicted bugger met with discriminatory reactions of a more ritualized character, these were related to an established concept of infamy and dishonesty attaching not only to the professions of the executioner and skinner but also to thieves and a broader category of dishonest deeds and professions. Infamy as flourishing among the craft guilds was also applied in legal doctrine as well as in quarrels and conflicts in the village.[36] Before the rise of any medical and psychiatric discourse on sexuality and sexual identity, this was only natural. Infamy/dishonesty (*oärlighet* in Swedish, *Unehrlichkeit* in German) seems to have been a superior concept for social discrimination and classification of behavior, corresponding in importance to the modern distinction between normal and deviant (perverse in terms of sexology).

[35]Court record, Västernorrlands län; Jämtland; Brunflo 27/7 1687, Östersund Provincial Archives (hereafter ÖLA).
[36]See Egardt.

Bodily Corruption

In the case of the bugger (and of the executioner and the skinner), the sense of physical defilement was not a simple derivation of infamy but, rather, of a direct and intimate physical involvement in an act of a most ambiguous and profane character, implying the reciprocal touch of intimate parts of the body and the mixture of bodily fluids. The correspondence to cannibalism consisted in the supposed mixture of human and animal seminal fluids, resulting in a "commixtio sanguinis." This was the essence of the defilement, "to corrupt the natural order and mix human blood with that of brute beasts and animal creatures."[37]

The result of such a mixture was the corruption of both human and animal nature and body. The mother of an accused bugger begged her son "with weeping tears" that "although he had corrupted his body" he might not cause her any further sorrow and "likewise destroy his soul" (by denying his sin).[38] When it came to the human aspect, bodily corruption could be felt most dramatically in continued sexual relations. A marital duty could be reversed into defilement. One married man felt uneasy and regretted with all his heart before the court that he had had sexual intercourse with his wife without her knowing of his now confessed bestiality.[39] In the aversion to and refusal of sexual intercourse, there is the indication closest to an "animalization" of the bugger as the basis of disgust. The wife of a peasant was beaten when she refused to go to bed with her husband after having surprised him in the stable; she told the court that every time her husband gained his will by force, "there was afterwards the smell and taste of mare in her mouth."[40] While it was possible to find authoritative support in the Bible for the defilement of the bugger, little is said about the animal, apart from the passage in Lev. 20:15–16, prescribing that the animal should be killed. In court sentences this was usually justified as being "to avoid further annoyance." And in the middle of the eighteenth century, when the executions reached their peak, one Swedish law commentator declared that the reason for killing the animal was not its supposed guilt but to obliterate the memory of the act. Defilement and bodily corruption were not mentioned.[41] But exactly what kind of reactions were aroused by the sight of such an animal?

In situations where the basis for an indictment was too weak (a solitary

---

[37]Court record, Västmanlands län; Norrbo 27/4 1708, ULA.

[38]Court record, Kristianstads län; Norra Åsbo 4/5 1752, LLA.

[39]Court record, Uppsala län; Löfstad och Hållnäs 7/6 1710, Renov. domb. Uppsala 86, Swedish National Archives (hereafter RA).

[40]Court record, Uppsala län; Sotholm 20/1 1651, Renov. domb. Uppsala 11 1/2, RA.

[41]David Nehrman, *Inledning til then swenska jurisprudentiam criminalem* (Stockholm, 1756).

witness or only strong suspicion and rumors) or before any denunciation was made, there were examples of witnesses and others expressing strong aversion toward the animal. A servant refused to hitch the mare to the coach when he was ordered to drive his mistress to church.[42] The sons of a disreputable father could not tolerate the cow because of all the talk.[43] Sometimes the owner anticipated an eventual trial and got rid of the animal; in one case, the cow was put to death and buried in the woods as soon as the owner was told what had happened.[44] When the suspected animal was bartered or sold, this could of course have been as much an anticipation of an economic loss as an expression of disgust. It was not until 1730 that the owner had the right to demand compensation from the convicted person's property.[45]

In court, the authorities often made strenuous and scrupulous efforts to identify every individual animal mentioned in the confessions, even if confessions were of a secondary character without witnesses to the act and the bugger himself was not sure of the time and place. Not infrequently this was done with the active cooperation and support of the probable owners. A twenty-year-old servant not only confessed his guilt on the suspected occasions but made further confessions concerning more than twenty cows, some identified, others not, in different cowsheds and villages. None of these acts, committed during the preceding three years, were known or suspected by anyone, but the current owners ordered the servant to point out the cows in question and declared in unison that "although they were poor and needed every cow, they would rather get rid of them than be left in a state of uncertainty and not be able to use them without mortification." When the servant entered the cowshed of his aunt, she begged him to show her all the cows that he recognized. "She would feel abomination to have such an animal in her house."[46]

Formally the animal was sequestrated, which meant that the owner was forbidden to kill, sell, or use it in any way. But behind the legal terms and arrangements, it is not difficult to discern a sense of the bodily corruption of the animal, especially obvious as an aversion to unclean food. From the first moments of strong suspicion or immediately upon the revelation of the act, there could be a refusal to drink the milk of the cow. The male servants on one farm declared that as long as the suspected bugger was not caught they would never taste a drop of milk in that house.[47] A female servant and

[42]Court record, Östergötlands län; Memming 12/6 1732, VLA.

[43]Court record, Kopparbergs län; Äppelbo 16/1 1686, Renov. domb. Kopparberg 22, RA.

[44]Court record, Västerbottens län; Umeå socken 11/5 1696, HLA.

[45]Almquist (n. 3 above), p. 31.

[46]Court record, Kopparbergs län; Orsa, Älvdalen, Ore dec., 1735, ULA.

[47]Court record, Jönköpings län; Tveta 30/5 1715, VLA.

witness threw the milking pail on the bench in front of the others, exclaiming, "The devil must eat that milk!"[48] The milk was given to dogs and other farm animals, or else milking was interrupted and stopped, long before the start of any legal proceeding. If she was correct, then the milk was "not good," an assistant vicar told a wife when she secretly confessed suspicions of her husband.[49] The milk and the meat were corrupt and "humanized," nauseating to eat except perhaps for the equally corrupt bugger. It was said of one suspected bugger that he did not want to drink any other milk than from the cow he had buggered.[50] In this aspect, cannibalism was not only a symbolic correspondence of bestiality but could also be a real consequence; a sergeant told the court that he had heard the suspected person not only confess to the priest but also say that the meat of the cow, which he had slaughtered afterward, "tasted rather sweet."[51] But again some reservations must be made clear. There are a few examples of owners who killed the animal and consumed the meat because of their great poverty. Poverty and hunger could obviously overcome the nauseated feeling and, in the late seventeenth century, the authorities changed the common practice from burying the dead animal at the place of execution to burning its body at a separate stake to prevent the hungry poor from digging it up.[52]

Monstrous Offspring

Disgust and nausea have been the characteristic reactions to bestiality as a boundary-crossing phenomenon. But the ultimate fear and consequence of this transgression and mixing of categories was not defilement and bodily corruption but the possible monstrous offspring. It has been debated whether contraceptive techniques were known and practiced to any extent in the old agrarian society. In cases of bestiality they certainly were. "Every time," one bugger said, "he had withdrawn his member and let the semen fall onto the ground, fearing that something living could be generated."[53] A young servant confessed that he did not dare to leave his semen in the mare, considering it most shameful if the mare should give birth to "something resemblant to himself."[54] Another very young bugger once heard the newborn kid of his father's goat bleat like a crying child. Later, during his intercourse with cows and heifers, he had been more careful, so as not to beget calves.[55]

[48]Court record, Kopparbergs län; Husby 18/3 1670, ULA.
[49]Court record, Västmanlands län; Våla 11/6 1754, ULA.
[50]Court record, Västernorrlands län; Hälsningland, Söderala 30/7 1684, HLA.
[51]Court record, Värmlands län; Kil 7/10 1752, GLA.
[52]Records of the Superior Court Göta Hovrätt, 28/11 1723.
[53]Court record, Västernorrlands län; Jämtlands län, Frösön 5/7 1695, ÖLA.
[54]Resolution of the Superior Court Svea Hovrätt, 19/3 1720.
[55]Court record, Västernorrlands län; Ångermanland, Sidensjö 27/8 1675, HLA.

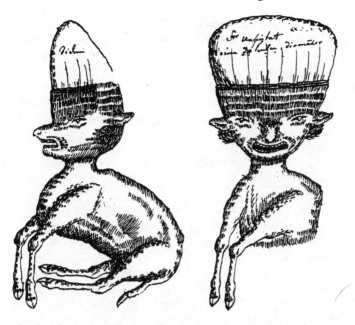

FIG. 2   A deformed calf fetus depicted and reported by Johannes Norlin, vicar in the parish of Skirö, February 1783, in Tabellverkets handlingar (Swedish Central Bureau of Statistics, Stockholm).

Stories about the birth of monsters, half-human and half-animal, occurred in learned publications as well as in broadsheets and oral tradition, always evoking great interest. In a discussion concerning the right of inheritance of newborn children who died before baptism or were born "partus monstruosus," the Chief Custodian of National Monuments informed the other members of the Law Committee that a monster had been born in a Swedish town in 1638, "half-human half-cow."[56] Bestiality was one of the explanations given for the occurrence of such monstrous births. This possible consequence infused the wife of a bugger with such apprehension and anxiety that she asked a female servant to intercede with God on her account, that she might die in childbed (the wife being in the last month of pregnancy) rather than live to see the appearance of the calf. According to the record her prayer was granted, but the calf showed no deformities.[57]

The sight of such a monster, associated with bestiality, was disgusting and perhaps more pitiable than frightening. In 1782 one cow gave birth to the man-like fetus depicted in figure 2. According to the notes of the vicar, the cow had been grazing all summer in the vicinity of a public road for

[56]Records of the Law Committee 28/2 1690, published by W. Sjögren in *Förarbetena till Sveriges rikes lag* (Uppsala, 1900), 1:160.
[57]Court record, Västernorrlands län; Ockelbo 19/3 1703, HLA.

travelers "and all sorts of individuals," which he had noted in case "any physical cause" could be derived from it. The owner of the cow allowed people to come to see and depict the fetus, until roaming dogs and swine broke into the room and devoured it.[58]

MALE AMBIVALENCE AND MASCULINITY

From the harsh punishments and from the disgust and condemnation in learned doctrines as well as in popular attitudes emerges a picture of a society where the symbolic and cultural meaning of human-animal sexual relations was of an extremely negative character. But social practice was not homogeneous. On the one hand, there was an increasing frequency of indictments, indicating a social network of control over and suspicion of male sexuality, a willingness and eagerness on the part of neighbors, masters, servants, and even family members to maintain the sanctions. On the other hand, there were persons who continued to find sexual gratification in bestiality in spite of the attitudes of disgust and repugnance and the risks of infamy, execution, or eternal damnation and association with the devil. Some of them were idiots or not completely sensible, but not very many. The overwhelming majority seem to have been just ordinary peasants, farm servants, soldiers, boatswains, craftsmen, and apprentices. Even one assistant vicar was charged and could not be acquitted without strong doubts. This suggests basic ambivalence in male relations to animals in seventeenth- and eighteenth-century Sweden, identifying bestiality as a focus in the problem of male sexuality. What were the cultural and social roots of this ambivalence?

"A Low Grade of Culture" or Sexual Frustration?

The pioneers of sexology in the late nineteenth and early twentieth centuries classified sexual relations with animals in two ways: either as a pathological perversion, "zooerastia," practiced by often intelligent and socially refined but highly "degenerate" persons, or as "bestiality," practiced by fairly normal persons "belonging to a low grade of culture." This low grade of culture was identified with "primitive peoples" and contemporary peasants. Bestiality was inherent and natural to peasant society, where the lack of cultural refinement in combination with a great familiarity with animals resulted in a weak or nonexistent barrier between man and animal: "For the peasant, whose sensibilities are uncultivated and who makes but the most elementary demands from a woman, the difference between an

---

[58]Johannes Norlin, vicar in the parish of Skirö, February 1783, Tabellverkets handlingar, Swedish Central Bureau of Statistics, Stockholm (hereafter SCB).

animal and a human being in this respect scarcely seems to be very great."[59]

This definition says something about the prejudices concerning peasants held by the early sexologists. But at the same time, paradoxically, in avoiding the label of perversity, this definition comes closer to a more dynamic concept of sexuality—as not just a natural instinct with built-in characteristics that can only be distorted, but as a force and desire whose goals and objects are to a large degree socially constructed and molded by culture and with a certain plasticity that permits different sexual acts without always being linked to a presupposed sexual identity.[60] In this sense this definition of bestiality as a cultural phenomenon provides the analysis with a proposition of "pull" factors: the great familiarity with animals in daily life as contrasted with the greater distance (at least to farm animals) in urban and "socially refined" life.

But the early sexologists also added some "push" factors—the absence of women or the inability to court them. This theme of sexual frustration has been taken up more recently in a debate among historians concerning the consequences of the pattern of belated marriage in early modern Europe. Perhaps dating back to the Middle Ages, people in western Europe married late and quite a few not at all. Given the religious and legal sanctions against sex outside marriage and the generally low rates of illegitimate births, particularly in the seventeenth century, the question of juvenile sexuality is raised. What did young people do with their sexual desires during the ten or more postpubertal years they had to wait before getting married? The most common answer has been that they were continent. Put into a quasi-Freudian framework, historians have argued that this resulted in outbursts of spectacular neurosis such as hysteria and witchcraft but also in sublimation, sexual asceticism and belated marriage functioning as a kind of family planning method inducing a spirit of matrimonial enterprise that complemented the puritan thrift in Weber's thesis concerning the origins of capitalism, or reducing sexuality and family life to a frozen iceberg with very little sex (manipulative, not expressive), affection, or empathy.[61]

[59]Havelock Ellis, *Erotic Symbolism*, vol. 5 of *Studies in the Psychology of Sex* (Philadelphia, 1919), chap. 4, pp. 71–88, quotation from p. 81; Ellis refers to and discusses the thesis and classification of another well-known pioneer, Richard von Krafft-Ebing (see his *Psychopathia Sexualis* [Stuttgart, 1886], p. 188).

[60]See Jeffrey Weeks, *Sex, Politics, and Society* (London, 1981), for a historical survey of the contemporary scientific debate concerning sexuality.

[61]This debate was started by an article of Jean-Louis Flandrin, "Contraception, mariage et relations amoureuses dans l'Occident chrétien," *Annales*, no. 6, (1969), pp. 1370–83, in which he criticized some statements made by Emmanuele Le Roy Ladurie in *Paysans du Languedoc* (Paris, 1966), p. 644. This was taken up by Andre Burguiere in "De Malthus à Max Weber: Le mariage tardif et l'esprit d'enterprise," in *Annales*, nos. 4–5 (1972), pp. 1128–39. Edward Shorter made another contribution in "Illegitimacy, Sexual Revolution, and Social Change in Modern Europe," *Journal of Interdisciplinary History* 2 (1971): 237–72, which he further developed in *The Making of the Modern Family* (New York, 1975).

Opposing the thesis of juvenile continence and sublimation, the French historian Jean-Louis Flandrin has argued that there were plenty of methods for sexual relief practiced without resulting in pregnancy and increasing illegitimacy rates. He mentions the use of contraceptives (mainly coitus interruptus) and masturbation, but also homoerotic contacts and bestiality, and he suggests that at the least masturbation and homoerotic contacts increased in early modern France.[62]

Applied to Swedish conditions, Flandrin's argument provides a potential explanation for the high frequency of bestiality charges. The great familiarity with animals combined not with a low grade of culture but with a high grade of sexual repression led young people to seek sexual satisfaction in bestiality. This explanation also suggests a reason for ambivalence. Bestiality was not an unproblematic and trivial behavior that could only be expected from uncivilized peasants, but an outcome of sexual frustration. This is, of course, an important argument and a partial explanation that could be supported by the age distribution of accused persons. In addition, the difficulty in marrying experienced by young people was explicitly mentioned in a memorial to the Swedish Parliament in 1741 as causing bestiality and infanticide.[63] However, there is a positive correlation between high frequency of prosecutions, high sex ratios (number of females per 1,000 males), and popular customs of bundling in the regional distribution of bestiality trials, which contradicts any simple relation between sexual frustration, committed acts of bestiality, and the number of trials.[64] Although of explanatory value, sexual frustration could not have been sufficient as a root cause of ambivalence.

[62]Jean-Louis Flandrin, "Mariage tardif et vie sexuelle," *Annales*, no. 6 (1972), pp. 1351–78; but this was a mere suggestion. Given the implicit definition of sexuality as a natural instinct that cannot be repressed (or successfully sublimated in most cases) but only distorted, he found that later adjustment to heterosexual family life after ten years of masturbation, homoerotic contacts, or bestiality was highly unlikely, which led him to argue that the main answer to the oppression was a development of sex without coitus within the traditional courting customs; see Jean-Louis Flandrin, "Repression and Change in the Sexual Life of Young People in Medieval and Early Modern Times," *Journal of Family History* 2 (1977): 196–210.

[63]Lars Johan Ehrenmalms memorial till 1740/41 års riksdag, Frihetstidens utskottshandlingar, Justitiedeputationen, R 2771, RA.

[64]In general, Sweden had a high sex ratio during the seventeenth and eighteenth centuries, but there were distinct regional variations due to both the recruitment and mortality of soldiers during wartime and the social and economic structure resulting in different demands for male and female servants. For example, in the northern county of Västernorrland, the annual rate of indictment per 100,000 of the population, 1745–54, was 4,2. The sex ratio, 1751, for the whole population was 1,210; among unmarried servants and children staying at home above the age of fifteen, 1,460. Corresponding figures for the southern county of Malmö were 1,8; 1,048 and 967. See population tables published by Nils Wohlin in *Emigrationsutredningen, bilaga* 9 (Stockholm, 1909).

Familiarity of Boys with Animals

There was a remarkable occurrence of very young boys below the age of fifteen being charged with bestiality—many of them only between nine and twelve years old and some even younger, the youngest only seven. These young boys could hardly be considered the frustrated victims of repressed premarital sexuality, impatiently waiting for a belated marriage to fulfill their desires. Rather they appear as curious and excited explorers, eager to find out the secrets of sexuality, belonging to adult and married life but present and visible in the life of farm animals. Several young boys told the court that they had been directly inspired and excited by the sight of farm animals mounting each other.[65] And this was only natural; in play and work children were socialized into men and women in close connection with the animals, providing a natural knowledge of covering and breeding as well as of slaughter. Children knew all the names and individual characteristics of the farm animals and learned how to handle them. In most parts of the country, herding was children's work, young boys and girls watching the cattle alone or sometimes together in the woods.[66] This was a game of dominance and affection, the larger animals challenging in their strength and intelligence and will, but also providing a basis for security and emotional ties—all this certainly resulting in familiarity.[67]

During the lonely hours of herding or in the search for consolation and affection away from a brutal master, familiarity could become too intimate. But also in play and high spirits, young boys could inspire each other. One servant related that when he was ten years old and playing with a friend of the same age, butting each other as oxen do, his friend said: "If you do it with cattle, you can't imagine how nice that is."[68] While bestiality in general was a solitary act, young boys not infrequently made their attempt in company: two twelve-year-old boys confessed that they had buggered the mare twice each, one of them teaching the other.[69] A ten-year-old boy agreed to hold the cow on condition that his thirteen-year-old friend would do the same for him.[70] The eight-year-old son of a boatswain had been in company with two nine-year-old boys. During the trial the boys revealed the names of another eight boys of about the same age whom they had seen practicing the same vice on different occasions.[71]

[65]See, for example, court records, Uppsala län; Lagunda 12/6 1661, Västmanlands län; Torstuna winter 1702, ULA, Västernorrlands län; Hedesunda 13/7 1725, HLA.

[66]Matyas Szabo, *Herdar och husdjur, Nordiska Museets handlingar* (Lund, 1970), chap. 3, "Den skandinaviska vallningsorganisationen."

[67]This is described in Ulla Lindström, "Landsbygdspojkar och husdjur," *Fataburen* (1986).

[68]Court record, Västmanlands län; Skinnskatteberg 20/10 1704, ULA.

[69]Court record, Uppsala län; Frötuna och Länna (date not available) 1707, ULA.

[70]Court record, Värmlands län; Philipstads bergslag 26/10 1726, GLA.

[71]Court record, Västmanlands län; Västerås rådstuga 23–30/6 1712, ULA.

Something of a boy's culture is indicated here. One of Sweden's most well known writers recalled in his autobiography the excited atmosphere, talk, and rumors among country boys during his adolescence in the early twentieth century: "Everyone seemed to have always known it. Nearly all the older boys talked about how boy so-and-so had mounted an animal. Almost never did they mention that it concerned themselves. . . . My grandpa had said that in former times they had never allowed other than female herders on the great manors. I had myself come to that age when I understood why. The rank smell of wool from the sheep and their inviting behavior was exciting. The soft furs of the young heifers, their climbing on each other out in the woods and fields, their open exposure of their sex and heat, was even more tempting."[72]

Of course the early sexologists were right. This was a bestiality-prone society irrespective of whether premarital sexuality was repressed or not. But the social, cultural, and psychological basis for this was not found in a general low grade of culture or dulled sensibilities, but in the socialization of boys.

It was the definite opinion of the authorities that bestiality was a boy's game sometimes growing into a man's habit. With this idea confirmed by the confessions of young boys and adult men testifying about their first temptations and attempts in boyhood, often during herding, the court could hardly believe a middle-aged man who claimed that this was the first time for him. In 1686 the Superior Court, Svea Hovrätt, complained in a letter to the king about the almost daily reports of bestiality charges. Very often these were said to concern young herdsboys, and the life of herding was described in the letter as a subculture of ignorance and abominable lust, where bestiality was held as a lesser vice than fornication—the young boys, living all summer in the woods together with the cattle, seldom or never attending church, lived a life no better than that of the brute animals. The court ordered the priests, diligently and with all possible efforts, to instruct these boys in Christianity, while at the same time it proposed a prohibition on the use of boys for herding cattle.[73] This resulted in a Royal Ordinance that same year, prescribing an obligation to employ, as far as possible, women instead of boys to herd cattle.[74] This ordinance was repeatedly read in public at the meetings of the county courts and in church. In 1723 it was supplemented with the prescription that all persons engaged as herders, irrespective of age and sex, must be able to read.[75]

---

[72]Ivar Lo-Johansson, *Pubertet* (Stockholm, 1978).

[73]Skrivelse till Kungl Majt. Svea Hovrätt till Kungl Majt, vol. 5, 1686–92, RA.

[74]Royal Ordinance to the Provincial Governors (Landshövdingar), November 17, 1686, Schmedeman, *Kongl stadgar, förordningar, bref o resolutioner* (Sthlm 1706), s. 1076. This ordinance was made into a special paragraph in the law of 1734: Byggningabalken 11:2, and remained in the written law until 1981.

[75]Wilksman, Swea rikes ecclesiastiqve werk 1781, s. 694.

The close association between boyhood and the roots of bestiality continued to attract attention in comments and ordinances. In the above-
mentioned memorial to the Swedish Parliament in 1741, the dangers of
herding were mentioned again, as offering opportunities for young boys to
watch the copulation of animals. But also receiving blame were a more general ignorance and lack of norms among youth as a result of negligent
upbringing, ignorance of basic Christian concepts, too much leisure, drinking, and the bad example of adults in demoralizing customs and lewd
talk.[76] Later in the eighteenth century, the authorities tried to restrict the
publicity and attention that bestiality trials attracted, in order to protect
other youths from being informed and instructed. Consequently one wife
was sentenced in 1755 to sit one Sunday in the stocks, because she had
taken her twelve-year-old son with her into the barn while investigating the
circumstances of her husband's crime, "even though such young people
should never hear of such abomination, even less watch how it could be
executed."[77]

There has been some discussion about the consequences of the ordinance of 1686, but probably it was not very effective. On a summer's day in
1720, one layman of a local county court in northern Sweden counted up
to seven boys, aged between six and twelve, herding cattle. The vicar assumed that if peasants living near the church openly ignored the ordinance,
then this was probably a general attitude in the more remote parts of the
parish. He also complained that it was hard to persuade women and female
servants to herd cattle.[78] The tradition of using young boys as herders was
deeply rooted in the social division of labor in most parts of the country.
On the shielings (special mountain dairy farms, used in summertime in
some areas) as well, young boys often assisted the female herders.[79]

Restricted Relations of Men to Cattle

The close and perhaps traditionally less problematic relation that boys
could have with farm animals was in contrast to that of adult males. Growing up, a boy's relation to cattle became more problematic as it came into
conflict with a similarly traditional concept of what constituted a man's
proper work and activity. The sexual division of labor in Swedish peasant
society was far from rigid, changing over time and varying from one region
to another. Much work had only vague gender connotations or none at all,
but in working relations to farm animals there existed some of the most
explicit, long-lasting, and general divisions between female and male.

[76]Lars Johan Ehrenmalms memorial.
[77]Court record, Västmanlands län; Våla 14/6 1754, ULA.
[78]Court record, Västernorrlands län; Gästrikland, Torsåker o Ovansjö 26/9 1720, HLA.
[79]Szabo (n. 66 above).

Apart from the institution of the village herder in the southern part of Sweden, adult male herders were rare and untypical, as was the male servant regularly tending the cattle in the cowshed.[80] The trial of a twenty-three-year-old servant confirms this. The young man had for a long time been forced by his father and stepmother to do all the cattle tending, for which he was mocked by the children and other servants, who called him *fäpojke* (cattleboy). According to the neighbors and one member of the village community, this servant was always sitting alone in a corner during haymaking feasts and other holidays, when the young people would be dancing and amusing themselves.[81]

The daily work in cowsheds belonged in general to the female sphere and was not done by men unless necessitated by the absence of the wife or the female servants.[82] Male visits to cowsheds without any special task or work attracted attention and could easily be considered suspicious; a milkmaid said that she was very astonished and became uneasy on finding one of the servants in the cowshed. The males on the farm never went there unless there was something to be repaired.[83] One woman often found her son-in-law in the cowshed. Not knowing what he was doing there, she drilled a hole in the door to find out. The son-in-law in defense said that males in that province (Dalarna) habitually did a lot of work in the cowshed because of the cold weather and gave the court details of some occupations.[84]

Milking carried the strongest female identification, approaching a male taboo. If herding represented the young boy's close relation with cattle, then milking was the symbol of the adult man's distanced and problematic relation. As a strictly female occupation entailing contact with a female animal's intimate parts, milking was considered improper for a man. On a dean's visitation, one soldier living alone was seriously exhorted to engage a woman to milk his cow and not to do it himself.[85] But in general, and above all, men considered milking to be shameful; to call another man "a cowmilker" was a serious offense that could be taken up in court.[86] A cot-

[80]Ibid., p. 205; and Orvar Löfgren, "Kvinnofolksgöra—om arbetsdelning i bondesamhället," *Kvinnovetenskaplig tidskrift* 3 (1982): 6–14; Pia Granath and Eva Strandberg, "Arbetsfördelningen i det norrländska bondesamhället" (University of Umeå, Department of History, 1981, mimeograph).

[81]Court record, Uppsala län; Lagunda 25/9 1739, ULA.

[82]For example, court records, Västmanlands län; Åkerbo 1/8 1711, Renov. domb. V-mlnd 64, RA. Kopparbergs län; Norrbärke 8/12 1714, Västmanlands län; Norrbo 27/4 1708, ULA. Elfsborgs län; Veden 9/10 1744, Värmlands län; Visnum 9/9 1728, GLA.

[83]Court record, Kopparbergs län; Brunnbäck 19/7 1697, Renov. domb. K-berg 36, RA.

[84]Court record, Kopparbergs län; Leksand 30/3 1693, ULA.

[85]Dean's visitation 1753 in Linghed, Kopparbergs län, published in Karl Linge, *Svärdsjö socken* (Stockholm, 1929).

[86]Court record, Västernorrlands län; Ångermanland, Grundsunda 20/2 1705, printed in Tyko Lundkvist, *Salva venia—Olåt och munbruk* (Härnösand, 1977).

tager who was seen in a cowshed, sitting beside a cow and "handling" the cow's udder, admitted "with great shame" that he had been overcome with "this foolishness" out of a sudden greed for milk.[87]

From a distance, the close position of a male milker to a cow immediately aroused suspicions of "abominable doings." A ship's assistant cook from Stralsund in Pommern was suspected by two male servants, who watched him standing close to a cow grazing on an islet. This young male suspect told the court that he had only been milking some drops into his cupped hand to drink. This was dubious, but there was little proof and the court believed him, noting that boatswains and other male persons "on the said place" were said to practice the habit of milking the cows (this could be interpreted in different ways, either as referring to thirsty persons passing to and from the ships out on the roadstead, or perhaps in more general terms to the customs of the assistant cook's home district).[88] Another servant found in a suspicious position close to a cow asserted, after some questioning and unsuccessful explanations, that he had intended to milk the cow to alleviate the burning in his throat, being too ashamed to confess this in the first place.[89]

The close association between females and cattle was most salient in the area of shielings in the western and northern parts of the country. In summer wives and female servants moved with the cattle to special dairy farms where all the cattle tending, milking, and herding were done. Living on the shielings, the women formed a close-knit female working culture based on a constant association with the cattle. Men did not usually stay permanently on the shielings, but occasionally fiancés and the young unmarried men of the village arranged visits during the holidays. Back again in the village, the symbolic ties between women and cattle were reinforced by the custom of girls and unmarried young women sleeping in barns and cowsheds during the warm season.[90]

Mares and Obscenities

If male relations to cows were problematic, their relations to horses on the other hand could be more relaxed and affectionate. Horses and stables belonged to the male sphere. The horse was a companion in work and a symbol of male status, even though oxen dominated as draft animals in much of the country. Stable work and the herding of horses was done by adult male servants.[91] But there was an ambiguity even in this relation; a

[87]Court record, Stockholms län; Närdinghundra 14/1 1752, ULA.

[88]Court record, Västernorrlands län; Gästrikland, Gävle rådstuga 7/6 1711, HLA.

[89]Court record, Västmanlands län; Skinnskatteberg 19/10 1731, ULA.

[90]Anna Johnson, *Sången i skogen* (Uppsala, 1986); Orvar Löfgren, "Från nattfrieri till tonårskultur," in *Fataburen* (Stockholm, 1969).

[91]Szabo (n. 66 above).

young servant related that when he was doing day work at the factory, driving his father's mare, this attracted attention and blame from various persons, who asked him if he had "had his way" with the mare in the woods.[92]

Men were vulnerable even in their relations to mares. This was perhaps most obvious in verbal abuse and desecrations. To be called by the name for the pudenda of a bitch, *hundsfått,* was most disparaging and could be used to insult men as well as women. The same could be said about the verbal usage of a mare's pudenda, but behind the insulting exhortation to kiss a mare's pudenda there was a tradition of male desecration; one man complained before the court that he was reputed to have kissed a mare when he visited a nearby village. He had been very drunk at the time, but whether any of his hosts had tricked him into doing this, he could not say.[93] During a revel a military officer and his boon companions amused themselves by tricking and forcing a male servant to kiss a mare.[94] In another case two servants forced a young man to kiss a mare first on the loin and then on the pudenda.[95]

The mare's position in the male sphere was ambiguous, with strong sexual and obscene associations, a subject not only for insults and desecrations but used also for blasphemous purposes. One soldier behaved like a man possessed when he was caught and put into the village jail, frothing at the mouth, spitting blood, biting the walls, shouting, and whistling for the devil to come. Later he cursed the day he was born, called the devil his master and brother, confessed bestiality with many animals, and, finally, catching sight of a mare while on his way to a place of custody, he asked the guards to release him so that he could flay that mare, but first he wanted to bugger her while she was dead.[96] This ultimate blasphemy expressed the whole range of ambiguity associated with horses in general and mares in particular.

Roots of Male Ambivalence and the Threat to Masculinity

It is now possible to make a more specific proposition of where to find the source of male ambivalence toward farm animals: boyhood in seventeenth- and eighteenth-century Sweden offered a natural and close relation with farm animals, providing the first demonstrations and knowledge of sexual functions and also opportunities for sexual experiences, and thus a psycho-

[92]Court record, Kopparbergs län; Söderbärke 15/6 1749, ULA.

[93]Court record, Örebro län; Sköllersta 26/3 1674, ULA.

[94]Court record, Östergötlands län; Skeninge rådstuga 22/2 1662, GHA Criminalia EVAA:41.

[95]Resolution of the Superior Court, Svea Hovrätt 25/4 1687, ULA.

[96]Court record, Västmanlands län; Snävringe 23/7 1726, ULA.

logical basis for continuing or later resumed sexual contacts with animals in adult life. This has presumably been known to most agrarian and stock-farming cultures, but the extent to which it became a problem has varied according to cultural and social traditions.

In Sweden this close relation was strengthened—and at the same time restricted primarily to boyhood—by the tradition of cattle herding as children's work, in combination with the definition of cattle tending and milking as belonging to the female sphere. It was the conflict between boyhood's close relations with farm animals and the adult males' restricted and problematic relations with cattle that constituted the roots of ambivalence and helped to make bestiality such a burning and ambiguous issue of male sexuality in seventeenth- and eighteenth-century Sweden.

This conflicting cultural pattern had probably existed for some time, long before the seventeenth century. In addition the intensified religious condemnation and legal persecution of bestiality was reinforced by an already existing watchfulness of male activities in cowsheds and pastures, and vice versa, making all signs of unexpected male visits to cowsheds not only remarkable but suspicious and most likely of an abominable character. Footprints in the snow leading to the cowshed or in the dung behind a cow upset many wives, maids, and masters and prompted them to carefully inspect the clothes and boots of the males, looking for compromising stains of dung and hair from the cattle. Gloves left behind or a dropped tobacco pipe could start a rumor. There was much peeping through knotholes and chinks, not only by women spying on men but by men spying on other men as well.

The activities of boys were harder to control, and in this aspect the cultural pattern counteracted the ambitions of the authorities in spite of royal ordinances and prescriptions. Indirectly, the strong association between young boys and herding as the roots of bestiality contributed to an increasing suspicion of adults. Given the tradition of cattle herding as a transitional stage of boyhood and the nonexistence of a professional corporation of male herders (aside from the southern part of the country) or a special transhumant male herding culture onto which the suspicions and fear of bestiality could be projected, the potential bugger could be any man and former herdsboy.

Thus bestiality consisted not only of the crossing of boundaries between man and animal but also of a transgression of masculinity. This was obvious in the reactions of ridicule; there was something ridiculous about a bugger. The laughter, smiling, and pointing fingers of witnesses and others indicate that bestiality threatened the male gender role. It was unmanly, but not in the same way as milking and cattle tending, which implied feminization. Did the threat emanate from boyhood? It seems probable that this was also a part of the cultural meaning of bestiality—the equation of the male bugger with an immature boy.

The Uniqueness of Sweden and Other Comparative Studies

To what extent was the intense problematization of bestiality unique to Sweden? Legal persecution of bestiality and homosexual acts was in process throughout Europe (and in New England) from the Middle Ages on, but is it possible to relate major regional differences to different human-animal relations and gender systems?

So far, scholarly attention to gender aspects of the early modern European sodomy trials has been concentrated on homosexual acts and their connection with concepts of masculinity and homosexual subcultures. The bugger of cows and mares has usually been left aside as the rustic and less problematic cousin of the largely urban sodomite. Mainly from English evidence, a number of scholars have argued that the increasing hostility and number of trials against sodomites in the eighteenth and early nineteenth centuries reflected a change in gender distinctions toward increasing rigidity and polarization accompanied by the emergence of a homosexual role exclusively associated with effeminacy. Before the eighteenth century the sodomite might not have lost masculine status as long as he played the dominant role (although he was punished as a grave sinner); later the concept of effeminacy changed to include all males interested in other males, regardless of what part they played. The permanent effeminate homosexual became a greater challenge to the more narrowly defined masculinity than the old-fashioned debauchee or libertine with his boy on one arm and his whore on the other.[97]

Bestiality has been taken into account with less consistency. In one interesting study on sodomy and male honor in eighteenth-century England, the author initially states that bestiality meant abandoning the male role and was one of the most serious threats to male sexual reputation. But the implications for the masculine reputation of the perpetrator are never discussed in further detail, perhaps due to fragmentary source material. In the end the reader is left with some general remarks on the violation of the distinction between man and animal and the traditional association with homosexual acts as unnatural confronted by a narrowing concept of masculinity as exclusively heterosexual in mind and action.[98] A lack of more specific and intricate connections with masculinity and a preponderance for

[97]Among the English scholars there is of course no perfect agreement on the nature and causes of the changing concepts of gender and sodomy. Here I am following Randolph Trumbach, "Sodomitical Subcultures, Sodomitical Roles, and the Gender Revolution of the Eighteenth Century: The Recent Historiography," *Eighteenth-Century Life* 9 (1985): 109–21.

[98]Polly Morris, "Sodomy and Male Honor: The Case of Somerset, 1740–1850," *Journal of Homosexuality* 16 (1988): 383–406. The author remarks that any speculation as to the meaning of the bestiality prosecutions must be based on very rudimentary data in contrast to the more abundant information concerning the prosecutions for homosexual acts.

the natural aspects of the challenge from bestiality might well have been relevant for early modern England and, it has been argued, even more so for the puritan colonies in America, but in Sweden the crossing of the boundaries between man and animal was closely interwoven with gender transgressions.[99] And this possibility must also be considered for a more complete analysis of the composite character of sodomy trials.

It is my ambition to continue this study in a more comparative perspective with special reference to Mediterranean culture and in particular early modern Spain. While criminal statistics could never give an accurate picture of the actual sexual behavior among the population, major cross-cultural variations and changes in the patterns of prosecutions could perhaps be a key to the history of gender. Certainly the early modern European sodomy trials, like the witchcraft trials, were the outcome of a complex process of interaction (some would say acculturation) within different judicial and social settings, between the endeavor of the ruling elite for social control and popular conformity to religious doctrines and morality, and popular notions and norms based on traditional patterns of culture. But among the factors affecting the willingness to prosecute as well as to report and witness before the court, gender-based prejudices and stereotypes certainly have been of considerable importance.[100] Given the presumption that different gender systems generate different kinds of challenges toward masculinity and femininity, the responses to criminalization of sexual behavior based on cross-culturally applied doctrines like the doctrine of sodomy would supposedly be modified in different ways.

In his book on popular culture in early modern Europe, Peter Burke recognizes three important regions in the variations of European popular culture: northwestern, southern (or Mediterranean), and eastern Europe. Mediterranean culture has been characterized by a value system laying great stress on honor and shame. It has been argued that, since the classical era, this system has resulted in a more intensive problematization of male-to-male relations, making homoerotic relations the burning issue of male sexuality.[101] At the same time the existence of male herding cultures would have affected the general attitudes toward bestiality.

[99]John Canup has in a brief essay argued that the special environmental circumstances of colonial America intensified the fear of dehumanization and thus the revulsion against bestiality; John Canup, "The Cry of Sodom Enquired Into," in *Bestiality and the Wilderness of Human Nature in Seventeenth-Century New England* (Charlottesville, VA, 1988). See also Bert F. Oaks, "'Things Fearful to Name': Sodomy and Buggery in Seventeenth-Century New England," *Journal of Social History* 12 (1978): 268–81.

[100]A more elaborated gender approach to sex-linked crimes in the context of European criminal history has been advocated by William Monter in his *Witchcraft in France and Switzerland* (London, 1976), pp. 196–97.

[101]David Law Cohen, "Society and Homosexuality in Classical Athens," *Past and Present*, no. 117 (1987), pp. 3–21.

Historical research on sodomy trials in southern Europe has just begun, but while charges of homosexual acts were very rare in early modern Sweden, they seem to have been fairly common in early modern Spain, and perhaps even more frequent than charges of bestiality. Recent historical research on the Spanish Inquisition has revealed large-scale prosecutions for sodomy during the late sixteenth and early seventeenth centuries. For example, in the kingdom of Aragon, prosecutions for bestiality were by far outnumbered by prosecutions for homosexual acts, with the exception of the sheep-raising area of Saragossa, where trials for bestiality and homosexuality were more equal in number, although with a clear dominance for bestiality.[102] It remains to be analyzed to what extent these differences in patterns of prosecution between Sweden and Spain were culturally exaggerated by different gender systems and human-animal relations.

Modern anthropological studies of gender could provide the historian with some theoretical perspectives on the problematization of masculinity, serving as a heuristic framework for a more comparative study. Following the approach of gender structures as prestige structures proposed by cultural anthropologists Sherry Ortner and Harriet Whitehead,[103] there is a general cultural tendency to define females in terms of relations with their menfolk (wife, mother, sister), while males tend to be defined in terms of status and role categories. In prestige terms this means that female prestige is more concerned with sexual reputation and shame, while male prestige is usually expressed in terms of social worth and honor. The same axes of symbols that distinguish male from female also crosscut gender categories and are used for internal gradation between males and females. The more polarized these distinctions are in terms of female passivity, chastity, and seclusion versus male activity, sexual freedom, and public performance, the greater the threat to masculinity from feminization and the greater the relevance for symbolic emasculation through metaphors alluding to the passive role in a homosexual relation. The theme of homosexual relations would be ambiguous and salient in the problematization of masculinity. The act of male bestiality, however, as unambiguously penetrating and dominant, would be less problematical.

In less genderized societies with less polarized gender distinctions as especially the northern parts of early modern Sweden (and probably also the early modern English plebeian sexual culture referred to by English scholars), the threat from effeminacy would be less articulated and prestige

102William Monter (personal communication, July 1990). I am very grateful to William Monter for permission to use material from his newly published but not yet available book, *Frontiers of Heresy: The Spanish Inquisition from the Basque Lands to Sicily* (Cambridge, 1990).

103Sherry B. Ortner and Harriet Whitehead, "Introduction: Accounting for Sexual Meanings," in *Sexual Meanings,* ed. Sherry B. Ortner and Harriet Whitehead (Cambridge, 1981).

structures centering on age and occupation of more relevance for gender. The prestige of a real man (*karl* in Swedish, as opposed to the more neutral *man*) would be vulnerable also for occupations and sexual practices that could be associated with boyhood and youth, such as cattle herding and bestiality in Sweden.[104]

To conclude, in his study of male sexual ideology in Andalusia, Stanley Brandes has described the theme of the threatening anal penetration and dishonor of the submissive man, commonly occurring in jokes and insults. Men in San Blas could state behind each other's back that they were going to order the rival to take it up the ass. The underlying meaning of this is the symbolic transformation of the antagonist into a woman[105] (so far I have found no examples of this kind of insult in early modern Swedish court records). This could be compared with the following insults between two quarreling peasant neighbors in a seventeenth-century Swedish village: "You are looking for trouble like a sow grubbing in mud," said the first one. "If I am the sow, then you are the boar," the other replied, "so come close to me." Then he turned his back, lowered his trousers, and invited his antagonist to look him in the arse.[106] At first instance these insults could be seen as ordinary examples of associating the antagonist with dung and human feces. But in old Swedish terms the words "come close to me" have an ambiguous meaning, and the context of metaphorical abuse of boar and sow provides the obvious second meaning of an invitation to the "boar" to mount his sow, waiting in the right position—an attempt to symbolically transform the antagonist into a bugger. Is there more than mere chance to these contrasting examples? The answer to that very intricate question is worth further research.

[104]Swedish ethnologist Ella Johansson has proposed a less dichotomized gender model as more appropriate, especially for the northern parts of Sweden. Ella Johansson, "Beautiful Men, Fine Women, Good Work People: Gender and Skill in Northern Sweden, 1850–1950," *Gender and History* 1 (1989): 179–91.

[105]Stanley Brandes, "Male Sexual Ideology in an Andalusian Town," in Ortner and Whitehead, eds.

[106]Court record, Västernorrlands län; Ångermanland Sidensjö 1639 HLA.

Sex, Gender, and Sexual Identity in Modern Culture: Male Sodomy and Female Prostitution in Enlightenment London

RANDOLPH TRUMBACH

Department of History
Baruch College, City University of New York

FEMALE PROSTITUTES and male sodomites were given in eighteenth-century London a similar public status. The purpose of this essay is
to ask why.[1] It will turn out that for a man to be labeled a sodomite had a
much more devastating and pervasive effect on his life than for a woman to
become a prostitute. But the support that public opinion and the law gave
to the outcast status of both these roles (into which individual men and
women must have been socialized by the circumstances of their particular
lives) will establish that these roles had become essential to the maintenance of the gender system that in the early and mid-eighteenth century
was being produced by the emerging culture of the modern western world.
This essay also aims to show that those roles which were the obverse of the
sodomite and the prostitute (and into which the majority of men and
women would have been socialized) similarly were maintained by the

---

[1] This essay is part of a larger research project, nearly completed, on "The Sexual Life of
Eighteenth-Century London." The archival sources on prostitution that are used in this article are detailed at length in that forthcoming book. They document the arrests of prostitutes
in the three jurisdictions of London (the City, Westminster, and Middlesex), as they are recorded in the magistrates' books, the lists of women committed to houses of correction or
dismissed with warnings, and the recognizances given by women who were able to arrange
bail. There are manuscript sources for the Lock Hospital and Asylum, but the Magdalen Hospital can be documented only by the printed reports, since the original records were destroyed
during World War II. From other manuscript collections, I have used material in the divorce
and defamation suits in the consistory court and from the Foundling Hospital admissions.
There is also a large miscellaneous body of printed materials: trials of whores for theft in the
Sessions Paper; biographies of whores; lists of whores arrested and whores available; tours of
the town; the tracts of the reformers; and the newspapers. Prostitution will be dealt with at
length in the forthcoming work. The documentation for sodomy can be found in my various
articles cited below.

This essay originally appeared in the *Journal of the History of Sexuality* 1991, vol. 2, no. 2.

changing patterns of the law's public prosecutions. The law, then, both reflected the culture and helped to shape it. But the cultural changes of the early eighteenth century occurred along many fronts. Modern society in its early Enlightenment phase seems to have arrived all at once in a single generation. Social relations inside the family, and more generally between the genders, and between the young and the old, were being changed by equality and individualism. Something similar occurred in political relations between adult men. The structures of government, war, and the economy were even more rapidly transformed under the influence of new financial institutions. It was traditional Christianity, however, that experienced the most profound disruption because of the decline in the belief in magic and the rise of modern scientific and historical thinking. The very imaginative structures of life shifted and produced in the new genre of the novel its perfect artistic embodiment.[2]

I shall be concerned in this essay only with the changing relations between sex and gender. It will appear that the old was never entirely replaced by the new, that the changes affected men more than women, that urban society changed faster than the rural (which is why I study London), and that the culture of the powerful who controlled the form and actions of the law was by 1750 more affected by the new modern culture than was the culture of the poor. But interestingly enough, while the poor by 1750 were not likely to read novels or own stock in the government debt and certainly still believed in magic, they were in London very likely to have accepted the modern relationship between sexual behavior and gender that the new sodomite's role required of all men.

The modern gender role for men presumed that most men desired women exclusively and that all masculine behavior flowed from such desire. This was a reversal of a long-standing European pattern in which the most

[2]The classic description of cultural change in the generation after 1690 is to be found in Paul Hazard, *The European Mind, 1680–1715* (Paris, 1935; English trans., London, 1952). This argument can be expanded for England by Margaret C. Jacob, *The Newtonians and the English Revolution, 1689–1720* (Ithaca, NY, 1976), and *The Radical Enlightenment* (London, 1981); Keith Thomas, *Religion and the Decline of Magic* (London, 1971); Henning Graf Reventlow, *The Authority of the Bible and the Rise of the Modern World* (London, 1984). On government and financial change, D. W. Jones, *War and the Economy in the Age of William III and Marlborough* (New York, 1988); P.G.M. Dickson, *The Financial Revolution in England* (New York, 1967); Geoffrey Holmes, *Augustan England* (London, 1982); John Brewer, *The Sinews of Power* (New York, 1989). The family and gender roles are discussed in Lawrence Stone, *The Family, Sex, and Marriage in England, 1500–1800* (New York, 1977); Randolph Trumbach, *The Rise of the Egalitarian Family: Aristocratic Kinship and Domestic Relations in Eighteenth-Century England* (New York, 1978); Susan Dwyer Amussen, *An Ordered Society: Gender and Class in Early Modern England* (New York, 1988). The prehistory of the novel can be found in Michael McKeon, *The Origins of the English Novel, 1600–1740* (Baltimore, 1987); J. Paul Hunter, *Before Novels* (New York, 1990).

daringly masculine men had had sexual relations with both women and adolescent males. The older pattern could still be found in London through the 1720s. But after that, it was only males in special gender-segregated environments, such as ships at sea, prisons, or colleges, who tended to be bisexual. In the early eighteenth century, the old pattern can be seen in the lives of aristocratic men such as Lord Stanhope, who headed the government, or the great philosopher Lord Shaftesbury, who liked both women and young men and did not suffer as a consequence. But after the 1720s aristocrats such as Lord Hervey or Lord George Germain were presumed to have married or to have had mistresses simply as a means of hiding what was really an exclusive sexual interest in males, whether adult or adolescent. And a man like Hervey, in his expressions of affection for the younger men in whom he was interested, cast himself in the passive effeminate role of the molly or he-whore.[3]

After 1750 aristocrats whose effeminacy was too obvious (for instance, Horace Walpole and Humphrey Morice) found that, while they were tolerated socially for their amusing tongues, they were very likely to be excluded from a share in real political power by those aristocratic men whose taste was now exclusively for women. These effeminate men were also likely to find themselves blackmailed by poorer men. Here the law came to their protection, since such aggression by the poor against their betters (whose greater elegance made them all seem sodomitical to poorer men) was not to be tolerated. A young unmarried aristocrat—Charles Fielding, for example—also found that his family, after they had rescued him from blackmail, were likely to force him to live abroad where his tastes would not embarrass them. Other married men, who overstepped the bounds of discretion and caused a scandal by seducing a young man, were separated from their wives and ostracized from the fashionable world. Even that famous libertine John Cleland, who produced the greatest pornographic novel of the century, discovered after 1750 that his apparent interest in female prostitutes did not save him from ostracism when his taste for sodomy with males became apparent.[4]

---

[3]Randolph Trumbach, "The Birth of the Queen: Sodomy and the Emergence of Gender Equality in Modern Culture, 1660–1750," in *Hidden from History: Reclaiming the Gay and Lesbian Past,* ed. Martin Bauml Duberman, Martha Vicinus, and George Chauncey, Jr. (New York, 1989), pp. 129–40; and "Sodomy Transformed: Aristocratic Libertinage, Public Reputation, and the Gender Revolution of the Eighteenth Century," *Journal of Homosexuality* 19 (1990): 105–24; Arthur Gilbert, "Buggery and the British Navy, 1700–1861," *Journal of Social History* 10 (1976–77): 72–98.

[4]Trumbach, "Sodomy Transformed," pp. 118–20; Randolph Trumbach, "London's Sodomites: Homosexual Behavior and Western Culture in the Eighteenth Century," *Journal of Social History* 11 (1977): 20; Henry Merritt, "A Biographical Note on John Cleland," *Notes and Queries* 226 (1981): 305–6.

During the Restoration (1660–1700), on the other hand, the position of aristocratic men who were sodomites had been quite different. Theirs had been the last generation of the old sexual culture, before the new way of conceptualizing the relationship of gender to sexuality in males had come into existence. Before 1700, in London and at court, wild rakes such as Lord Rochester had had wives, mistresses, and boys. Such characters could in the 1670s even be presented occasionally on the public stage. In *Sodom; or, The Quintessence of Debauchery,* Rochester (to whom it is now firmly attributed) wrote of sodomy with women and with boys as indifferently wicked and exciting. The play was printed probably twice, though never performed. But men like Rochester were put on the defensive beginning in the 1690s, and not so much at first by the fear of the new effeminate sod-omite's role as by the influence of ideas about romantic marriage and domesticity in family life. King William's taste for boys as well as women was not criticized in that decade so much as was the supposed sexual passivity of William Bentinck, the king's great friend, who was condemned as being too old to be a catamite—that was for boys. But bisexual libertinism ceased to be presented on the public stage in the 1690s, and Rochester's *Sodom* was printed for the last time in 1707.[5]

Between 1707 and 1730, public officials under the inspiration of the Societies for the Reformation of Manners launched a series of attacks against a new kind of effeminate sodomite among the London poor. These men constructed around themselves a protective subculture of meeting places and ritual behavior. A few men, who mainly seem to have been in-volved in prostitution, played out a largely feminine identity. They took women's names, spent nearly all their time in women's clothes, and almost consistently were referred to as "she" and "her" by their male and female acquaintances. Their male customers in some cases must have known that these prostitutes were genital males, but in other cases perhaps not, since some of these transvestite males worked the streets as members of a group of female prostitutes. The gender identity of these transvestite males was not entirely feminine, however, since they sometimes wore men's clothes and were prepared to take the active or inserter's role in sexual intercourse. They were, therefore, neither male nor female—they belonged instead to a third gender role that combined some characteristics from each of the other two legitimate genders. Such men may have existed before 1700, when

[5]Trumbach, "Birth of the Queen," pp. 131–32; J. W. Johnson, "Did Rochester Write *Sodom?*" *Papers of the Bibliographical Society of America* 81 (1987): 119–53; Trumbach, "Sod-omy Transformed," pp. 110–12; Dennis Rubini, "Sexuality and Augustan England: Sodomy, Politics, Elite Circles, and Society," in *The Pursuit of Sodomy: Male Homosexuality in Renaissance and Enlightenment Europe,* ed. Kent Gerard and Gert Hekma (New York, 1989), pp. 349–81.

they were likely to have been confused with the biological hermaphrodites who sometimes changed (though illegally) from the male or female gender to which they had been assigned at birth.[6]

After 1700, however, transvestite adult men who clearly possessed male genitalia and whose bodies showed no ambiguity were classified as part of a larger group of effeminate men who were supposed to desire sexual relations only with other males, who might be either adults or adolescents. These men, for whom the formal term was sodomite, were in the slang of the streets known as mollies, which was a term that had first been applied to female prostitutes. Many of them could not have been identified as sodomites outside the context of the molly-house, or sodomitical tavern or alehouse. Some of them were married, with children, and others provided themselves with female companions for the benefit of their neighbors. Once such men were inside the molly-house, they displayed many of the feminine characteristics of the male transvestite prostitute: they took women's names and adopted the speech and bodily movements of women. On some occasions, especially at dances, some of them dressed entirely as women. Some sodomites in the molly-houses played men to match the role of female prostitute that others took. But all of these men were obliged to play two roles, one in the public world in which they worked and must have spent most of their time and another in the molly-house. Some men, of course, could not sufficiently hide their effeminacy in public and as a consequence were abused or blackmailed. This suggests that they must have internalized their third gender role to such a degree that they were unable to hide it, even though it would have been very much to their advantage in the public world. In the public mind, all men in the molly-houses—as well as those who used the public latrines, the parks, or the cruising streets and arcades to find sexual partners—belonged to the same category, no matter what their behavior in the public sphere. All were members of a third gender that deserved to be treated with contempt. They were hanged in the few cases where anal penetration and seminal emission could be proven. Otherwise, they were fined, imprisoned, and sentenced to stand in the public pillory, where a few were stoned to death. But even the majority who survived the pillory must have had their lives ruined, since they usually were sentenced to stand in those neighborhoods where they previously had managed to hide their identities as sodomites.

Once this adult effeminate role was established in the public mind as the condition of all males who engaged in sexual relations with other males, it was no longer possible for adolescent males (as they had sometimes done in the seventeenth century) to play a role of sexual passivity with an older,

[6]Trumbach, "Birth of the Queen," pp. 125–39; "Sodomy Transformed," pp. 115–17; also Trumbach, "London's Sodomites"; Alan Bray, *Homosexuality in Renaissance England* (London, 1982), pp. 80–114. Bray tends to underplay the effeminacy of these men.

sexually active male. All males were now obliged to present themselves as sexually active and never passive once they had entered puberty, around the age of fifteen. Sexual passivity at any stage of life would permanently deprive a male of masculine status and cause him profound personal anxiety as well. This can be seen from the cases for sodomitical assault brought by boys or their parents. In almost all cases, the charges were brought by boys past puberty: there is little evidence of men interested in prepubescent children. The men charged were both young and old, married and unmarried. In many cases they seem to have been attracted to the sexual ambiguity of the male adolescent body, courting the boys as though they were girls, wanting to penetrate them, but in some cases fellating the boy. The boys themselves showed a variety of responses. Some ran for the constable after conversation and being touched. Other boys consented to a single act but resisted subsequent overtures. And still other boys seemed willing partners—in some cases they may have been future sodomites. None of the men seem to have been described as effeminate, but they were nonetheless classified as mollies at their trials. Some men who were arrested for soliciting other adult men were more clearly effeminate, often offering their bodies for penetration. Sodomites, in other words, might be more or less passive in their sexual behavior, but they were all classified as mollies. The boys who complained had to be careful themselves, especially after 1750 when the new effeminate role was fully established. A nineteen-year-old youth who told a fellow worker of his encounter with a sodomite when he was drunk was warned by his friend to be careful what he admitted in public, since, if he brought his charge to court, the judge might sentence him as well as the sodomite for having participated in the acts to the extent that he had. Charges of sodomitical assault and of attempting to blackmail a man for being a sodomite made up at least half of the sodomy cases in the London courts. Charges against sodomites for having sex with each other became the decided minority, especially after 1750. It is apparent that once the sodomite's role was established, the law's principal concern was to contain his behavior and insulate it from the rest of male society.[7]

Sexual relations between women, on the other hand, were never prosecuted in London. It is therefore difficult even to establish unambiguously that they occurred. They were occasionally described in imaginative or pornographic literature. The women were represented either as aristocrats or as prostitutes. But they were not described as cross-dressing or engaging in any other form of cross-gender behavior; and they usually expressed sexual

[7]Randolph Trumbach, "Sodomitical Assaults, Gender Role, and Sexual Development in Eighteenth-Century London," in Gerard and Hekma, eds., pp. 407–29; *Proceedings . . . at the Old Bailey*, no. 7, pt. 1 (1772), pp. 364–67. The terms "boy" and "girl" are used in conformity with eighteenth-century usage: they can refer to individuals between the ages of fifteen and nineteen, when puberty began at fifteen.

interest in men as well as in women. There were actual women who cross-dressed, and they were sometimes prosecuted for it; but their cross-dressing usually was undertaken as a means to pass safely in a male occupation rather than to sexually attract women. It was essential that their disguise be fully convincing, since any ambiguity that arose from the mixing of gender traits (as male sodomites did) would have led to their discovery and the failure of their purpose. Among some of these cross-dressing women, there were a few who eventually married women and perhaps even engaged in intercourse by using an artificial penis. These women had crossed the gender boundary and were condemned for it, but other women who lived as husbands to women for many years—but against whom no sexual charges were leveled—seem to have passed unscathed. After 1770 there were occasional examples of aristocratic women (sometimes singly, sometimes as part of a female couple) who were either romantically or sexually attracted to women and who cross-dressed: they were accepted when the romance was stressed and the sex vigorously denied, and they were condemned and ostracized when it was otherwise. It was, however, much more possible to be unaware that sexual relations between women existed in any form than it was not to know about effeminate male sodomites. One of the few prepubescent boys assaulted by a man was able to explain to his grandfather what had happened by saying that he had undergone what the two men had done to each other whom he had seen stand in the pillory in his neighborhood.[8]

It is likely, then, that sexual relations between women still occurred within the context that in the seventeenth century had applied to sexual relations between males as well—that is, persons who engaged in sexual relations with their own gender were presumed to be attracted to the other gender as well, and consequently their sexual acts with their own gender did not compromise their general standing as masculine or feminine individuals. Only two kinds of sexual acts endangered an individual's gender standing: sexual passivity in an adult male (but not in an adolescent) and sexual activity by a woman that included the use of an artificial penis or a supposedly enlarged clitoris. Such individuals, along with biological hermaphrodites, were likely to be viewed as dangerous, since they passed back and forth from active to passive rather than remaining in the passive female or active male conditions to which they had been assigned at birth. Only the temporary passivity of adolescent males whose bodies had not yet acquired secondary male characteristics did not threaten this system. It was the case that seventeenth-century society presumed that although there

---

[8]Randolph Trumbach, "London's Sapphists: From Three Sexes to Four Genders in the Making of Modern Culture," in *Body Guards: The Cultural Politics of Gender Ambiguity*, ed. Julia Epstein and Kristina Straub (New York, 1991), in press; and "Sodomitical Assaults," pp. 413–14.

were three kinds of bodies (men, women, and hermaphrodites), there were only two kinds of gender (male and female).[9]

After 1700 this system was replaced by another, for men but not for women. For eighteenth-century males, there were now two kinds of bodies (male and female) but three genders (man, woman, and sodomite)—since the sodomite experienced his desires and played his role as a result of a corrupted education or socialization and not because of a bodily condition. Hermaphrodites were described by some as being essentially male or female and not a third body type and by others as being, in effect, all women. With regard to women, the old system of three bodies and two genders could still be presumed, since there was for women as yet no public role equivalent to the third gender role of the molly, with his combination of male and female characteristics. But eighteenth-century men had entered a new gender system by changing the nature of their sexual relations with each other: men no longer had sex with boys and women—they now had sex either with females or with males. Those who desired males were obliged to accept assignment to a third gender role, which was held in great contempt and given a status similar to that which the female prostitute had among women. But the prostitute could be redeemed back into the general body of respectable women. The sodomite, on the other hand, could never be received among men. Nonetheless, the role of the sodomite played a very necessary part in the new relations between men and women that the emergence of individualism and equality were producing in eighteenth-century society. His role guaranteed that, however far equality between men and women might go, men would never become like women since they would never desire men. Only women and sodomites desired men, and this remained true for males throughout their lives from adolescence to old age.[10]

Men had entered the modern culture of gender equality by redefining their sexual relations with other men. Women entered this world by redefining their sexual relations with men, whether as virgins, wives, or prostitutes. They did not, in the eighteenth century at any rate, do so by significantly changing their sexual relations with other women. By the fifth decade of the century (which also produced the classic novels of the century), the new system for women began to be apparent in the changing patterns of prosecution for sexual offenses by women. Cases against

[9] Trumbach, "London's Sapphists"; and Randolph Trumbach, "Gender and the Homosexual Role in Modern Western Culture: The Eighteenth and Nineteenth Centuries Compared," in *Homosexuality, Which Homosexuality?* ed. Dennis Altman et al. (London, 1989), pp. 149–69.

[10] Trumbach, "London's Sapphists"; Randolph Trumbach, "Modern Prostitution and Gender in *Fanny Hill:* Libertine and Domesticated Fantasy," in *Sexual Underworlds of the Enlightenment,* ed. G. S. Rousseau and Roy Porter (Manchester, 1987), pp. 69–85.

women for committing adultery with other women's husbands began to decline and within twenty years entirely disappeared.[11] Defamation suits in the consistory court in which, typically, one married woman had called another a whore or a bitch (and thereby implied that she was adulterous) dropped to half of what they had been in the first decade of the century. By the end of the century they had fallen again by half, and they entirely ceased to be brought in the early nineteenth century.[12] It is unlikely that the decline of either of these two actions was a reflection of an actual change in the adulterous behavior of women, for at the same time the number of men who sought divorces from adulterous wives in the consistory court at least doubled. The number of women, though, who tried to divorce their husbands after 1750 in the consistory court was halved. In other words, before 1750 most divorce cases were brought by women, but after 1750 most were initiated by men. This is very curious, since in every other western divorce jurisdiction after 1750, women continued to bring more cases than men.[13]

Englishwomen were in fact being encouraged to settle their sexual and marital difficulties outside public forums. The number of private separations initiated on behalf of women do seem to have increased.[14] Male opinion and power, which controlled the courts, had come to believe in female delicacy and in the domestic, motherly tendencies of most women. Men were therefore anxious to prevent any public demonstration that women continued to be sexual beings. Sexuality in women was being swallowed up by motherhood for men of the elite. They wished to extend this ideal to women of all social ranks. For example, poor women who were accused of infanticide before 1750 were usually treated quite harshly. But after 1750 the tone of their trials changed, as everything was done to establish that the women—by providing baby linen or caring for other children—had demonstrated maternal feelings before the birth of their infants and therefore could not have intended to kill them. Women were

[11] In the house of correction lists for the three London jurisdictions (housed in the Greater London Record Office and the Corporation of London Record Office [hereafter CLRO]), as many as ten cases per year for adultery can be found until 1730, with two-thirds of the cases being brought against women. After 1740, the cases fall to one or more per year, and there are no cases at all after 1753.

[12] Randolph Trumbach, "Whores and Bastards: Women and Illicit Sex in Eighteenth-Century London" (paper presented at the meeting of the Northeastern American Society for Eighteenth-Century Studies, Toronto, October 10, 1979).

[13] Randolph Trumbach, "Kinship and Marriage in Early Modern France and England," *Annals of Scholarship* 2 (1981): 113–28. The history of divorce may now be followed in Roderick Phillips, *Putting Asunder: A History of Divorce in Western Society* (New York, 1988); Lawrence Stone, *Road to Divorce* (New York, 1990).

[14] Susan Staves, *Married Women's Separate Property in England, 1660–1833* (Cambridge, MA, 1990), pp. 162–95.

mothers and mothers did not kill babies. To make it less likely that they would, the Foundling Hospital was established to receive their children.[15] On the other hand, poor women who charged that they had been raped found that the courts became less and less sympathetic to their claims. This probably did not reflect a growing male callousness toward women but, instead, flowed from the presumption that a girl who behaved in a way appropriate to her future destiny as a mother was not likely to end up in a situation in which she would be raped.[16] Women clearly were charged with the greater responsibility for maintaining their status as mothers.

It was, after all, quietly accepted by legal authority after 1750 that some men were likely to need a sexual outlet that for whatever reason was not available to them in marriage. The constables therefore ceased to arrest men found with prostitutes in bawdy houses or in the streets, which they had regularly done until 1730. The only men arrested after 1750 were those who had scandalized public decency by engaging in sexual intercourse in a public place.[17] But though public opinion regularly professed to be shocked by the population of streetwalking prostitutes, who could be found on the great public thoroughfares throughout the city, it never really proposed that men be punished or otherwise socially discouraged from going to prostitutes. There were many inconveniences that arose from the presence of prostitutes—from the shock they caused to respectable women and children to the increasing spread of venereal disease. Men who became infected took the disease home to their wives and their unborn children. The disease spread from its traditional groups of gentlemen and soldiers to all of the London poor. To deal with the threat, a venereal disease hospital was established for the very poor. But a practical physician such as William Buchan, while advising washing as the best prophylactic, was reluctant to have any severe restriction placed on prostitution for fear that this would encourage men to turn to sodomy. When there were no natural outlets, unnatural ones would be sought. This was a very old piece of public wisdom. Even Thomas Aquinas had proposed tolerating prostitution so as to avoid sodomy. But to be a sodomite in the thirteenth century was to have sex with boys as an alternative to women, without losing one's status as a man. In the

[15]R. W. Malcolmson, "Infanticide in the Eighteenth Century," in *Crime in England, 1550–1800,* ed. J. S. Cockburn (Princeton, NJ, 1977), pp. 187–209; Peter C. Hoffer and N.E.H. Hull, *Murdering Mothers* (New York, 1981); Ruth K. McClure, *Coram's Children* (New Haven, CT, 1981).

[16]Antony E. Simpson, "Vulnerability and the Age of Female Consent: Legal Innovation and Its Effect on Prosecutions for Rape in Eighteenth-Century London," in Rousseau and Porter, eds., pp. 181–205; Anna Clark, *Women's Silence, Men's Violence: Sexual Assault in England, 1770–1845* (London, 1987).

[17]CLRO, Mansion House Minute Books, 1785–90; CLRO, Guildhall Justice Room Charge Books, 1752–95.

eighteenth century, to become a sodomite was to exile oneself from the majority of men and to take on the despised status of a third gender.[18]

Men therefore could not be expected to give up prostitution. Instead it had to be established that a girl became a prostitute from the peculiarities of her environment. If, however, she could be placed in a different and improved environment, it became likely that by the disciplines of work and religion she would be able to rejoin the domestic life for which women by their natures were intended. After 1750 the Magdalen Hospital and the Lock Asylum were established to provide just such environments. The idea for a house in which prostitutes could be employed and reformed seems to have appeared first in a pamphlet by Thomas Bray in 1698. Bray was one of the principal organizers of the Societies for the Reformation of Manners; his proposal was part of the reaction to the increase in streetwalking by prostitutes, which was first remarked in the late 1690s. Even the libertines, however, were struck by the need for some sort of institution. Christopher Johnson in 1724 recalled that, in his earlier days, many of the prostitutes would moan to him after sex about the way in which they had been deluded by their first seducers. They had taken to the streets because there was no other way to live after losing their reputation and their friends. "How often," he said, he had "wished we had such a provision for these unhappy females (and their offspring) as they have in other countries."[19]

In the 1750s a group of reformers, less inspired by a punitive religious zeal or the regrets of a superannuated rake, promoted the cause of an asylum for prostitutes. Robert Dingley, a successful London merchant in his early forties, married and the father of three children, took the lead. He seems to have been moved by civic pride in London's tradition of public charities, by humanitarian zeal ("humanity in its utmost efforts pleads their cause more powerfully than anything I can offer on the subject"), and by

[18]Randolph Trumbach, "Prostitution, Venereal Disease, and the Structure of Society in Eighteenth-Century London" (paper presented at the Columbia University Seminar on Eighteenth-Century European Culture, New York, February 15, 1990); William Buchan, *Observations Concerning the Prevention and Cure of the Venereal Disease* (1796; rpt., New York, 1985), p. 29.

[19]Thomas Bray, *A General Plan of a Penitential Hospital for Employing and Reforming Lewd Women* (London, 1698); Christopher Johnson, *The History of . . . Eliz. Mann* (London, 1724), pp. v–vi; *Satan's Harvest Home; or, The Present State of Whorecraft, Adultery, Fornication, Procuring, Pimping, Sodomy, and the Game at Flatts* (London, 1749), pp. 33–34. Modern histories of the institution: H.F.B. Compston, *The Magdalen Hospital* (London, 1917); S.B.B. Pearce, *An Ideal in the Working: The Story of the Magdalen Hospital, 1758 to 1958* (London, 1958); Stanley Nash, "Prostitution and Charity: The Magdalen Hospital, a Case Study," *Journal of Social History* 17 (1984): 617–28, and "Social Attitudes toward Prostitution in London from 1752 to 1829" (Ph.D. diss., New York University, 1980); Vern L. Bullough, "Prostitution and Reform in Eighteenth-Century England," in *'Tis Nature's Fault: Unauthorized Sexuality during the Enlightenment,* ed. Robert Purks Maccubbin (New York, 1987), pp. 61–74.

religious concern to be a "means . . . of rescuing many bodies from disease and death, and many souls from eternal misery." Dingley was soon joined by Jonas Hanway, his former partner and an active religious philanthropist. Saunders Welch and Sir John Fielding, the two London magistrates most active in trying to control street prostitution, joined the cause.[20]

Welch's proposals for the hospital neatly brought into focus the new attitude toward prostitution. He did not expect that the hospital would end prostitution. He thought that such an aim would be dangerous, in any case, since it might result in the increase of sodomy—"a horrid vice too rife already, though the bare thought of it strikes the mind with horror." His aim was simply to make prostitution less publicly apparent, by removing the young streetwalkers. Picking up these girls and sending them to the houses of correction had no long-term consequences: "Punishment only prevents for the time it operates, but hardly ever produced one reformation." A hospital, on the other hand, would educate the girls and send them out as apprentices or servants, thereby "striking at the root of the evil." If there were, in other words, no mass of poor girls to be seduced into prostitution, its more obvious manifestations in the street would be eliminated. Prostitution from Welch's point of view was objectionable when it was public and disorderly. But he presumed that it was needed as a means of affording men a sexual release that would otherwise seek its outlet in other men— though he found such an outlet almost impossible to contemplate. The behavior of men was therefore unlikely to change. It was the behavior of the prostitute that had to be modified. Punishing her in the way that had been done in the early eighteenth century had no long-term effect. She had to be reeducated into appropriate behavior. He clearly did not presume that a woman once fallen could never be redeemed. And it is likely that his hopefulness about her redemption was based on his acceptance of the view of women's nature that was becoming fashionable. But this he did not say in so many words. William Dodd, the chaplain to the new Magdalen Hospital, did: "Every man who reflects on the true condition of humanity, must know that the life of a common prostitute is as contrary to the nature and condition of the female sex as darkness to light: and however some may be compelled to the slavery of it, yet we can never imagine every line of right and virtue obliterated in the minds of all of them."[21]

---

[20]Robert Dingley, *Proposals for Establishing a Public Place of Reception for Penitent Prostitutes* (London, 1758), pp. 3, 6; Compston, pp. 23–36; Saunders Welch, *A Proposal . . . to Remove The Nuisance of Common Prostitutes from the Streets of This Metropolis* (London, 1758); Sir John Fielding, *An Account of the Origins and Effect of a Police* (London, 1758).

[21]Welch, pp. 16–19, 25–30; *An Account of the . . . Magdalen Hospital . . . Together with Dr. Dodd's Sermons* (London, 1776), p. 51. Some account of the changing position on women's nature at midcentury can be found in Felicity A. Nussbaum, *The Brink of All We Hate* (Lexington, KY, 1984), pp. 93, 136; Marlene Gates, "The Cult of Womanhood in Eigh-

The hospital, once it was established, could never have made much of a dent in the population of street prostitutes. It never had more than from sixty to one hundred women in it between 1758 and 1790. In its first twenty-five years, the hospital admitted 2,415 women, when there were a minimum of three thousand active prostitutes in London at any one time. It claimed that 65 percent of its young women were either reconciled to their parents or placed as servants. Twenty-five percent of the women left, either at their own request or at the insistence of the committee when they could not conform to the discipline of the house. (A few died or became lunatics, perhaps as a result of the mercury they had taken to cure venereal disease.) Some went back to prostitution, as did 20 (12 percent) of the 164 women discharged in the hospital's first three years. But by 1786 only 122 women (5.5 percent) out of a total of 2,197 had married or become mothers. This may overestimate the number of former prostitutes who married, since by 1786 the hospital had begun to take in girls who had been seduced by men and alienated from their families, but who had not yet "been publicly on the town." This policy may reflect the hospital's despair at an overwhelming task. Of the twenty to thirty-five girls who applied each month, it could admit only a few. Those who were venereally infected were sent to the venereal disease hospital and allowed to apply again. Some were supported until there was a vacancy in the Magdalen. Some were reconciled through the committee to their families and were never admitted. The committee took the point of view that a woman with relations or friends to care for her would never become a prostitute.[22]

Life inside the Magdalen Hospital recently has been compared to the regime of the modern penitentiary, but it might as fairly be regarded as a special kind of convent, where the nuns made promises to reform their lives and stayed until they were prepared to rejoin the world. When the girls entered, they were reminded that "it never was intended that you should pass your whole life here" or live in idleness. Instead, they were there to "be enabled to return into life with a reputation recovered," "with a habit of industry, and the means to procure honestly your own bread," and with a mind "resolved through God's grace to forfeit no more the blessed hope of everlasting life." They were to attend chapel twice on Sunday, when the chaplain preached and visitors were admitted by ticket to observe them. They were to wear a "downcast look" on such occasions and to remember

---

teenth-Century Thought," *Eighteenth-Century Studies* 10 (1976): 21–39; Kathleen M. Rogers, *Feminism in Eighteenth-Century England* (Brighton, 1982), pp. 119–47; C. J. Rawson, "Some Remarks on Eighteenth-Century 'Delicacy,' with a Note on Hugh Kelly's *False Delicacy* (1768)," *Journal of English and German Philology* 61 (1962): 1–13.

[22]*An Account of the . . . Present State of the Magdalen Charity* (London, 1761), pp. vi–xiii; John Butler, *A Sermon . . . [with the] General State of the Magdalen Hospital, 10 August 1758 – December 25, 1784* (London, 1786), pp. 4–5.

that a "bold and dauntless stare will give but mean ideas of reformation." They were to pray in private and read the Bible. In their conversation, they were to be meek to their superiors; and among themselves they were not to swear and never to "glory in your shame" by telling stories of their previous lives, "which should cover your faces with confusion."[23]

The Magdalen Hospital remained the only institution of its kind in London until 1789. In that year the Lock Asylum was founded. It received up to twenty penitent prostitutes at a time, after they had been cured of venereal disease in the Lock Hospital. The Lock Hospital had been founded in 1746 to cure the London poor of venereal disease. Half of its patients were women, and most of these were young prostitutes. The men, after their discharge, usually had their "places of abode or occupations" to which to return—the women had only prostitution. The Lock Hospital by the late 1760s began to give some girls either money with which to buy passage back to their families in the countryside or double sets of clothes, so that they could take places as servants in London. The money to do this came from theatrical benefits, from bequests, and from the funds collected in the chapel, which the Reverend Martin Madan had raised a subscription to build and to which his preaching drew a fashionable congregation.[24]

Madan had begun life as a libertine and a lawyer, but after a religious conversion, he took orders. In the 1750s he became chaplain to the Lock Hospital, which tended in its program to stress the cure of disease rather than the reformation of manners. After ten years as chaplain, Madan evidently became overwhelmed by the sense that neither sending a few women to the Magdalen Hospital nor locking up a great many more from time to time in a house of correction, where they helped to corrupt each other and came out more abandoned, would solve the problem of prostitution. Instead a way had to be found to discourage men from seducing girls in the first place. The answer he hit upon was mandatory polygamy— oblige every man to marry every girl he seduced. He began to talk about it to his friends, and, after fifteen years of studying the matter, Madan in 1780

[23]Stanley Nash, "Prostitution and Charity," made the comparison; the rules that described the daily life of women in the Magdalen Hospital may be found in most of the *Accounts* of the charity: the passages quoted here are from the 1776 edition, pp. 231–52, 307–27. It is possible that in the early nineteenth century, institutions such as the Magdalen Hospital came to be organized more like a penitentiary than a convent, but the convent seems the more likely model in the late eighteenth century. Horace Walpole, after a visit to the Magdalen Hospital, wrote that he "fancied myself in a convent" (W. S. Lewis et al., *Yale Edition of Horace Walpole's Correspondence* (New Haven, CT, 1937–83), 21:368.

[24]*An Account of the Institution of the Lock Asylum* (London, 1792); Royal College of Surgeons, Lock Hospital Manuscripts, General Court Book, 1773–89, p. 313; Lock Asylum Minutes, 1787–90; Board Minutes, 1768–70, pp. 23, 29, 54, 81, 153, 168, 172, 195, 214, 232, 241, 288, 299.

published his *Thelypthora, or a Treatise on Female Ruin,* to the delight of London's libertines and the pained shock of his evangelical friends.[25]

But preaching the gospel of traditional Christian asceticism, some argued, was the only way to end seduction and uncleanness. This was what the Reverend Thomas Scott, a subsequent chaplain to the Lock Hospital, intended to promote in the asylum for prostitutes that he set up in 1789. In theory, the asceticism of the gospel applied equally to men and women, but in practice it was easier to enforce on women. Madan's program of polygamy presumed that men needed to be made responsible for seducing women into prostitution. The Lock Asylum and the Magdalen Hospital held the prostitute responsible for her own condition and did not try to reach the behavior of the male libertine. This may, in part, have been because Christian asceticism did not yet accept the new, more positive evaluation of women's nature. The temptress Eve still had her power in the minds of the religious. Certainly Thomas Haweis had opposed Madan's idea because of its tendency "in the feebler sex to lessen the influence of conscience, and silence the pleadings of virtue against the violence of natural passion or persuasive seduction."[26]

The girls admitted to the Lock Asylum were those whom Scott had identified as the most tractable during the course of their cure for venereal disease in the Lock Hospital. One girl was rejected because she appeared "to be of such an artful disposition." The girls who seemed most promising were those who had been seduced, infected, and then deserted by a single man, but who had not yet gone on to "more general prostitution": "These are the most hopeful and proper objects of compassion . . . [and] may probably be almost all restored to society." The asylum, in its first eight months of operation and within its limit of twenty girls, chose about one in four (33 of 117) of those released by the hospital as cured.[27]

The women in the asylum spent their days in confined activities similar to those of the women in the Magdalen Hospital, and there was little recreation or interaction among them. They could have conversation only in the presence of the matron, who encouraged religious conversation and prevented other kinds. The women, except during working hours and in the matron's presence, were to spend as little time together as possible. This

[25]Richard Hill, *The Blessings of Polygamy* (London, 1781), pp. 157ff.; Thomas Willis, *Remarks on Polygamy* (London, 1781), p. vi; E. B. Greene, *Whispers for the Ear of the Author of Thelypthora* (London, 1781), p. xxiii.

[26]Hill, p. 71; Thomas Haweis, *A Scriptural Refutation of the Arguments for Polygamy* (London, 1781), p. viii.

[27]Royal College of Surgeons, Lock Asylum Minutes, 1787–90; *Account of the Lock Asylum,* pp. 12–13.

desire to separate the women from each other was a new departure, since it does not appear in any of the printed eighteenth-century rules for the Magdalen Hospital. Finally, the women's letters and boxes were subject to inspection. Not surprisingly, 40 percent (48) of the 120 women who went through this regime in its first five years were expelled for misbehavior or ran away from the house or, later, the employer with whom they had been placed. But as many girls (47) stayed with their employer. Nine girls died in the house. Only 16, however, were taken back by their families (though many of those admitted were probably orphans), and a few of these had married and borne children.

The founding of the Magdalen Hospital and of the Lock Asylum were the most innovative actions taken against prostitution after 1750, and they peculiarly reflected the new views of the elite on the role of women and the domestic affections, and of sentiment generally. But these houses were clearly failures, if for no other reason than the very small number of women with whom they dealt. Nonetheless, a magistrate such as Saunders Welch supported the Magdalen Hospital because he saw the failure of even the latest phase in the traditional response of arresting the prostitute and the bawdy-house keeper. This failure had occurred despite the rearrangement at midcentury of the relationship between the magistrate and the voluntary society of neighbors or religious reformers. In the early eighteenth century, the reformation societies had pushed the magistrates into action. But at midcentury, it was the magistrate who encouraged the reformer, and none more so than Sir John Fielding. It was largely through Fielding's efforts that two new acts made their way into the statute book in 1752 and 1774. But by 1758 Welch had already declared the 1752 act ineffective, and the act of 1774 did not fare much better.

The act of 1774 probably did account for the greater number of prostitutes arrested in the latter 1770s. But the surviving sources are not comprehensive enough to say so definitively. It is, however, possible to look at the treatment of all the prostitutes arrested in the City and brought to the Mansion House Justice Room in the years 1785–90. This is in fact the best such surviving source for the entire century. It allows us to see how the ideas about the reform of prostitution that became current after 1750 were put into force by a group of sober and responsible justices.

In the six years between 1785 and 1790, 798 women or girls were arrested as prostitutes and brought to the magistrates sitting in the Mansion House Justice Room. In 1785 and 1786 about one hundred women were arrested each year. In 1787 and the subsequent years about fifty more women per year were arrested, probably as a result of a new reform movement. Forty percent of the arrests were made in the months of May, July, and August, which probably reflected the increased level of streetwalking associated with the great London fairs. About 40 percent of the women were simply reprimanded and discharged, probably after promising not to offend again. About 50 percent were sent to the house of correction at Bridewell. Forty percent were sentenced to a fortnight, a third to a month, and 15 percent to a week or ten days. Thirteen percent of the women imprisoned were also whipped. (Compared with the early eighteenth century, the sentences were longer but fewer were whipped.) These varying dispositions probably reflected the magistrates' judgments as to whether they were dealing with a young, inexperienced girl or a habitual prostitute. But out of the 40 percent who were simply reprimanded, there were only three instances when a girl was clearly sent back to her family and three cases when she was sent to the hospital because her venereal infection was so evident. It is true that 14 percent of the women were passed to their parishes, but it is unlikely that in most cases the intention was to send them back to their families, since 70 percent of those passed had also been sentenced to a term in Bridewell. The relatively low number passed does confirm that few prostitutes were young girls fresh from the countryside: most of them must have been Londoners, or women with either a London settlement or no settlement at all. Some of those passed, in any case, were back on the streets as soon as they could manage it. Prostitutes in most cases therefore must have been passed to their parishes of settlement as a means of disposing of some of the incorrigible (Saunders Welch had recommended this) and not as a way of saving the young. That last aim was beyond the resources of most magistrates. They simply discharged the clearly inexperienced girl and hoped for the best.[28]

Such were the halfhearted attempts that men made in the second half of the eighteenth century to remove prostitution from the streets. These attempts were founded on a view of women's nature that arose from the system of gender relations that the late Enlightenment (or the sentimental movement) fostered throughout Europe. It was a system that presumed that men and women were close enough in the nature of their minds and feelings to meet each other in an intimate friendship that began to transform marriage and produced a new ideal of the couple's mutual care for their children. But it is apparent that a married man who went to whores did so in part because he wished to limit the degree of intimacy with his wife. The man without a wife who went to whores did so for a different but related reason. He was determined to show that his sexual interest was exclusively in women and that he was not an effeminate passive sodomite.

[28]CLRO, Mansion House Justice Room Minute Books, 1785–90; Welch, p. 28. On the theory that many of the young girls walking the streets were orphans, an asylum was set up in 1758 for girls whose parents could not be found and whose settlement was unknown, but like the Magdalen and Lock hospitals, it can have made very little practical difference; see *An Account of the Institution . . . for the Reception of Orphan Girls . . . Whose Settlement Cannot Be Found* (London, 1763).

Though it may not seem so at first, it is very likely that this fear of male passivity and the new sodomitical role that it had produced in the early Enlightenment was also a consequence of the anxieties induced by the new ideal of closer, intimate, more nearly equal relations with women. Men needed to establish that they could never be made passive as a result of intimate sexual relations. Adolescent males could no longer go through a stage of sexual passivity, and adult men who were passive were stigmatized as male whores. The changing sexual relations between men and women had transformed sexual relations between males. And since men's relations with each other were of much greater consequence to them in regard to questions of power than were their relations with women, the fear of sodomy was a stronger drive than the desire for intimacy with women. Men therefore could not give up prostitution. It was true that the figure of the prostitute contradicted all ideas about the natural domesticity of women. But she allowed men to establish that they were not sodomites. She also provided an escape from the demands of marital intimacy. Her public presence on the street was, however, an embarrassment—it flaunted too obviously the contradictions within the new system of gender relations. As a consequence, there were attempts to remove the women from the street and to reconstruct their lives. But these efforts never reached out to the male sexual desires on which the entire system of prostitution was founded. Those desires had to be left intact, since they were the bulwark men had built against equality with women. The sodomite and the prostitute guaranteed that ordinary men would never be transformed into women as a result of the intimacy or the passivity that might be produced by more nearly equal relations between men and women.

Colonizing the Breast: Sexuality and Maternity in Eighteenth-Century England

RUTH PERRY

Literature Faculty
Massachusetts Institute of Technology

But when mothers deign to nurse their own children, then will be a reform in morals; natural feeling will revive in every heart; there will be no lack of citizens for the state; this first step by itself will restore mutual affection. [Jean-Jacques Rousseau, *Emile*]

T HE INVENTION OF childhood, ascribed by Philippe Ariès to late seventeenth- and eighteenth-century Europe, inevitably involved a vast train of changes in the organization of the family, the politics of domestic life, the separation of public from private responsibility, and the revision of accepted conventions about human priorities.[1] If we want to know more

My thanks to research assistants Allen Grove and Heather MacPherson for their help on this project. This essay is a somewhat expanded version of a paper presented at the David Nichol Smith Memorial Seminar VIII, "Social Reform and Cultural Discourse in the Eighteenth Century," a conference held with the Australasian and Pacific Society for Eighteenth-Century Studies at Monash University, Melbourne, Australia, June 25–29, 1990. Papers from that conference will be published in a forthcoming special issue of *Eighteenth-Century Life* (vol. 16, no. 1) edited by Robert Purks Maccubbin.

[1] Philippe Ariès, *L'Enfant et la vie familiale sous l'ancien regime* (Paris, 1960; English trans., New York, 1962), was followed by John Demos, *A Little Commonwealth: Family Life in a Plymouth Colony* (New York, 1970); Lawrence Stone, *The Family, Sex, and Marriage in England, 1500–1800* (New York, 1977); and Randolph Trumbach, *The Rise of the Egalitarian Family: Aristocratic Kinship and Domestic Relations in Eighteenth-Century England* (New York, 1978), who have claimed that until the eighteenth century, childhood was not recognized as a stage of life distinct and separable from the rest of life. Children rather were assumed to be— and were treated as—miniature adults. These social historians infer this cultural fact from the way children were depicted earlier in paintings, with adult rather than infantine physical proportions, from the way they were dressed, and from the cultural assumption in printed sources that they were miserable sinners like their elders, rather than pure and plastic human material ready to be stamped with virtue, as John Locke thought, or guided tenderly toward

This essay originally appeared in the *Journal of the History of Sexuality* 1991, vol. 2, no. 2.

about the effects of modern child-raising patterns on the structure of Anglo-American families and gender identities, we would do well to investigate the historical effects of this "invention of childhood." Less frequently noted, but equally momentous, was the construction in that period of bourgeois motherhood—the dimensions of which current scholarship is establishing.[2] There is overwhelming literary evidence for the centrality of representations of motherhood to eighteenth-century English culture as a newly elaborated social and sexual identity for women.[3]

---

their best innate moral natures, as Jean-Jacques Rousseau thought. There is no question that by the middle of the eighteenth century there was an emerging literature on the socialization of children, as well as a new market evolving for children's toys and books. But the interpretation of these facts is by no means clear. Many historians of childhood argue that the meaning of these cultural developments is that parents were now taking their children more seriously and were more attached to them, because child mortality rates were falling and they could afford to invest themselves emotionally, so to speak, in their children. Others argue that childhood socialization took on an unprecedented severity in this period as a result of the new belief that children were especially impressionable. I leave it to historians of childhood to argue about whether or not parents really loved their children in the Middle Ages and the Renaissance in the absence of literary evidence to the contrary. That maternal sentiments were being newly recorded in the eighteenth century is undeniable—and this obviously contributes to the gestalt sometimes interpreted by cultural historians as a new interest in children and in childhood in general. My own position on this question is that of course parents of earlier periods loved their children, despite the perpetual anxiety and painful loss incurred by illness and the deaths of half of the children before they were five. It seems to me probable that what appears to us as increased parental concern for children in the eighteenth century is simply an artifact of the penetration of print culture into domestic life, in the form of diaries, memoirs, conduct books, and children's literature. Linda Pollock, in her excellent assessment of this literature, remarks acutely that what seems like increased interest in the *abstract* nature of childhood and in the methods used to socialize children might simply be increased "expertise with writing as a form of communication" rather than "any significant transformations in the parent-child relationship" (*Forgotten Children: Parent-Child Relations from 1500 to 1900* [Cambridge, 1983] p. 269).

[2] See Felicity Nussbaum, *The Autobiographical Subject* (Baltimore, 1989), chap. 9, especially pp. 205–12, as well as her "'Savage' Mothers: Narratives of Maternity in the Mid-Eighteenth Century," *Cultural Critique* (Fall 1991), in press.

[3] The construction of women *primarily* as caretaking mothers was suggested as early as 1978 by Randolph Trumbach in *The Rise of the Egalitarian Family*, although he interpreted this cultural shift as an advance for women. Ludmilla J. Jordanova in "Natural Facts: A Historical Perspective on Science and Sexuality," in Carol P. MacCormack and Marilyn Strathern, eds., *Nature, Culture, and Gender* (Cambridge, 1980), pp. 42–70, makes the enormously suggestive remark that "links between women, motherhood, the family and natural morality may help to explain the emphasis on the breast in much medical literature" (p. 49). What follows in this paper is a gloss on this observation. Valerie Fildes has done the definitive work on the history of breast-feeding and wet-nursing in England during this period. See her *Breasts, Bottles, and Babies: A History of Infant Feeding* (Edinburgh, 1986) and *Wet Nursing: A History from Antiquity to the Present* (Oxford, 1988). Susan Staves explained the enormous popularity of John Home's *Douglas*, first produced in 1756, as evidence of the new English interest in motherhood in the middle of the eighteenth century. See her "Douglas's Mother" in *Brandeis Essays*

I want to analyze one strand of this highly complex social phenomenon and to argue that motherhood was a colonial form—the domestic, familial counterpart to land enclosure at home and imperialism abroad. Motherhood as it was constructed in the early modern period is a production-geared phenomenon analogous to the capitalizing of agriculture, the industrializing of manufacture, and the institutionalizing of the nation state. In other words, these rearrangements in the psychological constellation of the family—the invention of childhood and the invention of motherhood—can be seen as adaptations of an existing social system to the new political and economic imperatives of an expanding English empire. The heady new belief in the rational manipulation of natural forces for greater productivity—whether in manufacture or in agriculture—can be traced in the operations of the family as well as in breeding cattle or in spinning cotton.

Eventually, as Anna Davin has argued crucially, the production of children for the nation and for the empire constituted childbearing women as a national resource.[4] Already in the eighteenth century there is some evidence of a growing demographic consciousness on the part of a nation in the process of industrializing and building an empire. More people were needed to keep up with the commercial and military interests of the state—more Englishmen were needed to man the factories, sail the ships, defend the seas, and populate the colonies. A petition presented to the House of

---

in Literature, ed. John Hazel Smith (Waltham, MA, 1983), pp. 51–67. Three pioneering articles about this new ideological dimension to the social construction of mid-eighteenth-century womanhood are Ruth Bloch, "American Feminine Ideals in Transition: The Rise of the Moral Mother, 1785–1815," *Feminist Studies* 4 (1978): 101–26; Mitzi Myers, "Impeccable Governesses, Rational Dames, and Moral Mothers: Mary Wollstonecraft and the Female Tradition in Georgian Children's Books," *Children's Literature* 14 (1986): 31–59; and Beth Kowaleski-Wallace, "Home Economics: Domestic Ideology in Maria Edgeworth's *Belinda,*" *Eighteenth Century* 29 (1988): 242–62. Nancy Armstrong describes this social phenomenon similarly but values it differently. She argues that this emerging definition of womanhood empowered women insofar as it created a new domain over which they were granted authority: "the use of leisure time, the ordinary care of the body, courtship practices, the operations of desire, the forms of pleasure, gender differences, and family relations." See her *Desire and Domestic Fiction* (New York, 1987), pp. 26–27. That women were in turn defined and constrained by this discourse seems to her an inevitable constitutive dimension of this new power. For French materials on motherhood, breast-feeding, and wet-nursing, see Elizabeth Badinter, *Mother Love: The Myth of Motherhood, an Historical View of the Maternal Instinct* (New York, 1981); George D. Sussman, *Selling Mother's Milk: The Wet-Nursing Business in France 1715–1914* (Urbana, IL, 1982), and Mary Jacobus, "Incorruptible Milk: Breast-feeding and the French Revolution" (paper circulated at the Center for Literary and Cultural Studies, Harvard University, Spring 1990).

[4]Anna Davin, "Imperialism and Motherhood," *History Workshop* 5 (1978): 9–65. Today, in contemporary debates about abortion, spokespersons on both sides of the issue—moral philosophers, legislators, and lawyers alike—refer unhesitatingly to the "state's interest in life."

Commons on March 10, 1756, asking for increased funds for London's Foundling Hospital shows evidence of this growing awareness. It argued that the country needed more troops for national defense and that it was in the national interest to save the lives of these abandoned children. Drafted by members of the board of governors of the Foundling Hospital, the petition pointed out that it was more cost-effective to save this native population than to hire mercenary soldiers, as had been so recently necessary to defend against a threatened invasion from France.

This connection between England's population needs and its evolving national identity as a commercial empire is patterned in the interests of the Foundling Hospital's chief administrator in 1756, Jonas Hanway.[5] Life-long campaigner for the rights of abandoned children—and a member of the commercial Russia Company—Hanway made explicit the connection between England's expanding colonial power and its need for more citizens. His instrumental reason for saving the lives of English orphans was linked to his vision of the imperial destiny of England. "Increase alone," he wrote, "can make our *natural* Strength in *Men* correspond with our *artificial* Power in *Riches,* and both with the Grandeur and Extent of the *British Empire.*"[6] Author of a history of the Caspian trade, of conduct books for women, and of treatises arguing for the Foundling Hospital, he had a financial stake in the Russia Company's brisk trade in raw silk for English wool and an emotional stake in socializing women to their proper stations, as well as in protecting abandoned children.[7] For him, national interest and morality alike urged that every effort be made to stop the appalling waste of infant life. More hands were needed to hold muskets, weave cloth, and people the empire. The "preservation of deserted children" was a patriotic duty, a cause "wherein morals, politics, and the noblest passions of the human soul, meet in a more harmonious concord."[8]

Hanway was governor of the London Foundling Hospital in 1756, on the eve of the Seven Years' War, when England was arming and anxious about having enough troops for the impending crisis. In this rising war

[5]See James Stephen Taylor, "Philanthropy and Empire: Jonas Hanway and the Infant Poor of London," *Eighteenth-Century Studies* 12 (1979): 285–306.

[6]Jonas Hanway, *Serious Considerations on the Salutary Design of the Act of Parliament for a Regular, Uniform Register of the Parish-Poor* (London, 1762), p. 26, quoted in Taylor, p. 294.

[7]Hanway's *Midnight the Signal: In Sixteen Letters to a Lady of Quality* (London, 1779) was a conduct book for gentlewomen, ostensibly the letters from a gentleman to his ward, inveighing against the dangers of keeping late hours and other bad habits of people of fashion. He also wrote a conduct book for servant women called *Advice from a Farmer to His Daughter in a Series of Discourses, Calculated to Promote the Welfare and True Interest of Servants,* 3 vols. (London, 1770), printed with a fascinating frontispiece that visually integrates the issues of gender roles, trade, government, religion, and agriculture.

[8]*Letters to the Guardians of the Infant Poor to Be Appointed by the Act of the Last Session of Parliament* (London, 1767), p. viii, quoted in Taylor, p. 293.

fever, the Foundling Hospital was reconceptualized by Hanway—and by Parliament—as a national resource for replenishing a population sure to be decimated in the coming conflict. The government rallied to save the lives of English infants and voted almost unlimited appropriations to the Foundling Hospital to establish a national network of rescue and care for abandoned children. All abandoned infants of a specified age (at first two months or younger, later six months, and then twelve months) were to be admitted to the hospital for medical attention and subsequently placed in the homes of wet nurses. The Foundling Hospital paid these women for their services and set up a system of inspection to evaluate their work and its results. Thousands of women were mobilized as surrogate mothers in this way, hired to play their unique part in the war effort.[9]

Eventually Hanway came to feel that this national effort to conserve infants for the state was ill-advised; the costs were exorbitant, and the waste of infant life was still very high. There were those, too, who felt that national revenues were being badly misspent in supporting these superfluous "bastards." In 1760, four years after the experiment had been initiated, the Foundling Hospital closed its doors to all but the foundlings of London, its mandate—and its budget—shrunk to a municipal service. According to James Stephen Taylor, "The last Parliamentary subsidy was paid in 1771; in sixteen years Parliament had expended over £500,000 to support some 15,000 children."[10]

The lesson learned by all concerned in this project was that commodification of motherhood on such a massive scale was too expensive. The nation simply could not—or would not—pay for maternal care on an individual basis. Even at £15 a year per woman, less than half of what a skilled (male) laborer might earn, the cost of subsidizing maternal care for unwanted children was greater than the national government was willing to pay. After a brief utopian attempt, this element of reproductive service was returned decisively to the private sphere. This episode is one chapter in the ideological appropriation of women as unpaid mothers for the nation. By the end of the century, even Mary Wollstonecraft seemed to believe that a woman's claim to citizenship depended on her willingness to "mother." Though she were faithful to her husband, Wollstonecraft wrote in 1792, the woman who "neither suckles nor educates her children, scarcely deserves the name of a wife, and has no right to that of a citizen."[11]

Henry Abelove, writing playfully but seriously about the population explosion in England during the late eighteenth century, has suggested that

[9]Fildes, *Wet Nursing*, pp. 174–87.

[10]Taylor, p. 293.

[11]Mary Wollstonecraft, *A Vindication of the Rights of Women*, vol. 5 of *The Works of Mary Wollstonecraft*, ed. Janet Todd and Marilyn Butler (New York, 1989), p. 217.

this demographic bulge was an effect of a new instrumentality characteristic of heterosexual relations—as of all other human behaviors. An increasingly utilitarian attitude toward human life and human production
dictated that "nonproductive" forms of sexuality were increasingly displaced and devalued during this period, replaced by a single standard of
sexual activity.[12] That the concept of bourgeois motherhood was essential
to this productive view of heterosexual relations seems to me obvious. I
want to argue that motherhood, that centrally important sentimental trope
of late eighteenth-century English literature, effected the colonization of
women for heterosexual productive relations. Following Joan Kelly's suggestion that sexual freedom is one index of women's power in other historical periods,[13] it is important to note that motherhood functioned in
this period to repress women's active sexuality. This is not to assert that
women's sexuality ever was encouraged culturally, although in earlier periods it was expected. Indeed, it could be argued that the image of women as
sexually active was as much a cultural construction as the subsequent image
of women as pure and sexless and served in its own way the male appropriation of female sexual and reproductive services. Nonetheless, it is worth
noting that in the eighteenth century, maternity came to be imagined as a
counter to sexual feeling, opposing alike individual expression, desire, and
agency in favor of a mother-self at the service of the family and the state.
This change, represented in both physiological and psychological terms,
would seem to be a paradox—the asexual mother, a contradiction in terms.
Even today these categories, the "sexual" and the "maternal," function as
mutually exclusive descriptive attributes, a formation that feminist intellectuals have puzzled over.[14] It is beyond the scope of this essay to establish
how this shift in the social construction of women's essential nature
meshed with other changes in English social identities. All I can do here is

[12]Henry Abelove, "Some Speculations on the History of Sexual Intercourse during the
Long Eighteenth Century in England," *Genders* 6 (November 1989): 125–31.

[13]Joan Kelly, "The Social Relations of the Sexes: Methodological Implications of
Women's History," in *Women, History, and Theory: The Essays of Joan Kelly* (Chicago, 1984),
pp. 1–19.

[14]Contemporary feminist theorists explain the fact that the "sexual" and the "maternal"
are constituted as mutually exclusive categories as an effect of women's exclusive care of children. See Susan Weisskopf Contratto, "Maternal Sexuality and Asexual Motherhood," in
Women: Sex and Sexuality, ed. Catharine Stimpson and Ethel Person (Chicago, 1980), pp.
225–40. In accounting for the complex interactions between parenting and sexuality and how
they affect the power relations between men and women, Ann Ferguson posits a system for the
production and socialization of children that she calls sex/affective production, analogous to
the economic production of material goods. See Ann Ferguson, "On Conceiving Motherhood and Sexuality: A Feminist Approach," in *Mothering*, ed. Joyce Trebilcot (Totowa, NJ,
1983), pp. 153–82, and *Blood at the Root: Motherhood, Sexuality, and Male Dominance*
(London, 1989).

locate one dimension of this change and connect it to the observations of other literary and cultural historians.

SEXUALITY

Students of eighteenth-century British fiction are often struck by the difference between the women imaginatively portrayed in the fiction of the earlier part of the century and the women imagined in the fiction of the latter half of the century.[15] The rakish heroines of Restoration drama, the self-advertising amorous adventurers of the love-and-intrigue novels of Aphra Behn, Delariviere Manley, and Eliza Haywood, and the freewheeling protagonists of Daniel Defoe's *Moll Flanders* and *Roxana* stand on one side of this cultural divide, while on the other side are those latter-day paragons of virtue, Evelina, Sidney Bidulph, and Emmeline, as well as Samuel Richardson's heroines—Pamela, Clarissa, and Harriet Byron—each one arguably more sexually repressed and sexually repressive than the one before.[16] This progressive desexualization of fictional heroines is further illustrated and amplified by an array of unrelenting plots punishing fictional women for what was rapidly becoming improper—and tragic—sexual behavior. Such characters as Sarah Fielding's adulterous Lady Dellwyn, Mrs. Inchbald's rebellious Miss Milner, Amelia Opie's convention-flouting Adeline Mowbray, or Mary Wollstonecraft's courageous and freethinking Maria are all severely punished in their respective texts for taking liberties with society's rules about female chastity.

Conduct literature, of course, since the seventeenth century had consistently counseled women against sexual flirtation—before or after marriage. I am not referring to prescriptive literature, however, but to fictional representations of women. In the earlier period, women's desire and sexual agency were portrayed in fiction with a tolerance, and even enjoyment, inconceivable in the later period. The rehabilitated prostitutes in John Dunton's series, *The Nightwalker* (1696–97),[17] or Aphra Behn's play, *The*

---

[15]See Ian Watt, *The Rise of the Novel* (Berkeley, 1957), pp. 161–73; Jane Spencer, *The Rise of the Woman Novelist from Aphra Behn to Jane Austen* (Oxford, 1986), especially chaps. 2 and 4; and Rosalind Ballaster, "Seductive Forms: Women's Amatory Fiction 1680–1740" (paper presented at Warren House Feminist Colloquium, February 24, 1989, Harvard University).

[16]Evelina, Sidney Bidulph, and Emmeline are the eponymous heroines of novels by Frances Burney, Frances Sheridan, and Charlotte Smith.

[17]For an argument about the positive literary construction of the women interviewed in John Dunton's *The Nightwalker*, see Shawn L. Maurer's "Reforming Men: The Construction of 'Chaste Heterosexuality' in the Early English Periodical," in *Historicizing Gender*, ed. Beth Fowkes Tobin (Urbana, IL), in press. Maurer points out that while Dunton's narrator begins by wanting to reform the nightwalking women whom he systematically ferrets out and interviews, he ends by documenting the repetitive detail of male sexual aggression and exploitation and female sexual victimization in their stories.

Rover (1677), for example, have no real counterparts in the fiction of the later period.[18] After about 1740, sexually promiscuous women—or even just lusty women—are never center-stage protagonists again, although they might be part of a colorful supporting cast. As Jane Spencer says, "In the typical woman's novel in the second half of the century, there may be a seduced woman but the heroine herself remains pure."[19]

Robert Bage was one late eighteenth-century author—a feminist of sorts—who several times portrayed a woman who had had a sexual mishap of one sort or another but who, though no longer a virgin, nevertheless went on to work or marry and live respectably.[20] Sir Walter Scott criticized this "dangerous tendency to slacken the reins of discipline" in an otherwise laudatory memoir of Bage. He noted that a number of respected authors—Henry Fielding and Tobias Smollett among them—"treated with great lightness those breaches of morals, which are too commonly considered as venial in the male sex." But Bage, he complained, "has extended, in some instances, that license to females, and seems at times even to sport with the ties of marriage."[21]

An anecdote in Scott's biography gives further evidence for a shift in cultural assumptions about women's sexuality in the course of the eighteenth century. To illustrate how changes in taste take place "insensibly without the parties being aware of it," Scott described the experience of his great-aunt reading Aphra Behn after an interval of sixty years. It seems that this woman, Mrs. Keith of Ravelstone, "a person of some condition" who "lived with unabated vigour of intellect to a very advanced age" and enjoyed reading "to the last of her long life," asked to borrow some novels by Aphra Behn from her literary nephew, for she remembered being much interested in Behn in her youth. When she perused the borrowed volumes, however, she was offended by the manners and language of the work and returned them to her nephew with the cheerful suggestion that he burn them. But she remarked at the same time: "Is it not a very odd thing that I, an old woman of eighty and upwards, sitting alone, feel myself ashamed to read a book which, sixty years ago, I have heard read aloud for the amusement of large circles, consisting of the first and most creditable society in London?"[22]

---

[18]For instance, Sukey Jones in Clara Reeve's *The Two Mentors* (1783) is betrayed into one sexual adventure but quickly repents and reforms; the heroine's mother in Robert Bage's *Mount Henneth* (1781) is raped by infidels. Neither participates in illicit sexual encounters of her own volition or out of sexual desire, as do the heroines of earlier texts.

[19]Spencer, p. 122.

[20]See n. 18 above.

[21]Sir Walter Scott, "Prefatory Memoir to Robert Bage," in Ballantyne's Novelist's Library, 10 vols. (London, 1821–24), 9:xxvii.

[22]J. G. Lockhart, *Life of Sir Walter Scott* (New York, 1848), pp. 390–91.

Thomas Laqueur has explained this cultural reconsideration of the nature of women's sexuality as part of a process establishing women's essential biological difference from men in a revolutionary context committed to sweeping clean all *socially* determined differences among people. In the context of late eighteenth-century revolutionary claims for equality between rich and poor, aristocrats and workers, men and women, the physiological differences between male and female had to be reinvented, so to speak, to offset potentially subversive claims women might make for political equality. Thus, the reexamination of women's bodies and their sexual subject position was an attempt to establish women's biological difference from men, including the possibility that women's desire—unlike men's desire—was not biologically necessary to reproduction and not "natural."[23]

The most striking aspect of this reinterpretation of the experiences of male and female bodies was the growing certainty on the part of the medical establishment that the female orgasm—or any other manifestation of women's sexual pleasure—was irrelevant to reproduction. Since male ejaculation was known to be essential for conception, the logic of physiological analogy had indicated that a female climax was also necessary for procreation—and medical authorities had always assumed women's symmetrical physiological response whenever conception took place. One appalling consequence of this assumption had been that if a raped woman became pregnant, her assailant could be acquitted on the grounds that her pregnancy proved her pleasure and hence her consent.[24] Once reproduction was recognized to be independent of women's sexual pleasure, however, the existence of women's active desire became a matter of debate.[25] Historically women had been perceived as lascivious and lustful creatures, fallen daughters of Eve, corrupting and corrupted.[26] But by the middle of the eighteenth century they were increasingly reimagined as belonging to an-

[23]Thomas Laqueur, "Orgasm, Generation, and the Politics of Reproductive Biology," *Representations* 14 (1986): 1–41.

[24]Alice Browne, *The Eighteenth-Century Feminist Mind* (Brighton, 1987), p. 63.

[25]Sometime around 1761, a liberal clergyman named Robert Wallace noted in his text "Of Venery" that "by a false, unnecessary, and unnatural refinement some would deny that there is any lust in modest women and virgins." He asserted that contrary to popular opinion, "every woman during certain seasons and a certain period of life is incited to lust" (Norah Smith, "Sexual Mores in the Eighteenth Century: Robert Wallace's 'Of Venery,' *Journal of the History of Ideas* 39 (1978): 419–35). That Wallace's point of view was a minority opinion by 1761, which he strenuously urged against a prevailing belief in women's "passionlessness," highlights the shift in cultural attitudes toward women's sexuality. For an analysis of "passionlessness" as it was fostered by conduct literature and by evangelical religion, see Nancy F. Cott, "Passionlessness: An Interpretation of Victorian Sexual Ideology," *Signs* 4 (1978): 219–36. I locate the transition somewhat earlier historically than Cott, but that might reflect the difference between an American and an English context.

[26]See Natalie Zemon Davis, "Women on Top," in *Society and Culture in Early Modern France* (Stanford, CA, 1975), pp. 124–51.

other order of being: loving but without sexual needs, morally pure, disinterested, benevolent, and self-sacrificing.[27]

The desexualization of women was accomplished, in part, by redefining them as maternal rather than sexual beings. It is this movement I want to focus on here—this double, interlocked, mutually exclusive relationship between sexuality and maternity as it was reconstructed in the middle of the eighteenth century. For in a remarkably short span, the maternal succeeded, supplanted, and repressed the sexual definition of women, who began to be reimagined as nurturing rather than desiring, as supportive rather than appetitive.

MATERNITY

Motherhood has not always carried with it associations of tenderness and unstinting nurture. Nor has it always been interpreted as a woman's ultimate fulfillment. According to Linda Pollock, until 1750 or so, pregnancy was treated as if it were a disease, an abnormal condition. Expectant mothers, for example, were bled when they felt unwell, like any other sick person.[28] The fact that women stopped menstruating during pregnancy was seen as a medical problem insofar as it left them without a regular purgative cycle; they had no outlet for "noxious humours," no way to void accumulated impurities.[29] But pregnancy was not yet really of much interest to the medical establishment. The texts that created the body of opinion about pregnancy and maternity in the sixteenth and seventeenth centuries were not medical but, rather, religious and legal. This discourse was designed to provide guidance on legal questions about marriage, legitimacy, and inheritance, and women were represented as disorderly and unruly beings whose sexuality needed to be controlled so that they would bear only legitimate children.[30] Herbal recipes and medical advice about what to expect during pregnancy or lying-in were directed not toward mothers but toward midwives, nurses, and medical practitioners.[31] Nor was this medical literature privileged: parents often as not rejected the advice of printed texts in favor of family lore and local customs.[32] Few detailed suggestions about the technique of breast-feeding—how to care for

---

[27]For an exploration of this phenomenon in the American context see Ruth Bloch, "The Gendered Meanings of Virtue in Revolutionary America," *Signs* 13 (1987): 37–58.

[28]Linda Pollock, *A Lasting Relationship* (Hanover, NH, 1987), p. 19.

[29]Linda Pollock, "Embarking on a Rough Passage: The Experience of Pregnancy in Early-Modern Society," in Valerie Fildes, ed., *Women as Mothers in Pre-Industrial England* (London, 1990), pp. 39–68, 59.

[30]Patricia Crawford, "The Construction and Experience of Maternity," in Fildes, ed., p. 6.

[31]Fildes, *Breasts, Bottles, and Babies,* p. 116.

[32]Pollock, "Embarking on a Rough Passage," in Fildes, ed., p. 59.

breasts and nipples, how often to feed an infant, how to hold the child, or when to put it to breast—can be found in this literature at all. Women were expected to learn these things from other women in a tradition of oral advice and lore. Motherhood was not yet the object of cultural control, and women were expected to muddle through it as best they could.[33]

By the middle of the century, however, motherhood became the focus of a new kind of cultural attention. Writers began to wax sentimental about maternity, to accord it high moral stature, and to construct it as noble, strong, and self-sacrificial. Admiration for mothers—and for maternal devotion—came to be a banner under which the newly constituted middle class marched. In literature, maternal sentiment began to emerge as an emotional force capable of moving a reading public, understood as the sign of an innately moral and uniquely female sensibility. In analyzing the power and popularity of John Home's famous tragedy, *Douglas* (1756), Susan Staves has argued that its success was due to the way it handled maternity, at that time a new cultural obsession. What was original in the play, particularly noted and appreciated by contemporary audiences, she says, was Home's "attempt to articulate and dramatize what was in 1756 a new sentiment: elaborated tenderness between mothers and children."[34]

Natural but learned, instinctive but also evidence of the most exquisitely refined sensibility, motherhood was celebrated in prose and poetry while medical men set about to advise women on dress, diet, and care for their children. Both scientists and moralists suddenly had a great deal to say about how women ought to behave as mothers. A complicated print culture arose, illuminating the evolving conception of motherhood—most of it directed at the women themselves, telling them how to act and how to feel.[35] Hugh Downman's poem, *Infancy; or, The Management of Children, a Didactic Poem in Six Books* (1774), is a good example of the popularity of this subject and of the way in which medical experts came to dominate the discourse. Downman himself was a physician, practicing in Exeter. His extremely popular poem, a repository in blank verse of the standard English attitudes toward motherhood in this period, went through at least seven editions by 1809. Being a doctor gave Downman special authority to pronounce on this subject, for motherhood was increasingly understood to be the province of the male medical establishment. Biologically grounded, a relationship "based in nature," motherhood was the outcome of a knowable physiological process. Maternal feeling, as the medical establishment increasingly made clear, was biologically determined; women who lacked it

[33]Patricia Crawford, "'The Sucking Child': Adult Attitudes to Child Care in the First Year of Life in Seventeenth-Century England," *Continuity and Change* 1 (1986): 26–51, 30, 42; Fildes, *Breasts, Bottles, and Babies*, pp. 117–18.

[34]Staves (n. 3 above), p. 53.

[35]Fildes, *Breasts, Bottles, and Babies*, p. 116.

were abnormal. "Is there a stronger principle infix'd / In Human Nature, than the zealous warmth / A Mother t'ward her Infant feels?" asked Downman rhetorically.[36]

By contrast, recall Alexander Pope's slanderous portrait of the novelist Eliza Haywood in *The Dunciad* as a sluttish mother ("Two babes of love close clinging to her waist"), heavily and even brutishly physical ("With cow-like udders, and with ox-like eyes").[37] These images clearly belong to an earlier period, before motherhood sanctified women and removed from them the taint of sexuality. Pope's images suggest a loose and instinctive sensuality—with nothing of the moral consciousness attributed to mothers later in the century. Such bovine sexual energy as Pope represented was fast disappearing from the cultural landscape by the 1760s, repressed as a motive in fictional heroines and antiheroines alike. Newer "feminine" sentiments were being elicited and demonstrated by the novels of the age—sentiments connected with maternity, such as pity, tenderness, and benevolence. Increasingly constructed as the higher good for which a woman must be prepared to sacrifice her sexual vanity, motherhood began to carry with it the suggestion of punitive consequences for sexual activity. If fictional women characters of the previous era had mated and bred casually—like Moll Flanders—maternity was now becoming a serious duty and responsibility.

The valorization of motherhood as it played into the domestication of Englishwomen in the late eighteenth century has been treated positively for the most part by cultural historians. Nancy Armstrong, for example, has argued that the cultural discourse of novels and conduct books created a new domestic domain over which women exercised authority as they were, in turn, constructed by this discourse.[38] More than a decade ago, Lawrence Stone's *The Family, Sex, and Marriage* claimed that this period witnessed the emergence of "companionate marriage" and argued that women's new role as their husbands' companions elevated women to a higher status within society. But companionate marriage is also interpretable as a more thoroughgoing psychological appropriation of women to serve the emo-

[36]Hugh Downman, *Infancy; or, The Management of Children, a Didactic Poem in Six Books* (London, 1774), bk. 2, lines 298–300.

[37]*The Dunciad* (London, 1728), bk. 2, lines 150, 156.

[38]See n. 3 above. Ann Ferguson's concept of a sex/affective production system is useful here. She argues that one needs to understand the social mechanisms for the production of "key human needs—sexuality, nurturance, children—whose satisfaction is just as basic to the functioning of human society as is the satisfaction of the material needs of hunger and physical security." Using this concept, one might describe the changes in families and social relations in eighteenth-century English society as changes in women's role in the sex/affective production system—changes in the arrangements society made for the satisfaction of sexual needs, needs for nurturance, and the care and socialization of children. See Ferguson, *Blood at the Root*, p. 83.

tional needs of men than ever was imagined in earlier divisions of labor by gender. Educating women to be more interesting companions for men rather than as individuals with their own economic or intellectual purposes is an ambiguous advance, not one that moves very far along the path toward equality. The bluestockings' achievement is usually represented in this light—as the ability to attract men to intellectual salons, to keep them at home in domestic space and out of the bachelor atmosphere of coffeehouses and taverns.[39] This reappropriation of female subjectivity for the sake of a new cultural discourse, which separated public from private, political from personal, and market relations from domestic relations, was a colonization of women far more thoroughgoing than any that had preceded it.

BREAST-FEEDING

As the processes associated with childbearing became the focus for a new cultural appropriation, the maternal rather than the sexual purposes of women's bodies were increasingly foregrounded in medical literature. Medical treatises multiplied on the subject of maternal breast-feeding, urging women to nurse their own children for a variety of medical, social, and psychological reasons. This outpouring was a novel phenomenon, created both by the existence of a print culture and by a seismic shift in cultural conceptions of family. Nothing like it existed earlier. The medical establishment seemed determined to convince women to nurse their own children—for their own sakes, for the health of their children, and often for the good of the nation.[40] The tone of the treatises was admonitory, with moral exhortations mixed in among the physiological descriptions and sci-

[39]Sylvia Harcstark Myers, *The Bluestocking Circle* (Oxford, 1990), corrects this misapprehension definitively, documenting the achievements of bluestockings as intellectuals and writers.

[40]A partial list of the treatises consulted follows: Nicholas Culpeper, *A Directory for Midwives: or, a Guide for Women, in Their Conception, Bearing, and Suckling Their Children* (London, 1651); John Maubray, *The Female Physician, Containing All the Diseases Incident to That Sex, in Virgins, Wives, and Widows* (London, 1724); William Cadogan, *An Essay upon Nursing, and the Management of Children, from Their Birth to Three Years of Age* (London, 1748); John Theobald, *A Young Wife's Guide, in the Management of Her Children* (London, 1764); Hugh Smith, *Letters to Married Women* (London, 1767); George Armstrong, *An Essay on the Diseases Most Fatal to Infants, including Rules to Be Observed in the Nursing of Children, with a Particular View to Those Who Are Brought Up by Hand* (London, 1767); William Buchan, *Advice to Mothers, on the Subject of Their Own Health, and on the Means of Promoting the Health, Strength, and Beauty, of Their Offspring* (London, 1769); William Moss, *An Essay on the Management, Nursing, and Diseases of Children, from the Birth: And on the Treatment and Diseases of Pregnant and Lying-in Women* (London, 1781); Michael Underwood, *A Treatise on the Diseases of Children, Part the Second: Containing Familiar Directions Adapted to the Nursery and the General Management of Infants from the Birth* (London, 1784).

entific explanations. Many followed Rousseau's *Emile* (1762), castigating women as selfish, callous, and unnatural who would not give themselves the trouble to nurse or waxing sentimental and voyeuristic at descriptions of lovely mothers suckling their infants. "Let not husbands be deceived: let them not expect attachment from wives, who, in neglecting to suckle their children, rend asunder the strongest ties in nature," warned William Buchan in his 1769 *Advice to Mothers*. No woman who was not able to nurse should breed; if she could not "discharge the duties of a mother . . . she has no right to become a wife."[41] Hugh Smith assured his women readers in 1767 that they would lose nothing by nursing. "O! That I could prevail upon my fair countrywomen to become still more lovely in the sight of men! Believe it not, when it is insinuated, that your bosoms are less charming, for having a dear little cherub at your breast."[42] Even Mary Wollstonecraft echoed this promise of domestic devotion when she recommended maternal nursing in *A Vindication of the Rights of Woman:*

> Cold would be the heart of a husband, were he not rendered un-natural by early debauchery, who did not feel more delight at seeing his child suckled by its mother, than the most artful wanton tricks could ever raise; yet this natural way of cementing the matrimonial tie . . . wealth leads women to spurn. To preserve their beauty, and wear the flowery crown of the day, which gives them a kind of right to reign for a short time over the sex, they neglect to stamp impressions on their husbands' hearts that would be remembered with more tend-erness when the snow on the head began to chill the bosom, than even their virgin charms.[43]

Wollstonecraft reinscribes here the mutually exclusive nature of sexuality and maternity, the choice women were expected to make between trying to hold their husbands with "wanton tricks" or with the spectacle of suckling an infant—a sight to which only the most debauched of men failed to respond. Yet women of means were still choosing to hire wet nurses, choos-ing the ephemeral "flowery crown of the day" rather than the more "natural way of cementing the matrimonial tie." For both were not pos-sible: either one stamped lasting impressions on a husband's heart with the image of one's maternal devotion and self-sacrifice or with one's "virgin charms," one's sexual attractions. The former was natural, appealing to all but the most degraded tastes, while the latter was "wanton" and un-naturally sexualized.

By the time Wollstonecraft wrote this passage, sentimental exhortations

[41] Buchan, pp. 217–18.
[42] Smith, p. 76.
[43] Wollstonecraft (n. 11 above), p. 213.

like hers had been appearing since the middle of the century, together with an increasing number of fictional representations of model maternal behavior and medical arguments for the "scientific" benefits of maternal breastfeeding. This discourse—in conduct books, novels, magazine essays and stories, children's books, and medical treatises—erupting as it did in the middle of the eighteenth century is testimony to the intensifying cultural significance of motherhood. The medical focus on maternal breast-feeding can be interpreted as the beginning of the physiological colonization of women's bodies corresponding to the psychological colonization of women's subjectivity in both companionate marriage and motherhood.

The locus—both symbolic and real—of this new appropriation of women's bodies for motherhood and for the state was the maternal breast. Distinctions between fathers' and mothers' parental roles, as well as male expertise about women's reproductive capacities and bodily processes, were joined here. It was as if this organ became the site of the struggle over the maternal definition of women, staged in opposition to the sexual definition of women. Increasingly, as the second half of the century unfolded, maternal breast-feeding became a moral and a medical imperative for women of all classes.

The cultural climate surrounding childbearing and breast-feeding had been noticeably different in the previous century. Not only had there been little prescriptive literature on the subject, as I have noted, but that little was directed not at mothers but at midwives and medical practitioners. Wet-nursing was so widespread in England, taken so much for granted in the seventeenth century, that aside from a few eccentric exhortations to mothers to nurse their own children, the controversy about breast-feeding focused not on who nursed the child (a wet nurse or a birth mother) but on whether or not breast-feeding was preferable to artificial feeding. According to Valerie Fildes, there was a fad during the last quarter of the seventeenth century in England among aristocrats for bypassing nursing altogether, a "radical change in ideas and practice of infant feeding among some of the wealthier classes."[44] Medical experts of that period advocated raising infants "by hand" or "dry-feeding" them, which meant eschewing breast milk altogether and feeding them water or milk gruels made with breadcrumbs, sugar, and sometimes butter or other forms of grease. This lethal practice was encouraged by James II, who, on the advice of his royal physicians in 1688, decided to dry-feed his heir in this manner. Apparently numbers of aristocrats followed suit, despite the ill success that attended this method of feeding.

[44]Fildes, *Breasts, Bottles, and Babies,* p. 288. For a fuller discussion of this practice among the upper classes, see also pp. 106, 288–92. Trumbach (n. 1 above) also discusses this phenomenon, pp. 197–208.

This extraordinary medical advice must be understood as a backlash to what was in fact a very widespread practice of wet-nursing. For despite the peculiar desire of the wealthiest classes to raise their children "by hand," English wet-nursing was at an all-time historical high in this period.[45] Mothers from a wide spectrum of classes—the wives of merchants, farmers, scholars, lawyers, physicians, and clergymen, as well as aristocrats and gentry—regularly hired wet nurses to breast-feed their newborns in the late seventeenth and early eighteenth centuries.[46] The aristocratic interest in raising infants "by hand" may have been motivated by a desire to distinguish their practices from those of the less wealthy classes, or by a shortage of wet nurses, or by a distaste for the lowborn women to whom they had to resort for this service. But it is noteworthy that dry-feeding had the sanction of "medical science" in this period and was considered to be the latest advance. What these phenomena demonstrate—both the enthusiasm for "dry-feeding" and the practice of hiring wet nurses—is that women's sexual identity was not yet defined, independent of class, by their willingness to give themselves to their reproductive tasks. In 1689 Walter Harris lamented that "so many *Mothers,* not only of high Rank, but even of the common Sort, can with so much Inhumanity, and more than Brutish Cruelty, desert their tender Offspring, and expose them to so many Dangers of mercenary Nurses."[47]

In 1711 Richard Steele created a cranky male reader in one of his *Spectator* columns who complained that mothers of all ranks were delegating to wet nurses the task of breast-feeding their own children. He referred to the "general Argument, that a Mother is weakened by giving suck to her Children" and observed that it was a common excuse for hiring a wet nurse. "For if a Woman does but know that her Husband can spare about three or

[45]Fildes, *Wet Nursing* (n. 3 above), p. 79. For a contemporary satire on the aristocratic practice of bringing up a child "by hand" see Richard Steele, "On the Birth of an Heir," *The Tatler,* no. 15 (May 12, 1709).

[46]Fildes, *Breasts, Bottles, and Babies,* p. 99.

[47]Walter Harris, *A Treatise of the Acute Diseases of Infants,* trans. J. Martyn (London, 1689), pp. 18–19; quoted in Beth Kowaleski-Wallace, "Monster or Mother? Eighteenth-Century Medical Discourse on Maternal Breast Feeding" (paper presented at the meeting of the American Society for Eighteenth-Century Studies, Cincinnati, April 1987). The satiric author of an early eighteenth-century medical treatise blames both the fashionable mother and the mercenary, neglectful wet nurse in the scene he imagines in the wet nurse's cottage, when the mother has been notified that her child is ill. "Down comes Madam the mother, furbulo'd, with an erect rump (crying and bellowing) and running about half mad, like a cow stung with a gad flie, and with her maid laden with pots, glasses, venice treacle, Goody Kent's powder, goat-stone, black cherry-water, etc. And after her, easie, her husband with a coach and four, with, perhaps, a brace of doctors, or some famous child's apothecary, etc." (E. Baynard, *The History of Cold Bathing: Both Ancient and Modern, Part II* [London, 1706], pp. 149–50, quoted in Fildes, *Wet Nursing,* p. 93). The cowlike attributes of this mother are meant to suggest that she ought to be nursing her own child.

six Shillings a Week extraordinary . . . she certainly, with the Assistance of her Gossips, will soon persuade the good Man to send the Child to Nurse . . . by pretending Indisposition."[48] Steele's description conjures up a picture of wet-nursing as a widespread service in England, available to those with even a small surplus. For that segment of the population with an extra three shillings a week or more—a proportion of the population one might call the middle class—breast-feeding moved, in the course of the century, from being paid labor to being unpaid reproductive labor. That is, if there is truth in Steele's description, then women's bodily services were commodified and purchased across class lines in the early part of the eighteenth century, while in the second half of the century, those services were redefined as the unpaid labor that women owed their husbands, their families, and even the state.

By 1784, a medical treatise on childhood diseases and the "general management of infants from the birth," filled with self-congratulations to the enlightened age for "recent examples among persons of rank" of maternal nursing, observed that maternal breast-feeding had become by then a new social expectation for women. "That tyrant, Fashion," remarked the author dryly, "has prevailed over the good sense and natural feelings of many whose maternal affections can be, in no other instance, suspected."[49] By the 1770s and 1780s, then, breast-feeding was no longer being determined by class but by gender. "That tyrant, Fashion" had changed the way women conceived of their roles as mothers. A historian, using information in diaries, claims that 67 percent of mothers in the eighteenth century breast-fed their own infants as compared to only 43 percent in the seventeenth century, a proportion of breast-feeding mothers never equaled before or since.[50] No longer was nursing considered quite so detachable a bodily service, available for wealthier women to hire from poorer women in order to spare themselves and make their lives easier. By the end of the eighteenth century, this bodily service came to be constructed as part of all women's unpaid reproductive labor.

A comparison of Steele's discussion of breast-feeding in *The Spectator* with later discussions of the subject when it became the vogue shows how unsentimental a tone he took about motherhood and maternal nursing in the early part of the century. Females ought to nurse because it was their duty to sustain what they brought forth, as "the Earth is called the Mother of all Things, not because she produces, but because she maintains and nurses what she produces." Steele did not argue the naturalness of tender

[48]*The Spectator,* no. 246 (December 12, 1711).
[49]Underwood, p. 173.
[50]Pollock, *Forgotten Children* (n. 1 above), p. 215. According to Susan Contratto (n. 14 above), as recently as 1980 in the United States "fewer than 25 percent of all newborns [were] nursed, even for the five days of the usual hospital stay" (p. 236).

t

maternal feelings, the advantages in nursing of establishing a deep and primal bond of love between mother and child, or the peculiar suitability of women for the office of mothering; these beliefs came later. He concentrated instead on the character of the nurse and argued that mothers should not hand over their infants to "a Woman that is (ten thousand to one) neither . . . sound in Mind nor Body, that has neither Honour nor Reputation, neither Love nor Pity for the poor Babe, but more Regard for the Money than for the whole Child."[51]

Steele's class-based objection to wet-nursing is characteristic of the earlier period: an unsuitable dependence on women of another class and a revulsion from those commonly hired to do that work—coarse country breeders or unwed mothers. With phrases that go back at least to Nicholas Culpeper's 1651 treatise on midwifery, Steele's cranky gentleman asked whether a child sent out to nurse might not "imbibe the gross Humours and Qualities of the Nurse, like a Plant in a different Ground, or like a Graft upon a different Stock? Do we not observe, that a Lamb sucking a Goat changes very much its Nature, nay even its Skin and Wooll into the Goat Kind?"[52] In this view, women were not all alike; their milk was not interchangeable. Class was still a more important determinant in this most intimate of matters than biological sex.[53]

Mary Astell's incidental reference to wet-nursing is another example of this class-based argument in the late seventeenth century. In her 1694 *A Serious Proposal to the Ladies* she argued for maternal breast-feeding as a check on aristocratic pride rather than as a medically superior practice or an act of solidarity with working-class women. She enjoined those upper-class women to whom she always addressed herself, "how *Great* soever they are," not to "think themselves too *Good* to perform what Nature requires, nor thro' Pride and Delicacy remit the poor little one to the care of a Foster Parent. Or, if necessity enforce them to depute another to perform their Duty, they would be as choice at least in the Manners and Inclinations, as they are in the complections of their Nurses, least with their Milk they

[51]*The Spectator,* no. 246 (December 12, 1711).

[52]These phrases are repeated in the 1794 treatise written by the man-midwife John Maubray (n. 40 above), p. 329.

[53]No one save the Countess of Lincoln in the seventeenth century seemed aware of the other implication of a class-based system of wet-nursing: that the child of the wet nurse might starve. "Bee not accessary to that disorder of causing *a poorer woman to banish her owne infant,* for the entertaining of *a richer womans child,*" she wrote (original emphasis) (Elizabeth Clinton, Countess of Lincoln, *The Countesse of Lincolnes Nurserie* [Oxford, 1622], p. 19, quoted in Crawford, "The Construction and Experience of Maternity" [n. 30 above], p. 24). Later in the eighteenth century, this concern can also be found in Michael Underwood's treatise. In urging women to try nursing their own children before looking for a wet nurse to undertake that office, he refers to "the sacrifice that poor women make in going out to suckle other people's children, the sad consequences of which are often severely felt by their own" (p. 174).

transfuse their Vices, and form in the Child such evil habits as will not easily be eradicated."[54] Astell's Christian asceticism, her cheerful belief in effort, and her invocation of "the natural" foreshadows later cultural attitudes about women's "duty." People should do whatever life required of them, and nursing one's own children was one of those things. Following the medical practitioners of her time, Astell understood breast milk to be a bodily fluid, like blood, that carried and transmitted one's essential nature. The class of one's wet nurse mattered, for habits, vices, manners, and inclinations might be transmitted to the child along with maternal milk.

By the middle of the eighteenth century, these ideas had changed. Mothers no longer were reproached for the class of caretakers to whom they turned over their own flesh-and-blood but for mistakenly preferring their own independence of movement, social life, looks, or figures to the duties—and the joys—of motherhood. When William Cadogan published *An Essay upon Nursing, and the Management of Children, From Their Birth to Three Years of Age* in 1748, it was not to attack wet-nursing on the grounds of class difference. The vanity he attacked in mothers who hired wet nurses was not the vanity of class but the vanity of sexual attractiveness. He urged every woman to "prevail upon herself to give up a little of the Beauty of her Breast to feed her Offspring." From the start, his language revealed that this maternal practice was defined in opposition to female sexual vanity and was expected to contain it. The tradeoff for "beauty" was a pleasanter domestic situation to offer one's husband, a bourgeois vision of a happier home life. He pictured to men the pleasures of having their children at home rather than sent away to nurse and appealed to them to encourage rather than forbid this practice. "The Child, was it nurs'd in this way, would be always quiet, in good Humour, ever playing, laughing or sleeping. In my Opinion, a Man of Sense cannot have a prettier Rattle (for Rattles he must have of one kind or other) than such a young Child."[55] Arguing for middle-class domestic values as a substitute for decadent aristocratic pursuits, Cadogan implied that maternal nursing was the key to a quiet moral revolution.

Since this extremely influential treatise marks the beginning of medical preoccupation with maternal breast-feeding, it is worth analyzing in some detail. Written to instruct the governors of the London Foundling Hospital and adopted as its official medical guidelines, Cadogan's *Essay upon Nursing* went through at least eleven editions in French and English before the end of the century. As I have said, the class of wet nurses was not an issue for Cadogan; indeed, he took a sentimental liberal view of class: "That Mother who has only a few Rags to cover her Child loosely, and little more than her own Breast to feed it, sees it healthy and strong, and very

[54]Mary Astell, *A Serious Proposal to the Ladies* (London, 1694), pp. 28–29.
[55]Cadogan, p. 24.

soon able to shift for itself; while the puny Insect, the Heir and Hope of a rich Family lies languishing under a Load of Finery, that overpowers his Limbs, abhorring and rejecting the Dainties he is crammed with, till he dies a Victim to the mistaken Care and Tenderness of his fond Mother."[56]

What the enlightened doctor cared about in wet nurses was not class or morals but their condition as healthy animals. He recognized that there were cases in which it was necessary to engage wet nurses; there were families in which the birth mother was unable to nurse; moreover, wet nurses were needed to feed the hundreds of abandoned infants at the London Foundling Hospital. He advised selecting a woman who was between twenty and thirty years old and newly lactating, ideally having been delivered herself within two or three months. As with valued livestock, her diet was to be supervised: she was to be fed a "proper Mixture of Flesh and Vegetables . . . with a good deal of Garden Stuff, and Bread." She was to be prohibited from drinking wine or strong liquors.[57]

"If we follow Nature," asserted Cadogan, "instead of leading or driving it, we cannot err." What he meant by nature in this context was "women's nature," whose "natural" characteristics consistently had revealed themselves to male physicians and not to "unlearned women" who blindly passed along the "Customs of their Great Grand-mothers" received in turn from "the Physicians of their unenlighten'd Days."[58] One by one he dismantled the standard arguments for wet-nursing and other common practices in raising infants. The assertion that nursing was debilitating to women "too weak to bear such a Drain, which would rob them of their own Nourishment," Cadogan disposed of with the observation that disease is caused not by "Want" but by "too great a Fulness and Redundancy of Humours." Therefore, since nursing was purgative for both mother and child (the colostrum was thought to have a laxative effect on the newborn), its good effect for both was assured. He inveighed against "Herbs, Roots, and Drugs," swaddling, "superstitious Practices and Ceremonies," and feeding an infant more frequently than two or three times in twenty-four hours.[59] He assured his readers that if his plan were followed, it would reduce the terrible mortality of children. "Half of the People that come into the World, go out of it again before they become the least Use to it, or themselves," he remonstrated. "Yet I cannot find, that any one Man of sense, and publick Spirit, has ever attended to it at all; notwithstanding the Maxim in every one's Mouth, that a Multitude of Inhabitants is the greatest Strength and best Support of a Commonwealth."[60] It was about time that "men of sense" took an interest in this national problem.

[56]Ibid., p. 7.
[57]Ibid., p. 27.
[58]Ibid., p. 3.
[59]Ibid., pp. 14, 17.
[60]Ibid., p. 6.

Cadogan was convinced that women needed to be reeducated by medical men like himself to recognize where their real duty lay. The "plain natural Plan I have laid down, is never followed," he complained, "because most Mothers, of any Condition, either cannot, or will not undertake the troublesome Task of suckling their own Children."[61] He asserted the need for male control of the process in order to set it on its "natural" track. "It is with great Pleasure I see at last the Preservation of Children become the Care of Men of Sense," he wrote. "In my Opinion, this Business has been too long fatally left to the Management of Women who cannot be supposed to have proper knowledge to fit them for such a Task, notwithstanding they look upon it to be their own Province."[62] He recommended that every father have his child suckled under his own eye and that he "make use of his own Reason and Sense in superintending and directing the Management of it."[63] Although against dry-feeding in general, he believed that it was possible for a good physician to manage it properly but warned that it required "more Knowledge of Nature, and the animal Oeconomy, than the best Nurse was ever Mistress of." He was confident that in time his plan would "convince most Nurses, Aunts, Grand-mothers etc. how much they have hitherto been in the wrong."[64] Cadogan argued for the instruction of women by a male medical establishment for the sake of domestic quiet and family life. As a century earlier it was believed that women's unruly and insatiable sexuality needed to be governed by men, so now it was believed that women needed bodily instruction in matters of childbearing. "Nor to the dictates plain of candid Truth / Thy antient Nurse's doating saws prefer," warned Hugh Downman's *Infancy*.[65]

CULTURAL REPRESENTATIONS

Representations of the breast and of maternal breast-feeding in the fiction of Samuel Richardson and others corroborate the historical periodization of this phenomenon that I have presented here and the shift in cultural attitudes toward it. Richardson's *Clarissa* provides one of the most interesting examples of these changing attitudes about sexuality and maternity, as

[61]Ibid., p. 23.
[62]Ibid., p. 3.
[63]Ibid., p. 24.
[64]Ibid., p. 5.
[65]Downman (n. 36 above), bk. 2, lines 108–9. In 1781 William Moss (n. 40 above) warned against preferring the wisdom of wet nurses to the advice of physicians: "It is an opinion, very generally adopted, that the care and direction of women and children upon these occasions is most properly submitted to the management of nurses; who, from their constant practice and experience are supposed sufficiently qualified to direct it; and that it is a province in which they ought not be controlled. These arguments, which have originated in ignorance and superstition, are supported upon no other or better ground than prejudice; as daily experience proves their fallacy" (p. 11).

they crystallize in a scene in volume 2. Published about the same time as Cadogan's *Essay upon Nursing,* this scene illustrates the cultural ambiguity about sexual and maternal definitions of women and clearly places the breast at the center of that ambiguity.

The relevant sequence begins at a moment when it appears that at last Lovelace will marry Clarissa and end his dangerous game. Lulling her— and us—into a false sense of security with respectful remarks about her family, sensible arrangements for obtaining a marriage license and drafts of the settlements, and repeated proposals of particular days for the happy event, he reclines his head upon her shoulder and begins to kiss her hands. "Rather bashfully than angrily reluctant," he writes to Belford, "her hands sought to be withdrawn; her shoulder avoiding my reclined cheek—apparently loath, and more loath, to quarrel with me." He then snatches away her handkerchief, and with "burning lips" he kisses "the most charming breast that ever my ravished eyes beheld." She struggles angrily out of his grasp, saying "*I see there is no keeping terms with you.* Base encroacher!"[66]

Later in the letter Lovelace writes this paean to the breast—and the woman—he has tried to appropriate by stealth and force: "Let me perish, Belford, if I would not forego the brightest diadem in the world for the pleasure of seeing a twin Lovelace at each charming breast, drawing from it his first sustenance; the pious task, for physical reasons, continued for one month and no more!"[67] The sexual breast briefly experienced earlier in the day is here transformed into the maternal breast, property of Lovelace the conqueror. His fantasy of possession is not a fantasy of erotic pleasure, but a fantasy of territorial claim. To discover Clarissa's sexual charms is to imagine colonizing them, domesticating them, rather than voluptuously enjoying them. He would rather own this one woman than be crowned with "the brightest diadem," he asserts. Moreover, this kingdom of one has the capacity to reproduce him—in duplicate—to create a society in his image and to nurture it singlehandedly, in an image of bountiful and even heroic nature.

The oddly medical addendum to this fantasy, the recommendation that the nursing mother continue "for one month and no more," calls our attention to the new prestige for professional medical expertise in these matters and to Richardson's own particular interest in questions of maternal breastfeeding. In the third edition of *Clarissa,* published three years later, he specifically reminds us of his earlier treatment of this subject with a footnote referring the reader to the debate in the sequel to *Pamela* published in 1741, *Pamela II,* "between Mr. B. and his Pamela, on the important subject of mothers being nurses to their own children."[68] There, Richardson had

[66]Samuel Richardson, *Clarissa; or, The History of a Young Lady,* 4 vols. (London, 1747–48; rpt. New York, 1962), 2:476.

[67]Ibid., p. 477.

[68]Ibid. I am grateful to Florian Stuber for calling this footnote to my attention.

represented Mr. B. as forbidding Pamela to nurse their child, although she wanted to and argued with him. Whereas in most other things Mr. B. is enchanted by Pamela's unerring sense of honor and obligation, in this matter he disputes her judgment and insists that she follow his command rather than her own conscience—precisely because his rights in her sexual person are at stake. Richardson depicts their dispute and Pamela's capitulation in a series of letters Pamela writes to her parents from London, where she has come for her first lying-in. For Pamela and her parents in 1741, nursing was a moral duty—even a sentimental pleasure—but not yet a medical imperative. More significant, it was still seen as less urgent than a woman's duty to sexually serve her husband. Mr. B. argues that breast-feeding will engross Pamela's time in an office that was now beneath her and disturb her rest. He also objects to it on the grounds that it will interfere with his enjoyment of "her person" and the pleasing sight of her "personal graces." Her first responsibility is to his sexual satisfaction, and he is sure that nursing will interrupt his "honest pleasure" and ruin her figure. Women were not supposed to engage in sexual relations when they were nursing a baby, for it was believed it would spoil the milk—curdle it and make it sour. Physiologically, sexuality and maternity were understood to be mutually exclusive if a woman was nursing—which must account in part for the widespread use of nurses in families that could afford them.

The argument between Mr. B. and Pamela about maternal breast-feeding in the last volume of *Pamela II* is only the most prominent in a series of transactions whose effect is to separate Pamela's maternal self from her sexual self, that is, to redefine her as an ardent mother and not as Mr. B.'s sexual object. Once Pamela surrendered her long-defended chastity in legitimate marriage, Richardson had to recast the narrative conflict in the last volume as a dramatic opposition between sexuality and maternity. The emotional business of the last volume is precisely to detach motherhood from sexual desire and to reorient Mr. B.'s love accordingly. From the entertainments to which Pamela is introduced when she enters London society for the first time, to Mr. B.'s jealous competition with his infant son for Pamela's attention, to the stabilizing of their monogamous marriage through Pamela's renunciatory turn from sexual wife to chaste mother in her psychological duel with the Countess Dowager of ———, the incidents of this last volume all work to clarify for us the emotions of a mother and to distinguish them from the emotions of a wife or sexual partner.[69]

---

[69]The literary anatomizing of these two conflicting roles begins with the plays Pamela sees, the first she has ever attended: a tragedy (Ambrose Philips's *The Distressed Mother*) and a comedy (Richard Steele's *The Tender Husband; or, The Accomplished Fools*). Both plays dramatize potential dangers to matrimonial fidelity, a foreshadowing of Mr. B.'s flirtation with the Countess Dowager of ———. In *The Distressed Mother*, an adaptation of Racine's *Andromaque*, Andromache must choose between saving her son by marrying Pyrrhus—thus betraying her

The antithetical relation between nursing and sex as it was understood undoubtedly had some basis in the mild contraceptive properties of lactation, which were relatively well known.[70] It is simply less possible for a woman to conceive when she is nursing. Whether or not this commonly held opposition found both in the medical literature and in old wives' tales constituted a cultural taboo against the sexual activity of a nursing mother is a matter of dispute.[71] But Mr. B.'s refusal to share his wife's bodily services with an infant is probably typical of his historical location and his class and was an attitude that had long existed in English culture. Husbands' desire to resume sexual relations with their wives led to minimizing the maternal role—and to the general use of wet nurses. As William Gouge wrote in 1622, "Husbands for the most part are the cause that their wives nurse not their own children,"[72] and both Linda Pollock and Valerie Fildes confirm this attitude into the early eighteenth century.[73] Even as late as 1792 Mary Wollstonecraft remarked, in *A Vindication of the Rights of Women,* that there were "husbands so devoid of sense and parental affection, that during the first effervescence of voluptuous fondness they refuse to let their wives suckle their children."[74] Here Wollstonecraft emphasized the appropriation of women's sexual services as an earlier social formation than the maternal practices of her contemporary society.

The medical discourse on breast-feeding in the second half of the eighteenth century did not dwell on the biological mechanisms that made it inadvisable to nurse while engaging in sexual activity—but the opposition continued to be implied in the accusation that women were sacrificing their children to the decadent pleasures of the social whirl. It was also argued that careless wet nurses, who pretended to but did not actually

---

fidelity to her dead husband, Hector—or preserving that wifely vow and sacrificing her son. The play demonstrates emblematically the double bind involved in being a wife and a mother and foreshadows the dilemma in store for Pamela. In its symbolization and its action, the narrative of this volume accentuates, explores, unsettles, but eventually ratifies Pamela's transition from being an eighteenth-century Cinderella heroine to being a model bourgeois mother and wife.

[70]Dorothy McLaren, "Nature's Contraceptive: Wet Nursing and Prolonged Lactation: The Case of Chesham, Buckinghamshire 1578–1601," *Medical History* 23 (1979): 426–41; Fildes, *Breasts, Bottles, and Babies,* pp. 107–8.

[71]Valerie Fildes argues that by the seventeenth and eighteenth centuries, the belief that nursing mothers should abstain from sex, which goes back at least as far as Galen, was very much attenuated (*Breasts, Bottles, and Babies,* pp. 104–5, 121). Linda Pollock, on the other hand, argues that "it was believed that women who were feeding should abstain from sex, on the grounds that intercourse curdled the milk, and that if the mother became pregnant her milk supply would dry up" (*A Lasting Relationship* [n. 28 above], pp. 53–55).

[72]William Gouge, *Of Domesticall Duties* (London, 1622), quoted in Fildes, *Wet Nursing* (n. 3 above), p. 84.

[73]Pollock, *Forgotten Children* (n. 1 above), p. 50; Fildes, *Wet Nursing,* p. 84.

[74]Wollstonecraft (n. 11 above), p. 142.

abstain from sexual relations while engaged to nurse another's newborn, could ruin their milk supply and endanger their charges if they became pregnant again.[75] Even eighteenth-century medical men who explicitly denied the necessity for continence while nursing recommended waiting several hours after intercourse before nursing and encouraged general sexual moderation.[76]

The cross-cultural evidence that mothers in some societies practice sexual abstinence while nursing suggests a possible psychological or emotional basis for the strain between these two deployments of the body.[77] Feeding a newborn on demand, giving oneself over to the rhythms of the child, can be exhausting and leaves little energy for sexual play. Moreover, the erotic symbiosis between infant and mother can be so absorbing as to leave the mother uninterested in other libidinous contact. William Buchan hints at this erotic satisfaction in *Advice to Mothers* (1769): "The thrilling sensations, as before observed, that accompany the act of giving suck, can be conceived only by those who have felt them, while the mental raptures of a fond mother at such moments are far beyond the powers of description or fancy."[78] Finally, the combination of total power and selfless responsibility experienced in caring for an utterly dependent infant may be at odds with the helpless hungers of sexual desire as we know it.

The ambiguity about the function and definition of the breast as maternal or (hetero)sexual seems pivotal to me here. The locus of many a modern woman's role strain during the first year of her child's life, the breast seems to have represented for eighteenth-century women the mutually exclusive nature of motherhood and sexual desire.[79] In our own culture, the breast is defined as the quintessence of female sexuality, symbolic in its externality of both the pornographic and erogenous possibilities of female flesh. From *Playboy* bunnies to silicon implants, the culture invests the breast with great power as a sexual stimulus. For women in twentieth-century America, breasts often emblematize their femininity and their success or failure as sex objects and hence as women.[80] In eighteenth-century England, a woman who used her breasts to nurse her children literally suspended other erotic

---

[75]Hugh Smith (n. 40 above), p. 73.

[76]See, for example, treatises by John Maubray (1724) and John Theobald (1764) (n. 40 above).

[77]Gabrielle Palmer, *The Politics of Breastfeeding* (London, 1988), pp. 92–103.

[78]Buchan (n. 40 above), p. 210.

[79]On the role strain between maternal nursing and sexual play, see Palmer, pp. 28–31, 92–103. For another statement of the centrality of breasts to eighteenth-century definitions of women's sexual nature, see Julia Epstein, *The Iron Pen: Frances Burney and the Politics of Women's Writing* (Madison, WI, 1989), pp. 78–79.

[80]Daphna Ayalah and Isaac J. Weinstock, *Breasts: Women Speak about Their Breasts and Their Lives* (New York, 1979).

bodily practices until the child was weaned. Psychologically as well as physically, motherhood cancelled a woman's (hetero)sexuality. Either a woman
sent away her children to nurse (if she could afford to) and resumed her
earlier social and sexual identity, or she gave herself over to the business of
mothering.

Lovelace's fantasy of a domesticated Clarissa (together with Richardson's footnote to his treatment of these issues in *Pamela II*) locates this
cultural ambivalence toward breasts in the middle of the eighteenth century and connects it to the new interest in maternity. The medical
addendum—"for physical reasons, continued for one month and no more"
—indicates how scientized these arguments had become in the years since
Mr. B. worried that breast-feeding would alter Pamela's "genteel form." As
if to complete the sequence of ideological conversion, Richardson wrote a
third time about maternal breast-feeding in his last novel, *Sir Charles Grandison* (1753), in a manner that suggests that medical opinion about the
benefits of breast-feeding for both infant and mother had by that time prevailed. Indeed, Richardson's successive treatments of maternal breast-
feeding can be read as stages in an advancing belief system whose tenets
included the following: that women's essential nature was to be mothers;
that men's rights in women's bodies extended to their reproductive functions and, indeed, that men's ascendancy over women was based on
women's "natural propensity" for motherhood; that maternal feeling was
antithetic to sexual desire; and that men's heterosexual desire was an immature expression of the ultimate desire to procreate and to "have" a family.
From Mr. B. who does not want his wife's reproductive labors to interfere
with her sexual services, to Lovelace who fantasizes his ultimate conquest
of Clarissa not as raping her but as making a mother of her, to Charlotte
Grandison, Sir Charles's witty and irrepressible sister, newly softened and
"feminized" by motherhood, Richardson's characters reflect the growing
preoccupation with women as reproducers.

In *Sir Charles Grandison*, Charlotte Grandison is tamed by motherhood,
and the scene in which she nurses her "little marmoset" celebrates her tri-
umphal entry into true womanhood with her delighted spouse's approval
and relief. This time there is no demur, whether about the optimal duration
of nursing or any husbandly objection to a woman's decision to take on that
office herself. The lively Charlotte Grandison is brought into line by childbearing, made to see her true nature, calmed, and fulfilled: "matronized" is
Richardson's word. When she nurses her newborn infant for the first time,
her husband throws himself at her feet in raptures and insists on watching,
providing dramatic evidence for Hugh Smith's specular argument in *Letters to Married Women* (1767) that "though a beautiful virgin must ever
kindle emotions in a man of sensibility; a chaste, and tender wife, with a
little one at her breast, is certainly, to her husband, the most exquisitely en-

chanting object on earth."[81] In Richardson's last novel, breast-feeding brings the lively woman to heel, not the authority of her husband. Perfect Pamela may think her moral duty lies in nursing her own child, but her parents advise her that her sexual services to her husband come first, and her wifely obedience is proved by hiring a wet nurse. But by the time of *Sir Charles Grandison*, a woman's wifely obedience was guaranteed by her re-productive services, her willingness to undertake the lowly task of nursing her own child.

As fiction began to valorize maternal feeling, women's physiological needs increasingly were seen as focused in the desire for a child, and other sexual urges were interpreted as perverse. Jane Austen's *Lady Susan* records the incompatibility of these two modalities, the sexual and the maternal, insofar as its heroine is of the earlier sexual sort, caught in the moral context of the later period. A throwback to those earlier creations of Behn or Haywood, Lady Susan is as confidently sexy and verbally brilliant as a Res-toration heroine. But she is out of place in the moralized and domesticated world of late eighteenth-century fiction.[82] Her incongruence in this world is detected by her insufficiently maternal behavior toward her daughter Frederika.

Other novels as well were part of the discourse that desexualized the female breast and redefined women's physiological nature for domestic life. A scene in Clara Reeve's *The Two Mentors* (1783) reinscribes the husbandly adoration of maternal breast-feeding foreshadowed in *Sir Charles Gran-dison* and promised by a number of medical treatises and conduct manuals. Framed as a narrative about a young lord who secretly marries and impreg-nates a penniless gentlewoman of whom his parents disapprove, the inter-polated tale tells of their interrupted flight when the young wife goes into labor. Although the best that can be done for them is done, the young woman dies tragically, soon after giving birth to a daughter. The next day Bennet, the narrator, seeking his own wife all over the house in which these events have transpired, finds her in the nursery. In his own words: "I found her—oh divine benevolence! emanation of the Divinity! first of the Chris-tian virtues!—I found her giving her own breast to the poor little orphan child, while the tears rolled down her cheeks in compassion for it. I kneeled involuntarily to her as to a superior being.—Oh Maria! my angel wife! This action is worthy of thee, and few besides thee would have performed it." The divine Maria then asks his forgiveness for performing this office with-out first asking his permission, for her reproductive services are his to

[81]Samuel Richardson, *Sir Charles Grandison*, 7 vols. (London, 1753–54), 7:209–13; Smith, p. 77.

[82]For a discussion of whether *Lady Susan* was written in the 1790s or between 1800 and 1805, see B. C. Southam, *Jane Austen's Literary Manuscripts* (London, 1964), pp. 136–48.

command. To this he replies: "Excuse you! my love . . . I adore you for it."
He then informs the new father of this turn of events, which makes possible
another sentimental scene: "Tears and blessings spoke his gratitude for
it."[83] Three times the worshipful husband bows down before his domestic
madonna: when he first finds her in the nursery, when she asks his permission to continue nursing the orphan, and when he tells the bereaved
husband about the angelic wet nurse of his new child. This is Mrs. Bennet's
moment of glory, a moment emphasized by the text, a moment very much
belonging to its particular historical context—when practices commodified earlier as services performed for wages by working-class women are
remunerated ideologically (with adoration) when performed voluntarily
by middle-class women.

The movement to promote breast-feeding in the latter part of the eighteenth century has always been understood as the sane light of reason
penetrating the dark corners of superstitious compulsion. Randolph
Trumbach has argued that breast-feeding and maternal care lowered the
aristocratic death rate in the second half of the eighteenth century and that
it was "one of the finest fruits of the Enlightenment."[84] What I have been
trying to suggest is that this movement involved an unprecedented cultural
use of women and the appropriation of their bodies for procreation. A discourse including sentimental fiction and medical treatises functioned as a
new way to colonize the female body and to designate within women's experience a new arena of male expertise, control, and instruction.

RESISTANCE

There is at least literary evidence that the English craze for breast-feeding in
the last half of the eighteenth century, which had men kneeling to their
wives, was a matter of some ambivalence to women. Maria Edgeworth's
Belinda thematizes anxiety about the breast and its functions in a powerful
narrative of loneliness and fear. Lady Delacour, an intelligent woman driv-
en by love of admiration to extravagance and affectation, tells her history to
Belinda. Like Austen's Lady Susan, she is impudent and entertaining as a
character from the Restoration stage. But though all gaiety on the outside,
she fears she is dying of breast cancer, the culmination of the mess she has
made of domestic life. A failed mother, her first child was born dead "because I would not be kept prisoner half a year." A second starved to death at
her breast: "It was the fashion in that time for fine mothers to suckle their
own children. . . . There was a prodigious point made about the matter; a
vast deal of sentiment and sympathy, and compliments and enquiries. But

---

[83]Clara Reeve, *The Two Mentors* (London, 1783), pp. 175–76.
[84]Trumbach (n. 1 above), p. 191.

after the novelty was over, I became heartily sick of the business; and at the end of three months my poor child was sick too—I don't much like to think of it—it died."[85] Her husband, estranged by her notorious conduct, kills a man in a duel defending her honor, and the victim's grieving mother haunts her dreams. Finally, as a result of a blow on the breast during a transvestite adventure with a dueling pistol, she so injures herself that when her remaining daughter embraces her, she screams with pain and pushes her away. Thus, in stubbornly clinging to her sexual self—and refusing the responsibilities of domestic life—she does real damage to her maternal organ.

Behind a locked dressing room door, amidst the vials of ill-smelling medicines and rags, she confesses to Belinda her terror of breast cancer, from which she fears she is dying. Beth Kowaleski-Wallace has interpreted the meaning of her disease as guilt over her failure to nurse her child: "The injured breast . . . is the center of her excruciating hurt, the psychic wound which she suffers in connection with her inability to perform the mother's role."[86] But Lady Delacour's history could also be read as festering resentment at the colonization of her body, represented synecdochically by the breast that poisons her life. Her adventures and friendship with the crossdressing Harriot Freke are attempts to escape women's domestic roles and retain an independent life. But her body is never her own, as its traumas register vividly; her desires pervert its natural functions, and its health is beyond her capacity to understand or maintain. When at last she confesses to her husband that the secret of her locked boudoir is not a lover but a diseased breast and permits a famous doctor to examine her, she finds that her injury is not mortal after all. When she accedes at last to the wisdom of male medical professionals, she is cured. But the irreducible horror of her fear and suffering remain—a record of her alienation from her female body and its vulnerability to male control. In its preoccupation with issues of women's power and domesticity, as they are contested on the site of the female breast, *Belinda* documents an extraordinary historical moment in the social construction of woman's nature.

The Memoirs of Miss Sidney Bidulph (1761), by Frances Sheridan, is another novel with an emblematic scene about breast disease. An unrelenting representation of miserable, obsessive, filial obedience, the novel has at its center an interpolated tale about a young woman with a diseased breast, who lives in Sidney Bidulph's neighborhood. The circumstances that the sufferer first bruised this tender part of her anatomy while reaching for a book, that her ensuing illness interrupted her correspondence with her lover of choice, and that this lover was a physician whose skill might have

---

[85]Maria Edgeworth, *Belinda* (London, 1801; rpt. London, 1986), p. 33.
[86]Kowaleski-Wallace, "Home Economics" (n. 3 above), p. 250.

prevented the disease are, in the context of the main plot of the novel, crucially symbolic. They constitute a subtext that simultaneously critiques the masochistically passive protagonist while it reinforces the message that women's bodies are vulnerable to male control and their health dependent on male knowledge. In contrast to Sidney Bidulph's suicidal docility and her obstinate obedience to her undeserving mother and husband, this young woman's firmness—her belief in her choice and judgment—saves her breast, saves her life, and most certainly saves her marriage.

The anecdote begins and ends with the wedding of the deserving young woman told by Sidney Bidulph in a letter to a friend. It seems that the bride's father had left a will stating that if she married without her brother's consent she could not inherit her fortune, but at the age of twenty-one she "had the power of bequeathing her fortune by will to whom she pleased." She falls in love with a young physician, against whose family her brother bears a grudge. It is at this juncture that she injures her breast, symbol of her jeopardized womanhood, torn between lover and brother. Her brother, angry at her refusal to marry a rich man, retains an inferior doctor who, after inflaming the infection for three months, prepares to amputate the breast. Our heroine, with a fortitude, independence, and foresight that Sidney Bidulph stood in great need of, summons her brother and her lover to the scene of her surgery to announce that, since she is now twenty-one and her life is in danger, she is willing her fortune to her lover. Whereupon this sagacious young man examines her breast and announces that her state is the result of medical bungling and that her wound can be cured and the breast spared without endangering her life. A second opinion is sought from an eminent Bath surgeon, who concurs with the physician-lover. In a simultaneous triumph of advanced urban medical knowledge and men's superior knowledge of women's reproductive bodies, the young woman perfectly recovers her health in five weeks' time.[87]

Once again, the breast is the locus of women's vulnerability to male control, the site of her sexual definition and dependence and of the struggle between men over her sexual uses. That her lover uses his superior science to save her breast—and thereby win her as his wife—seems only fair. Medicine and romantic love together construct the woman as sexual property in this sequence.

It is not merely coincidence that novels dealing with breast disease, written by women, appeared in roughly the same period as medical treatises advocating maternal breast-feeding and such sentimental scenes of maternal nursing as I have noted in the novels of Richardson and Reeve. All of these texts participated in the new cultural discourse constructing women's

[87]Frances Sheridan, *The Memoirs of Miss Sidney Bidulph*, 3 vols. (London, 1761), 2:266–81.

bodies as maternal rather than sexual, symbolized in reconceptualizing the function of the breast. Thus, the debate over the "natural" sexual or reproductive purposes of the female body found fictional representation in scenes focusing on the female breast, whether to revere it as a site of maternal self-sacrifice or to fear and loathe it as a site of inexplicable disease. If Richardson's scenes involving breast-feeding in his successive novels illustrate the cultural appropriation of women's bodies for reproductive purposes, then the novels of Frances Sheridan and Maria Edgeworth dramatize women's resentment at this new colonization of their bodies. The scenes and images of breast disease in their novels may express how women felt victimized by their female bodies and by their new dependence on superior male medical knowledge of those bodies. These fictional representations are the other side of the new reverence for motherhood, record of a growing feeling among women that they no longer controlled their own bodies, no longer believed they could understand their own physiological processes, no longer believed in their shared medical and herbal knowledge, no longer expected to exercise independent judgment about how to deploy their bodies.

Science, national interest, "natural" feeling, and morality all concurred in the judgment that maternal practice was at the heart of real femininity. It became less and less acceptable for women to delegate their reproductive services to hired labor, to wet nurses. In other words, the effect of erasing class differences among women in this matter was to universalize the meanings and purposes of the female body and to reduce the degrees of freedom in interpreting women's sex roles. Gender—not class—increasingly defined a woman's duties. And the dimensions of gender were being redefined by medical treatises on motherhood and childcare, by conduct literature, and by the novel. Thus, the "invention" of childhood, the new sentimentality about motherhood, and the representation of the female breast in fiction of the later eighteenth century are all different aspects of the same cultural phenomenon: the reconfiguration of class and gender within English society and the colonization of the female body for domestic life.

Incest or Survival Strategy?
Plebeian Marriage within the Prohibited Degrees in Somerset, 1730–1835

POLLY MORRIS

Department of History
University of Wisconsin—Milwaukee

In EIGHTEENTH- and nineteenth-century England, the legal definition of incest bore very little relation to what we now think of as an intrafamilial sexual crime. Sexual relations between closely related family members did not become a criminal offense in England until 1908. Instead, canon law treated incest as an aspect of the church's regulation of marriage and dealt with it in the ecclesiastical courts. The definition of incest enforced in these courts was bilateral and forbade marriage with relatives by blood or marriage to the fourth degree. Canon law also limited punishment of the incestuous couple to an order to separate and to perform penance; where the marriage was challenged from within by a spouse or other private individual, successful litigation ended in an annulment ab initio. Moreover, prior to the passage of Lord Lyndhurst's Act (5 & 6 Will. 4, c. 54) in 1835, these marriages were merely susceptible to annulment during the lifetime of both parties and remained valid until voided in court.

The variety of incest with which the church courts concerned themselves was public and found expression in marriages within the prohibited degrees solemnized in church and, more rarely, in consensual unions that resembled marriages. Illicit sexual relations were also punished under canon law but as fornication or adultery.[1] In theory, the courts did not

I would like to thank Randolph Trumbach and the anonymous readers for the *Journal of the History of Sexuality* for their comments on earlier drafts of this essay.

[1] I am not suggesting that incestuous sexual relations did not occur, then as now, and at all levels of society. In the period under discussion, such cases were perhaps at their least visible, due to the state of the law and the unwillingness of the church courts to continue regulating matters of sexuality. Incest causes are more widely studied for the seventeenth century, when both marriages and illicit sexual relations were more likely to be presented to the courts. Un-

This essay originally appeared in the *Journal of the History of Sexuality* 1991, vol. 2, no. 2.

distinguish between incestuous and nonincestuous intercourse. (In practice, the courts did take up a few cases of incest in which the marriage was in doubt, though technically such couples could only be charged with committing adultery or fornication.) Finally, the great majority of the incestuous unions subjected to ecclesiastical scrutiny involved marriage between affines, or people previously related by marriage rather than by blood. (I will follow contemporary practice and refer to unions as incestuous whether they involved affines or consanguines.) Such marriages often occurred after a spousal death and may have helped to provide for children who had recently lost a parent.

Incest in the sense of sexual relations between close blood relatives, whether consensual or not, certainly did occur, but—given its typically clandestine nature and the lack of legal recourse—it has left fewer traces in the records. Prior to 1908, incestuous relations within the family came to the attention of local authorities haphazardly, most commonly when an unmarried mother swore her child before the magistrates.[2]

From 1835, incest in all its forms moved outside the direct jurisdiction of the courts. There is no indication that this legal anomaly in any way

---

fortunately, scholars who have looked at this material have tended to aggregate the two kinds of causes, and they have not always taken care to distinguish between affinal and consanguineous incest. The best study is Martin Ingram, *Church Courts, Sex and Marriage in England, 1570–1640* (Cambridge, 1990), especially pp. 245–49. See also A.D.J. Macfarlane, "The Regulation of Marital and Sexual Relationships in Seventeenth-Century England, with Special Reference to the County of Essex" (M.Phil. diss., London School of Economics, 1968), p. 49: Macfarlane found thirty-seven incest causes (as compared to eight hundred witchcraft causes) in the Essex records between 1560 and 1680. G. R. Quaife, *Wanton Wenches and Wayward Wives: Peasants and Illicit Sex in Early Seventeenth-Century England* (London, 1979), suggests that the majority of causes in that period were affinal (father-stepdaughter being the most common), but he does not make it clear whether he is discussing sex or marriage (p. 72). The state of the law in the eighteenth century certainly contributes to the impression that more weight was attributed to sexual incontinence than to incest where it is clear that no marriage occurred. See Chapman and Burge v. Fisher, Beake (D/D/C [1786]; D/D/Ca 397, 437 [1786]), in which a couple is accused of living in adultery. It is only from the parish registers that we learn that the relationship between William Fisher and Mary Beake was incestuous as well as adulterous (Beake was Fisher's stepdaughter) and that the couple had baptized three children between 1779 and 1784 (D/P/w.zoy. 2/1/4 and 2/1/5). Beake's mother did not die until 1798; she had borne two children for Fisher, in 1774 and 1776. Unless specified otherwise, all manuscript sources cited in this essay are found in the Somerset Record Office, Taunton, England. The documents are cited with the following designations: D (ecclesiastical records); D/D/C (papers in causes); D/D/Ca (act books); D/P/parish abbreviation (parish registers); D/D/P pb (prebendary records).

[2]Births issuing from these illicit unions occasionally were noted in parish registers (see, for instance, D/P/w.st.c. 2/1/2 and D/P/w.zoy. 2/1/4 and 2/1/5). For a discussion of the difficulties of studying incest within the family and the belated intervention of the state, see Anthony S. Wohl, "Sex and the Single Room: Incest among the Victorian Working Classes," in Anthony S. Wohl, ed., *The Victorian Family: Structure and Stresses* (New York, 1978), pp. 197–216.

reflected popular indifference toward incestuous sexual relations; in addition, there is substantial evidence, drawn from middle- and upper-class sources, that opinion on the nature of incestuous marriage was divided. Public questioning of the prohibition against one type of affinal marriage (that with a deceased wife's sister) began with the passage of Lord Lyndhurst's Act. The original purpose of the bill had been to establish the legitimacy and protect the inheritance of a son of such a union and to reduce the uncertainty surrounding incestuous marriages by limiting the period in which they were voidable. In its amended form it went so far as to protect all affinal marriages celebrated before its passage, but it effectively ended incest litigation in the ecclesiastical courts by declaring all subsequent marriages within the prohibited degrees of affinity or consanguinity void ab initio. Many had supported the amended bill on the assumption that another, permitting marriage with a deceased wife's sister, would follow.[3]

This was not the case, but the agitation in favor of such a bill continued, maintained by the thousands of middle- and upper-class couples who had taken advantage of their wealth and the more lenient laws of other countries to contract affinal marriages abroad.[4] Between 1835 and 1907, when marriage with a deceased wife's sister finally was legalized, a series of royal commissions were appointed to inquire into the prohibited degrees. The first commission, with which we are concerned here, was appointed in 1847. It limited itself to relations of affinity and, in effect, to the marriage with a deceased wife's sister among the middle and upper classes.[5] The witnesses, lay and clerical, arrayed on either side reflect the unsettled state of educated opinion on the issue. Much opposition to reform of the prohibited degrees was based on the belief that affinal incest would lead directly to toleration for consanguineous incest, an argument Nancy Anderson relates to the nature of Victorian family relations. Proponents were equally wary of justifying their marriages on the grounds that only consanguineous unions were incestuous and simply characterized marriage with the deceased wife's sister as a special case.[6]

[3]Nancy F. Anderson, "The 'Marriage with a Deceased Wife's Sister Bill' Controversy: Incest Anxiety and the Defense of Family Purity in Victorian England," *Journal of British Studies* 21 (1982): 67–86; and Cynthia Fansler Behrman, "The Annual Blister: A Sidelight on Victorian Social and Parliamentary History," *Victorian Studies* 11 (1968): 488.

[4]Anderson, pp. 68, 73, 80–81; and Behrman, pp. 490–91. These unions became voidable if the couples returned to reside in England.

[5]"First Report of the Commissioners Appointed to Inquire into the State and Operation of the Law of Marriage, As Relating to the Prohibited Degrees of Affinity, and to Marriages Solemnized Abroad or in the British Colonies," from Parliamentary Papers, 1847–48, 28, reprinted in the Irish University Press Series of British Parliamentary Papers, *Marriage and Divorce* (Shannon, 1969), 1:13–14.

[6]Anderson, pp. 80–81, and Sybil Wolfram, *In-Laws and Outlaws: Kinship and Marriage in England* (New York, 1987), p. 36. Wolfram argues that it was not until the early twentieth

Educated opinion and practice was divided—but what of plebeian opinion and practice? One of the claims made by proponents was that legal reform belatedly would recognize a situation that existed among the lower classes, where poor widowers relied on the unmarried sister of a deceased wife to raise their children and subsequently became intimate enough to desire or require marriage.[7] This behavior was seen as part of a more universal plebeian amorality, the general sentiment being that the life of the poor—except in some tiny Arcadian parish—was hidden from view and that lower-class morality, if it existed at all, was at best different and at worst defective. The most that many parliamentary witnesses felt they could do for these couples was to regularize their situation by offering legal marriage. The Reverend John Garbett, rural dean of Birmingham and rector of a parish with more than twenty thousand inhabitants, was one of the few to contend, on the basis of personal experience, that "it is a mistake to suppose that the people generally, are reckless about these things." More typically, the commission's investigator for the West Country stated that the lower orders lacked the "delicacy of feeling" required to oppose marriage with a deceased wife's sister on the grounds that it was incestuous.[8]

How did the plebs define incest and how did it affect their marriage choices? Did they enter into incestuous marriages out of ignorance or did they, like some members of the middle and upper classes, no longer view affinal kinship as a bar to marriage? Was incestuous marriage a survival strategy among the plebs, as the parliamentary witnesses implied, and, if it was, did it take the form suggested? What role was played by the state (in this case, most frequently embodied in the local parson) in countenancing or even encouraging what were—from the parochial point of view—marriages of convenience?

In the pages that follow I will use the diary of William Holland, a parson in Somerset, and the prosecutions in the county's church courts between 1730 and 1835 to explore plebeian attitudes and practice.[9] Both sources shed some light on how the plebs perceived kinship and made their marriage choices. Holland's diary is particularly helpful in examining the

---

century that the distinction between affinity and consanguinity was finally accepted, which partially accounts for the legislative activity of those years (p. 142), though it remains to be explained why Lord Lyndhurst's Act made exactly that distinction.

[7] Both Behrman, pp. 490–91, and Anderson, pp. 80–81, reject the working-class rationale for passing the bill. Anderson notes that it was rejected at the time because the agitation for reform was seen to emanate from among the middle- and upper-class couples who had married abroad.

[8] "First Report of the Commissioners," 1:97, 16.

[9] Jack Ayres, ed., *Paupers and Pig Killers: The Diary of William Holland, A Somerset Parson, 1799–1818* (Gloucester, 1984). For the records and procedures of the ecclesiastical courts in the diocese of Bath and Wells, which shared the county's boundaries, see Polly Morris, "Defamation and Sexual Reputation in Somerset, 1733–1850" (Ph.D. diss., University of Warwick, 1985), chap. 3.

parochial context of incest and in distinguishing between motives that might have contributed to clerical acceptance of incestuous unions.

The Somerset material suggests that though some couples may have entered affinal unions out of ignorance, others chose to reject the canonical definition of incest and took steps to avoid detection when they solemnized their incestuous marriages. It also suggests that the plebs entered into affinal unions for different reasons than did the upper and middle classes. Plebeian affinal unions were unique in being determined in part by the widowed woman's economic dependence, rather than solely by the widower's need for a woman to run his household and raise his children. Finally, given the fact that these marriages were solemnized in parish churches, often in small parishes, it seems possible that they may have been tolerated or even encouraged by local authorities.[10] The pursuit of the questions raised by this material—about kinship, marriage, and the nature of official tolerance—will, I hope, enlarge our understanding of plebeian sexual culture in the eighteenth and nineteenth centuries.

I

It seems incontrovertible, given the ambiguous status of incestuous marriages under law until 1835, that many incestuous couples enjoyed long marriages free from official interference. The length of time many of the Somerset unions endured prior to prosecution certainly supports that conclusion. Although it is at least as difficult to determine the reasons for the survival of individual incestuous marriages as it is to discover what led to the eventual termination of a handful of them in court, we do know that a clergyman officiated at each of these marriages. Nor did the pivotal role of the parson begin and end with the marriage ceremony: it was the parson who registered births and deaths and who, because of his personal knowledge of his parishioners, was able to instruct churchwardens to prosecute couples in the ecclesiastical courts. To understand the plebeian practice of incestuous marriage we need to know how clergymen reacted to incestuous sexual relations and marriages within the prohibited degrees within their own parishes.

Clerical supervision was uneven in eighteenth-century Somerset. Bath and Wells was as beset by the evils of nonresidence, dilapidation, and inadequate compensation as any other diocese. Likewise, class antagonisms were

---

[10]The Somerset incest material supports John Gillis's contention that plebeian marriage preferences generally were determined by women's relative economic independence. It is also worth considering the role of local authorities in countenancing these unions in the context of what Gillis sees as a widely implemented policy (in the Southeast, at any rate) of forced marriage for the poor: see John Gillis, *For Better, For Worse: British Marriages, 1600 to the Present* (New York, 1985), pt. 2.

increasingly exacerbated by the clergy's role in administering systems of criminal law and poor relief that were seen as averse to the lower orders.

Yet the fact that many incestuous couples, in Somerset and elsewhere, married outside their parishes suggests that they might encounter clerical resistance at home. Again, the state of the law obscures the nature of that resistance. Clergymen quick to note incestuous births in their registers— and among those who did, there is no evidence that they routinely distinguished between affinal and consanguineous incest—do not seem to have presented the couples at Wells Court for either sexual incontinence or marrying within the prohibited degrees.[11] Where clergymen did join incestuous couples in marriage, there is some question as to whether canon law was being violated out of ignorance or with official complicity. If a clergyman did not act out of ignorance, did he agree to the marriage because he believed that the poor (and the parish) could ill-afford the luxury of enforcing the fine points of Christian morality, or because he no longer considered affinal marriage to be incestuous?

The diary of William Holland, the vicar of the western Somerset parish of Overstowey, illustrates some of the dilemmas facing clergymen at this time. Holland, whose diary covers the years 1799–1818, was a farmer-parson in the eighteenth-century paternalist mode. He resided, visited the sick, personally distributed food to the needy, and fed the poor in his kitchen every Christmas. Nor did he neglect the souls in his care, tending to his sermons and expressing his religious and moral views freely. He abhorred fornication, promoted charity, championed marriage as a sacred and desirable institution (his own was very happy), and maintained an egalitarian belief in salvation. The marriages of the poor were as sacred and as necessary to him as those of the rich: he acted quickly to ensure that cohabiting couples married but refused to profane the sacrament by officiating at weddings arranged by parish officers who failed to gain the consent of bride and groom. Overstowey was itself a rather traditional parish, despite the residence of Tom Poole, the Radical, in the neighborhood, and its streets still rang to the sound of rough music in the time of Holland's incumbency. His

[11]The cases I have found of clergymen registering births as incestuous all involve father-stepdaughter incest. While the daughter may have been punished by the magistrates for bearing a bastard and the father may have been forced to provide support, they could not be punished for their incestuous sexual relations. It was only when a couple lived together without marrying that they could be brought before the ecclesiastical courts for committing adultery or fornication. This assumed a consensual relation; indeed, there was little room, in the contemporary scheme of things, for the idea of nonconsensual sexual relations within the family—though it is clear enough that such things occurred (Quaife, p. 72). Rape, even the rape of children, was hedged with a great many qualifications—I have not yet found a case of intrafamilial rape in the Somerset criminal records. See below for a discussion of a case of father-daughter incest in William Holland's parish in which it is assumed that the daughter was equally culpable.

social life was conducted among the local elite, but he did not entirely es-
chew popular festivities, and his slightly anachronistic view of society and
his role in it eased relations with all his parishioners, from the farmers who
manned the vestry to the broom-makers who squatted on the heath.[12]

In the absence of the records of the western archidiaconal court it is difficult to know whether Holland or his churchwardens ever employed the
church court to punish moral offenses, but he certainly never mentions
doing so. Holland was apt to deal with local problems locally, providing
the remedy himself or seeking out a magistrate. In this he was not unlike his
neighbors, who punished adulterers with rough music rather than presenting them to the courts.[13]

Though Holland was an active parson and claimed to have a good
knowledge of his parishioners, he was not immune to the problems of expanding population, geographical mobility, and the rise of Dissent. The
size of the parish (461 souls in 1811) and its scattered pattern of residence
over an extensive territory would have made regular personal contact difficult.[14] Except during his occasional canvasses of the entire parish when he
felt that church attendance was being affected adversely by competition
from the Methodists, Holland was most closely involved with those who
attended church. When it came to marriage, as the parliamentary report of
1847 makes clear, even a conscientious clergyman in a large parish had little
choice but to take a couple's word for their fitness to marry, and elsewhere
parish clerks and clergymen were not always zealous in pursuing these
questions.[15]

Nevertheless, it may have been that the hard times of the early nineteenth century brought Holland into closer contact with the poor, both at

[12]Some of Holland's traditionalism may be attributed to his Welsh origin. The ties between Somerset and South Wales were strong, and Holland and his fellow countrymen
continued to celebrate St. David's Day long after they had left Wales. Holland was also typical
in holding two livings, one at Overstowey and one at Monkton Farley, near Bath. Though
Holland had resided at Monkton Farley for six years, after he moved permanently to Overstowey the parish was left in the hands of a curate, and Holland limited his direct contact to an
annual visit mostly concerned with collecting rent and tithe. Holland is far closer in temperament and social views to his diary-keeping predecessor, James Woodforde, than to their
successor, John Skinner. See James Woodforde, *The Diary of a Country Parson, 1758–1781,*
ed. John Beresford (London, 1924), and John Skinner, *Journal of a Somerset Rector: Parochial
Affairs of the Parish of Camerton, 1822–1832,* ed. Howard Coombs and the Reverend Arthur
N. Bax (London, 1930). Neither Woodforde nor Skinner discusses incest, but Skinner was an
active and willing participant in forced marriages of bastard-bearers, while Woodforde was
not. See also Gillis, *For Better, For Worse,* p. 115.

[13]Ayres, ed., pp. 241–42.

[14]John Collinson, *The History and Antiquities of the County of Somerset,* 3 vols. (Bath,
1791), 1:259–60.

[15]The Reverend John Garbett was speaking of Birmingham when he testified that "banns
are utterly unsuited to the present state of society," but there was wide sympathy with this
view: "First Report of the Commissioners," 1:97; see also pp. 15, 26, 34–35, 52, 62, 75.

the poorhouse and at his own back door. In his official capacity as an administrator of the poor law Holland became involved with the Porter family, longtime residents of the parish poorhouse and members of what might be described as a local underclass.[16] The man Holland frequently referred to as "Villain" Porter first appeared early in the diary as the "madman in the Poorhouse."[17] His behavior, which included terrorizing the other inmates and periodically breaking out and rampaging through the village, was the subject of vestry meetings and other less formal consultations. Four years after the commencement of the diary—years during which Porter received sporadic mention, as threatening villagers, being arrested for theft, and generally causing trouble—Holland wrote one Sunday: "That Villain Porter had the impudence to come [to church], it disconcerted me much. His own daughter confesses herself to be with child by him. Oh Abominable Villain. I will punish him if there is any law to be had."[18]

Three days later his hopes were dashed: "That horrid woman Porter was brought to bed of a dead child this morning, by her own father. Oh Horrid Deed, and this circumstance I fear prevents our moving against him in a legal way for now we cannot compel the girl to swear to the father of the child. I hope there has been fair play."[19] In the absence of a live birth and a criminal statute against incest, there was no legal redress at all.

This did not mark the end of Holland's relations with Porter. For the clergyman, whose previous experience of consanguineous incest seems to have been limited to the occasional play at Bath, the revelation of Porter's deed conferred a peculiar fascination on him that was to last until the man's death. Holland had written of a performance of *God Speed the Plow* that it was a play with "good morality in it," but "the Plot was horrible and shocking in itself:—Murder and Incest, repentance and reconciliation," and he was determined to reintroduce good morality into the local drama by helping Porter to repent.[20] He visited Porter on his first deathbed, later in the same year, and noted that "that Shocking Sinner Old Porter . . . had a child by his own Wicked Daughter . . . [and] did not seem to have much

---

[16]There are some difficulties in disentangling the members of the clan because Holland habitually refers to them by epithets ("Old," "Scoundrel," or "Villain" Porter) rather than by their Christian names. Unlike the broom-makers who kept to themselves and only frequented the parish church for funerals, the Porters considered themselves members of the congregation and, in an elaborate ritual of confrontation, went out of their way to solicit the parson's services. Holland reports disgustedly on the appearance of Thomas Porter's daughter in church, "dressed out in a very gay manner," after she had been let off by the Wells magistrates for stealing "some articles of apparel." "The father had some Psalms given out for singing, expressive of his case as he foolishly imagined," Holland notes, adding that this "has given offence to the whole Parish" (Ayres, ed., pp. 229–30).

[17]Ibid., p. 21. His exploits at the poorhouse are also described on pp. 22, 38, 57, 69, and 101.

[18]Ibid., p. 77.

[19]Ibid., p. 78. Holland may have suspected that the child was killed at birth.

[20]Ibid., p. 31.

sense of guilt on his mind, but I spoke to him in Strong Terms." In a later account, he described their conversation: "He shocked me by his insensibility on speaking of the shocking crime he had been guilty of. He answered that he hoped God would forgive him. I replied that I hoped so too but that it was a crime of a most heinous Nature. There are others as bad as me he answered quick. I did not approve of his answers at all."[21]

Porter survived and continued to terrorize the parish, but not until the end of 1805 did he seriously discomfit Holland. It was Sunday again, and Holland wrote: "That Villain Porter who had a child by his only daughter attempted to stay [for the sacrament] but I gave him to understand that he must not. Indeed the man may repent and in that case forgiveness is promised to any offence, but I feel there is no real repentance in this man, neither does he see his crime in its true light, and moreover he should have come to me beforehand to talk to me before he presumed to come to the Sacrament."[22]

The final entries came a year later, in early 1807, at the time of Porter's death. Holland regretted missing Porter's last deathbed, and he wrote as much on the man's death and what he saw as his greatest sin as he did on almost any other parishioner. Some of Holland's commentary on the man was concerned with local opinion and where it diverged from or coincided with his own. An early entry derides his fellow vestrymen, solid farmers struggling with Porter's fits and outbursts, for suspecting that "there is something more in it than madness." They believed he was "possessed by the Devil or bewitched." In recounting the incident over the sacrament Holland described himself as "shocked and surprized" and concluded, "I was not prepared for him neither were the congregation." Yet there was no evidence that the congregation interfered with Porter's churchgoing, for "he attended Church very regularly some time before his death," and the bell tolled at his death as it did at any other. Perhaps Holland recognized that Porter exercised the same fascination over his neighbors as he did over his clergyman. When Porter broke loose from the poorhouse in late 1803, after the incestuous episode, Holland noted: "and all the Parish after him." They were all there one last time, in 1807, for "the Church was very full" at Porter's burial.[23]

Two years later Holland first wrote about a couple whose relation was affinal rather than consanguineous. The contrast is striking:

> I met the Botany Bay man who lived at the Workhouse. He has had another child by his Sister in Law and in short they have lived together and the husband is in Botany Bay. He asked me about marry-

[21]Ibid., pp. 86, 137–38.
[22]Ibid., p. 126.
[23]Ibid., p. 21 (on the vestry), p. 126 (on the sacrament), p. 88 (on his escape), and pp. 137–38 (on Porter's death and burial).

ing her but I said that she ran a risk if the Husband should come home, besides she was by law his sister. But he said such do marry and that it could not in the Sight of God be worse than it is now. I was staggard but replied that I begged he would not ask me any questions on that head as I could not consent to anything or advise anything but what the Law directs. I would not marry him nor have anything to do with him. He says it is his wish to live soberly and honestly and maintain his family. I replied that it was what I could wish to do. He walked with me and wished to know whether it was more sinful in the Eye of God than living in the manner he did with her. I answered that he knew what the Law was and that I could say no more. I asked him whether he had any sense of Religion. He said he had and knew there was another World. In short he spoke sensibly. It was a difficult case to determine but certainly marriage of any kind is some sanction rather than to live together as they do without any sanction in a Moral Sense.[24]

It was not until 1817 that Holland mentioned the man again. On one of his missions to reclaim his parishioners from the clutches of the Methodists, he wrote: "One man I went to see was a fierce looking man. He lives with his brother's wife and has many very fine children by her. . . . I could not marry him because I knew the case yet it is better he was married than to live in this uncomfortable way."[25]

Though the Botany Bay man posed a dilemma for Holland, he excited none of the shock or horror of Villain Porter. As Holland pointed out, marriage involved two dangers for the couple. First, the union would be bigamous and should the convicted husband return unexpectedly from the penal colony ("she ran a risk if the Husband should come home"), the wife could face serious legal consequences. Second, the affinal relationship ("she was by law his sister") would make the marriage incestuous. Given his law-abiding nature, Holland had to refuse marriage. Yet he made it clear that were it a question not of law but of moral scruple he would have viewed neither a permanently absent first husband nor an affinal relationship as an obstacle to marriage, if the choice lay between marriage and a consensual union. The alternative, forcing the couple to separate by prosecuting them in the church court for living in adultery, does not seem to have occurred to Holland. Unable to marry them, Holland baptized their children, describing them as "base born," his "mildest term of censure."[26]

[24]Ibid., p. 190. Botany Bay was the penal colony to which English felons were transported for varying periods of time. Presumably the brother who had returned had served a shorter sentence, and the husband had been transported for life.

[25]Ibid., p. 282.

[26]Ibid., p. 308 n. The relationship Holland tolerated was with a deceased (or absent) husband's brother, one that many felt was condemned specifically in Leviticus, unlike the marriage with a deceased wife's sister, which was condemned only by analogy. This suggests

In the matter of affinal incest, William Holland's tolerance was based upon knowledge, sympathy, and a sense of morality that did not distinguish among classes. His justice took only passing account of the state of the law and operated independently of the church courts; in the case of the Botany Bay man, it took the form of taking no action at all. What clergymen like Holland did distinguish between—most definitely—was consanguineous incest and affinal incest. Without that distinction, it would be impossible to justify setting aside secular law in the interest of a higher law.

II

On Sunday, March 24, 1765, Joan Sturges entered the chapel of Edington, a small Somerset parish of farmers and turf-cutters, wearing a white sheet and carrying a white wand in her hand. She and her husband, William, similarly attired, stood before the reading desk throughout divine service, and after a sermon or homily against incest (as the penance ordered) they each repeated an acknowledgment, "word for word after the Minister." This is Joan Sturges's penance:

> I Joan Sturges do hereby acknowledge and confess that I have most grievously offended the divine Majesty of Almighty God and the laws Ecclesiastical of this Realm by living and cohabiting with William Sturges lawful Brother of John Sturges my late deceased Husband and having been delivered of three Children by him Incestuously begotten on my body. And I do protest I am heartily sorry for the same and do ask God's forgiveness for this my heinous offence and evil example to you in this behalf given and promise from hence forth not to be guilty of the like offence, But on the Contrary to behave myself as becomes a good Christian and dutiful Subject. And I entreat You all here present to pray with me and for me to Almighty God that it may please him of his Infinite goodness to forgive me.

Then, "meekly and penitently kneeling down," Joan and William rehearsed the Lord's Prayer.[27]

These incest penances of Joan and William Sturges are the only ones that survive among the ecclesiastical court records of the diocese of Bath

---

that Holland regarded all affinal marriage as nonincestuous. By the time of the parliamentary inquiry in 1847, some clergymen openly had abandoned the levitical degrees. Joseph Butterworth Owen described them as "part of the moral law of a peculiar people under peculiar circumstances" in "First Report of the Commissioners," 1:73. A fellow witness, an Irish clergyman, directly addressed the issue of wife-abandonment by asserting that in his country incestuous marriages "chiefly originate in emigration and desertion" (ibid., p. 158).

[27]Sturges v. Sturges, Sturges (D/D/C [1761–5] [for 1765]; D/D/Ca 429 [1765]). For Edington see Collinson, 3:433.

and Wells for the hundred years following 1730. Yet they draw our attention to factors common to many of the cases of incest that came before the Somerset courts in that period. Incestuous marriage was affinal: it involved couples previously related through marriage rather than by blood. It was public: couples celebrated their marriages in church or lived openly in consensual unions that resembled marriages. Finally, half the incestuous couples who ended up in Wells Court came from small rural parishes with populations well under five hundred (the population of Edington was 284 in 1801, the nearest census date). Couples from towns, particularly the cloth-working center of Frome, were prosecuted in the first half of the eighteenth century, but thereafter incestuous couples were shielded by the anonymity and lack of ecclesiastical supervision to be found in larger urban areas.

The records of twenty-one incest causes, the first in 1736 and the last in 1823, survive among the papers of the diocesan court of Bath and Wells and the archidiaconal court of Wells.[28] These cases, because they involve solemnized marriages, tell us more about popular perceptions of kinship and the way they influenced marriage choices than about sexual relations within the family. Although the laws relating to incest did not alter in this period, church court procedures did. These alterations were the result of the courts' withdrawal from the active regulation of sexuality and tended to shift the burden of prosecution away from public officials and onto private individuals. These procedural ambiguities merely indicate that the church was unwilling to surrender its jurisdiction over marriage. While ready enough to abandon its responsibility for adulterers and fornicators, leaving it to the magistrates to punish the bastard-bearing poor, the church courts remained halfheartedly involved with the crime of incest, primarily in its guise as a transgression against marital prohibitions. There was no chronological divide between unions challenged through the vigilance of outsiders (most commonly churchwardens) and those dissolved from within. Throughout this period we are looking at men and women who—aware or not that they were forbidden to marry—married and lived openly as married couples beneath the gaze of parson, churchwardens, and neighbors.[29]

[28]This does not account for all the incest detected in the county in this period, and certainly not for all the incest practiced. In addition to causes lost in gaps in the records and causes that may have been heard in the archidiaconal court of Taunton (the records are lost) or handled at visitations, incest came within the jurisdiction of peculiar courts. The presentation of sexual misbehavior in these smaller jurisdictions, dependent as it was on the zeal of many individual officials whose policies might deviate from those adopted at Wells and for whom close personal supervision of their jurisdictions was a real possibility, was often more thorough and certainly continued long after it had ceased for the diocesan jurisdiction (Morris [n. 9 above], chap. 3).

[29]The continuity between ex officio and instance causes is borne out by persistent procedural anomalies. The causes waver uncertainly between disciplinary, or ex officio, actions

III

Like other ecclesiastical court documents, the incest cause papers provide some biographical data on the litigants and, depending on the length and complexity of the suit, information on the legal outcome. Where depositions survive, it is possible to determine the way in which spouses were related, to reconstruct their marital histories, and to catch glimpses of local reaction to their unions. In the sections that follow I will use this material to examine the ways in which plebeian marriage within the prohibited degrees differed—in form, content, and motive—from the incestuous marriages of the middle and upper classes and from the picture presented in the parliamentary inquiry.

Occupational information for participants in these causes typically is sparse and, again typically, participants of a higher social class, both litigants and witnesses, are identified more readily in cause papers. The occupation of the promoter of the cause or the plaintiff is not necessarily relevant; some causes were promoted by churchwardens or by individuals whose relation to the defendants is unknown. Nonetheless, there are indications that many defendants were drawn from the lower orders. Defendants and their relatives include cloth-workers, a private in a foot regiment, the wife of a laborer, a cordwainer, and a woman who died in the local poorhouse.

Defendants of a higher social class can be recognized by their behavior in court as well as by their status or occupational tags. By the mid-eighteenth century, members of the middle and upper classes made minimal use of the ecclesiastical courts in Somerset, resorting to them only when necessary, as in matters of marriage or probate. When upper-class couples were cited involuntarily, as they might be in incest causes, they did not appear personally at Wells but entered their pleas through their proctors, or ecclesiastical lawyers. They also had the time and money to engage in the lengthier and more costly forms of litigation—thus their preponderance in causes of nullity—and to pursue appeals to the Court of Arches in London.

Moreover, the propertied had different reasons for entering into and

---

and instance litigation, which was a form of suit between parties. They also shift between summary and plenary proceedings. The identities of the plaintiffs, too, are sometimes at odds with judicial practice. In seven ex officio causes churchwardens acted as plaintiffs (the earliest causes were promoted by the office of the judge, but after about 1736 the Somerset courts began to require churchwardens to promote the causes they presented at visitations). More peculiarly, churchwardens were listed as the plaintiffs in a cause for nullity commenced in 1814. Other identifiable plaintiffs included an acknowledged relative and three spouses (all in causes of nullity) and two people who shared a surname with the accused couple, one in each type of cause. In six causes, the connection between plaintiff and defendant is unknown. The procedural anomalies that arise in incest causes are most noticeable when one compares them with divorce proceedings or causes for sexual incontinence. See Morris (especially chaps. 3 and 4) on the cessation of ecclesiastical involvement in lay sexuality.

dissolving their marriages with close relatives. The marriage of affines could have served to preserve or consolidate property, but, unlike the perfectly legal unions of first cousins, affinal marriages were vulnerable to legal attack by disgruntled heirs.[30] Children of a prior marriage anxious about their right to parental property could bastardize and disinherit their half-siblings by challenging the more recent marriage in court. This may have been the case with Ann Williams, who married her late husband's nephew—a farmer substantial enough to be identified as a yeoman—in 1761, fifteen months after her husband died. By the time that James Bryant, Esquire, of neighboring Withiel Flory, brought a case against Ann and her husband six years later, Ann's children from her first marriage may have been old enough to be anxious about the existence of their half sister.[31]

Prosecutions explicitly founded on the financial self-interest of plaintiffs or those they represented are not easy to identify, though the dissolution of marriages involving property, as the Williams marriage probably did, must have been advantageous to some parties. Contention over mercantile property may have been at issue when Abraham Gadd, a Bristol maltster and brewer, took John Keate, another maltster and brewer, to court for marrying two of Gadd's daughters in succession.[32] Reginald Bean, the rector of North Perrott, brought before the bishop in 1736 and charged with incestuously marrying Margaret Pysing, the sister of his deceased wife, was alone in pointing a finger at his accusers. He contended that Benedict Pysing, one of the many clerical witnesses arrayed against him, would be released from a debt he owed Bean if the marriage were annulled.[33]

If propertied individuals could use charges of incestuous marriage to challenge decisions about inheritance, those without property could use the same charges against an adversary as part of a larger strategy of legal harassment. While there is evidence that popular opinion treated affinal incest far less severely than consanguineous incest, it was still a sufficiently

---

[30]On affinal marriage among the aristocracy, see Randolph Trumbach, *The Rise of the Egalitarian Family: Aristocratic Kinship and Domestic Relations in Eighteenth-Century England* (New York, 1978), pp. 18–23, 27, 31–32.

[31]Bryant v. Williams, Williams (D/D/Ca 430, 431, 432 [1767]). For births, see D/P/luxb. 2/1/1 and 2/1/2. The Withiel Flory registers include many Williamses in this period (D/P/wi.f. 2/1/1 and 2/1/2).

[32]Gadd v. Keate (D/D/C [1782]; D/D/Ca 436, 497 [1782]).

[33]Browne v. Bean, Pysing (D/D/Ca 415, 416, 418 [1736]); Bean v. Browne (D/D/Ca 416, 417, 418 [1737]). The causes were promoted by a proctor (Browne) and heard, at least initially, before the bishop as local judicial custom demanded in cases of clerical discipline. The investigation into Bean's affairs was very thorough. Witnesses—depositions do not survive—included Bean's servants and an array of clergymen. Bean's occupation, the zealousness of the Reverend Benedict Pysing (Bean also contended that several of the witnesses had already testified on Pysing's behalf in various tithe causes), and the serious interest the court took in matters of sexual correction in the early eighteenth century may have contributed to the shape of the proceedings.

serious offense, and the consequences of voiding a marriage momentous enough, to lead to malicious prosecution. Causes promoted by private individuals with no obvious relation to the incestuous couple were the least likely to succeed: of the six plaintiffs whose connection to the defendants is uncertain, five failed in prosecution. Three such causes failed at the outset because the plaintiffs did not post bond guaranteeing that they would pay costs if they were nonsuited. William Jenkins, a Frome cloth-worker, brought two causes against William Oram in 1759, both dismissed for lack of guarantees. Jenkins first accused Ann Gifford, and then Mary Harvey, of taking Oram's name and pretending to be his wife. The citations to Wells Court were part of a larger feud involving men and women with the same surnames that leaves traces in quarter sessions and assizes records as well as among the cause papers of the ecclesiastical courts. Jenkins's failure to stipulate suggests that the charges were not well-founded.[34]

Though the failure of many incest causes may indicate a high level of unfounded prosecution, it may also show a strong disinclination on the part of the courts to interfere with solemnized marriages.[35] We know very little about why so many causes failed. How much was it attributable to malice or misjudgment on the part of plaintiffs, how much to caution on the part of court officials, and how much to the indifference of defendants? While some defendants seem to have come to accept the canonical definition of incest, once apprised of it, the actions of other prosecuted couples reflect ambivalence or indifference to the legal proceedings at Wells.

[34]Jenkins v. Oram, Gifford calling herself Oram, Harvey calling herself Oram (D/D/Ca 426 [1759]). See also quarter session indictments (hereafter Q/SI) 379 (1759), Wells; Q/SI 381 (1761), Ilchester; and Public Record Office, London, Western Circuit Assizes (hereafter ASSI) 24 41 process book (Winter 1761); ASSI 23 7 gaol book (July 1761). The Frome registers are not helpful in untangling the relationships because Oram, Gifford, and Harvey were all common surnames in the large parish. However, we cannot exclude the possibility that Jenkins took this opportunity to expose a previously tolerated irregularity and was too poor to post bond. For another cause that failed for want of stipulation, see Collins v. Sheppard, White calling herself Sheppard (D/D/Ca 419 [1740]).

[35]Overall, three annulments were granted, five couples were dismissed, one couple performed penance, two were excommunicated for failing to appear initially, and two others suffered the same penalty at some point after they had confessed. In four causes the outcome is unknown, and in another three litigation ceased before a decision was reached. The charge that the church courts acquiesced in this form of annulment in the period before the prohibited degrees had been limited to four, and thus provided a form of divorce allowing remarriage in a formally divorceless society, has been debated; see R. H. Helmholz, *Marriage Litigation in Medieval England* (Cambridge, 1974), p. 75, and Jack Goody, *The Development of the Family and Marriage in Europe* (Cambridge, 1983), pp. 142–46. In the absence of cause papers it is impossible to know whether Ann Ware was seeking just such a divorce from her husband, Thomas, when she tried to have her marriage annulled on the grounds of incest in 1764 (Ware v. Ware, D/D/Ca 429 [1764]). The court dismissed the cause after a long period of litigation. Given that women had fewer grounds for divorce than men, it is possible that women occasionally made use of prior relationship to achieve divorce.

In some cases, indifference to the crime is difficult to distinguish from indifference to the ecclesiastical courts. Samuel and Anne Brint of Martock were presented at Ilchester Visitation for cohabiting incestuously, but when their cause was forwarded to the archidiaconal court in 1736 Samuel, at least, was excommunicated for failing to appear and answer the charges against him.[36] Whether an individual chose to ignore the court's decrees, as Samuel Brint did, or whether the attempts of one or both members of an incestuous union to comply with them were frustrated, the result was the same. Once excommunicated, in the years before subsequent imprisonment became common, a couple might continue to cohabit unless driven apart by local pressure or a personal sense of wrongdoing.

In the first half of the period, defendants ready enough to confess their crimes might balk at the penances they were expected to perform. The severity of these penances remained constant for all sexual offenses and declined over time, but incestuous couples who had married in the parish church might be unenthusiastic about being subjected to the same punishment, in public, as adulterers or fornicators.[37] In 1736, Elizabeth Harvey of Frome sought absolution within a month of being excommunicated for failing to respond to a citation. She admitted to living incestuously with John Harvey, her deceased husband's nephew. She had borne him several children and was, at the time of her confession, "with Child by him." Harvey was ordered to perform penance on three successive Sundays, taking the parishes of Frome, Beckington, and Road in turn. That the penance was to be performed only before the ministers and churchwardens in each parish was perhaps a concession to her pregnancy, but it was not enough to convince Elizabeth Harvey to comply. She was excommunicated once again for failing to prove that she had performed this elaborate penance.[38]

Incestuous couples might also find their defenders out of court, as John Kington of Winscombe learned. Kington abandoned his action against John Rattle and Elizabeth Fuller (calling herself Rattle), of the same parish, when "being terrified and overawed by the menaces of some person or persons to him well known . . . [he] thought it not proper to proceed any further in the prosecution." According to Ralph Sutton, the proctor who later sued Kington for failing to pay his fees in the cause, Kington "was very resolute and intent" on prosecuting Rattle and Fuller ex officio for liv-

---

[36]Office of the Judge v. Brint, Brint (D/D/Ca 466 [1736], Archdeaconry of Wells [hereafter AW]). There are many Bryants and Baileys in the Martock parish registers, but a Samuel Bryant married Anne Bailey on February 19, 1733/4 (D/P/mart. 2/1/3).

[37]Penance, while still favored by certain elements of the plebs, long had been eschewed by the upper classes of Somerset. The cause James Bryant brought against Ann and David Williams ran into difficulties when he demanded that they perform traditional penance in his parish church. Such a punishment for a couple of their status would have been most unusual by this point in the eighteenth century, and even the ecclesiastical judge seems to have taken extra time to consider the request.

[38]Tesser and Hayward v. Harvey, Harvey (D/D/Ca 466 [1736], AW).

ing incestuously. Sutton acted for Kington from December 1756 until he was told to "desist from further prosecution." During that time, Sutton traveled to Winscombe to meet Kington and inspected the parish register at his request; he exhibited articles that were then contested and he received the names "of some certain witnesses which he . . . John Kington thought were proper to prove the contents of the [articles] and did direct that the said witnesses should be cited to appear to give their testimony and when they appeared did attend with them and at his own expence entertain them." Kington withdrew from the cause in April 1757, leaving a bill of more than 50 shillings with Sutton. Sutton gave Kington until 1758 to pay before prosecuting him.[39]

Though malice may have motivated some of the incest suits brought to Wells that were subsequently dismissed or abandoned, the progress and outcome of others reflect an uncertainty about kinship, marriage, and the status of relationships. This uncertainty could account for the local solemnization of what in retrospect appear to be incestuous marriages, as well as some of the lengthy intervals between solemnization or cohabitation and presentment. In at least two causes the defendants arrested the legal process by simply denying the charges against them. John and Honor Griffin were taken to the archidiaconal court in 1773 by the churchwardens of Bruton, but the Griffins denied that they were living incestuously, and the cause was ended by mutual agreement.[40] William Crabb, a churchwarden of Road, took William Moger of neighboring Woolverton to court in 1763. He charged him with marrying Anna Kington ten years previously, eight or nine years after the death of her sister Jane, Moger's first wife. Moger allegedly had cohabited with each of his wives at Woolverton and had children by both of them. The cause ended when Moger denied the charge and Crabb failed to provide proof.[41]

IV

The most obvious point about the couples brought before the ecclesiastical courts in Somerset, of whatever class, is that they had entered into affinal or

---

[39]There is no record of the incest cause in the act books of either church court. There is a gap in the episcopal acta from October 1756 to October 1758, but it is covered by a draft act book; there is no record among the cause papers. All we know of it comes from Sutton v. Kington (D/D/C [1758]). The outcome of this cause is further obscured by a perhaps unrelated cause brought by Sutton in 1762 against a John Kington, a yeoman late of Winscombe, and Ann Chard, a widow of High Ham, again for subtraction of fees (D/D/C [1762]). In a city such as Bath, if a plebeian man married his deceased wife's sister he might benefit from broad public sentiment in his favor ("First Report of the Commissioners," 1:13–14).

[40]Chaffin and Hazard v. Griffin, Griffin (D/D/Ca 471 [1773], AW).

[41]Crabb v. Moger (D/D/C [1763]; D/D/Ca 428 [1763]). It was very unusual to prosecute only one partner in an incestuous couple. The facts that Moger threatened to appeal the cause and that he had married his deceased wife's sister suggest that the Mogers were not plebeian litigants.

quasi-affinal unions. These unions fall into a pattern that suggests that, alongside the canonical definition of incest, there existed a popular definition that was far less restrictive and distinguished very clearly between affinity and consanguinity.[42]

The degree of relationship between partners is stated or discernible in thirteen causes. Four widowers married the sisters of their deceased wives, three widows married the brothers of their deceased husbands, and two widows married the nephews of their deceased husbands. In addition, one widower married his stepdaughter, another married his son's widow, and two pairs of half siblings married or lived together incestuously.

I have chosen to describe these pairings, where possible, from the perspective of the widowed partner in order to emphasize differences in plebeian strategies of remarriage. As the surprising number of causes in which affinal marriage united two bereaved families suggests, Somerset widows were as likely to be looking for husbands as widowers were to be looking for wives. Furthermore, the marriages I confidently can identify as involving defendants of a higher social class most commonly took the form of a marriage with a deceased wife's sister. When plebeian widowers sought new wives among their affines, they were far more likely to look to the generation beneath them: to stepdaughters, daughters-in-law, or nieces. Some of these marriages would have been particularly distasteful to members of the upper classes, whose ideas of incest were more closely related, in the nineteenth century, to feelings about the sanctity of the home and of affective relations within the nuclear family.[43]

The horror inspired by incest is strikingly absent from the depositions in incest causes, where one might expect to find it. (Indeed, the penance assigned to Joan and William Sturges, for all its strong language, is exactly like the penances meted out to adulterers and fornicators.) This does not indicate popular indifference to incest but suggests that affinal sexual relations inside or outside marriage were not uniquely stigmatized. Marriage with an affine was marriage nonetheless, and having nonmarital sexual relations with an affine was one of many variations on adultery. Horror was reserved for sexual relations between blood relatives.

An examination of defamatory language (and defamation causes in Somerset were an almost entirely plebeian phenomenon) confirms this distinction between affinity and consanguinity. In 1733 a man defamed a woman he identified as "my brother's wife" by saying that he had lain with her several times. This man, and presumably those who overheard his de-

[42]For an anthropological view of the relationship between endogamy and sexual offenses and descent systems, see Jack Goody, *The Development of the Family*, pp. 291, 293, 304, and his "A Comparative Approach to Incest and Adultery," *British Journal of Sociology* 7 (1956): 286–305. See also Helmholz, pp. 79–80, on the strategies employed to avoid consanguineous incest.

[43]Anderson (n. 3 above), pp. 73, 77–78.

famatory speech, ignored the incestuous implications of his words for himself as well as for his sister-in-law. He was merely verifying his brother's cuckoldry by citing his personal experience. Similarly in 1776 Anthony White confessed to saying that Mary the wife of James Ashman, a Bruton innholder, was "a whore to her brother in law and to all the world beside."[44] In both cases, the main concern is with adultery; the affinal relations are used to confirm and describe the woman's promiscuity. In contrast, two other defamers took pains to identify the woman's sexual partner as a blood relative and to draw attention to the conception of a child. (This emphasis on the progeny of consanguineous unions was surely not accidental, but evidence of the persistence of popular fears of monstrous births, their meaning, and their causes.)[45] In 1727 a man performed penance for accusing a woman of lying with her father and being with child by him. More than a century later, William White, watching the wife of a fellow butcher walk by, called out to him: "There goes thy old Bawd that had a son by Charles Wills her own Brother." The words of these two men suggest that consanguineous incest was a crime apart, one that might be attended by consequences that reflected the heinousness of the deed.[46]

Though the distinction between affinity and consanguinity appears to have been widely recognized by the plebs, there is at least one case that hints at further variations in the definitions of kinship that dictated marriage preferences. In a society where marriages frequently were broken by death and remarriage was not unusual, half siblings abounded. Little is known about the ways in which half kinship was perceived, but if relations between half siblings were straightforward at most times, the death of their parents could create dependencies that were strengthened by differences in age and gender.[47] In Somerset, two pairs of half siblings were prosecuted

[44]D/D/C penances, box PB9 (1733); Ashman v. White (D/D/Ca 471 [1776], AW).

[45]See Wolfram (n. 6 above), pp. 137–46 and especially p. 156, n. 3, for the evolution of the association between incest and idiot births from a religious to a "scientific" concept. Though she is convinced that the English distinguished between sexual relations with affinal and consanguineous relatives, she is unsure whether the association extended to affinal marriages.

[46]D/D/C penances, box PB9 (1727); Vowles v. White (D/D/C [1832]; D/D/Ca 452 [1832]).

[47]Kinship terminology is not always the most reliable guide in these matters. Generational differences sometimes obscured the degree of relationship (see Morris, pp. 529–47), and affinity, though usually acknowledged, was described in different ways (daughter-in-law used for stepdaughter, for instance). Even in the two causes that follow, Margaret Hobbs is described as John Hobbs's "Sister," while Harriott Sweet is William Sweet's "Sister of the half blood." This may have reflected change over time, but see also Mary Edwards's description of her half brother, below. Louis Crompton, *Byron and Greek Love* (Berkeley, 1985), pp. 223–24, notes that sibling incest was enjoying a certain artistic vogue at the time Byron was accused of having an affair with his half sister. Crompton does not distinguish between full and half siblings (nor did Byron's social peers, it would seem) but argues that it was sodomy and not incest that exercised Byron's contemporaries.

for living incestuously, and in neither case did simple coresidence provoke suspicion. Rather, both women gave birth to children reputed to be bastards. Margaret Hobbs performed penance for her lapse in 1754, and in 1823 William Sweet submitted to a maintenance order for the child of his half sister, Harriott.[48] What distinguishes the two cases from each other, and what calls into question any simple definition of incest, is the fact that Margaret Hobbs and her half brother were assumed to have married.

While some half siblings were close in age and were raised together, others spent their childhoods apart, living with relatives or separated by age or the requirements of service. We do not know how much Margaret Hobbs saw of her elder half brother, John, during the lifetime of her parents. When she was orphaned by the death of her father, Richard Hobbs, in 1747, she began or continued to live in the same house with John at Hemington. Her mother, Mariabella, had died ten years earlier, and Margaret, baptized in 1724, was probably her only surviving child. Richard Hobbs had been married previously; his first wife had died in 1717, leaving behind five children including John, who was baptized in 1707.[49] According to the churchwardens of Hemington and the witnesses they called, John and Margaret "are and always have been and now are commonly accounted reputed and taken to be lawful son and daughter of . . . Richard Hobbs." Yet from the time of their father's death, it was alleged, John had cohabited with his "Sister" and in July 1751 they had been married at the Bedminster parish church. Margaret had baptized a daughter, Phebe, at Hemington in 1749 and another, Sarah, early in 1754. Margaret is the only parent listed in the parish register, a common way of indicating bastardy. Within a month of Sarah's birth, Margaret was cited to Wells Court and accused of committing adultery, incontinence, or fornication. She confessed to delivering a bastard, performed "open and solemn penance" in the Hemington church, and was excommunicated in May for failing to pay £1 in costs.[50]

By this time she and John were embroiled in an incest cause—they were cited a week after she had performed penance in February—again at the instigation of the churchwardens. John Hobbs confessed to part of the charge (he may have admitted some or all aspects of his kinship to Margaret, or he may have acknowledged the marriage), and Margaret Hobbs denied all the articles when they appeared in court. Of the four witnesses called, only two gave testimony. They confirmed the kinship of John and Margaret and acknowledged that there was a report current in the parish encompassing all the charges against the couple, but they offered no elaboration. Margaret Hobbs had already confessed to bearing a bastard, and

[48]Hales and Brownjohn v. Hobbs, Hobbs (D/D/C [1754]; D/D/Ca 425 [1754]); Yeeles and Evill v. Sweet, Sweet (D/D/C [1823]; D/D/Ca 451 [1823]).

[49]Hales and Brownjohn v. Hobbs, Hobbs (D/D/C [1754]; D/D/Ca 425 [1754]; D/P/hem. 2/1/3).

[50]Hales and Brownjohn v. Hobbs (Margaret) (D/D/Ca 467 [1754]).

no proof of the alleged marriage was offered in court. Not surprisingly, the cause ground to a halt at this point. It is within the realm of possibility that she shared a house with her half brother and her bed with someone else. Similarly, it is not inconceivable that Margaret, presented with the choice between fornication and incest, chose to confess to the former offense.

What is significant is that the couple were believed to have married three years previously and to have left the parish to do so. This suggests that the union was a consensual one and that the couple knew it was within the prohibited degrees, and yet they felt their degree of relatedness to be sufficiently diminished to allow them to marry.[51] The progress of the cause— perfunctory depositions joined with the failure of half the witnesses to appear frequently indicates a lack of popular support for a prosecution—and the length of time between the alleged marriage and the prosecution suggests that their neighbors may have agreed.

The case commenced sixty-nine years later against another pair of half siblings, William and Harriott Sweet, is free of such ambiguities. Their crime was detected quickly, and again the birth of a child appears to have brought the couple to the attention of the local authorities. Their father, Thomas Sweet, married his first wife in Bristol in 1776 and William (who was baptized in 1819 at the age of thirty-eight, when he was described as "late Private in the 40th Regiment Foot") was born five years later. Thomas Sweet remarried in Bathford in 1790. He and his second wife baptized their daughter Harriott in 1799. Thomas probably predeceased his second wife, for he was certainly dead at the time of the cause, and the burial of Elizabeth Sweet of Bathford poorhouse, age fifty-two, is recorded in January 1822. William and Harriott were accused of cohabiting incestuously from about this time, and, according to the charges against them, it was rumored that when Harriott bore a child sometime after that, William submitted to a maintenance order. When an officer of the ecclesiastical court caught up with him in July 1823, William was at Shepton Mallet. He had departed the scene like many another father of a bastard who wished to avoid paying for its support. William may have appeared at Wells to hear the charges against him but Harriott never did, and their contumacy was signified to Chancery at different points in the second half of the year.[52]

---

[51]Gillis (n. 10 above), p. 116, notes the importance of matrilineal kinship in protoindustrial areas, but the focus on matrilineage may have been peculiar to plebeian culture in the southwest of England and not merely an epiphenomenon of protoindustrialization.

[52]Yeeles and Evill v. Sweet, Sweet (D/D/C [1823]; D/D/Ca 451 [1823]). This was the only ex officio cause for living incestuously heard at court after 1773 and the charges of adultery, incontinence, and fornication—increasingly rare in the nineteenth century—were added to the accusation of incest because William and Harriott had never married. William was not necessarily eighteen years older than Harriott, for she was baptized at the same time as a brother who may not have been a twin. See Bathford bishops' transcripts, Somerset Record Office, pre- and post-1813.

At first glance, these two causes come closest to the violations of consanguinity we identify as incest. Both liaisons occurred in the wake of parental deaths, and both involved women who were much younger than their male partners. In the case of William and Harriott Sweet there is no suggestion of marriage, and what little we know from the documents that survive does nothing to modify a picture of exploitation and abandonment. Certainly the unusual behavior of the churchwardens in commencing an ex officio cause, or disciplinary prosecution, in the church court at that late date, when such prosecutions were unheard of, indicates strong negative feeling in Bathford. Whether it originated among the gentry, the poorer population that serviced neighboring Bath, or their clergyman, we do not know.[53]

It is worth considering whether the union between John and Margaret Hobbs in fact conformed to certain rules governing the formation of plebeian marriages—rules that defined a descent system that differed in several respects from the one sanctioned by the church. John and Margaret Hobbs shared a father rather than a mother. If the Hobbses and their neighbors differentiated not only between affinity and consanguinity, but also between maternal and paternal descent within the family unit, they may have felt their relatedness to be diminished within acceptable bounds. We cannot help noticing that Margaret Hobbs, who did not balk at performing penance in her parish church, as well as many of the other plebeian participants in incestuous marriages honored some of the social and religious conventions of their society. Most significant of all, these couples sought out legal marriage, properly solemnized in a parish church.

V

Unlike William and Harriott Sweet, nearly all the incestuous couples that came before the church courts had married, many legitimizing new family units formed in the wake of spousal death. Did these couples marry out of ignorance or preference? Were they abetted by local authorities—clergymen, parish clerks, and churchwardens—or could they at best count on a degree of ignorance or a lack of interest in the details when they formed these unions? The size of the parish and the likelihood of the clergyman knowing the couple had a significant impact on a couple's ability to marry locally. If the clergyman was, like William Holland, unwilling to flout the law, a couple aware of their relationship would have to leave their parish to marry. This generally meant going to the largest parish in the neighborhood.

Where churchwardens intervened rapidly in the affairs of parishioners

<hr>

[53]For Bathford, see Collinson (n. 14 above), 1:111–16.

who had taken the precaution of marrying outside the parish, aggravating circumstances probably contributed to suspicion. Foremost among these was the birth of a child of uncertain legitimacy, and this was compounded when the parents were of widely disparate ages. Marriages between young and old were popularly condemned on the grounds of propriety and aesthetics. Where children of previous unions were involved, generational confusions might arise—particularly between a young stepmother and her older stepchildren—that challenged notions of domestic hierarchy. When Samuel Watts of Frome married Hannah Hyatt, his stepdaughter, less than a year after her mother had died, he may have been forming a conspicuously ill-assorted union. Watts had married Hyatt's mother in 1740 in the adjacent parish of Elm, and he returned to Elm and to the Reverend Joseph Francis in 1746 for his second wedding. The churchwardens of Frome, a large textile center, did not trouble the couple until 1747; the birth of an "incestuously begotten" child may have brought Hyatt to their attention. Watts and Hyatt confessed immediately and were ordered to perform penance and to separate by or before Easter, a time more than half a year away. (The sentence was far less punitive than those handed down in the previous decade.) Though they promised to live apart, a gap in the act books leaves their compliance in doubt.[54]

In a more notorious case, Henry Plenty married Eleanor Plenty by banns at Bedminster on September 5, 1814, a year after the death of his septuagenarian first wife and two years after the death of George Plenty, Henry's son and Eleanor's husband. Mary Edwards, the "Natural Daughter" of Henry's first wife, drew attention to the household's ambiguities when she deposed that George and Eleanor, married in the parish church in 1804, had had three children, "all of whom are now living in . . . Chewton Mendip with . . . Henry Plenty their grandfather and Eleanor Plenty his wife their mother."[55]

The witnesses acknowledged the births, deaths, and marriages that established the affinal relation. They also made it clear that Henry and Eleanor Plenty had no trouble presenting themselves as a married couple in Chewton Mendip, an extensive parish with lead and lapis mines in its hilly sections, and that the churchwardens' legal action had not prompted them to separate.[56] Anna Gould had known Henry and Eleanor all twelve years

[54]Bull and Rossiter v. Watts, Hyatt (D/D/C [1747]; D/D/Ca 423, 386 [1747]). On Francis's long tenure at Elm, see Collinson, 2:206–7.

[55]Hippisley and Gait v. Plenty, Plenty (D/D/C [1794–1815] [for 1814] and D/P/chewt.m. 2/1/4). Only two of the children were registered locally, Charlotte in 1805 and John in 1810.

[56]Collinson, 2:115–20. Somerset's miners were traditionally viewed as an immoral lot, and Hannah More had chosen the Mendips as the field for her moralizing activity in the 1790s. It is certainly possible that the couple had been denied the opportunity to marry in Chewton Mendip and had gone to Bedminster in search of anonymity. The marriage between

she had been in the parish, and she described going to Bedminster "very early in the morning" on September 5 to celebrate their marriage. They all returned home immediately, and the Plentys "ever since lived and cohabited together as Man and Wife." The sentence read against them in May 1815 stated that Henry and Eleanor Plenty "did thro' their ignorance of the Law" contract a marriage "or rather Effigies of a Marriage." It was dissolved, and they were ordered to separate.

William and Joan Sturges, who performed penance in Edington, married after the nearly simultaneous deaths of their spouses. Twenty years passed before they were cited to Wells Court for living incestuously. The parish registers of Edington and Moorlinch provide an unusually clear picture of the marital history of the Sturgeses.[57] In October 1733 John Sturgas married Joane Morres, and seven months later his brother William Sturgas married Elizabeth Deane. Over the next twelve years William and Joan each had at least six children with their respective spouses. On August 15, 1745, William's wife Elizabeth was buried; two months later John and Joan buried their eldest daughter Joanna (a daughter baptized less than a month later was given the same name). On November 22 John Sturges, "Father of the to [two] above said Joanna's," was buried. The widowed Joan buried another child three weeks later.

Having lost their spouses within a few months of each other, Joan and William began a new life together. The record of their reproductive history left in the registers indicates that though Joan and William fell immediately into the birth pattern of their previous marriages, some uncertainty about their marital status remained until the period between 1750 and 1753. By that time they had either formally married or their union was recognized as legitimate. The baptism, in 1747, of "Joane Daughter of Joane Sturges" is followed in 1750 by that of "Priscilla Daughter of Wm Sturgas and Joan Sturgas" (Priscilla was the name of the second child Joan had buried in 1745). In 1753 came "Thomas son of William Sturgas and Jone his wife." Their childbearing over, Joan and William continued to live as man and wife at Edington for another twelve years.[58]

John and Margaret Hobbs, if it ever did take place, was also said to have been solemnized in Bedminster, fifteen miles from Hemington. It is remotely possible that the Hobbses, like the Wattses, had a family tradition of marrying outside the parish, because neither of Richard Hobbs's marriages are recorded at Hemington. Miners were among the groups Gillis describes as following their own marital traditions, again based on the economic independence of women (chap. 4).

[57]Sturges v. Sturges, Sturges (D/D/C [1761–5] [for 1765]; D/D/Ca 429 [1765]). Edington, the Sturgeses' parish, was a chapelry of Moorlinch and at different times Edington baptisms, marriages, and burials, clearly noted as such, took place at the mother church (D/P/ed. 2/1/2; D/P/morl. 2/1/4).

[58]How long Joan and William waited before commencing sexual relations is uncertain, because Joan presumably was nursing her baby Joanna, and possibly Elizabeth's youngest

It was only in 1765 that John Sturges of neighboring Chilton Polden, a man who well could have been a son from either of their first marriages— Joan had baptized a son John in 1741 and William had done so at the end of 1739—promoted a cause against Joan and William in the diocesan court. If Joan and William and those around them had been living in genuine ignorance until some time in 1765, they then may have employed one of their grown children to bring a suit at Wells. This would have provided them with the opportunity to publicly confess, apologize, and separate. Their immediate compliance with the court's decrees and the fact that no costs were assigned in their very rapid suits would be consonant with such a strategy. Such attention to propriety and publicity would be of a piece with most of their other behavior, the official status of their relationship between 1745 and 1753 being a possible exception. It would also add weight to the characterization of penance as a ritual intended to restore wrongdoers to the community, for Joan and William continued to live in Edington until their deaths many years later.[59]

Only three marriages were contested from within on the grounds of incest in this period.[60] Elizabeth Adams claimed that George Adams, her deceased husband's elder brother, "by false and artful insinuations and taking advantage of . . . [her] ignorance in the Law" had persuaded her to marry him by banns at Bath in 1814. She had married James Adams, a cordwainer, by license at East Harptree in 1811 and lived there with him until his death two years later, their only child dying soon after birth. Shortly after her marriage to the widowed George Adams, Elizabeth "was informed by her Father and some of her Friends and acquaintances that the . . . Marriage was unlawful and incestuous and that as soon as . . . [she] was convinced of the illegality of such Marriage by reason of Incest

---

daughter Anne, and may have remained infertile for about a year. Similarly, the confusion over their marital status—in the years before Lord Hardwicke's Act (1754) made solemnization in church a necessity—may have reflected a reliance on the older procedures, where a promise to marry followed by consummation made a marriage legally valid if irregular.

[59]William and Elizabeth had buried a "man Child" five months after their marriage, but this may have been a miscarriage—the child was not christened—rather than a prenuptial conception. Joan was buried in 1770 and William in 1788. What may have been a characteristically plebeian use of the church courts in this cause may be contrasted with what has been described as a legal strategy of incestuous couples of a higher social class. Prior to 1835, these couples could protect their marriages (and the legitimacy and right to inherit of their children) by persuading a friendly party to commence a suit challenging their marriage, which could then be tied up in the church courts until the death of one partner (Behrman [n. 3 above], p. 488). This might explain the participation of some Somerset plaintiffs of a higher rank, but close relations could be equally interested in annulling marriages if they thought they might benefit.

[60]Adams v. Adams (D/D/C [1817]). The two other causes, for which no papers survive, are Ware (Ann) v. Ware (Thomas) (D/D/Ca 429 [1764]) and Dyer (Edward) v. Dyer otherwise Fowler (Sarah) (D/D/Ca 440 [1807]).

she . . . did leave the Company and society of . . . George Adams and has not accompanied and lived with him since." She separated from him in 1815 and sought an annulment two years later, when she was living at Compton Martin and George was living in Ston Easton.

The identity of the five witnesses called by Elizabeth Adams supports the idea that there were a number of friends and relatives who were aware of her two marriages and might have counseled her against the second. Even the wording of the documents suggests that Elizabeth had entertained doubts, which George allayed, and that her family and friends were not at all ignorant about the prohibited degrees. John Adams, age 74 (the father of James and George) and William Kingman, age 70, his brother, testified to living in nearby Farrington for many years. Kingman had been present when James was buried there, in the parish of his birth. Elizabeth's brother, William Hatch, was a lifelong resident of East Harptree. He witnessed her first marriage, claiming to have known James Adams many years and to have attended his funeral. William Stephens, a gentleman who also witnessed the first marriage, had been born in East Harptree and lived there at that time, as had Elizabeth and James. (It is possible that Stephens had an independent connection with the Adams family, for both he and George Adams moved to Ston Easton around the same time.) Even Charles Russell, the parish clerk who witnessed the Bath wedding, asserted that he had known George Adams for many years. His claim to have known Elizabeth prior to the marriage may have applied only to the three weeks during which banns were read; in any case, he mentioned no difficulty in arranging for the banns or in witnessing the marriage.

George Adams admitted the incestuous marriage and the subsequent separation but denied that he had tricked Elizabeth into marrying him. His reasons for marrying outside the Mendips were not necessarily devious: he may have been living and working in Bath at the time (his long friendship with Russell supports a connection with the city); or he may have chosen, as many did, to solemnize his second marriage quietly, away from the immediate neighborhood of family and friends. Indeed, Elizabeth's status as a widow, even a young one, offers a plausible explanation for the incestuous marriage going forward unopposed. As a widow, she was free to marry without the direct knowledge or approval of her family.

A sentence was read dissolving the marriage two months after the libel, or charge, was given in. The rapid termination of the cause, despite the summoning of five witnesses, and the willing participation of George's kin suggest that the Adamses and their friends had determined to end the marriage. (George's seeming resistance probably amounted to no more than an unsuccessful effort to avoid paying costs.) Their reasons for doing so at Wells are not clearly linked to a desire for public expiation, as they may have been with the Sturgeses. Elizabeth Adams waited two years before seeking an annulment, a procedure that did not entail the performance of penance anyway. Yet, like Joan and William Sturges, she was troubled enough by the knowledge she received to separate from her husband, in her case within five or six months of their marriage.

Ignorance, genuine or asserted, was essential to the undertaking of a nullity cause, such as Elizabeth Adams's, because couples applying for a marriage license or for banns to be read were queried as to their knowledge of impediments to their marriage. Ignorance of the full extent of the prohibited degrees was probably not unusual. Even those who could read and who attended church might find themselves in a church where the table of kindred and affinity was missing from its place on a pillar, as did the parishioners of East Harptree in 1751.[61] Yet all the couples who came before the Wells Court were closely related, many shared surnames, and a great many took the precaution of marrying outside their own parishes, where their kinship would be unknown.

Where a spouse did not promote the litigation, there was no necessity to allege that the marriage had been contracted through ignorance. Henry and Eleanor Plenty and their friends, relations, and neighbors may have been truly ignorant, or ignorance may have been a more palatable explanation for their conduct than indifference. There is nothing in the cause papers to support the conclusion reached in the sentence, and it seems more likely that the Plentys were aware of the impediment and deliberately took the precaution of going outside their parish to the populous town of Bedminster to solemnize their marriage. Couples who married in their home parish, such as the Sturgeses, were the most likely to have acted out of ignorance. Joan and William Sturges seem genuinely to have been ignorant of their transgression, and they took it seriously enough when it was finally brought to their attention to submit promptly to the decrees of the church court and to publicly terminate their long-established union.[62]

The Sturges marriage, and its lengthy survival in a small parish, returns us to the question of official complicity in the formation of incestuous marriages. Was the parson who regularly registered the births, deaths, and marriages of the Sturges clan in Edington unaware of the impediment to

---

[61]Visitation presentments of the prebend of East Harptree (D/D/P pb, box 9 [1751]); the book of homilies was also missing. The table was supposed to be posted in every church and printed in the Book of Common Prayer. Whether or not the situation was rectified, the churchwardens of East Harptree, a peculiar jurisdiction, presented couples for contracting incestuous marriages in 1823 and 1841.

[62]Clergymen who testified before the commission were divided, in their anecdotal evidence, on the degree of ignorance of the lower classes, but it is possible that in a city like London or Birmingham the alienation of the poor from the church was sufficiently long-standing to have produced a widespread ignorance of the prohibition against affinal marriage: "First Report of the Commissioners," 1:32, 60, 74–75, 96–97.

their marriage? Was the Reverend Joseph Francis of Elm, a parish of about three hundred souls, unaware that it was Samuel Watts's first wife's daughter he had brought as a bride when he returned to have his second marriage solemnized by the same clergyman? Was the parish clerk who arranged for the banns to be read for the incestuous marriage of Elizabeth and George Adams ignorant, or was he willing to take George Adams's word—just as the Bedminster parish clerk took Henry Plenty's word—when he alleged that there was no impediment to his prospective marriage on the basis of consanguinity, affinity, or precontract?

The marriages in Edington and Elm were both attended by special circumstances that obscure the general issue. Though Edington itself had a population of 284 in 1801, it was merely a chapelry of neighboring Moorlinch, and so clerical supervision was spread over the inhabitants of more than one parish. Samuel Watts and his two wives were resident not in Elm but in the neighboring town of Frome. Moreover, there was a six-year gap between the two marriages. Similarly, with parish clerks it is difficult to know whether we are looking at something more than the routine neglect that affected all large parishes. Charles Russell was a friend of George Adams's and may have sympathized with him; Benjamin John Room was performing his menial job in an acceptably perfunctory manner.[63]

Official tolerance could stem from knowledge and a sense of justice, as it did with William Holland. But it also operated in the grey area between ignorance and expediency. Proximity and dependence after spousal death (or permanent absence) undoubtedly played a role in propagating incestuous unions, and official tolerance may have been extended more readily in situations where these events brought about the coresidence of related adults and an irregular marriage promised to provide for widows and orphans, who might otherwise fall on the parish. Official connivance in these arrangements cannot be proved, but even among the handful of Somerset couples who ended up in court, some lived together without interference prior to presentment, and some benefited from the strict construction of ecclesiastical justice afterward, winning dismissals on grounds unrelated to their guilt or innocence.

VI

How accurately did the royal commission characterize plebeian marriage within the prohibited degrees? The Somerset material, Holland's diary, and the incest and defamation causes suggest that while the commission overlooked certain similarities between plebeian and middle- or upper-class

---

[63]In Somerset, the inquiries into impediments seem to have been left to the parish clerk. William Holland is very clear about the low status of parish clerks; he called all of his "Mr. Amen" and employed them about his farm as odd-job men (Ayres, ed. [n. 9 above]).

attitudes and practices, it also ignored the significant differences. A small number of people of all social classes married within the prohibited degrees. They seem to have done so out of choice rather than ignorance, and their consistent preference for affinal partners demonstrates that the canonical definition of incest had been rejected by some people at all levels of society. However, the reasons for entering these marriages, the strategies employed to solemnize them, and the risks to the couple and their children varied from class to class.

There is every indication that incest with blood relatives was perceived negatively among the plebs—except perhaps among those, such as the Porter clan, on the very margins of society—but the defamation material suggests that these perceptions were shaped by traditional fears of divine retribution rather than by feelings about the nuclear family.[64] Attitudes toward affinal marriage probably varied, as they did among the educated. While a clergyman like William Holland may have come to accept that affinal unions were not incestuous and registered parish births accordingly, some of his colleagues continued to adhere to the canonical system when describing these children. Just as wealthy couples, whose concern was with the legitimacy of their children and their right to inherit, married outside England, plebeian couples went to the large towns of Bedminster and Bath to regularize their consensual unions. When they did so, they were entering marriages that they knew were illegal but did not consider incestuous. The Sturgeses genuinely may have been ignorant of the incestuous nature of their marriage, and their withdrawal from it may have been motivated by religious scruples or by a more general law-abidingness, but marriage patterns suggest that in general the plebeian couples based their marriage choices on a view of kinship that distinguished clearly between consanguineous and affinal relationship.

The reasons for entering into an affinal marriage and the partner chosen were closely related to social class. The reformers' focus on a single form of affinal union, the marriage with a deceased wife's sister, left them blind to the variety of affinal marriage among the plebs. Upper- and middle-class men required women to raise their children if their wives died, as they so frequently did in childbirth; and given the demographic configuration of

---

[64]Whether indifference to incest was a characteristic feature of the sexual life of the very poor remains unknown. The Porters, according to Holland, had produced incestuous children in at least two generations, though the earlier incident seems to have involved sexual relations with a husband's brother before marriage, thus creating a bar to their subsequent marriage by reason of affinity. Holland does not refer to the incestuous implications of this incident; he may have ceased to view nonmarital sexual relations as a way of creating affinity. He mentions the incident late in the diary while describing the problems of the child, long grown and, after a round of theft and other dubious activities, about to become a charge on the parish (Ayres, ed., pp. 230–31).

middle-class families there was likely to be an unmarried woman, quite probably a sister of the dead woman, already on hand.[65] Among the plebs, we find widows looking for husbands and perhaps fathers to raise their children. This reflected, no doubt, the limited possibilities for women's survival outside a family economy. We have also seen that plebeian widowers were more likely to seek out mates of a younger generation, even marrying stepdaughters and daughters-in-law.[66]

Incestuous marriage was a marginal phenomenon among all classes. Its status as a marriage strategy confined to specific circumstances is confirmed not only by its rarity in the court records, but also by the fact that many of the plebeian defendants in incest causes operated on the fringes of plebeian sexual culture as a whole, participating in sexual and marital irregularities that persisted across generations. Mary Edwards, who described herself as "the Natural Daughter of the late Mary Plenty" and who was baptized as "Mary the base born daughter of Mary Smith," recalled her spinster mother's marriage to Henry Plenty, when she was eight or ten years old, and the birth of their son George, "whom she always called Brother." George was prenuptially conceived: his parents married four or five months before his birth. Margaret Hobbs's two daughters, Phebe and Sarah, who were certainly illegitimate if not the products of an incestuous union with her half brother, married men with the same name, possibly a father and son, within a few years of each other. Joanna Sturges, the youngest child of Joan and John Sturges who was raised in the family unit formed after the deaths of John Sturges and Elizabeth Sturges, baptized a bastard daughter in 1771. She named her Sarah, the name of one of William and Elizabeth Sturges's daughters, born three years before her and buried in 1752.[67]

These sexual and marital irregularities were incorporated into a familiar pattern of social and family life. Naming customs and the regularity with which couples solemnized marriages in church and baptized their children located these women and men in the mainstream of plebeian sexual culture, just as their bastard-bearing, prenuptial conceptions and incestuous marriages pushed them toward its fringes. Moreover, this ability to pick and choose between the rites of the established church, to determine their tim-

[65]Anderson (n. 3 above), pp. 80–81; Behrman (n. 3 above), pp. 490–91.

[66]Plebeian marriage may have been following a more traditional pattern: Goody, *The Development of the Family* (n. 35 above), pp. 62–63, argues that affinal unions were used to provide for widows and orphans among other cultures and at various times in the past.

[67]Hippisley and Gait v. Plenty, Plenty (D/P/chewt.m. 2/1/3); Hales and Brownjohn v. Hobbs, Hobbs; Sturges v. Sturges, Sturges (D/P/ed. 2/1/2, D/P/morl. 2/1/4). Joan and John had a daughter in 1747 named Joane, but it is more likely that her older half sister was the mother of the child, baptized in 1771 and buried in 1772. The Beakes of Westonzoyland may have been another family with a history of irregularities—a Betsy Beake performed penance for giving birth to a bastard in 1760 (D/D/C penances, box PB9).

ing, and to invest them with their own meaning was an identifying trait and persistent strength of plebeian sexual culture.[68]

By the nineteenth century, the church was engaged in its own battle to retain control over the institution of marriage. That control was gravitating steadily into the hands of the civil authorities. For this reason, and because at the local level marriage was often seen as an attractive alternative to poor relief, clerks and parsons may have been unwilling to inquire too closely into the legality of certain marriages. In practice, this may have become easier as the debate over affinal marriage became more public and as it became increasingly acceptable for clergymen to profess ignorance of the mass of their parishioners.[69] What Jack Goody has called the "dual economy of kinship, one at the level of rules, one at the level of practice," was surfacing around the problem of affinal marriage, but the middle- and upper-class reformers, clergymen among them, were ill-placed to make use of the longstanding plebeian practice.[70] Plebeian marriage within the prohibited degrees remained an unexamined element in the hidden sexual life of the poor.

[68]William Holland's diary provides many examples of this; he is also quite open about the way the clergy might exploit it, particularly in their dealings with sectarians (Ayres, ed., p. 58). For more on plebeian sexual culture in Somerset see Morris (n. 9 above).

[69]In only one instance in Somerset was the clergyman who performed an incestuous marriage charged with profaning matrimony: see Gadd v. Keate (D/D/C [1782]; D/D/Ca 436, 397 [1782]) and Gadd v. Browne (D/D/C [1782]; D/D/Ca 436 [1782]). Gadd claimed that Browne, "having been apprized of and well knowing the said marriage to be illegal and contrary to the Laws Spiritual and temporal of this realm," went ahead with the ceremony unlawfully. Gadd and Keate were from Bristol and there may have been an element of clandestinity in crossing the county border to marry. Both causes were dismissed but not necessarily on the merits, and it is notable that it was the interested private individual, and not a church official, who brought the prosecution.

[70]Goody, *The Development of the Family*, p. 182.

Sexual Politics and Public Order in Late Eighteenth-Century France: The *Mémoires secrets* and the *Correspondance secrète*

JEFFREY MERRICK
Department of History
University of Wisconsin—Milwaukee

WHEN THE comtesse de Mirabeau asked the Parlement of Aix for a marital separation from her dissolute husband in 1783, her lawyer denounced the future Revolutionary orator as a "bad son, bad husband, bad father, bad citizen, and dangerous subject."[1] It made sense to lump the count's transgressions against his relatives and his sovereign together in this manner, not only because the combination of charges made the indictment more damning but also because the social and political structures of the ancien régime made simple distinctions between private and public affairs impossible. In early modern France the family was regarded as a miniature kingdom, and the kingdom was regarded as an extended family. The household and the realm embodied the same principles of order dictated by patriarchalism, absolutism, and Catholicism. Law and theology endorsed the customary assumptions about the physical, mental, and moral inferiority of the female sex that subordinated women to men and relegated them to the home. The father ruled his wife, children, and servants like a domestic monarch, and the divinely ordained monarch ruled his subjects like a royal father. Disobedience and impropriety in the household were regarded as public offenses because families provided the model for the hierarchical relations of subordination and authority that ordered French society.

My thanks to Elizabeth Colwill, Susan Dunn, Sarah Hanley, Penelope Johnson, Gary Kates, Paul Lucas, Sarah Maza, and Randolph Trumbach for comments on drafts of this article.

[1]*Mémoires secrets pour servir à l'histoire de la république des lettres en France depuis 1762 jusqu'à nos jours,* 36 vols. (London, 1777–89), 35:278. Hereafter abbreviated *MS* and cited in the text.

This essay originally appeared in the *Journal of the History of Sexuality* 1990, vol. 1, no. 1.

The metaphorical assimilation of household and kingdom left its mark on the jurisprudence as well as the rhetoric of the ancien régime.[2] Monarchs and magistrates protected the interests of families and strengthened the authority of fathers by outlawing clandestine marriages, criminalizing female adultery and infanticide, and imprisoning wayward wives as well as rebellious children. Served by sword and robe families intent upon advancing their own dynastic fortunes, sanctified by clergy intent upon implementing the disciplinary reforms of the Council of Trent, the crown punished sexual license in order to ensure the inheritance of estates by legitimate progeny and enforce the standards of conduct defined by the Catholic church. Divine-right absolutism, aided and abetted by the Counter-Reformation, made the king responsible for the moral rectitude as well as the religious orthodoxy of his subjects. The church identified vaginal intercourse within marriage for the purpose of procreation as the only legitimate use of human sexuality. The monarchy condemned various forms of nonprocreative and extramarital sexual activity—masturbation, sodomy, bestiality, prostitution, adultery, bigamy—that violated the precepts of the church, undermined the stability of the family, and disturbed the public order of the kingdom.

In theory, French men and women mastered their sinful passions and performed their assigned roles in the patriarchal system of politics and procreation constructed by family, state, and church. In reality, they undermined the hegemony of the authoritarian household, Bourbon absolutism, and Counter-Reformation rigorism in the eighteenth century. Paternalism displaced patriarchalism in conceptions of the family and the monarchy, and the secular authorities withdrew from the business of en-

---

[2]Works on early modern French family history and political history—such as Jean-Louis Flandrin, *Familles: Parenté, maison, sexualité dans l'ancienne société* (Paris, 1976); and Roland Mousnier, *Les institutions de la France sous la monarchie absolue, 1598–1789,* 2 vols. (Paris, 1974–80)—inevitably mention the relationship between paternal and royal authority, but there is no sizable, systematic, and searching study of the French case comparable to Gordon Schochet, *Patriarchalism in Political Thought: The Authoritarian Family and Political Speculation and Attitudes, Especially in Seventeenth-Century England* (New York, 1975); and Jay Fliegelman, *Prodigals and Pilgrims: The American Revolution against Patriarchal Authority* (Cambridge, 1982). On the connections between patriarchal order in the household and the kingdom, see Sarah Hanley, "Family and State in Early Modern France: The Marriage Pact," in *Connecting Spheres: Women in the Western World, 1500 to the Present,* ed. Marilyn Boxer and Jean Quataert (New York, 1988), pp. 53–63, "Engendering the State: Family Formation and State Building in Early Modern France," *French Historical Studies* 16 (1989): 4–27, and "Engendering the State: The Family Model of Authority Propagated in Early Modern France" (paper delivered at the Shelby Cullom Davis Center, Princeton University, Princeton, NJ, November 1989); as well as Susan Amussen, "Gender, Family, and the Social Order, 1560–1725," in *Order and Disorder in Early Modern England,* ed. Anthony Fletcher and John Stevenson (Cambridge, 1985), pp. 196–217, and *An Ordered Society: Gender and Class in Early Modern England* (Oxford, 1988).

forcing standards of morality defined by the clergy.[3] Commoners, nobles, clergy, and royalty frequently succumbed to temptation, and the magistrates routinely failed to apply the letter of the laws designed to preserve domestic and social order.[4] Reports about moral misdemeanors and sexual scandals fill many pages of the *Mémoires secrets* and the *Correspondance secrète,* the two most voluminous and informative compilations of news and gossip from Paris and Versailles collected and published in the last decades of the ancien régime.[5] The *Mémoires secrets* (covering the years 1762–87 and published in thirty-six volumes between 1777 and 1789 by the prolific *nouvellistes* Pidansat de Mairobert and Moufle d'Angerville) emanated from the Parisian salon of Madame Doublet, peopled by abbés, academicians, artists, poets, philosophes, physicians, and parlementaires. Louis-François Mettra, formerly employed as a Prussian commercial and diplomatic agent in Paris, produced the *Correspondance secrète* (covering the years 1774–85 and republished in eighteen volumes between 1787 and 1790) in the German principality of Neuwied.

More substantial than contemporary memoirs and less objective than modern newspapers, the *Mémoires secrets* and the *Correspondance secrète* collected news from many sources and published it selectively. They often fixated on sensationalistic stories, sometimes confused fact and fiction, and frequently editorialized by making comments about "public opinion."[6]

[3]On changing conceptions of the family, see, e.g., Cissie Fairchilds, *Domestic Enemies: Servants and Their Masters in Old Regime France* (Baltimore, 1984); and Randolph Trumbach, *The Rise of the Egalitarian Family: Aristocratic Kinship and Domestic Relations in Eighteenth-Century England* (New York, 1978).

[4]See my "Patterns and Prosecution of Suicide in Eighteenth-Century Paris," *Historical Reflections/Réflexions historiques* 16 (1989): 1–53, and "The Religious *Police* of the Ancien Regime and the Secularization of Jurisprudence in Eighteenth-Century France," in *Proceedings of the Nineteenth Annual Consortium on Revolutionary Europe, 1750–1850,* ed. Louise Parker (in press).

[5]On the *Mémoires secrets,* see Robert Tate, *Petit de Bachaumont: His Circle and the "Mémoires secrets," Studies on Voltaire and the Eighteenth Century,* vol. 65 (1968); and Louis Olivier, "Bachaumont the Chronicler: A Doubtful Renown," *Studies on Voltaire and the Eighteenth Century* 143 (1975): 161–79. On the *Correspondance secrète,* see Johann Johansson, *Sur la Correspondance littéraire secrète et son éditeur* (Göteborg, 1960); Martin Fontius, "Mettra und seine Korrespondenzen," *Romanische Forschungen* 76 (1974): 405–21; and Cécile Douxchamps-Lefèvre, "Un magasin de la cour de France au début du règne de Louis XVI," *Revue historique* 549 (1984): 95–108. Jean Sgard, ed., *Dictionnaire des journalistes, 1600–1789* (Grenoble, 1976), contains articles on Bachaumont, Pidansat de Mairobert, Moufle d'Angerville, and Mettra. The *nouvelles* reveal more about these editors than they do about their Parisian, provincial, and foreign readers, who have not yet been systematically investigated and identified. The printed editions presumably reached a wider public than the manuscript versions, but the cost of the *nouvelles* obviously restricted their audience.

[6]On the problem of "public opinion," see Keith Baker, "Politics and Public Opinion under the Old Regime: Some Reflections," in *Press and Politics in Pre-Revolutionary France,* ed. Jack Censer and Jeremy Popkin (Berkeley and Los Angeles, 1987), pp. 204–46; and Mona Ozouf,

Unlike periodicals licensed by the crown, these *nouvelles* generally escaped royal censorship. They informed provincial and foreign subscribers not only about the latest news in the world of arts and letters but also about political developments and causes célèbres in the capital and at court. They described spectacles intended to glorify the monarchy, but they also condemned ministerial despotism and endorsed the constitutional claims of the parlements. They documented the vogue of sentimental paintings and melodramas on domestic subjects, but they also reported many violations of gender codes, sexual norms, and domestic concord.[7] Commonly cited piecemeal and rarely studied systematically by historians, the *Mémoires secrets* and the *Correspondance secrète* are not only more impressionistic but also more discursive and more accessible than criminal records. They do not contain quantifiable series of cases, but they do contain a running commentary on sexual politics and public order in the form of reports about homosexuality, unmanly men and unwomanly women, unruly and unchaste wives, marital separations, and misconduct involving members of the royal family, first Louis XV and his mistresses, then Louis XVI and Marie Antoinette. More often than not, the *nouvelles* commented negatively on behavior that contradicted conventions about gender, sex, and family embodying fundamental relations of subordination and authority in the household and the kingdom. Like the slanderous *libelles* that proliferated in the last decades of the ancien régime, they invested what might look like private affairs with public significance and underscored the association of sexual and political disorder in contemporary perceptions of the breakdown of customary social and political structures.[8]

The *Mémoires secrets,* lacking the vocabulary developed in the nineteenth century to describe male and female homosexuality, recognized that "pederasty" and "tribadism" had always been popular among men and women, respectively, but reported in 1784 that "pederasts" and "tribades" had never before paraded their "vices" so scandalously (*MS* 27:116).[9] Previously

---

"L'opinion publique," in *The Political Culture of the Old Regime,* ed. Keith Baker (Oxford, 1987), pp. 419–34.

[7]On familial imagery in contemporary art and literature, see Carol Duncan, "Happy Mothers and Other New Ideas in French Art," *Art Bulletin* 55 (1973): 570–83, and "Fallen Fathers: Images of Authority in Pre-Revolutionary French Art," *Art History* 4 (1981): 186–202; and D. G. Charlton, *New Images of the Natural in France: A Study in European Cultural History, 1750–1800* (Cambridge, 1984).

[8]On the production and political content of *nouvelles, libelles,* and clandestine publications more generally, see Robert Darnton, *The Literary Underground of the Old Regime* (Cambridge, MA, 1982); as well as Jeremy Popkin, "The Prerevolutionary Origins of Political Journalism," in Baker, ed., pp. 203–24, "Pamphlet Journalism at the End of the Old Regime," *Eighteenth-Century Studies* 22 (1989): 351–67, and *News and Politics in the Age of Revolution: Jean Luzac's Gazette de Leyde* (Ithaca, NY, 1989).

[9]The *nouvelles* also referred to "pederasts" as "berdaches," "nonconformists," or "sodomites" and attributed "antiphysical" or "ultramontane" inclinations to them. On these terms,

associated with aristocrats and wits, "pederasty" had allegedly become so fashionable that it now "infected" the entire social hierarchy, from dukes to the common people (*MS* 22:241). Both *nouvelles* regaled their readers with anecdotes about the notorious marquis Charles de Villette and described the gruesome crime and punishment of the defrocked monk Jacques-François Pascal. Villette, derided in satirical verses for attacking the English during the war for American independence with nothing more than epigrams and for "instinctively" turning his back to the enemy,[10] exemplified the relatively new conception of male homosexuals as sexually passive and effeminate individuals. Pascal, who repeatedly stabbed a boy who resisted his advances, exemplified the much less common (in these sources) but much more menacing conception of sexually aggressive and predatory "monsters" (*CS* 15:167). Given the violence involved in this unrepresentative case, the authorities made an example of Pascal by executing him in the Place de Grève on October 10, 1783. In general, however, the police and the magistrates deliberately avoided public punishments that had the effect of "making the sin against nature more common by making it known" (*MS* 22:241). They usually confined themselves to exiling, imprisoning, or merely chastising "pederasts," depending on their social status and the circumstances of their offenses. The *nouvelles* did not condone but also did not condemn "pederasty" as such, as least not in traditional religious terms. They denounced the exceptional Pascal as vociferously as they did because he attempted not only to seduce but also to murder his victim. They made fun of the more typical Villette and other unmanly "pederasts" because they violated conventional assumptions about masculinity and femininity.

When the *nouvelles* named names, they identified "pederasts" from a variety of backgrounds but consistently located "tribades" in the theatrical milieux frequently associated with prostitution and pornography. Year after year they chronicled the professional tribulations and amorous escapades of the noted actress Françoise-Marie-Antoinette-Joseph Saucerotte, better known as Mademoiselle de Raucourt, who "declaims like she loves,

---

see Claude Courouve, *Vocabulaire de l'homosexualité masculine* (Paris, 1985). On male homosexuality, see Claude Courouve, *Les assemblées de la manchette: Documents sur l'amour masculin au XVIIIe siècle* (Paris, 1987); D. A. Coward, "Attitudes toward Homosexuality in Eighteenth-Century France," *Journal of European Studies* 10 (1980): 231–55; Maurice Lever, *Les Bûchers de Sodome* (Paris, 1985); Michel Rey, "Parisian Homosexuals Create a Lifestyle, 1700–1750: The Police Archives," in *'Tis Nature's Fault: Unauthorized Sexual Behavior during the Enlightenment,* ed. Robert Maccubbin (Cambridge, 1987), pp. 179–91, and "Police and Sodomy in Eighteenth-Century Paris: From Sin to Disorder," in *The Pursuit of Sodomy: Male Homosexuality in Renaissance and Enlightenment Europe,* ed. Kent Gerard and Gert Hekma (New York, 1989), pp. 129–46. On female homosexuality, see Marie-Jo Bonnet, *Un choix san équivoque: Recherches historiques sur les relations amoureuses entre les femmes, XVIe–XXe siècles* (Paris, 1981).

[10] *Correspondance secrète, politique et littéraire,* 18 vols. (London, 1787–90), 8:180. Hereafter abbreviated *CS* and cited in the text.

and it's always in the wrong way" (CS 8:364). Raucourt, who enjoyed the protection of Marie-Antoinette, allegedly dressed like a man when sexually involved with women and like a woman when sexually involved with men (CS 8:327). She reportedly "married" the singer Sophie Arnould (CS 1:209) and supposedly slept with men, when short of cash, only in order to get all the money she could out of them (CS 3:302). When the prince de Montbarrey discovered Madame Desmahis, whom he had lavished with gifts, in Raucourt's arms, he admitted, according to the *Mémoires secrets,* that he was not capable of bringing about her "conversion" and left the two women to their "shameful embraces" (MS 34:18). The *Correspondance se-crète,* however, insisted that the unconventional females it referred to at least once as "lesbians" could not stifle the "natural inclination" of women for men. The *nouvelles* suggested that "tribades" were more commonly bisexual by inclination and also more commonly motivated by mercenary considerations than "pederasts." While "pederasts" disobeyed traditional gender codes, "tribades" defied the traditional double standard that tacitly allowed men, but not women, to seek sexual pleasure outside marriage. They also betrayed their "natural" destiny as wives and mothers. The *Correspondance secrète* noted that the laws did not criminalize "tribadism" as such, inasmuch as they did not recognize that women could have sex without men, but it nonetheless condemned this "vice" as "fatal to society, which it divides, and to propagation, which it destroys" (CS 14:397). "Un-natural" relationships between women, in the last analysis, disrupted the patriarchal and familial order of French society by diverting or extricating women from marriage, which institutionalized their "natural" subordina-tion to men and their "natural" procreative functions.

The *nouvelles* ridiculed unconventional celebrities like the chevalier d'Eon and Madame de Genlis, as well as passive "pederasts" and independent "tribades," for flouting the more inflexible differentiation of gendered roles discernible in the eighteenth century. After d'Eon, soldier, diplomat, and man of letters, identified himself as a woman, the crown ordered him to put away his military uniform and put on female attire.[11] The *Correspon-dance secrète* commended this convert to the "fragile sex" for his "manly strength of body and mind" (CS 7:384) but snickered at him for begging Louis XVI to allow him to rejoin the army after the 1778 alliance with the rebellious American colonies. It assumed that the effeminate Villette, on the one hand, was not capable of fighting the British like a man and that the "female" d'Eon, on the other, had no business going off to battle like a man. Marie-Antoinette reportedly refused to support his suit because she did much not care for what she called "women-men" (CS 8:187). D'Eon lost

[11]On d'Eon, see Gary Kates, "D'Eon's Books: The Library of an Eighteenth-Century Transsexual," *Primary Sources* (in press), and other forthcoming work by Kates.

his masculine prerogatives when he surrendered his male identity; Madame de Genlis usurped masculine prerogatives when the duc de Chartres (the future Philippe-Egalité) named her, instead of some suitable male, to the position of tutor to his sons in 1782. The *nouvelles* characterized Genlis, known both as her patron's sometime mistress and the author of prudish books, as a "hermaphrodite."[12] With her "feminine" body and "masculine" mind, she played the role of "mister in the schoolroom" and "madam in the boudoir" (*CS* 12:332; *MS* 20:77). When he heard the news about the unprecedented nomination, Louis XVI, who had a son and nephews of his own to inherit the throne, allegedly dismissed the next duc d'Orléans with the disapproving remark that he could do whatever he wanted with his sons (*MS* 20:27). The Parisian public, accustomed to booing the notorious Raucourt on stage, responded more aggressively than the king by hooting and hissing Genlis during a performance of Molière's play *Les Femmes savantes,* which seemed to condemn her unwomanly pretensions (*MS* 20:188).

Perpetuating traditional stereotypes about female sexuality and feminine shortcomings, the *nouvelles* portrayed women in general as silly, fickle, unruly, lustful, treacherous creatures likely to disrupt households and society as a whole.[13] The *Mémoires secrets,* to be sure, applauded the women who took an uncharacteristic interest in public affairs and excluded supporters of chancellor Maupeou's despotic suppression of the parlements from their society (*MS* 19:269). But the *Correspondance secrète* scoffed, more typically, that women hardly knew what extravagant fashions to settle their "little notions" on (*CS* 2:342) and lamented that they still believed in astrological nonsense because of "the weakness of their constitutions and the flightiness of their minds" (*CS* 4:234). Their proverbial volatility made them "more dangerous than men" in the bread riots of 1775 (*CS* 1:341), and their carnal passions made them equally unmanageable at home. The comtesse d'Harcourt, the model of conjugal fidelity, installed a wax effigy of her deceased husband in a dressing gown in an armchair next to her bed

---

[12]The *nouvelles* made disparaging comments about the literary activities of other female authors as well. The *Mémoires secrets* criticized Madame Elie de Beaumont for writing about "matters that a woman shouldn't touch" (*MS* 2:75). The *Correspondance secrète* suggested that the poet Claude-Joseph Dorat had written the plays attributed to the comtesse de Beauharnais, his sometime mistress, and warned that the theater, like the crown, should not fall to the distaff side (*CS* 2:153).

[13]On the stereotype of disorderly women, see Pierre Darmon, *Mythologies de la femme dans l'ancienne France, XVIe–XVIIIe siècles* (Paris, 1983); Natalie Davis, "Women on Top," in her *Society and Culture in Early Modern France* (Stanford, CA, 1975), pp. 124–51; Joan Landes, *Women and the Public Sphere in the Age of the French Revolution* (Ithaca, NY, 1988); Ian Maclean, *The Renaissance Notion of Woman: A Study of the Fortunes of Scholasticism and Medical Science in European Intellectual Life* (Cambridge, 1980); Pierre Ronzeaud, "La femme au pouvoir ou le monde à l'envers," *Dix-septième siècle* 108 (1975): 9–33.

(*CS* 9:108), but most wives supposedly had no qualms about disobeying and cuckolding their spouses while they were still very much alive. Some women reportedly enjoyed "the act of Venus" so much that they frequented the infamous bawd Madame Gourdan in order to satisfy their sexual appetites with strangers (*CS* 2:169).

The *nouvelles,* of course, criticized members of both sexes for debauchery and recognized that predatory males sometimes victimized innocent females, but they blamed women, more often than not, for extramarital escapades. They rarely pitied unhappy wives incarcerated in convents by their husbands with royal lettres de cachets, but they repeatedly denounced unfaithful wives who managed to outfox their spouses.[14] The comte de B—— apprehended his wife flagrante delicto with another man and charged her with adultery, but she succeeded in getting him locked up by claiming he was insane (*CS* 9:312). The marquis de Saint-Hurugue suffered the same fate after his dissolute wife, a former actress, accused him of murder and infanticide. He spent several years in the asylum at Charenton while she squandered his fortune (*MS* 35:288). Traditional characterizations of women did not credit them with enough cleverness to dispose of their husbands in this way but did suggest that they were naturally capricious, unsubmissive, libidinous, and untrustworthy. Confused on this score, like so many other eighteenth-century sources, the *nouvelles* chastised women for following what conventional wisdom described as their natural inclinations and at the same time expected them to conform to the domesticated and desexed conception of women's nature articulated most memorably by Rousseau.[15]

In the time of the Gauls, sighed the *Correspondance secrète,* husbands had had the power of life and death over their wives. In the eighteenth century,

[14]On the use of lettres de cachets against wayward spouses, see the cases documented in Arlette Farge and Michel Foucault, eds., *Le désordre des familles: Lettres de cachet des archives de la Bastille* (Paris, 1982). Both *nouvelles* discussed the baron de Breteuil's 1784 instructions to intendants restricting the use of these royal orders (*CS* 17:140; *MS* 27:117–27).

[15]On the muddled question of women's nature, see my "Royal Bees: The Gender Politics of the Beehive in Early Modern Europe," *Studies in Eighteenth-Century Culture* 18 (1988): 7–37; as well as Maurice Bloch and Jean Bloch, "Women and the Dialectics of Nature in Eighteenth-Century French Thought," and L. J. Jordanova, "Natural Facts: A Historical Perspective on Science and Society," both in *Nature, Culture, and Gender,* ed. Carol MacCormack and Marilyn Strathern (Cambridge, 1980), pp. 25–41 and 42–69, respectively; Paul Hoffmann, *La femme dans la pensée des lumières* (Paris, 1977); Samia Spencer, ed., *French Women and the Age of Enlightenment* (Bloomington, IN, 1984). For giving me much food for thought on this score, I am indebted to the authors of the three papers I commented on at the annual meeting of the American Historical Association in San Francisco in December 1989: Jennifer Jones, "Le luxe des vêtements: Women and the Debate on Luxury in the Ancien Regime"; Elizabeth Colwill, "Salonnière to Ménagère: The Transformation of Women's Empire in Revolutionary France"; Judith DeGroat, "The Redefinition of Women's Work in Post-Revolutionary France."

the same source lamented, husbands hardly had the right to complain about their wives, let alone punish them for their misbehavior (*CS* 9:329). Women, on the one hand, "abused their empire" by regarding customary male deference "as a prerogative of their sex" and treating men like "slaves" (*CS* 16:112). On the other hand, they did not hesitate to denounce their spouses as "despots" (*CS* 18:80) in order to convince the magistrates to grant them marital separations. Ecclesiastical and secular law, of course, did not allow for outright divorce but did authorize judicial separation on specific grounds, including serious mistreatment. Both *nouvelles* were astonished and appalled by the apparent proliferation of separation cases in the 1770s and 1780s.[16] In 1775 the *Correspondance secrète* reported that the Parlement of Paris intended to handle such cases strictly, so as not to encourage "the sex already too prone to changes" to cast "all marriages" into "extreme disorder" (*CS* 2:167). By 1780 the same source complained that the parlementaires, moved by misguided "pity for the weak and seductive sex," granted separations on "the most frivolous pretexts" and thereby emboldened more women "to trouble the peace of families" (*CS* 9:427).

When the magistrates ruled against Madame de Champbonas, who had complained of mistreatment by her husband and decided to plead her own case because of her physical charms (*CS* 1:265), "the public" allegedly applauded (*CS* 2:167). "The young women of Paris," however, "were quite shocked" (*MS* 31:346). They supposedly flocked to the Palais de Justice when lawyers argued separation cases in order "to learn the means they must employ" (*MS* 29:150) to get rid of their spouses when they had their own days in court. In reporting dozens of these cases, the *Mémoires secrets* and the *Correspondance secrète* suggested that (naturally or unnaturally) unruly and unchaste women subverted the principles of order common to household and society by betraying their husbands, breaking up their marriages, and claiming "unnatural" independence for themselves. By invoking the language of "slavery" and "despotism," key words in contemporary political polemics, the *nouvelles* underscored the political implications of marital contestations, dramatically played out in the well-publicized Kornmann affair in the 1780s.[17] This tangled affair combined

[16]See *CS* 1:265, 2:167, 9:426–27, 18:80; *MS* 8:326, 29:149, 31:320. On separations, see Alain Lottin et al., *La désunion du couple sous l'ancien régime: L'exemple du Nord* (Lille, 1975); and Roderick Phillips, *Family Breakdown in Late Eighteenth-Century France: Divorces in Rouen, 1792–1803* (Oxford, 1980); as well as the cases documented in Isabelle Vissière, ed., *Procès de femmes au temps des philosophes ou la violence masculine au XVIIIᵉ siècle* (Paris, 1983).

[17]On the political implications of eighteenth-century causes célèbres, see Sarah Maza, "Domestic Melodrama as Political Ideology: The Case of the Comte de Sanois," *American Historical Review* 94 (1989): 1249–64, as well as her "Le tribunal de la nation: Les mémoires judiciaires et l'opinion publique à la fin de l'ancien régime," *Annales* 42 (1987): 73–90, and "The Rose Girl of Salency: Representations of Virtue in Pre-Revolutionary France," *Eighteenth-Century Studies* 2 (1989): 395–412.

charges of adultery against the wife, who had demanded separation from her husband, with charges of abuse of authority against the police, who had sequestered her from him and allegedly conspired with the enemies who had tried to ruin him financially.

The *nouvelles* had already associated debauchery with despotism during the reign of Louis XV.[18] His profligacy gave new meaning to the words "living royally," which became synonymous, according to the *Mémoires secrets*, with "being a whoremonger" (*MS* 19:275). Once the king installed the notorious Madame du Barry at court, "the most respectable women" reportedly had no more scruples about frequenting "the most resolute whores" (*CS* 1:20). Courtiers, meanwhile, imitated their sovereign's example by preying on innocent females. When the duc de ——— set a poor couple's house on fire in order to ravish their daughter, Louis XV, far from reprimanding him, simply advised him to be "a bit more moderate" in the future (*CS* 1:50). French law, on paper, prescribed punishments for sexual assault, but French society, in practice, allowed not only the king but also noblemen and untitled men as well to take advantage of women, especially women of the lower classes, with impunity. The *nouvelles* probably expected Louis XV to play the field, sexually speaking, just like his Bourbon ancestors, but he paraded his virility less publicly than Henry IV and Louis XIV. Confined to the private apartments and Parc aux cerfs at Versailles, his sexual excesses seemed squalid and dangerous because they seemed to subject him to domination by women. In reporting gossip about licentiousness at court, the *Mémoires secrets* and the *Correspondance secrète* did not question what they regarded as the legitimate sexual and political power of men over women. On the contrary, they decried the sexual and political power of women over men, which betokened disorder in the household and the kingdom.

The Louis XV described in these sources made a mockery of the familial ethos of French kingship by setting a bad example for his subjects and ruling them like a despot rather than a father.[19] The *nouvelles* assigned much of the blame to his meddlesome mistresses: Madame de Pompadour, "who reigned so despotically over the mind of the king" (*CS* 1:25), and Madame

[18]On Louis XV, see Michel Antoine, "Les batârds de Louis XV," reprinted in his *Le dur métier du roi: Etudes sur la civilisation politique de la France d'ancien régime* (Paris, 1986), pp. 293–313, and *Louis XV* (Paris, 1989); as well as Jean-Pierre Guicciardi, "Between the Licit and the Illicit: The Sexuality of the King," in Maccubbin, ed. (n. 9 above), pp. 88–97; and Jean de Viguerie, "Le roi et le public: L'exemple de Louis XV," *Revue historique* 563 (1987): 23–35.

[19]On popular disaffection, expressed in posters, verses, and *mauvais discours*, see Arlette Farge and Jacques Revel, *Logiques de la foule: L'affaire des enlèvements d'enfants, Paris, 1750* (Paris, 1988), pp. 126–36; Pierre Rétat et al., *L'attenat de Damiens: Discours sur l'événement au XVIIIᵉ siècle* (Lyon, 1979), pp. 167–96; Dale Van Kley, *The Damiens Affair and the Unraveling of the Ancien Regime, 1750–1770* (Princeton, NJ, 1984), pp. 226–65.

du Barry, who allegedly acquired the Van Dyck portrait of Charles I now in the Louvre in order to encourage the king to bully the unsubmissive parlementaires who challenged royal authority (*CS* 1:402–3; *MS* 6:15–16).[20] Dominated by his mistresses and misled by his ministers, he degraded the *lit de justice* (literally "bed of justice"), the ceremony in which the crown imposed its will on the magistrates, by forcing them to register declarations that they regarded as contrary to the welfare of the realm. The verses about the king's misuse of this ritual of absolutism recorded in the *Correspondance secrète* graphically underscored the linkage of sexual and political disorder in contemporary reprobation of Louis XV:

> Do you know what they say in Paris?
> Lady Justice is disconsolate.
> The king sat down on her bed.
> They say he raped her.
>
> [*CS* 1:69][21]

Given their support for the parlementaires, the *nouvelles* privileged the theme of royal profligacy not simply for the sake of titillation but because it provided them with a vehicle for criticizing abuses of royal authority.

After Louis XV died of smallpox, supposedly contracted from one of the many young females rounded up and "cleaned up" for his pleasure (*CS* 1:48), the *nouvelles* reported that Paris was flooded with scurrilous wisecracks about Louis "the Beloved." According to one disrespectful story, the late king, or rather his departed soul, encountered Saint Denis (martyred by decapitation) and then Mary Magdalen. He asked them both how to get to paradise, and they both pointed him in the wrong direction. When he finally reached paradise and explained why it had taken him so long to get there, Saint Peter scoffed that he had always made the mistake of taking advice from "men with no brains and whores" (*CS* 1:41). When Louis XVI ascended the throne in 1774, he distanced himself from his deceased grandfather by dismissing the unpopular Maupeou (the headless Saint Denis), exiling the hated du Barry (the wanton Magdalen), and having himself inoculated for smallpox. He restored the rule of law by recalling the parlements suppressed by Maupeou and restored morality by defending gender distinctions, sexual regularity, and domestic order at court and throughout his realm. If Louis XV, identified with sexual promiscuity and

---

[20]On the mistresses, see the summary discussion in Susan Conner, "Women and Politics," in Spencer, ed., pp. 49–63.

[21]The rhyming version, with the original punctuation:
> Sais-tu ce qu'on dit à Paris!
> Dame Justice est désolée,
> Le roi sur son lit s'est assis;
> On prétend qu'il l'a violée.

royal despotism, embodied patriarchalism in the old style, Louis XVI, identified with sexual monogamy and royal justice, embodied paternalism in the new style.[22]

The young king exiled several noblemen apprehended in compromising positions with members of their own sex (*MS* 27:57), squelched the chevalier d'Eon's attempt to rejoin the army, snubbed the duc de Chartres for entrusting his sons to Madame de Genlis, and condemned marital infidelity as well as prostitution. He encouraged women to breastfeed their children (*CS* 1:134) and discouraged them from breaking out of their "natural" roles in the family, defined by their subordination to men and their reproductive functions. He granted no more *brevets de dames* authorizing unmarried daughters to abandon their parents and join the court (*MS* 21:121), and he no longer permitted women to escape their domestic obligations by enrolling in the company of opera singers and dancers without the consent of "their natural superiors," that is, their fathers or husbands (*CS* 1:200).[23] When Louis XVI was crowned in 1775, one Parisian woman, according to the *Correspondance secrète*, left for Reims to witness the festivities without her husband's permission. When she suggested in her own defense that he would be "a very bad Frenchman and a subject unworthy of the ruler God has given us" if he lost his temper, he rebuked her for her impertinence. Their king, he reminded her, had no intention of allowing wives to disobey their husbands, especially if they ran off, as she had done, with their husbands' money in their pockets and in the company of other men (*CS* 1:423). Louis XVI signed a lettre de cachet for the detention of the princesse de Monaco, involved in an adulterous affair with the prince de Condé, because he wanted to preserve order in the household and promote "the conservation of morals." "A woman not living with her husband," he declared, "could not remain in society" (*MS* 27:309). Given these gestures and sentiments, "the few people who love morality and virtue" began to hope that "the king's example" would influence his subjects (*CS* 2:235) and save the kingdom from the corruption countenanced by his predecessor.[24]

Louis XVI sounded like the complete "family man," except for the fact

[22]On Louis XVI, see François Furet, "Louis XVI," in *Dictionnaire critique de la Révolution française*, ed. François Furet and Mona Ozouf (Paris, 1988), pp. 268–77; and Evelyne Lever, *Louis XVI* (Paris, 1985).

[23]The police were instructed to return women who joined the company without the necessary permission "to the power of those to whom they are subordinate" (*MS* 7:258).

[24]For other reports of enthusiasm about the young king, see "Chronique secrète de Paris sous le règne de Louis XVI (1774)," *Revue retrospective* 3 (1934): 29–96, 262–96, 375–415; and "Lettres de M R—— à M M—— concernant ce qui s'est passé d'intéressant à la cour depuis la maladie et la mort de Louis XV jusqu'au rétablissement du parlement de Paris," in *Mélanges publiés par la Société des bibliophiles français*, 6 vols. (Paris, 1820–29), vol. 5, separately paginated.

that he apparently failed to consummate his own marriage for a number of years. The *nouvelles,* having recorded complaints about Louis XV's turpitude and exaggerated the number of his illegitimate offspring, recorded gossip about his grandson's impotence and wondered about his ability to produce an heir to the throne. Saluting the future Louis XVI and his wife in 1773, three years after their marriage, the Parisian *poissardes* stretched out their "long, thick, plump, stiff forearms" and wished him "one like this." "It's not too much for such a pretty wife," they added (*MS* 7:11). As the market women waited and waited to celebrate births in the royal family, the king's sexual capabilities became a subject of speculation and satire.[25] When he restored the power of the disgraced (and allegedly impotent) Maurepas, the sympathetic minister allegedly wished he could do the same for his sovereign (*CS* 1:4). Distressed by rumors that Louis XVI had to have an operation to make him "more fit for progeniture" (*MS* 33:350), a concerned abbé threw himself on his knees before the king in order to communicate to him "a secret for perpetuating his august race" (*MS* 9:336). When Marie-Antoinette finally gave birth to a daughter in 1778, her grateful husband provided dowries for a hundred Parisian girls and promised further subsidies to support their first children. Within months he let it be known that he was doing his best to produce a son, and this news reportedly delighted "the public" (*MS* 3:323). The birth of the long-awaited Dauphin in 1781 filled "all French souls" (*CS* 12:113) with "patriotic ecstasy" (*MS* 18:119). The *poissardes* rejoiced by congratulating their sovereign on the virility of his newborn son, which promised the perpetuation of the Bourbon dynasty. The earthy verses in which they claimed to have seen the child's "little thing" erect supposedly embarrassed some women at court,[26] but the king applauded them appreciatively (*CS* 12:138). He fulfilled his reproductive obligation to his ancestors and his people, but the rumors about his impotence lingered.

[25]On the market women, see Elizabeth Colwill, "Rites of Subjection and Bonds of Sex: Women's Public Behavior in France, 1770–1789," forthcoming in the proceedings of the French Revolution bicentennial meeting of the Consortium on Revolutionary Europe in Tallahassee, FL, in October 1989.

[26]The colloquial verses as printed in the *Correspondance secrète:*

> Notre charmante Antoinette
> Vient de faire un petit bout,
> Et j'avons vu la broquette
> De nôt' Dauphin à tretous;
> Elle levait
> Elle dressait,
> Oh, ce fera un compère;
> Elle levait
> Elle dressait,
> C'a vous promet un maître clou.

Louis XVI, who showed "all the sensibility of the best of fathers" (*MS* 18:96), tried to make his own family a model of domestic felicity and devoted himself to the happiness of his subjects, whom he regarded as an extended family (*MS* 18:117).[27] Good father to his children (*CS* 1:39; *MS* 30:167), both biological and figurative, he gave the Dauphin farming lessons to prepare him for the responsibility of looking after the people's daily bread (*MS* 29:36). Good brother to his siblings, he told the comte d'Artois and the comte de Provence to continue to call him by his first name (*CS* 1:40) and invited them and their wives to share his dinner table at Versailles (*CS* 1:102). Good husband to his wife, he strolled the gardens with her arm-in-arm without "asiatic pomp" (*MS* 27:264) and remodeled the private quarters in the palace so as to make it possible for him to make his way to her bedroom without letting "the public" know what he was doing (*MS* 8:143). In his personal life Louis XVI embraced conjugal companionship and domestic privacy and at the same time renounced husbandly authoritarianism and the double standard. Supposedly separated from the queen only when he went hunting or attended meetings of the royal council (*CS* 1:106), he had no inclination and little opportunity for extramarital adventures. When he happened to dine without Marie-Antoinette one night in 1779 and took notice of a young woman among the onlookers, some courtiers, according to the *Mémoires secrets,* tried to kindle illicit passions in his heart. "Good patriots," remembering the bad old days of Louis XV and his mistresses, were "very distressed" by these wayward glances (*MS* 4:289), but this king, as the *Correspondance secrète* exulted, took no mistress other than Truth (*CS* 1:109).

Hailed as the reincarnation of the beloved Henry IV during the early years of his reign,[28] Louis XVI ended up vilified like his grandfather. Louis XV could not control his libido, and his grandson, it turned out, could not control his wife. Louis XVI chided Marie-Antoinette for gambling, taking part in plays at court, wearing too much makeup and jewelry, popularizing extravagant coiffures, and spending too much money, but the *nouvelles* suggested that he lacked the "masculine" strength of character necessary to bridle her "feminine" frivolity and resist her "feminine" importunities. The *Mémoires secrets* commented on the king's unusual "sensibility" as early as

[27]On the polemical uses of paternalistic rhetoric, see my "Patriarchalism and Constitutionalism in Eighteenth-Century Parlementary Discourse," *Studies in Eighteenth-Century Culture* 20 (1990), in press.

[28]As Madame de Pompadour pointed out to Louis XV in a fictitious dialogue printed in the *Correspondance secrète,* Henry IV, too, "loved women excessively," but he always remained "the father of his people" (*CS* 1:121). On Henriolatry, see George Armstrong Kelly, *Mortal Politics in Eighteenth-Century France* (Waterloo, ON, 1986); Jean Meyer, "Mythes monarchiques: Le cas Henri IV aux XVIIᶜ et XVIIIᶜ siècles," in *La monarchie absolutiste et l'histoire de France* (Paris, 1987), pp. 169–96; Marcel Reinhard, *La légende de Henry IV* (Saint Brieuc, 1935).

1774, when he reportedly developed a fever after having seen a workman fall and fracture his skull (*MS* 29:324). When Turgot's deregulation of the grain trade provoked rioting around Paris in 1775, Louis XVI gave in to "the first impulse of his heart" and lowered the price of bread, but he subsequently yielded to the comptroller general's objections (*MS* 30:244). The king's "sensibility" ennobled him by making him benevolent but also weakened him by making him impressionable, impulsive, ineffectual. When Marie-Antoinette complained in 1786 that she did not get to see the deer because a peasant riding a donkey had blocked her way during the hunt, her devoted husband angrily ordered the arrest of the disrespectful peasant, but he later regretted his hasty command and had the man released (*MS* 33:187). By 1787 the *Mémoires secrets* noted that Louis XVI, overwhelmed by the problems facing the monarchy, often broke down and cried (*MS* 35:428). Despite his admirable intentions, his "unmanly" weakness of character allegedly made him incapable of discharging his royal responsibilities and left him vulnerable to manipulation by his treacherous wife.

Marie-Antoinette, of course, was included in the adulation that surrounded Louis XVI at the time of his accession to the throne. She reportedly did her best to second his efforts to restore moral order in the royal household, at court, and throughout the kingdom. She refused to allow the adulterous princesse de Monaco to be presented to her, for example, on the grounds that she did not see "women separated from their husbands" (*CS* 1:9). She also refused to allow plays starring the dissolute actress Mademoiselle Hus to be staged at Fontainebleau, in order "to cooperate with her august husband in the preservation of decency and morality" (*MS* 32:355). As for herself, like a good wife and good queen, Marie-Antoinette supposedly wanted nothing more than to present her husband and his subjects with a son. In 1775 she shed "tears of regret" because she was not pregnant like her sister-in-law, the comtesse d'Artois (*MS* 8:178).[29] Because she felt the first "sign of maternity" in 1778 upon hearing the news of a French naval victory, she felt sure she was carrying a son (*CS* 6:378), presumably destined for martial exploits. When she gave birth later that year, she was allegedly "so struck by being only the mother of a princess" that the doctors feared she might suffocate (*CS* 7:195). Her own devaluation of royal daughters underscored her sexual and political role as the vehicle for the perpetuation of the male line. During her second childbirth in 1781, she again feared, this time mistakenly, that she had "only produced a daughter" (*MS* 18:95).

When Marie-Antoinette attended the services in Notre Dame cathedral to give thanks for the birth of her second son in 1785, she wondered why

[29]See the revealing passages on the reproductive and political rivalries between Louis XVI and Marie-Antoinette, on the one hand, and the comte and comtesse d'Artois, on the other, in *MS* 8:149 and 35:413.

the Parisian populace greeted her with so little enthusiasm. The *nouvelles* attributed her unpopularity to the proliferation of "licentious songs" and "clandestine and calumnious writings" that taught the people "to respect less that which previously had been the object of their veneration and their love" (*CS* 18:154).[30] As far back as 1774 the *Correspondance secrète* commented on the circulation of anonymous writings that criticized Marie-Antoinette for walking alone in the gardens at Versailles and for "running here and there to indulge in the dissipation so suitable to her age" (*CS* 1:74). In 1776 the *Mémoires secrets* condemned some "execrable verses" that questioned the king's virility and "criminally" misrepresented the queen's friendship for the princesse de Lamballe (*MS* 9:54). Hostile gossip about Marie-Antoinette originated in court circles, but published attacks on her character reached a much wider public. The *nouvelles* did not discuss this slanderous literature title by title, but they did document changes in "public opinion" about the queen and mention most of the standard accusations against her during the years preceding the Revolution. She supposedly squandered the revenues of the crown and cared nothing for the French people, who had welcomed her to their country with open arms. Unnaturalized and also "unnatural," she was a disobedient daughter, irresponsible mother, and unfaithful wife. Given the king's impotence, she allegedly satisfied her voracious sexual appetites with lackies, ladies-in-waiting, the cardinal de Rohan, and the comte d'Artois, often identified as the father of her children. She not only deceived her husband but also meddled in his business, the administration of the kingdom. Ministers, neglecting their responsibilities, kowtowed to her, and no one got anything at court "except through her" (*CS* 18:106).

Even if Louis XVI was not really impotent, he nonetheless looked impotent, in spite of his progeny and his paternalistic devotion to the welfare of his subjects, because of his troubling inability to manage his troublesome wife and his troubled realm. He set out to cleanse France of the immorality and injustice that besmirched the reign of his predecessor, but he, too, found himself entangled in domestic and public disorders. The *nouvelles*, having associated the debauched and despotic Louis XV with sexual and political excess, associated the inadequate and ineffectual Louis XVI with

---

[30]On the defamation of Marie-Antoinette, see Vivian Cameron, "Gender and Power: Images of Women in Late Eighteenth-Century France," *History of European Ideas* 10 (1989): 309–32; Elizabeth Colwill, "Just Another Citoyenne? Marie-Antoinette on Trial, 1790–1793," *History Workshop* 28 (1989): 63–87; Jacques Revel, "Marie-Antoinette," in Furet and Ozouf, eds. (n. 22 above), pp. 286–97; Chantal Thomas, "L'héroïne du crime: Marie-Antoinette dans les pamphlets," in *La Carmagnole des muses: L'homme de lettres et l'artiste dans la Révolution,* ed. Jean-Claude Bonnet (Paris, 1988), pp. 245–60, and *La reine scélérate: Marie-Antoinette dans les pamphlets* (Paris, 1989); as well as Lynn Hunt, "The Many Bodies of Marie-Antoinette: Political Pornography and the Problem of the Feminine in the French Revolution," in *Eroticism and the Body Politic,* ed. Lynn Hunt (Philadelphia, in press).

sexual and political weakness. The old king represented the abuses of patriarchalism, and the new king represented the failure of paternalism. Both kings, despite the obvious differences in their personal lives and their styles of kingship, had at least one thing in common: they were allegedly dominated, even emasculated, by women.[31] The grandfather was dominated by his homegrown mistresses, and the grandson was dominated by his Austrian wife, who seemed to combine many of the worst qualities of Madame de Pompadour and Madame du Barry—not to mention Mademoiselle de Raucourt, Madame de Genlis, and the shameless women who cuckolded or demanded marital separations from their husbands—with the insatiable libido of Louis XV himself.

The lustful, bisexual, pretentious, meddlesome, and unruly Marie-Antoinette caricatured in *nouvelles* and *libelles* reincarnated the familiar stereotype of the disorderly female. She subverted the principles of gender distinction, sexual regularity, and domestic propriety that Louis XVI hoped to exemplify in his own life and inculcate in his subjects. The hysterical vilification of the unfortunate queen makes somewhat more sense when considered not simply by itself but in the context of the perceived breakdown of social and political structures documented by the *Mémoires secrets* and the *Correspondence secrète*. These sources, unlike the contemporary *Journal des dames,* constantly confused the categories of sex and gender.[32] They endorsed pejorative characterizations of women and blamed them for many of the problems in the royal family, other families, and the familial kingdom as a whole. Well before the Jacobins undertook the task, the *nouvelles* suggested that the regeneration of France required that women be put back in their place in the home under male tutelage. As Joan Landes has suggested, this redomestication of the female sex, enshrined in revolutionary and Napoleonic legislation, played a determinative role in the modern differentiation of private and public spheres.[33] At the same time, it perpetuated the assumption, shared by the *nouvelles,* that private violations of socially defined and politically sanctioned conventions about gender, sex, and family deserved public reprobation because they threatened public order.

[31]See Maza, "Domestic Melodrama as Political Ideology" (n. 17 above), p. 1259; and Colwill, "Just Another Citoyenne?" p. 72.

[32]See Nina Gelbart, *Feminine and Opposition Journalism in Old Regime France: Le Journal des Dames* (Berkeley and Los Angeles, 1987).

[33]On the revolutionary fate of political patriarchalism, see Landes (n. 13 above); Darline Gay Levy, Harriet Branson Applewhite, and Mary Durham Johnson, eds., *Women in Revolutionary Paris, 1789–1795* (Urbana, IL, 1978); and Lynn Hunt, "The Political Psychology of Revolutionary Caricatures," in *French Caricature and the French Revolution, 1789–1799,* ed. James Cuno (Berkeley and Los Angeles, 1988), pp. 33–40, and "The Sacred and the French Revolution," in *Durkheimian Sociology: Cultural Studies,* ed. Jeffrey Alexander (Cambridge, 1988), pp. 25–45.

Tribades on Trial:
Female Same-Sex Offenders in
Late Eighteenth-Century Amsterdam

THEO VAN DER MEER

Faculty of Law
The Free University, Amsterdam

In 1792 the criminal court in Amsterdam exiled a woman named Bets Wiebes for six years from the city because she had lain upon another woman "in the way a man is used to do when he has carnal conversation with his wife."[1] It was the first such verdict in that city and probably in all of the Republic of the United Provinces. In contrast, sodomy trials were not uncommon, beginning in 1730 when a wave of persecutions of sodomites swept the country. Other series of sodomy trials occurred in 1764 in Amsterdam and in 1776 in the province of Holland. Three years after the first trial for "tribadism," yet another series of trials began that lasted until 1798, not only in Amsterdam but in several other cities as well.[2] During these three years, a number of women—called "tribades" by one judge in his private annotations[3]—were tried for engaging in "caresses and filthy

A shorter version of this article was presented as "Evil Malignities, Malign Evils: Tribades on Trial in Eighteenth-Century Amsterdam" at the Homosexuality, Which Homosexuality? Conference at the Free University in Amsterdam in December 1987. I owe many thanks to Sjoerd Faber, Joseph Geraci, Dorelies Kraakman, Randolph Trumbach, Martha Vicinus, Gary Waterspoon, and the editors of the *Journal of the History of Sexuality* for their comments on a first draft of this article. Thanks also to my colleague Wim Heersink for providing some of the material used here. Of course, the responsibility for any error, misunderstanding, or incongruity in the text is mine alone.

[1] Gemeente Archief Amsterdam (Municipal Archive, Amsterdam) Rechterlijk Archief (Judicial Archive) (hereafter GAA RA) Secreet Confessieboek 5061-538, p. 252.

[2] Theo van der Meer, *De wesentlijke sonde van sodomie en andere vuyligheeden* (Amsterdam, 1984), and "The Persecutions of Sodomites in Eighteenth-Century Amsterdam: Changing Perceptions of Sodomy," in *The Pursuit of Sodomy: Male Homosexuality in Renaissance and Enlightenment Europe,* ed. Kent Gerard and Gert Hekma (New York, 1989), pp. 263–310. See also Wayne R. Dynes, *Homosexuality: A Research Guide* (New York, 1987), pp. 127–31.

[3] GAA RA Crimineel Register 5061-640A.

This essay originally appeared in the *Journal of the History of Sexuality* 1991, vol. 1, no. 3.

things," "sodomitical filthiness," or "evil malignities," as the accusations were alternately called.

Prosecutions for same-sex offenses in the Netherlands throughout the eighteenth century involved somewhere between six hundred and eight hundred people.[4] Including the 1792 tribadism case, twelve women were prosecuted for these kinds of acts, which represented approximately 5 percent of the total number of people prosecuted for same-sex acts in Amsterdam between 1730 and 1811. In the latter year, the introduction of the French penal code in Holland abolished prosecution of same-sex acts. However, between 1795 and 1798, the number of women involved in such trials amounted to 28 percent of the cases (eleven of a total of thirty-nine).[5]

Before 1792, although there were no prosecutions for it, the phenomenon of women having sex with other women was not unknown in the Republic. In 1750 two Amsterdam women, aged fifty and sixty, were indicted by their former landlady, who accused them of "living as if they were man and wife . . . feeling and touching one another under their skirts and at their bosoms . . . yes, she had even seen how in broad daylight while committing several brutalities Mooije Marijtje lay down on Dirkje Vis, having both of them lifted their skirts and their front bodies being completely naked, Marijtje made movements as if she were a male person having to do with a female."[6] For reasons discussed later in this essay, these women were not prosecuted. Additionally, a number of cases are known from both the seventeenth and the eighteenth centuries in which women, dressed as men, enlisted in the army or the navy, or engaged in other male professions. In some of these cases the women married other women and had sexual relations with them.[7]

It was the trial of Hendrikje Verschuur in the first half of the seventeenth century that became something of a cause célèbre. Dressed in male attire, Verschuur had been a soldier in the army of Prince Frederic Henry of Nassau and had taken part in the siege of Breda in 1637. After her real sex was discovered, she was examined by Dr. Nicolaas Tulp, a physician immortalized in Rembrandt's painting of the "anatomical lesson." In one of his published studies on medicine he described the case.[8] Hendrikje Ver-

---

[4]See van der Meer, *De wesentlijke sonde,* apps. 1, 2; and Arend H. Huussen, Jr., "Sodomy in the Dutch Republic during the Eighteenth Century," in *'Tis Nature's Fault: Unauthorized Sexuality during the Enlightenment,* ed. Robert Purks Maccubbin (Cambridge, 1987), pp. 174–75.

[5]See van der Meer, *De wesentlijke sonde,* apps. 1, 2.

[6]GAA Notorial Archive (hereafter NA), deposition before Cornelis Stael 13131, no. 183.

[7]Rudolf M. Dekker and Lotte C. van de Pol, *The Tradition of Female Transvestism in Early Modern Europe* (London, 1989), pp. 58–63.

[8]Nicolaas Tulp, *De drie boeken der medicijnsche aenmerkingen* (Amsterdam, 1650), p. 244.

schuur "had the clitoris the size of a child's penis and thickness of half a little finger and with that had carnal conversation with several women, amongst others with Trijntje Barends . . . and they had been so besotted with one another that they would have liked to marry if it had been possible."[9] In punishment for her actions Hendrikje Verschuur was whipped (although not publicly) and exiled for twenty-five years.[10] In the eighteenth century Dr. Tulp's description was quoted at least twice in private annotations of judges concerning sodomy cases, one of which involved a man who had sodomized his wife.[11]

The difference between these "transvestite" women and those women involved in same-sex trials after 1795 was that the latter were tried specifically for their sexual encounters. The trial of Bets Wiebes for tribadism in 1792 had come about as a result of another crime (as happened frequently with sodomy trials), in this case nothing less than murder in a female ménage à trois.

The research on which this article is based is part of a larger project examining sodomitical subcultures in seventeenth- and eighteenth-century Holland. I have assembled the research data through the use of criminal court records, records of civil lawsuits, minutes and correspondence of criminal courts, as well as sworn affidavits, prison archives, and prosopographic data.

Like the court records of their male counterparts, the records of tribades are detailed and explicit about the sexual acts for which these women were prosecuted. From what we know of same-sex behavior among women in history, this is rather unusual. Most of our knowledge about such conduct in the early modern period comes to us through popular literature, pornography (written for males), and gossip about court circles such as those of Marie-Antoinette in France and Queen Mary and Queen Anne in England.[12] Few facts are known even about those "passing women" who were

---

[9]Quoted from the manuscript of Maarten Weveringh, "Aantekeningen betreffende het verhandelde in de Schepenbank gedurende de jaren 1765–1768, 1771, 1772, 1776, 1777" (GAA Collection of Handwritings, no. 55, p. 297).

[10]Dekker and van de Pol, p. 79.

[11]The heterosexual sodomy case was that of Willem de Boer (1702). For the annotations, see GAA RA 5061-640i-2. The other annotations are those in the manuscript of the judge, Maarten Weveringh (n. 9 above).

[12]Lillian Faderman, *Surpassing the Love of Men: Romantic Friendship and Love between Women from the Renaissance to the Present* (London, 1985), pp. 23–46; Marie-Jo Bonnet, *Un choix sans équivoque* (Paris, 1981). See also Martha Vicinus, "They Wonder to Which Sex I Belong: The Historical Roots of the Modern Lesbian Identity," in Dennis Altman et al., *Homosexuality, Which Homosexuality?* (Amsterdam, 1989), pp. 171–98; Dennis Rubini, "Sexuality and Augustine England: Sodomy, Politics, Elite Circles, and Society," in Gerard and Hekma, eds., pp. 363–73.

involved in sexual relations with other women, though rumors of unusually large clitorises or the use of dildos abounded.[13] The sources used
here reveal a small if unique body of material that demands more extensive
consideration. Following a description of the trials, a closer study will be
made of the physical and emotional relations between these women, their
social background, and the ways in which their behavior was perceived by
their contemporaries. I also will address the question of why these women
were prosecuted at all, and—in contrast to their male counterparts—why
these prosecutions occurred only late in the eighteenth century. Finally, the
matter of sexual identities needs to be raised, especially since in the historiography of sexuality it has become a virtual paradigm to consider such
identities as molded by historical and cultural circumstances.

THE TRIALS

The trial of Bets Wiebes in 1792 was a rather touching story of loyalty and
betrayal. Wiebes was arrested in that year on suspicion of murdering her
friend Catharina de Haan.[14] Only after several months of examinations
was it determined that it was not Wiebes but another woman, with whom
Wiebes lived, who had killed de Haan. Bartha Schuurman, after a stormy
outburst of jealousy over Wiebes's relationship to de Haan, stabbed de
Haan to death in front of Wiebes. Schuurman was first arrested but accused Wiebes of the murder and was consequently released.[15] After the
murder Wiebes cut her hair and, dressed as a man, went into hiding for a
week because she did not want to testify against Schuurman. Once arrested, Wiebes claimed that on the evening of the murder the three women
had been arguing but that she had been too drunk to remember what actually had happened. Wiebes's mother indeed made a deposition in which she
said that Wiebes engaged in heavy drinking.[16] After the court denied the
request of the prosecutor to apply torture to force a confession from
Wiebes, Schuurman was again arrested. However, she continued to accuse
Wiebes of the murder and managed to escape torture herself by claiming

[13]Brigitte Eriksson, trans., "A Lesbian Execution in Germany, 1721: The Trial Records,"
in *Historical Perspectives on Homosexuality*, ed. Salvatore J. Licata and Robert P. Petersen (New
York, 1980/81), pp. 27–40.

[14]Data on this case unless otherwise indicated are to be found in GAA RA Confessieboek
5061-468, pp. 79–442, and 5061-469, pp. 228–357; and GAA RA Secreet Confessieboek
5061-538, pp. 251–56.

[15]GAA NA, deposition before L. Beels 17979 no. 13.

[16]Ibid., deposition before C. W. Decker 17099 no. 76. Such a sworn affidavit could be
submitted to the court and be used in the trial (Wim Heersink, "Eenakter uit het ruige leven:
Notarissen, criminaliteit en conflictregeling, in het bijzonder te Amsterdam, 1600–1800," in
A tort et à travers: Liber amicorum Herman Bianchi, ed. René van Swaaningen, Bert Snel,
Sjoerd Faber, and Erhard Blankenburg [Amsterdam, 1988], pp. 261–72).

that she was three months pregnant. It was not until three months after her arrest that Wiebes, examined at her own request, told the court that Schuurman was the murderer. The court delayed two more months to determine that Schuurman was not pregnant, and then, under threat of torture, Schuurman confessed to the killing. When asked why she had persisted in making such untrue and vague statements during that time, Wiebes answered, "To avoid burdening Bartha Schuurman, who is a woman with a child."[17] Two days after her confession, Schuurman voluntarily stated "that the envy she had entertained against Catharina was situated in a strong jealousy, born from the dirty lusts that had taken place between Bets Wiebes and Catharina and between Bets Wiebes and herself."[18] She also claimed that "during the time they had lived together, Bets Wiebes many a time had lain upon her in the way a man is used to do when he has carnal conversation with his wife and that they had known one another in this way."[19] Wiebes denied the "dirty lusts" and claimed "never to have done such things nor to have been present at that and never to have had such things in mind."[20] She qualified this denial by telling the court that "if ever something indecent had happened between her and Bartha Schuurman, she must have done it without being aware."[21] She vigorously denied accusations by neighbors that she used to caress Schuurman's breasts and put her head in her lap.

The court did not really try to find out what happened between Schuurman and Wiebes. Bartha Schuurman was garroted at the scaffold, the usual capital punishment for female offenders, and hanged at the gallows field, "given up to the influences of air and birds."[22] Bets Wiebes was exiled from the city for six years.

The immediate causes for the arrests of eleven women later in the decade were not at all similar to the Wiebes murder trial in 1792, but some were sensational enough in their own way. Of four women arrested in 1796, it is not possible to determine how their activities were discovered.[23] Two were arrested by nightwatches, so they may have been caught in flagranti.[24] A more immediate cause may have been that neighbors had complained about the house these four women occupied. It was rumored to be a place where disreputable people gathered—perhaps it was even a brothel. Anna

[17]GAA RA Confessieboek 5061-468, pp. 429–30.
[18]Ibid., 5061-469, p. 240.
[19]GAA RA Secreet Confessieboek 5061-538, p. 254.
[20]Ibid., p. 252.
[21]Ibid., p. 255.
[22]GAA RA Sententieboek 5061-619 no. 1.
[23]The women were Gesina Dekker, Willemijntje van der Steen, Pietertje Groenhof, and Engeltje Blauwpaard (GAA RA Secreet Confessieboek 5061-538, pp. 339–52).
[24]GAA RA appendixes to the Bailiff's Bill, Lieutenant A. Hardenberg 5061-130 (1796).

Grabou was arrested in 1797 after complaints by female neighbors about verbal aggression they had suffered.[25] Christina Knip, arrested that same year, was caught after raping a fourteen-year-old girl with a dildo.[26] Perhaps most spectacular were the arrests of five women in 1798, who were saved by constables from a mob riot.[27] The sexual activities between at least two of these women had come to light through the efforts of neighbors, who had suspected Anna Schreuder and Maria Smit for a considerable time of "malign actions." One afternoon one of the neighbors heard a noise in the attic and went to find out what was happening. Through a hole in a wall she saw both women making love. She called in the other neighbors and each of them took turns peeking through the hole. One neighbor estimated that both women had been occupied in lovemaking from four until six o'clock in the afternoon. All that time the neighbors had been peeping, but finally one could not restrain herself anymore and shouted through the hole: "Yes, you foul whores, we can see you, why don't you get up yet, didn't you foul long enough?"[28] Schreuder and Smit departed, but the neighbors did not leave it there. They set out to investigate further and caused such an uproar that a crowd assembled in front of the house. The constables who hurried to the scene found Anna Schreuder naked under her cupboard-bed; they threw a cloak around her shoulders and took her to the Corps du Guarde, a local police office. The other four women had to be rescued from the crowd by the constables and were then taken to the Corps du Guarde as well.[29] As their neighbors did not neglect to mention at the trial, these women together sang a song—though a rather cryptic one—about the House of Orange, which was driven out in 1795. Pro-Orangist utterances at this time could cause major disorder and could lead to prosecution as well. (In their case it was only mentioned.) At the police office Schreuder confessed everything, but at the trial she revoked her confession and stated that she had only pleaded guilty because the lieutenant had threatened to cut off her breasts.

Only three of the women arrested between 1795 and 1798 confessed to the accusations. The prosecutor tried to obtain permission to force Anna Grabou, Christina Knip, and two of the five women arrested in 1798 to confess by means of whipping. The remaining three women arrested in that year were all released "*cum capitulo gravissimo,*" with a serious warning.

25GAA NA, deposition before P. Lijndraijer 18588 no. 225. Court records: GAA RA Confessieboek 5061-481, pp. 302–3; and GAA RA Secreet Confessieboek 5061-539, pp. 29–39.

26GAA RA Secreet Confessieboek 5061-539, pp. 17–22.

27The women were Anna Schreuder, Anna de Reus, Catrina Mantels, Anna Schierboom, and Maria Smit (ibid., pp. 91–137).

28Ibid., p. 112.

29GAA NA, deposition before P. Lijndraijer 18589 no. 147.

Their arrests perhaps were due to the fact that they all shared the same apartment and at first were held equally suspect. On all occasions the use of corporal violence was denied to the prosecutor. With or without confessions all the other women—the four arrested in 1796, the two arrested in 1797, and two of those arrested in 1798—were found guilty and sentenced to jail, the verdicts varying from two years' confinement (Anna Grabou) to twelve (Christina Knip).

THE RELATIONSHIPS

Court records of sodomy and tribadism trials only offer a rare glimpse into the bonds between those involved. Trials, after all, were meant to establish whether criminal (sexual) acts had taken place. References to emotional attachments were only used when they could help to "persuade" a suspect. The trial of Bartha Schuurman and Bets Wiebes was an exception. Yet the records of this trial showed only one aspect of the emotional bonding between these two women: the jealousies.

It may be enlightening to take a closer look at the case of Bets Wiebes, the woman whose conviction for tribadism in 1792 arose through her shielding of her friend from charges of murder. In 1789 at the request of her mother, Wiebes, then twenty-two, was confined by the court to the New Workhouse, a correctional institute in Amsterdam, for outrageous drunkenness. Reportedly, she daily used strong liquor, sold her mother's possessions, and slandered and brutalized her mother.[30] After seventeen months Wiebes was released and according to her mother seemed to have mended her ways.[31]

Wiebes first returned to her mother's house. But the mother, a widow, had remarried during her absence and Wiebes could not get along with her mother's new spouse. She left to live with Bartha Schuurman, who offered lodgings. In 1791, when Schuurman received news that her husband had died on board an East India Company ship, both women and Schuurman's child moved to a basement and tried to live on their earnings by selling news broadsides.

Wiebes paid regular visits to an older woman, Catharina de Haan, whom she had gotten to know in the workhouse. These visits aroused Schuurman's jealousy. One afternoon early in March 1792, Wiebes was drinking a glass of liquor at de Haan's home when Schuurman burst in. She rebuked Wiebes for drinking again and started to quarrel with de

[30]Ibid., deposition before Pieter Berkman 17624 no. 307; GAA RA Confessieboek 5061-463, p. 474, and 5061-464, p. 2.

[31]GAA Inschrijfboek der Schouts- en Geldgasten Private Archive (hereafter PA) 347-127; deposition of Bets Wiebes's mother before the notary C. W. Decker, GAA NA 17099 no. 76.

Haan by accusing her of the theft of a sieve. Wiebes defended her friend: "She has suffered too much from poverty herself to be a thief."[32] This defensive reaction was not at all effective in calming Schuurman. After leaving de Haan, Wiebes and Schuurman continued to quarrel all day, scolding one another and slapping each other's face. Schuurman said several times that she would put an end to the situation.

Two days later, quarreling again, Schuurman shouted at Wiebes, "The moon may consume me if I don't make short work of this now."[33] Wiebes was surprised when, that afternoon, Schuurman again came to de Haan's home, now in a cheerful mood. She even offered de Haan her snuff. Wiebes was suspicious of Schuurman and asked her, "Why should thou do a thing like that, thou does not mean this and thou does not do this with a kind heart." Nevertheless, Wiebes left the two women and when she returned to de Haan's later that afternoon, she was greatly surprised to learn that de Haan was visiting Schuurman, despite, in Wiebes's words, "those two not being friends at all and Bartha always finding fault with Catharina."[34] She went over to the basement she shared with Schuurman and, at the moment of her arrival, witnessed Schuurman stab de Haan to death.

The reason why Schuurman acted as she did on Wiebes's entrance may have been something more than mere jealousy. According to the forensic report, the city doctor who examined de Haan's corpse in the hospital found her with her upper body naked.[35] Of course she may have been undressed in the hospital, but could it be that Schuurman and de Haan had started lovemaking and that Schuurman panicked when she heard Wiebes enter?

From what has been said earlier about the way Wiebes tried to protect Schuurman while she herself was put on trial, one may infer a remarkable compassion on her part, even to the point where she herself suffered serious consequences. Usually, people who were put on trial for whatever reason showed a great readiness to accuse or involve others. In Wiebes's case compassion seems to have been a character trait. After being banished from the city she returned illegally, was arrested again, and confessed to having stolen a silver clasp, which she had pawned, from the people with whom she had found shelter. She had written a note to the people whom she had robbed, explaining that she had not done so out of a lust to steal but because of her need for liquor. She also let them know in which pawnbroker's shop they could find their clasp and that her mother was willing to make restitution.[36]

[32]GAA RA Confessieboek 5061-469, p. 232.
[33]Ibid.
[34]Ibid., 5061-468, pp. 429, 432.
[35]GAA RA Chirurgijnsrapport 5061-640 G.
[36]GAA RA Confessieboek 5061-471, pp. 434, 449–52. This time she was imprisoned for

The case of Anna Grabou in 1797 showed that she was another passionate woman, albeit of a different nature. According to her maid she had a "restless, evil and fickle temper, which made her every now and then say all kinds of coarse and indecent things."[37] Grabou was supposed to have approached a woman living next to her with the statement: "I love you so much, you should always be without your bonnet, then I love you so much. I shall take care that my old fellow leaves town, then you should sleep with me, then we shall have pleasure. . . . If you change your clothes you should come to me, but we should be alone together, because I want to see you naked and if you do what I like, I shall support you. I shall give you anything your heart desires, because if I have drunk a glass of wine I am hot as fire."[38] A sister of this neighbor claimed to have been assaulted by Grabou, whom she accused of having said: "Pretty flower, you're not as pretty above your skirt as below. I don't feel any hair. It is as if it's grown with cotton."[39] A third witness said that once, when she and Grabou had been looking at a boy swimming naked in a canal, Grabou had told her, "You do have something in your being that attracts both male and female. If I just see you I shoot and if you have me whipped tomorrow and branded the day after, I shall yet love you for it."[40]

A fourth witness's testimony was not used in court, though hers went beyond mere statements by Grabou. According to this witness Grabou had boasted to her about the beauty of her maid and told her that she used to wake her up every morning "to scratch her poverty" and that her maid preferred her to do it rather than a man.[41] In addition, one of these witnesses testified that Grabou had once tried to lock her in a room with obvious intent, which resulted in a hand-to-hand fight.

In a deposition in 1798 that never resulted in a trial, Susanna Marrevelt and her maid were accused by her husband's uncle. One evening he had seen how his nephew's wife and her maid had embraced one another and made

---

four years. During the turbulent days of the French invasion in 1795 Wiebes was able to escape from prison, but once again she was caught. Instead of the six years' imprisonment the prosecutor now requested for her sentence, she received eight months (GAA RA Confessieboek 5061-477, pp. 258–59, 267). Two months later, in January 1796, the remainder of her sentence was remitted, though she still had to fulfill her years of exile (GAA RA Af- en opslagboek van Tuchtelingen 5061-636). It is not possible to verify whether she stayed away from the city during those years. At least she had no other confrontations with the court; her name is not mentioned in the eighteenth-century inventory of the court records 5061-562 (W). But she did return to Amsterdam and died there in 1808 (GAA Doop-, Trouw- en Begraafboeken [henceforth DTB] 1184/118v).

[37] GAA RA Secreet Confessieboek 5061-539, p. 37.
[38] Ibid., pp. 29–30.
[39] Ibid., p. 33.
[40] Ibid., p. 35.
[41] GAA NA, deposition before P. Lijndraijer 18588 no. 225.

"unnatural movements." His cleaning woman also said that she had seen how Susanna and her maid used to embrace and bare their lower bodies and touch each other's "shameful place." Moreover, one day when the cleaning woman was standing on a ladder, the maid had said, "Goddammit, I should see, I should feel what she has under her skirts," and the maid carried out her intention. The cleaning woman was deeply startled and complained to the nephew, which resulted in a "frightful hatred" from the maid. When several days later she was shown out by this maid, the maid pushed her down the steps. Her fall caused her so much pain that she was unable to work for three months and was denied an income.[42]

In all the other cases the physical acts between the women involved were described explicitly. One of the four women arrested in 1796, Gesina Dekker, twenty-four, had left her husband and children to live in the house of Willemijntje van der Steen, a place where not only "bad people" reportedly came but also a number of women who used to caress and kiss one another and feel each other under their skirts. She admitted that she "was lying on the floor with Engeltje Blauwpaard next to her, and when they were caressing one another, Engeltje Blauwpaard had put her finger in her womanliness, moved that finger up and down, which lasted about a quarter of an hour."[43] Van der Steen confirmed that she had been present when Dekker and Blauwpaard had their "improper conversation." Blauwpaard denied everything. A fourth woman, Pietertje Groenhof, admitted to having taken part in caressing after having been seduced with coffee and alcohol. She also stated that Blauwpaard "was very jealous over Gesina Dekker."[44]

In the early summer of 1797, Christina Knip, forty-two, invited a fourteen-year-old girl she had met in the street to come to her room. Once inside she reportedly threw the girl on her bed, "after which she took a black object, looking like a big finger, from her pocket, which she tied around her body with a string. Lying across the body of the girl she put the thing with her hand in the girl's womanliness and moved it to and fro for about half an hour, which caused the girl great pain."[45] In court Knip admitted to having taken the girl to her room but denied the rape.

The most elaborate description of sexual acts between women came from the neighbors of Anna Schreuder and the other four women arrested with her in 1798. They had seen how these women had "lain with their lower bodies nude and had kissed and caressed one another, like a man is used to do to a woman."[46] According to the neighbors they had lain upon

[42]Ibid., 18589 no. 72.
[43]GAA RA Secreet Confessieboek 5061-538, p. 341.
[44]Ibid., p. 347.
[45]Ibid., 5061-539, p. 19.
[46]Ibid., p. 112.

one another, had moved up and down, and one of them "had lifted her leg across the shoulder of the other" and "had licked the womanliness of the other with her tongue."[47]

SOCIAL ORGANIZATION

Like many men prosecuted as sodomites, a number of the women described here either were or at least had been married. Gesina Dekker, who had left her husband prior to her arrest, had married when she was only eighteen.[48] She had given birth to two children.[49] Anna Grabou had married a much older man and also had several children.[50] Of the five women arrested in 1798 two were still married and one was a widow.[51]

While most of the prosecuted sodomites engaged in occupations—as shopkeepers, peddlers, footmen—that offered them a great mobility and opportunities to meet other men, the women (with the exception of Anna Grabou) lived in deep poverty. Some held jobs that came close to begging or were alternated with begging. At least one of them depended on the charity of the Reformed Church. Some had a background of prostitution. Willemijntje van der Steen, who owned the house of ill repute where she and the other women arrested in 1796 had their sexual encounters, was punished with ten years' imprisonment. With the exception of Christina Knip (the rape case of 1797) it was the harshest verdict of all the women involved, though she was never accused of specific sexual acts and had merely acknowledged that she had been present when other women engaged in sexual activities. She seems to have been tried as a whorekeeper rather than as a tribade. The fact that it was explicitly mentioned that "bad people" used to come to her house also seems to refer to a brothel. In her confession (later revoked) of 1798 Anna Schreuder had referred to her background of prostitution and related that her mother had put her up to it when she was only fourteen. The lieutenant who took her into custody mentioned "street-whoring" as a reason for her arrest, while he recorded the names of the others by the phrase "evil malignities."[52] Her mother, Anna de Reus (also arrested), indeed had had a past as a prostitute.

Some of the women shared another background: like Bets Wiebes, Pietertje Groenhof and Anna Grabou had spent time in the New Work-

---

[47]Ibid.

[48]GAA DTB 634, fol. 354.

[49]Ibid., 85, fol. 45, and 113, fol. 133.

[50]Anna Maria Grabou and Richard Langerhans married October 10, 1790. He was forty, she twenty-one (ibid., 635, fol. 193). In 1792 she had a stillborn child (ibid., 1265, fol. 450); in 1793 the couple had a son (ibid., 276, fol. 60); and in 1795 a daughter (ibid., 276, fol. 52).

[51]See Appendix.

[52]GAA appendixes to the Bailiff's Bill (n. 24 above).

house. Groenhof was sent there at the request of her brother because of her excessive drinking.[53] Anna Grabou's case had been different: in 1793 her husband had filed a complaint with the court because on several occasions she had threatened to kill him with a knife, she had openly had an affair with another man, and her behavior toward not only her husband but her neighbors as well often was "as if crazy." Though the court decided to confine Grabou for a year her husband took her out of the New Workhouse after several weeks.[54]

There is a striking difference between the men persecuted as sodomites in the eighteenth century and the women tried in the last decade of that century. Most of the men had a recognizable sodomite role, which included recurrent sexual behavior, effeminacy (though never as extreme as in England), codes, slang, particular rituals, and expectations about their future behavior. They took part in more or less extensive sodomite networks and had numerous private and public places to meet one another and carry on their sexual activities.[55]

Only in the case of the four women tried in 1796 is there a mention of a meeting place where women had sexual encounters (van der Steen's house). The other women the court examined in these years seem to have been rather isolated. Perhaps some of them, like the women who were arrested in 1798, formed a small group, but one could hardly speak of a network. What these women shared seems to have been their poverty rather than a specific sexual interest.

CONTEMPORARY ATTITUDES AND PERCEPTIONS

When in 1730 the first wave of persecutions of sodomites swept the country, many people were either ignorant of the practice of sodomy or were unaware that sodomy was a criminal offense. Later in the eighteenth century, when this was no longer true, most people did not show a great willingness to turn sodomites over to the authorities. When they did, it was usually only after they had suffered verbal or physical aggression. Many people who were arrested on same-sex charges had been known to be sod-

---

[53]GAA RA Confessieboek 5061-470, pp. 208–9, 218; GAA NA, deposition 18051 no. 13 (at the back of the Protocol). GAA Inschrijfboek Schout- en Geldgasten PA 347-127, fol. 89.

[54]GAA RA Schepen Minuut Register met Requesten 5061-1279, fol. 71r–72r; Inschrijfboek Schout- en Geldgasten PA 347-127, fol. 92.

[55]Theo van der Meer, "Zodoms zaat in de Republiek: Stedelijke homoseksuele subculturen in de achttiende eeuw," in *Soete minne en helsche boosheit: Seksuele voorstellingen in Nederland, 1300–1850,* ed. Gert Hekma and Herman Roodenburg (Nijmegen, 1988), pp. 168–96.

omites for years. It was primarily at the end of the eighteenth century that some individuals set out to discover the places where sodomites met or to entrap them. However, all through the eighteenth century many citizens had preferred to settle things outside the law, with violence and mob beatings. Usually these citizens would beat sodomites only if they themselves were solicited or if the sodomites were caught in flagranti.

As far as the same-sex activities of women were concerned, ignorance seems to have prevailed. One of the neighbors of Anna Grabou claimed that at first she had not understood what Grabou wanted of her and that it only gradually dawned upon her that she wanted "unnatural things."[56] Frequently these women were the subject of ridicule. Christina Knip, who had raped the fourteen-year-old girl in 1797, had long been considered by her neighbors to be out of her mind, "on account of which she is the subject of mockery by boys and others."[57] One of her neighbors gave an example of Knip's supposed madness. She reported that once she had said to her teasingly, "Chris, it amazes me that you don't marry." If anything, Knip's answer had been straightforward: "Just to fuck? If that's all I'm missing I can do it myself."[58]

The neighbors who in 1798 watched Anna Schreuder and the other woman for two hours may not have intended initially to have them arrested. The arrests were actually a consequence of the mob riot in front of their house. When in 1798 Hendrik Brouwer and his cleaning woman indicted his nephew's wife and her maid, he went to the authorities only after the cleaning woman had recovered from the fall caused by the maid, three months after the incident had happened. Before that he had complained to his nephew, who told him, "My wife can do as she wants. If I'm satisfied, it's nobody's business. It's none of your concern." Upon hearing this reply, Brouwer threatened to throw the nephew and his wife out of his house.[59]

Nevertheless, some of the women faced other consequences. While she was in prison Gesina Dekker's husband initiated proceedings to obtain a "separation from bed and board," which was granted him. He also received custody of their one surviving child.[60] After Anna Grabou was sentenced, her husband may have decided that he had had enough of his wife's follies. He requested and received copies of the affidavit as well as copies of the court records to use in a divorce proceeding.[61] However, there is no record of such a divorce. Only a short time later he supported his wife's requests

---

[56]GAA NA, deposition before P. Lijndraijer 18588 no. 225.
[57]GAA RA Secreet Confessieboek 5061-539, p. 21.
[58]Ibid.
[59]GAA NA, deposition before P. Lijndraijer 18589 no. 72.
[60]GAA RA Schepen Minuut Register met Dispositien, 5061-1985, fol. 120v.
[61]Ibid., 5061-1106, fols. 131r–132r, 202v–203v, 206v–207r.

for extra refreshments and a reopening of her trial, which were both denied.[62]

Still, the criminal court seems to have considered tribadism as a less serious crime than sodomy. The average penalty imposed on these women was six years' confinement, as compared to twelve for men.[63] Furthermore, all the women received a reduction of their sentences.[64]

In 1730 theology and jurisprudence began to provide an etiology of sodomy, on both an individual and a collective level. Individuals, it was purported, were prone to fall victim to sodomy by seduction, once they had gone down successive steps in sinfulness: gambling, swearing, slander, whoring, and other lewdness. And since the Dutch by that time were supposed to have lost the sobriety of their ancestors that had made the country great, and since they copied all the sins of Sodom—indulgence in pride, and copious food, and the lack of enemies of the state—they also had begun to indulge in another atrocious sin: sodomy.[65] Sodomy represented the world turned upside down—it was an inversion of the sexes. This behavior also was at odds with matters that at a symbolic level represented manliness: honor, cleanliness, the outside world. It was only in the last quarter of the eighteenth century that manliness directly became equated with the strength of the state and sodomites were presented as a species deviant from their gender roles, as monsters or freaks.[66]

A Dutch historian supposed that women were not prosecuted on same-sex charges until the end of the eighteenth century because such activities were considered to be a source of erotic attraction for men.[67] On the other hand, "phallocentric" attitudes toward sexuality could only conceive of sexual relations involving women in terms of an actual penetration—hence the ideas about large clitorises or the use of dildos. Such opinions may have been confirmed by Christina Knip's rape of a girl. People who participated in the mob riot that caused the arrest of Anna Schreuder in 1798 shouted questions to her about the instrument she used; her supposed answer— that she had no need for such a thing but could do it with her body—may have caused some bewilderment.

[62]GAA Notulen Regenten Werkhuis PA 347-2, fols. 84, 94, 96–97. It may be of some significance that when Richard Langerhans died in 1822, his death was registered by a neighbor and an acquaintance (GAA DTB 1822-4, fol. 43), while Anna's death twelve years later at a different address was registered by her son-in-law (GAA DTB 1834-10, fol. 98).

[63]See van der Meer, *De wesentlijke sonde* (n. 2 above), app. 1.

[64]GAA RA Op- en Afslagboek van Tuchtelingen 5061-636 and appendix.

[65]See van der Meer, *De wesentlijke sonde,* pp. 27–31.

[66]Theo van der Meer, "Acts, Actors, and Authorities: Sodomite Networks and the Perception of Sodomy in the Eighteenth-Century Republic" (paper presented at the seventeenth International Congress of Historical Sciences, Madrid, August 1990).

[67]Arend H. Huussen, Jr., "Strafrechterlijke vervolging van sodomie in de Republiek," *Spiegel Historiael* 17 (1982): 551.

Even though legal tradition in Europe provided for the punishment of sexual acts between women,[68] such acts were not perceived as equivalent to the acts of sodomites, not least of all because apparently they were not seen as representing the kind of threat that sodomy did. Sodomy, after all, was supposed to incur the wrath of God and thus would cause the destruction of the country, as happened in Sodom and Gomorrah. Moreover, sodomy threatened to challenge well-defined gender roles.

But how, then, was tribadism perceived? It may shed some light on this question to examine some of the words and their meanings that pertain to women engaging in same-sex erotic behaviors. Of course the word *lesbian* did not yet exist in the eighteenth century. However, for women involved in same-sex acts, a whole series of classical terms existed: *faemina tribades, fricatrices, subigatrices, clitorifantes.* These mainly seem to refer to a specific sexual technique. But these terms were only used in legal or theological comments.[69] The terms that were used by the court or members of the court and the public at large were *tribadism, evil malignities,* the no longer existing Dutch verb *lollen* (to foul), and *sodomitical filthiness.* Only on one occasion did a lieutenant constable use a derivation of *sodomy* (*sodomieterije*) in reference to a woman.[70] In strictly legal terms this was not correct, since it was only applied to anal intercourse or bestiality. However, the verb *lollen* and its stem *lol* especially should be noted. The stem returns in words such as *lolhoeren* (foul whores), for which the last group of tribades to be arrested were decried, *lolder* (sodomite), and *lolhuis* (literally foul house, brothel). There was later the word *lollepot*, which, possibly as early as the nineteenth century and certainly in the twentieth century, referred to lesbians (the word *pot* nowadays means dyke). The exact meaning of *lol* is ambiguous at best. In present-day usage it means fun but in the eighteenth century it definitely had a negative connotation. In the words mentioned above it sometimes explicitly referred to same-sex acts (*lollen*) or men engaged in such activities (*lolder*), sometimes to sexual misconduct in general (*lolhuis, lolhoeren*).[71] While sodomites both in judicial and theological discourse were becoming a separate category, tribades seem to have been perceived as women who misbehaved in general. Neither the court nor the women

---

[68] Louis Crompton, "The Myth of Lesbian Impunity: Capital Laws from 1270–1791," in Licata and Petersen, eds. (n. 13 above), pp. 11–25. Judith Brown, *Immodest Acts: The Life of a Lesbian Nun in Renaissance Italy* (New York, 1986), pp. 3–20.

[69] P. Loens, *Regtelijke aanmerkingen omtrent eenige poincten concernerende de execrabele sonde tegens de natuur* (Rotterdam, 1760), p. 10.

[70] GAA appendix to the Bailiff's Bill (n. 24 above).

[71] Similar to *bugger,* the eighteenth-century Dutch equivalents of which (*buggeren, boggeren*) were derived from *bougre;* originally both referred to heresy—Manichaeism—and same-sex activities. *Lollen* and its derivations may come from the Lollards, a heretical sect in thirteenth- and fourteenth-century England and Holland.

themselves (as far as they said anything at all) saw tribadism as an autono-
mous phenomenon but, rather, as acts resulting from prostitution, alcohol
abuse, and social background. While it was only prior to the emergence of
an effeminate sodomite role at the end of the seventeenth century that men
were considered to be capable of desiring both men and women, this concept probably held true for women well into the nineteenth century.[72]

PROSECUTIONS REVIEWED

A bill against sodomy was passed in the province of Holland in 1730. It did
not mention women explicitly, though in 1731 the prosecutor of the Court
of Holland, reflecting on this subject, concluded that sexual activities between women were comparable to mutual masturbation between men and
in his opinion likewise deserved the death sentence.[73] However, in actual
practice capital punishment was never demanded or applied in cases of mutual masturbation but only in cases where anal intercourse could be proven.
The question of why women (such as Mooije Marijtje and Dirkje Vis in
1750) were not prosecuted until the end of the eighteenth century is to a
large extent answered by the previously described perception of same-sex
activities among women and the general ignorance on the subject.

One reason why the women arrested between 1795 and 1798 were prosecuted may have been because they all caused public nuisances: it should be
noted again that Willemijntje van der Steen most likely was convicted because she kept a "bad house," always a major nuisance to neighbors; Anna
Grabou had been aggressive to quite a few neighbors; Christina Knip was
found guilty of rape. The women involved in the 1798 arrests had become
the focus of a mob riot, which was no doubt exacerbated by the singing of a
pro-Orangist song by the women, a punishable offense at this time. Yet
there are other possible factors that may help to explain why the women
described here were prosecuted: personal zealousness on the part of the
prosecutor and a changed attitude toward behavior that now was characterized as deviant.

In 1795 the invasion of French troops put an end to the ancien régime
and brought a new, "enlightened" government to power. In Amsterdam the
newly installed members of the local court—and especially its public prosecutor, the conservative Maurits Cornelis van Hall[74]—probably gained

---

[72]Randolph Trumbach, "Gender and the Homosexual Role in Modern Western Culture:
The Eighteenth and Nineteenth Centuries Compared," in Altman et al. (n. 12 above), pp.
149–69.

[73]Algemeen Rijks Archief Hof van Holland, Criminele Sententien 5661, fols. 113v–
114r.

[74]Simon Schama, *Patriots and Liberators: Revolution in the Netherlands, 1780–1813*
(London, 1977), p. 214.

more credit for their revolutionary zeal than for their judicial expertise. In the years between 1795 and 1798 when van Hall acted as prosecutor, more people than ever before were tried on suspicion of same-sex sexual activities. The zealousness on the part of van Hall is not without irony, since his colleague responsible for public order, Mayor Carel Wouter Visscher, was in more than one instance identified as a possible sodomite.[75] The trials may even have had to do with rivalry between the two officials, since they belonged to different revolutionary cabals.[76]

Moreover, during the time that van Hall was the prosecutor, suspicion of soliciting was deemed sufficient to try a man for sodomy, with a conviction leading to several years' imprisonment, while van Hall's predecessors prosecuted only when statements from either witnesses or accomplices in definite sexual acts were available.[77] As a lawyer in 1730 stated, the desire to perpetrate sodomy could not be prosecuted.[78] Though not an explanation per se, the personal zealousness on the part of van Hall and his rivalry with Visscher may have contributed to a climate in which women in Amsterdam were more likely to be prosecuted when suspected of same-sex offenses. Such trials—both for tribadism and for soliciting—either did not occur at all or occurred rarely elsewhere in the Republic.

There is yet another element to be considered. At both the beginning and the end of the eighteenth century, prosecutions for moral offenses were the majority of all criminal cases against women and even increased in the last decade of that century.[79] Moral offenses included many different things: adultery, a sexual relationship with a Jew, tribadism, prostitution, exposure of children, neglect of a household and family, running away from parents, and bad behavior in general. A substantial part of such criminal cases from 1790 on involved a so-called confinement on request. It was applied when (like Bets Wiebes, Pietertje Groenhof, and Anna Grabou before

[75]Van der Meer, "Zodoms zaat in de Republiek" (n. 55 above), p. 182.

[76]Whereas van Hall was a conservative, Visscher definitely was much more of a radical. In 1798, after a radical coup d'état, van Hall was temporarily removed from office because of his moderate views (Schama, p. 329).

[77]See van der Meer, *De wesentlijke sonde,* pp. 123–28. In some cases van Hall asked and received permission to apply "mild" torture to force a suspect to confess. According to the rules, however, torture could only be applied when the court had evidence at its disposal to show that a capital crime (anal intercourse) had occurred. This contradicts the avowed "enlightened" discomfort at using torture to obtain confessions. But van Hall did not consider whipping to be torture (Sjoerd Faber, *Strafrechtspleging en criminaliteit te Amsterdam, 1680–1811: De nieuwe menslievendheid* [Arnhem, 1983], pp. 121–26). On several occasions I was able to ascertain that van Hall's judicial knowledge was faulty.

[78]*Requeste en deductie mitsgaders advisen en bylagen in de zake van Jan Lucas Bouwens ingedaagde in persoon* (1730).

[79]Hester Lunsingh Scheurleer, "Diefstal, prostitutie en andere slechtigheden: Vrouwen in Amsterdamse Confessieboeken uit de achttiende eeuw," in *Jaarboek voor vrouwengeschiedenis 1984,* ed. Jeske Reys et al. (Nijmegen, 1984), pp. 24–26.

their arrests for tribadism) a person was considered to be a nuisance to his or her surroundings because of immoral behavior, and relatives and neighbors requested that such a person be confined. Though this procedure was applied all through the century, in the last decade the number of such requests increased.[80]

However, at the end of the eighteenth century, prostitution constituted a smaller percentage of the moral offenses brought before the court than at the beginning of the century. Most likely, it was the result of a major change in the organization of prostitution. Earlier, prostitution was primarily the business of *hospitas,* who kept two or three women whom they took to playhouses and inns to solicit customers, and whores who cruised the streets. In the last part of the eighteenth century the playhouse owners themselves kept women, according to some sources as many as twenty-five. While prosecution of women working in a more or less controlled environment such as a brothel was rare, it was more vigorously imposed on "street-whores," often at the request of relatives.[81]

Given the connection between tribadism and prostitution, at least in the perception of those involved—the prosecutor, the judges, and perhaps the women—this modification in policing moral offenses may also account for the trials of the women described here.

The change in attitude has been explained by Dutch historians as resulting from a major shift in the psychology and perception of morality. Beginning in the last quarter of the eighteenth century, conjugal fidelity, sobriety, honorable citizenship, and domesticity were strongly emphasized, a middle-class ideology intended to filter down to the lower classes. If these ideals were to concern both man and wife, it was women on whom the virtue of domesticity was particularly imposed. Moreover, as Randolph Trumbach has pointed out, in northwestern Europe, as a result of the emergence of a definite effeminate sodomite role, in the course of the eighteenth century it became more and more important for men to avoid effeminacy. For women, on the other hand, it was the avoidance of any association with prostitution that became pivotal in the development of their gender roles.[82] "Criminal justice and the requests for confinement could be seen as efficient means of a moral offensive"[83]—and especially to impose a more

---

[80]Ibid., pp. 31–32.

[81]Lotte van de Pol, "Van speelhuis naar bordeel? Veranderingen in de organisatie van de prostitutie in Amsterdam in de tweede helft van de 18de eeuw," *Documentatieblad werkgroep achttiende eeuw* 17 (1985): 157–72; Scheurleer, pp. 26–31, 35.

[82]Randolph Trumbach, "The Birth of the Queen: Sodomy and the Emergence of Gender Equality in Modern Culture, 1660–1750," in *Hidden from History: Reclaiming the Gay and Lesbian Past,* ed. Martin Duberman, Martha Vicinus, and George Chauncey, Jr. (New York, 1989), pp. 129–40; also Trumbach, "Gender and the Homosexual Role" (n. 72 above), pp. 149–69.

[83]Scheurleer, p. 34. Compare D. J. Noordam, "Zedeloos Nederland? Seksuele losban-

vigorous control on women, one might add. Tribadism, both as a form of lascivious behavior and because of its supposed relation with prostitution, was no longer considered by men to be a desirable erotic attribute of women.

POSSIBLE DEVELOPMENT OF LESBIAN IDENTITIES

A modern lesbian identity is supposed to have emerged from late nine-teenth-century medical discourse. The historiography on lesbianism in the early modern period has focused on two elements that, proceeding through a stage of butch/femme roles in the nineteenth century, are theorized as the roots from which a modern lesbian identity sprang: the tradition of roman-tic friendships and that of female transvestism.[84] Both traditions are recorded in Dutch history.

The romantic friendship between Betje Wolff and Aagje Deken, en-lightened authors of epistolary novels who lived together from 1777 until their deaths in 1804, was the most well known. Prior to and during the time they lived together the two friends courted other young women.[85] Wolff favored amiable young women who appreciated her intellectual su-periority and whom, rightly or wrongly, she considered to be aspiring poets. In her youth she had been the focus of a rousing scandal with a young man and then had married an elderly vicar in another part of the country (within days after his death, Aagje Deken came to live with her). Though in favor of marriage for young women, on her own part she re-jected sexuality.[86] Deken seems to have sought a mutual spiritual understanding that would allow for an independent life, intellectual stim-ulation, and moral rectitude and that would overcome whatever physical sensuality might exist.[87]

Though Wolff was called the Dutch Sappho by some contemporaries, according to her biographer it had only a literary connotation.[88] It is in-deed unlikely that Wolff and Deken perceived their relationship as in any way similar to that of the tribades prosecuted in the late 1790s in Amster-dam. Nor was their relationship perceived in that manner by others, at least not by van Hall, the prosecutor who showed such zealousness in prosecut-ing sodomites and tribades. From 1798 until their deaths he befriended both women and administered a fund for the impoverished authors.[89]

---

digheid rond 1800: Visies, remedies, realitait," in Hekma and Roodenburg, eds. (n. 55 above), pp. 197–209.

[84]Vicinus (n. 12 above), pp. 174–75.

[85]P. J. Buijnsters, *Wolff en Deken: Een biografie* (Leiden, 1984), pp. 151–54, 215–16; Myr-iam Everard, "Tribade of zielsvriendin," *Groniek* 16 (1984): 16–20.

[86]Buijnsters, pp. 215–16.

[87]Everard, "Tribade of zielsvriendin," p. 18.

[88]Buijnsters, p. 153.

[89]Ibid., pp. 300–301.

In their study of some 120 women who in seventeenth- and eighteenth-century Holland dressed as men, Rudolf Dekker and Lotte van de Pol were able to attribute sexual motives to a small number of them. These few women married other women and (though not in all cases) had sexual relations with them. Some of these spouses were not aware of the actual sex of their "husbands." A case is known in Germany in which a "passing woman" is supposed to have fooled her "wife" by using a dildo.[90]

According to Lillian Faderman a romantic friendship such as the one between Wolff and Deken, an "all-consuming emotional relationship in which two women are devoted to each other above anyone else," is "lesbian."[91] Dekker and van de Pol argue that in the absence of a same-sex role a woman who fell in love with another woman would perceive herself to be a man and experience "gender confusion." They see this confusion as a stage in the development of a modern lesbian identity.

Clearly, the women put on trial in the last decade of the eighteenth century in Amsterdam fit into neither the transvestite tradition nor that of romantic friendship. The final question to be answered here is, where do they fit, then? Indeed, I would like to suggest that there was a third tradition that played a major role in the development of a modern lesbian identity—that of a connection between prostitution or lewdness and same-sex behavior, as a stage parallel to or perhaps even more important than romantic friendship and female transvestism.

Lillian Faderman has been taken to task for ignoring or trivializing sexuality between women, especially in view of the fact that the very concept of "lesbianism" as it emerged in the late nineteenth century centered upon sexual acts between women.[92] Dekker and van de Pol, even if their observations may be true for some of the transvestite women they describe, can be criticized for equating sex with love and basically ignoring the role of the female spouses of the transvestite women. Both Faderman's and Dekker and van de Pol's work assumes the existence of a timeless, exclusive lesbian desire, which in the case of the transvestite women preceded the transformation from woman to man, whereas Randolph Trumbach argues that prior to the emergence of a lesbian role a woman could desire both men and women. He also argues that until the mid-eighteenth century a woman could do so without suffering any detriment to her gender status but that this changed significantly between 1750 and 1880, still without producing

[90]Dekker and van de Pol (n. 7 above), pp. 58–63; Eriksson, trans. (n. 13 above), pp. 27–40.

[91]Faderman (n. 12 above), p. 19.

[92]Lisa Duggan, "Eleanor Roosevelt—Was She or Wasn't She? The Problem of Lesbian Definition in Lesbian History," in Homosexuality, Which Homosexuality? Conference Papers (Amsterdam, 1987, typescript), 2:5–17.

a distinctive lesbian role.[93] As a consequence one might argue that the sexual activities of the tribades in Amsterdam—and perhaps also those of some of the women who changed gender roles—came about as a result of actual circumstances instead of resulting from a clear-cut and timeless lesbian desire.

A Dutch scholar, Myriam Everard, has also criticized Faderman for ignoring matters of class. Everard theorizes that while middle- or upper-class women tried "to kill off lusts," lower-class women actually entered into sexual relationships with one another. She also refers to the fact that both in nineteenth-century France and in Holland it was reported that many tribades were involved in prostitution. Perhaps, Everard posits, the modern lesbian did not emerge from romantic friends but from the tribade, the prostitute, and the transvestite.[94]

However, while the tradition of female transvestism vanished in Holland in the early nineteenth century (though it may have been replaced by butch/femme roles), medical practice in the Netherlands in the late nineteenth and early twentieth centuries virtually ignored romantic friendships as evidence of lesbianism. Instead it focused on the tribade as a lewd or morally degenerate woman.[95] It is my view that the tribades described here indeed may represent the more—if not the most—important and direct predecessors of the modern lesbian.

APPENDIX
CASES OF TRIBADISM, 1751–98

1751   Deposition against *Mooije Marijtje*.
        Deposition against *Dirkje Vis*.
1792   *Elizabeth Frederica Wiebes*, age 23, sells newspapers. Exiled for six years.
        Bartha Schuurman, age 31, widow, one child, sells newspapers. Garroted for the murder of Catharina de Haan.
1796   *Gesina Dekker*, age 24, married to Jan Hendrik Willing, two children, divorced in 1798. Six years' confinement in Spinhuis; released in 1800.
        Willemijntje van der Steen, age 37, seamstress. Ten years' confinement in Spinhuis; released in 1801.
        Pietertje Groenhof, age 46, supported by the parish. Four years' confinement in Spinhuis.
        Engeltje Blauwpaard, age 27, helps her father trundling a wheelbarrow. Six years' confinement in Spinhuis; released in 1800.

[93]Trumbach, "Gender and the Homosexual Role" (n. 72 above), pp. 158–59.
[94]Everard, "Tribade of zielsvriendin," pp. 18–19.
[95]Myriam Everard, "Lesbianism and Medical Practice in the Netherlands, 1897–1930," in Homosexuality, Which Homosexuality? Conference Papers, History Supplement, pp. 73–84.

1797   *Christina Knip,* age 42, sews caps. Twelve years' confinement in Spinhuis; died in 1799 in prison.

        Anna Grabou, age 27, married to Richard Langerhans, two children. Two years' confinement in New Workhouse; released in 1799.

1798   *Anna Schreuder,* age 17, born out of wedlock, gathers wood. Five years' confinement in Spinhuis; released in 1801.

        Anna de Reus, age 55, mother of Anna Schreuder, married to Johannes Jochems, sells newspapers. Released with a serious warning.

        Maria Smit, age 46, married to Johannes Mantels, widow since 1792, one child. Five years' confinement in Spinhuis; released in 1801.

        Catrina Mantels, age 49, sister-in-law of Maria Smit, married to Jan Lauterbeek, two children, sells newspapers. Released with a serious warning.

        Anna Schierboom, age 31, no occupation. Released with a serious warning.

        Deposition against *Susanna Marrevelt,* married to Albert Limpers, two children. No trial.

        Deposition against *Elizabeth Tuijn,* maid of Susanna Marrevelt, married in 1801. No trial.

Definition and Control:
Alexander Walker's Trilogy on Woman

ROBYN COOPER

Department of Fine Arts
University of Sydney

IN THE 1830s and early 1840s a trilogy on "woman" by Alexander Walker, a Scottish physiologist, was added to the mounting stack of publications on this subject. From the latter half of the eighteenth century "woman" had become a major preoccupation, predominantly, although by no means exclusively, for male minds. Vast quantities of mental effort and textual toil were expended by philosophers, clergymen, men of science, and men of letters generally on the subject of woman—her nature, her role, her body, mind, and soul, as well as her relationship with her other half, man. This preoccupation was connected with the dramatic and dislocating social, economic, and political transformations arising out of the development of industrial capitalism, the formation of the urban bourgeoisie, intent on establishing its identity and power, and the spread from the Enlightenment and the French Revolution of ideas of freedom and equality. The decades in which Walker's texts were published were especially disruptive. But in all areas of life, changes and challenges were accompanied by efforts to know, understand, define, and control.

The "woman" investigated and defined in response to these transformations is the subject of this essay. She is the product of an intricate and interconnecting network of ideas current in scientific and other discourses. Her encasement in quotation marks here is to signal that she represents not an actualized lived body but a generalized body and an ideological construct. The locus of my analysis is Walker's trilogy, and the full titles of the

I would like to thank Carole Adams, Barbara Caine, Anthea Callen, Ludmilla Jordanova, Ornella Moscucci, and Roy Porter for their assistance with this essay. None but myself, however, can be held responsible for the final product. An earlier version of this essay was first presented at a conference, "Women in the Nineteenth Century," Research Centre for Women's Studies, Adelaide, Australia, 1985.

This essay originally appeared in the *Journal of the History of Sexuality* 1992, vol. 2, no. 3.

books provide their contents: *Beauty: Illustrated Chiefly by an Analysis and Classification of Beauty in Woman* (1836); *Intermarriage; or, The Mode in Which, and the Causes Why, Beauty, Health, and Intellect Result from Certain Unions, and Deformity, Disease, and Insanity from Others* (1838); and *Woman Physiologically Considered as to Mind, Morals, Marriage, Matrimonial Slavery, Infidelity, and Divorce* (1839).

The importance of these texts lies both in the extraordinary range of their investigation into woman and in their historical location. In their construction and analyses of woman the books draw on art and aesthetics, philosophy, history, literature, biomedical science, sexual selection, and the pseudosciences of phrenology and physiognomy. They extend widely over time, drawing on classical sources, Sir Thomas More, Francis Bacon, David Hume, and John Milton, and an extensive range of eighteenth- and early nineteenth-century material (British, French, and German). There are nearly a hundred sources cited and often extensively quoted in the books. In other words, the woman represented in these texts is not in any way idiosyncratic. Supported by this body of knowledge, the texts offer an exhaustive investigation into woman, her nature and role, her mind, her anatomy and physiology, her health and disorders, and her education. I am not aware of any other nineteenth-century publication in English as comprehensive in its investigation of woman as the Walker trilogy. The total oeuvre constitutes a particularly rich case study of the exercise of men's knowledge for the definition and control of women and the ambiguities and contradictions within such an exercise.

In addition, the trilogy is of interest and value in terms of its historical location. At the time of its publication, a particular image of woman had been set in place. Middle-class and evangelical in its origins, it represented woman in terms of her domestic role and charged her with the preservation of moral and spiritual values by precept and example within the home environment.[1] This image was enshrined in works such as Sarah Ellis's *The Women of England* (1839), Mrs. John Sanford's *Woman in Her Social and Domestic Character* (1837), and James Green's *Woman; or, The Excellence, Duties, and Influence of the Female Character* (1844). Central to this image of woman was the idea of her "purity," her sexual innocence and passivity. The woman represented in the Walker texts is in many ways the opposite of this "pure woman," since she is entirely defined by and identified with her sexualized body. Her being and purpose are determined by nature rather than by God. The relationship of this sexualized woman to the pure woman, as well as her reception, are questions that will be investigated below.

It is important to establish at the outset that Walker's trilogy, while little

---

[1] See Leonore Davidoff and Catherine Hall, *Family Fortunes: Men and Women of the English Middle Class, 1780–1850* (London, 1987), especially chaps. 1–3.

known now, cannot be considered a marginal work. The books were "re-spectable" publications, published by well-established houses such as Henry Bohn, and they went through several editions in England and the United States.[2] *Beauty* appears to have been particularly successful, pub-lished in a deluxe edition in 1851 with tinted plates and a gold-embossed leather binding, as well as in a cheap condensed version.[3] Copies of the books even reached the shores of the Antipodes.[4] The books were accom-panied by dedications to prominent men of the period—George Birkbeck, founder of the Mechanics' Institute and University College, and Sir Anthony Carlisle, vice president of the College of Surgeons. They were extensively and for the most part favorably reviewed.[5] Walker's trilogy thus fit into the mainstream of Victorian publishing.

I

Before proceeding to my analysis of the trilogy, I need to consider the ori-gins of the woman represented in these works, the science that provides the foundation for her nature and function in society, and the purpose of the publications. Alexander Walker was born in Scotland in 1779 and studied at the Edinburgh Medical School, although he does not appear to have received a degree. In his books he describes himself as a "lecturer in anatomy and physiology" and as a "physiologist." But his career was mainly literary and his publications were as much addressed to the general reader as to the man of science.[6] Walker's intellectual formation was in the late

[2]Walker's publishing history is provided in Paul F. Cranfield's introduction to Walker's *Documents and Dates of Modern Discoveries in the Nervous System* (1839; rpt., Metuchen, NJ, 1973). Walker seems to have been particularly popular in the United States. The advertise-ment to the American edition of *Beauty* (New York, 1845) states that the publisher has responded to public demand in issuing this work sooner than planned. It also states that *Intermarriage,* the first of the trilogy to be published in the United States, went through six editions in eighteen months, while *Woman Physiologically Considered* had been scarcely less suc-cessful (p. v).

[3]This was published under the title *The Book of Beauty; with Modes of Improving and Preserv-ing It in Man and Woman.* The book, however, makes no reference to the preservation of beauty in man. An American edition, based on the fifth London edition, was published in 1843.

[4]The trilogy is advertised among a "Splendid Importation of Books" in the *Sydney Gazette* (March 3, 1842).

[5]There are a number of reviews cited in Dr. Adolph Carl Peter Callisen, *Medizinisches Schriftsteller-Lexicon der jetzt lebenden Verfasser, Aertze, Wundärtze, Geburtschelfer, und Natur-forscher aller gebildeten Völker,* 33 vols. (Copenhagen, 1830–45), 33:205–6. Quotations from reviews are also to be found at the back of *Intermarriage* and *Woman Physiologically Considered.*

[6]Not much is known about Alexander Walker. Some biographical information can be found in Cranfield and in *Dictionary of Scientific Biography,* s.v. "Alexander Walker." The inter-nal evidence of the texts indicates that philosophically Walker was a naturalist, that he was a secularist and anticlerical, and that politically he was identified with middle-class radicalism.

Scottish Enlightenment with its deep commitment to the development of a science of "man" and its belief that "man" and his environment could be both studied and controlled.[7] The Scottish Enlightenment had close French connections, and Walker quotes extensively from French as well as English and German luminaries.[8] From the eighteenth century also comes Walker's commitment to a naturalist explanation of human phenomena. The nature-determined and sexually defined woman of the Walker texts is a product of this Enlightenment background.[9]

The sciences that Walker brings to his analysis are anatomy and physiology, incorporated into a system in which the division of organs and functions in animals is tripartite: the locomotive organs control movement; the nutritive or vital organs control digestion, circulation, and generation; and the mental organs control sensation, thought, and volition. These organs are hierarchically ordered, ascending from the feet and legs (locomotive organs) to the trunk (vital organs) to the head (mental organs). Thus there is no separation between mind and body, the mind being as physiologically determined as the body.[10]

Three more observations must be made about Walker's system. In the first place he identifies his system as "natural," the laws determining its operations being nature's laws. The eighteenth century witnessed an elevation in the status of nature as the source "whereby society, morals, education, even medicine, are to be reformed and purified."[11] The law of nature was given a status and authority equal to the law of God. In his placement of woman within his system, Walker claims to be following nature's laws. These laws are both descriptive and prescriptive: what is and what should be are conflated. And their transgression is attended by

[7]On the Scottish Enlightenment see Gladys Bryson, *Man and Society: The Scottish Enquiry of the Eighteenth Century* (Princeton, NJ, 1945); Nicholas Phillipson, "The Scottish Enlightenment," in *The Enlightenment in National Context*, ed. Roy Porter and Mikulás Teich (Cambridge, 1981), pp. 19–40; and Anand Chitnis, *The Scottish Enlightenment and the Evolution of Victorian Society* (London, 1986).

[8]Among the French writers on woman that Walker quotes extensively are Jean-Jacques Rousseau and the medical scientists De Lignac, Pierre Roussel, Pierre J. G. Cabanis, and Georges Buffon. Paradoxically, Walker's debt to French luminaries is combined with traditional British francophobia, no doubt exacerbated by the Napoleonic Wars.

[9]On women and the French Enlightenment, see Paul Hoffmann, *La Femme dans la pensée des lumières* (Paris, 1977); Yvonne Knibiehler and Catherine Fouquet, *La Femme et les medécins* (Paris, 1983); and Philippe Perrot, *Le Travail des apparences; ou, les transformations du corps feminin XVIIIe au XIXe siècle* (Paris, 1984).

[10]On the emergence of a physiology of the mind in the late eighteenth century see, especially, Karl M. Figlio, "Theories of Perception and the Physiology of the Mind in the Late Eighteenth Century," *History of Science* 13 (1975): 117–212.

[11]Maurice Bloch and Jean H. Bloch, "Women and the Dialectics of Nature in Eighteenth-Century French Thought," in *Nature, Culture, and Gender*, ed. Carol P. MacCormack and Marilyn Strathern (Cambridge, 1980), pp. 25–41, quotation on p. 31.

punishment and denaturing. The conflation of description/prescription reveals the social, cultural, and ideological bases of Walker's natural laws, since if the laws were simply descriptive of what is there would be no need to introduce the prescriptive "should." I shall have more to say further on about nature in relation to woman. At the moment I simply want to show the way in which Walker establishes the authority of his system through its identification with nature.

Second, it is a system that can be "read." It is laid out visually in a "Natural Arrangement of Organs."[12] The secrets and mysteries of the body and mind can be uncovered, given the requisite knowledge, since the internal organization reveals itself on the surface of the body. The body is thus a sign system whose meanings can be decoded. The other tools that Walker brings to his investigation of woman's body are the visually based pseudosciences of physiognomy and phrenology.[13] The organ to be used in deciphering the body is the eye. The act of seeing is to be transformed into the informed look. Walker deplores the way we "merely see objects without knowing what we see."[14] It is the visibility of the body's meanings, once the code has been mastered, that provides access to knowledge of the body for the nonspecialist.

Finally, this system cannot be considered apart from the various determinants on the gender relationships it establishes or the social and political purposes of the texts. Science and society are closely linked, as has been argued in recent writing on the history of science, in terms both of the knowledge produced and of its utilization. Scientific knowledge can thus be seen as culturally and socially contingent.[15] Walker's woman is as much confined as defined within Walker's science, whose articulation is an exercise of power and control as well as explication.

What, then, were the purposes of these publications on woman? Walker sets them out clearly in the advertisement at the beginning of *Beauty*: "There is perhaps no subject more universally or more deeply interesting than that which is the chief subject of the present work. Yet no book, even pretending to science or accuracy, has hitherto appeared upon it. The forms

[12]Walker's system and method are set out in his *The Nervous System, Anatomical and Physiological: In Which the Functions of the Brain Are for the First Time Assigned* (London, 1834), p. 12.

[13]Walker wrote a book entitled *Physiognomy, Founded on Physiology, and Applied to Various Countries, Professions, and Individuals* (London, 1834).

[14]Walker, *Documents and Dates*, p. 10.

[15]See, for example, Eveleen Richards, "Darwin and the Descent of Woman," in *The Wider Domain of Evolutionary Thought*, ed. David Olroyd and Ian Langham (Dordrecht, 1983), pp. 57–111, quotation on p. 58; Ludmilla J. Jordanova, "The Social Sciences and the History of Science and Medicine," in *Information Sources in the History of Science and Medicine*, ed. Pietro Corsi and Paul Weindling (London, 1983), pp. 81–127; Evelyn Fox Keller, ed., *Body/Politics: Women and the Discourse of Science* (New York, 1990).

and proportions of animals—as of the horse and the dog, have been examined in a hundred volumes. Not one has been devoted to woman, on whose physical and moral qualities the happiness of individuals and the perpetual improvement of the human race, are dependent."[16] It will be seen that the books have the two-fold purpose of increasing individual happiness and advancing the human species—two key items on the Enlightenment agenda.[17] The advancement of the species was to be a preoccupation of the nineteenth century, evident in other publications of the Walker period, such as Orson Fowler's *Hereditary Descent: Its Laws and Facts Applied to Human Improvement* (1840), and more widely in later nineteenth-century writing on evolutionism and eugenicism by Charles Darwin, Herbert Spencer, Alfred Wallace, and others.[18]

The responsibility for species advancement through selective breeding lies with the middle class. If Walker's intellectual origins are in the eighteenth century, his politics are the middle-class radicalism of the 1830s and 1840s.[19] His science is being used in the service of politics, as well as sexual politics. It is to the middle classes that the texts are specifically addressed. The laboring classes are trapped in their social position, lacking the education and knowledge to breed themselves out.[20] The aristocracy, on the other hand, are feminized, enfeebled, and degenerate as a result of inbreeding, dissolute habits, and the withering away of their mental organs through disuse. As Foucault observes in *The History of Sexuality,* the nineteenth-century bourgeoisie was making its own class system, not through the aristocratic lineage of blood but through the health of its progeny. "The bourgeoisie's blood was its sex. . . . The concern with genealogy became a preoccupation with heredity."[21] The importance of the subject for individual happiness as well as species advancement is illustrated in *Beauty*

[16]Alexander Walker, *Beauty: Illustrated Chiefly by an Analysis and Classification of Beauty in Woman* (London, 1836), p. vii.

[17]See Peter J. Bowler, *Evolution: The History of an Idea* (Berkeley, CA, 1985).

[18]There is a reference to Walker's *Intermarriage* by Darwin in an annotation to a letter he had received on April 5, 1839. See Charles Darwin, *The Correspondence of Charles Darwin,* ed. Frederick Burckhardt and Sydney Smith, 3 vols. (Cambridge, 1988–90), 2:185 and n. 3.

[19]Walker states that in his early life he had "listened to the earnest and eloquent arguments of the excellent Godwin in behalf of the perfectibility of man!" (*Intermarriage; or, The Mode in Which, and the Causes Why, Beauty, Health, and Intellect Result from Certain Unions, and Deformity, Disease, and Insanity from Others* [London, 1838], p. 232). William Godwin, a novelist and political theorist, was one of the leading radicals of the eighteenth century. On late eighteenth and nineteenth-century radicalism, see M. C. Jacob, *The Radical Enlightenment: Pantheists, Freemasons, and Republicans* (London, 1981); and Paul Adelman, *Victorian Radicalism: The Middle-Class Experience, 1830–1914* (London, 1984).

[20]Walker's ideas about the place of workers within his theories of sexual selection are ambiguous, since he also suggests that education would enable them to improve themselves.

[21]Michel Foucault, *The History of Sexuality: An Introduction,* vol. 1 of *The History of Sexuality,* trans. Robert Hurley (New York, 1980), p. 124.

by the example of a man who has devoted his life to the improvement of bantam fowls and curious pigeons. And yet he married a madwoman, whom he confines to a garret and by whom he has insane progeny.[22]

The books are in effect guidebooks. They were part of the expansion of nonspecialized popular literature to cater to the needs and demands of a mass reading public that developed in the 1790s.[23] They also participated in the popularization of science, that is to say, popularization in the sense of making this area of knowledge available to the literate but uninformed reader, not in the sense of vulgarization.[24] In a review in 1839 of two recent works on physiology in the *Athenaeum,* the reviewer commented on the importance of physiological instruction as an element of knowledge, referring also to the problems of making scientific knowledge accessible to the uninformed.[25] Walker himself declared—and his reviewers often remarked—that his books were addressed to the general reader as well as the man of science.[26] Such works assisted the middle class in its self-definition as a class morally superior to the classes above and below and helped it gain access to power through access to knowledge.

Furthermore, these works in themselves were part of the endeavor by Walker and other middle-class intellectuals and professionals to establish "the validity of their vision of the world, and their right to debate social issues."[27] *Beauty* is dedicated to George Birkbeck, fellow Scotsman and alumnus of the Edinburgh Medical School, and the founder of the Mechanics' Institute and University College. Birkbeck is lauded in *Beauty* as "the inventor of the best mode of diffusing scientific knowledge among the most meritorious and most oppressed classes of society."[28] The dedication also includes a bitter attack on the Stamp Tax, decried as a "tax upon knowledge." A tax on all publications, it was reduced in 1836 and finally abolished in the 1870s.

What are the respective roles of men and women within this all important goal of species advancement? These are clearly set out in the second chapter of *Beauty,* where Walker defends his choice of the form of woman

[22]Walker, *Beauty,* p. 10.

[23]See Richard Altick, *The English Common Reader: A Social History of the Mass Reading Public, 1800–1900* (Chicago, 1957).

[24]See Roger Cooter, *The Cultural Meaning of Popular Science: Phrenology and the Organization of Consent in Nineteenth-Century Britain* (Cambridge, 1984); and Ludmilla J. Jordanova, "The Popularization of Medicine: Tissot on Onanism," *Textual Practice* 1 (1987): 68–79.

[25]*Athenaeum,* no. 586, January 19, 1839, pp. 46–47.

[26]For example, one review of *Intermarriage* refers to the author's attempt to adapt his subject "to the taste and capacity of the public" (*British and Foreign Medical Review* 1 [April 1839]: 37).

[27]Ludmilla J. Jordanova, "Natural Facts: A Historical Perspective on Science and Sexuality," in MacCormack and Strathern, eds. (n. 11 above), pp. 42–69, quotation on p. 64.

[28]Walker, *Beauty,* p. iii.

for his examination, "because it will be found, by the contrast which is per-petually necessary, to involve a knowledge of the form of man, because it is best calculated to ensure attention from men, and because it is men who, exercising the power of selection, have alone the ability thus to ensure indi-vidual happiness and to ameliorate the species; which are the objects of this work." He continues: "Let it not be imagined that the views now taken are less favourable to woman than to man. Whatever ensures the happiness of one ensures that of the other; and as the variety of forms and functions in man requires as many varieties in woman, it is not to exclusion or rejection of woman that this work tends, but to a reasoned guide in man's choice, to the greater suitableness of all intermarriages, and to the greater happiness of woman as well as man, both in herself and in her progeny."[29]

It can be seen from these passages that, while the knowledge of the meaning of beauty in woman is of supreme importance for the happiness of both sexes and the progress of the species, it is man who activates this knowledge. Nature has allotted to man the power of reason, of selection, so he must be instructed in making a "reasoned" choice. Woman attracts and man acts.

II

Having considered the purpose of Walker's trilogy, the origins of the woman it investigates, and the anatomical/physiological system in which she is located, I want now to turn to the texts themselves and the woman that they construct. In *Beauty* Walker declares his general theories of beau-ty, founded on the "immoveable basis of science," and expounds his three types of beauty, which are visual representations of his system, namely, lo-comotive, nutritive or vital, and mental. Beauty in woman is not simply a cause of visual pleasure but a sign of her reproductive fitness. In *Intermarriage* Walker sets out the "natural" laws of heredity, determining the precise forms and qualities of progeny. Since Walker's evolutionism is Lamarckian, he also considers habits and behavior, acquired characteristics, even the state of mind at the moment of conception, as being passed on to the "ens" (embryo). As well, he expounds his ideas on sexual development at puberty, sexual desire and pleasure, marriage, and procreation. The last volume of the trilogy, *Woman Physiologically Considered*, discusses "philo-sophically the moral relations of the sexes as founded on physiological principles."[30] Woman is examined in relation to her mind, morals, matri-monial relationship, and divorce. While the first two books are specifically

[29]Ibid., pp. 12–13.
[30]Alexander Walker, *Woman Physiologically Considered as to Mind, Morals, Marriage, Matri-monial Slavery, Infidelity, and Divorce* (London, 1839), p. vi.

directed toward species improvement, *Woman Physiologically Considered* looks at its subject more in terms of her domestic role and relationships.

Who is the woman constructed in the texts? First and foremost she is entirely defined by her biology. "I must observe," states Walker, "that the reproduction of the species is, in woman, the most important object of life, and everything in her physical organization has evident reference to it."[31] Thus the highest class of beauty in woman is vital/nutritive beauty, because this relates to the organs in Walker's system of anatomy and physiology that are peculiarly hers—the organs controlling generation and nutrition. Vital/nutritive beauty is distinguished by softness, moderate plumpness, rounded forms, light and graceful movements, "qualities which please, because they announce the good condition of the individual who possesses them, and the greater degree of aptitude for the functions which that individual ought to fulfil."[32] The beauty of woman is not simply for visual enjoyment but has a function of great social and political significance.

There are several consequences of woman's construction and definition in terms of her reproductive purpose. To begin, Walker says, she is physiologically constituted—physically and mentally—in such a way that the desire for love (that is, sexual love) is preeminent in her. Indeed woman is more highly sexed than man, although the role that nature has allotted her is one of modesty and resistance. However, she is allowed a "natural coquetry," which is distinguished from captivating coquetry. Being more highly sexed, girls mature more quickly than boys and consequently require more restraint during puberty. Erotic excitement can lead to masturbation, "uterine epilepsy," "sapphic tastes," and nymphomania. For this reason girls are to be kept away from those artifices and activities of civilization that overstimulate the imagination and the senses, such as fashionable novels, paintings, music, balls, theaters. One of the "accidental causes" of nymphomania are "obscene paintings and engravings."[33] The nonappearance of "catamenia" (menstruation) is equally dangerous, leading to what was known as "chlorosis" (green sickness), the symptoms of which are avid eating of plaster, charcoal, sealing-wax, and other non-nutritive substances. This disorder, however, is cured by reading fashionable novels and going to balls and theaters, that is, by the stimulation of the imagination and the senses. On the other hand, nineteenth-century etiquette manuals were universally opposed to the sensual stimulation of girls. They were more concerned with dampening pubescent sexual development and did not concern themselves with the problems of and solutions to the nonappearance of menstruation. Because of the problems of sexual development

[31]Ibid., p. 242. For an extended analysis of women and reproduction, see Emily Martin, *The Woman in the Body: A Cultural Analysis of Reproduction* (Boston, 1987).

[32]Walker, *Woman Physiologically Considered*, p. 244.

[33]Walker, *Intermarriage*, p. 97.

in puberty, particularly for girls, Walker was an advocate of early marriage at a time when middle-class marriages were being postponed in the interests of economic security.[34]

On the employment of the sexual organs in marriage, Walker is insistent on moderation in frequency as well as in performance. Moderation in marital encounters (as indeed in all behavior) was promoted as a quintessentially middle-class virtue, distinguishing it from the debaucheries of the upper class and the animal excesses of the lower class. Moderation in the Walker texts has a physiological as well as a moral foundation. The body's capital is fixed, and overexpenditure in one sector is at the expense of others. It is for this reason that sexual expenditure has to be moderate and carefully invested in acts of generation, where there would be a return on the investment.[35] Moreover, given that what is in the parents' state of mind at the moment of conception can be passed on to the child, the product of wild passion will be weak and feeble.

Man wastes more in acts of reproduction and is more fatigued, which is why his life is shorter than woman's. For woman, excessive employment of her reproductive organs results in "erotomania" and ultimately death. On the other hand, absolute continence in woman also causes hysteria, insanity, and death (a gloomy prognosis for single women!). Even though woman's sexual development is attended by dangers and excessive use of her sexual organs brings on disease, it cannot be argued that Walker finds the condition of being a woman pathological, as was pronounced by a number of Victorian medical practitioners.[36] Nature, after all, had designed woman for her reproductive destiny, and to find intrinsic faults in woman's system would be to find faults in nature's design. Thus menstruation, far from being a "morbid condition," is indispensable to health.[37] But woman's highly sensitive nervous organs and the continuous variations in

---

[34]See Davidoff and Hall (n. 1 above), pp. 222–23.

[35]See, for example, Walker's quotation from the naturalist philosopher Joseph Priestley: "Every act of indulgence before marriage is a deduction from this most valuable stock of happiness" (*Woman Physiologically Considered,* p. 355). For the use of economic metaphors in relation to the body, see G. F. Barker-Benfield, "The Spermatic Economy: A Nineteenth Century View of Sexuality," *Feminist Studies* 1 (Summer 1972): 45–74.

[36]On the Victorian medical profession and women, see Lorna Duffin, "The Conspicuous Consumptive: Woman as an Invalid," in *The Nineteenth-Century Woman: Her Cultural and Physical World,* ed. Sarah Delamont and Lorna Duffin (London, 1978), pp. 26–56; and Barbara Ehrenreich and Diane English, *For Her Own Good: 150 Years of Experts' Advice to Women* (Garden City, NY, 1978). See also Ludmilla J. Jordanova, "Conceptualizing Power over Women," *Radical Science Journal* 12 (1982): 124–28 (for a critique of Ehrenreich and English).

[37]Elaine and English Showalter, "Victorian Women and Menstruation," in *Suffer and Be Still: Women in the Victorian Age,* ed. Martha Vicinus (Bloomington, IN, 1972), pp. 38–44, especially p. 40.

her vital organs resulted in a certain derangement, which could end in insanity (woman being more susceptible to insanity than man). The treatment of these derangements does not require medical intervention but, rather, changes in her habits and environment. As far as nymphomania is concerned, Walker considers it a disorder of puberty caused by unsatisfied sexual desire and cured by marriage, although for many in the Victorian medical profession it was the result of the very presence of sexual desire in a woman.

On the subject of sexual pleasure, Walker once again reveals his Enlightenment roots, sharing its belief "that Nature had made men to follow sex, that sex was pleasurable, and that it was natural to follow one's urges."[38] On woman's capacity for sexual pleasure, Walker is in no doubt. Given her larger vital organs and the association of her whole life with her reproductive functions, it follows that everything connected with love is more essential for a woman and that she must derive "far higher pleasure than man" from the employment of her reproductive organs.[39] Woman needs frequent and enduring, although always moderate, employment of these organs for her health and survival, even after menstruation has ceased. This is only "natural justice." Walker's insistence on woman's pleasure in intercourse also connects with the belief (dating back to classical antiquity) that female orgasm was necessary for conception, the reason being that the body of woman was colder than that of man and needed heating to provide a receptive place for the product of their union.[40]

Another consequence of woman's definition in terms of her reproductive function relates to her mind. Walker maintains that there is a sex of mind.[41] In woman the organ associated with reason is less developed, as is the organ of will, except for the will to please. More developed are the organs connected with sensibility, observation, imagination, and feeling. Woman's mind is thus designed by nature for the fulfillment of her reproductive destiny. It is patently evident, states Walker, "that love, impregnation, gestation, parturition, lactation and nursing have little, or nothing to do with reason and are almost entirely instinctive."[42] Woman's proneness to derangement also prevents her from attaining reasoning power.[43]

---

[38] Roy Porter, "Mixed Feelings: The Enlightenment and Sexuality in Eighteenth-Century Britain," in *Sexuality in Eighteenth-Century Britain,* ed. Paul-Gabriel Boucé (Manchester, 1982), p. 4.

[39] Walker, *Intermarriage,* pp. 76–77.

[40] See Thomas Laqueur, *Making Sex: The Female Body and Gender from the Greeks to Freud* (Cambridge, MA, 1990), pp. 98–103.

[41] Walker, *Woman Physiologically Considered,* p. 11.

[42] Ibid., p. 23.

[43] Ibid., pp. 37–38.

Woman's morals are also a direct consequence of her reproductive destiny. Walker refers to her "DEPENDENCE ON AND KNOWLEDGE OF MAN, as preliminary to love, and her morals [are] related either to it or its consequences."[44] This in turn arises out of "her natural sensibility, feebleness and timidity." Woman's morals are therefore associated with politeness, coquetry, vanity, caprice, and sympathy. She is incapable of justice, since her benevolence and pity interfere, and she is incapable of friendship, which is an "intellectual passion," as opposed to love, which is a "vital passion" and therefore her "empire."[45] Woman's morals have nothing to do with virtue, and they are good only insofar as they are associated with functional effectiveness.[46] Furthermore, her morals are directed to the particularities of her situation and not to the larger sphere. Woman's biology determines that her "natural" sphere is the domestic, and she "necessarily remains much in the interior of the house, in which alone her chief duties can be performed."[47] Woman's "natural duties" in the family include her "perpetual readiness to treat her husband with kindness"[48] and to take care of her children (for which she is peculiarly fitted, being a child herself), and preparation of food and clothing. These duties are natural, not sacred, and no special value is attached to them, as they were to the pure asexual woman, the "angel in the house." Woman has no place in the public sphere. "PHILANTHROPY, PATRIOTISM, and POLITICS, not being matters of instinct, but of reason, are unsuited to the mind of woman."[49] The exclusion of woman from philanthropy makes an interesting contrast to the Victorian acceptance of philanthropy as the appropriate public sphere for women because it was perceived as an extension of their duties in the home.

The biologically determined woman of the Walker texts is defined in terms of her difference from man, a difference that is a polarized opposition ostensibly founded on biology, in which man is the measure. By the mid-eighteenth century the definition of woman as an inferior version of man had been replaced by one that emphasized sexual difference. "The anatomy and physiology of incommensurability replaced the metaphysics of hierarchy in the representation of women in relation to men." A two-sex model of male and female bodies replaced the earlier one-sex model.[50] But female

[44]Ibid., p. 83.

[45]Ibid., pp. 64, 96.

[46]On the identification of goodness with functional fitness, see Christine Pierce, "Natural Law, Language, and Women," in *Woman in Sexist Society,* ed. Vivian Gornick and Barbara K. Moran (New York, 1971), pp. 242–57.

[47]Walker, *Woman Physiologically Considered,* p. 140.

[48]Ibid.

[49]Ibid., p. 67.

[50]See Laqueur, *Making Sex;* and Londa Schiebinger, "Skeletons in the Closet," in *The Making of the Modern Body,* ed. Catherine Gallagher and Thomas Laqueur (Berkeley, CA, 1987), pp. 42–82, and *The Mind Has No Sex? Women in the Origins of Modern Science* (Cambridge, MA, 1989).

inferiority survives in this new model. There was also a basic asymmetry in the construction of difference in the Walker texts, since woman was entirely defined by her biology, as I have shown.

Walker's laws of sexual selection in *Intermarriage* are founded on difference. The mother and father contribute different organs to the child. In the choice of a partner difference, not similarity, must be the guide. What assists these choices is a natural attraction toward the opposite, a love of difference. "Man consequently looks for delicacy, flexibility and gentleness in his mate; woman, for strength, firmness and power."[51] Not only are there differences between the sexes, but there are also differences within the sexes. A little man should choose a tall woman. An "effeminate man is better matched with a masculine woman, though for him it is a despicable position."[52] Difference is essential to the progress of the species, since the union of people of similar temperament leads to quarrels and sterility.[53]

Throughout the texts the inferiority and subordination of the sexually differentiated woman is made patent. Beauty in woman is inferior to that in man, since it is the beauty of the nutritive system and not of the higher thinking system.[54] Because feebleness is a necessary part of her constitution, woman is distinguished by "beauty and grace" while man possesses "force and grandeur."[55] Moreover, "beauty and grace, as has been observed, seem to demand of nature less labour and time than attributes of force and grandeur."[56] Girls mature more quickly than boys, but this is because the making of boys requires more effort on nature's part. As regards woman's feebler muscular power, "no education will remedy these defects, or rather change these organic differences."[57] Among the enervating effects of polygamy on society is the production of more girls than boys, rendering the less powerful sex more superabundant.[58] If the pleasures of love are more essential to a woman's organization and more exquisitely enjoyed, these pleasures are also less determined and more easily suspended because of the necessary weakness of will in her mental organization, apart from her will to please man. Woman may have more pleasure in sex than man, but her urges are not as compelling. Woman cannot therefore be the initiator in her marital encounters ("cannot" being both descriptive and prescriptive), and she is thus "passively voluptuous." It is not altogether clear, either, what Walker means by woman's sexual pleasure, since it excludes "spasmodic convulsions" succeeded by "weakness and relaxation."[59]

[51]Walker, *Intermarriage*, p. 118.
[52]Ibid., p. 376.
[53]Ibid., pp. 124–25.
[54]Walker, *Beauty*, p. 351.
[55]Ibid., p. 171.
[56]Ibid., p. 167.
[57]Walker, *Woman Physiologically Considered*, p. 32.
[58]Ibid., p. 309.
[59]Walker, *Intermarriage*, p. 381.

Sexual difference determines the roles and relations of man and woman. In terms of species improvement, as I have already stated, it is man who has the power of selection in the choice of partner. With regard to the relations between husband and wife, "It is evident that the man, possessing reasoning faculties, muscular power, and the courage to employ it, is qualified for being a protector: the woman, being little capable of reasoning, feeble and timid, requires protection. Under such circumstances, the man naturally governs, the woman as naturally obeys."[60]

Walker claims that sexual difference is founded on nature. Certainly there are differences between the bodies of men and women. Women do bear children, and for this reason there are differences in their body structure. A woman is in general smaller than a man, she has a relatively larger pelvis, and her cranium is smaller. But it does not follow from this that women are necessarily weaker than men, that their destiny is solely maternal, or that their intellectual capacities are diminished. Other aspects of Walker's science are pure fiction, such as his sexing of the organs of the mind. The biological differences between men and women, actual and fictive, have been mediated and interpreted through historically and socially contingent ideologies of gender. I use the word "ideology" advisedly because it implies the naturalization of relationships that are based on power. The shift in scientific conceptions of the relations between men and women found correspondences in social institutions and practices, and their supporting ideologies, with the establishment of two spheres, the public and the private—the workplace and the home—and the roles assigned to men and women within them. Gender difference and its organization was indeed central to the establishment of the industrial urban middle class. Ideologies of gender were also important in relation to the sexual politics of the time, used to secure married middle-class women in the home and to prevent the leakage of Enlightenment and revolutionary ideas of freedom and equality to women.

Woman Physiologically Considered is the site for taking on "the passionate and unreasoning writers about the rights of woman."[61] "Mrs. Wolstonecraft's" argument that women must have reason to perform any duty properly is dismissed as "nonsense" and evidence of her ignorance of science, since woman's performance of her duty is instinctive, requiring no reason.[62] Walker also dismisses her arguments for women's political rights and mockingly imagines a parliament of members competing for the attentions of the pretty female representatives, with midwives present to attend to the accidents affecting their health.[63] As historical proof of woman's in-

---

[60]Walker, *Woman Physiologically Considered*, p. 129.

[61]Ibid., p. 134.

[62]Ibid., p. 25. Walker refers, of course, to Mary Wollstonecraft, *A Vindication of the Rights of Woman* (London, 1792).

[63]Ibid., p. 69.

capacity to govern, he gives a devastatingly critical account of Elizabeth I (inspired also, one suspects, by Scottish nationalist sentiments, since her chief sins were committed against Mary, Queen of Scots).[64]

In addition, the Walker texts contain dire warnings to women who transgress their nature-determined roles, particularly through the excessive use of their mental organs, which results in the deterioration of the vital system, central to woman's identity, and of "natural attraction."[65] Indeed, "a learned and philosophical lady is as monstrous a deformation of nature as a eunuch."[66] These warnings about the disastrous effects of women's excessive use of their mental organs must be interpreted as responses to early feminist demands and to the fear of women's claiming access to the political sphere, exacerbated by the extension of the vote to sections of the male middle class in 1832. Thus Walker combines ridicule and science to keep women within their sphere.

One finds in Walker the familiar association of a feminized society with disorder and decline. Maintenance of the division between the sexes is thus essential to order and progress. But there would not be the need for this continual insistence if the sexual boundaries were indeed secure. Within the texts themselves there are ambiguities with regard to ideas of gender division and separate spheres. Gender relations are perceived in terms of complementarity as well as difference, but complementarity does not signify equality, as I have shown above.

It must also be pointed out that the two spheres in reality were not as separate as their ideology, and the divide was crossed by interconnections.[67] For Walker, women were located in the private sphere, as were the acts of procreation between husband and wife. Yet reproduction and childrearing were activities of great public significance—hence the need for intervention in the most private activity in the most private room of the house. Moreover, there was the continuous threat of women attempting to escape from the sphere to which they had been assigned. As a result Walker is ambiguous about women's education. On the one hand women need to be educated, since uneducated women "communicate lower mental faculties to their children."[68] This declaration does not appear to fit with his concerns about the masculinizing effects of intellectual exercise on woman. However, the solution to the problem would appear to be that woman's education was to be within the limits of her familial functions as a companion to her husband and an instructor of her children.

---

[64]For a discussion of the subversive capacities of women within the political order, see Carole Pateman, "'The Disorder of Women': Love and the Sense of Justice," *Ethics* 91 (1980): 20–34.

[65]Walker, *Woman Physiologically Considered,* p. 38.

[66]Ibid., p. 142.

[67]Davidoff and Hall (n. 1 above), p. 33.

[68]Walker, *Intermarriage,* p. 435.

In two areas alone did Walker's politics and sexual politics operate in favor of women: divorce and marital infidelity. In *Woman Physiologically Considered* Walker has much more to say about unhappy than happy marriages, and he writes at length on the subject of "matrimonial slavery," the current indissolubility of unhappy marriages, and the infidelity and prostitution that result from this situation. The larger part of the book is given over to vehement arguments in favor of divorce, describing the damaging effects of its impossibility in England for all but the most wealthy. The matrimonial slavery of women is worldwide, except in republics; England, as an aristocracy, is one of the worst cases. Wives have "no property either in their fortunes, their persons, their children."[69] The wife's condition is one of slavery, no less degrading to her tyrant/husband than to herself. Walker is writing at a time of considerable public debate over married women's property rights, in relation to the case of Caroline Norton, although Walker does not mention it.[70] His condemnation of matrimonial slavery comes out of his political radicalism and his belief in "natural justice."[71] What is not recognized, however, is the extent to which "matrimonial slavery" relies on the dependent and subordinate wife he has presented. Nor does he comment on the anomalies of a financially independent subordinate wife, who, despite her intellectual deficiencies, has command over her own property.

One of the consequences of marital slavery is infidelity. A woman deprived of the love that is essential to her being has a "natural right" to seek compensation elsewhere.[72] Walker's views on infidelity are fairly tolerant, since its foundation is in nature, novelty and variety being "essential to the high enjoyment of every natural pleasure."[73] Infidelity is as natural in a woman as in a man. Walker's criticism is directed less toward infidelity per se than toward the double standard that punishes women for what men are forgiven—all the more unjust given woman's greater need for love. Infidelity does not necessarily injure domestic affections, unless it results in jealousy and persecution. One of the reasons why Walker can be so fair-minded about women's marital infidelity is because the paternity of progeny is no problem for him. His "laws of resemblance" in progeny, which he outlines in *Intermarriage,* would easily identify the father.

Of prostitution and courtesanship Walker is rather less tolerant, con-

[69]Walker, *Woman Physiologically Considered,* p. 150.

[70]See Lee Holcombe, "Victorian Wives and Property," in *A Widening Sphere: Changing Roles of Victorian Women,* ed. Martha Vicinus (Bloomington, IN, 1980), pp. 3–28, especially pp. 8–9.

[71]Cf. Jeremy Bentham, who advocated divorce to free women from the tyranny of sexual slavery. See Porter, "Mixed Feelings" (n. 38 above), p. 7.

[72]Walker, *Woman Physiologically Considered,* pp. 169–71.

[73]Ibid., p. 182.

demning them as "vicious practices."[74] This is less for moral reasons than because they are a waste of reproductive fluid, since prostitutes rarely conceive. At the same time he does not condemn prostitutes themselves, seeing them as victims, not as sinners. Both infidelity and prostitution primarily are consequences of indissoluble marriages. Canonical law in England forbade divorce, and annulment could be attained only through an act of Parliament, which the middle and lower classes could not afford to do. He argues vehemently for the right to dissolve unhappy marriages, except when children are in need of care. Again, the possession of this right is natural justice. For Walker, then, marriage is a civil contract that can be broken, not a divinely ordained lifelong union. It might also be argued that there is a third area of Walker's sexual politics that is favorable to women, the allowance of sexual pleasure. But the texts' accounts of woman's sexual pleasure are ambiguous, sexual pleasure being more essential to woman yet more easily suspended. Furthermore, as I will show in relation to rape, woman's sexual pleasure can be turned against her.

The separation of the sexes and the different roles assigned to each are determined by nature. Throughout the texts, nature is the authenticating voice for the validity of what is spoken. Nature, as Christine Pierce states, "must be among the most enigmatic concepts ever used. Often, when the 'natural' is invoked, we are left in the dark as to whether it is meant as an explanation, a recommendation, a claim for determinism, or simply a desperate appeal, as if the 'natural' were some sort of metaphysical glue that could hold our claims or values together."[75] These ambiguities are present in the Walker texts. They are compounded by the complexities of the perceptions of the relationship between woman and nature and of the gendering of nature as feminine.[76] Nature and the body of woman have long been identified—positively in the analogy of fecundity and caring, negatively in the analogy of excess and uncontrolled destructiveness. These positive and negative identifications reveal men's profound uncertainties and anxieties around women's sexuality.

Woman is closer to nature than man because of her functions of bearing and nurturing children. Walker's texts show a deep ambivalence regarding this identification. On the one hand woman is worshipped, even envied, as the favored child of nature. Walker writes of his deserving the gratitude of

[74]Ibid., p. 326.

[75]Pierce (n. 46 above), p. 242.

[76]On the relationship between woman and nature, see Sherry B. Ortner, "Is Female to Male as Nature Is to Culture?" in *Woman, Culture, and Society,* ed. Michelle Z. Rosaldo and Louise Lamphere (Stanford, CA, 1974), pp. 67–87; Carol P. MacCormack, "Nature, Culture, and Gender: A Critique," pp. 1–24, Ludmilla J. Jordanova, "Natural Facts," and Bloch and Bloch, all in MacCormack and Strathern, eds. (n. 11 above). See also Carolyn Merchant, *The Death of Nature: Women, Ecology and the Scientific Revolution* (San Francisco, 1983).

the female sex "by showing, that nature, for the preservation of the human species, has conferred on woman a sacred character, to which man naturally and irresistibly pays homage, to which he renders true worship—that nature has, therefore, given to woman prompt and infallible instinct as a guide in all her gentle thoughts, her charming words, and her beneficent actions, while man has only slow and often erring reason to guide his cold and calculated conduct, and that hallucination of mental supremacy which, vain as he may be, only enables him blindly to protect and support woman, and makes him proud to promote her desires."[77]

At the same time it is evident in the texts that woman's instinct and lack of reason are also signs of her inferiority and the potential disorderliness of her nature. There is a further twist in the nature/woman connection. Instinct is considered to be entirely natural, and sexual desire is perceived to be instinctual. Being closer to nature, woman's sexual desires are stronger and can become voracious and destructive. Similarly woman's lack of reason leads to superstition, religious zealotry, and other irrational beliefs and activities. This nature-identified woman thus constitutes a threat to the rationally ordered world that the texts seek to create and in whose creation her role is so central. Consequently this woman, who is the object of man's admiration and envy, must also be confined and controlled. But there is a real paradox here. Women are denied reason because a rational woman would be a threat to men's gender preeminence and power, but an irrational woman is a threat to the power of reason itself.

There is a further analogy between woman and nature in their relationship to man, although again the relationship is ambivalent. From Francis Bacon on, scientific knowledge itself was conceived as mastery over a feminized nature, encapsulated in his famous declaration, "I am come in very truth, leading to you Nature with all her children to bind her to your service and make her your slave."[78] These words resonated down the centuries. This is the nature who is to be penetrated and possessed by the man of reason, forced to reveal her secrets and to submit herself to his power.[79] Yet Bacon's metaphor of mastery and domination over nature is less simple than first appears. He also wrote: "For man is but the servant and interpreter of nature: what he does and what he knows is only what he has

[77]Walker, *Woman Physiologically Considered,* pp. v–vi.

[78]Quoted in Genevieve Lloyd, *The Man of Reason: "Male" and "Female" in Western Philosophy* (London, 1984), p. 12.

[79]For example, Sir Humphry Davy (who became president of the Royal Society in 1820) stated that the man of science, not content "with what is found upon the surface of the earth . . . has penetrated into her bosom, and has even searched the bottom of the ocean for the purpose of allaying the restlessness of his desires, or of extending and increasing his power" (quoted in Brian Easlea, *Science and Sexual Oppression: Patriarchy's Confrontation with Woman and Nature* [London, 1984], p. 127).

observed of nature's order in fact or in thought; beyond this he knows nothing and can do nothing. For the chains of causes cannot be broken, nor can nature be commanded except by being obeyed."[80] In other words, man has mastery over nature only through the discovery of and submission to her laws. "Science controls by following the dictates of nature and mastery over nature depends on obedience to her."[81] Simultaneously nature is master over and servant to man.

Yet while both sexes must adhere to nature's laws, only man with his power of reason has the capacity to discover and articulate these laws. Knowledge is in the possession of man. Mrs. Sanford, in her *Woman, in Her Social and Domestic Character* (1837), writes: "There is no possession, of which men are so tenacious, as that of learning. Perhaps it is, because knowledge is power, that they are therefore not disposed to share it with woman; or perhaps it is, because instead of her improving her acquirements for good purpose, she sometimes only uses them as a plea for assumption."[82] With regard to the Walker trilogy, addressed to a general readership, it would appear that the intention was not to deny women access to its knowledge. A reviewer of *Beauty* thought that wives as well as husbands would profit from the book.[83] *Intermarriage*, the most sexually explicit of the texts, does not contain the detailed descriptions and illustrations of sexual organs that one finds in texts addressed to a scientific or medical readership. Nonetheless, the reaction of some—but not all—reviewers to the propriety of this publication and *Woman Physiologically Considered* signaled a shift in the moral environment. One reviewer of *Intermarriage* stated that, despite Birkbeck's defense of the purity of the work, "it is of a nature which forbids our entering upon a particular review of it."[84] Similarly a reviewer of *Woman Physiologically Considered* shortened his account of Walker's investigations, "which may be pure to the pure, but are not very fit for the general reader."[85] The censoring and censuring of these books in reviews does not necessarily mean that women did not have access to them. What is clear, however, is the denial of woman's participation in the making of the knowledge they purveyed. Woman was closer to nature yet unable to speak nature. She was subject to laws that she had no part in making. Women's claims about their own bodies and experiences were dismissed because they were not founded on reason and knowledge.

[80]Quoted in Evelyn Fox Keller, *Reflections on Gender and Science* (New Haven, CT, 1985), p. 36.

[81]Ibid., p. 37.

[82]Mrs. John Sanford, *Woman in Her Social and Domestic Character*, 5th ed. (London, 1837), p. 25.

[83]*Court Magazine and Belle Assemblée* 9 (July 1836): 42.

[84]*Literary Gazette and Journal of Belles Lettres, Arts, and Sciences*, no. 1131, September 22, 1838, p. 596.

[85]*Tait's Edinburgh Magazine* 6 (May 1839): 344.

Take, for example, the subject of rape. With the support of other authorities Walker argues against the possibility of "violence" (that is, rape) unless narcotics have been administered, several men are engaged, or a strong man attacks a pre-pubescent girl. No healthy grown woman can be taken against her will. Women's assertions to the contrary are of "no weight."[86] Similarly there are women who claim to conceive without pleasure, but "women are not remarkable for truth on this point."[87] Since pleasure is necessary for conception, it follows that a woman who becomes pregnant cannot have been taken against her will.

Women were excluded from the community in which the knowledges about their bodies and nature were being formulated, while the women who questioned these knowledges were denigrated and ridiculed. Because of their exclusion from the scientific community, women, as Londa Schiebinger states, "had little opportunity to employ the methods of science in order to revise or refute the emerging claims about the nature of women. As science gained social prestige in the course of the nineteenth century, those who could not base their arguments on scientific evidence were put at a severe disadvantage in social debate."[88]

For all their ambiguities and ambivalences, the texts in the end must be seen as an exercise of masculine knowledge and power over women.

III

Finally, I want to look at the Walker texts not as products whose sources lie in the Enlightenment but as publications of the 1830s. By the 1830s a woman who seemingly was the opposite of Walker's woman had been set in place. Her origins also lay in the eighteenth century. But she was the product not of the discourses of the philosophes and the men of science, but of the writings of middle-class Protestant religious revivalism, particularly evangelicalism. This woman was pure, asexual, the "angel in the house." She was the guardian of moral and religious values, the regenerator of a corrupt society. The home she presided over was a "sacred place."[89] If love was central to her being, it was love as "domestic affection," not love as sexual desire. Her moral superiority over man derived from her very lack of

[86]Walker, *Intermarriage*, p. 135.

[87]Ibid., p. 420.

[88]Schiebinger, "Skeletons in the Closet" (n. 50 above), p. 43; for an extended analysis of women's exclusion from modern science, see her *The Mind Has No Sex?* (n. 50 above). Trevor Fawcett argues that it was rare for women to be allowed into anatomical lectures. See Davidoff and Hall (n. 1 above), p. 538, n.141.

[89]On Victorian domestic ideology and the pure woman, see Nancy Cott, "Passionlessness: An Interpretation of Victorian Sexual Ideology, 1790–1850," in *Signs* 4 (1978): 219–36; Catherine Hall, "The Early Formation of Victorian Domestic Ideology," in *Fit Work for Women*, ed. Sandra Burman (London, 1979), pp. 15–32; and Davidoff and Hall, chap. 3.

"carnal motivation"; she was "passionless." The passionless woman had support in science, with the discovery of spontaneous ovulation in mammals in 1843, leading to the conclusion that "ovulation could occur without coition and thus presumably without orgasm."[90] Sexual pleasure and orgasm lost their reproductive status.

This pure woman signaled a shift away from the relatively uncomplicated eighteenth-century notions of sex and pleasure to attitudes that were more complicated, particularly in the area of female desire. Desire and pleasure were not necessarily natural and innocent, even when enjoyed moderately within the sanctioned space of the home. They could be a sign of man's animal nature and his fall from grace, a fall instigated by the woman Eve. To speak openly of sex and pleasure was to run the risk of arousing those animal urges that had to be regulated and controlled.[91] I have already referred to the hesitancy of some reviewers of the Walker texts. Walker himself felt obliged to defend the purity of his undertaking—the exposure of female nudity—in *Beauty*, while George Birkbeck defended the delicacy and propriety of Walker's impartment of his knowledge in his introductory letter to *Intermarriage*.

The coexistence of these two types of woman points to the complexity of the representations of women in the nineteenth century. The pure asexual woman did not replace the sexualized woman of the Walker texts, who had a continued existence in later editions of his trilogy and in biomedical publications, in which, however, women's sexual pleasure is both affirmed and denied.[92] Nor were the two types of womanhood necessarily opposed; their naturalist and religious values could intermingle. Thus Michael Ryan's book, *The Philosophy of Marriage* (1837), considers procreation, sexual activity, and pleasure (described very explicitly). Like the Walker publications, Ryan's book emphasizes the procreative purpose of marriage and gives women a more insatiable sexual appetite than men. But the views expressed on sex and marriage are also shaped by evangelical values. Thus Ryan states that "the chief characteristics of a good husband or wife are piety, love, meekness, reasonableness, application to duties and a love of

---

[90]Laqueur, *Making Sex* (n. 40 above), p. 9.

[91]On nineteenth-century sexuality see Jeffrey Weeks, *Sex, Politics, and Society: The Regulation of Sexuality since 1800* (London, 1981); and Foucault (n. 21 above).

[92]The question of Victorian women's sexual pleasure has been the subject of considerable debate recently. See F. Barry Smith, "Sexuality in Britain, 1800–1900: Some Suggested Revisions," in Vicinus, ed., *A Widening Sphere* (n. 70 above), pp. 182–98; Peter Gay, *The Bourgeois Experience: Victoria to Freud—Volume 1, Education of the Senses* (New York, 1984); and M. Jeanne Peterson, "Dr. Acton's Enemy: Medicine, Sex, and Society in Victorian England," *Victorian Studies* 29 (1986): 569–90. For a good review of this revisionist writing, see Carol Zissowitz Stearn and Peter N. Stearn, "Victorian Sexuality: Can Victorians Do It Better?" *Journal of Social History* 18 (1985): 625–34.

home, 'sweet home.' "[93] What is apparent is that there is no single dominant representation of womanhood, but competing and often conflicting
representations and discourses. The question to be asked is whether it is
possible to find common ground in these differences and conflicts. Before
attempting to answer this question, I want to look more closely at the evan-
gelically derived woman who was firmly in place by the 1830s.

To describe this woman in relation to the woman of the Walker trilogy, it
is not necessary to move out of the Walker ambit. She is to be found in the
long appendices to the American editions of *Woman Physiologically Considered* (1840) and *Beauty* (1845), written by the editor, "An American
Physician"—nearly two hundred pages for *Woman Physiologically Considered*, forty-three for *Beauty*. From the start it is clear that God, Christianity,
and divine law have a powerful presence in these appendices. The editor is
critical of Walker's exclusively naturalist approach to his subject and his exclusion of the "spiritual principle."[94] The mind is not simply matter (as we
find in Walker), but spirit added to matter. He also draws attention to what
is conspicuously absent in the Walker trilogy—the soul. There is more to
beauty than "physical goodness," since there is a soul as well as a body of
beauty, visible in expression, especially in the eyes, and in behavior.[95]
Woman's religious enthusiasm is not dismissed as superstition and cred-
ulity, evidence of her weak reasoning powers. Rather, it is "chiefly owing to
the superior sensibilities of woman, that religion has, in modern times,
shed its benign influence over the human family."[96] The "natural" role of
woman is not simply procreative and nurturant. Of even higher importance
are her educative, moral, and religious duties within the sphere of the home
and the family. "The moral destinies of the world, then, depend upon
moral influence, yea, maternal influence; for it is this which forms the mind,
the prejudices, the virtues of nations, as it unquestionably does of families,
of which nations are composed."[97]

What we find here is the ennoblement of woman through her moral role,
a role for which nature has peculiarly fitted her: "But nature has in general
assigned to the female intellect a different sphere, and to herself a different
calling. Endowed with the milder virtues, and those graces which are cal-

[93]Michael Ryan, *The Philosophy of Marriage* (London, 1837), p. 77. Like Walker, Ryan had
to defend the propriety of his undertaking. His book went through several editions but one
reviewer, at least, was outraged at its intrusion "on modest eyes all that civilized people agree
to conceal with decent care"(*British and Foreign Medical Review* 5 [April 1838]: 443.

[94]Alexander Walker, *Woman Physiologically Considered as to Mind, Morals, Marriage, Matrimonial Slavery, Infidelity, and Divorce*, edited by an American Physician (New York, 1840),
p. 315. This edition is hereafter cited as *Woman* (1840 ed.).

[95]Alexander Walker, *Beauty: Illustrated Chiefly by an Analysis and Classification of Beauty in
Woman*, edited by an American Physician (New York, 1845), p. 346.

[96]Walker, *Woman* (1840 ed.), p. 329.

[97]Ibid., p. 379.

culated to cheer, and soften and humanize the rougher sex, she is eminently fitted by her organization to fulfil her destiny, and shed the light of love and happiness over a degenerate race.—A higher destiny she could not seek; a loftier sphere she could not fill! may woman ever feel, that herein lies her highest glory,—that this constitutes her noblest aim!"[98] Whereas for Walker woman's importance lay in the improvement of the human species, for the American editor her role is one of moral salvation.

This ennobled view of woman and her function is accompanied both by a deemphasis on the importance of sexual activity to human health and happiness and by a much stronger emphasis on the moral criminality, as well as the sinfulness, of sexual transgression. Walker saw chastity as being as unnatural and unhealthy as promiscuity, but for the American editor it is a viable alternative to marriage. He completely disagrees with Walker on the subject of marital infidelity, condemning his views as "lax."[99] The consequences of infidelity are licentious conduct and the destruction of the home.

The American editor also condemns Walker's "reasonings" on divorce as "fallacious and unsound," since marriage is not only a civil contract, but also an "institution of *divine ordinance*."[100] Unhappily married couples should submit themselves to a fate they have voluntarily chosen. He denies that marital infidelity is the result of indissoluble marriages and that it is founded on nature, as Walker argues; rather, it springs from the violation of natural laws (an excellent instance, one might add, of the plasticity of nature's laws).

The American editor also disagrees with Walker on the subject of "matrimonial slavery," arguing that because husband and wife become one in marriage, the wife's financial independence would be a threat to "a happy and permanent union."[101] Certainly he exposes the anomalies in Walker's argument for woman's freedom in a marriage in which she is the subordinate partner. Whether her independence "does not destroy that authority which nature and the laws would seem to give a man over his wife, as well as that obedience and subjection which the rules of the gospel prescribe in the deportment of the wife, we leave to the judgment of the reader."[102] It is clear how the reader is expected to judge. But the editor is unaware of the anomalies in his own representation of a subordinate woman with a high mission, which sets up a "tension between subordination and influence, between moral power and political silence."[103]

[98]Ibid., pp. 323–24.
[99]Ibid., p. 413.
[100]Ibid., p. 390.
[101]Ibid., p. 394.
[102]Ibid., p. 396.
[103]Davidoff and Hall (n. 1 above), p. 183.

What is the relationship between the "woman" in the Walker trilogy and the "woman" in the American appendices? It is clear that—for all their differences—the two are fundamentally connected. Both are defined in terms of a sexual politics of gender difference that places them in a position of dependency and subordination, despite their supposed elevation as reproducers or redeemers. Both are confined to the private, domestic sphere. Both are excluded from participation in public and civic life. The women who try to enter this alien field are denounced and derided, in the words of the American editor, as "female brawlers."[104] Finally, both may be seen as instruments in the middle-class drive to establish its identity and authority, whether as sexual generators or moral regenerators.

Yet this is not the final conclusion to this essay, which would be all too gloomy and depressing for women. Rather, I want to end on a more positive note by considering the possibilities for actual women contained in the texts by Walker and the American editor. With regard to Walker, there is allowance of sexual pleasure (albeit an ambiguous allowance), his critique of "marital slavery," and his support of divorce. However, concerning women's reaction to the sexual politics of the text, he offers no position other than one of direct opposition, which would be dismissed on "scientific" grounds. On the other hand, for all their moral and religious conservatism, the American appendices allow women an agency denied in the Walker texts. Middle-class women seeking a place in the public sphere utilized the rhetoric of the morally superior, passionless woman for their own social and political purposes. They did not challenge the ideas of woman's nature and role within evangelical domestic ideology, but they used them to justify their entrance into the field of philanthropy (for which, it will be remembered, the woman of the Walker texts is unfitted), which was seen as an extension of woman's caring role in the family. The organizational skills and experience in public speaking that they acquired through their involvement in philanthropy were applied to the various campaigns that women—employing the rhetoric of their moral superiority—engaged in during the nineteenth century. Passionlessness was perhaps not such a high price to pay for these enabling possibilities.

104Walker, *Woman* (1840 ed.), p. 374.

Homosexual Behavior in the Nineteenth-Century Dutch Army

GERT HEKMA

Department of Sociology
University of Amsterdam

In THIS ARTICLE I undertake to examine manifest homosexual behavior and its repression in the nineteenth-century Royal Dutch Army.[1] Before going into my research material in detail, I will consider a few related issues concerning gay and military historiography. First, the debate over the various historical forms of homosexuality will be summarized. A different topic, homosexual behavior within homosocial arrangements, is dealt with in the following section. The main section sketches the organization of the Dutch army in the nineteenth century and sets forth my research material, the sex crimes brought to trial before the military court in Haarlem. This is followed by an overview of all sex crimes, of which homosexual cases make up the majority. The final sections provide pertinent information about homosexual behavior in the Dutch army, and in conclusion I offer some answers to the questions raised.

FORMS OF HOMOSEXUALITY

It has become increasingly clear from the work of Leo Boon, Arend H. Huussen, Jr., Dirk Jaap Noordam, and Theo van der Meer that a subculture of sodomites was emerging in the Dutch republic in the eighteenth century, as was the case in other urbanized centers of northwestern Europe.

My thanks to James D. Steakley for his comments on this article.

[1] See Gert Hekma, *Homoseksualiteit, een medische reputatie: De uitdoktering van de homoseksueel in negentiende-eeuws Nederland* (Amsterdam, 1987), for the history of the introduction of the term and concept of "homosexuality" in the Netherlands in the nineteenth century. When I use the terms "homosexual" and "homosexuality" here, they refer to homosexual behavior and not necessarily to fixed preferences or psychological states.

This essay originally appeared in the *Journal of the History of Sexuality* 1991, vol. 2, no. 2.

Because of the decriminalization of sodomy in 1811 in the Netherlands and the lack of action by the Dutch police in the realm of sexual crimes in the first half of the nineteenth century, little can be stated with certainty about the continuance of the Dutch sodomitical subculture of that era. Such a subculture clearly reemerged at the close of the nineteenth century.[2] Other authors indicate that the same was true for France, England, and Germany, so it is generally presumed that the subcultures, having come into being in the early 1700s, survived the intervening period, although only scant traces of these subcultures exist for the first half of the nineteenth century.

The character of these subcultures and these sodomites has been subject to close scrutiny. Randolph Trumbach has stated in two provocative articles that since about 1700, the sodomite's identity properly ought to be characterized as effeminate and that his object-choice was exclusively oriented toward the male sex: "I would propose that the most salient characteristic of the homosexual role from about 1700 to the present day has been the presumption that all men who engage in sexual relations with other men are effeminate members of a third or intermediate gender, who surrender their rights to be treated as dominant males, and are exposed instead to a merited contempt as a species of male whore." By contrast, the sodomite of the preceding period did not transgress gender lines but was instead a real male who made love to both women and boys. The "queen" identity of sodomites survives, according to Trumbach, to the present.[3]

In earlier articles treating the Netherlands of the second half of the nineteenth century, I have discussed the existence of different types of "wrong loves" and different subcultures of "wrong lovers" (in Dutch, *verkeerde liefdes* and *liefhebbers*). The most important were the casual forms of sexual

[2]See Dirk Jaap Noordam, "Sodomy in the Dutch Republic, 1600–1725," pp. 207–28; Leo Boon, "Those Damned Sodomites: Public Images of Sodomy in the Eighteenth-Century Netherlands," pp. 237–48; Arend H. Huussen, "Prosecution of Sodomy in Eighteenth-Century Frisia, Netherlands," pp. 249–62; and Theo van der Meer, "The Persecutions of Sodomites in Eighteenth-Century Amsterdam: Changing Perceptions of Sodomy," pp. 263–307, all in Kent Gerard and Gert Hekma, eds., *The Pursuit of Sodomy: Male Homosexuality in Renaissance and Enlightenment Europe* (New York, 1989); and on nineteenth-century Netherlands, see Gert Hekma, *Homoseksualiteit*, and "Wrong Lovers in the Nineteenth-Century Netherlands," *Journal of Homosexuality* 13, nos. 2/3 (1986/87): 43–56.

[3]See Randolph Trumbach, "Gender and the Homosexual Role in Modern Western Culture: The Eighteenth and Nineteenth Centuries Compared," in Dennis Altman et al., *Homosexuality, Which Homosexuality?* (Amsterdam, 1989), pp. 149–69, quotation on p. 153; and "The Birth of the Queen: Sodomy and the Emergence of Gender Equality in Modern Culture, 1660–1750," in Martin Bauml Duberman, Martha Vicinus, and George Chauncey, Jr., eds., *Hidden from History: Reclaiming the Gay and Lesbian Past* (New York, 1989), pp. 129–40. For a parallel argument, see Philippe Ariès, "Réflexions sur l'histoire de l'homosexualité," *Communications* ("Sexualités occidentales," ed. Philippe Ariès and André Béjin) 35 (1982): 56–67.

encounters of the streets and of all-male institutions such as the prison and the army; boy love, which often took the form of prostitution but sometimes remained chaste; and male love among men of the same age group. In my estimate, it was especially among this last group that effeminate identities existed, upon which the medical invention of homosexuality was based.[4]

Different forms of male love existed in the eighteenth, nineteenth, and twentieth centuries alongside each other; the one was not superseded by the other, and different styles developed in and among themselves. It seems apparent, for example, that male-male love in the form of romantic friendship was an important mode in which homosexual feelings were experienced in the first half of the nineteenth century, foremost in Germany and the Netherlands, but also elsewhere, and notably during the period for which data on the "queen" subcultures are missing.[5] It is, according to Ellen Moers, also the time that the dandy is appearing on the public stage, a figure steadily becoming more homosexual during this century.[6] The casual forms, typical for the lower classes, were rampant throughout the eighteenth and nineteenth centuries and provided an important resource of love and sexual relations for both boy and male lovers of the middle and upper classes.[7] The queens constituted a conspicuous presence among male lovers, but certainly they did not always dominate their circles, for example, at the time of the exaltation of romantic friendship. In his diaries, the German poet August von Platen (1796–1835), an ardent apostle of friendship, does not discuss effeminacy in relation to himself or any of his many loves, or indeed in any other context.[8] Concerning the Vere Street

[4]See Hekma, *Homoseksualiteit,* and Gert Hekma, "Sodomites, Platonic Lovers, Contrary Lovers: The Backgrounds of the Modern Homosexual," in Gerard and Hekma, eds., pp. 433–55.

[5]Hans Dietrich Hellbach, *Die Freundesliebe in der Deutschen Literatur* (Leipzig, 1931); Harry Oosterhuis, "De gave om gestalte te geven aan de vriendschap is een van de schoonste Duitse deugden," *Homologie* 12 (March/April 1990): 8–12; and Paul Derks, *Die Schande der heiligen Päderastie: Homosexualität und Öffenlichkeit in der Deutschen Literatur, 1750–1850* (Berlin, 1990). For England, see Jeffrey Richards, "'Passing the Love of Women': Manly Love and Victorian Society," in J. A. Mangan and James Walvin, eds., *Manliness and Morality: Middle-Class Masculinity in Britain and America, 1800–1940* (New York, 1987), pp. 92–122. For North America, see Michael Lynch, "'Here Is Adhesiveness': From Friendship to Homosexuality," *Victorian Studies* 29 (1985): 67–96; and Robert K. Martin, "Knights-Errant and Gothic Seducers: The Representation of Male Friendship in Mid-Nineteenth-Century America," in Duberman, Vicinus, and Chauncey, eds., pp. 169–82.

[6]Ellen Moers, *The Dandy: Brummell to Beerbohm* (New York, 1978).

[7]See, for example, Jeffrey Weeks, "Inverts, Perverts, and Mary-Annes: Male Prostitution and the Regulation of Homosexuality in England in the Nineteenth and Early Twentieth Centuries," in Duberman, Vicinus, and Chauncey, eds., pp. 195–211.

[8]August von Platen, *Tagebücher,* ed. Rüdiger Gönner (Zurich, 1990). I did not see the complete edition (*Tagebücher,* ed. G. von Laubmann and L. von Scheffer, 2 vols. [Stuttgart,

scandal in 1810 in London, one author claims, after citing many names of queens: "It is a generally received opinion, and a very natural one, that the prevalence of this passion has for its object effeminate delicate beings only: but this seems to be . . . a mistaken notion."[9] It would be equally mistaken to conclude from the publicity given to queens that their style actually set the tone for all homosexual subcultures, be it in practice or in opinion.

In the 1860s, Karl Heinrich Ulrichs initially defined homosexuals (in German, *Urninge,* or Uranians) as male bodies with female souls, but in the course of his investigations he eventually had to admit that many did not show the presumed signs of effeminacy. When, in 1897, Magnus Hirschfeld began a homosexual movement and set forth his theory of homosexuals as a third sex different from both men and women, others such as Benedict Friedländer and Hans Blüher opposed his claim, arguing that homosexuals were precisely examples of masculinity.[10] The French literature beginning with Claude François Michéa in 1849 may provide numerous instances of femininity in homosexual males, but on the other hand such an important author as Ambroise Tardieu had very little to offer in this regard among his many cases of "péderastie."[11] In the early works dealing with "psychopathia sexualis," there were certainly many cases of queens, for example in the work of Hieronimus Fränkel, Johann Ludwig Casper, Karl Friedrich Otto Westphal, and Richard von Krafft-Ebing. But only haltingly was the theory developed that homosexual behavior and effeminacy were closely linked, and it would not go uncontested.

The notion that, ever since the eighteenth century, received opinion

---

1896–1900]), but there is little chance that seeing it would change my claim. See also two biographies of adherents of German friendship, "Zur Seelenkrankheitskunde," in *Magazin zur Erfahrungsseelenkunde,* vol. 8 (Berlin, 1791), pt. 1, pp. 6–10, and pt. 2, pp. 100–106. For an overview of the friendship tradition, see Hekma, "Sodomites, Platonic Lovers, Contrary Lovers," pp. 435–40.

[9]Robert Holloway, *The Phoenix of Sodom; or, The Vere Street Coterie: Being an Exhibition of the Gambols Practised by the Ancient Lechers of Sodom and Gomorrha, Embellished and Improved with the Modern Refinements in Sodomitical Practices by the Members of the Vere Street Coterie, of Detestable Memory* (London, 1813), p. 13; reprinted in Randolph Trumbach, ed., *Sodomy Trials: Seven Documents* (New York, 1986).

[10]See James D. Steakley, *The Homosexual Emancipation Movement in Germany* (New York, 1975), and Hubert C. Kennedy, *Ulrichs: The Life and Works of Karl Heinrich Ulrichs, Pioneer of the Modern Gay Movement* (Boston, 1988).

[11]See Hekma, *Homoseksualiteit,* pp. 57–58. The French psychiatrist Claude François Michéa was the first to develop a biological theory of homosexuality in which effeminacy held a central place; see his "Des déviations de l'appétit vénérien," *Union médicale* (July 17, 1849), pp. 338–39; Ambroise Tardieu, *Etude médico-légale sur les attentats aux moeurs,* 5th ed. (Paris, 1867), pp. 171–221, the third chapter of which was entitled "De la pédérastie et sodomie." See also Jean-Paul Aron and Roger Kempf, *Le pénis et la démoralisation de l'Occident* (Paris, 1978); and Pierre Hahn, *Nos ancêtres les pervers: La vie des homosexuels sous le II empire* (Paris, 1979), both containing many documents of the period.

about homosexual males has held them to be effeminate cannot be substantiated on the basis of either theories about male love or sources concerning homosexual subcultures. Granted, the opinion that homosexuals are effeminate has become more widespread since the late nineteenth century, and it even appears that ever more men have lived according to this stereotype; but other forms have existed alongside the effeminate forms. Especially for the early nineteenth century, Trumbach's thesis lacks proof both in practice and in theory, whereas it is clear that another form, male-male friendship, existed and was also defended on an intellectual level. And it was definitely not an ascetic tradition. This sort of friendship may have constituted a transitional stage in gay history, temporally situated between the Mary-Annes and mollies of the eighteenth and the Uranians of the late nineteenth centuries. But certainly the effeminate type gradually became the prototype of homosexual love in the medical and popular literature of the times. Even for the eighteenth century, the factual material on which Trumbach's assertions are based seems rather slim, for the effeminate sodomite was only one figure among many others. For the time being, the universality of this type in the eighteenth century remains to be proven, and the presence and importance of any style of homosexuality have yet to be ascertained for other periods.

Gay history needs more sophisticated theories than have been used until now. It has to move beyond social constructionism and a facile critique of an essentialism that is actually defended by no one.[12] Social constructionism originated with a focus on the medicalization of homosexuality at the end of the nineteenth and the beginning of the twentieth centuries.[13] Later, eighteenth-century specialists asserted that "the making of the modern homosexual" ought to be traced back to the eighteenth century, as Trumbach does with his elevation of the queen to the dominant type of homosexual since the 1700s.[14] Both approaches slight the diversity and development of homosexual styles and the related ways to theorize these forms. In the following, I aim to enter this debate on the basis of research findings concerning sex crimes in the Dutch army from 1830 to 1899. To what extent are certain types of homosexuality discernable in this setting?

[12]See, for example, John Boswell's proposal to move beyond constructionism: "Concepts, Experience, and Sexuality," in Edward Stein, ed., *Forms of Desire: Sexual Orientation and the Social Constructionist Controversy* (New York, 1990), pp. 133–74.

[13]See Michel Foucault, *The History of Sexuality: An Introduction,* vol. 1 of *The History of Sexuality,* trans. Robert Hurley (New York, 1978); Jeffrey Weeks, *Sex, Politics, and Society: The Regulation of Sexuality since 1800* (London, 1981); Kenneth Plummer, ed., *The Making of the Modern Homosexual* (London, 1981); and Hekma, *Homoseksualiteit.*

[14]The first to state this was Mary McIntosh, "The Homosexual Role," in *Social Problems,* vol. 16 (Fall 1968), which was reprinted in Plummer, ed., pp. 30–44; Alan Bray, *Homosexuality in Renaissance England* (London, 1982); and Trumbach's many articles, two of which are cited in n. 3 above. For the Netherlands, see the articles by van der Meer and Noordam in n. 2 above.

SEX IN HOMOSOCIAL ARRANGEMENTS

Male homosexual behavior in homosocial (all-male) institutions is clearly an underresearched subject. There are a few books on English boarding schools, and Barry R. Burg has given some disputable suggestions concerning sodomy among pirates. John Chandos has claimed that homosexual practices were rampant in some nineteenth-century English boarding schools, while others remained relatively free of them. Burg's material on pirates is not especially reliable because his speculations about sexual behavior were distilled from present-day literature on homosocial arrangements.[15] Arthur N. Gilbert has conducted research on male sexual behavior in the British navy from the seventeenth through the nineteenth centuries, and Jan Oosterhoff has investigated the Dutch East India Company ships of the eighteenth century.[16]

Gilbert arrived at the conclusion that the British navy responded very harshly to cases of buggery, especially in time of war. In the periods 1756–1806 and 1810–16, he found that there were nineteen and twenty-six capital sentences, respectively. He attributed the sharp decline in executions in the nineteenth century following the Napoleonic wars both to the more humane outlook of that era and to the growing awareness that homosexual behavior could be a result of insanity. He explained the vehement persecution of sodomy in different ways. In the first place, Gilbert underlined the importance of discipline, especially because sodomy was considered "somehow symptomatic of lack of discipline and control in all areas of life." But he gave more weight to vaguer arguments, such as the Bataillian one that "sexuality has always been one mode of affirming life in the face of death," and stressed societal abhorrence of anality.[17] Oosterhoff noted that more than two hundred men were tried for sodomy before the Court of Justice in Cape Town during the period 1705–92. Most of them were transferred to the court from the ships of the Dutch East India Company while making a stop in Cape Town on their voyage between the Dutch East Indies and the Netherlands. Here death penalties were carried out only in cases of recidivism.[18]

[15]See John Chandos, *Boys Together: English Public Schools, 1800–1864* (London, 1984), chap. 14; and Danny Danziger, *Eton Voices: Interviews* (London, 1988), for fascinating contemporary material; Barry R. Burg, *Sodomy and the Perception of Evil: English Sea Rovers in the Seventeenth-Century Caribbean* (New York, 1983).

[16]Arthur N. Gilbert, "The Africaine Courts-Martial: A Study of Buggery and the Royal Navy," *Journal of Homosexuality* 1, no. 1 (1974): 111–22; and "Buggery and the British Navy," *Journal of Social History* 10 (1976/77): 72–98; Jan Oosterhoff, "Sodomy at Sea and at the Cape of Good Hope during the Eighteenth Century," in Gerard and Hekma, eds., pp. 229–36. See also Frank Arnal, "Le vice marin," in Patrick Cardon, ed., *Actes du Colloque International, Sorbonne décembre 1989* (Lille, 1990), 2:10–16, on the French naval base at Toulon in the 1920s.

[17]Gilbert, "Buggery and the British Navy," pp. 85–88.

[18]Oosterhoff, pp. 229–30, and personal communication, February 1991.

George Chauncey has offered a fine analysis of a homosexual scandal in the American naval base at Newport in 1919–20, at a time when the definitions and boundaries of sex and gender were undergoing rapid change. A homosexual drag subculture existed in Newport, with queens (primarily civilians) taking a place of prominence. Many soldiers participated in this subculture as "husbands" of the queens. In the elaborate minutes of the criminal proceedings, only once a new medical term for homosexuality— "invert"—was mentioned. Particular interest attached to the role of the clergymen involved: their professional attitude was considered effeminate and homosexual by the naval authorities, whereas the church endorsed it as exemplary behavior.[19] Just as the boundaries of masculinity became narrower at the time, so the definition of effeminacy was broadening. More men could thus be defined as effeminate.[20] The question arises whether these drag practices and these "queer" self-definitions were also present in the Dutch army.

Little may be known about sex in the military, but considerable research has been devoted to prison sexuality. The practice of "the unmentionable sin" (clearly to be understood as homosexual behavior) within jails became a political issue in the nineteenth-century Netherlands. As elsewhere, the advantages and disadvantages of shared versus solitary confinement were hotly debated. The Netherlands ultimately opted for solitary confinement, and one of the most important reasons behind this decision was the incidence of sodomy in the sleeping quarters. The authorities were persuaded that onanism in solitary confinement was less dangerous than homosexual seduction in the dormitories. Within the homosocial arrangement of prison, discipline had to be strictly enforced and became an issue of great concern for the government.[21] In contemporary sociological literature, there is some discussion of sex in prisons, especially with reference to the United States, where a considerable amount of prison homosexuality is reported.[22] To my knowledge, there are no such records of the incidence of homosexuality in the military. Researchers concerned with the history and persecution of sodomy have paid little or no attention to the military, or for that matter to monasteries.[23] Thus the following findings on the sex lives

[19]George Chauncey, Jr., "Christian Brotherhood or Sexual Perversion? Homosexual Identities and the Construction of Sexual Boundaries in the World War I Era," in Duberman, Vicinus, and Chauncey, eds., pp. 294–317. See also Lawrence R. Murphy, *Perverts by Official Order: The Campaign against Homosexuals by the United States Navy* (New York, 1988).

[20]For male gender boundaries, see Joe L. Dubbert, *A Man's Place: Masculinity in Transition* (Englewood Cliffs, NJ, 1979).

[21]Hekma, *Homoseksualiteit*, pp. 112–20.

[22]Wayne S. Wooden and Jay Parker, *Men behind Bars: Sexual Exploitation in Prison* (New York, 1982). In this study, 65 percent of the prison inmates reported homosexual behavior, whereas 21.5 percent considered themselves homosexual or bisexual.

[23]In Gerard and Hekma, eds., there is nothing on the topic, but there is an article on sodomy in a homosocial arrangement (Oosterhoff). On the borders of friendship and homo-

of soldiers in the nineteenth-century military opens up new territory in the history of sexuality.

My interests focus on the kind of sex crimes that were prosecuted, the social structure of homosociality and homosexuality, how the military and the soldiers arranged sexuality in an all-male environment, and how discipline was enforced.

THE DUTCH ARMY

The Dutch army consisted in the nineteenth century of approximately sixty thousand soldiers, mostly conscripts. Each year, eleven thousand eighteen-year-old men, about one-fifth of their age cohort, were conscripted into the army by the drawing of lots. Conscription was a despised system, introduced under Napoléon I for his many campaigns, yet nevertheless continued in the Kingdom of the Netherlands after Napoléon's defeat. The conscripts had to serve five years, but often they were furloughed before they finished their service time. A young man from a well-to-do family could escape military service by paying for a *remplacant,* another young man who took his place. Many youngsters from the upper classes did so because of the lengthy term and the bad living conditions of the soldiers. The Dutch army also made use of hirelings, often foreigners, especially for service in the colonies. The French poet Arthur Rimbaud was one of the more famous soldiers of the Dutch East Indies army, one who deserted, however, as soon as he reached his destination.[24]

Most soldiers tried before the military court in Haarlem were Dutch. The archives of this court form the basis of this article on sex crimes in the Dutch army, covering the period 1830–99. The tribunal had jurisdiction over the approximately twenty thousand soldiers who were encamped in the two northwestern provinces of the Netherlands, Northern Holland

---

sexuality more has been written; see, for example, Giovanni Dall'Orto, "'Socratic Love' as a Disguise for Same-Sex Love in the Italian Renaissance," pp. 33–65; and George S. Rousseau, "'In the House of Madame Van der Tasse, on the Long Bridge': A Homosocial University Club in Early Modern Europe," pp. 311–47, both in Gerard and Hekma, eds.; and Alan Bray, "Homosexuality and the Signs of Male Friendship in Elizabethan England," *History Workshop* 29 (Spring 1990), pp. 1–19. See also n. 5 above. For the military, we have to use present-day material, as furnished in Allan Bérubé, *Coming Out Under Fire: The History of Gay Men and Women in World War Two* (New York, 1990); and Colin J. Williams and Martin S. Weinberg, *Homosexuals and the Military: A Study of Less than Honorable Discharge* (New York, 1971). For monastic life, most research concerns convents; see Judith C. Brown, *Immodest Acts: The Life of a Lesbian Nun in Renaissance Italy* (New York, 1985); and Odile Arnold, *Le corps et l'âme: La vie des religieuses au XIXe siècle* (Paris, 1984).

[24]There is no good history of the nineteenth-century Dutch army. Most information has been collected from *Bepalingen en voorschriften omtrent organisatie, garnizoensindeeling en mobilisatie van het leger* (The Hague, 1883).

and Utrecht. The most important garrisons were Amsterdam, Haarlem, Den Helder (a naval base), Utrecht, and Amersfoort. Most of the cases brought before the Haarlem court, perhaps one hundred a year, concerned insubordination and theft, both from the army itself as well as from fellow soldiers. An incriminated soldier occasionally had already been convicted of the same crime in a civil court proceeding if he had been arrested outside his garrison. In such cases, the prosecution was repeated in the court-martial for specific supplementary penalties. Thus a convicted soldier could receive a dishonorable discharge from the army after serving his prison sentence.

The sexual crimes of which the soldiers were convicted were defined as such in the Dutch criminal law, which was the same as the French penal code until 1886. This meant that only public indecencies and sexual assault constituted crimes. On December 31, 1845, the minister of war promulgated a special order concerning "unnatural fornication," stating that soldiers who could not be convicted of transgressions or inclinations should not be discharged from the army but instead placed in the second disciplinary class. This was a form of military detention from which the soldier could be advanced to the first disciplinary class if he behaved well. The detention had to be carried out in solitary confinement under strict surveillance. Only after a thorough investigation into the possibility of prosecution under criminal law had been undertaken could this procedure be implemented. Such soldiers were not to be discharged from the army, for to do so would apparently reward illicit behavior.[25] This measure stands in sharp contrast to the policy followed by the United States military since World War II. According to Allan Bérubé, the United States Army considers homosexuality entirely incompatible with the military and therefore discharges homosexuals.[26] The Dutch minister of war made the opposite choice. He linked unnatural fornication not with effeminacy or unmanliness but with the danger of seduction in the barracks, and he therefore called for solitary confinement. On the level of state policy in the Netherlands, Trumbach's model of the queen was strikingly absent one hundred years after it should have become general.

In my research I have not been able to locate regulations for soldiers concerning their daily furloughs. It is clear that soldiers had the opportunity to visit prostitutes, because in the late 1850s the minister of war demanded that the cities with garrisons introduce medical control of prostitution to combat the high incidence of sexually transmitted diseases among the military.[27] The court archives also indicate that many soldiers succeeded in

[25]In *Recueil militaire, bevattende wetten, besluiten en orders betreffende de Koninklijke Nederlandsche Landmagt* [for 1845], pt. 2 (The Hague, 1846), pp. 197–99. I did not find other references to regulations concerning unnatural lewdness.

[26]Bérubé, chap. 1.

[27]Hekma, *Homoseksualiteit*, p. 154.

leaving camp without permission. It appears that control and discipline were not strictly enforced in the Dutch army. Soldiers were given the chance to go on leave from their garrisons. But even if they did so, they would have found it difficult to consort regularly with prostitutes because of their low pay.[28] Prostitution cannot have been the sole sexual outlet of the soldiers. Many men found sexual outlets elsewhere: in masturbation, with their fellow soldiers, or with animals.

SEX CRIMES

When I began my research on sex crimes in the Netherlands of the nineteenth century, I was struck by the proportion of sex crimes in the military as compared to those recorded among the civilian population: between 1850 and 1870, one of every six men convicted for public indecency was sentenced before a court-martial. In later years, this proportion changed because of the higher number of civilian convictions. We must remember, however, that until the 1870s, the number of reported sex crimes in the Netherlands was quite low. In the 1860s, there was a total of 371 cases of public indecency, which was the most common sex crime of the time (the Netherlands had sixty thousand soldiers in a population of three million in 1850).

My research covers all the cases brought before the court in the period 1830–99. The court dealt with a total of 104 men charged with sex crimes, most of whom were accused of public indecency. This included all indecent behavior in public, from swimming in the nude or exposing one's genitals to actually engaging in sexual relations. Indecencies that occurred in private but could be seen from a public place (for example, through a window) could also be prosecuted. As military establishments, including their barracks, were considered public places, most sex crimes came under this heading.[29] But there were also several cases of aggravated assault, rape, and sexual assault against minors and dependents, such as lower-ranking soldiers, and these crimes could be and were punished far more severely than public indecency. Until 1860, most of those convicted for public indecency were sentenced to a year or eighteen months of imprisonment, which was

[28]For the history of prostitution in nineteenth-century Netherlands, see Hekma, *Homoseksualiteit,* pp. 149–64; An Huitzing, *Betaalde liefde: Prostituées in Nederland, 1850–1900* (Bergen, 1983); F. A. Stemvers, *Meisjes van plezier: De geschiedenis van de prostitutie in Nederland* (Weesp, 1985), pp. 36–76; and Diet Sijmons, "Een noodzakelijk kwaad, maar voor wie? Prostitutie in Nederland in de tweede helft van de negentiende eeuw," *Jaarboek voor Vrouwengeschiedenis* (Nijmegen, 1980), 1:65–110.

[29]On the definition of sex crimes, see Gert Hekma, "'Bewaar mij voor den waanzin van het recht': De jurisprudentie met betrekking tot homoseksueel gedrag in Nederland, 1811–1911," *Hollandse Studiën* 22 (1989): 115–24.

reduced to six months after 1860, when solitary confinement was introduced and equated with one full year in shared confinement. After 1880, the average sentence was approximately three months, although sentences for assault were often more severe, especially when children were involved. The longest sentence given was ten years for a twenty-one-year-old trumpeter who had forced a younger soldier to perform oral sex and had sexually violated a girl with his finger. But in another case, a captain who had abducted a fourteen-year-old girl was sentenced to only three months in jail.[30]

Some seventy-two soldiers (and possibly seventy-four) were tried for homosexual offenses,[31] fourteen for heterosexual offenses, one for both homosexual and heterosexual offenses, fourteen for bestiality, and one for exhibitionism. Many of the cases of bestiality concerned cavalrymen who had sexual relations with horses (six), while other cases involved dogs (three), goats (three), and sheep (two). Of the one hundred and four soldiers, twenty were acquitted; of these, fifteen cases involved homosexuality, four bestiality, and one heterosexuality. We cannot conclude from these numbers that homosexuality was rampant in the barracks, but it must have been rather widespread to have been tried so often in comparison with other sex crimes. On the other hand, many heterosexual crimes may have been brushed aside by the authorities. In eight of the homosexual cases, the soldiers and petty officers were convicted not of public indecency but of assault or aggravated assault on dependents, and they received sentences varying from three months to five years. All charges of bestiality were prosecuted as public indecencies, while eleven of the fourteen heterosexual cases were prosecuted as aggravated assaults. The punishments were as severe as in the homosexual cases. It is interesting to note that nine of the fourteen heterosexual indictments concerned girls between four and fourteen years of age. Whereas most of the homosexual and bestial crimes took place in the barracks or within the garrison, the heterosexual ones often happened outside the camp. And finally, all the cases involving homosexuality and bestiality concerned the lower ranks, while the heterosexual defendants included a captain and a lieutenant, both of whom got off with very light sentences (three months and one month, respectively).

Table 1 shows the temporal distribution of the cases. The rise in the

[30]The cases discussed here are found in the Rijksarchief (State Archive) North Holland in Haarlem, Archief Auditeur-Militair Haarlem (hereafter AAMH), maps 86–155, covering the period 1830–99. I cite the cases with the date on which the higher military court in The Hague judged in appeal or confirmed the judgment of the military court in Haarlem. The two cases mentioned here, respectively, are AAMH, September 4, 1867, and AAMH, February 9, 1883.

[31]Two men were acquitted together for public indecency in 1836, so we can presume they were suspected of a homosexual relation, but the archives do not give sufficient information in this respect. AAMH, October 28, 1836.

TABLE 1 Number ~f Persons in Courts-Martial Accused of Crimes Involving Homosexuality, Heteros   ~ty, and Bestiality (Convictions and Acquittals)*

Convict Acquit						
	Homosexuality		Heterosexuality		Bestiality	
Decade	Convict	Acquit	Convict	Acquit	Convict	Acquit
1830–39	—	2**	—	—	1	—
1840–49	6	1	1	—	—	—
1850–59	3	—	—	—	4	1
1860–69	8	6	1	—	1	—
1870–79	24	4	2	1	1	2
1880–89	13	—	5	—	1	1
1890–99	5	2	4	—	2	—
Total	59	13 (15?)	13	1	10	4

Source—Rijksarchief North Holland (Haarlem), Archief Auditeur-Militair Haarlem, maps 86–155.

*The mixed homosexual/heterosexual and exhibitionistic cases are omitted.

**Two men also were acquitted together for public indecency in 1836, so we can presume that they were suspected of a homosexual relation, but the archives do not give sufficient information to confirm it.

number of homosexual prosecutions among the military in the period 1850–80 coincided with the increase of such cases brought before civilian courts; but while the number of prosecutions there continued to rise, the number in the military courts declined sharply after 1880.[32] I can offer no explanation for this shift. The decline is even more remarkable in light of the fact that the revised Dutch criminal law of 1886 extended the number and definition of sex crimes, which helps to explain the increase in the number of heterosexual cases.

HOMOSEXUAL BEHAVIOR BROUGHT BEFORE THE MILITARY COURT IN HAARLEM

In 1870, a marine, Mijas Schaap, tried to touch the genitals of his mate on the next cot, and when the man rebuffed his advances, the accused went on to the next bed. This scene was repeated twice, until finally with the fourth marine Schaap had his way, joining the man on his cot. The other soldiers heard them whispering and moving, but only when the noise awakened another marine did the bunk-mates of the sodomites decide to take action, on the initiative of this last marine.[33] The ease with which Schaap approached his comrades is as amazing as their slow reaction. Also, the

[32] See Hekma, *Homoseksualiteit,* p. 106.
[33] AAMH, May 6, 1870.

willingness of one marine to give in to his desires is remarkable. How often had Schaap seduced his mates before he was der̶̶̶ced? We will never know, but other similar cases indicate that it was not too difficult to find sex partners in the barracks or elsewhere within the garrison. Men who were more prudent than Schaap would not often have run into trouble.

Two other soldiers were even less inhibited than Schaap. André Leroy assaulted three mates in succession, and Bernard Bongenaer was condemned for having pursued other soldiers in "several places such as the detention room, the train wagon, the guardhouse, the stockade, the yard of the barracks, and its public convenience."[34] The stockades of the barracks are often mentioned in these indictments. This suggests that some soldiers addicted to the pursuit of this pleasure were rather heedless in seducing their comrades and ran into problems only in new situations, such as the stockades. It is also possible that bunk-mates were disinclined to denounce the soldiers with whom they had lived for some time in the barracks unless there were aggravating circumstances. Such a balance, of course, did not exist in the stockades.

In certain ways the barracks produced homosexual behavior. Fully half of the charges of public indecencies on the part of soldiers involved this setting. Sex was possible, in the first place, because the barracks dormitories were unlighted and crowded with young men who, moreover, were often drunk. Intoxication was mentioned in connection with twenty-five defendants, and of seventy-two men indicted for homosexual indecencies, fifty were between the ages of twenty and twenty-nine, which is considered to be a male's sexually most active age. Even if other soldiers wanted to denounce their bunk-mates, it was often difficult to prove what had actually happened. For a conviction, the courts required two witnesses to testify that they had seen the defendant commit the act, unless he confessed his crime. In many cases, the defendants were acquitted because the witnesses could not swear to have seen the bare genitals. In some cases involving a defendant who had tried to seduce various mates and had groped their private parts, the serial indecencies could not be proved because there was only one witness for each assault, which fell short of the evidentiary requirements for a conviction. Also, many of the accused seeking acquittal claimed they had been drunk or seduced by their comrade. In most instances, such exculpatory or extenuating circumstances did not sway the courts, although in exceptional cases they were accepted. Because of the difficulties in arresting the sodomites, their mates tried in some cases to entrap them. Joseph Bendix, for example, had wanted to seduce his two bunk-mates to "dishonorable acts." On the next night, the soldiers decided to feign sleeping. Bendix waited until everything was silent, then asked his

[34]AAMH, November 17, 1869; AAMH, March 27, 1847.

neighbor if he were asleep, and when he got no answer he started to open the man's trousers and fondle his genitals. At that moment, the soldier jumped up and punched Bendix; an indictment followed.[35]

In cases when an accusation could not be proven, there was another method of handling the case at the disposal of the authorities. Accompanying some court proceedings is a copy of the confidential report on the accused. From these reports, it appears that soldiers who could not be convicted were indeed placed in the second disciplinary class, in accordance with the order of the minister of war. It was the severest penalty possible outside the criminal law.[36] Jan Willem Assie was accused of public indecency with a drunken fellow soldier, but he was acquitted because he only had laid his hand on his companion's thigh. Two years later, his superiors again suspected him of buggery in an instance that could not be proven. He nonetheless was consigned to the second disciplinary class, upgraded to the first class after three months, and finally released as a common soldier after another four months. A year later, Assie was apprehended flagrante delicto with a cavalryman and this time was sentenced to twelve months in prison. It is in connection with this sentence that we learn about Assie's former status in the first and second disciplinary classes.[37] By implementing this approach, it was possible for officers to mete out sentences as severe as the solitary confinement of the courts and to do so even if an accusation could not be proven. Another soldier, Vitus de Birk, spent seven months in the two disciplinary classes because his superiors were convinced that he practiced unnatural crimes.[38] From this supplementary source we also have information concerning a sergeant who was convicted for mutual masturbation with a corporal, and who had previously been in the disciplinary class for a sexual assault on a young woman.[39] His desires certainly were not exclusively homosexual, and we may surmise that the same is true for many other indicted soldiers. One soldier, convicted for having sexual intercourse with a horse, was asked by the court why he did not go to prostitutes, to which he replied that he did not have the money to do so.[40] Homosexual behavior, or bestiality for that matter, was a cheap and easy way to have sexual pleasure.

Most of the accused did not succeed in consummating their sexual deeds, as they were caught in the act. The precise acts that were being perpetrated often cannot be ascertained, both because in many instances the men had only started touching each other and because the terms used in the

[35]AAMH, May 8, 1878.
[36]As explained above, p. 274.
[37]AAMH, October 19, 1865; AAMH, December 10, 1869.
[38]AAMH, November 3, 1865.
[39]AAMH, June 4, 1886.
[40]AAMH, November 23, 1875.

court archives are vague, such as *ontucht* (vice or lewdness) and "loathsome posture." The specific sexual acts mentioned most frequently are anal penetration and mutual masturbation; fellatio is mentioned only rarely. The type of act apparently had no influence on the severity of the sentence.

Nearly half of the cases (twenty-nine men) involved consensual sex. Most of these relations were consummated in the sleeping quarters of the barracks, but pairs of soldiers were also arrested in other places. These men were the most ingenious in presenting excuses, such as having been intoxicated. In the case of a sergeant and a corporal who were arrested in an Amsterdam park, the sergeant testified that he had been drunk, while the corporal stated that he had been forced by his partner. They did not succeed in convincing the court of their innocence.[41] But two young marines who were found in "loathsome postures" in another Amsterdam park were acquitted, because they claimed they had only been relieving themselves. This was confirmed by a police officer who had been dispatched to the park following their arrest, for he indeed found their stools on the spot. According to the testimony, the marines also made remarks after their arrest that suggested culpability. The younger one confirmed to the arresting officer that he had been the "wife." And both marines apparently even tried to bribe the night watchmen not to arrest them.[42]

Precise investigative work was key in another case. A sergeant and a corporal were arrested on the ramparts on Naarden. There was only one witness, but the responsible under-officer immediately set off for the scene of arrest and thus was able to testify that the grass was downtrodden at that spot and that he had even found a substance looking most like "the raw white of an egg." The court held this to be definite proof of public indecency.[43]

Regrettably, information on the sexual discourses of the soldiers is documented in only a few cases. In one, a trumpeter named Torrer complained that another soldier wanted to "queer" him (*flikkeren,* which as a verb is nonexistent in Dutch).[44] "Queer" (*flikker*) was also used as a noun.[45] One soldier remarked to bystanders that another soldier wanted to "sodomize" him (*sodomieteren,* also unknown as a verb in Dutch).[46] Two twenty-one-year-old infantrymen mutually masturbated each other on a cot, and witnesses heard them say, "You have to strip naked," "Aren't you ready?" and "Yes, I am ready, feel it."[47] When trying to seduce a trumpeter, the drunken

[41]AAMH, June 20, 1875.
[42]AAMH, March 30, 1874.
[43]AAMH, June 4, 1886.
[44]AAMH, August 13, 1895.
[45]AAMH, February 11, 1887.
[46]AAMH, November 18, 1861.
[47]AAMH, February 24, 1891.

corporal Andreas Enders said to him, "What a lovely little trumpeter you are," and "Let me feel your little sweet one," whereupon he tried to touch the trumpeter's genitals. The object of his desire then turned around, which the corporal understood not as a refusal but as an indication that the trumpeter was embarrassed in this situation, so he continued his advances and proposed to the trumpeter, "Come on to the street, then we can do a little thing, I'm so horny."[48] Several years earlier, the following utterance was reported of two soldiers who enjoyed each other's company in a berth: "You are my best cock." The men lay naked against each other and embraced each other "as a man a woman."[49] This gender metaphor also appears in other indictments. In the same year, a soldier testified that the accused had touched his genitals "as if he were a girl."[50]

Such gender metaphors are also documented in other archival sources. There are at least two ways of interpreting these metaphors. On the one hand, it may refer to the traditional sex/gender system of the sodomite: men who were approached felt themselves put in the passive (non-male) sex role and were afraid to be penetrated. In my opinion, this was the case in both the military and the civilian court cases where this gender metaphor was used. The second possibility is that anxiety about being put in the female role actually referred to being considered a queen and having a homosexual identity, if we assume that homosexual behavior and effeminacy were conflated, as in Trumbach's sex/gender system. This seems less likely in these cases. According to an Amsterdam court proceeding of 1830, a man was approached by someone described as a "sodomite" and as "being known to commit unnatural fornication"; here, the metaphor of effeminacy was applied not to the sodomite, but to the solicited man who had been put in a passive, unmanly role. The gender of the sodomite was certainly not questioned. The use of the gender metaphor can indicate both sex/gender systems, and it is not always possible to disentangle its references.[51]

Not only cases of public indecency were prosecuted, but also aggravated assaults, assaults on minors, and sex with dependents. A fifteen-year-old trumpeter was caught in the act of rubbing his penis against the buttocks of a three-year-old boy. Probably because of his age, he was given a light sentence: three months in prison.[52] Another soldier convicted of touching two boys, age fifteen and twelve, was sentenced to five years.[53] The severest sentence in this series was handed down in the case of a twenty-one-year-old trumpeter, Petrus Wittebol, who had touched the bare buttocks of a girl

[48]AAMH, April 15, 1877.
[49]AAMH, August 30, 1861.
[50]AAMH, April 19, 1861.
[51]Hekma, *Homoseksualiteit*, p. 236.
[52]AAMH, September 19, 1884.
[53]AAMH, October 7, 1873.

(no age indicated) and violently assaulted another soldier (no age indicated, but probably in his late teens). Wittebol was condemned to ten years.[54] Four out of seven assault cases were tried after the introduction of the revised criminal code in 1886, which extended the definition of sex crimes. The sentences were less severe than earlier, but more consistent. The hardest sentence after 1886, for a prison term of three years, was handed down in the case of a soldier in a hospital, who had masturbated two soldiers "until a seminal discharge took place." The young men were asleep in the barracks where the accused was on guard duty. How he succeeded in bringing them to climax without awakening them was not explained.[55]

In contradiction to the supposition of Gilbert that homosexuality increasingly was considered insanity and was therefore prosecuted less severely, psychical abnormalities are never mentioned in the Dutch material, and the court officials never sought the expert testimony of psychiatrists. The same was true of contemporary civil courts, which only started to rely on psychiatric expertise in the final decade of the nineteenth century. Nor was medical testimony concerning the clinical evidence of sodomy requested by military courts, and rarely so by civil courts.[56]

Sexual slanders were brought before the military courts in addition to sex crimes. One soldier was charged with slander after telling his fellow soldiers in the barracks that a certain captain had "obliged him to come to his quarters and that the captain forced him to do things and committed acts against him of a very obscene and vicious nature." Although these slurs were contrary to military discipline and were of a sort that would "expose [the captain,] if true, to the contempt and hatred of the citizenry," the court ruled that the barracks did not constitute a public place, and thus the soldier had not committed a crime.[57] This is a remarkable decision, because the court never hesitated to consider indecencies in the barracks to be public deeds. And it is also remarkable that they did not shield the captain, surely a fellow officer, from this defamation.

One soldier, who was being taken into custody for an unrelated crime, resisted the arresting sergeant, shouting at him, "Keep off my body, you dirty hound, I'll grab your sodomite! [Not a standard Dutch noun—he meant cock.] This is really a sodomitical thieves' gang here." He was sentenced to be drummed out of the military.[58] But how true was his characterization of the barracks, and how routine was homosexual behavior in the sleeping quarters?

[54]AAMH, September 4, 1867.
[55]AAMH, June 12, 1895.
[56]Hekma, *Homoseksualiteit,* pp. 228–30, and Gert Hekma, "Een reeks schandalen in Enkhuizen," *Homologie* 12 (March/April 1990): 13–15, especially 14.
[57]AAMH, September 23, 1872.
[58]AAMH, April 30, 1847.

OTHER SOURCES

The archives of Dutch psychiatric institutions dating from the last decade of the nineteenth century contain fascinating material pertaining to homosexuality, suggesting that life in the army garrisons may well have created homosexual and gender anxieties for some soldiers. It is not uncommon to find stories of men who suffered from delusions relating to pederasty or sodomy. These delusions take two different forms: some patients are afraid of being sodomized, and others are afraid of being regarded as pederasts. In the psychopaths' asylum of Medemblik, founded in 1884, twenty-four case histories from the period 1884–95 refer to homosexual practices or delusions. Six of these case histories involve former soldiers, of whom five suffered from such delusions. In all five of the cases, they were afraid of being considered pederasts, and in one case the man also feared being sodomized.[59] These delusions indicate that homosexual conduct was becoming increasingly incompatible with the male gender role, probably most so for effeminate men with a predilection for passive sexual behavior, who had good reason to fear being regarded as pederasts. These case histories also suggest that Trumbach's queen model of the homosexual was indeed on the advance, compelling soldiers unsure about their sexual inclinations and living in an all-male environment to reflect on their sexual and gender identity. Nothing is revealed about the soldiers' actual conduct in these case histories. Such delusions, specifically among soldiers, are evidence that these anxieties concerned foremost the military and its sleeping quarters. Judging by the cases from the courts-martial, we can affirm that these fears were very real as far as the possibility of homosexuality in the barracks is concerned: some soldiers lost no opportunity to have sex with their bunk-mates.

This is confirmed by an autobiographical memoir of a navy officer. Having been discharged from the navy at the end of the century after being suspected of homosexual relations, this "Uranian" (his own term for a "born" homosexual, implying that he was familiar with the medical literature of the period) sent his life story to the first Dutch professor of psychiatry, Cornelis Winkler. One of Winkler's students published it as a case study in a psychiatric journal. It is a valuable document, because the officer relates how many sexual encounters he enjoyed in the navy, with Uranians as well as with heterosexuals—or so the officer claimed. During two and a half years in Indonesia, he had sex with forty-one Indonesians, and when he later served for twenty months on a naval vessel, he had sex with thirty European sailors, many of whom he saw several times. In the three following months, he stayed at the naval base in Hellevoetsluis, near Rotterdam, and he had sexual relations with six other sailors. On his next

[59]Hekma, *Homoseksualiteit*, pp. 230–31 and 254–57.

tour of duty aboard a vessel, he found a steady lover, but he was forced to resign from the navy when other sailors accused him of being a pederast. Given the number of sexual partners this officer was able to find, his autobiography indicates that homosexual behavior was quite widespread in the navy. It also indicates that most homosexual behavior was casual, with a few men being true Uranians, as the officer claimed. His awareness of his homosexual predilection in the all-male environs of the navy posed many problems for him, and it comes as no surprise that he had to leave the navy. Others no doubt did better at surviving in such a homoerotic situation.[60]

A similar account of sex life in the navy was written by a professor of public hygiene, a former naval doctor who, when discussing the regulation of prostitution, warned against the dangers of onanism and homosexuality. If we forbid prostitution, he claimed, many men will seek sexual fulfillment by themselves or with other men, as happened on board the naval vessels on which he had served. He stated: "Thousands of men and women do not want to restrain their sexual urge looking for natural satisfaction outside of marriage, contrary to the thousands who secretly satisfy themselves in solitude or with someone of the same sex."[61] The navy may have been a more totally segregated institution and may have produced more homosexual behavior than the army; it was, nevertheless, a comparable homosocial environment in which the same social and sexual mechanisms were at work.

Another source of material on sexual behavior in the army and the navy is the published jurisprudence, which includes several cases from courts-martial. The most interesting and earliest one, dating from 1838, concerns the captain of a naval ship who himself initiated a proceeding before the high military court to save his honor, probably after he had been summoned before a lower court. He had had sexual relations with several cabin boys and was observed by one of the other sailors through a small window of the captain's cabin. He was acquitted because his cabin was considered a private place, notwithstanding the fact that other personnel could see into it from the deck. Later, jurisprudence became more strict in this sort of case, condemning as public indecencies any such sexual activities observable from a public place. The captain did not deny having sex with the cabin boys, so it remains questionable whether his honor was indeed saved. Other cases of jurisprudence provide scant additional information on homosexual behavior in the army. One indicted soldier said he had been

---

[60]Pierre F. Spaink, "Bijdrage tot de casuïstiek der urningen," *Psychiatrische Bladen* 11 (1893): 143–65.

[61]Gillis van Overbeek de Meijer, review in *Nederlandsch Tijdschrift voor Geneeskunde* 36 (1892): 421–22; see also his "Geneeskundig toezicht op de prostitutie," in *Nederlandsch Tijdschrift voor Geneeskunde* 33 (1889): 60–63, especially 63. For the debate on the medical regulation of prostitution in the Netherlands and its importance for the discussion of the "perversions," see Hekma, *Homoseksualiteit,* pp. 149–64.

introduced to this kind of immorality in a youth prison, where—so he claimed—it was rampant.[62]

CONCLUSIONS

At the age when young men join the army, they are in their most active sexual period. It therefore comes as little surprise that the soldiers described above were prone to sexual crimes; and because they were nearly all of the time living in an all-male environment, it is not surprising that most of their sex crimes were homosexual. Because of the prevailing negative attitudes toward homosexual behavior (the death penalty for sodomy was not abolished in the Netherlands until 1811), it is also understandable that acting out homosexual pleasures entailed many difficulties and fears. Some soldiers tried to entrap their mates who were indulging in such practices, and other soldiers went insane with delusions and anxieties connected with pederasty. The manliness of the soldiers was threatened by homosexual behavior, especially when they were forced into a "female" position, as the gender metaphors that appear in the archives indicate. But when soldiers took the male part in sodomy, problems with their masculinity did not have to arise—on the contrary, it seems to have affirmed their male standing. There was also a group of soldiers apparently unconcerned about either homosexual conduct or their masculinity: they could assume either role and enjoy it.

It is my claim that homosexual behavior was widespread in the army, but I know my proofs are not totally convincing. The base of evidence is too small, so additional research has to be done. A comparison with onanism may be illuminating. Homosexual behavior was despised somewhat more than masturbation was by officials and doctors in nineteenth-century Netherlands, but masturbation never came to the attention of the military courts, although it must have been quite general. The military authorities were very lax in implementing sexual discipline, which explains the low number of convictions for homosexual behavior in the army. Sodomy was a crime not to be named, which made it very difficult for the authorities to initiate prosecutions. Only in the more extreme cases, such as in prisons, could the wall of silence be broken down. But I have to admit that many questions remain unanswered for the moment.

What bearing does this material concerning the nineteenth-century Dutch military have on the debate over the "making of the modern homosexual"? There is precious little data about men identifying themselves as homosexuals or having clearly effeminate roles. The minister of war's 1845

[62]Hekma, "Bewaar mij voor den waanzin van het recht" (n. 29 above), the cases being discussed on pp. 116 and 123.

order concerning unnatural fornication indicates that the authorities were concerned primarily about the problem of seduction, not about effeminacy or unmanliness. The naval officer's autobiography bespeaks a clear consciousness of a homosexual identity, but effeminacy is only mentioned perfunctorily. The officer claimed not to like "boys' games," a topos he may well have taken from the medical literature with which he was acquainted. The gender metaphors that appear sporadically in the archival sources probably refer to passive sexual behavior, not to any supposed homosexual identity of the soldiers. They do not appear to confirm the queen model of the homosexual. Only in the case studies from psychiatric asylums is there any indication that male effeminacy is becoming an issue in the military, but here less so for the authorities than for the soldiers themselves. Dating from the very last decade of the nineteenth century, the psychiatric material does offer some support for the queen model set forth by Trumbach. On the other hand, the overwhelming majority of the homosexual behavior in the military presented above clearly falls into the category of casual homosexuality, with indications of both friendship and effeminacy nearly altogether lacking. Thus the making of the modern homosexual properly ought to be regarded as a gradual process, with different developments among distinct social groups and social classes in distinct countries, and with a variety of individual forms. Gay history has been preoccupied with general trends, such as the making of the homosexual or the queen model, where specific historical and local trends are disregarded. The types of homosexuality that existed in the barracks differed from those in the urban centers of that era, and it is improbable that the sodomites' identity and subculture of the eighteenth century survived unchanged until 1900.[63]

The dearth of sexual violence in this material is also remarkable. Modern studies of homosexuality in the military indicate that group violence and sexual humiliations are quite commonplace.[64] The nineteenth-century situation, with soldiers living for long tours of duty in crowded barracks, would seem to be especially conducive to acts of sexual violence and degradation, but they are not documented in the archives of the military courts in Haarlem during the period under consideration, neither among the sex crimes nor among the crimes of violence. Did the authorities tolerate such behavior even more than they do at present, or were the soldiers more disciplined and it simply did not occur? These possibilities seem implausible. Or could instances of sexual violence have been handled by superiors in the same manner with which they dealt with unproven cases of homosexual

[63]See John Marshall, "Pansies, Perverts, and Macho Men: Changing Conceptions of Male Homosexuality," in Plummer, ed. (n. 13 above), pp. 133–54, who takes the position that the modern homosexual became general only after World War II.

[64]Marcel Bullinga, *Het leger maakt een man van je: Homoseksualiteit, disciplinering en seksueel geweld* (Amsterdam, 1984).

behavior—assignment to the disciplinary classes? This is a puzzling matter that may be illuminated by further archival research.

An additional puzzle surrounds the strict surveillance of homosexual behavior in a different, even more segregated, institution in the same period, namely, in prisons. Beginning in the 1830s, Dutch prison authorities debated the best prison system. Many issues were raised, including the utility of forced labor, but especially the benefits of shared versus solitary confinement. Solitary confinement came to be considered preferable and was instituted from the 1850s on; confinement in the cell was meant to weigh on the conscience of the prisoners but also to prevent their social and sexual promiscuity. The unmentionable sin played an important role in the discussion. One prison reformer argued that the onanism occurring in single cells was less heinous than the homosexual behavior of prison dormitories.[65] Thus the disciplining of prisoners bore clear consequences for homosexual promiscuity. It is possible that the order of the minister of war of December 1845 was inspired by the debate on the prison system and on solitary confinement, but that is all we find for the army. Why did contemporary military authorities not concern themselves more with the issue of sexual discipline? The simplest answer has to do with the emergence of a prison reform movement at the beginning of the nineteenth century, whereas no such movement existed for the army. Moreover, the prison is a more segregated institution than the army, soldiers having more social and sexual freedoms than prisoners at that time. But it remains remarkable that the discussion on prison promiscuity was not also transferred to the military realm, in light of the similarity in both settings of more or less compulsory homosociality.

Thus the military authorities devoted scant attention to sexual discipline in the barracks. Sex crimes were brought up rarely—but then condemned fairly harshly. In the Dutch military courts of the nineteenth century, most cases involved minor thefts and insubordination. The charges had to do with infractions of the hierarchy and with breaches of property relations: between the army and the soldiers (for example, when the men sold their uniforms), but also between soldiers, who had very little private space and little possibility of locking away their possessions. But sexual discipline was imposed only in a haphazard way. The standards of the Dutch army cannot have been very strict in those times, given the slackness with which the authorities combated undisciplined sexual behavior as well as drunkenness. The Victorian age has recently lost its reputation as an age of sexual repression,[66] and the material from the courts-martial can only con-

[65] Hekma, *Homoseksualiteit*, pp. 112–20.

[66] See Foucault (n. 13 above); and Peter Gay, *The Education of the Senses*, vol. 1 of *The Bourgeois Experience: Victoria to Freud* (New York, 1984).

firm this view. Homosexuality may not have been rampant in the barracks, but neither was it extremely repressed or persecuted. Neither the authorities nor the soldiers were bothered too much about homosexual behavior so long as it was not too flagrant and did not subvert gender roles.

The situation in the military was conducive to homosexual behavior, but fairly few cases were prosecuted, and sexual discipline was not strictly implemented. To arrive at a more complete picture of the system of sexuality, violence, and discipline, and the structure of male homosociality and homosexuality in the military, more research must be done, not only for the Netherlands, but also for other countries. As it appears now, the army was not a paradise of pleasure for most soldiers, least of all for men aware of their unmasculine behaviors or same-sex preferences.

Sexual Politics in Wilhelmine Germany: The Male Gender Crisis, Moral Purity, and Homophobia

JOHN C. FOUT

Department of History
Bard College

W RITING IN HIS memoirs, *Von einst bis jetzt: Geschichte einer homo-sexuellen Bewegung* (From then until now: History of a homosexual move-ment), published in 1922–23, Dr. Magnus Hirschfeld, the pioneering German sexologist and homosexual rights activist, described the challenge that his movement faced when it began its activities in late Imperial Ger-many. "It was certainly an extremely difficult road," he wrote, "rich in aborted hopes and bitter disappointments, often even from quarters that one least expected, and yet if we compare the present with the circum-stances then, one would have to conclude that the work was worthwhile and that it was not in vain." The movement, he argued, despite fierce op-position had fought vigorously to convince the government and society at large through a program of education that the sexual activities of homosex-uals did not deserve the assignation of "sodomy" or "unnatural vice" in the German criminal code under §175. Moreover, Hirschfeld believed that de-spite the countercurrents, "new scientific findings about homosexuality have become dominant and point to new assessments of the problem, which appear very valuable."[1]

Indeed, Hirschfeld and his followers justifiably could claim that their

I would like to thank Ann Taylor Allen, James Steakley, and Randolph Trumbach, who all read an earlier draft of this article and offered many helpful comments.

[1] Magnus Hirschfeld, *Von einst bis jetzt: Geschichte einer homosexuellen Bewegung, 1897–1922,* ed. Manfred Herzer and James Steakley (Berlin, 1986), pp. 7, 10. Unless otherwise noted, all translations of German materials in this essay are my own. For a general study, see James D. Steakley, *The Homosexual Emancipation Movement in Germany* (New York, 1975). For a recent study, see Hans-Georg Stümke, *Homosexuelle in Deutschland: Eine politische Geschichte* (Munich, 1989), especially the chapter entitled "Magnus Hirschfeld und die kaiser-lichen Urninge" (pp. 21–52), which is based uncritically on limited homosexual sources and breaks no new ground.

This essay originally appeared in the *Journal of the History of Sexuality* 1992, vol. 2, no. 3.

participation in Wilhelmine political life had brought about a fascinating cultural response, namely, a protracted public discussion of homosexuality that was both more extensive and more acrimonious than the modern world had yet seen. One of the questions that will be addressed here was whether Hirschfeld's claim was overstated. Had his movement's efforts improved the lot of the homosexual? These activists had focused their efforts on a demand for the decriminalization of male homosexual acts growing out of their portrayal of the homosexual as an innocent victim of legal and social discrimination; his sexual life was the behavioral consequence of a hereditarily determined nature. Unfortunately, Hirschfeld and the leadership had an inadequate understanding of the mechanisms of sexual politics and developed no effective response to the sustained, vicious, and politically effective counterattacks of the moral purity movements. These attacks proved most productive in successfully undermining the endeavors of homosexuals to bring about an end to social and legal discrimination. The moral purity leaders crafted a strategy that circumvented the reformers' attempts to redefine gender roles and reform penal laws. In the fierce struggle, in fact, to dominate the discourse on sexuality, one result was a substantial "restatement"—rather than a radical transformation—of the dominant sexual and gender paradigm in the period after 1890, and the moral purity movements were a central force in shaping that restatement to meet their own ends. The revised sexual ethic and the interconnected assumptions about acceptable gender roles were still diametrically opposed to the interests of homosexuals and women.

Before turning to a brief discussion of the political strategy of the Hirschfeld activists and a longer discussion of the response from the moral purity organizations before 1914, some additional information should be provided about the historical context for these findings. In ongoing research on sexual politics in Wilhelmine Germany, I have juxtaposed sexual reform, feminist, and homosexual rights movements against the broad counterreform endeavors of the moral purity organizations; to investigate only the limited issues surrounding the homosexual experience and the larger disputation over the meaning of homosexuality is an approach that would be conceived too narrowly, given the complexities of sexual politics.[2] I have also concluded that the period beginning around 1890 is a "new," historically specific stage in the history of sexuality (concurrent with trends across the industrialized west), continuing to 1945, with subphases from 1914 to 1933 and from 1933 to 1945, given the exigencies of the German experience. The period from the mid-1860s through the late

---

[2]This study is part of an ongoing project on sexual politics in Wilhelmine Germany; my first book to come out of this research has a working title of "The Moral Purity Movement in Wilhelmine Germany: The Male Gender Crisis and the Concern about the Regulation of Masculinity."

1880s was probably a transitional era. Therefore, this analysis is framed by the emergence of a revised dominant paradigm associated with what has been characterized as the "modern era," which manifested a unique set of cultural norms lasting through to the Holocaust; that contrasts with a set of values and norms revised yet again in the postmodern era.

There were a host of controversial issues central to sexual and gender politics from about 1890 on, and those questions and the vocabulary used to discuss them were unique to that moment in time. An array of complex economic, social, and political changes helped shape both the reform ideas and the counterreform impulse in Germany, including broad political mobilization after 1890,[3] as well as ongoing parliamentarization of a semi-authoritarian regime; the ever more explicit discussion of sexual behavior as a result of the emergence of sexology, which provided a vocabulary for discussing sexual activities and a set of norms for determining "normal" and "abnormal" behavior in those matters; the debate over female prostitution and the growing apprehension over the increasingly rapid spread of venereal diseases, for which the female prostitute bore the blame; the call for decriminalization of various sexual acts between consenting adults (going beyond just §175) and other sexual reform demands on the part of the sexual reformers and, conversely, the demand for increased criminalization of these same and other acts by the moral purity forces; the controversy over abortion and the increased discussion and awareness of birth control and the availability of inexpensive condoms, at a time when many on the political Right became consumed with the notion that there was a declining birthrate that threatened Germany's future as a great power.

While it is conventional to emphasize the medicalization of sexuality[4]—and it is a central issue and one that shaped modernism—I will also argue that the complex factors already articulated and the role played by the Protestant moral purity organizations were certainly as important, if not more so. Purity activists, supported by their church-based claim of moral authority, preached their vision of a moral order, which countered the demand for sexual diversity with a pronounced emphasis on the centrality of heterosexual marriage and family as defined by their interpretation of "Christian values." They contrasted those values with the perversity of all other forms of sexual behavior, most decidedly male homosexual acts. In close alliance with the Protestant churches in Germany, the moral purity organizations increasingly saw their role as championing the existing—and, in their minds, divinely ordained—gender order. In fact, it will be argued here that the leadership of the Protestant churches reaffirmed in the modern era what

[3]David Blackbourn and Geoff Eley, *The Peculiarities of German History: Bourgeois Society and Politics in Nineteenth-Century Germany* (New York, 1984).

[4]See, for example, Jeffrey Weeks, *Sex, Politics, and Society: The Regulation of Sexuality since 1800* (New York, 1981), pp. 141–59.

they believed was the church's traditional role as the arbiter and upholder of the gender order, a logical position since they sought to maintain a monopoly on the regulation of heterosexual marriage and family life. A similar role was played by the Roman Catholic church in those areas of Germany where the population was predominantly Catholic; in other words, moral purity organizations surfaced in all geographic areas of Wilhelmine society.[5]

To be sure, the moral purity advocates located their discourse explicitly in a broad range of "sexual sins" in their assaults on what they perceived as declining morality and the dangerous demands of the sexual reformers, but their concerns went far beyond the question of sexual mores. I would argue that the debate was only outwardly about the sins of sexual vice; in reality it reflected an implicit crisis in gender relations, primarily in the form of growing concern about eroding gender boundaries on the part of a large segment of the middle-class male population as well as a part of the male working class (mostly, the limited evidence would suggest, better-paid skilled workers). Instead of seeing the steady, if not dramatic, increase in the number of women working for pay outside the home as positive, these men became increasingly alarmed about this development and, in turn, about the appropriate role for men in society.

At the same time, many men in the latter half of the nineteenth century, which was a period of especially intense misogyny, saw women in an ever more negative and threatening light, and it became commonplace for men to depict women through "fantasies of feminine evil," whether it was as an idol of perversity, the invalid, the lesbian vampire, the daughter of Dracula, or the virgin whores of Babylon.[6] Men's groups, then, evolved out of a context where the gains made by women brought into question the roles played by men. Though the moral purity organizations epitomized such groups, there were other like-minded organizations as well, such as the *Deutsche Bund zur Bekämpfung der Frauenemanzipation* (German league in the struggle against women's emancipation); these men's groups actually had as their real aim the reversal or the prevention of any further gains for women. The editor of the above-mentioned antifeminist league's publication articulated the group's views in the inaugural issue—and they were

---

[5]See *Volkswart: Organ des Verbandes der Männervereine zur Bekämpfung der öffentlichen Unsittlichkeit* (The people's guardian: Voice of the men's associations in the struggle against immorality), which began in 1908 and was the magazine of Catholic adherents of the moral purity movement. While these organizations officially were interfaith ones and less dominated by clergy, they were located in cities with predominantly Catholic populations (Cologne and Munich, among others), and most publications listed in this periodical carried the imprimatur (the printer was Görres-Druckerei, a Catholic press in Coblenz).

[6]These are some of the many images of women presented in Bram Dijkstra's brilliant study of this phenomenon in *Idols of Perversity: Fantasies of Feminine Evil in Fin-de-Siècle Culture* (New York, 1986). His work is drawn primarily from the paintings of male artists across the industrialized west in the latter half of the nineteenth and early twentieth centuries.

representative, I believe, of the dominant male mentality in the modern era: "We want to preserve the division of labor of the sexes as it has developed historically in the culture, given that it has been a blessing to the nation as a whole. The woman should reserve the household and the family as her sphere of activity, and women's employment outside the home should only be seen as an exception or an economic necessity and should be made superfluous if at all possible. The man should not have to experience any interference from women in his profession and in his work in the community and for the state."[7]

A last crucial point must be made in these introductory remarks. If one proceeds from the supposition that to understand sexual politics one must understand the sexual values expressed by the dominant culture at a given moment in time and, in turn, the relationship between the regulation of sexuality and those governing values, then one must enunciate the mechanism for controlling the two. In the Wilhelmine era, the key elements in the equation were assumptions about appropriate gender roles and how those roles defined acceptable sexual behavior. By the late nineteenth century, theories about gender were deeply embedded in a biological worldview that clearly associated gender behavior with an essentialist imperative. At the same time it was widely believed that such imperatives determined characteristics of individuals who were members of various racial groups or who suffered from certain mental or physical illnesses; ultimately such views shaped the science of eugenics.[8] Men were men and women were women because of the inherent nature of their bodies. Therefore, what was chaste or what was sinful, normal or abnormal, evolved from the relationship between sexual acts and acceptable activities for the female or male gender. Perhaps the most articulate spokesman of that mentality was Richard Freiherr von Krafft-Ebing, professor of psychiatry and neurology at the University of Vienna and one of the most prominent European sexologists of the late nineteenth century. Before Freud, his views undeniably were the most influential of all the "medical experts." In his study *Psychopathia Sexualis*, first published in 1886, he discussed the fundamental correlation between normal sexual behavior and innate male and female gender traits. He started with the hypothesis that sexual activity within the confines of monogamous heterosexual marriage, especially for procreative purposes, was the standard for determining what defined "normal sexuality" in higher civilizations. In his mind, "episodes of moral decay always

---

[7] Their magazine, *Monatsblatt des Deutschen Bundes zur Bekämpfung der Frauenemanzipation*, began publication in January 1913; for the quotation, see "Frauenbewegung und Frauenbildungsfrage," *Monatsblatt* 1 (January 1913): 1.

[8] See Ann Taylor Allen, "German Radical Feminism and Eugenics, 1900–1918," *German Studies Review* 11 (1988): 31–56; Robert Proctor, *Racial Hygiene: Medicine under the Nazis* (Cambridge, MA, 1988).

coincide with the progress of effeminacy, lewdness, and luxuriance of the nations."[9] Therefore, corrupt sexuality had to be understood as behavior that grew out of perversions of the gender order, when men and women did not engage in those forms of sexuality acceptable for their gender.[10] Krafft-Ebing's views on homosexuality will be spelled out in greater detail at a later point in this essay.

Finally, the last section of this essay will bring together the various elements of the analysis to advance a theoretical perspective on the male gender crisis of the modern era and on the crucial function that the debate over homosexuality played in that controversy. It is not enough simply to reiterate the views of the two opposing camps, the moral purity movement and the homosexual rights activists. What I shall attempt is an explanation of why this debate took place at this particular moment in time. I shall contend that the sexual politics of the modern era were shaped by a specific shift in male and female gender relations overall in western culture. The rapid pace of economic and social change in Germany exacerbated the problem there, and, as a result, Wilhelmine culture and society was on the front line in the battle of the sexes at the beginning of the twentieth century.

HIRSCHFELD AND THE HOMOSEXUAL RIGHTS MOVEMENT

In examining the debate over sexuality, a logical starting point is to contrast the Hirschfeld wing of the predominantly male homosexual rights movement with the male organizations of the moral purity movement. (The women in the latter movement, the *Deutsch-evangelischer Frauenbund* [German evangelical women's league], were concerned in the main with very different issues, and they developed their own discourse, which must be considered in its own right.)[11] It must be emphasized that these movements under consideration here were but two of many that sought to

[9]Richard von Krafft-Ebing, *Psychopathia Sexualis: With Especial Reference to the Antipathic Sexual Instinct: A Medico-Forensic Study,* trans. Franklin S. Klaf (from the 12th German ed. [Vienna, 1903]) (New York, 1965), pp. 3–4.

[10]It is interesting to note the fascination of Hirschfeld and the moral purity movement with Krafft-Ebing. See the commentary on Krafft-Ebing's work by a medical doctor, A. Roemer, in the first issue of a pamphlet series that began publication in Berlin in 1892: "Das Sittengesetz vor dem Richterstuhl einer ärztlichen Autorität," *Streitfragen: Wissenschaftliches Fachorgan der deutschen Sittlichkeitsvereine* (Controversial subjects: The scientific professional journal of the German moral purity organizations) 1 (1892): 5–15. Moral purity commentators generally agreed with Krafft-Ebing's findings about sexual behavior, but his views on decriminalization of sexual activities between consenting adults they saw as hateful.

[11]See Richard J. Evans, *The Feminist Movement in Germany, 1894–1933* (Beverly Hills, CA, 1976), pp. 195–201; Barbara Greven-Aschoff, *Die bürgerliche Frauenbewegung in Deutschland, 1894–1933* (Göttingen, 1981).

reshape the discourse on sexuality after 1890. It is possible, in actuality, to identify most of the participants in the debate over sexuality in late Imperial Germany, from the medical authorities who were concerned about curbing the spread of venereal disease and the nudists who idealized the body[12] to the *Christliche Verein Jünger Männer* (CVJM)—the German branch of the Young Men's Christian Association (YMCA), an organization that sought to shape a redefinition of the masculine role as well as to regulate the masculinity of young men—and from the *Bund für Mutterschutz und Sexualreform* (League for the protection of motherhood and sexual reform) to the opponents of sexually explicit material. Any comprehensive study of sexual politics must take these and other such groups and their political agendas into account to understand the intense preoccupation with sexuality.

In 1897 Magnus Hirschfeld and his newly created *Wissenschaftlich-humanitäres Komitee* (Scientific humanitarian committee, or WhK) petitioned the Reichstag to reform §175 of the German penal code, which criminalized sexual acts between males, as well as bestiality. That paragraph, which was both short and vague, read as follows: "Sodomy, when it is perpetrated by persons of the male sex or by people with animals, is to be punished by imprisonment; and [it] can be recognized as justification for the loss of civil rights."[13]

In contrast, it must be emphasized, there was a major endeavor made by the moral purity organizations in the period before 1914 to revise and expand §175 and all the other morality clauses in the German criminal code, but nothing came of those efforts.[14] Though a major reform of the legal code was proposed, it was never adopted, and thus the so-called morality clauses remained unchanged. The moralists even sought the criminalization of lesbian sex, but they never made a robust attack on lesbianism because, it seems to me, such a posture might have given credence to the notion that women had sexual desires; the women's movement also vigorously attacked those who advocated criminalization of female homosexuality.[15] The Nazis would expand the definition of "sodomy" for men when they revised § 175 in 1935, and they were able to carry out in prac-

---

[12]Corona Hepp, *Avantgarde: Moderne Kunst, Kulturkritik, und Reformbewegungen nach der Jahrhundertwende* (Munich, 1984); Wolfgang R. Krabbe, *Gesellschaftsveränderung durch Lebensreform: Strukturmerkmale einer sozialreformerischen Bewegung im Deutschland der Industrialisierungsperiode* (Göttingen, 1974).

[13]*Strafgesetzbuch für das Deutsche Reich,* 20th ed. (Leipzig, 1912), pp. 53–54.

[14]For a discussion of the changes proposed in the morality clauses, see Professor D. Mahling, "Die gegenwärtige Stand der Sittlichkeitsfrage," *Vierteljahrsschrift für Innere Mission* 36 (1916): 3–123, and especially pp. 3–32 for a discussion of homosexuality.

[15]See, for example, Helene Stöcker, "Die beabsichtigte Ausdehnung des §175 auf die Frau," *Die Neue Generation* 7 (1911): 110–22.

TABLE 1   Persons Charged with Sodomy under §175, 1890–1905

Year	Arrests (N)	Convictions (N)
1890	730	412
1895	790	484
1900	799	535
1905	860	605

Source.—*Statistik des Deutschen Reichs, Kriminalstatistik,* n.s., 58:154 (1890); 89:142 (1895); 139:162 (1900); and 176:244 (1905) (rpt. Osnabrück, 1975–76).

tice what had been the sexual politics goals of the moral purity movements.[16]

Interestingly, convictions for sodomy under §175 before World War I were not all that high. Comparing statistics from 1890, 1895, 1900, and 1905, it is apparent that the number of arrests and convictions were relatively few (see table 1).

While it would appear that the number of cases and convictions were steadily increasing, by 1905 a further breakdown of the figures was given by the authorities responsible for keeping the criminal statistics, and it is most revealing. Of the arrests, 374 were for sodomy and 486 for bestiality, and of the convictions, 289 were for sodomy and 316 for bestiality.[17] Research on the question of bestiality in Imperial Germany has not yet even begun. But as far as male homosexuality was concerned, 289 convictions in one year for all of Germany for violation of §175 was a rather negligible figure, given that in 1900 the population of Imperial Germany was just over fifty-six million and by 1910 had risen to almost sixty-five million.[18] By comparison, the prosecution of sodomy during the Nazi regime increased dramatically; in 1934, there were 1,091 cases brought to trial, with 948 convictions, and, in 1938, there were 9,479 cases brought to trial, with 8,562 convictions.[19]

In seeking the decriminalization of homosexual acts (and presumably bestiality) in the petition of 1897, Hirschfeld and his supporters constructed one of the basic cornerstones of their movement, and the language

[16]For the revised Nazi law, see *Deutsche Strafgesetze,* ed. Leopold Schäfer (Berlin, 1943), p. 100.

[17]For detailed figures, see *Statistik des Deutschen Reichs, Kriminalstatistik,* n.s., 58 (1890): 154; 89 (1895): 142; 139 (1900): 162; and 176 (1905): 244 (rpt., Osnabrück, 1975–76).

[18]Koppel S. Pinson, *Modern Germany: Its History and Civilization,* 2d ed. (New York, 1966), p. 221.

[19]Länderrat des Amerikanischen Besatzungsgebiets, *Statistisches Handbuch von Deutschland, 1928–1944* (Munich, 1949), p. 634.

of the plea revealed much about their intent and beliefs.[20] The petition took the political high road, as did Hirschfeld himself throughout his active career, appealing to science, logic, and justice for the homosexual.[21] The document emphasized that such acts were not criminalized elsewhere (for example, in France, Italy, or Holland) and that, from classical civilization to the present, homosexuals were among the ranks of the most gifted in western culture, a theme reiterated over and over in the homosexual activist literature.[22] However, the petition (like most of Hirschfeld's writings) reflected a view of the homosexual and homosexuality that was problematic at best and would be the source of vicious condemnation of the homosexual rights movement by the moral purity leaders. Science, the petition argued, had clearly proven that homosexuality was a phenomenon that was "a widely appearing manifestation across time and place and therefore must grow out of a deep internal constitutional disposition"—that is, homosexuality truly was an inborn condition. Therefore, since the cause of the "puzzling phenomenon" was developmental, "no one with such a disposition should be judged as committing a moral wrong." It also posited that the "same-sex disposition manifests itself in as great as or often in greater degree than in the normal." Such a consistent choice of words was unfortunate indeed. The petition even suggested that "anal and oral sex (that is, the use of nonsexual bodily orifices for sexual purposes) are acts in sexual-contrary sex seldom engaged in, or are no more extensive than in normal sex."[23]

The petition went on to suggest that since §175 was against all progressive scientific knowledge, the authors, "inspired by the striving for truth, justice, and humanity," advocated its abolition. Sexual acts between persons of the same or opposite gender, they suggested, should no longer be against the law except in cases where force was used, when a person was under sixteen, or in cases of public prostitution. In addition, in an appendix to the document, the authors argued the legal merits of overturning the law. They maintained that the state should not punish sexual acts engaged

[20]The petition was reprinted in an important political pamphlet of the homosexual rights movement published by the WhK, *Was muss das Volk vom dritten Geschlecht wissen! Eine Aufklärungsschrift* (Leipzig, 1901), pp. 15–23 (though not in its entirety). The petition also appeared in Hirschfeld's *Jahrbuch für sexuelle Zwischenstufen unter besonderer Berücksichtigung der Homosexualität* 1 (1899): 239–80, under the title "Petition an die gesetzgebenden Körperschaften des deutschen Reiches behufs Abänderung des §175 des R.-Str.-G.-B. und die sich daran anschliessenden Reichstags-Verhandlungen." This yearbook will henceforth be cited as *JfsZ*.

[21]For the only biography of Hirschfeld, see Charlotte Wolff, *Magnus Hirschfeld: A Portrait of a Pioneer in Sexology* (London, 1986). This study is hopelessly uncritical.

[22]See Eugen Wilhelm [Dr. jur. Numa Praetorius, pseud.], "Michel Angelo's Urningtum," *JfsZ* 2 (1900): 254–67; Dr. O. Kiefer, "Hadrian und Antinous," *JfsZ* 8 (1906): 565–82.

[23]"Petition," *JfsZ* 1 (1899): 239–41.

in by consenting adults in private. They also underscored the ongoing difficulties the courts had in interpreting the law. Generally, the petition
maintained, the courts only found individuals guilty when it was proven
that emission had taken place inside the body or as a result of bodily fric-
tion. Mutual masturbation, for example, was not penalized under the law.
Finally, the document lamented the fact that the legislators, who had drawn
up the law decades earlier, had not understood at that time what "inborn
contrary sexual desire" was all about. If they had, they would not have
punished those who, despite all efforts to the contrary, were driven to have
sex with individuals of their own gender. Nor was it then known, they argued, that anal sex or sex with children "were as uncommon among
contrary sexuals as with those of a normal sexual inclination." Finally, the
petitioners sought to make legislators aware that the law had driven "hundreds to other lands, where the urning [homosexual] law does not exist,"
and continued to rob the fatherland of many talented people. The law
branded many innocent individuals as criminals only because of their
nature, and as a result many chose suicide.[24] The message, then, was a para-
doxical one at best: homosexuals, even if they were not normal, were just
like everyone else, and therefore they deserved equal treatment before the
law.

It might be useful to discuss even more blatant (at least from our late
twentieth-century perspective) contradictions in two other major publications, a political pamphlet written by the WhK, *Was muss das Volk vom
dritten Geschlecht wissen!* (What people should know about the third sex),
originally published in 1901, and Hirschfeld's magnum opus, *Die Homosexualität des Mannes und des Weibes* (Male and female homosexuality), which
he published in 1914.[25] In the latter, Hirschfeld commented on the first
decade and a half of the committee's existence and stressed the importance
of its activities for the establishment of self-confidence in the homosexual;
the petition was, according to Hirschfeld, a turning point in the history of
the homosexual rights movement. He also emphasized that, other than the
decriminalization effort, the two most important goals had been to educate
public opinion about all aspects of homosexuality and to carry out scientific
research.[26] It must be said that Hirschfeld and his followers made a unique
contribution in these areas. Their movement was the first of its kind in the
modern era, and their educational efforts contributed much to our knowledge of the homosexual experience.[27] Hirschfeld played as important a role
as any of the sexologists in "creating" the modern homosexual role, but one

[24]Ibid., pp. 239–41, 266–70.
[25]Magnus Hirschfeld, *Die Homosexualität des Mannes und des Weibes* (Berlin, 1914).
[26]Ibid., pp. 973–75, 1004.
[27]See, for example, Magnus Hirschfeld, *Berlins Drittes Geschlecht* (Berlin, 1904).

has to ask whether his creation was a Frankenstein monster that would soon turn on its creator.

Indeed it was Hirschfeld's research and his intellectual perspective that was responsible for the unfortunate limitations of his leadership. Throughout he spoke of the *"Beseitigung der Urningsverfolgung,"* the end to the persecution of urnings. Yet the very strategy that he and his leadership adopted too often provided the ammunition to attack the legitimacy of the movement. That was not necessarily Hirschfeld's fault; it was, after all, the moral purity leaders who sought to discredit the homosexual rights movement. Yet Hirschfeld must be criticized for the flaws in his logic, stemming from his biologically determined definition of homosexuality. He created a tension between an appeal for justice, on the one hand, and the desire to depict homosexuality as an innate pathology, something other than normal, on the other. It is fascinating to observe that Hirschfeld, in our own contemporary terms, adopted an essentialist position, arguing that homosexuality was deeply rooted in a biological imperative. Thus for the homosexual, there was no escape from inevitable sexual desires for individuals of the same sex. Hirschfeld and the other sexologists were responsible for imposing a most restricted definition of homosexuality on homosexuals as a whole.

In *Was muss das Volk vom dritten Geschlecht wissen!* positive opinions were juxtaposed against negative self-images. "What this brochure intends," it read, "is to explain to the public about the 'third sex,' so that they can make a correct judgment about a subject where there are widespread prejudices and incorrect opinions." It was the authors' hope that "whoever reads this little booklet intelligently and without preconceived ideas will recognize that we are not talking about the promotion of immorality but rather the redress of a grave injustice against unfortunate individuals." There were homosexuals to be found everywhere, it stressed, among the upper and lower classes and among the best and least educated; they could be found in big cities and in little towns as well. Moreover, "the love that they have for their own sex can be as pure, tender, and noble as that for the opposite sex and therefore is different only in direction, rather than in kind." Readers must understand, the pamphlet asserted, that urnings had desires as powerfully directed to their own sex as the lawmakers who drafted §175 had for the opposite sex. Such men naturally sought intercourse with women; similarly, homosexuals found such love unnatural and were forced to seek lifelong relations with men.[28]

The major component, therefore, in Hirschfeld's homosexual pathology was the argument that a third sex existed, and it was to be found somewhere

---

[28]*Was muss das Volk vom dritten Geschlecht wissen!*, pp. 1–2, 10–11. Wolff (n. 21 above) argues that Hirschfeld himself wrote this pamphlet (p. 57).

between the two dominant genders. Individuals of this third sex, he believed, should be understood to be homosexuals. Though they might have the physical body of one gender, their personality often manifested behavioral characteristics and sexual desires of the opposite. Thus the gender assumptions that society held about men or women did not apply to very effeminate males or overtly masculine females, where these strange contrary emotions were the norm. Such individuals were unfortunate souls who constantly were misunderstood and oppressed by the people around them. Therefore, it was wrong for opponents to hold that there were too many of these individuals, "even if their number is rather small in comparison to those who have normal tendencies"; too many argued that those who were born contrary should be dispatched to "prisons, insane asylums, or other special institutions."[29] Here Hirschfeld paraphrased an oft-repeated argument of the moral purity organizations, which consistently argued for institutionalization of all homosexuals.

"Anyone who has a normal disposition," the pamphlet exhorted, "should some time put himself in the role of an urning." Such "an unfortunate condition, for which he is not in the least responsible, is thought of by his fellow human beings as simply something that does not exist or is a burden; people do not believe that others can feel any differently than they themselves do." Therefore, homosexuals suffered from a variety of negative circumstances, including unhappiness over their passion and daily persecution. Many urnings were bitter individuals, because society punished them when they expressed their feelings. Yet "every urning should see it as his inescapable duty to fight for his honor and freedom, the most sacred possessions we have." The world should understand "that we do not struggle against Christian moral principles, toward which all people should strive. Rather, we are against those who would brand us as criminals, which is not what Christianity is about at all."[30]

One other consistent theme of the Hirschfeldites that should at least be mentioned was an ongoing complication in the daily lives of homosexuals, namely, the fear of discovery and blackmail. That debilitating problem was often discussed in essays and reports in Hirschfeld's annual, *Jahrbuch für sexuelle Zwischenstufen unter besonderer Berücksichtigung der Homosexualität* (Yearbook for sexual intermediate types, with special consideration of homosexuality), the first volume of which appeared in 1899. One of the earliest articles to appear was Ludwig Frey's "Zur Charakteristik des Rupfertums"—the German noun *Rupfertum* is a derivative of the verb *rupfen*, which means to fleece or to skin someone.[31] Frey stressed that anyone who

---

[29]*Was muss das Volk vom dritten Geschlecht wissen!*, pp. 4–5, 8–9.
[30]Ibid., pp. 11–14.
[31]Ludwig Frey, "Zur Charakteristik des Rupfertums," *JfsZ* 1 (1899): 71–96.

wanted to know something about homosexuality must understand "the misery of the social conditions in which the contrary sexual [*Konträrsexuale*] languishes." He decried that breed of lower-class criminal who lived off this ugly and exploitative trade. "They seek out their prey," he wrote about blackmailers in Berlin, "in the early evening or at night in the region of public toilets in various quarters of the city or in the Tiergarten, especially in the neighborhoods around the Brandenburg Gate." Frey recounted many examples and enumerated the many lives destroyed or threatened by these scurrilous attempts at blackmail—in other cases, the victims were robbed or even killed—that were reported frequently in the public press. Too often, he lamented, the press not only discussed the blackmailers but cast aspersions on their victims as well. Moreover, the courts, while they often sentenced the blackmailers to long prison terms, generally also imprisoned the homosexual victim.[32]

Finally, it is interesting to observe the lengths to which Hirschfeld took his notion of a third sex, namely, that male or female urnings, like heterosexual men and women, were not only a product of an inborn hereditary condition but actually exhibited "visible" physical differences, which further proved his thesis, he believed, that homosexuality was wholly an innate rather than an acquired condition. In a lengthy commentary he wrote for his *Jahrbuch* in 1903, entitled "Ursachen und Wesen des Uranismus" (Causes and character of uranism), he spelled out those assumptions and even provided illustrations of the body types of the three sexes (see figs. 1, 2, and 3). While he admitted that there were circumstances in which individuals who were not innately homosexual would engage in homosexual acts (such as prostitution, lack of access to members of the opposite sex—in prisons, monasteries, military bases, and in schools—and for reasons of friendship, gratitude, or even sympathy), only true homosexuals were not free to make such a choice.[33] The reason was clear—it was because of the *Unausrottbarkeit der Homosexualität*, the ineradicability of homosexuality. Therefore he challenged all those who argued that individuals could "become" homosexual. Hirschfeld decried the convictions of the German sexologist Iwan Bloch, who believed, for example, that men could become homosexuals by working in occupations with a feminine character; having abnormalities of the genitals; engaging in masturbation, opium use, and chronic alcoholism; using effeminate dress or manners; watching animals engage in sex; looking at obscene pictures or going to museums with naked statues; or being around homosexuals in same-sex institutions; and that women could become lesbians if they engaged in mutual masturbation or oral sex, dressed in men's

[32]Ibid., pp. 72–73.
[33]Magnus Hirschfeld, "Ursachen und Wesen des Uranismus," *JfsZ* 5 (1903): 1–193; for this material, see p. 15.

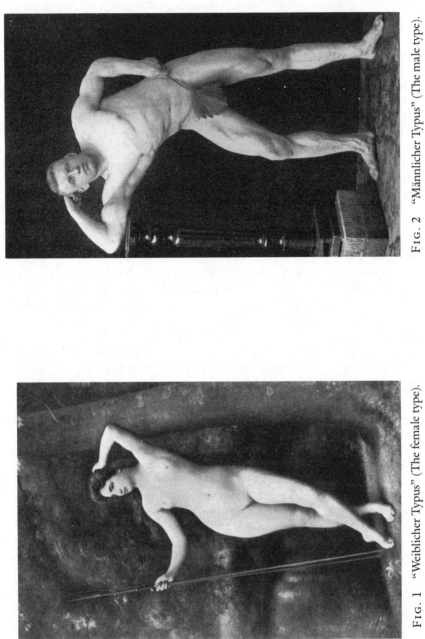

FIG. 2 "Männlicher Typus" (The male type).

FIG. 1 "Weiblicher Typus" (The female type).

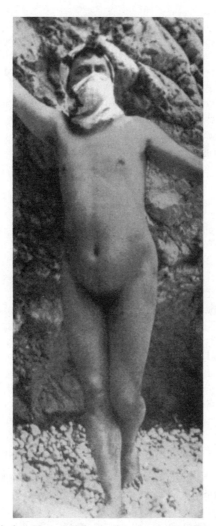

FIG. 3   "Urnischer Typus" (The urning type). Dr. Magnus Hirschfeld illustrated the body types of the three sexes in his article entitled "Ursachen und Wesen des Uranismus" (Causes and character of uranism), published in his *Jahrbuch für sexuelle Zwischenstufen mit besonderer Berücksichtigung der Homosexualität* in 1903.

clothes, or became involved in the women's movement.[34] Too many real homosexuals, Hirschfeld lamented, prayed endlessly to God to be saved from their condition, but the end result was only their loss of faith and their ultimate rejection of enforced chastity.[35] Homosexuals definitely deserved sympathy.

[34]Ibid., pp. 118–22.
[35]Ibid., pp. 110–12.

To summarize, the homosexual rights movement sought to educate the public about homosexuality and to illustrate in graphic detail the legal and social discrimination under which the homosexual lived. It also had as its goal the education of society about the true pathology of homosexuality, a pathology that was responsible for creating this third gender. Individuals with that nature were innocent victims of their condition, and thus they deserved equal treatment before the law. Certainly, the movement also hoped to convince the opponents of homosexual rights that homosexuals—decent people in every way—as a result of their innate condition engaged in sexual activities that were completely normal to them, given their own objects of desire. To argue, as Hirschfeld and his supporters did, that homosexuality was not a sin was most significant. Hirschfeld, in fact, always had an optimistic conviction about the efficacy of modern science to bring about a more just society. In contemporary terms, then, this was the first homosexual civil rights movement, and it began a tradition that has lasted for a hundred years in the west, despite some major losses, with many victories. It was also the first time that a self-liberating political movement was organized by homosexual men, and it was accomplished in the political context of the parliamentarization of late Imperial Germany and the emergence of a range of reform-minded parties and groups, exemplified by the phenomenal growth of the Social Democratic party after 1890. Nevertheless, Hirschfeld and his followers, though they made a poignant appeal for justice and acceptance, addressed homosexuality from such a limited perspective that they only exposed themselves to greater persecution and homophobia. Fortunately, later permutations of the movement, even in Germany, would jettison many of those troublesome features.

MORAL PURITY AND THE BATTLE AGAINST "VICE"

Before describing the counterattack by some of the major moral purity organizations and offering a brief overview of their development and ideals, it would serve the purpose of this essay to return to Krafft-Ebing and his views on male homosexuality. While he and many of the sexologists supported the abrogation of §175 and he, most of all, was credited with providing part of the ideological ammunition for the homosexual rights movement, it must not be forgotten that his views on homosexuality were negative in the extreme, and he thereby contributed as much to homosexual persecution as to liberation. It is ironic that Hirschfeld and his movement lionized him as "the most distinguished champion of our movement.[36] Homosexuals, Krafft-Ebing emphasized, had feelings that represented an "abnormal congenital manifestation," and "the essential feature of this strange manifestation of the sexual life is the want of sexual sensibility for the opposite sex, even to the extent of horror, while sexual

[36]For Krafft-Ebing's obituary, see "Jahresbericht 1902/3," *JfsZ* 5 (1903): 1292–97.

inclination and impulse toward the same sex are present."[37] Krafft-Ebing, much earlier than Kinsey, anticipated him in his observations on a range of homosexual behavior, from the mildly tainted male to the extremely effeminate ones, the true homosexuals.[38] Interestingly, it was in those latter cases that Krafft-Ebing scrutinized the men who personified this new homosexual role.

In general, all these tainted males, he stressed over and over again, were hypersexual—to the point that even the touch of another male could bring them to ejaculate. They were subject to neurasthenia, which meant that they were predisposed to fatigue, emotional disorders, and a lack of motivation; they often pursued "artistic" interests; and they were prone to periodic insanity—in other words, they totally violated their appropriate gender roles.[39] These men often could be found in occupations designated as women's work, and many were effeminate. Effeminacy, in fact, was the most exaggerated example of the male homosexual and illustrative of the most profound congenital disturbance; it was "characterized by the degree in which the psychical personality, especially in general manner of feeling and inclinations, is influenced by the abnormal sexual feeling." Krafft-Ebing went on to describe such homosexuals as men who actually felt they were women and, of course, they were only interested in the passive role in sexual intercourse. Krafft-Ebing also emphasized that such men were not pederasts—there was no inclination for boy-love. These were adult men who only wished to engage in sexual intercourse with other adult men.[40] Put together, the composite picture of the male homosexual emerged, a despicable, unacceptable male role that grew out of a degenerate masculinity, reflecting a pattern of behavior that was in total violation of assumptions about "normal males"; it was all too suggestive of the dreaded female.

While the moral purity movement might have agreed with many of Krafft-Ebing's findings, its political agenda, as we shall see, was quite different. One of the first of many moral purity associations in Germany, called *Sittlichkeitsvereine,* was established in 1885, and by 1890 a national organization was created, the *Allgemeine Konferenz der deutschen Sittlichkeitsvereine* (General conference of German morality organizations), with headquarters in Berlin.[41] These groups took up a series of controversial "moral

[37]Krafft-Ebing (n. 9 above), p. 221.

[38]I refer here to Kinsey's "heterosexual-homosexual rating scale"; see Alfred C. Kinsey, Wardell B. Pomeroy, and Clyde E. Martin, *Sexual Behavior in the Human Male* (Philadelphia, 1948), pp. 638–41.

[39]Krafft-Ebing, pp. 221–23.

[40]Ibid., pp. 253–57.

[41]See, for example, *25 Jahre der Sittlichkeits-Bewegung: Bilder aus der Geschichte des Westdeutschen Sittlichkeitsvereins und der Allgemeinen deutschen Sittlichkeits-Konferenz,* ed. D. Weber and P. Ellger (Lüttringhausen, n.d. [1910?]).

issues," which, they argued, threatened the fundamental values of Christian marriage and family life. The *Allgemeine Konferenz,* in conjunction with local associations, published materials that were widely distributed across Germany, primarily by church-related organizations, throughout the prewar period. The *Allgemeine Konferenz* published its own monthly newspaper, *Korrespondenzblatt zur Bekämpfung der öffentlichen Sittenlosigkeit* (Reports on the battle against public immorality), as well as pamphlets, fliers, lectures, essay collections, stenographic reports of their annual meetings, and numerous books.[42] In any given year, they published many small publications, in tens of thousands of copies. They sent endless petitions demanding state intervention or revisions in the penal codes to local, state, and national government officials in their quest for increased state control of morality and sexual behavior.

A brief look at the leadership and the membership of the moral purity movement is informative. Not surprisingly, the top leadership generally—in local branches or the national organization—were Protestant ministers, and that group was dominated by individuals in the circle of Inner Mission activists around Adolf Stoecker, a fact that has been all but entirely ignored in the literature on the Christian Social movement. Stoecker was also a rabid anti-Semite, and many of the moral purity attacks on Hirschfeld were of a fundamentally anti-Semitic character—homosexuals were always depicted as outside the bounds of society. Key figures such as Dietrich von Oertzen, who published a biography of Stoecker, and Reinhard Mumm, who edited some of Stoecker's writings, played a dominant role in the moral purity movement of the Wilhelmine and Weimar periods.[43] Many other prominent figures in the movement were involved in various Inner Mission social welfare organizations (there were hundreds of these institutions across Germany), and thus there were extensive connections at all levels of the Protestant church in Germany to the moral purity movement; special Sundays were set aside each year by the churches to collect funds for the movement's activities and publications.

Annual meetings of Inner Mission leaders and Protestant church synods regularly carried moral purity issues on their agendas, and thus all the Protestant churches and their affiliated organizations were closely associated with and supporters of the moral purity ideology. Often, church assemblies passed proclamations in support of the moral purity movement's efforts, as

---

[42]*Korrespondenzblatt zur Bekämpfung der öffentlichen Sittenlosigkeit* was one of many names for the newspaper; shortly before World War I it again changed its name, to *Zeitschrift des deutsch-evangelischen Vereins zur Föderung der Sittlichkeit.* It began publication on May 15, 1887, and continued until 1930. It will be cited hereafter as *Korrespondenzblatt.*

[43]See Dietrich von Oertzen, *Adolf Stoecker: Lebensbild und Zeitgeschichte,* 2 vols. (Berlin, 1910); and Adolf Stoecker, *Reden im Reichstag,* ed. Reinhard Mumm (Schwerin, 1914).

was the case in a 1904 synod resolution of the Royal Consistory of Brandenburg, which mandated its church officials as follows:

> We trust that ministers in collaboration with all other church officials will continue to carry on steadfastly the battle against immorality, this most terrible enemy in our nation's midst.
>
> Above all else it will matter a great deal if the ministry awakens and sharpens the conscience through prayer, pastoral care, and education, and through advice, exhortation, and admonition, and bears witness in an open and determined way to the indifference and laxity in wide circles about the sins of immorality that destroy the body's power and health, do terrible damage to mental and emotional life, paralyze the resilience of the mind, estrange the heart from the Lord God and his promise of salvation, shatter family life, and as a result bring about temporal and eternal destruction.[44]

These were tough words, and they reflected the intensity of the church's concern about violations of the sexual and gender order. What was important here was the uniformity of the message of the moral purity movement and the church's governing bodies, which added great weight and prestige to the efforts of the moral purity advocates. In fact, it was their ubiquitous relationship to the churches that ultimately made it possible for them to play such an authoritative role in the restatement of the dominant sexual and gender paradigm.

A further examination of moral purity membership lists is revealing of the movement's raison d'être. The great majority of the members came from elite male professions and occupations: they were educators, pastors, government officials, military officers, and businessmen. Some of these occupations were already under siege by women and feminists, such as medicine and teaching, while other professions represented the last all-male bastions.[45] I believe that there was a direct connection between the occupational categories and the ultimate rationale for these men to become involved in moral purity organizations. Of the 348 members of the Berlin

[44]Quoted in an unpublished 1909 report by Councillor von Rohden of the Royal Consistory of the province of Brandenburg to the Protestant High Consistory in Berlin, "Maßnahmen zur Bekämpfung der Unsittlichkeit" (Measures in the struggle against immorality), February 25, 1909, Evangelisches Zentralarchiv, Berlin (hereafter cited as EZiB), Bestand 7/3805.

[45]See three important studies by James C. Albisetti, "Could Separate Be Equal: Helene Lange and Women's Education in Imperial Germany," *History of Education Quarterly* 22 (1982): 301–17, "The Fight for Female Physicians in Imperial Germany," *Central European History* 15 (1982): 99–123, and *Schooling German Girls and Women* (Princeton, NJ, 1988). For a comparative perspective see, for example, Michael Grossberg, "Institutionalizing Masculinity: The Law as a Masculine Profession," in *Meanings for Manhood: Constructions of Masculinity in Victorian America,* ed. Mark C. Carnes and Clyde Griffen (Chicago, 1990).

Männerbund zur Bekämpfung der Unsittlichkeit (Men's league in the battle against immorality) in the early 1890s,[46] approximately 33 percent were church officials, 20 percent were government bureaucrats, 7 percent were teachers and professors, 4 percent were military officers, 2 percent were medical doctors, and another 4 percent were other professionals—engineers, architects, and the like. At least 70 percent of the membership, therefore, had university educations. There were another 10 percent who were in business, and 9 percent were skilled workers. Only about 4 percent of the sample had working-class occupations, and a very small number were retired or listed no occupation. Membership lists from other branch organizations showed all but identical occupational backgrounds.[47] The executive committee of the Hamburg *Verein zur Hebung der öffentlichen Sittlichkeit* (Association for the promotion of public morality), for example, in 1896 was made up of four pastors, three doctors, two teachers, a professor, a judge, an art dealer, a print-shop owner, a book dealer, a cashier, a master shoemaker, and a master woodturner.[48]

Leaders of the various moral purity organizations barnstormed the nation year after year, speaking in church pulpits and lecture halls. By doing so, they effectively eclipsed public opinion in this fashion alone. Groups in opposition either were effectively silenced or were co-opted into responding to an agenda that was identified and defined by the moral purity advocates. Even the language of the cultural discourse as a whole was largely fashioned by them. Words such as *Unzucht* (vice), *widernatürliche Unzucht* (sodomy or unnatural vice), *gewerbsmässige Unzucht* (prostitution), *Reinheit* (purity), and *Keuschheit* (chastity) were used by the moral purity movement to focus the discussion on issues of their choosing—words that were heavily laden with tacit philosophical and religious assumptions. Intellectuals and feminist reformers really did not respond to or question these terms. The moral purity movement had a free hand to use them as the basic weapons to shape a "restatement" of the dominant sexual paradigm. Titles of numerous pamphlets and books were carefully crafted

    [46]This undated Mitglieder-Verzeichniss (membership list) is in the Archiv des Diakonischen Werkes der Evangelischen Kirche in Deutschland, Berlin (hereafter cited as AdDWdEKD), Bestand ADW, CA 528 II, with other material that would date it between 1890 and 1892.

    [47]See, for example, *Bericht über den Verein zur Hebung der Sittlichkeit mit dem Sitz in Dresden (E.V.) auf das Jahr 1904* (Dresden, 1904). The organization in Dresden claimed a membership of 855 for that year.

    [48]A printed petition that the association sent to government leaders was signed by a group that included thirteen ministers, five judges, five doctors, two teachers, two professors, three administrators, a hospital director, and a director of an orphanage. See *Fünfter Jahres-Bericht des Hamburger Vereins zur Hebung der öffentlichen Sittlichkeit für das Jahr 1895* (Hamburg, 1895), Staatsarchiv Hamburg, Politische Polizei, V 324, "Verein zur Hebung der öffentlichen Sittlichkeit in Hamburg 1890–1914," unpaginated.

to arouse the appropriate concern: *Kampf gegen die Schund- und Schmutz-literatur* (Battle against trash and smut literature), which generally was the prewar German term for pornography; *Der Einfluss der Unsittlichkeit auf Erkrankung und Sterblichkeit* (The influence of immorality on sickness and death); *Die Fürsorge für die heranwachsende weibliche Jugend* (The concern for growing girls); or, simply, *Der Kampf wider die Unzucht* (The struggle against vice).[49]

The moral purity movement was founded on certain basic suppositions about sexuality, gender roles, marriage, and the family—primarily, that the sex act was only for procreation and only should be engaged in by hetero-sexual couples within monogamous marriages. All other forms of sexual behavior were either immoral, illegal, illicit, perverse, abnormal, dan-gerous, unhealthy, or even anti-German. It was the French or the Italians who regularly engaged in perversions or immoral vice; as one moral purity author put it, in an article entitled "Entsittlichte Völker sinken" (Depraved nations decline): "Moral recklessness is a fundamental error of the French."[50] Further, all people were expected to marry, and the rigid bound-aries between appropriate female and male gender roles were to be maintained at all cost. Women, idealized as sexually passive, obedient, chaste, and motherly, were to provide a loving home and a Christian atmo-sphere and morality for the good German family.

While sexual reformers, feminists, and homosexual rights advocates ar-gued in favor of sexual reform, especially for the rights of women and homosexuals to express themselves freely in sexual matters, the moral pu-rity movement was a response first and foremost to the changing nature of society, and then secondarily to the threats posed from these so-called radi-cal reform movements. The churchmen were the self-proclaimed arbiters of public morals and saw themselves fighting an ever more dangerous battle against the evil forces of vice. But were those "unnatural vices" the real cause of their outrage? I would argue that they were only incidental con-cerns. Rather, the moral purity movement was in reality a male-dominated, clerical-led response to the growing presence of women of all classes in the workplace and in the public domain. Due to the rapid pace of industrializa-tion in the latter half of the nineteenth century, by 1907 there were almost ten million working women in Germany, out of a total female population of just over thirty-one million. Of that group, 223,676 were members of trade

---

[49]*Kampf gegen die Schund- und Schmutzliteratur,* Zeit- und Streitschriften zur Sitt-lichkeitsfrage, n.s., no. 6 (Plötzensee, 1910); Dr. med. Höffel, *Der Einfluss der Unsittlichkeit auf Erkrankung und Sterblichkeit* (Berlin, n.d. [1894/95?]), EZiB, Bestand 7/3803; Richard Vetter, *Die Fürsorge für die heranwachsende weibliche Jugend* (Berlin, 1904); Lic. Weber, *Der Kampf wider die Unzucht* (Gotha, 1891).

[50]"Entsittlichte Völker sinken," *Korrespondenzblatt* 2 (1888): 74–75, 82–83, 91–92, quotation on p. 92.

unions, and only 6.5 percent were employed as white-collar workers or public officials—most women were to be found in poorly paid, unskilled jobs. Furthermore, the women's movements experienced especially rapid growth from the 1890s on and could rightfully claim some real gains for women; it has been estimated that in 1913, about 470,000 women were members of organizations affiliated with the *Bund deutscher Frauenvereine* (League of German women's associations).[51] Thus morality issues were the thin veneer of bourgeois respectability that, it was hoped, would make the moral purity attack on women and the women's movement more palatable—an openly antifeminist, antiwomen stance would have been too revealing of their ultimate motivations. Also lurking behind the facade of morality was the declining role for the church in a pluralistic society: to stand as the paragon of public virtue was to reclaim an "important" role for the church.

In that vein, the attack on male homosexuality played a crucial role in the strategy. The concern was "to keep men on top" literally and figuratively, and that meant the preservation of the myth of male sexual dominance and female submissiveness in all things sexual. Male homosexual rights activists threatened the role that male-defined heterosexuality played in the traditional sexual discourse. Homosexuality conveniently served to delineate as well the differences between "normal" and "abnormal" sexual behavior for the moral purity advocates, and it reiterated the central importance, according to the moralists' perspective, of male sexual power in a class and gender sense. Similarly, they sought to preserve the inequality of the sexes, especially in the case of the male monopoly on clerical power. Thus for the moralists, there were high stakes in the struggle, and they pulled out all the stops.

The moral purity leaders created an ever-expanding network of interrelated organizations, most of which were connected with the Inner Mission; they played a prominent role in a range of social welfare institutions, especially homes for fallen women or unwed mothers, orphanages, and youth organizations. Under the guise of preserving public decency, for example, the organization known as *Der Volksbund zur Bekämpfung des Schmutzes in Wort and Bild* (People's league in the battle against filth in word and picture) was one of many parallel groups saturating society with their views on morality—in this instance using the charge of pornography

---

[51] See Ute Frevert, *Women in German History: From Bourgeois Emancipation to Sexual Liberation* (New York, 1988), pp. 329–34. For works on German women, especially in English, see John C. Fout, "Current Research on German Women's History in the Nineteenth Century," in *German Women in the Nineteenth Century: A Social History,* ed. John C. Fout (New York, 1984). See also Helena Cole, ed., with Jane Caplan and Hanna Schissler, *The History of Women in Germany from Medieval Times to the Present: Bibliography of English-Language Publications,* Reference Guides of the German Historical Institute, no. 3 (Washington, DC, 1990).

as a rationale for an assault on the views of the sex reformers.[52] Or one could mention *Der Akademische Bund »Ethos«* (Academic league "Ethos"), which limited its membership to university students and had as its goal "the advancement of a deeper and more refined conception of sexual life, the purification of the moral code of honor, and a battle against sexual debauchery." Members were obligated "through their deeds and behavior to stand for chastity in and outside marriage" and "to protect their comrades from sexual influence and to protect women and girls whenever possible from molestation."[53] Thus, such organizations were able—with the strong stamp of approval of the churches—to disseminate their message ever more effectively in Wilhelmine society.[54]

Much of the moral purity propaganda was directed to youth, growing out of a concern, I believe, to educate young men and women about their proper gender roles.[55] It was also linked to broad anxiety in western culture about the importance of youth for the future of the nation.[56] Another national moral purity organization, *Der Bund vom Weißen Kreuz* (League of the White Cross), was founded in 1890 and was directed to young men under the age of nineteen; it was an affiliate of the CVJM, which itself had been founded in Berlin in 1883 based upon the American model of the YMCA.[57] A 1910 report indicted that there were 311 White Cross local organizations in Germany with a total of 4,476 members.[58] To become a member, a youth had to take the following pledge (*Gelübde*):

1. To treat all women and girls with respect and to protect them with all one's strength against injustice and degradation.

[52]See, for example, the *Flugschriften des Volksbundes zur Bekämpfung des Schmutzes in Wort und Bild*, nos. 1–6, published between 1906 and 1911. The first four pamphlets were published in Leipzig and the last two in Berlin.

[53]See the "Satzungen des Akademischen Bundes 'Ethos,'" AdDWdEKD, Bestand ADW, CA 526.

[54]See, for example, the fascinating article by Karin Hausen, "Mother's Day in the Weimar Republic," in *When Biology Became Destiny: Women in Weimar and Nazi Germany*, ed. Renate Bridenthal, Atina Grossmann, and Marion Kaplan (New York, 1984), pp. 132–52. In her discussion of the organizations that played such a role in developing Mother's Day, Hausen focuses on the *Arbeitsgemeinschaft für Volksgesundung*, one of the many organizations that developed out of the moral purity movement in Imperial Germany.

[55]For a typical publication of the CVJM, see a pamphlet by the general secretary, Johannes Levsen, *Die Bewahrung und Rettung der heranwachsenden Knaben und Jünglinge: Referat für den Kongreß des Bundes vom Weißen Kreuz am 16–19. September 1899 in Bielefeld* (Berlin, n.d. [1900?]).

[56]See, for example, Derek S. Linton, *"Who Has the Youth, Has the Future": The Campaign to Save Young Workers in Imperial Germany* (New York, 1991), pp. 98–117.

[57]Ibid., p. 99.

[58]See "Verzeichnis der Weißkreuz-Gruppen," *Weißes Kreuz: Zeitschrift des Sittlichkeits-Bundes vom Weißen Kreuz für Deutschland und die Schweiz* 17 (1910): 48–53. Many of the local leaders were listed, and their dominant occupations were church officials and teachers.

2. To forgo the use of all unchaste language, as well as off-color jokes and gestures.
3. To recognize that the law of chastity applies equally to man and wife.
4. To instill these principles among those comrades of one's own age and also to look after and aid the younger brothers.
5. To hold ardently to God's Word and sacrament in order to fulfill the commandment: Keep yourself chaste![59]

The implications in such a set of principles are fascinating indeed. Men, not women, controlled sexuality, it should be clear, and women were the object of that control.[60] Boys must be taught these truths at an early age. The traditional stereotype of the woman as either virgin or whore was reincarnated in the moral purity literature as either the good mother or the syphilitic prostitute.

Ultimately the moral purity movement was influential because it managed to associate its own position with behavior that supposedly had characterized traditional sexual and family life in western culture. The moral purity leaders successfully appealed to existing male-defined bourgeois norms. They were able as well to give credibility to their program by locating their attack on the sexual behavior of the working class. That class, they hoped to demonstrate, was the real source of public immorality and was to be found in the crowded urban centers of Germany, places that were associated in the bourgeois mind with filth, crime, and deviance of a variety of kinds, including radical political ideologies such as Marxist socialism. George Mosse was especially effective in drawing those connections in his important study, *Nationalism and Sexuality: Respectability and Abnormal Sexuality in Modern Europe.*[61]

From my own perspective, the emphasis on working-class vice, especially the supposed loose morality and licentiousness of the women of that class, was a convenient weapon that also served as a warning to and a means of manipulating the sexual behavior of middle-class women.[62] In

---

[59]See "Was Wir Wollen," an article by the editor, Pastor F. Patzschke, in the first issue of the league's newspaper (*Weißes Kreuz* 1 [1894]: 1–3). Another article, "Das Weiße Kreuz im Christlichen Verein Junger Männer in Berlin" by Chief Forester von Rothkirch, noted that the Berlin organization had 530 members, including 198 workers (ibid., p. 4).

[60]An early pamphlet that personified the notion of male control of sexuality was G. Weitbrecht, *Die Sittlichkeit des Mannes Ehre: Ein Wort an die deutschen Männer und Jünglinge* (The morality of man's honor: A word for German men and young lads) (Stuttgart, 1889), AdDWdEKD, Bestand ADW, CA 528 I.

[61]George L. Mosse, *Nationalism and Sexuality: Respectability and Abnormal Sexuality in Modern Europe* (New York, 1985).

[62]See, for example, Karin Walser, "Frauenarbeit und Weiblichkeitsbilder—Phantasien über Dienstmädchen um 1900," in *Frauen in der Geschichte VI*, ed. Ruth-Ellen B. Joeres and

addition to the endless barrage of attacks on prostitutes, another effective way to denigrate working-class women was to locate the morality problem in women's work; hence waitresses, domestic servants, female factory workers, and other working-class women workers were singled out repeatedly in the literature. In an 1899 pamphlet, *Denkschrift über das Kellnerinnen-Wesen* (Memorandum on the waitress problem), Adolf Henning, the general secretary of the *Allgemeine Konferenz,* spoke out against the dangers of women serving men in public.[63] Henning cleverly characterized the problem to fit his own agenda. While he admitted that there were economic and social problems that contributed directly to large numbers of waitresses eventually becoming prostitutes or contracting a venereal disease—low wages, family poverty, and so forth—those were only passing concerns to Henning. The real threat for him was women who could not control their own sexuality, and too often, he argued, they sought to substitute work for marriage and family—the very concern the moral purity advocates had about women of their own class. Henning therefore drew the parallel between waitressing work for women (male waiters never had such problems) and prostitution. Quoting an unnamed authority, Henning reminded his readers that "female waitresses are a true plague on the whole country."[64] What happened, he reasoned, was that countless fine young men came into contact with these women and were ruined. Henning's solution was a common one for the moral purity movement—more government legislation. He lent his support to those who advocated such measures as restriction of this work to those over twenty-one, police surveillance of the sleeping quarters of waitresses, and, among others, a rule that waitresses not be allowed to work after ten or eleven in the evening. The implication was clear; if women could not control themselves, the state should.[65]

It is in this context of the moral purity attack on working-class women that we must view the moral purity movement's attack on homosexuality. I believe that in the struggle between the competing ideologies in the Wilhelmine era, there was surely real gender and sexual anxiety reflected in sexual politics, especially on the side of the moral purity leadership, and

---

Annette Kuhn (Düsseldorf, 1985). See also Elisabeth Meyer-Renschhausen, *Weibliche Kultur und soziale Arbeit: Eine Geschichte der Frauenbewegung am Beispiel Bremens 1810–1927* (Cologne, 1989); part of this material is available in English, in Meyer-Renschhausen, "The Bremen Morality Scandal," in Bridenthal, Grossmann, and Kaplan, eds., pp. 87–108.

[63]Adolf Henning, *Denkschrift über das Kellnerinnen-Wesen* (Berlin, 1899).

[64]Ibid., p. 16.

[65]Ibid., pp. 9–10. This material is discussed in greater detail in John C. Fout, "The Protestant 'Moral Purity Movement' in Wilhelmine Germany and Its Assault on Feminist Sexual Politics" (paper presented at the Eighth Berkshire Conference on the History of Women, Rutgers University, June 10, 1990).

indeed there was deep-seated homophobia, further stimulated by the attacks of church and moral purity leaders, but that does not adequately explain the tirades that the movement mounted against middle-class homosexuals and working-class women. While there was a clear desire to maintain a society where patriarchy ruled supreme, the moral purity message was directed mainly at men, and what we see was an attempt to "redefine" appropriate masculine behavior in an age when women's activities and women's organizations prompted men to rethink their own male role. In other words, the male response to the women's movement was to create a men's movement to counter the efforts of middle-class women to enlarge their sphere and gain equality with men.

The attacks on homosexuality, I believe, also illustrate real concern about the kind of masculinity that the male homosexual had come to represent. He was now clearly perceived as some novel but unacceptable masculine creature, who manifested behavior that contradicted a newly emerging redefinition of hypermasculinity. Moral purity advocates and others hoped that the new male would reinvigorate the classic male prototype; men should remain as the quintessential and dominant sex in gender relations. The male homosexual was portrayed as sickly, effeminate, perverse, and out of control, just the opposite of the "normal" male, who was physically strong and active, the head of the family, dominant in the public world of politics at home and abroad, and in complete control of his sexuality and his emotions. The male homosexual only personified female characteristics, such as passivity and physical and emotional weaknesses.

Homosexuality was frequently presented by the moral purity advocates as closely akin to and a product of another evil, namely, masturbation, or self-abuse; certainly masturbation was seen as another excessive and dilatory activity, which might lead to homosexuality or perhaps insanity. The difficult question to answer, however, was why the horrors of masturbation were of such concern to the moral purity organizations such as the CVJM and their auxiliary organization, the White Cross? Why was masturbation such a dangerous threat to both boys and men? Obviously, it symbolized the horror of being sexually out of control, which was not a socially acceptable or normal male trait, the moral purity movement asserted, and it signaled the abuse of the chaste and healthy body that would likely bring on physical and emotional weakness and even neurotic debility, behavior associated with effeminacy and the despised female role. Masturbation could dilute the very essence of maleness—strength of purpose and mind. Moreover, masturbation also suggested, like homosexual activity and sexual intercourse with prostitutes, a sexual outlet for men outside the confines of marriage and the family, sites of heterosexual male domination.

I would like to refer briefly to a pamphlet from the CVJM entitled *Offener Brief an Jünglinge* (An open letter to young lads), which decried the debilitating outcome of masturbation. The pamphlet was often reprinted, after its initial printrun of 100,000. The young reader was reminded again and again that self-abuse was indeed a terrible sin and that "God punishes the sins of unchastity." But, thank goodness, if a boy saw the evil of his ways, God would forgive those weak moments. After all, it implied, men did not suffer the same plight as the fallen woman, who was lost forever.[66] Nonetheless, the pamphlet suggested an analogy between the wounding of a young sapling and the act of masturbation. Once cut, "the sap of life flows out, the leaves wilt, the branches hang down . . . and when the winter with its frost and its storms arrives, then the sapling will die." The same would happen to young people who engaged in this filthy act. Instead of experiencing the joy of becoming a strong man, a youth who masturbated would begin his own demise. "Your face becomes pale; your lips lose their fresh redness; your eyes become dull, weak, and hollow; your earlier, so lively gait becomes sluggish, your fresh voice trembles, and your whole character is broken and old before its time."[67] Such were the terrible visions presented to youth, but, I believe, their aim was clear: namely, to intimate that the end result of masturbation was the loss of one's manhood and, even worse, the taking on of those features that they believed defined the female—illness, passivity, and an existence shaped by inactivity.[68]

With this background in mind, let us consider further some of the actual discussion about sexuality and homosexuality mounted by the moral purity movement. The leadership often responded to specific homosexual publications, and thus it is not surprising that they printed a counterpetition to the WhK's plea to abolish §175. "It is extremely important" to oppose this petition, the moral purity advocates wrote, "in the interest of the welfare of the German people, in the name of religion, morality, and order." Homosexuality sounded threatening indeed. They went on to describe sodomy as "the worst and filthiest aberration of sexual life," as well as an example of the deepest moral decline that a people could experience. Only the worst calamities stemmed from it, the counterpetition argued, such as the "disappearance of one's own moral responsibility and a further decline in the family life of the nation." Since, as indicated earlier, it was assumed that the family was male-led, a decline in the centrality of the family meant for moral purity another possible loss of a male-dominated institution. The

---

[66]*Offener Brief an Jünglinge*, AdDWdEKD, Bestand ADW, CA 526, p. 1.

[67]Ibid., p. 2.

[68]Part of this masturbation material is taken from John C. Fout, "The Male Gender Crisis in Wilhelmine Germany: Moral Purity and the Attempt to Regulate Masculine Behavior" (paper presented at the Men's Studies Conference, Tucson, AZ, June 6, 1991). For a brief review of some of the literature on masculinity and homophobia, see Leonard L. Duroche, "Men Fearing Men: On the Nineteenth-Century Origins of Modern Homophobia," *Men's Studies Review* 8, no. 3 (1991): 3–7.

eventual organic damage to those committing such acts, the counterpetition continued, in reproduction led to the degeneration of the race and thus was a threat to the nation's welfare. If the law drove these individuals from the land, so much the better—the fatherland would be relieved of this terrible plague. If not, then all means should be used to rid the nation of this burden, including the state's right and responsibility to uphold Christian moral authority.[69]

A pamphlet countering the arguments in *Was muss das Volk vom dritten Geschlecht wissen!* was also published by the moral purity movement. "Any person who has the welfare of his nation at heart should have knowledge of the depravity of such efforts," they stated. After all, the abolition of §175 would give a free hand to pederasts, and it would allow degenerates to go unpunished. "Whoever has the misfortune from birth onward to be perverse," they proclaimed, "must be treated as a sick person," because sexual attraction to persons of one's own sex was a sign of generations of developmental degeneration. "Nature created only two genders, and the so-called 'third sex' is a filthy sickness, a result of a severe decadence." So §175 must not be overturned because society, and especially its youth, must be protected from these pederasts, and the rakes themselves must be penalized.[70]

Throughout the literature on sexuality published by the moral purity movement and other commentators on sexuality, one finds sexual activities outside marriage consistently equated with sickness and early death. Here the perversion of the pseudoscience of gender abounds, as medical authorities were cited to substantiate Christian moral teachings of "normal" versus "abnormal" sexuality, pure rather than sinful sexual activities. In a lecture entitled *Der Einfluss der Unsittlichkeit auf Erkrankung und Sterblichkeit* (The influence of immorality on sickness and death), a medical doctor named Höffel reiterated these themes at the sixth annual meeting of the *Allgemeine Konferenz* in 1894. He argued that there were two forms of suicide, one sudden and the other slow but inevitable, because of the "pursuit of pleasure, alcoholism, and sexual dissipation." Therefore, immorality was the ultimate cause of early death for many in society. Too often, he wrote, venereal disease was a certain source of disaster that prevented men from getting married. In fact, single people who failed to remain chaste naturally would fall into ruin. "Weak, sick, deaf, blind, crippled individuals, the idiots, and the insane are almost always to be found among the ranks of those who do not marry." But those who did marry and have chil-

---

[69]Der Vorstand der Allgemeinen Konferenz der deutschen Sittlichkeitsvereine, *Gegen-Petition betreffend die Beihaltung des §175 des R.-Str.-G.-B.* (Berlin, 1898), AdDWdEKD, Bestand ADW, CA 526, unpaginated.

[70]*Was soll das Volk vom dritten Geschlecht wissen? Auch eine Aufklärungsschrift herausgegeben gegen das 'Wissenschaftlich-Humanitäre Komitee,'* AdDWdEKD, Bestand ADW, CA/GF13525, originally published in *Volkskraft* 3, no. 7 (n.d. [1901?]): 3–5.

dren, he suggested, were likely to be among the ranks of the healthy people in society who would enjoy a long life regulated by high moral principles. Therefore, "the individual is obligated to control himself, to avoid immorality, and to struggle against it in others." For the doctor, self-control was the watchword for appropriate male behavior.[71]

Similar sentiments were expressed by a director of a sanatorium in his study, *Krankhafte Richtungen der geschlechtlichen Sinnlichkeit und ihre Entstehungsgesetze* (Pathological tendencies of sexual sensuality and their origins). People could and must be in control of their sexual desires, he argued; it was a sign of our higher intellectual and moral capacities. Errors in our sexual lives were manifestations of pathological symptoms, and there existed two types of such pathologic individuals. "There are congenital severe forms of degeneration, the offspring from sick families, the progeny of continued vice, the children of syphilis, and those who are the result of ecstasy of drunkenness—these severe congenital neuropaths naturally exhibit signs of degeneration of their sexual lives even in early youth. They are lewd and immoral because they are sick." Additionally, there were those who were sexual psychopaths because they were unable to control their own sexual desires. They lost complete control of their sex drive, which led them into a degenerative state. Homosexuality, he suggested, was a product of both of those pathologies. It certainly represented "a hereditary perversity, a kind of error of nature in the developmental history of the individual." This led to mental problems, problems in the individual's sex life, and even physical deformities of the sex organs. But individuals need not be prisoners of their bodies; out of their innate characteristics could develop acquired characteristics. The homosexual, pathologically weakened, was unable to resist the weaknesses of the flesh and succumbed to ongoing sexual excitement that soon controlled his entire personality, with no thoughts for anything else. Society must realize the threats posed to the youth of the nation. Young boys were vulnerable to the aggressive sexuality of adult male homosexuals, especially; the mental faculties of the young were not yet sufficiently developed to protect them. Individuals were molded in early puberty, this moral purity writer believed, and their sexual life could be determined by the first sexual contacts in those years. The availability of filthy pictures and extensive masturbation began a process that led to the decline of the normal sexual drive. As a result, same-sex activity brought on continual sexual excitement, and the individual sadly would fall into depravity because his whole sexual sensibility was mired in smut; the rest of his adult life was an outgrowth of these early perversions.[72]

[71]Höffel (n. 48 above), pp. 3–4, 7, 14.
[72]Dr. J. Marrinowski, *Krankhafte Richtungen der geschlechtlichen Sinnlichkeit und ihre Entstehungsgesetze*, Flugschriften des Volksbundes zur Bekämpfung des Schmutzes in Wort und Bild, no. 1 (Leipzig, 1906), pp. 5–10.

In contrast to Hirschfeld, then, and to the widely accepted medicalized view of homosexuality in general, the moral purity movement's argument was what we would now describe as a social constructionist one, a belief that individuals and society—and the value systems they hold—shape and define appropriate sexual behavior. While homosexuals in part may have been victims of their biological makeup, the individual's intellectual and moral capacities made it possible to overcome the body; one's moral faculties could and must overpower the physical imperative. The moralists claimed that such control of the sex drive defined and in fact represented the measure of a "real man." The conquering of the "sins of the flesh" also was a reflection of individuals with higher moral values and Christian ethics, they explained, which were powerful arguments that the moral purity movement used effectively. One moral purity writer put it this way: "We are of the conviction that only the moral and strong-willed influence of the Christian faith can keep a man who is afflicted with a contrary sex drive from abnormal gratification, and if this passion is killed, [his faith] can lead him to victory on the way to self-mastery and in the battle over himself."[73]

A THEORETICAL PERSPECTIVE

What remains is to bring the threads of the argument together. In his now classic article, "The Birth of the Queen: Sodomy and the Emergence of Gender Equality in Modern Culture, 1660–1750," Randolph Trumbach argued that "in traditional European societies, men who did not restrict their sexual experience to marriage usually had sex with both adolescent boys and female whores."[74] However, a change took place in the sex/gender system after 1700, he posited, as modern society evolved, and "the appearance of the English molly and his European counterparts would therefore indicate that male and female roles had begun to grow more nearly equal." Building on the work of Lawrence Stone, Trumbach contended that this development represented a major shift in attitudes toward male homosexuality and that it occurred within the context of the emergence of companionate marriage and the domesticated family in western culture. Now "the molly could not find licit partners among the majority of adult males. The molly was therefore a wall of separation between the genders rather than a bridge." Finally, Trumbach suggested that society perceived

[73]Professor J. Ludwig, "Paragraph 175 des Deutschen Strafgesetzbuches: Eine Kritische Studie," in *Streitfragen: Wissenschaftliches Fachorgan der deutschen Sittlichkeitsvereine*, no. 1, ed. Pastor Philipps (Berlin, 1892), p. 26.

[74]Randolph Trumbach, "The Birth of the Queen: Sodomy and the Emergence of Gender Equality in Modern Culture, 1660–1750," in *Hidden from History: Reclaiming the Gay and Lesbian Past*, ed. Martin Bauml Duberman, Martha Vicinus, and George Chauncey, Jr. (New York, 1989), pp. 129–40, quotation on pp. 130, 140.

the molly as a "new kind of sodomite who was identified principally by his effeminate manner."[75]

Gert Hekma in a recent essay, "Homosexual Behavior in the Nineteenth-Century Dutch Army," challenged aspects of Trumbach's findings. He suggested that evidence for the "queen model" was only to be discovered in the last decade of the nineteenth century in the Netherlands and that it was only one of "a variety of forms. Gay history has been preoccupied with general trends, such as the making of the homosexual or the queen model, where specific historical and local trends are disregarded."[76] The argument that a variety of forms existed was made even in the Wilhelmine era in Germany, as Max Katte suggested in his article "Die virilen Homosexuellen" (Virile homosexuals), which, interestingly enough, was published in Hirschfeld's *Jahrbuch* in 1905. Challenging the idea of Karl Heinrich Ulrichs (an early homosexual writer who suggested, in the 1860s, that a male homosexual was a female soul in a male body) that all homosexuals were effeminate, Katte responded that the existence of virile male homosexuals could not be denied. What about the possibility of the homosexual who had a "male soul in a male body"? How were those men distinguished, he asked, from heterosexual men who preferred women? Katte's answer was confusing, to say the least, but clearly the question was widely debated in this period.[77] The Hirschfeldites also were opposed by another homosexual group, the *Gemeinschaft der Eigenen* (Community of the Other), which was founded in 1902 and led by Adolf Brand, Benedict Friedländer, and others, and which idealized male friendship and overtly masculine men; it was a misogynist organization at best. Their periodical, *Der Eigene: Ein Buch für Kunst und männliche Kultur* (The Other: A book for art and male culture), for the most part contained adventure stories, accounts of male friendships, and pictures of naked virile men and teenage boys—it was an intriguing part of the men's movement as a whole and one that deserves further study.[78]

While Trumbach's views evidently were correct for London, though perhaps not for the rest of Great Britain, why did the "effeminate homosexual role" apparently not appear until the late nineteenth century in the Netherlands or Germany? My research suggests another possible set of explanations, different from those articulated by Trumbach. The emergence

[75]Ibid., p. 140. See Lawrence Stone, *The Family, Sex, and Marriage in England, 1500–1800* (New York, 1977), especially pp. 325–404.

[76]Gert Hekma, "Homosexual Behavior in the Nineteenth-Century Dutch Army," *Journal of the History of Sexuality* 2 (1991): 266–88.

[77]Max Katte, "Die virilen Homosexuellen," *JfsZ* 7 (1905): 85–106, quotation on p. 95.

[78]As an example, see the story by Ludmilla von Rehren, "Pentti und Hannu," *Der Eigene: Ein Buch für Kunst und männliche Kultur* 6 (1906): 173–79; the volume contains many illustrations.

of the "queen model" may well be the product of a particular moment of crisis in gender relations and a specific set of economic and social conditions. It is therefore not necessarily a linear development from the eighteenth through the early twentieth centuries, as Trumbach's interpretation suggests. If modern society emerged in eighteenth-century London, it still may not have emerged until the Wilhelmine era in Germany. Moreover, while I would agree that companionate marriage and the domesticated family was a dominant form of family organization in late nineteenth-century Germany, I certainly would not posit that "male and female roles had begun to grow more nearly equal"—just as I am skeptical that they were very nearly equal in eighteenth-century London, either. On the contrary, I would argue that the emergence of the notion of the effeminate male homosexual, who naturally only engaged in "passive" sexual intercourse, may be the fantasy of extreme heterosexual male anxiety and a strategy to convince society that there were only two genders. While men and women existed in their separate spheres, the male was to be the dominant gender in both (such an interpretation does not deny, of course, that in reality there are effeminate men, and that those men can be heterosexual or homosexual in their sexual preferences). Such a siege mentality may also reflect male concern that gender parity was all too possible and therefore to be fought at all costs.

Whatever else it was, the moral purity movement reflected considerable gender and sexual anxiety, and the fear of homosexuality was rampant in that society as a whole—homophobia was the norm. At the same time, that fear cannot be separated from the larger concerns about eroding gender boundaries that were evident in the culture of the late nineteenth and early twentieth centuries, which surely signaled a perceived crisis in gender relations. The attack on homosexuality was only one element among many concerns that the male moral purity advocates exposed through the wide range of moral issues they claimed to represent. In that context, they sought to sustain the myth of two separate and immutable genders. Homosexuality, as they defined it, provided society with evidence of the disaster that comes with the perversion of the natural order when gender differences are transgressed. Indeed the male homosexual was "a wall of separation between the genders rather than a bridge," but that wall was intentionally constructed to prevent any further erosion of gender boundaries or loss of male gender power. If my theoretical argument has validity, then it must necessarily force scholars of homosexuality to assess the implications of such an important factor in the ongoing debate over sexuality in general and in the lives of homosexuals in particular. Intense homophobia is perhaps a direct consequence of a male gender crisis, where heterosexual men are profoundly fearful of the effeminization of society and the loss of male preeminence.

As a strategy, then, the attack on homosexuality was a necessary component in the moral purity movement's attempt to counter the gains made by women in society. The supposed menace of homosexuality helped to sustain the myth of a world where only male sexuality was considered significant. It was also a rationale for claiming that there was indeed a real threat to traditional marriage and family, where "normal" men and women maintained their appropriate, God-ordained gender roles in the nuclear family. The primary rationale for the moral purity advocates' mobilization was their belief that the gains made by women and the women's movement had gone too far and must be reversed at all costs. The battle over vice was really a battle of the sexes over gender roles in public and private life. If homosexuality had not existed, the movement would have had to invent another convenient excuse to maintain that traditional male and female gender boundaries were necessary to preserve order in society. But homosexuality did exist—and it could only be characterized by the moral purity leaders as a perverted version of male or female sexuality, outside the norm of a universal Christian sexual ethic, which, they argued, defined morality.

Some tentative conclusions about the impact of the moral purity movement on the discourse over sexuality in Wilhelmine Germany, as well as their vilification of homosexuality, are now in order. If nothing else, the movement's attack on homosexuals and the homosexual rights movement surely was an important source of ongoing homophobia that grew ever more intense after 1890. The daily life of the average homosexual must have worsened—with the exception perhaps of those involved in or influenced by the homosexual rights movements, who found these ideas liberating. The activist men who went public must have garnered considerable sustenance from their activities. Most homosexuals, however, probably continued to live a life in the shadows, ever fearful of exposure or imprisonment. Despite the efforts of Hirschfeld and his followers to educate the public about homosexuality, the plea for the decriminalization of homosexuality and the end to social discrimination fell on deaf ears, given the virulent attack of the moralists (against which no strategy may have had a chance for success). In the absence of an effective counterstrategy from Hirschfeld, the moral purity advocates were able to portray homosexuality as a sickness, rather than the pathology of nature that he had described. Moreover, it was not just homophobia that caused homosexuals to suffer in their private lives; the intense social pressure to marry and live a heterosexual life-style must have been extremely difficult. As one moral purity writer put it, "Immorality is any form of sexuality in or outside marriage that does damage by thought or deed to marriage."[79]

The sexual diversity advocated by the sexual reformers was attacked

---

[79]See *Bericht über den Verein zur Hebung der Sittlichkeit* (n. 47 above), pp. 14–15.

strenuously throughout the Wilhelmine period and after, and the moral purity leaders managed to "restate" a sexual ethic that idealized traditional sexual practices, gender relations, and family organization. Undoubtedly the strong institutional support of the Protestant churches added great prestige to the moral purity censure of homosexuality. The churches had taken up once again their conventional role as the supporter of the male-defined gender order. Moreover, the intense hatred of homosexuality and vicious rebuke of homosexual life-styles must be understood to represent the heterosexual male fear of a new gender role for men that threatened, they believed, the traditional role for men in society. The emergence of this unacceptable homosexual role nonetheless can be clearly recognized by the spirited denunciation of it, just as the moral purity movement vigorously condemned the increasing presence of women in public life and in the workplace. Such men and women, it was feared, would not marry and would live outside the male-dominated organization of the family, the church, and society—especially if the state did not act to criminalize their behavior.

Forbidden by God, Despised by Men: Masturbation, Medical Warnings, Moral Panic, and Manhood in Great Britain, 1850–1950

LESLEY A. HALL

Contemporary Medical Archives Centre
Wellcome Institute for the History of Medicine

M ASTURBATION IS a sexual manifestation extremely common in the male sex and almost universal in the male adolescent, at least in modern western societies. Its construction as a disease entity and the rise of the concept of masturbatory insanity in the wake of the publication of *Onania* and of Tissot's work in the eighteenth century has already been described.[1] Such attitudes to the practice were not monolithic, however, even though self-abuse was constructed as physically and mentally deleterious as well as sinful, not only by the medical profession but by groups with interests ranging from the religious to the commercial. The varying attitudes to this common sexual manifestation during a particular historical period in a particular society are worth consideration, especially in the context of what men themselves felt about a practice universally stigmatized but nevertheless indulged in by them.

This study therefore looks at beliefs about male masturbation that were promulgated in Britain from the middle of the nineteenth century, the height of the Victorian era and allegedly also the high-water mark of anx-

I am very grateful to my fellow participants in the conference on "The Role of the State and of Public Opinion in Sexual Attitudes and Demographic Behavior since the Eighteenth Century," Madrid, August 31–September 1, 1990, for the discussion on an earlier version of this essay and to the editor and the anonymous referees of the *Journal of the History of Sexuality* for their helpful comments on the draft of this expanded version.

[1] E. H. Hare, "Masturbatory Insanity: The History of an Idea," *Journal of Mental Science* 108 (1962): 1–25; Robert H. MacDonald, "The Frightful Consequences of Onanism: Notes on the History of a Delusion," *Journal of the History of Ideas* 28 (1967): 423–31; H. Tristram Engelhardt, Jr., "The Disease of Masturbation: Values and the Concept of Disease," *Bulletin of the History of Medicine* 48 (1974): 234–48; Alex Comfort, *The Anxiety Makers: Some Curious Preoccupations of the Medical Profession* (London, 1967), pp. 69–113.

This essay originally appeared in the *Journal of the History of Sexuality* 1992, vol. 2, no. 3.

iety over masturbation, to the middle of the twentieth century, by which time the notion that scaremongering about the habit did more harm than the habit itself had become prevalent. The impact of varying views of the subject on the man in the street between the two world wars, a period of transition, will be illustrated from correspondence received by Marie Stopes, whose book *Married Love*, first published in 1918, generated thousands of letters from the sexually troubled and bewildered of both sexes and all social classes for the subsequent thirty years.

The discourses on masturbation discussed below are discourses about male sexuality, its nature and its control. Men's attitudes toward masturbation were attitudes toward the nature of their own male sexuality, unmediated through the female. Writers of sex advice occasionally might warn young women against endangering male purity by provocative dress or by conduct leading to the arousal of desires that could only be slaked by masturbation or fornication, but men were subjected to a barrage of anxiety over solitary sexual activity, both willed (as in self-abuse) and unwilled (as in nocturnal emissions).[2] The negative feelings about sexuality that might also have been projected in misogyny were here directed by men against themselves.

I

William Acton's famous and much discussed *The Functions and Disorders of the Reproductive Organs in Youth, Adult Age, and Advanced Life, Considered in their Physiological, Social, and Psychological Relations,* first published in 1857, is often considered to be the definitive Victorian work on sexual functioning. Was it not pointed out by Havelock Ellis as an exemplar of all that was wrong in Victorian attitudes to sex?[3] For Acton, sexuality was a

[2]Winfield Scott Hall, M.D., with Jeannette Winter Hall, *Sexual Knowledge: In Plain and Simple Language; Sexology or Knowledge of Self and Sex for Both Male and Female; Especially for the Instruction of Youths and Maidens, Young Wives and Young Husbands, All Fathers and All Mothers, School-Teachers and Nurses, and All Others Who Feel a Need of Proper and Reliable Information on Sex Hygiene, Sex Problems, and the Best Way and the Best Time to Impart Sexual Knowledge to Boys and Girls about to Enter into Manhood and Womanhood* (Philadelphia, 1913; rpt., London, 1926), pp. 184–85; Norah March, *Towards Racial Health: A Handbook for Parents, Teachers, and Social Workers on the Training of Boys and Girls,* with a foreword by J. Arthur Thomson, 4th ed., rev. (London, 1920), p. 175.

[3]William Acton, *The Functions and Disorders of the Reproductive Organs in Youth, Adult Age, and Advanced Life, Considered in Their Physiological, Social, and Psychological Relations,* 3d ed. (London, 1862); Havelock Ellis, *The Erotic Rights of Women and the Objects of Marriage,* British Society for the Study of Sex Psychology, no. 5 (London, 1918), p. 9. See also Havelock Ellis, *Eonism and Other Supplementary Studies,* vol. 7 of *Studies in the Psychology of Sex* (Philadelphia, 1928).

constant source of danger to the male. The pleasure of orgasm was too intense to be safely experienced often. While arguing that a man accustomed to gratifying his urges by self-abuse was undermining his self-discipline and therefore was less likely to be able to resist other temptations, Acton believed that waste of the vital spermatic fluid (even in legitimate marriage) itself could lead to debilitating disease. Masturbation was only one of the lurking perils of manhood, but far from the least of them.

Some historians have suggested that Acton was neither influential nor representative of the medical profession at large.[4] But Victorian doctors, even if they did not subscribe completely to Acton's views on the subject, commonly were convinced of the physical as well as the moral evils of self-abuse. In his *Dictionary of Practical Medicine,* a more general guide than Acton's specialist work, Dr. James Copland was vehement about the dangers of "pollutions," in particular those produced by "manustupration," to which he attributed the decreased life expectancy and greater morbidity of those who remained unmarried. His views had considerable and enduring circulation.[5]

Sir James Paget's clinical lecture on "Sexual Hypochondriasis" published in 1875 (though presumably given earlier) admittedly contradicts the picture of every Victorian doctor threatening a string of ailments ending in insanity and death as the inevitable outcome of onanism. Paget, even though he wished that he "could say something worse of so nasty a practice; an uncleanliness, a filthiness forbidden by God, an unmanliness despised by men," was emphatic that masturbation did no more harm than any other indulgence in excess and certainly did not lead inevitably to the lunatic asylum.[6] While, as Jeanne Peterson has argued, Paget's ideas must have influenced his students, his writings on this subject had considerably less circulation than Acton's.[7] *Functions and Disorders* was issued in three editions in its first five years and continued to be reprinted well after

---

[4]F. B. Smith, *The People's Health, 1830–1910* (London, 1979), pp. 294–315, and "Sexuality in Britain, 1800–1900: Some Suggested Revisions," in *A Widening Sphere: Changing Roles of Victorian Women,* ed. Martha Vicinus (Bloomington, IN, 1977); M. Jeanne Peterson, "Dr. Acton's Enemy: Medicine, Sex, and Society in Victorian England," *Victorian Studies* 29 (1986): 569–90, and "No Angels in the House: The Victorian Myth and the Paget Women," *American Historical Review* 89 (1984): 677–708; Peter Gay, *The Education of the Senses,* vol. 1 of *The Bourgeois Experience: Victoria to Freud* (New York, 1984).

[5]James Copland, *A Dictionary of Practical Medicine: Comprising General Pathology, The Nature and Treatment of Diseases, Morbid Structures, and the Disorders Especially Incident to Climates, to the Sex, and to the Different Epochs of Life,* 4 vols. (London, 1844–58), 3: 441–48; *British Medical Journal,* 1881, no. 2:904.

[6]Sir James Paget, "Sexual Hypochondriasis," in *Clinical Lectures and Essays,* 2d ed. (London, 1879), pp. 275–98.

[7]Peterson, "Dr. Acton's Enemy."

Acton's death. While Paget represented one significant alternative to the Actonian view, it was clearly not the only, or even the predominant, trend of thought upon masturbation among the Victorian medical profession.

Even otherwise radical medical writers on sex condemned self-abuse. Dr. George Drysdale's Malthusian work *Elements of Social Science* (first published anonymously in 1854) advocated early marriage with the use of contraceptive measures, anathematized by most of the contemporary medical profession as "conjugal onanism." For Drysdale, a secularist and rationalist, the unnatural restraints society placed on the indulgence of natural urges during the years of youthful vitality led inevitably to the evils of masturbation, a practice that he was convinced was essentially pernicious.[8] Horror over onanism was not merely about a distinction between non-procreative and potentially reproductive sexual activity. Drysdale warned against "injurious habits of self-pollution," which he believed would lay the foundations of lingering disease during the vulnerable period of puberty.[9] Doctors and authorities who might disagree on everything else could nevertheless agree on this.

The application of brutal remedies for self-abuse is a charge often laid to the Victorian medical profession. Certainly, in 1870 *The Lancet* recommended, for cases of sexual debilitation, "guarding the penis for a time against improper manipulation" by "keeping up slight soreness of the body of the organ . . . sufficient to render erection painful." Cauterization might be routinely prescribed for "over-sensitivity" of the organ.[10] But remedies that made erection uncomfortable were not the province of the orthodox profession alone. The "American remedy," consisting of "a ring of common metal, with a screw passing through one of its sides, and projecting into the centre, where it had a button extremity . . . to be applied to the 'part affected' at bed-time," was an expedient probably "extensively used," but it was purchased by sufferers at disproportionate expense from purveyors of quack nostrums, not imposed by doctors upon victimized patients.[11] The horror over masturbation and the related phenomenon of nocturnal emissions was widespread in popular belief. It was intensified and exploited by quacks and charlatans.

Wise to the widespread market for their wares, quacks found all sorts of niches to attract the attention of the sexually troubled: posters, handbills, and newspaper advertisements, as well as catchpenny "anatomical museums." Exploiting a desire for information as much as prurient voyeurism,

[8]George Drysdale, *Elements of Social Science; or, Physical Sexual and Natural Religion, An Exposition of the True Cause and Only Cure of the Three Primary Social Evils: Poverty, Prostitution, and Celibacy, by a Doctor of Medicine* (London, 1905), pp. 80–81.

[9]Ibid., pp. 77–78.

[10]*The Lancet*, 1870, no. 2:159.

[11]*The Lancet*, 1857, no. 2:537.

these establishments displayed wax models of the dreadful consequences of onanism next to those depicting venereal disease and horrific portrayals of monstrosities and of childbirth. The museums were also centers for the dissemination of quack pamphlets and "cures."[12] The tracts put about by the vendors of patent devices and drugs painted lurid pictures of the dangers of self-abuse, nocturnal pollutions, and "spermatorrhoea." They would then offer the poor victim hope of restoration through the use of "vegetable compounds," or such devices as "Pulvermacher's World Famed Galvanic Belts" and the "Electric Life Invigorator."[13] In a climate of sexual ignorance, guilt, and fear, the quacks were able to build a profitable edifice on the site of masturbation, giving shape to inchoate male anxieties.

Concern about masturbation had several aspects. It was a "filthiness forbidden by God," morally reprehensible and a habit that decent men were united in believing to be disgusting. It was widely supposed to be depleting to health. Sometimes it was condemned as the first step in a course of impurity leading to fornication, disease, and death, eroding self-discipline and self-control. According to the Honorable Edward Lyttelton, a clergyman and a pedagogue, in *The Causes and Prevention of Immorality in Schools,* "the least defilement by hand enormously increases the difficulties of continence in manhood."[14]

Opinions varied, particularly among the medical profession. In a pamphlet containing "The Testimony of Medical Men," published and circulated by a purity organization called the White Cross League, some

[12]For general attacks on quacks offering cures for sexual disorders and their wiles, see *The Lancet,* 1870, no. 1:880, 889, and no. 2:72, 89–90, 124–26, 159–60, 224–25; *British Medical Journal,* 1885, no. 2:303–4; *The Lancet,* 1885, no. 2:350; *British Medical Journal,* 1892, no. 2:753. For the involvement of anatomical museums with the dissemination of quack remedies during the nineteenth century, see *British Medical Journal,* 1879, no. 1:823–24; British Medical Association Archives, Contemporary Medical Archives Centre (hereafter CMAC), Wellcome Institute for the History of Medicine, London, "Medico-Political" files, "Birth Control and Indecent Advertisements: Correspondence, c. 1929–1955" file (CMAC, SA/BMA/C.483) contains a description of such a museum, which had survived well into the 1950s and was still doing business without any attempt to update the exhibits, the descriptions, or the catalog.

[13]S. Gould, E.B.P. (medical herbalist), *A Brief Treatise on Venereal Disease and Spermatorrhea, Its Cause and Cure. (For Private Circulation Only. Entered at Stationers' Hall.) Manhood, How Lost, by Acquired Diseases; How Regained, by Vegetable Compounds* [?Bradford, c. 1910]; "A Graduate," *A Lecture to Young Men on the Preservation of Health and Personal Purity of Life,* 7th ed., published by Pulvermacher's World Famed Galvanic Belt Company (London, 1892); *Nature's Revelations for the Married Only,* printed for private circulation only by Electric Life Invigorator Company, G. W. Ventnor, The Limes, Painswick Road, Gloucester [?1904], contains, besides advertisements for the eponymous Electric Life Invigorator and other appliances, details of other publications issued by G. W. Ventnor, including *Startling Revelations for Men Only.*

[14]Edward Lyttelton, *The Causes and Prevention of Immorality in Schools,* printed for private circulation by the Social Purity Alliance (London, 1887), p. 15.

medical authorities agreed with Lyttelton that masturbation was the high road to a career of diverse debauchery. They contended that "the precocious indulgence of boyhood may . . . ripen into the ungovernable passion of manhood and become responsible for the support of prostitution."[15] Others believed that the vice of masturbation itself would become an overriding obsession: "the habit of solitary sin, learned and contracted at school, and not discontinued even in later and more mature years," would ultimately "become the one absorbing and uncontrollable passion of life."[16]

This latter view led to the apocryphal prescription of fornication as the remedy for self-abuse. So harmful was masturbation supposed to be that copulation was often supposed to be the "cure." In spite of the purity literature warning against medical men who advocated fornication as essential for male health, it is exceptionally hard to find evidence of doctors (or anyone) actually recommending this remedy. One elderly man (age seventy-six in 1924) did write the following account to Marie Stopes about his own younger days during the Victorian era: "The doctor . . . strongly advised me to drop masturbation. He even suggested certain houses where I might meet women of a better class, and advised the use of sheaths or injections. . . . The doctor even advised woman as a lesser evil than the risk of disease in masturbation."[17] This advice, remarkably, was proffered during treatment of the patient for "a clap" contracted during earlier (unprotected) application of such remedy. Such an account, given in a private communication, is hardly evidence of widespread prescription of such a remedy by the medical profession, although there are reports in the same correspondence of (perhaps jocular) hints by doctors in the interwar years to men suffering from the strains of continence that they should "find a woman."[18] Dr. J. Charsley Mackwood, M.C., qualified in 1910 and therefore of a younger generation than the above correspondent, suggested in 1920 that the campaign to make the horrors of sexually transmitted disease more widely known was such a success that "the convert practices self-abuse rather than risk infection," and this could be considered "a crime against humanity."[19] This is tenuous evidence compared to the fulminations—not only by purity campaigners but by doctors influenced by the purity movement—against the prescription of fornication. The influence of man-to-man, subcultural, almost folkloric communications on this subject, however, should not be discounted.[20]

[15]F. Le Gros Clark, quoted by Arthur T. Barnett, "The Testimony of Medical Men," in *The Blanco Book* (London, 1913), p. 223.

[16]C. G. Wheelhouse, quoted in ibid., p. 226.

[17]Marie Stopes Papers, CMAC, PP/MCS/A.1/25.

[18]CMAC, PP/MCS/A.19 DHB, A.165 DML, A.205 HWP.

[19]*British Medical Journal,* 1920, no. 1:130.

[20]Consider the persistence of the superstition (reported at least as late as the Second World War) that venereal disease could be cured by "passing it on" to a virgin.

There was another, still somewhat hydraulic, model of the male sexual function. This model too assumed an inevitable build-up of pressure within the male genital system requiring release but promulgated the theory that, in a state of health, nocturnal emissions occurring infrequently (monthly, paralleling menstruation in women) were "Nature's way" of dispelling pent-up sexual tensions. Anything more frequent was indicative of a general state of impurity and signaled the undermining of health. Deliberate masturbation would undermine health and probably lead to excessive involuntary emissions as well by stirring up feelings and functions best left in quiescence.

II

In the 1880s a growing concern over the need to protect the young from sexual danger produced a new genre of warning against masturbation. The works previously described were written either by medical men at least implicitly for other members of the profession, by individuals (radical medical men or proponents of alternative health systems) who wished to enlighten adult members of the public, or by quacks anxious to make a quick profit out of ignorance and anxiety. In the wake of the campaign against the Contagious Diseases Acts, leading to the formation of a self-conscious, though far from monolithic, purity movement, arose a discourse on masturbation emanating from figures of establishment authority (doctors, clergymen, educators) and directed principally at the young or those with responsibility for them. Tension between perception of an urgent need to warn of impending dangers and fear of putting undesirable ideas into formerly untouched minds meant that this departure was far from universally accepted as being necessary or desirable.[21] However, the amount of literature produced in this connection and its wide dissemination would perhaps suggest that the era of greatest masturbation anxiety was not (as is usually thought) the mid-Victorian period but the late Victorian to Edwardian era, indeed up to the outbreak of World War I.

Organizations such as the White Cross League and the Alliance of Honor emerging out of the anti–Contagious Diseases Acts campaigns published numerous pamphlets aimed at youths and young men, with the intention of inculcating a high and single standard of chastity. These attained wide dissemination: *True Manliness* by J.E.H. (purity worker Jane Ellice Hopkins) had sold over one million copies by 1909, presumably not including its further circulation in *The Blanco Book,* a compilation of White Cross League pamphlets produced for issue to troops.[22]

[21]*British Medical Journal,* 1881, no. 2:904; 1885, no. 2:303–4; 1892, no. 1:1266–67; *The Lancet,* 1885, no. 2:350–51.

[22]Edward Bristow, *Vice and Vigilance: Purity Movements in Britain since 1700* (Dublin, 1977), p. 138.

True Manliness, as its title suggests, portrayed an ideal of the true male as pure and chivalrous, emphasizing the virile struggle that the maintenance of continence required. The sexual dangers faced by men were depicted by dramatic metaphors: man was "an intelligent being mounted on a spirited horse," which he had to master. Would the young man "run the risk of tainting your blood and making it a fountain of corruption, till you have to loathe your body, the temple you have made into a charnel-house, reeking with the very breath of the grave," or would he "play the man, and fight against everything low and beastly, determined that your life shall have no shameful secrets in it"? Medical messages were blended with the religious and moral: "stored-up passion" would generate "splendid energy." The literature warned against quacks but suggested that reputable medical men were to be consulted if advice were needed. "Dirty, shameful, secrets in your life" may have subsumed both fornication and masturbation, but "a forbidden pleasure within your reach, forcing itself on your notice," surely must allude to self-abuse.[23]

Anxiety over self-abuse began at an early age. Child-rearing manuals warned parents to be on the lookout for the early manifestation of autoeroticism in infants, but it is not easy to establish the extent to which the recommendations of stringent preventive methods were carried out.[24] Warning literature, or literature aiding parents in giving warnings to their offspring, targeted younger and younger age groups, in spite of fears that warnings would put ideas into innocent minds. By the 1890s a number of such books were available. One of the most popular and typical was *What a Young Boy Ought to Know,* by Sylvanus Stall, an American divine. After forty-seven pages on "God's purpose in endowing plants, animals and Man with reproductive organs," it moved straight on to the danger of abusing the reproductive organs.[25] Stall attributed this danger to the existence of the hand: "Man is possibly the only animal which persistently pollutes and degrades his own body, and this would not have easily been possible if God had not given him hands, which He designed should prove useful and a means of great help and blessing to him in his life upon the earth." Stall threatened (echoing quacks) "idiocy . . . early decline and death . . . consumption . . . total mental and physical self-destruction" to those who failed to resist this temptation.[26] Even when the unfortunate victim of the pernicious habit lived to manhood and managed to become a father, the "inferior quality" of his "sexual secretion" would be manifested in his off-

[23]J.E.H., *True Manliness,* in *The Blanco Book,* pp. 115–43.

[24]Christina Hardyment, *Dream Babies: Child Care from Locke to Spock* (London, 1983), pp. 137–38.

[25]Sylvanus Stall, *What a Young Boy Ought to Know,* Self and Sex Series (Philadelphia, 1897), pp. 25–72.

[26]Ibid., pp. 80–83.

spring.[27] Stall's prescriptions for avoidance of self-abuse, and for recouping strength if succumbed to, involved life-style rather than patent remedies: wholesome light diet, healthy exercise, early rising, hard beds, the pursuit of mental improvement, cold baths. The book is nevertheless a horrifying and prurient work, with its detailed description of the vice it so roundly condemns.

Works such as Lord Baden-Powell's *Scouting for Boys* (1908) and *Rovering to Success* (1922), which aimed to regenerate the imperial race with a much broader program, probably reached an even wider audience than books specifically on sex education. Initially reserved to the "Notes for Instructors" in the appendix of *Scouting for Boys*, the remarks on "Continence" advised dealing with this problem in a frank and open manner, giving "clear and plain-spoken instructions." Self-abuse, according to Baden-Powell, "brings with it weakness of head and heart, and, if persisted in, idiocy and lunacy."[28] In later editions the cautions were given directly to scouts themselves: "There is one temptation that is pretty sure to come to you at one time or another and I want just to warn you against it."[29]

For a somewhat older age group, Baden-Powell produced *Rovering to Success*. "Rocks you are likely to bump on" included "Women," but during the "rutting season" masturbation was at least as dangerous as actual relationships with women.[30] Readers were reminded that "the Germ is a Sacred Trust for carrying on the race." The best precaution against excessive nocturnal emissions or the temptation to self-abuse was to keep "the organ clean and bathed in cold water every day."[31] At least Baden-Powell was convinced that recuperation was possible through leading a healthy scouting life. His ideas on the deleteriousness of masturbation remained the same over the years during which his works continued to be republished and were not influenced by the changing ideas discussed below. Like many other individuals and organizations involved in the field of sex education, he received "a heavy burden of correspondence with young men."[32] Among those letters which survive are several dealing with that particular "Rock."[33]

Although the importance of eschewing self-indulgence in solitary vice in order to build up self-discipline to resist later temptations was often em-

---

[27]Ibid., p. 113.

[28]Lord Baden-Powell, *Scouting for Boys: A Handbook for Instruction in Good Citizenship* (London, 1908), p. 279.

[29]Ibid., 10th ed. (London, 1922), p. 209.

[30]Lord Baden-Powell, *Rovering to Success: A Book of Life-Sport for Young Men* (London, 1922), p. 103.

[31]Ibid., p. 104.

[32]Bristow, p. 147.

[33]Baden-Powell Papers, Scout Association Archives, Baden-Powell House, London, "*Rovering to Success* Correspondence, c. 1922," TC/2.

phasized, enormous weight was given to the deleteriousness of the habit itself. The practice was supposed to be dangerously depleting to the vital forces of the adolescent at a time of life when these were needed for the maturing process, but it was equally pernicious for the mature male. In this period the middle-class male was often not in a position to marry before the age of thirty or so, and despite claims made by the works of advice that men were not fully mature and fit for marriage and reproduction until the age of twenty-five at least, there was a profound awareness of the strains such prolonged continence caused and the dangers that might ensue.

While there was intense anxiety about these "evil habits" being learned from "evil companions" during schooldays, rather surprisingly the fears were not of creating a permanent homosexual or "inverted" tendency through adolescent homoerotic experimentation. The anxiety seems to have been far greater that mutual experimentation would lead to solitary self-abuse. Homosexuality sometimes might be attributed to a continued habit of masturbation, just as it sometimes was seen as the ultimate vice into which the worn-out heterosexual debauchee would decline, the end of all "excess."[34] But the prime danger of self-abuse usually was perceived as the establishment of a habit of dangerous indulgence in sensual pleasure, eroding self-discipline and leading to a career of self-gratification likely to involve fornication with harlots, ending in venereal disease.

This apparent paradox may be related to the rise of concepts of a distinct "invert" identity, mutual and group masturbation being recognized as too prevalent among male adolescents to be connected with what was coming to be perceived as a congenitally anomalous, physically distinctive minority.[35] Another factor may be the persistent association of homosexuality in many minds with the specific act of buggery, or anal intercourse. While writers on gay sexual practice and history have indicated that within the subculture a considerable range of sexual practices would have been pursued, common assumptions, slang, and jokes connect homosexuality with this one particular sexual act.[36] Masturbation, singly or with "evil compan-

[34]For example, this would seem to be what Acton (n. 3 above) was implying, very covertly, in his descriptions of ancient debauchees "pandering to their vile desires and gratification of every sensuality" (pp. 198–99).

[35]Jeffrey Weeks, *Sex, Politics, and Society: The Regulation of Sexuality since 1800,* Themes in British Social History (London, 1981), pp. 96–121.

[36]Barry R. Burg, *Sodomy and the Perception of Evil: English Sea-Rovers in the Seventeenth-Century Caribbean* (New York, 1983), pp. 135–38; R. Davenport-Hines, *Sex, Death, and Punishment: Attitudes to Sex and Sexuality in Britain since the Renaissance* (London, 1990), pp. 77–83. The latter argues that the association of buggery with the sodomite identity enabled many men to distance themselves from the latter; however, see Jeffrey Weeks, "Discourse, Desire, and Sexual Deviance: Some Problems in a History of Homosexuality," in *The Making of the Modern Homosexual,* ed. Kenneth Plummer (London, 1981), in which he argues the very loose and inexact connotations (legally and popularly) of buggery. Brigid McConville and John Shearlaw, *The Slanguage of Sex: A Dictionary of Modern Sexual Terms* (London, 1984), cite a number of terms that imply buggery, for example, "arse bandit."

ions," was seen as one of a variety of deleterious habits to which male adolescents were prone, such as smoking, swearing, talking smut, and hanging about streetcorners.

The danger of some form of seduction by older men was sometimes recognized as a distinct threat. A work entitled *What a Boy Should Know* included the dangers threatened by "men who take an evil delight in telling young boys about this habit," and in such a way as "to encourage them to commence or continue this injurious habit." Such men, it was feared, "will lead you further, and towards more injurious and disgusting practices," which certainly sounds like a covert warning against homosexual advances. The reader should be prepared, in such a case, to "punch his head."[37]

What the authors were alluding to (though only to condemn it) was a wholly different discourse about masturbation, in which the practice was created as a site not of fear and guilt but of manly pride. Wicked men would not only declare that "it will do you no harm," but they even would assert that "it will make a man of you."[38] This faint hint of a persistent subcultural, even folkloric, set of beliefs about masturbation is also found in occasional remarks made in the letters to Stopes: "I was told by grown men that it was good for me and that kind of thing made a man of one."[39] How much this has to do with masturbation being seen as a necessary adolescent stage in sexual development, which would shortly be transcended and possibly even condemned if continued beyond that stage, is even harder to confirm than the existence of this alternative viewpoint on the practice.

Attitudes toward solitary pleasure were bound up with assumptions about masculinity. A "real man" had sexual urges, or at least the potential for them; however, a true man was able to control these. He was in charge of what his body did, not its victim. If this dynamic were reversed it boded ill, reflecting upon his very manhood. Masturbation was a temptation many men found themselves unable to resist, while involuntary emissions, apparently being completely beyond the effort to achieve conscious control, were experienced as even more threatening, a kind of "automatism."[40]

It might be argued that opinions about the ill effects of masturbation and "pollutions" in general simply were effusions by the medical profession, clergymen, and schoolmasters, and that all these diatribes had little effect upon the average young man. Such an argument ignores the fact that masturbation was equally, or even more strongly, represented as pernicious by underground and alternative sexual advice. It cannot be assumed that contact with either purity leaflets or quack pamphlets had no effect upon

[37]Dr. A. R. Schofield and Dr. P. Vaughan-Jackson, *What A Boy Should Know*, Questions of Sex Series (London, 1913), p. 50.

[38]Ibid.

[39]CMAC, PP/MCS/A.107 CHG.

[40]See, for example, G. Stanley Hall, *Adolescence: Its Psychology and Its Relations to Physiology, Anthropology, Sociology, Sex, Crime, Religion, and Education* (London, 1904), p. 457.

individuals, or that young men could ignore a climate of opinion that blamed masturbation for a variety of ailments from warts on the fingers to impotence, consumption, convulsions, insanity, and death for the man himself, as well as the corruption of his posterity. The existence of these pervasive discourses suggests that masturbation was a practice with the potential for generating enormous anxieties connected with manhood, strength, and sexuality.

III

While the production of anxiety-generating literature about masturbation continued, however, some authorities began to suggest that the guilt and shame aroused by purity literature and quack horror stories also were damaging. As early as the 1880s Sir T. S. Clouston, writing on the "Insanity of Masturbation," thought the quack scare advertising to be as productive of insanity as the vice itself, and similar arguments from time to time were expressed in the columns of the medical press.[41] This did not mean, however, that self-abuse was perceived as completely harmless.

A new perspective on masturbation began with Havelock Ellis's *Auto-Erotism*, part of volume 1 of *Studies in the Psychology of Sex*, first published in 1899. Ellis turned a radically critical gaze on the received wisdom concerning masturbation and commented: "It seems to me that this field has rarely been viewed in a scientifically sound and morally sane light, simply because it has not been viewed as a whole. . . . The nature and evils of masturbation are not seen in their true light and proportions until we realize that masturbation is but a specialized form of a tendency which in some form or in some degree affects not only man but all the higher animals." He went on to explode contemporary myths that autoerotic practice was inevitably physically, mentally, or morally debilitating, a uniquely human trait, and a sad side effect of civilization. Boys, he thought, particularly were prone to the risk of internalizing very negative attitudes toward masturbation, through encountering prevalent attitudes that it was an "unmanly" practice, as well as "exaggerated warnings and quack literature."[42]

Ellis was by no means altogether in favor of deliberate masturbatory practices. But while he attributed the traditional "morbid heightening of self-consciousness without any co-ordinated heightening of self-esteem" to the practitioner, it was only in the case of the persistent and habitual masturbator.[43] Although Ellis certainly did not ignore the possibility of

[41]Sir T. S. Clouston, "The Insanity of Masturbation," in *Clinical Lectures on Mental Diseases*, 6th ed. (London, 1904); see also n. 12 above.
[42]Havelock Ellis, *Auto-Erotism*, vol. 1 of *Studies in the Psychology of Sex* (Philadelphia, 1910), pp. 98, 263.
[43]Ibid., p. 261.

undesirable results in certain cases of masturbation (prolonged, habitual, or combined with a morbid constitution), his view of masturbation as inevitably deleterious only in specified circumstances, rather than universally, must have put many minds at rest. His writings on the subject foreshadowed changing attitudes toward masturbation. Given the limited circulation of *Studies in the Psychology of Sex,* however, their direct effect must have been somewhat circumscribed.

Well after the publication of Ellis's work, the old beliefs continued to be propounded in works of sex education. Norah March in *Towards Racial Health* gave prescriptions for discouraging "sexual laxity and distress" in the growing boy, which, in spite of the lip service she paid to Freud, had a familiar ring: "[He] should absolutely free himself from the dominion of eroticism. . . . The male mental attitude should be pure and cool enough to refrain from susceptibility. . . . The more frequently he exerts his willpower to triumph, the more easily will it act for him in the day of sudden emergency."[44] While the stress was on mental attitude rather than physical measures, the underlying attitude about the need for and the struggle involved in control was still there. March reiterated the usual exhortations about early rising, hard beds, wholesome diet, and cold baths. In dealing with masturbation in infants, she advocated making sure the hands were outside the bedclothes and distracting any child engaged in "unhealthy pursuits."[45] This policy of distraction seems to have been the new idea of the post–World War I period: some authorities even suggested that, as far as possible, the genital aspect was to be played down and preventive measures made to seem general rather than localized.[46]

As late as 1925, *For Men Only,* a work purporting to be written by "A Physician," discussed "Secret Habits and Vices" in terms that echoed the medical views canvassed by the White Cross League nearly fifty years earlier, with the imagery of "patches of deceptive quivering slime" threatening to engulf the unwary after a single misstep. The author warned of "a secret and hideous travesty of the marriage embrace that is practised alone under the cloak of night, a travesty more exhausting and more demoralising than any excess in married life," and added that "many a youth has had his life utterly ruined by this habit."[47]

However, a less gruesome view of the outcome of onanism was being disseminated by sex educators. (At this period most sex educators were to be found among those with an overall commitment to the ideals of the purity movement, anxious to promote a single standard of sexual morality.) In

[44]March (n. 2 above), p. 175.

[45]Ibid., p. 54.

[46]Hardyment (n. 24 above), p. 204.

[47]*For Men Only, by a Physician, author of "How to Be Healthy" and "For Women Only"* (London, 1925), pp. 73–81.

a volume by the Reverend A. Herbert Gray issued by the National Sunday School Union during the 1920s, it was clearly stated that masturbation "does not permanently injure physical vigour, sexual power, or mental capacity." Nevertheless, it was "a bad habit" and liable to have "mischievous" psychological effects. Furthermore it militated against "full efficiency and full nervous vigour."[48]

Similar views were debated in a textbook for the medical profession on *Male Disorders of Sex,* in which the genitourinary specialist Kenneth M. Walker argued that masturbation in the mature male was dangerous only because of "the mental conflict it engenders and the excess that it encourages." He was inclined to believe that in the young, and if "practised to excess, . . . physical health and growth may suffer." For Walker, masturbation was "an unpleasant and unsatisfactory practice," and in some cases, where great strain was being caused by continence, he was prepared to advocate coitus as being the preferable outlet for unbearable sexual desire. He emphasized, however, that for many patients, however good for health, coitus would be counterproductively fraught with guilt. Another expedient he suggested for the patient "overwhelmed with ungratified sexual desire" was "a single act of masturbation, deliberately undertaken." This would "cause no harm" if seldom resorted to; it should not be employed as a "source of pleasure."[49]

There is some evidence that counselors of young men (clergymen, schoolteachers, and youth workers) had sometimes recommended this occasional hygienic outlet in private interviews. One of Baden-Powell's correspondents, writing about his son's difficult struggle for continence, said that his son had been told by religious, medical, and educational authorities that fortnightly self-abuse was consistent with leading a pure life.[50] It is not much before the 1920s that such a view was advocated in print, and usually with the proviso that it should not be in any way a sensual indulgence.

Although some writers claimed that the idea that masturbation was harmless was gaining entirely too much acceptance,[51] most writers on the subject seem to have been trying to tread a fine line between exploding the old scaremongering myths about masturbation and continuing to discourage the practice. For all their up-to-date parlance of "repressions" and "sublimation" and their self-consciously modern appeals to the science of

[48]A. Herbert Gray, *Sex Teaching* (London, [n.d.]), pp. 50–57.

[49]Kenneth M. Walker, *Male Disorders of Sex* (London, 1930), pp. 100–111.

[50]Baden-Powell Papers (n. 33 above), TC/2.

[51]Meyrick Booth, *Youth and Sex: A Psychological Study* (London, 1932), p. 102n.; Marie Stopes, *Enduring Passion: Further New Contributions to the Solution of Sex Difficulties, Being the Continuation of "Married Love,"* 2d ed. (London, 1929), pp. 62–63.

psychology, these writers still were in the business of issuing warnings against self-abuse. Serious repercussions upon eventual normal sex life were threatened, either through establishing negative mental connotations with sexual arousal[52] or (according to Marie Stopes) by accustoming the organ to a particular type of stimulus coarsening to the sensitive response of the nerves.[53] These warnings, however, applied only to a persistent habit: the dangers of occasional lapses were minimized.

An often almost unconscious repugnance to the idea of masturbation was still prevalent. Although the possibility of microscopic study of semen for investigations into fertility had been known since at least the beginning of the twentieth century, doctors seem to have been extraordinarily reluctant to employ it. The mechanisms of fertility were little understood, but nonetheless doctors were happy to recommend and perform major abdominal operations of sometimes dubious value on women to correct infertility, while neglecting to perform a simple and noninvasive test upon their husbands. While this was part of a nexus of attitudes regarding male reproductive functioning as a simple healthy matter, unlike the innately pathological female system, is it fanciful to imagine that there was also a repugnance toward the mode of obtaining the specimen?[54] The somewhat scanty evidence presented by Stopes's correspondents on this subject appears to indicate that men, reluctant to submit their wives to the knife unless it were strictly necessary, were less horrified at the prospect than their doctors, in occasional cases actually raising the possibility of such an examination themselves.[55]

Advocates of artificial insemination for eugenic purposes, one must assume, must have come to terms sufficiently with a procedure regarded in most circles with repugnance or horrified condemnation to recommend it or even regard it as more desirable than the usual haphazard method of increasing the race. Nevertheless they went through enormous convolutions in working out how such desirable genetic material might be obtained, apart from what one would imagine to be the obvious method of "crude masturbation."[56]

Sex education continued to adhere to the new orthodoxy on the subject. By the late 1940s Cyril Bibby was writing in *Sex Education* that "the

[52]Gray, p. 52; Walker, p. 108; Leonora Eyles, *Commonsense about Sex* (London, 1933), pp. 38–39.

[53]Stopes, *Enduring Passion*, pp. 65–67.

[54]See Naomi Pfeffer, "The Hidden Pathology of the Male Reproductive System," in *The Sexual Politics of Reproduction*, ed. Hilary Homans (Aldershot, 1985).

[55]CMAC, PP/MCS/A.36 B, A.38 HHB.

[56]See correspondence between Herbert Brewer and C. P. Blacker, general secretary of the Eugenics Society, in Eugenics Society Archives, CMAC, SA/EUG/C.43.

trouble is not so much in the habit of masturbation . . . as in the mental conflict which may arise from its condemnation."[57] Dr. Eustace Chesser in *Grow Up—and Live,* while stating that masturbation "has no ill-effects, physical or mental" and speaking out against "those bruises which may be caused to the young mind when the child . . . is made to have a feeling of guilt and shame," nevertheless considered that although "it is not wrong . . . it is something you might make an effort to do without." While "masturbation may be regarded as quite 'normal' . . . it is wise and healthy to consider the reasons for doing your best to refrain." Chesser, a prolific and popular writer on sex matters, offered similarly ambiguous advice in his most famous work, *Love without Fear.*[58]

Such constant reassurance suggests that notions of the harm caused by masturbation were still widespread, which perhaps is not surprising. A mail-order lending library operating in North London and specializing in works on sex continued to circulate all sorts of Victorian horrormongering volumes in 1949, such as Walling's *Sexology* or MacFadden's *The Virile Powers of Superb Manhood.*[59] Readers who came into contact with such works, or even sought them out for prurient purposes of their own, did not necessarily realize that they were—or ought to have been—"amusing museum relics," as Cyril Bibby described them.[60] Underground tales of sexual mythology doubtless persisted and must have gone on producing their own horrors.[61] Even relatively enlightened works of sex advice and education, in spite of their stated intention of setting minds at rest, were profoundly ambivalent about self-abuse.

IV

It is possible to make some essay toward ascertaining how men actually thought and felt about masturbation during an era when attitudes were undergoing considerable change. In 1918 Marie Stopes, a scientist (not a

[57]Cyril Bibby, *Sex Education: A Guide for Parents, Teachers, and Youth Leaders* (London, 1946), p. 109.

[58]Eustace Chesser, *Grow Up—and Live* (Harmondsworth, 1949), p. 237; *Love without Fear: A Plain Guide to Sex Technique for Every Married Adult* (London, 1942), pp. 91–100.

[59]This catalog is to be found among the papers of the Mass Observation "Sex Survey" in the Tom-Harrisson Mass Observation Archive, University of Sussex, A.9 file 16/A, "Sex Survey 1949: Advertising and Publications: Published Material on Sex." Bernarr A. MacFadden, *The Virile Powers of Superb Manhood: How Developed, How Lost, How Regained* (New York, 1900); and W. H. Walling, *Sexology* (Philadelphia, 1902), both give gruesome accounts of the outcome of masturbation and the dangers of sexual "excess."

[60]Bibby, p. 128.

[61]Regrettably, the Mass Observation "Sex Survey" of the late 1940s (see n. 59 above) did not ask questions about attitudes toward masturbation. However, numerous pejorative comments about the male subculture, within which many men first learned about sex, deplored the "smutty" and unpleasant associations thus acquired.

doctor of medicine), published at her own expense a little volume entitled *Married Love*.[62] In spite of her publisher's lack of confidence in the work and war restrictions, the book became a runaway best-seller, reprinting several times within the first year and selling over half a million copies within seven years, more than famous fiction best-sellers of the period. She subsequently produced other works of sex advice: *Wise Parenthood,* giving detailed instructions on the subject of birth control; a short pamphlet clearly explaining to working-class women how to protect themselves from weakening pregnancies; a book of advice for mothers entitled *Radiant Motherhood;* a sex education manual, *Sex and the Young;* a short volume containing *The Truth about Venereal Disease;* and a textbook on *Contraception* aimed at the medical profession.[63]

These books sold well, by which we can make some assumptions about the need for sexual instruction during the period, although salacious interest cannot be excluded entirely as a motive for their purchase. (One young man admitted that he had initially purchased *Married Love* for autoerotic stimulus.)[64] But reader response went beyond purchase or perhaps recommendation to others. From the first publication of *Married Love* Stopes received a torrent of correspondence from nearly all social classes that continued until her death in 1958, although it declined radically after World War II. Several thousand of these letters survive. Over 40 percent of her correspondents were men.[65] In spite of what appears to the present-day reader as her explicit bias in favor of monogamous heterosexual marriage at an early age, consequent upon a chaste youth, what seems to have struck her contemporaries was her sympathy on the seldom-discussed topic of sex. Men confessed their premarital and extramarital affairs, mercenary or otherwise, and revealed their anxieties over masturbation as well as problems affecting sex life within marriage. She was even consulted by a few men describing themselves as homosexual or at least as having "effeminate" or "inverted" sides to their nature in the expectation of a certain sympathy, and even the hope that she might write something particularly geared toward their problems.[66] The overwhelming majority of her correspondents, however, implicitly were heterosexual and either married or hoping to be.

We therefore have at our disposal a collection of letters revealing at-

[62]Marie Stopes, *Married Love: A New Contribution to the Solution of Sex Difficulties, with a Preface by Dr. Jessie Murray, and Letters from Professor E. H. Starling, F.R.S., and Father Stanislaus St. John, S.J.* (London, 1918).

[63]Peter Eaton and Marilyn Warnick, *Marie Stopes: A Checklist of Her Writings* (London, 1977); Billie Melman, *Woman and the Popular Imagination in the 1920s* (London, 1988), p. 3.

[64]CMAC, PP/MCS/A. 168 AMM.

[65]Lesley A. Hall, "The Stopes Collection in the Contemporary Medical Archives Centre of the Wellcome Institute for the History of Medicine," *Bulletin of the Society for the Social History of Medicine* 32 (1983): 50–51.

[66]CMAC, PP/MCS/A.240 CDW, A.159 PL, A.174 CTM.

titudes to sex and to sexual conduct from thousands of men of all social classes, covering the period 1918–45. Most of these men had grown up with exposure to the traditional Victorian and immediately post-Victorian views on marriage, sex, and the roles of the sexes. They were also exposed to the new ideas being promulgated by Stopes herself and by other writers reacting against "Victorianism." Thus they are a valuable source for study of changing (or persisting) attitudes during an age of transition. While these letters obviously represent a self-selected sample, on the basis of the other issues about which correspondents consulted Stopes it seems reasonable to assume that they were typical of a considerable proportion of the population, distinguished largely by the determination to do something about their problems that led them to write to Stopes.

The majority of the men who wrote to Stopes displayed a remarkable enthusiasm for her ideals of marriage. In some cases with a certain hesitation, they were receptive to her doctrines concerning birth control within marriage, and they were passionately engaged by her vision of sex within marriage as a mutual and reciprocal pleasure. Apparently, therefore, they were very receptive to the new morality of the 1920s, if in many cases they had difficulties with the practicalities, from actually obtaining contraceptive devices to locating the clitoris.[67] It is possible, of course, that preceding attitudes toward marriage were less Victorian and less patriarchal than is often assumed.

This attitude toward marriage and its possibilities contrasts surprisingly with the way correspondents presented problems relating to masturbation. Sufferers (in their own eyes it was suffering) decried "that pernicious and shameful habit, self-abuse" and "the exquisite but pernicious soul and body-destroying sin of masturbation."[68] They declared of themselves, "I was a slave to the vile practice," and "I have been a weak and miserable rotter."[69] Such pejorative terms suggest considerable internalization of prevalent attitudes toward the solitary vice. The practice was said to have been picked up from "undesirable and debased characters" or "a rotten set."[70] (Those who stated that they had acquired the habit as the result of homosexual seduction [or "degradation"] at an early age at school seem in all cases to have been approaching Stopes about a habit they found themselves unable to overcome, not about any particular sense of having thus become "inverted" by nature.)[71] Self-abuse was described as "folly," a "mistake," even

---

[67] See Lesley A. Hall, *Hidden Anxieties: Male Sexuality, 1900–1950* (Oxford, 1991), chaps. 3 and 4, for discussion of the changing ideology of marriage at this period and the response of Stopes's correspondents.

[68] CMAC, PP/MCS/A.157 ML, A.220 WS; similar feelings were often expressed: see also A.228 AGS, A.245 MW, A.168 AMM, A.17 CH, A.128 JSH, A.244 WPW, A.64 GWC.

[69] CMAC, PP/MCS/A.183 JM, A.157 FJL.

[70] CMAC, PP/MCS/A.54 C, A.32 B.

[71] CMAC, PP/MCS/A.115 HPH, A.244 WPW, A.232 CT, A.157 ML, A.65 C.

a "disease,"[72] and it was presented to Stopes as something of which the sufferer was a victim: "The urge got a great hold on me until finally I was unable to hold myself in."[73] One man claimed that he had been "edected [*sic*]" to it.[74] In some cases ignorance was pleaded: "[I] was denied such knowledge as a boy, abused myself, was never warned"; "I did not know the dangers of it and became, I suppose, fascinated."[75] Some claimed that their eyes had finally been opened by sex education literature: "Somehow I got hold at the age of nineteen of a book called 'What a Young Man Ought to Know.' Having read it, and with a violent assertion of will-power, I overcame the vice of masturbation, and have kept free from it ever since."[76]

Men described the feelings and symptoms they experienced as a result (so they believed) of the practice. For some it was a matter of its effects on the "nerves": "This has given me a great feeling of nervousness, shame and remorse." One correspondent wrote, "When I was about twenty-two I had a nervous breakdown and the doctor who attended me said case was taken just in time and the I was on that verge of Petit Mal . . . It was not until I read that book that I realised what harm I had been doing to my health through self-abuse." Another noted, "Nervous system all to pieces."[77]

Others believed it had had deleterious effects upon the organ itself, either by restricting its growth ("My penis is far too small. . . . This I realise . . . is due to abuse")[78] or precisely the opposite, as with "'too frequent erection,' a certain 'flabbiness' and possible 'overenlargement' of the male organ" attributed to "youthful indulgence in solitude."[79] Varicocele (a cluster of varicose veins on one testicle) widely was supposed to be another effect.[80] One working-class man believed that "eventually nature's desire and masturbation turned me insane in my opinion," the traditional penalty.[81] A young railway clerk produced a compendium of symptoms reading like a quack pamphlet's warnings on the subject: "As a result I am very pale and awfully depressed, I cannot interest myself in anything, I am unfit for my work, sometimes I feel so depressed that I wish I was dead. I am perfectly certain that my present condition is due to my awful folly as described above. . . . My chief ailments are: increasing headaches, aching eyes, and I have a throbbing in my body that seems to make my whole being give a little automatic jump, the jump keeping exact time with my

[72]CMAC, PP/MCS/A.176 MM, A.183 WN, A.107 GHG, A.232 CT, A.239 CW.

[73]CMAC, PP/MCS/A.132 HPH.

[74]CMAC, PP/MCS/A.126 JGH.

[75]CMAC, PP/MCS/A.194 TCP, A.176 MM; see also A.252 AEW, A.222 PDS, A.222 JHS, A.123 HPH, A.117 CH.

[76]CMAC, PP/MCS/A.32 JJB.

[77]CMAC, PP/MCS/A.126 JGH, A.107 CHG, A.64 GWC.

[78]CMAC, PP/MCS/A.222 JHS.

[79]CMAC, PP/MCS/A.208 AWR.

[80]CMAC, PP/MCS/A.194 TCP, A.89 F.

[81]CMAC, PP/MCS/A.65 C.

pulse and veins, the throbbing is greatly pronounced near the temple and ears."[82] Another man was so convinced of the deleterious effects of the habit that he attributed all his troubles at the age of twenty-nine to self-abuse carried on twelve years previously, for a period of five months and then abandoned.[83] Masturbation was also blamed for eczema between the legs and a dripping after urination.[84] Others, while noticing no particular adverse effects, were concerned that it might have disastrous repercussions on their abilities when they married or even affect any children they might father.[85] Some wondered if sexual problems they experienced during marriage could have been caused by it.[86]

Heroic remedies for this ailment (as it was perceived) were demanded: "Would you advise me to be circumcised? . . . If you advise circumcision could I do it myself as I don't wish to approach a doctor on the subject as I am thoroughly ashamed of myself."[87] "Now will you tell me if vasectomy will cure my loss of semen, for I confess that even yet I get at intervals the terrible craving to indulge in this sin, and sometimes have nocturnal losses."[88] The belief that vasectomy was a cure for "sexual weakness" is also found among enquiries received by the Eugenics Society about this operation.[89]

One or two of Stopes's readers did venture to voice a certain skepticism about the alleged horrendous effects of self-abuse: "I know it should be discouraged but all boys do it and nothing ever happens"; "I feel sure [it] is not so harmful as generally thought but is obviously unpleasant and undesirable."[90] Some considered it a "lesser evil" than fornication: "I was told and I believed, that the only possible alternative to this was to go with prostitutes, and that this alternative was more degrading than the other."[91]

The commonsense approach that regulated self-relief could be a permissible expedient—morally and even hygienically preferable to fornication—was advocated by the clergymen among Stopes's correspondents rather than by doctors, presumably on grounds of comparative morality. One, conceding that "it cannot be discussed in public prints," suggested that if

[82]CMAC, PP/MCS/A.189 WN.

[83]CMAC, PP/MCS/A.128 JSH.

[84]CMAC, PP/MCS/A.228 AGS, A.232 EB.

[85]CMAC, PP/MCS/A.239 CW, A.220 WS, A.63 C, A.80 SGE; similar anxieties are also to be found in A.252 AEW, A.222 PDS, A.183 JM, A.120 OLH, A.107 CHG, A.43 PAB.

[86]Both impotence and premature ejaculation were attributed to this cause: CMAC, PP/MCS/A.185 AGM, A.89 F, A.37 WB, A.64 GWC, A.88 FWF, A.157 ML, A.109 EG.

[87]CMAC, PP/MCS/A.239 CW; see also A.132 LACH (Royal Air Force).

[88]CMAC, PP/MCS/A.220 WS.

[89]Eugenics Society Archives, CMAC, SA/EUG/D.210–12, "Voluntary Sterilisation: Enquiries."

[90]CMAC, PP/MCS/A.248 Sgt. HTW (in India), A.42 Lt. Col. WWB.

[91]CMAC, PP/MCS/A.109 Major GCGG, A.200 JP.

masturbation "is only availed of for relief and self-regulation (like the bowels, as an eminent London medical man once said to me) say once a week or in ten days, I not only see no sin or fault in this but an act of self-denial, of escape, and probably of unselfishness towards another. It is certainly better than either seducing a girl, or availing of prostitutes."[92] Stopes was inclined to agree with the clergyman's point of view. Such an attitude contrasts, however, with the tales of those men who were so horrified by their practice of self-abuse that they sought fornication as a cure, an expedient that did not necessarily work: it might even exacerbate the problem. "Before I was married I used to have unions three and four times a night, two or three times a week with different girls in the hope of curing myself but it was of no use."[93]

Obviously, masturbation was surrounded for many men by guilt and fear, which extended to cover emissions that were not produced voluntarily. The use of the term "pollutions" to describe these emissions would seem to have embodied the emotions they raised. So adverse were the feelings about these phenomena that even the sexual sensations aroused by contact with an intended wife sometimes were perceived as frightening as well as sinful. One young man was so horrified by the emissions he experienced while embracing his fiancée, he informed Stopes, that he had returned to the front during the First World War almost hoping that he would not return.[94]

Profound worries over the use of contraception seem to have been bound up with these anxieties. The most commonly used method at that time was coitus interruptus, often known as "onanism" (and correctly so: it is a misnomer when applied to masturbation).[95] The practice of birth control in general sometimes was condemned as "conjugal onanism"; thus, the shrinking men felt ("as from sodomy," one remarked) perhaps was not surprising.[96] The stigma around masturbation also caused considerable inhibition in conjugal lovemaking. Even when men had come to recognize the role of clitoral stimulation in female arousal and satisfaction, they were inclined to question whether this might be "too indecent to the nicely minded woman" or "savour of perversion or prove harmful."[97] How men themselves felt about being handled and stimulated is a subject about

[92]"An Old Priest," quoted in *Dear Dr. Stopes: Sex in the 1920s,* ed. Ruth Hall (London, 1978), p. 65.

[93]CMAC, PP/MCS/A.33 WWDB (in New Zealand).

[94]CMAC, PP/MCS/A.65 C; see also A.145 BJ, A.118 SNCH, A.54 HC, A.132 HDH, A.138 LRI, A.165 HGL, A.92 F, A.230 LT, A.157 WAL, A. 240 JW.

[95]See Genesis 38:9 for the origins of the word; for its use at this period to denote coitus interruptus (in the context of the expression of anxieties over the prevalence of the practice), see Arthur Cooper in *British Medical Journal,* 1914, no. 1:478.

[96]CMAC, PP/MCS/A.15 A.

[97]CMAC, PP/MCS/A.156 THL, A.56 RC.

which Stopes's correspondents on the whole were silent. Very occasionally, a man seeking further information about Stopes's comment on the woman "playing an active part" might mention something such as "she never 'handles' me and I never receive those kisses and caresses that I am anxious to bestow."[98] One can readily imagine that this was a subject shrouded in a complex of taboos. The very possibility that male arousal might not be automatic but require a certain degree of stimulation by his partner was almost never mentioned by writers of marriage advice manuals.[99]

On the evidence of the Stopes correspondence, therefore, it would appear that the horror of masturbation so often associated with the Victorians was exceptionally persistent. It prevailed throughout a period during which well-meaning writers of sexual advice—who, unlike the quacks, had no investment in fostering anxiety on the subject—were producing books that over and over reiterated the message that masturbation did not necessarily have the appalling results attributed to it. The underlying ambiguities in such writers' messages, and the continuing circulation of the older ideas, seem to have combined with the existing negative potential of masturbation to continue to generate enormous fears. Correspondents writing to Stopes during World War II were just as concerned as those who had written during the last months of World War I.

In spite of the half century elapsed since Ellis's *Auto-Erotism* and twenty years of a new orthodoxy on masturbation purporting to dispel Victorian fears and horrors, in 1946 Cyril Bibby could cite the following examples of questions asked by boys of thirteen to fifteen: "Does self-abuse make you lose blood? . . . lose strength? lose weight?" "Does masturbation cause insanity [or] . . . consumption, venereal disease, paralysis, pimples, etc.?" "If you do it, will you be able to marry?"[100] Nearly fifty years later, sex educators of the 1980s found boys believing that masturbation could cause impotence.[101] Anxieties about the possible effects of masturbation appear to have persisted with a life of their own, distinct from what respectable and reputable sources of authority were saying.

The evidence suggests that even while messages about masturbation and its dangers apparently were becoming more benign, the practice itself caused men profound anxiety. They were readily threatened by any hint that it might have deleterious effects and that a short moment of solitary pleasure might bring about dire repercussions. The act was and still is surrounded by a burden of derogatory associations ("wanker" continues to be

[98]CMAC, PP/MCS/A.220 JLS, A.88 F.

[99]One of the few who did was Dr. Isabel E. Hutton, in *The Hygiene of Marriage*, 4th ed. (London, 1933), pp. 65–66.

[100]Bibby (n. 57 above), p. 157.

[101]Carol Lee, *The Ostrich Position: Sex Schooling and Mystification* (London, 1983), p. 80.

an insult). During the period under discussion, sex was perceived as an area of danger generally. In the works cited above, men's sexual drives and sexual organs typically were depicted as both hard to control (only, if at all, by major efforts of will) and ultimately fragile, readily damaged by a moment's carelessness. So loaded was the subject with negative connotations that any reassurances seem to have been far less audible than the slightest hint of potential harm.

The Voluntary Sterilization Campaign in Britain, 1918–39

JOHN MACNICOL

Department of Social Policy
Royal Holloway and Bedford New College
University of London

In all advanced industrial societies, the unfolding of the twentieth century witnessed two interrelated demographic trends that had social, economic, and political implications of enormous magnitude—the growing use of birth control to limit fertility and the aging of populations through a rise in the proportion of elderly citizens. Taken together, these constituted a "quiet revolution" that fundamentally changed the demographic expectations of all men and women. Increasingly, parenthood could be voluntary and planned to fit the career and personal aspirations that accompanied improved chances of survival to adulthood and old age. In one respect, therefore, birth control was liberationist, bestowing on citizens the right to reproduce as they wished. Population growth could reflect the freely exercised choices of ordinary people.

Yet birth control also opened up the possibility of eugenic social engineering by a coercive state. Advanced industrial economies were increasingly complex and thus demanded control by a more intrusive, authoritarian state and progressively higher levels of skill and adaptability on the part of their work forces. Hence the contribution of each citizen—worker or mother—came under increasing scrutiny. Should the right to reproduce be enjoyed by all citizens, regardless of their value to society? This was the urgent question posed by eugenists, on the basis that social worth was determined genetically. But implementing eugenics in the form of social policy required the resolution of an enormously difficult political dilemma: the transition to the twentieth-century liberal state had brought about the progressive extension of democratic rights, and the right to reproduce was seen as part of that package of entitlements. Yet for eugenic social engineering to be effective, it had to violate those rights. In a liberal

This essay originally appeared in the *Journal of the History of Sexuality* 1992, vol. 2, no. 3.

capitalist democracy, coercive eugenic measures (such as compulsory sterilization) would upset that delicate balance of stability and legitimation; the social benefits promised by eugenists seemed too speculative and dubious to warrant the political risks involved. Only in totalitarian states could eugenics succeed as practical policy.

The eugenics movements that developed in all advanced industrial societies at this time were complex and held a variety of meanings for their loyal ideologues. But in essence they represented the possibility of forging a strategy of antisocialist reformism that would achieve social betterment without altering the existing ownership and distribution of wealth. As such, eugenics was an ideology with both "radical" and "conservative" implications, promising a true meritocracy but usually equating social worth with social class. As will be shown in this essay, the radical aspects of eugenics held a tantalizing appeal for some liberal and socialist intellectuals; but this was more than balanced by the opposition of organized labor movements, which correctly deduced that in practice eugenics would operate punitively against the lowest stratum of the working class.

In Britain, the eugenics movement reached a peak of activism and influence between the two world wars. The story of how it did so has now received the considerable attention of social historians, who have performed excellent work in their explorations of the seductive appeal of eugenics to individuals of widely differing ideological positions. But there still remains the vexed question of why eugenics in Britain achieved relatively little success in terms of policy. Why did such a powerful ideology, promising so much social improvement, fail to translate itself into specific eugenic legislation?

The question is puzzling because, on the one hand, the influence of eugenics appears to have been enormous. We simply cannot deny what Richard Soloway, in his magisterial new study, has called "the pervasiveness of qualitative biological evaluations that fell under the broad mantle of eugenics. . . . Eugenics permeated the thinking of generations of English men and women worried about the biological capacity of their countrymen to cope with the myriad changes they saw confronting their old nation in a new century."[1] A broad range of social debates—on education, birth control, public health, unemployment, and the overall population problem—were underpinned by widely held assumptions about the importance of heredity. For the first half of the twentieth century, a British citizen who wished to achieve upward social mobility had to pass through an extraordinarily complex series of filters built into the education system, the labor force, and societal attitudes, designed to let through only

---

[1]Richard A. Soloway, *Demography and Degeneration: Eugenics and the Declining Birthrate in Twentieth-Century Britain* (Durham, NC, 1990), pp. xi, xvii–xviii.

the fanatically determined or the exceptionally talented. In an essay such as this, space does not permit extensive citation of impressionistic evidence; but it should not in any case be needed, for no one can deny that the discourse of high politics was littered with quasi-eugenic assumptions. To take but one example, from innumerable ones that could be produced, in 1943 the secretary of state for India, Leo Amery—Tory reformer, advocate of family allowances, and strong supporter of welfare measures to improve the health and nutrition of the nation's children—could seriously offer the following solution to the Indian problem: "If India is to be really capable of holding its own in the future without direct British control from outside, I am not sure that it will not need an increasing fusion of stronger Nordic blood, whether by settlement or intermarriage or otherwise. Possibly it has been a real mistake of ours in the past not to encourage Indian Princes to marry English wives for a succession of generations and so breed a more virile type of ruler."[2] That such a statement could be made by a cabinet minister would seem to support Soloway's contention.

Yet, on the other hand, when its achievements are measured against the early hopes of its leaders, the British eugenics movement must be judged a failure. By the early 1940s, its political confidence had been shattered by the combined onslaught of several social forces. In the 1930s, the revelations of Nazi "race hygiene" policies had done more than anything else to discredit negative eugenics and had caused acute embarrassment to the leaders of the Eugenics Society. Particularly devastating was the fact that Britain was fighting a war with the most crudely eugenic regime in world history.

Again, as the 1930s evolved, the emergence of a middle-way, liberal reformist consensus—represented by bodies such as Political and Economic Planning (PEP) and the Next Five Years Group—increasingly seemed to offer the possibility that a "caring capitalism" could be achieved through corporatist state intervention and long-term planning. The cautious optimism of the "reform eugenists" who transformed the Eugenics Society in the late 1930s (notably, Dr. C. P. Blacker, A. M. Carr-Saunders, and Julian Huxley) was in stark contrast to the bleak pessimism of the old guard of the early 1920s, but it was also a sign that many of the political concerns that had driven the movement in the 1920s now had disappeared. However, this created real problems. The more accommodating eugenics became, the more it lost its meaning. There was undeniable plausibility in the reform eugenist position that nurture was not incompatible with nature, in that as the environment was improved, so could genetic inequality be identified more easily and appropriate measures taken. As Maurice Newfield argued, it should be possible to "contemplate the problems of nature and nurture in

[2]Leo Amery to Lord Linlithgow, October 1, 1943, quoted in M. J. Akbar, *Nehru: The Making of India* (London, 1989), p. 360.

explicit terms, not as antithetical factors but as variables within conditions that can be defined with increasing precision."[3] But this could be seen as a recipe for eternal delay, for when *would* the perfect environment be achieved? At what point would the ground have been cleared for eugenic measures?

The reform eugenics position was also a recipe for confused thinking, in which lip service was paid to the two notionally opposed positions of nature and nurture. Thus the draft report produced by the Population Policies Committee of the research organization called Political and Economic Planning (a committee containing both Blacker and Carr-Saunders) made strongly eugenic noises in arguing that a raising of the birthrate would only be socially beneficial if children were "born to the right parents—i.e., are free from avoidable hereditary defects," but in the same breath it urged investigation of the important question, "To what extent is there excessive inequality of opportunity? Use material from Wedgwood, Daniels and Campion on inheritance and ownership of capital, Moshinsky, Gray and Leybourne on educational opportunity, etc."[4]

Another weakness very evident by the end of the 1930s was the inability of eugenists, after several decades of research and propaganda work, to come up with convincing proof of the mechanics of Mendelian inheritance in human populations. Reputable estimates of the proportion of mental defectives who owed their condition to heredity ranged from 5 percent to 80 percent. This weakness was exploited ruthlessly by vocal critics within the scientific community (notably Lancelot Hogben and J.B.S. Haldane), who portrayed eugenics as a pseudoscientific apologia for naked class self-interest.[5] It is instructive to contrast the stagnant scientific development of eugenics with the rapid expansion of the "newer knowledge of nutrition"—a discipline that was about as old as eugenics and, by the 1930s, was having an enormous influence on a whole range of social debates. By contrast, the claims of eugenists remained speculative, unconvincing, and suspiciously self-seeking.

Thus when viewed from a landmark of the early 1940s, the British eugenics movement appears in complete disarray. The Eugenics Society's secretary, Dr. C. P. Blacker, was engaged on military service with the Royal Army Medical Corps. Deprived of his charismatic leadership and experiencing the disruptions of London in the blitz, the society's reliance on a small group of socially and politically well-connected propagandists was revealed even more clearly. In the confusion of wartime, the *Eugenics Re-*

---

[3]Quoted in Soloway, p. 317.

[4]Political and Economic Planning (PEP), Population Policies Committee, *Report on Population Policies,* chap. 4, "Foundations of Population Policy for a Free Community," June 19, 1940, Political and Economic Planning Archives, London School of Economics and Political Science, PWS 1/4.

[5]See, for example, Lancelot Hogben, *Dangerous Thoughts* (London, 1939).

view had been captured by the liberal clique of Maurice Newfield, Richard Titmuss, and François Lafitte, and it was becoming a forum for their idiosyncratic amalgam of eugenics, demography, and social reform. The hegemony of the 1930s "between Cobden and Lenin" middle-way reformism and the sudden wartime shift leftward in the British political mainstream was epitomized in the publication in 1942 of the Beveridge *Report on Social Insurance and Allied Services.* The society's most recent experiment in eugenic social engineering—the "homes in Canada" scheme, whereby children of eugenically desirable families would be placed with appropriate foster parents across the Atlantic—had ended as yet another tragicomic fiasco.

A list of the tangible achievements of the British eugenics movement does not look impressive. The Eugenics Society claimed a lobbying victory when in 1927 income tax rebates for children were increased in amount; but this was merely in line with the "new Conservatism" policy of tax cuts for the middle class and social insurance for the working class that had already been established by Winston Churchill's first budget of 1925. The society was also the leading organization publicizing the demographic concerns of the 1930s, playing a large part in the establishment of the Population Investigation Committee and claiming some credit for the 1938 Population (Statistics) Act; but civil servants and government ministers remained largely unconvinced by the Cassandra-like warnings about impending race suicide. In the late 1930s, the Eugenics Society provided a unique forum for discussion of the population question, providing employment and research facilities for individuals, such as David Glass, who were subsequently to become influential figures in British social science; but, again, there is the problem of deciding whether it was eugenic ideology that attracted such individuals or whether they were merely taking advantage of the intellectual stimulation, career-advancing political networks, and financial support offered by the society at a time when the academic discipline of demography was struggling to establish itself in British universities. Most telling of all, the society's campaign for the legalization of voluntary sterilization of mental defectives—seen by its leaders as crucial to the wider success of eugenics—came to nothing.[6]

Most historians of the eugenics movement have worried away at the question of precisely why eugenics should have appealed—in part or in full—to individuals of diverse and notionally opposed political interests, particularly some on the Left. But this should not surprise us: an ideology is not some kind of table d'hôte menu, to be accepted or rejected in full. It is instead a cluster of interrelated beliefs and value systems, from which individuals select a portion and to which they apply their own subjective

[6]John Macnicol, "Eugenics and the Campaign for Voluntary Sterilization in Britain between the Wars," *Social History of Medicine* 2 (1989): 147–69. This article contains a much more detailed account of the campaign and the issues raised by it.

criteria of political acceptability. Today many aspects of eugenics (for example, genetic screening for diseases such as cystic fibrosis or sickle-cell anemia) would be endorsed warmly by liberals as an enhancement of personal freedom, just as some socialists in the 1930s believed that science (including the science of human genetics) could be harnessed in the service of democratic progress. Diane Paul has demonstrated convincingly that many socialist and Marxist intellectuals in the 1930s envisaged the possibility of a "classless" eugenics and were prepared to accept that heredity played some part in the causation of social problems; their principal objection to eugenics was that it was usually deployed as a justification for capitalist inequalities.[7] Hence the Marxist Lancelot Hogben could declare in 1931 that "the legitimate claims of the eugenist" had validity and were "not inherently incompatible with the outlook of the collectivist movement"; likewise, the Swedish sociologists Gunnar and Alva Myrdal could advocate a eugenic policy that would "root out all types of physical and mental inferiority" but would not be based on criteria of class, religion, or race; again, when we find T. H. Marshall declaring to Blacker that he was "fully in sympathy with the aims of the Society," we need to balance this against his published writings in which eugenics did not exactly loom large.[8]

If this is true of a relatively arcane and elitist ideology such as eugenics, attracting most of its support from a small, London-based, medicopolitical clique, then it is even more true of political ideologies, which are subjected to all the compromises of electoral whim and the policy process. Had eugenics ever reached the statute book, this process of ideological dilution would have become even more apparent. The really interesting question, then, is not why a few liberal or socialist intellectuals occasionally appeared to flirt with eugenics: it is why the movement failed, for analysis of its failure reveals the balance of social and political forces that pulled Britain through the potentially devastating challenges of mass democracy, the rise of socialism, and the interwar economic depression.

THE VOLUNTARY STERILIZATION CAMPAIGN

In examining the origins of the voluntary sterilization campaign in Britain, we must note that it was part of a wider movement as eugenics gained credibility in all advanced industrial societies. Sterilization legislation was

[7] Diane Paul, "Eugenics and the Left," *Journal of the History of Ideas* 45 (1984): 567–90.
[8] [Lancelot Hogben], "Sterilization of Defectives," *New Statesman and Nation*, July 25, 1931; Walter A. Jackson, *Gunnar Myrdal and America's Conscience: Social Engineering and Racial Liberalism, 1938–1987* (Chapel Hill, NC, 1991), p. 78; T. H. Marshall to C. P. Blacker, July 3, 1945, Eugenics Society Archives, Contemporary Medical Archives Centre (hereafter CMAC), Wellcome Institute for the History of Medicine, London, EUG/C.227.

passed in countries such as Denmark (1929), Norway (1934), Sweden (1935), Iceland (1938), Germany (1933), and in several states in the United States. In all such societies, discoveries in human genetics led to the application of Mendelian laws of inheritance to human populations. Simultaneously, the growth in the power of the medical profession provided eugenics with a constituency of support. Sterilization held an attraction on several levels, for not only would it radically limit the procreation of the "residuum" or "social problem group," but also it would legitimate the power of the doctor. By a simple act of operative intervention, enormous social betterment would be achieved through racial purification.

In Britain before the First World War, there were implicit demands from eugenists that the breeding of the unfit should be restricted, but it was only after the war that a concerted campaign emerged to tackle the problem of racial degeneration via legislation.[9] The legal status of the operation to sterilize was unclear, and thus the immediate aim of the interwar campaign was to secure parliamentary legislation that would establish its legality. But, as I have argued elsewhere, the voluntary sterilization campaign must also be seen as part of a carefully planned, three-stage strategy by the Eugenics Society.[10] First, studies were to be conducted to provide clear proof that mental deficiency and other categories of "mild social inefficiency" that characterized individuals in the social problem group had a hereditarian basis, and then this evidence was to be deployed in such a way as to instill a "eugenic conscience" within political, scientific, and public opinion. Second, an intensive campaign was to be directed at Parliament to achieve the passage of a bill legalizing voluntary sterilization of mental defectives only, subject to a host of safeguards that would reassure public opinion that the measure was truly libertarian. The final stage was the most controversial and could only have been achieved once voluntary sterilization had been operating effectively for several years: to secure the passage of legislation for the compulsory sterilization of all categories in the social problem group.

The chronology of the campaign can be quickly summarized. In the early 1920s, the Eugenics Society began the first phase of this three-part strategy, launching several social problem group enquiries. Simultaneously, eugenists sought to influence the Mental Deficiency Committee, appointed in 1924 under the chairmanship of Sir Arthur Wood (who had been assistant secretary to the Medical Branch of the Board of Education). The committee originally had been set up for fairly mundane managerial reasons—to review the procedures for ascertaining mental defectives that had

---

[9]See, for example, Leonard Darwin, *Eugenics and National Economy* (London, 1913).
[10]Macnicol, pp. 154–55.

been established by the 1913 Mental Deficiency Act. But it became caught up in the much-emphasized concern that the incidence of mental deficiency was increasing (from 4.6 per one thousand population in 1908 to 8.56 in 1927), and that this represented a real increase rather than one artifactually produced by improved procedures of ascertainment and registration. By this reckoning, there were three hundred thousand mental defectives in England and Wales, only one-fifth of which had been ascertained. Containing several eugenists (Sir Cyril Burt, Evelyn Fox, Dr. A. F. Tredgold, and Dr. Douglas Turner), the Wood committee published a three-volume report in 1929 that discussed the relative merits of segregation, socialization, and sterilization in the social control of mental deficiency and gave strong support to the social problem group thesis.[11]

From 1929 on, the Eugenics Society redoubled its efforts and set up the Committee for Legalizing Eugenic Sterilization, with the aim of drawing up a sterilization bill and forming a coalition of support from relevant organizations in social work, public health, and mental care. Chaired by the society's president, Sir Bernard Mallet, the membership included Lady Askwith, C. P. Blacker, A. M. Carr-Saunders, A. G. Church, M.P., R. A. Fisher, Cora Hodson, Julian Huxley, and E. J. Lidbetter.[12] From the beginning, the committee labored under one great disadvantage: despite nearly ten years of effort, no convincing evidence had been produced of the biological basis of social problem group membership. The much-trumpeted surveys of the 1920s had only resulted in one study, E. J. Lidbetter's *Heredity and the Social Problem Group, Volume I.* When the committee began its work, this study had not yet been published: it was to appear only in 1933, after some difficulties in publication, and its tentative and speculative conclusions were to offer little comfort to eugenists. Thus the Committee for Legalizing Eugenic Sterilization was, in effect, an attempt to launch the second stage of the society's three-part strategy before the first had even properly commenced.

A crucial event in testing the mood of Parliament occurred on July 21, 1931, when a member of the committee, Major A. G. Church, tried to introduce a motion (under the ten-minute procedural rule) seeking leave to present a bill to Parliament. In a brief exchange of speeches, Church was utterly crushed by his fellow Labour M.P. and avowed anti-eugenist Dr. Hyacinth Morgan, who portrayed the voluntary sterilization movement as fundamentally anti–working class. In the resulting division, Church's motion was defeated, 167 votes to 89.[13]

[11]*Report of the Mental Deficiency Committee, being a Joint Committee of the Board of Education and Board of Control,* 3 vols. (London, 1929).

[12]C. P. Blacker, "The Sterilization Proposals," *Eugenics Review* 22 (1931): 239–40.

[13]*Parliamentary Debates* (Commons), 5th ser., vol. 255 (1931), cols. 1245–56.

Seeking to bypass the hostility of the House of Commons, particularly the strong opposition by the Labour party, the Eugenics Society turned to more sympathetic quarters—the bureaucrats in the Ministry of Health and Board of Control. Pressure on both departments by the more easily managed method of persuasion—the "representative" deputation from bodies such as the Central Association for Mental Welfare, the National Council for Mental Hygiene, the Association of Municipal Corporations, and the County Councils' Association—succeeded in the establishment of a Departmental Committee on Sterilization under the chairman of the Board of Control, Sir Lawrence Brock. Interestingly, Blacker admitted in private that the lobbying technique of the society was to make it appear as if the demand for an official enquiry emanated from these large bodies, whereas in fact it was the society that was masterminding the campaign.[14]

Originally, the Eugenics Society had hoped that a full Royal Commission on Sterilization would be appointed. This would have given great kudos to the cause of eugenics; but a royal commission would have had to include a plausible balance of opinion on the issue, including anti-eugenists who would have exposed the empirical weaknesses in the hereditarian analysis of mental deficiency. A departmental committee was easier to influence, especially one chaired by an official who was so sympathetic to the society's aims. (An example of this covert assistance is the fact that Brock met confidentially with Blacker and gave him advice on how to improve the wording of the society's draft sterilization bill.)[15]

Between June 1932 and January 1934 the Brock committee held thirty-six meetings and interviewed sixty witnesses. Dominated by its chairman, who pulled every string to assist the society in its campaign (thus flagrantly violating civil service neutrality), the committee's report recommended the legalization of voluntary sterilization for three identifiable categories of patient—mental defectives or the mentally disordered, persons suffering from a transmissible physical disability (for example, hereditary blindness), or persons likely to transmit mental disorder or defect. A list of extraordinary safeguards was proposed: two medical recommendations were required; no operation could take place without the written authorization of the minister of health (reinforced by consultation with an advisory committee in doubtful cases); patients had to have understood the full implications of the operation; and operations could not take place in a mental hospital where other patients were being cared for.[16]

The publication of the Brock Report was about as far as the voluntary sterilization campaign progressed. Intensive lobbying by the Eugenics So-

[14]C. P. Blacker to Lord Dawson, January 2, 1936, CMAC, SA/EUG/D.219.
[15]C. P. Blacker to A. G. Church, April 20, 1931, CMAC, SA/EUG/C.67.
[16]*Report of the Committee on Sterilization*, Cmd. 4485 (1934).

ciety for the remainder of the 1930s—including the formation of a large Joint Committee on Voluntary Sterilization and the exertion of renewed pressure on the Ministry of Health—produced a cool reaction from Whitehall. Mindful of the hostility toward eugenics among certain sections of public opinion (notably, the Labour party and the Roman Catholic church) and aware of the contradictory views within the medical community on the inheritance of mental deficiency, the ministry backed off from the issue. Though personally supportive, Sir Hilton Young (minister of health from 1931 to 1935) was very unwilling to take up such a contentious issue. His successor as minister of health (1935–38) was Sir Kingsley Wood, who likewise saw the issue as too "thorny and controversial" and was reluctant to alienate Roman Catholic voters.[17] For the remainder of the 1930s, the Eugenics Society got nowhere on the issue.

THE CAMPAIGN'S FAILURE

Why did the campaign fail? In the first place, the medical profession was deeply divided on the question of how far mental deficiency was an inherited condition; most thoughtful authorities realized that its causes were multifactorial. Having been defined by the 1913 Mental Deficiency Act in broad "social competence" terms, there was also much room for disagreement on the balance of clinical and behavioral indicators that should be used to assess the condition. Hence the British Medical Association refused to back Blacker's campaign.

Similar unease was felt within organizations representing those who cared for the mentally ill and retarded. The Board of Control was cautious in providing official support for a measure that seemed to threaten the custodial and curative role of the psychiatrist and which, A. F. Tredgold warned, could be interpreted as a callous, cost-cutting alternative to proper institutional care.[18] Mindful of this criticism, the Eugenics Society went out of its way to emphasize that sterilization could only ever be envisaged as a complement to humane methods of segregation, but anti-eugenists such as Lancelot Hogben portrayed supporters of voluntary sterilization as motivated by the self-interested, parsimonious "reformism" of the tax-paying classes.

Overwhelming opposition came from the Roman Catholic church, which, although representing only about 6 percent of the population, was a presence in society that ministers of health did not wish to offend. The 1930 papal encyclical *Casti Connubii* had voiced, in theological reasoning, the reservation felt by many in the medical profession—that still too little

[17]C. P. Blacker, "Memorandum of a Conversation with Sir Lawrence Brock, April 6th 1936," CMAC, EUG/D.50.

[18]A. F. Tredgold to Sir Bernard Mallet, November 24, 1930, CMAC, SA/EUG/C.337.

was known about the mechanics of inheritance for eugenics to have any predictive ability: it was impossible to say, in advance of conception, birth, and growth to adulthood, that two mentally defective parents would invariably produce a mentally defective child. The encyclical cast this in terms of the operation to sterilize violating mankind's natural right to enter the state of matrimony and produce an offspring to God's ordinance.[19] Whatever they may have thought about the theology, Ministry of Health officials were in no doubt about the strength of the Roman Catholic church's hostility.

Even more important was the opposition of the labor movement. Eugenics may have seduced a few left-wing intellectuals, as has already been noted. And like other fads of the 1930s—from Buchmanism to Social Credit—it was discussed on the Left as one of many recipes for social betterment. It is thus quite easy to find occasional instances of prominent labor intellectuals (such as Sidney Webb, H. G. Wells, Harold Laski, or—even more so—Frieda Laski) who displayed a modicum of interest and then violently wrench such small pieces of evidence out of their broad context. But, despite the claims by some historians, the central tenets of eugenics were seen as fundamentally anti–working class.[20] Dr. Hyacinth Morgan (a Roman Catholic) spoke for many in the labor movement when he voiced the fear that voluntary sterilization in practice would only be used on the poor. Blacker realized this and made several attempts to woo Labour M.P.s and trade union leaders—with a dismal lack of success. He was particularly vexed that "the Catholic opposition is in the fortunate position of being able to enlist the support of a formidable and influential body of opinion, namely the Labour Party," since on the birth control question the two bodies were opposed to each other.[21]

The fact remains, therefore, that a yawning gap existed between the eugenics movement and organized labor. The small clique of London-based intellectuals and propagandists who publicized the population problem in the late 1930s and involved themselves in groups like PEP or the Population Investigation Committee contained no one from the labor movement; indeed, one suspects that uncompromising socialists were specifically excluded. From reading the *Eugenics Review,* one might imagine that the Trades Union Congress (TUC) did not exist; from reading TUC *Annual Reports,* that the Eugenics Society did not exist. When their worlds did collide, labor leaders took a strongly anti-eugenics stand, as when the Independent Labour party stalwart Patrick Dollan angrily replied to one of

[19]Letetia Fairfield, *The Case against Sterilization* (London, n.d. [c. mid-1930s]).

[20]The most recent example of an attempt to portray eugenics as compatible with mainstream socialism is the controversial book by Stephen Trombley, *The Right to Reproduce: A History of Coercive Sterilization* (London, 1988), which nevertheless gives a very detailed account of the interwar campaign.

[21]C. P. Blacker to Lord Dawson (n. 14 above).

Sir William Beveridge's many speeches in the late 1930s on the population problem: Dollan argued that the answer lay in saving working-class lives at birth through social reforms and not, as Beveridge had maintained, with pronatalist policies to raise the birthrates of the middle and upper classes.[22]

However, the fascinating exception to this was the interest shown by some sections of labor women. In 1936 the National Conference of Labour Women passed a motion in favor of voluntary sterilization by six hundred votes to eleven, and support also came from the Women's Co-operative Guild. The reasons for this interest must lie in gender-differentiated attitudes: nonlabor female organizations such as the National Council of Women and the National Council for Equal Citizenship also passed resolutions in favor, and Lady Askwith claimed to have noticed a much greater interest from women than from men.[23] As I have argued elsewhere, analysis of the responses by audiences of working-class women to prosterilization speeches by representatives from the Eugenics Society reveals that women made an intuitive but confused connection between voluntary sterilization and broader issues of maternity, birth control, and even the punishment of male sexual offenders, believing that a sterilization operation curbed the male sex drive.[24] No doubt this reveals the dark and unhappy side of female working-class sexuality that could be voiced on very few occasions.

Even without this unfavorable balance of political forces, there were major legal problems raised by voluntary sterilization. The broad consensus of informed legal opinion was that an operation performed for therapeutic and curative reasons (for example, in the case of testicular disease) would probably be legal, but the status of a nontherapeutic one was very uncertain. A lower-grade mental defective could be judged non compos mentis by the courts, which would invalidate any consent the individual might have given. In the case of a higher-grade defective, the position was unclear. Even if valid consent were obtained, a prosecution could be brought (for example, by an aggrieved relative) on several grounds, such as "unlawful wounding" under the 1861 Offences against the Person Act. The bolder spirits in the voluntary sterilization movement argued that many nontherapeutic operations (such as cosmetic surgery) were performed every day; and even more telling was the fact that the wealthier classes could obtain sterilizations privately. But Blacker was perplexed as to the right tactics to pursue, sensing that to push the legal issue too far might result in a judg-

[22]P. J. Dollan, "The Decline in Population: A Reply to Sir William Beveridge," *Foreward*, July 3, 1937.

[23]C. P. Blacker, "Voluntary Sterilization: The Last Sixty Years," *Eugenics Review* 54 (1962): 15.

[24]Macnicol, p. 164.

ment outlawing all nontherapeutic operations unless consent from a clearly compos mentis patient were obtained.

The legal difficulties were symbolic of a wider political problem. A crucial issue raised by the voluntary sterilization campaign was one that affected the whole population debate in the interwar years—the impossibility of reconciling the coercive policies required if eugenic social engineering was to be effective with the framework of legal checks and balances that protected the liberty of the individual and contributed to the stability of British society. This was a problem much discussed in progressive liberal circles in the 1930s—and by commentators as different as Harold Macmillan and Joseph Schumpeter—in the context of the wider question of whether state planning was compatible with democracy. For long-term planning to work, it had to violate the rights of minorities, on a fascist model. But for plans to be introduced as policy, they had to pass through Parliament, and, as Blacker noted gloomily in 1938, "there seems to be no argument to which members of the House are more sensitive than that a given measure infringes the liberty of the individual."[25]

The dilemma was well understood by the politically centrist research organization Political and Economic Planning when it tried to work out the basis of a population policy for a democratic state such as Britain. The spread of contraception had created the situation where parenthood was increasingly voluntary, argued PEP. This could work advantageously, in that more children would be "wanted children"; but without proper education, many couples now could decide whether or not to have a child "without any thought of what would be in best interest of community." However, any interference with the rights of citizens to voluntary parenthood either would not work (as in some European countries) or would be resented strongly; as a PEP memorandum summarized it: "Idea and practice of individual control of parenthood part and parcel of western-democratic culture and concept of personal liberty. Attempts to uproot it certain to be regarded as intolerable invasion of personal liberty and likely to meet with violent opposition. Coercive policy likely to defeat its own ends. Unacceptable to a free community except *in extremis*."[26] In a democracy, therefore, the only line of advance could be through gentle persuasion, via policies of economic assistance to parenthood and strengthening the effective desire for children through the creation of a "population consciousness." Any restriction of the breeding of the "social problem group" thus could only be achieved through provision of birth control or by persuasion or education: compulsory methods were "out of question at present."[27]

[25]C. P. Blacker to E. Neill Hobhouse, April 6, 1938, CMAC, SA/EUG/D.234.
[26]PEP Population Policies Committee, *Report on Population Policies* (see n. 4 above).
[27] Ibid.

Voluntary sterilization was a particularly sensitive issue because, of course, it involved a medical operation on the patient's reproductive system and in the public mind often was confused with castration. Supporters of the campaign labored hard to present the proposal as essentially libertarian: mental defectives could be deinstitutionalized, marry, and lead more normal lives. Mental institutions thus would become "flowing lakes," with patients passing through, rather than "stagnant pools" in which defectives languished all their lives in misery and isolation. Unfortunately for them, however, eugenists were particularly inept in letting slip on a number of occasions the revelation that their ultimate goal was compulsory sterilization of the unfit. (For example, A. G. Church said this in the House of Commons, thereby destroying any chance his motion might have had.)[28]

As stated earlier, the Brock committee's recommendation was that voluntary sterilization procedures should be hedged in with numerous legal safeguards. These were necessary to assuage public concerns, and no doubt the intention was to remove them eventually; but they would have rendered any legislation unworkable in practice. Supporters of sterilization were repeatedly frustrated by this seemingly insurmountable obstacle—by the fact that, as Sir Hilton Young revealingly put it, the constraints of democracy would "not allow such a question to be decided on its merits."[29] After the fiasco of Church's motion in 1931, campaigners tried to circumvent Parliament and go directly to the Ministry of Health. But there they found that the ministers and officials who had offered them succor and covert advice were acutely sensitive to the mood of the Commons, especially on the issue of the rights of the individual, and in political terms regarded voluntary sterilization as of relatively minor importance.

The inherent incompatibility of eugenics and democracy is revealed even more clearly if one examines the situation in Germany, for the massive eugenic program launched by the Nazis after 1933 was only possible within the totalitarian political structure of fascism. A Social Darwinist movement had existed in Germany since the late nineteenth century, and a eugenics movement steadily developed in the 1920s: some sterilization operations took place semilegally, a focus for activity was established in 1927 in the form of the Kaiser Wilhelm Institute for Anthropology, Human Genetics, and Eugenics (under the direction of Eugen Fischer), and a Reich Sterilization Law was drawn up in 1932. We can see, therefore, that developments in Germany were comparable to those in Britain. As Jeremy Noakes has observed, the Nazis' 1933 Sterilization Law was not abruptly

[28]*Parliamentary Debates* (Commons), 5th ser., vol. 255 (1931), col. 1249.

[29]Sir Hilton Young to Sir Arthur Robinson, January 15, 1932, Public Record Office PRO MH 58/103.

new: instead, it represented the culmination of more than thirty years' activity by the German eugenics movement.[30] But until 1933, the progress of the movement was held in check by the restraints of political democracy.

After 1933, however, developments rapidly escalated, and, as the structure of the fascist state was established, so was it possible for a full program of negative eugenics to be introduced. Whereas in Britain citizenship remained a legalistic concept, under the Nazis the concept of "biological citizenship" was developed. Experiments were undertaken to try to discover a medicalized basis for race by criteria such as blood type; the shape of the teeth, gums, and tongue; the half-moon at the base of the fingernails; or the physiognomy of the outer ear. Restrictions on racial intermarriage and pronatalist policies for those judged "pure Aryans" were designed to consolidate the purity of this biologized citizenship, while an escalating program of compulsory sterilization led inexorably to genocide.[31] Clearly all of this was possible only because of a rupturing of those legal safeguards on the rights of citizens that remained intact in Britain and by the successful formulation of new, coercive apparatuses of political control. Revealingly, Theodor Geiger commented in 1933 on the opposition to compulsory sterilization that "concern about personal freedom rests on the liberal ideal of personal self-determination, an ideal which both in fact and in law has been too eroded to be maintained as a principle. Heroic collectivism is overcoming this attitude to life and making it appear superfluous. If a measure is recognised as socially necessary and useful, there is no point in criticising it with such arguments."[32] Thus in Germany, the erosion of citizenship rights took the form of a violent physical intrusion into the body—from the surgeon's knife to the gas chamber. By contrast, in Britain the campaigners for voluntary sterilization never even managed to surmount the legal obstacles.

CONCLUSION

The final question to be answered, therefore, is a simple but important one: was the eugenics movement the driving force behind those wider assumptions about the inheritance of intelligence, ability, and social worth that were so undeniably pervasive in the first half of the twentieth century—or was it the other way round? In a sense, the question is artificial, for the relationship was symbiotic. But posing it helps us to understand why so

[30]Jeremy Noakes, "Nazism and Eugenics: The Background to the Nazi Sterilization Law of 14 July 1933," in *Ideas into Politics: Aspects of European History, 1880–1950*, ed. Roger J. Bullen, Hartmut Pogge Von Strandmann, and A. B. Polonsky (London, 1984), p. 87.

[31]Robert Proctor, *Racial Hygiene: Medicine under the Nazis* (Cambridge, MA, 1988).

[32]Quoted in Noakes, p. 88.

many leading figures of the political ruling class in Britain appeared to es-
pouse eugenics—and yet the movement failed.

Richard Soloway recently has argued that the eugenics movement was
the driving force behind many aspects of the population debate in the
1870–1940 period.[33] At the risk of being overeconomistic, I would like to
argue the reverse. The decline in the British birthrate that commenced in
the late 1870s had multifactorial causes, all of them rooted in the transition
of the economy to a late-industrial stage of development. This transition
took place in a highly class-stratified, unequal society, whose rulers had to
cope with the potentially destabilizing forces of emerging socialism, the
irresistible pressure for mass democracy, and the slowing down of Britain's
economy.

The ideological context within which this peaceful transition took place
was one dominated by a seamless web of shared assumptions justifying the
existence of class divisions. Everywhere one looks, one finds such a view
pervasive—from the languid entrance requirements of Oxford and Cambridge universities, whereby the children of the wealthy and powerful,
however unintelligent, virtually were guaranteed a place, to the almost he-
reditary-baronial way that skilled apprenticeships were kept within certain
families. It was the pervasiveness of these assumptions that so frustrated
R. H. Tawney, when he described the existing education system as "class
stratification and the curious educational ritual which in England is an-
nexed to it."[34]

But this institutionalized inequality was balanced and legitimated by a
framework of legal rights and a flexible parliamentary democracy that protected the liberty of the subject and, more important, created conditions of
social order. By the mid-1930s, it was obvious that this delicate balance of
forces had steered Britain through the politically troubled waters of the
post-1918 situation and was successfully accommodating both the potential social tensions of three million unemployed and the restructuring of
the economy's industrial base. Whatever personal sympathy may have existed toward eugenics on the part of the political ruling class, the dubious
benefits of a measure such as voluntary sterilization simply were not worth
the price that might have to be paid in terms of political stability. For a eugenic program to have reached the statute book, a substantial and flagrant
violation of the notion of individual rights would have had to occur, perhaps fatally disturbing this political equilibrium. Indeed, the case of
Germany shows that only massive political upheaval, with the introduction
of a totalitarian state apparatus, would have rendered eugenics viable.

[33]This is the central thesis of Soloway (n. 1 above).
[34]R. H. Tawney, *Secondary Education for All: A Policy for Labour* (London, 1922; rpt., London, 1988), p. 65.

Thus, as argued earlier in this essay, we can find endless examples of major public figures who made quasi-eugenic utterances at one time or another and yet played no part in the movement. Eugenics may have provided them with a scientific justification of their class loyalties, but it was not the driving force behind the formation of those loyalties. Only one such example need suffice. In his Birmingham days, Neville Chamberlain had shown some interest in eugenics, even joining the Eugenics Education Society; and in the 1930s he was one of the few senior politicians who expressed concern over the population problem. Lofty in manner, immensely hard-working, and with an iron will, Chamberlain was the personification of the new post-1918 professional politician who was determined to refashion Conservatism into a powerful force, capable of maintaining the political status quo, defeating socialism by electoral appeal, and simultaneously modernizing the economy. As we now know from the work of historians such as David Dilks and John Ramsden, Chamberlain's personality was complex, but it would not be unfair to say that his view of the working class, especially their political representatives, was often close to disdain. His diaries and letters are full of disparaging references to the ineptitude of the Parliamentary Labour party in the 1920s, and he made no attempt to hide his feelings from his victims. An indication of Chamberlain's views may be obtained from his verdict on the 1923 general election result, which removed the Conservatives from office: "The new electorate contains an immense number of very ignorant voters of both sexes whose intelligence is low and who have no power of weighing evidence."[35] But was Chamberlain driven by eugenic concerns? If so, we would expect that during his extraordinarily energetic and reformist tenure at the Ministry of Health in 1924–29, he would have been receptive to the advances of the Eugenics Society. However, his attitude was identical to that of his ministry—a modicum of personal sympathy, but nothing more. Quite simply, there were innumerable other social problems that took precedence over the need to restrict the breeding of the unfit. Modernizing British capitalism in the new conditions of mass democracy, coping with a strong labor movement, and achieving social betterment on Conservative lines—these were objectives that could be attained by other means. Historians of eugenics should bear in mind the sobering thought that, for this paragon of the new politics, rating and valuation reform was far more urgent an issue than reversing the trend toward race suicide.

[35]Diary, December 9, 1923, Neville Chamberlain Papers, University of Birmingham Library, NC 2/21.

Pornography, Fairy Tales, and Feminism: Angela Carter's "The Bloody Chamber"

ROBIN ANN SHEETS
Department of English and Comparative Literature
University of Cincinnati

B RITISH AUTHOR Angela Carter holds a problematic place in the debates about pornography that have polarized Anglo-American feminists,
originally over issues of sadomasochism and other sexual practices, and
more recently over questions of artistic representation. In Carter's case,
much of the controversy has come to center on *The Sadeian Woman and the
Ideology of Pornography* (1978). Carter defends Sade because "he treats all
sexual reality as a political reality" and he "declares himself unequivocally
for the right of women to fuck" as aggressively, tyrannously, and cruelly as
men.[1] In this essay, I propose to reassess Carter's stance on pornography by
reading *The Sadeian Woman* in conjunction with "The Bloody Chamber"
(1979), one of her most brilliant "adult tales," and by situating both works
in relationship to the feminist debates on pornography that began during
the mid-1970s and continue to the present. Such an approach makes two
assumptions: (1) that fiction constitutes an important part of the contemporary discourse on sexuality; and (2) that an interdisciplinary approach is
necessary for reading imaginative literature about sexuality. Recent works
by feminist philosophers, psychologists, and film critics furnish new insights into the issues Carter explores in "The Bloody Chamber," such as the
link between sexually violent imagery and male aggression, the meaning of

I would like to thank Michael Atkinson, Gisela Ecker, Tom LeClair, and Ellen Peel for their
helpful suggestions. I would also like to express my appreciation to the Taft Foundation for a
summer grant to support the initial research for this essay.

[1] Angela Carter, *The Sadeian Woman and the Ideology of Pornography* (New York, 1978),
p. 27; further references to this work, abbreviated *SW,* will be included in the text. The book
was published a year later in London under the title of *The Sadeian Woman: An Exercise in
Cultural History.*

This essay originally appeared in the *Journal of the History of Sexuality* 1991, vol. 1, no. 4.

masochism for women, and the relationship of pornography to other literary and artistic forms.

After providing a brief account of *The Sadeian Woman,* I will analyze the relevant issues in the feminist pornography debates, including the arguments about sadomasochism that were so divisive in the late 1970s and early 1980s and the discussions about representation that became increasingly prevalent during the 1980s. Because the written debate was earlier, more extensive, more explicit, and more theoretical in America than in Great Britain,[2] I rely primarily on American polemicists, such as Andrea Dworkin, Robin Morgan, Gayle Rubin, and Pat Califia, for matters of sexual practice. For issues of representation, I draw upon British and American film theorists and cultural critics, such as Laura Mulvey, Annette Kuhn, Susan Kappeler, Mary Ann Doane, and Linda Williams. In offering a detailed study of one story, I am striving for the "fully realized feminist thematic reading" of pornography advocated by Susan Rubin Suleiman.[3]

I

In 1978 *The Sadeian Woman* seemed isolated and idiosyncratic. Sade existed as "a potent vacancy" in British literary circles because publication of his books had been curtailed in response to a highly publicized murder trial.[4] Public discussion of pornography was shaped by two opposing factions, neither of which was particularly helpful to feminists: (1) the liberal consensus represented by the Williams Committee on Obscenity and Film Censorship, which in its 1979 report allowed the circulation but not the display of pornographic materials; and (2) the religiously based, right-wing, pro-censorship lobby led by Mary Whitehouse and the National Fes-

---

[2]Many British commentators base their theoretical analyses of pornography on American texts. For example, in their article about lesbian sadomasochism, Susan Ardell and Sue O'Sullivan decry the "almost complete absence of talking or writing about sex" in England ("Upsetting an Applecart: Difference, Desire and Lesbian Sadomasochism," *Feminist Review* 23 [June 1986]: 41). A. W. B. Simpson, a member of the Williams Committee, notes that "virtually everything which has been produced by the radical feminist movement on the subject is American" (*Pornography and Politics: A Look Back to the Williams Committee* [London, 1983], p. 67).

[3]Susan Rubin Suleiman, "Pornography, Transgression, and the Avant-Garde: Bataille's *Story of the Eye,*" in *The Poetics of Gender,* ed. Nancy K. Miller (New York, 1986), p. 130.

[4]*Justine* was first published in mass-market paperback in 1965 and quickly went through four editions. But when the press covering the Brady-Hindley trial revealed that the murderers had tortured their victims in imitation of particular scenes in Sade's novels, some politicians and editorial writers urged that respectable publishers refuse to handle Sade's works. According to John Sutherland, "Since 1966, no British publisher has been prepared to put his name to the Divine Marquis's more notorious books" (*Offensive Literature: Decensorship in Britain, 1960–1982* [London, 1982], p. 72).

tival of Light.[5] In the late 1970s, representatives of various women's groups testified before the Williams Committee, critiques of pornography appeared in magazines like *Spare Rib,* and "Reclaim the Night" marches began in London and other cities. Rejecting traditional definitions that emphasize content (the explicit representation of sexual organs or activities) and intention (to arouse the audience, generally assumed to be male), feminists sought to redefine pornography as a form of violence against women and to classify as pornographic those representations which eroticize male domination. Organized attacks on sex shops and "adult" bookstores would begin in 1980, and the 1981 publication of books by Andrea Dworkin and Susan Griffin, feminists active in the American antipornography movement, would bring new urgency to the discussions in Great Britain.[6]

Unlike literary critics in France and America, Carter was not interested in defending pornography in aesthetic terms. She did not follow traditional political approaches—liberal or conservative; nor did she pursue arguments being formulated by feminists active in the early phases of the antipornography movement. Yet in retrospect, publication of *The Sadeian Woman* marked the beginning edge of a controversy that would be at the center of feminist discourse for more than a decade.

Although Carter assumes that most pornography is reactionary because it serves "to reinforce the prevailing system of values and ideas in a given society," she envisions the possibility of a "moral pornographer" who would use the genre "as a critique of current relations between the sexes." As a critic, the moral pornographer would "penetrate to the heart of the contempt for women that distorts our culture." As a visionary hoping to transform society and human nature, such a person would create "a world of absolute sexual licence for all the genders" (*SW,* pp. 18–20). Carter acknowledges Sade's misogyny—his fantasies of "woman-monsters" and his "hatred of the mothering function"—but she commends Sade "for claiming rights of free sexuality for women, and in installing women as beings of power in his imaginary worlds" (*SW,* pp. 25, 36). Sade invented·women who suffer, most notably the innocent and always abused Justine, but he also invented women who cause suffering, such as Justine's sexually aggressive, whip-wielding sister, Juliette. Sade believed "it would only be through the medium of sexual violence that women might heal themselves

[5]For a feminist critique of the Williams Committee, see Susanne Kappeler, *The Pornography of Representation* (Minneapolis, 1986), pp. 19–34; for further information on Mary Whitehouse, see Rosemary Betterton, ed., *Looking On: Images of Femininity in the Visual Arts and Media* (London, 1987), p. 145; and especially Ruth Wallsgrove, "Between the Devil and the True Blue Whitehouse," in Betterton, ed., pp. 170–74.

[6]Sutherland, p. 143.

of their socially inflicted scars, in a praxis of destruction and sacrilege" (*SW*, p. 26). Asking that we "give the old monster his due," Carter asserts that Sade "put pornography in the service of women, or, perhaps, allowed it to be invaded by an ideology not inimical to women" (*SW*, p. 37). Initial reviews were positive, but as the feminist antipornography movement gained momentum in England and North America, *The Sadeian Woman* was denounced by Andrea Dworkin as "a pseudofeminist literary essay."[7]

II

When Robin Morgan characterized women who opposed the antipornography movement as "Sade's new Juliettes," she revealed how deeply the issue had divided feminists of the early 1980s. According to Morgan, writers like Ellen Willis, Gayle Rubin, and Pat Califia have no right to call themselves feminists. By supporting pornography, they have chosen a sexual practice based on domination, aligned themselves with Juliette, the power-mad protagonist of Sade's novels who enslaved others in pursuit of her own pleasure, and given up "all hope of connecting with *real* sexual energy."[8]

Morgan's scornful comment about other women writers is typical of the intensely acrimonious debate in its sense of rigid oppositions—"for" or "against," "feminist" or "antifeminist"—and in its reliance on unstated assumptions about woman's nature. No matter how the conflicting positions are labeled, each side perceives the other "as falling into the dominant view of women associated with the right or left: virgins or whores, prudes or sexual objects, victims or consenting participants."[9] Feminists who defend pornography, such as Willis, Califia, and Rubin, often present themselves as "bad girls," adventurous sexual outlaws daring to break restraints. They

[7]Andrea Dworkin, *Pornography: Men Possessing Women* (New York, 1981), p. 84.

[8]Robin Morgan, *Anatomy of Freedom: Feminism, Physics, and Global Politics* (New York, 1982), pp. 116–17, my emphasis.

[9]Ann Russo, "Conflicts and Contradictions among Feminists over Issues of Pornography and Sexual Freedom," *Women's Studies International Forum* 10 (1987): 106. Critics have utilized a variety of terms to define the opposing positions in the feminist pornography debates: "anti-porn" versus "pro-porn" (Russo); "radical" versus "libertarian" (Cheryl H. Cohen, "The Feminist Sexuality Debate: Ethics and Politics," *Hypatia* 1 [1986]: 71–86); "cultural feminists" versus "radical feminists" (Alice Echols, "The Taming of the Id: Feminist Sexual Politics, 1968–83," in *Pleasure and Danger: Exploring Female Sexuality*, ed. Carole S. Vance [Boston, 1984], pp. 50–72); "puritans" versus "perverts" (Joanne Russ, *Magic Mommas, Trembling Sisters, Puritans and Perverts: Feminist Essays* [Trumansburg, NY, 1985]); "good girls" versus "bad girls" (Lisa Orlando, "Bad Girls and 'Good' Politics," *Voice Literary Supplement* [December 7, 1982], pp. 1, 16–19); "anti-pornography feminists" versus "social constructionists" (Linda Williams, *Hard Core: Power, Pleasure, and "The Frenzy of the Visible"* [Berkeley, 1989]).

depict the antipornography essayists as "good girls"—sentimental, naive, and sexually repressed. These "new Juliettes" regard Morgan and other antipornography activists as the "new Justines": by their constant complaints against male brutality, they make themselves into perpetual victims.

Robin Morgan issued the rallying cry of the feminist antipornography movement during the mid-1970s: "Pornography is the theory, and rape the practice."[10] Some activists distinguished between "pornography," condemned as cause of women's oppression, and "erotica," celebrated by Gloria Steinem as "a mutually pleasurable, sexual expression between people who have enough power to be there by positive choice."[11] More radical feminists, such as Andrea Dworkin, opposed all heterosexual relationships, claiming that the violence and aggression of pornography are essential characteristics of male sexuality. According to antipornography feminists, pornography does not produce sexual pleasure; instead, it displays male power—"the power of the self, physical power over and against others, the power of terror, the power of naming, the power of owning, the power of money, and the power of sex."[12] Pornography is not simply a form of expression; rather, it is an action against women.

Although some critics have attempted to center discussion on a category called "violent pornography,"[13] many argue that *all* pornography is violent: in its content—which involves scenes of bondage, rape, mutilation, and torture—and in its structures of representation, which silence, objectify, and fragment the female. In the pornographic scenario analyzed by Susanne Kappeler, "The woman object is twice objectified: once as object of the action of the scenario, and once as object of the representation, the object of viewing."[14] Drawing upon theories of the male gaze introduced by filmmaker Laura Mulvey and defining sadomasochism quite broadly "as any sexual practice that involves the eroticization of relations of domination and submission,"[15] these feminists maintain that pornography encourages sadomasochism by placing the male viewer/reader in the sadist's active position while assigning the masochist's passive role to the female viewer/reader.

Antipornography feminists decry the harm done to women in the pro-

---

[10]Robin Morgan, *Going Too Far: The Personal Chronicle of a Feminist* (New York, 1977), p. 174.

[11]Gloria Steinem, "Erotica and Pornography: A Clear and Present Difference," in *Take Back the Night: Women on Pornography*, ed. Laura Lederer (New York, 1980), p. 37.

[12]Dworkin, *Pornography*, p. 24.

[13]See, for example, the essays anthologized in *For Adult Users Only: The Dilemma of Violent Pornography*, ed. Susan Gubar and Joan Hoff (Bloomington, IN, 1989).

[14]Kappeler (n. 5 above), p. 52.

[15]Sandra Lee Bartky, "Feminine Masochism and the Politics of Personal Transformation," *Women's Studies International Forum* 7 (1984): 323.

duction and circulation of pornographic materials: as performers whose bodies are exploited on stages and in film studios; as victims of men whose misogynistic attitudes and hostile actions have been encouraged by their consumption of pornography; and as readers/viewers whose autonomy and self-respect are threatened by exposure to the genre. Calling for personal and political reform, Dworkin insists that "freedom for women must begin in the repudiation of our own masochism."[16] She and Morgan urge women to rid society of pornographic images by participating in "Take Back the Night" marches, joining organizations such as Women against Violence in Pornography and Media (WAVPM), teaching, and lobbying in support of antipornography ordinances.[17]

In opposing the antipornography movement, the writers Morgan denounces—Ellen Willis, Pat Califia, and Gayle Rubin—claim that pornography, even sadomasochistic pornography, is a possible source of erotic pleasure; they deny the right of WAVPM or any other group to limit women's fantasies or proscribe their practices. Willis declared that women should be free to experience sex as "an expression of violent and unpretty emotion": "A woman who is raped is a victim; a woman who enjoys pornography (even if that means enjoying a rape fantasy) is in a sense a rebel, insisting on an aspect of her sexuality that has been defined as a male preserve. Insofar as pornography glorifies male supremacy and sexual alienation, it is deeply reactionary. But in rejecting sexual repression and hypocrisy—which have inflicted even more damage on women than on men—it expresses a radical impulse."[18] Advocates of pornography argue that the genre serves women's interests by offering them an escape from the repressions of bourgeois ideology: it counteracts romantic love, undermines heterosexual monogamy, and subverts procreative sex.

Morgan's reference to the "new Juliettes" reveals the extent to which the problem of sadomasochism has permeated the discussions. When the National Organization of Women (NOW) condemned pornography at its 1980 convention, the resolution appeared under the rubric of "Lesbian Rights." It appeared to be directed at specific sexual minorities, for it also condemned sadomasochism, public sex, and pederasty as "issues of exploi-

[16]Andrea Dworkin, *Our Blood: Prophecies and Discourses on Sexual Politics* (London, 1982), p. 111.

[17]The best known campaigns were those in support of the MacKinnon-Dworkin ordinances in Minneapolis (1983) and Indianapolis (1984). The legal complexities of the MacKinnon-Dworkin argument are beyond the scope of this article. Interested readers should see Donald Alexander Downs, *The New Politics of Pornography* (Chicago, 1989); and Catharine A. MacKinnon, *Feminism Unmodified: Discourses on Life and Law* (Cambridge, MA, 1987).

[18]Ellen Willis, "Feminism, Moralism, and Pornography," in *Powers of Desire: The Politics of Sexuality,* ed. Ann Snitow, Christine Stansell, and Sharon Thompson (New York, 1983), p. 464.

tation and violence" rather than sexual or affectional preference.[19] The protests of Pat Califia, Gayle Rubin, and other members of Samois, a self-defined "group of feminist lesbians who share a positive interest in sadomasochism," helped shape arguments against the antipornography movement. Although proponents of sadomasochism insist that power is an integral part of sexual relationships, they deny that one person keeps the other in a state of submission. Emphasizing fantasy, theatricality—scripts, costumes, and props—and play, they present sadomasochism as "an eroticized exchange of power negotiated between two or more sexual partners."[20] Under the terms of this analysis, sadomasochism does not replicate the structures of oppression. Rather, it is "the quintessence of non-reproductive sex" and "the most radical attempt in the field of sexual politics to promote the fundamental purpose of sex as being simply pleasure."[21]

Although concerns about sexual practices dominated the early phases of the debates, by the mid-1980s questions about representation were becoming equally divisive, especially in artistic and academic communities. Using increasingly broad definitions of pornography, antipornography feminists challenged the lines between hard-core and soft-core, pornography and art, popular culture and high culture; they also cut across historical boundaries. For example, in her analysis of objectification—a key characteristic of pornography—Dworkin links the philosophy of Ernest Becker, "every soap and cosmetic commercial," the prose of Norman Mailer, and the poetry of John Keats.[22] Although such juxtapositions are often provocative, polemicists like Dworkin and Griffin tend to ignore variables of genre, audience, and context.

Moreover, when Catharine MacKinnon declares that pornography "*is* a form of forced sex," she identifies the representation of a rape with the rape itself.[23] There is no difference between image and act: "When a man looks at a pornographic picture—pornographic meaning that the woman is defined as to be acted upon, a sexual object, a sexual thing—the *viewing* is an *act,* an act of male supremacy. . . . Pornography is not imagery in some relation to a reality elsewhere constructed. It is not a distortion, reflection, projection, expression, fantasy, representation, or symbol either. It is sexual

[19]Pat Califia, "A Personal View of the History of the Lesbian S/M Community and Movement in San Francisco," in *Coming to Power: Writings and Graphics on Lesbian S/M,* ed. Samois (Boston, 1982), p. 270. Many feminists who defend sadomasochism speak from a lesbian viewpoint.

[20]Samois, ed., p. 288.

[21]Jeffrey Weeks, *Sexuality and Its Discontents: Meanings, Myths and Modern Sexualities* (London, 1985), pp. 239–40.

[22]Dworkin, *Pornography* (n. 7 above), p. 115.

[23]MacKinnon, *Feminism Unmodified,* p. 148, my emphasis.

reality."[24] In *The Pornography of Representation,* Susanne Kappeler insists that the pornographer and the artist do the same thing "in terms of representation, and with respect to the objectification of the female gender. . . . What feminist analysis identifies as the pornographic structure of representation—not the presence of a variable quality of 'sex,' but the systematic objectification of women in the interest of the exclusive subjectification of men—is a common place of art and literature as well as of conventional pornography." Given current political conditions, Kappeler concludes that a committed feminist cannot be a committed artist.[25] The problem is clear. As Kathy Myers has argued, if feminists accept such "perceptual essentialism" and agree that all forms of representation are harmful to women, then they will lose the ability to communicate, relinquish the right to represent their own sexuality, and deny themselves pleasure.[26] "Good girls" will have neither voice nor vision; all the artists will be "bad girls."

Although scholars in several disciplines now express dissatisfaction with the generalized and ahistorical pronouncements of the feminist antipornography movement, the most promising recent work has come from film critics who also refute some of the traditional tenets of psychoanalytic theory while giving careful attention to economic and social contexts. Convinced that previous theories of representation and audience response have proved to be inadequate, Gaylyn Studlar, Tania Modleski, and Kaja Silverman call for a reconceptualization of the pleasures of masochism. Determined to understand what masochism means to women, Mary Ann Doane, Carol J. Clover, and Linda Williams propose careful distinctions among different types of materials and narrow their focus to a particular genre, such as the "paranoid woman's film" of the 1940s, the slasher film of the 1970s and 1980s, or the stag film; in analyzing audience response, they seek a theory of the spectator that has historical and sexual specificity. Like many other critics of the visual arts, they object to Mulvey's account of the male gaze because it reduces the woman to object and denies her pleasure. As an alternative theory, Doane suggests that viewers might identify with the female protagonists who exercise "an active investigating gaze" in gothic films.[27] Rejecting the concept of a fixed viewing position, Williams and Clover discover multiple and fluid cross-gender identifications. Ac-

[24]Ibid., pp. 130, 149.

[25]Kappeler (n. 5 above), pp. 102–3. Kappeler does, however, encourage "the active participation of women (and other non-experts) in cultural practice." For the future, she envisions a feminist cultural practice that would arise "from a changed consciousness of what culture and its practices are" and "from a different social and economic organization" (pp. 221–22).

[26]Kathy Myers, "Towards a Feminist Erotica," in Betterton, ed. (n. 5 above), p. 200.

[27]Mary Ann Doane, "The 'Woman's Film': Possession and Address," in *Re-Vision: Feminist Essays in Film Criticism,* ed. Mary Ann Doane, Pat Mellencamp, and Linda Williams (Frederick, MD, 1984), p. 72.

cording to Williams, a female viewer of a torture scene might not identify with the character being beaten: "She may also, simultaneously, identify with the beater or with the less involved spectator who simply looks on. And even if she does identify only with the tortured woman, she might identify alternately or simultaneously with her pleasure and/or her pain." Williams urges feminists to recognize that male and female spectators "find both power and pleasure in identifying not only with a sadist's control but also with a masochist's abandon."[28] Sadomasochistic pornography can serve women's interests.

Williams turns from women spectators to women producers in her account of Femme Productions, a film company formed by Candida Royalle and other well-known female porn stars. The representation of mothers as sexual subjects in *Three Daughters* (Candida Royalle, 1986) and other Femme Production films is particularly important in suggesting ways that women might learn to express their desire. Working from psychoanalyst Jessica Benjamin's theories of female identity, Williams treats penis envy as a social problem. A young girl needs to identify "with a sexual agent—an agent who could just as well be the mother if the mother was also associated with the outside and articulated as a sexual subject of desire." Pornography for women can be an important arena for change, "especially if it is a pornography that can combine the holding and nurturing of motherhood with sexual representation."[29]

By demonstrating that representation need not encode structures of domination and by describing terms whereby women artists and audience members might pursue their own pleasures, feminist film critics can help the parties in the pornography debates move beyond their current oppositions; by offering new perspectives on such issues as masochism and motherhood, they also provide strategies for resolving some of the interpretive dilemmas in Angela Carter's work.

III

In her protests against the repression of women's sexual desire, her determination to break the ideological link between sex and romance, and her apparent willingness to accept sadomasochism as an eroticized exchange of power negotiated between partners, Carter anticipates many of the arguments made in support of pornography during the 1980s. Indeed, in *The Sadeian Woman,* Carter appears to be one of the new Juliettes, a "bad girl" promoting an aggressive, power-oriented sexuality. James Sloan Allen describes Carter as an "author of pornography"; Amanda Sebestyen calls her

[28]Williams (n. 9 above), pp. 215, 217.
[29]Ibid., p. 259.

"the high priestess of post-graduate porn."[30] According to Avis Lewallen, Carter is caught in Sade's scheme of binary oppositions; according to Kappeler, she has fled to a "literary sanctuary" where she treats Sade as a cultural artifact beyond the reach of political criticism.[31]

In contrast, I will argue that Carter is practicing intensely political criticism. Her stance on pornography resists easy categorization. Indeed, the thematics of "The Bloody Chamber" align her with the antipornography feminists who have been among her most vehement critics. In this story, male sexuality is death-oriented: the male murders with his eye, his penis, his sword. Pornography becomes a display of male power, expression *and* cause of men's aggression against women. The pornography represented in the story does not offer the woman a way to be a sexual rebel; instead, it subjects her to harm. Has Carter become one of the "good girls," repudiating pornography, even at the risk of ending heterosexual relationships? Or does she seek to escape from dichotomies altogether, including the "good girl/bad girl" dichotomy that has divided feminists at both the practical and the theoretical levels?

In her collection, *The Bloody Chamber and Other Adult Tales* (1979), Carter retells such well-known fairy tales as "Bluebeard," "Beauty and the Beast," "Puss in Boots," and "Little Red Riding Hood." "I was using the latent content of those traditional stories," she told an interviewer. "And that latent content is violently sexual."[32] Carter associates traditional tales with the "subliterary forms of pornography, ballad and dream."[33] "The Bloody Chamber," the first story in the volume, continues—but also qualifies—the analysis of sexuality and culture that Carter had begun a year earlier in *The Sadeian Woman*. Drawing upon that study, I will read "The Bloody Chamber" against three kinds of fiction: (1) the fairy tale of "Bluebeard" and the interpretive traditions surrounding it during the nineteenth and twentieth centuries; (2) pornographic fiction, especially *Justine* (1791), the Sade novel Carter describes as "a black, inverted fairy tale" (*SW*, p. 39); and (3) Freud's theory of female development, which is, according to Carter, an account "of such extraordinary poetic force that . . . it retains a cultural importance analogous . . . to the myth of the crime of Eve" (*SW*, p. 125).

Carter takes the basic elements of her story from Charles Perrault's "La

[30]James Sloan Allen, "Where Ego Was," *Nation* 229 (October 6, 1979): 312; Amanda Sebestyen, "The Mannerist Marketplace," *New Socialist* 47(March 1987): 38.

[31]Avis Lewallen, "Wayward Girls but Wicked Women? Female Sexuality in Angela Carter's *The Bloody Chamber*," in *Perspectives on Pornography: Sexuality in Film and Literature*, ed. Gary Day and Clive Bloom (New York, 1988), p. 146; Kappeler, p. 134.

[32]Kerryn Goldsworthy, "Angela Carter," *Meanjin* 44 (March 1985): 6.

[33]Angela Carter, "Afterword," in her *Fireworks: Nine Profane Pieces* (London, 1974), p. 122.

Barbe Bleue" (1697), which is the earliest written version of the Bluebeard tale. In Perrault's seventeenth-century *conte*, a young girl is revolted by her suitor's blue beard and suspicious about the mysterious disappearance of his previous wives. But she is so dazzled by his extravagant wealth and the seemingly endless pleasures of his parties that she soon marries him. Shortly after the marriage, Bluebeard subjects his wife to a test: he departs from the mansion, giving her the keys to all the rooms but warning her against entering a "little room . . . at the end of a dark little corridor." Consumed, almost immediately, with "the desire to open the door of the forbidden room," the wife finds corpses of his murdered wives strewn about the chamber. In her horror, she drops the key on the blood-clotted floor and is unable to remove the stain. When the husband discovers the bloody key, he immediately realizes what has happened. Enraged at his wife's transgression, Bluebeard orders her to prepare for death. But just as he lifts his cutlass to behead her, her brothers burst through the door and kill him. The wife inherits her husband's money, which she uses to help her sister and brothers and "to marry herself to an honest man who made her forget her sorrows as the wife of Bluebeard."[34]

According to folklorists, oral versions of this tale were widespread throughout Europe long before Perrault composed his *conte*. In one version, the maiden waits for her brothers to rescue her from the murderous ogre; in another, a clever young woman tricks the ogre, secures her own escape, and saves her sisters from his rage.[35] These oral tales, which are lacking in didacticism, provide little commentary on the characters' actions. When Perrault developed the first literary version of the Bluebeard tale, he chose the helpless heroine rather than the clever one. He also appended two sophisticated *moralités* in verse: the first, presumably addressed to his women readers, cautions against the dangers of curiosity; the second warns husbands against making impossible demands on their wives. Although the moral lesson of this prohibition/transgression tale is "somewhat ambiguous,"[36] it does seem that Perrault is as much concerned with the husband's jealousy as with the wife's curiosity.

However, by the early nineteenth century, "the rich ambiguities attending the curiosity of Bluebeard's wife in Perrault's tale are sorted out and funneled into two separate tale types by the Grimms. . . . By the time that the *Nursery and Household Tales* appeared [in 1812], 'Bluebeard' had branched off into two separate narratives: one a cautionary fairy tale about the hazards of curiosity [such as "Mary's Child"], the other a folk tale de-

[34]Charles Perrault, "Bluebeard," in *Sleeping Beauty and Other Favourite Fairy Tales,* trans. Angela Carter (New York, 1984), pp. 20, 34, 39.

[35]Antti Aarne, *The Types of the Folktale,* trans. and enlarged by Stith Thompson (Helsinki, 1964), pp. 101–2.

[36]Jeanne Morgan, *Perrault's Morals for Moderns* (New York, 1985), pp. 110–11.

picting the triumph of a clever young woman over a bloodthirsty villain [such as "Fowler's Fowl"]."[37] Tales of female triumph abound in the folk tradition,[38] but it was the other type—the didactic story warning against female curiosity—that gained popularity on the stages and in the bookstalls of nineteenth-century Europe. Maria Tatar has found that "nearly every nineteenth-century printed version of 'Bluebeard' singles out the heroine's curiosity as an especially undesirable trait."[39] Thus by the nineteenth century the wife's disobedience had become a much more serious issue than the husband's violence.

Twentieth-century sympathizers with the wife have sometimes recast her transgression as a heroic search for knowledge.[40] But in the most influential modern interpretation of the story, psychoanalyst Bruno Bettelheim emphasizes the wife's wrongdoing, which he defines in explicitly sexual terms. According to Bettelheim, the blood on the key "seems to symbolize that the woman had sexual relations" with the castle's guests. For Bettelheim, this is "a cautionary tale which warns: Women, don't give in to your sexual curiosity; men, don't permit yourself to be carried away by your anger at being sexually betrayed."[41]

Writing *against* the interpretive tradition that emphasizes the wife's illicit sexual curiosity, Angela Carter makes four important changes in the tale. First, she depicts the husband, whom she renames "the Marquis," as a patron of the arts and collector of pornography, thereby demonstrating a cultural foundation for his sadism and suggesting a relationship between art and aggression. Second, she grants moral complexity and narrative control to the wife, who tells the tale from her own point of view. Third, she develops the character of the second husband so that he stands as an alternative to the type of masculinity represented by the Marquis. Fourth, she restores to prominence a figure who is strikingly, ominously, absent from

[37]Maria Tatar, *The Hard Facts of the Grimms' Fairy Tales* (Princeton, NJ, 1987), pp. 171, 178.

[38]Tales of triumphant women include the English "Mr. Fox," where Lady Margaret outwits her wife-murdering suitor before the marriage; the Italian "Silver Nose," where a young girl recognizes the demonic male and rescues her sisters from the hellish fires of his forbidden chamber; and the Grimm brothers' "Fowler's Fowl," where the heroine finds the mutilated bodies of her sisters in the secret room, magically restores them to life, and tricks the bloodthirsty wizard into taking them home to their parents.

[39]Tatar, p. 158.

[40]See, for example, Maeterlinck's play *Ariadne et Barbe-Bleue* in Maurice Maeterlinck, *"Sister Beatrice" and "Ariadne and Barbe Bleue,"* trans. Bernard Miall (New York, 1910) and Sylvia Townsend Warner's short story, "Bluebeard's Daughter" (in her *The Cat's Cradle Book* [New York, 1940]).

[41]Bruno Bettelheim, *The Uses of Enchantment: The Meaning and Importance of Fairy Tales* (New York, 1977), pp. 301–2.

fairy tales, from pornographic fiction, and from the Freudian theory of female development: the strong, loving, and courageous mother.[42]

Although Carter follows her seventeenth-century source by making the husband wealthy, she moves beyond Perrault by depicting the husband as a devotee of opera, an admirer of Baudelaire, and a collector of books and paintings. Here she draws upon the popular French tradition of associating Bluebeard with Gilles de Rais (1404–40), companion-in-arms to Joan of Arc, Marshal of France under Charles VII, refined patron of the arts, *and* child-murderer.[43] Interest in Gilles de Rais had "suddenly revived" during the nineteenth century, exactly when it could be fitted into a new category of crime: sex-killing.[44] With his atrocious crimes *and* his aesthetic sensibilities, Gilles de Rais became an important figure in decadent literature, most especially in J. F. Huysman's *Là-bas* (1891), a copy of which is lavishly displayed in the Marquis's library. The Marquis's shimmering castle by the sea seems to come from an imaginary world. But by locating it in Brittany and by describing the villagers' fears of the bloodthirsty Marquis, Carter also evokes the brutal feudalism of the historical Gilles de Rais. Unfortunately, abuses of male power—social, economic, cultural, political, and sexual—are not confined to past societies. The Marquis's purchases, such as the wardrobe by Poiret, bring the story into "more democratic times,"[45] the early part of the twentieth century. References to the telephone, the stock market, and the international drug trade identify the Marquis as a modern businessman and establish the economic basis of his art collection.

With his wealth, the Marquis can offer the young woman tickets to *Tristan*, a Bechstein piano, an early Flemish primitive of Saint Cecelia. From courtship through consummation, he uses art to aid in seduction. Thus Carter situates the story in the tradition of "aesthetic sadomasochism": works that center on the "education of one person in the sexual fantasy of another through complex role playing cued to works of art and

[42]In some variants of the Bluebeard tale, the mother is the cause of the daughter's enslavement. The story begins when the mother is imprisoned and decides to give her daughter to the tyrant in order to save her own life.

[43]According to Reginald Hyatte, Perrault did not base his characterization of Bluebeard on Gilles de Rais. Rather, it was the people of Brittany who traditionally associated the historical child-murderer with the fictional wife-murderer (*Laughter for the Devil: The Trials of Gilles de Rais, Companion-in-Arms of Joan of Arc* [Rutherford, NJ, 1984], p. 25). Comorre the Cursed (ca. 500), a Bretton chieftain who murdered his wives when they became pregnant, has also been suggested as a historical antecedent for Bluebeard.

[44]Deborah Cameron and Elizabeth Frazer, *The Lust to Kill: A Feminist Investigation of Sexual Murder* (New York, 1987), p. 22.

[45]Angela Carter, *The Bloody Chamber and Other Adult Tales* (New York, 1981), p. 36; subsequent references to this work, abbreviated *BC*, will be incorporated into the text.

imagination."[46] As the bride is being undressed, she realizes that her husband has arranged their encounter to resemble an etching. "And when nothing but my scarlet, palpitating core remained, I saw, in the mirror, the living image of an etching by Rops from the collection he had shown me . . . the child with her sticklike limbs, naked but for her button boots, her gloves, shielding her face with her hand as though her face were the last repository of her modesty; and the old, monocled lecher who examined her, limb by limb" (*BC*, p. 12). The gentleman displays age, wealth, experience, and the power of the eye; the child-like female is reduced to an object of the male gaze. Perhaps the narrator calls this the "most pornographic of all confrontations" (*BC*, p. 12) because she realizes that by giving herself to be looked at, she has entered what Jonathan Elmer calls "the classic pornographic contract."[47]

Later that day, the young wife is shocked by illustrations in one of her husband's books: "I had not bargained for this, the girl with tears hanging on her cheeks like stuck pearls, her cunt a split fig below the great globes of her buttocks on which the knotted tails of the cat were about to descend, while a man in a black mask fingered with his free hand his prick, that curved upwards like the scimitar he held. The picture had a caption: 'Reproof of curiosity'" (*BC*, p. 14). Through the caption, Carter links the flagellation scene, a staple of nineteenth-century pornography, to the Bluebeard tale. Moreover, by representing the male as a Turkish sultan raising his scimitar, Carter acknowledges the orientalizing of the tale which occurred among dramatists and illustrators.[48] Another engraving, "Immolation of the wives of the Sultan," stimulates the groom to take his bride to bed in a mirror-lined room in broad daylight. "All the better to see you," he says (*BC*, p. 15).

In both episodes—the disrobing and the defloration—the contrast between the husband's action and the wife's immobility seems to support the theory of the male gaze articulated by film critic E. Ann Kaplan: "To begin with, men do not simply look; their gaze carries with it the power of action and possession that is lacking in the female gaze. Women receive and return a gaze, but cannot act on it. Second, the sexualization and objectification of women is not simply for the purposes of eroticism; from a psychoanalytic point of view, it is designed to annihilate the threat that woman (as cas-

[46]Williams (n. 9 above), p. 224.

[47]Jonathan Elmer, "The Exciting Conflict: The Rhetoric of Pornography and Anti-Pornography," *Cultural Critique* 8 (Winter 1987–88): 67.

[48]As examples of the way the tale has been orientalized in England, Juliet McMaster discusses George Coleman's popular pantomime, *Blue-beard, or Female Curiosity* (1798) and William Thackeray's illustrations to *The Awful History of Blue Beard* (1833) (see her "Bluebeard: A Tale of Matrimony," *A Room of One's Own* 2 [Summer/Fall 1976]: 10–19).

trated, and possessing a sinister genital organ) poses."[49] According to Laura Mulvey, "the woman as icon, displayed for the gaze and enjoyment of men, the active controllers of the look, always threatens to evoke anxiety." The male unconscious might escape from this castration anxiety by becoming preoccupied with "the re-enactment of the original trauma"; Mulvey calls this reaction, which involves investigating and demystifying the woman, "voyeurism": "Voyeurism . . . has associations with sadism: pleasure lies in ascertaining guilt (immediately associated with castration), asserting control and subjecting the guilty person through punishment or forgiveness. This sadistic side fits in well with narrative. Sadism demands a story, depends on making something happen, forcing a change in another person, a battle of will and strength, victory/ defeat, all occurring in a linear time with a beginning and an end."[50] Carter's voyeuristic Marquis is indeed a sadist—in terms of his sexual practices and in terms of his control of narrative: he has arranged the setting, written the script, and set the plot in motion.

According to the bride, the initial sexual encounter taught her the truth of Baudelaire's statement: "There is a striking resemblance between the act of love and the ministrations of a torturer" (*BC*, p. 29). The husband's poetic allusions and his penchant for forcing his nude wife to wear a jeweled collar show his allegiance to Baudelaire, while his title, his sexual practices, and the furnishings in his forbidden room link him to Sade. The Marquis's bloody chamber recalls several rooms in *Justine,* such as the monks' pavilion, which is reached through a winding underground tunnel and filled with "scourges, ferules, withes, cords, and a thousand other instruments of torture,"[51] and Roland's subterranean cave, which is hung with skulls, skeletons, bundles of whips, and collections of sabers. Carter's Marquis bears a

[49]E. Ann Kaplan, "Is the Gaze Male?" in Snitow, Stansell, and Thompson, eds. (n. 18 above), p. 311. Some psychoanalytic critics such as Susan Lurie ("Pornography and the Dread of Women: The Male Sexual Dilemma," in Lederer, ed. [n. 11 above], pp. 159–73) question whether the boy is traumatized by the possibility of his mother's castration; as Linda Williams explains, a boy's real fear may be that his mother is *not* mutilated. Thus, the notion of woman as castrated man may be "a comforting, wishful fantasy intended to combat the child's imagined dread of what his mother's very real power could do to him" (Linda Williams, "When the Woman Looks," in Doane, Mellencamp, and Williams, eds. [n. 27 above], p. 89). The theory of the male gaze is being questioned, revised, and refuted, especially by feminist film critics trying to find a place for the female spectator. I emphasize Laura Mulvey ("Visual Pleasure and Narrative Cinema," *Screen* 16 [Autumn 1975]: 6–18) and Kaplan ("Is the Gaze Male?" and *Women and Film: Both Sides of the Camera* [New York, 1983]) because their theories have the most explanatory power for "The Bloody Chamber" and *The Sadeian Woman.*
[50]Mulvey, pp. 13–14.
[51]D. A. F. de Sade, *Three Complete Novels,* trans. Richard Seaver and Austryn Wainhouse (New York, 1965), p. 567.

particularly close resemblance to the Comte de Gernande, the aristocrat in *Justine* who equips his apartment with straps to bind his wives and surgical devices to bleed them to death. Both the Marquis and Gernande have already killed three wives; both have a lust for blood. Unlike most libertines, they are committed to torturing women within marriage.

For these male characters, sex does not appear to be a pleasurable experience. According to Carter, the libertine's orgasm is "annihilating, appalling," marked by screams, blasphemies, and fits; it requires him "to die in pain and to painfully return from death" (*SW*, pp. 149–50). The bride of "The Bloody Chamber" gives a similar description of her husband: "I had heard him shriek and blaspheme at the orgasm." For this "one-sided struggle," the Marquis brought his bride to "the carved, gilded bed on which he had been conceived"—and presumably born (*BC*, p. 15). Immolating the woman upon his ancestral bed becomes an act of protest against his mother. In *The Sadeian Woman* Carter explains that the libertine feels "greed, envy and jealousy, a helpless rage at the organs of generation that bore us into a world of pain where the enjoyment of the senses is all that can alleviate the daily horror of living. . . . Sade's quarrel, therefore, is not only with the mother, who can deprive him of love and sustenance at will; it is the very fact of generation that he finds intolerable" (*SW*, p. 135). Perhaps the Marquis, like the Sadeian libertine, "cannot forgive the other, not for what she is, but for what she has done—for having thoughtlessly, needlessly inflicted life upon him" (*SW*, p. 135). This animosity toward the mother also helps account for the emphasis on the Marquis's gaze. According to Kaplan, "The domination of women by the male gaze is part of men's strategy to contain the threat that the mother embodies, and to control the positive and negative impulses the memory traces of being mothered have left in the male unconscious."[52]

While the husband is defeated, reduced even before death to one of "those clockwork tableaux of Bluebeard that you see in glass cases at fairs" (*BC*, p. 45), the wife survives to tell the story of her moral development. Unlike the women in the illustrations, she is not trapped in a visual representation. Because she has a voice, she can be heard without being seen. To be sure, the use of a female narrator does not in and of itself constitute a challenge to the conventions of pornography. As Kappeler has argued, the "assumption of the female point of view and narrative voice—the assumption of linguistic and narrative female 'subjectivity'—in no way lessens the pornographic structure, the fundamental elision of the woman as subject."[53] Sade's Juliette personifies "the whore as story-teller," using narrative to entertain her captors and evade death (*SW*, p. 81). Yet unlike the

[52]Kaplan, "Is the Gaze Male?" p. 324.
[53]Kappeler (n. 5 above), p. 90.

female narrators who have such a prominent place in the history of pornographic fiction, Carter's narrator is not using language to provide sexual entertainment for male readers.[54] Roland Barthes would see the protagonist's control of language as evidence of a shift in power: "The master is he who speaks, who disposes of the entirety of language; the object is he who is silent, who remains separate, by a mutilation more absolute than any erotic torture, from any access to discourse, because he does not even have any right to receive the master's word."[55] Susan Griffin would see the female voice as constituting a challenge to pornography, a genre which assumes male control of language and "expresses an almost morbid fear of female speech."[56]

The young woman not only escapes from silence; she also avoids the dichotomized treatment of female characters in fairy tales and pornographic fiction. In *The Sadeian Woman,* Carter argued that Sade's "straitjacket psychology"—his belief that virtue and vice are innate—"relates his fiction directly to the black and white ethical world of fairy tale and fable" (*SW,* p. 82). Fairy tales, as Andrea Dworkin indicates, offer only "two definitions of woman": "There is the good woman. She is a victim. There is the bad woman. She must be destroyed. The good woman must be possessed. The bad woman must be killed, or punished. Both must be nullified."[57] The woman in "The Bloody Chamber" is not modeled after either of the protagonists in the traditional Bluebeard tales described by Maria Tatar: the victim who is rightly punished for her curiosity or the avenger, the triumphant heroine who singlehandedly defeats the tyrant. Nor does she fit the Sadeian categories, for she is neither Juliette, the aggressor, nor Justine, the helpless martyr who aspires to be "the perfect woman." According to Carter, Justine defines virtue in passive terms of obedience and sexual abstinence. Unable to act, unchanged by experience, she is "the heroine of a black, inverted fairy-tale":

---

[54]The narrator addresses the reader as "you" at seven points in the story. On two occasions, the narrator recognizes the reader's right to judge her and issues a modest plea for leniency (*BC,* pp. 9, 17). On two other occasions, she doubts her ability to convey the quality of her experience to the reader: she cannot transmit the intensity of horror she felt upon seeing her husband's car return (*BC,* p. 36); nor can she find anything in the reader's experience comparable to the strange sight of her mother riding to her rescue (*BC,* p. 45). In two places, she assumes that she and the reader have some common experiences: the reader has seen "clockwork tableaux of Bluebeard" at fairs (p. 45); the reader might also share some knowledge of practices in the brothel. But the narrator does not want the reader to indulge in too much fantasy: in the next paragraph, she tells the reader not to imagine "much finesse" in her husband's ritualistic foreplay (*BC,* p. 12).

[55]Roland Barthes, *Sade, Fourier, Loyola,* trans. Richard Miller (New York, 1976), p. 31.

[56]Susan Griffin, *Pornography and Silence: Culture's Revenge against Nature* (New York, 1981), p. 89.

[57]Andrea Dworkin, *Woman Hating* (New York, 1974), p. 48.

To be the *object* of desire is to be defined in the passive case.

To exist in the passive case is to die in the passive case—that is, to be killed.

This is the moral of the fairy tale about the perfect woman. [*SW*, pp. 76–77]

In Carter's analysis, "Justine marks the start of a self-regarding female masochism"; *she,* not Sade, personifies the pornography of the female condition during the twentieth century (*SW*, p. 57). In contrast, the protagonist of "The Bloody Chamber" learns that she is not a perfect woman; she has the right to act, to experience the consequences of her decisions, to learn from error. Hence she achieves a much more complicated sense of morality than Bluebeard's wife or Sade's Justine.

That morality is, however, founded on her sense of "shame" (*BC*, p. 46).[58] In Sade's novel, the ever pure Justine was able to have the brand on her shoulder removed by a surgeon. In contrast, Carter's young bride must bear a permanent mark on her forehead: a "heart-shaped stain" from the bloody key (*BC*, p. 40).[59]

Reflecting on her experiences, the narrator feels ashamed of the materialism that drove her to marry the Marquis and of her complicity in sadomasochism. Carter casts her protagonist in genteel poverty to show "relationships between the sexes are determined by . . . the historical fact of the economic dependence of women upon men" (*SW*, pp. 6–7). Raised by a widowed mother who "beggared herself for love," the young woman wears "twice-darned underwear" and "faded gingham" so that she can continue her study of music (*BC*, pp. 2, 6). When the Marquis appears offering opera tickets and an opal ring, the protagonist willingly forsakes her mother's shabbiness for his extravagance: "This ring, the bloody bandage of rubies, the wardrobe of clothes from Poiret and Worth, his scent of Russian leather—all had conspired to seduce me" (*BC*, p. 8). She later realizes that she sold herself for "a handful of colored stones and the pelts of dead beasts" (*BC*, p. 16). At the end of Perrault's tale, the protagonist kept Bluebeard's money to further her happiness and that of her family; Carter's protagonist distributes her inheritance to charity, retaining only enough to start a small music school.

The narrator's understanding of sexuality also changes. Her mother had

[58]Instead of recognizing a painful but ultimately human pattern of moral growth, Avis Lewallen (n. 31 above) argues that it is "unfair" for the woman to be "branded as guilty" (p. 152).

[59]Kari E. Lokke, who interprets the story as a challenge to sadomasochism, argues that the heart is "also a badge of courage . . . evidence of the unconditional power of love, both the indomitable love of the mother and the total acceptance of the gentle male partner" (*"Bluebeard* and *The Bloody Chamber:* The Grotesque of Self-Parody and Self-Assertion," *Frontiers* 10 [1988]: 11).

given her a legacy of romance and a bit of factual knowledge. "My mother, with all the precision of her eccentricity, had told me what it was that lovers did; I was innocent but not naive," she recalls (*BC,* p. 14). During the engagement, she discovers her "potentiality for corruption" when she attends the opera wearing the ruby choker given to her by the Marquis:

> I saw him watching me in the gilded mirrors with the assessing eye of a connoisseur inspecting horseflesh, or even of a housewife in the market, inspecting cuts on the slab. I'd never seen, or else had never acknowledged, that regard of his before, the sheer carnal avarice of it; and it was strangely magnified by the monocle lodged in his left eye. . . . And I saw myself, suddenly, as he saw me, my pale face, the way the muscles in my neck stuck out like thin wire. I saw how much that cruel necklace became me. And for the first time in my innocent and confined life, I sensed in myself a potentiality for corruption that took my breath away. [*BC,* p. 7]

Aspects of this scene are repeated later during the disrobing. Again, he is the purchaser; she, the commodity, the piece of meat, "bare as a lamb chop." He examines her through his monocle; she watches in the mirror. "And, as at the opera, when I had first seen my flesh in his eyes, I was aghast to feel myself stirring" (*BC,* p. 12).

To understand why she might take sexual pleasure in being objectified, it is helpful to turn to the psychoanalytic account of women's castration anxiety. According to Kaplan:

> The entry of the father as the third term disrupts the mother/child dyad, causing the child to understand the mother's castration and possession by the father. In the symbolic world the girl now enters she learns not only subject/object positions but the sexed pronouns "he" and "she." Assigned the place of object (since she lacks the phallus, the symbol of the signifier), she is the recipient of male desire, the passive recipient of his gaze. If she is to have sexual pleasure, it can only be constructed around her objectification; it cannot be a pleasure that comes from desire for the other (a subject position). . . . Women . . . have learned to associate their sexuality with domination by the male gaze, a position involving a degree of masochism in finding their objectification erotic.[60]

Given that this position involves a "degree of masochism," it is not surprising to find the protagonist clinging to the man who impaled her, "as though only the one who had inflicted the pain could comfort [her] for suffering it" (*BC,* p. 16). The Marquis disgusts her, but she craves him like

---

[60]Kaplan, "Is the Gaze Male?" (n. 49 above), pp. 315–16, 324.

pregnant women crave "for the taste of coal or chalk or tainted food" (*BC*, p. 21).

In his absence, she searches the castle for "the evidence of his real life" (*BC*, p. 25). Like the heroines in the "paranoid Gothic films" of the 1940s—films like *Gaslight* and *Secret beyond the Door*, which are linked to the Bluebeard tale through Robertson Stevenson's version of *Jane Eyre* (1944)—the narrator becomes an active investigator, bringing light into the darkened corridors.[61] She approaches the forbidden room through a gallery hung with Venetian tapestries depicting "some grisly mythological subject," possibly the rape of the Sabine women (*BC*, p. 28). When she enters the bloody chamber, she finds "a little museum of his perversity," a collection of deathly artifacts—Etruscan funerary urns, a medieval rack and great wheel, an "ominous bier of Renaissance workmanship" (*BC*, p. 29). Here, within the bloody chamber, she discovers her ties to other women. Driven by her "mother's spirit . . . to know the very worst," she examines the physical remains of the Marquis's former wives: the embalmed corpse of the opera singer, the veiled skull of the artist's model, the still-bleeding body of the Romanian countess (*BC*, pp. 29–30).

Like the wife in a "paranoid Gothic film" who finds mutilated traces of other wives in her house, the narrator sees herself "slowly becoming another, duplicating an earlier identity as though history, particularly in the case of women, were bound to repeat itself."[62] She sobs with pity for "the fated sisterhood" of her husband's other victims and with anguish for her own lost innocence (*BC*, p. 30). As Philip Lewis says in his stimulating reading of Perrault, the bloody floor subsumes "the blood of consanguinity, the bloodshed of violence and death, and . . . the red blood of womanhood"; it is "the double agent of the dual perception the wife experiences in discovering herself, and that Bluebeard experiences in his turn when the blood appears to his eyes as a tarnish or a taint on the magic key."[63] The revelation that she, like the other women, has chosen death shocks the protagonist into life. Masochism may have served her interests during the courtship and the initial sexual encounter: perhaps she assumed a passive role as a way to disguise her curiosity about sex and her desire for wealth. But she did not contract for death. "My first thought," she says, "when I saw the ring for which I had sold myself to this fate, was how to escape it" (*BC*, p. 31). Unfortunately, with her husband's sudden reappearance, she seems to be trapped in his deadly plot.

Attired only in the ruby choker, her hair drawn back as it was for the

[61]Mary Ann Doane, *The Desire to Desire: The Woman's Film of the 1940's* (Bloomington, IN, 1987), pp. 123–54.

[62]Ibid., p. 142.

[63]Philip Lewis, "Bluebeard's Magic Key," in *Les Contes de Perrault; La contestation et ses limites; furetière,* ed. Michael Bareau et al. (Paris, 1987), p. 42.

sexual encounter, the bride anticipates her beheading. She is saved, not by her brothers but by her mother, who bursts through the gate, with one hand on the reins of a rearing horse, and the other clutching her husband's military revolver which she has removed from her reticule. The mother shoots the Marquis, frees her daughter, and restores her to a life of emotional and moral integrity. Through this witty and flamboyantly triumphant ending, Carter rewrites Perrault's fairy tale, the Gernande section of *Justine,* and the Freudian account of female development. In Sade's novel, the Comtesse de Gernande, whose husband was trying to bleed her to death, asked Justine to carry a letter to her mother; she felt certain that her mother would "hasten with all expedition to sever her daughter's bonds."[64] But Gernande thwarted that plan: strong and loving mothers do not appear in Sade.

In Freud the mother is rendered powerless—to herself and to her daughter—by her lack of a penis. "The turning away from the mother is accompanied by hostility; the attachment to the mother ends in hate," hypothesizes Freud (*SW,* p. 125). According to Carter, the "psychic fiction" of women's castration does not just affect individual development; it pervades our culture and helps to account for the recurrence of sexual violence. "The whippings, the beatings, the gougings, the stabbings of erotic violence reawaken the memory of the social fiction of the female wound, the bleeding scar left by her castration, which is a psychic fiction as deeply at the heart of Western culture as the myth of Oedipus. . . . Female castration is an imaginary fact that pervades the whole of men's attitude towards women and our attitude to ourselves, that transforms women from human beings into wounded creatures who were born to bleed" (*SW,* p. 23). In "The Bloody Chamber," the mother certainly does not act like a wounded creature born to bleed. Indeed, her courage sustains the young bride who realizes that she has inherited her "nerves and a will from the mother who had defied the yellow outlaws of Indochina" (*BC,* p. 29). The mother has performed legendary feats of male and female heroism: "Her mother had outfaced a junkful of Chinese pirates, nursed a village through a visitation of the plague, [and] shot a man-eating tiger with her own hand" (*BC,* p. 2). Similarly, Carter equips the mother with male and female Freudian symbols, making several references to the father's gun kept in the mother's reticule. This parent is powerful enough to serve as father and mother to the young woman. Instead of rejecting her, the daughter and her new husband join the mother to form a new family.

Since the theories of individuation that permeate our culture stress the necessity of renouncing the bond with the mother—that dangerous, archa-

[64]Sade (n. 51 above), p. 651. Jane Gallop discusses Sade's treatment of mothers in *Thinking through the Body* (New York, 1988), pp. 55–71.

ic force who would "pull us back to what Freud called the 'limitless narcissism' of infancy"[65]—some readers see the protagonist's reunion with her mother as a regression. But I think that Carter, like psychoanalyst Jessica Benjamin, is challenging the Oedipal models of development which privilege separation over dependence. Benjamin urges women "to reconceive the ideal" of motherhood, not by idealizing female nurturance but by acknowledging the mother as an independently existing subject, one who expresses her own desire.[66] The mother in "The Bloody Chamber" has experienced autonomy and adventure in the world; she has also acted according to her desires, having "gladly, scandalously, defiantly" married for love (BC, p. 2). Carter seems to anticipate the recent work of women filmmakers and critics who believe that "some part of Motherhood lies outside of patriarchal concerns . . . and eludes control"[67] and that recognizing the mother as sexual subject might provide a solution to the representation of desire, especially if she is also granted access to the outside world of freedom.

In addition to criticizing the position of the mother in pornography, popular literature, and psychoanalytic theory, Carter also challenges definitions of masculinity based on domination. In Perrault's "Bluebeard," the second husband seemed to be an afterthought, part of the reward accorded to the wife at the end of the story. In "The Bloody Chamber," he appears as the bride's humble friend and confidant. A poor piano tuner, Jean-Yves has neither the power of the Marquis nor the glamor of a fairy tale prince. Because of his blindness, he will never look at the materials in the Marquis's library; nor will he see the mark of shame on the narrator's forehead. Jean-Yves is not perfect: when he tells the bride that she, like Eve, should be punished for her disobedience, he reveals that his attitudes have been shaped by myths of feminine evil. Despite this limitation, he is a sympathetic listener, loyal, tender, and sensitive, as he offers to "be of some comfort . . . though not much use" to the despairing bride (BC, p. 42). The Marquis treated the narrator's musical talent as a stylish accomplishment to be displayed in his mansion; Jean-Yves expresses reverence for her art. The Marquis took the young woman away from her mother; Jean-Yves helps open the courtyard gate so that the mother might return.

However, in a culture that eroticizes domination, it is not surprising that some readers are reluctant to accept Jean-Yves as the hero. His relationship with the narrator does not appear to have a sexual dimension. According to Patricia Duncker, "while blindness, as symbolic castration,

[65]Jessica Benjamin, *The Bonds of Love: Psychoanalysis, Feminism, and the Problem of Domination* (New York, 1988), p. 135.

[66]Ibid., p. 82.

[67]Kaplan, *Women and Film* (n. 49 above), p. 206.

may signal the end of male sexual aggression, it is also mutilation. As such it cannot be offered as the answer, the new male erotic identity."[68] In rejecting pornography, did Carter feel compelled to eliminate all signs of a physical attraction? Must women choose between a dangerous but exciting sexuality based on male dominance, or a sweet, safe, and utterly asexual relationship between equals? And does that "equality" demand that the male be disfigured?

Perhaps if Carter were to continue the story, she would develop a male sexuality centered on smell, touch, and sound; indeed, this is already implicit in Jean-Yves's extreme sensitivity to music. After the narrator relinquishes her position as object of the male gaze, she may eventually glimpse the "benign sexuality" that eluded Justine (*SW*, p. 49). But in assuming the subject's position, she has not yet found the language to express her desire. In other words, the new relationship may have erotic possibilities that the narrator does not know how to represent and that we do not know how to read. Perhaps Jackie Byars's argument pertains: we need to learn to recognize a tradition of mutual gazing that "expresses a 'different voice' and a different kind of gaze that we've not heard or seen before because our theories have discouraged such 'hearing' and 'seeing.' "[69] In the meantime, mother and daughter will be the only members of this household who can gaze lovingly at one another.

Has Angela Carter become a "moral pornographer" exposing the misogyny that distorts our culture and envisioning a new world of sexual freedom? Although "The Bloody Chamber" does, I think, use pornography as a critique of the current relations between the sexes, Carter's hopes for a world of "absolute sexual licence" seem subdued and her attitude toward Sade more critical than in *The Sadeian Woman*. Carter refuses to define pornography as the primary cause of women's oppression, for she believes that complicated economic, social, and psychological forces contribute to the objectification, fetishization, and violation of women. But in "The Bloody Chamber" Carter moves closer to the antipornography feminists: she assumes that pornography encourages violence against women and that the association of sex, power, and sadomasochism in pornography is part of society's common prescription for heterosexual relations. Like the feminists opposed to pornography, she urges women to challenge assumptions about female masochism and to define a sexuality outside of dominant-submissive power relations.

[68]Patricia Duncker, "Re-Imagining the Fairy Tale: Angela Carter's Bloody Chambers," *Literature and History* 10 (Spring 1984): 11.

[69]Jackie Byars, "Gazes/Voices/Power: Expanding Psychoanalysis for Feminist Film and Television Theory," in *Female Spectators: Looking at Film and Television*, ed. E. Deidre Pribram (London, 1988), p. 124.

"The Bloody Chamber" ultimately fulfills Kappeler's definition of feminist critique: "It shows up and criticizes the folklore nature of the pornographic plot, the rearticulation of an unchanging archetype, reiterated in the patriarchal culture at large, which recites the same tale over and over again, convincing itself through these rearticulations of the impossibility of change."[70] Carter refuses to isolate pornography—as a genre or as a social problem. Instead of treating pornography as a specialized subgenre appealing to a small group of male consumers, Carter employs a complex series of allusions to link pornography to fairy tales, psychoanalysis, and other forms of fiction. With Catharine A. MacKinnon, she treats psychoanalysis and pornography as "epistemic sites in the same ontology," "mirrors of each other, male supremacist sexuality looking at itself looking at itself."[71] Thus Carter achieves Annette Kuhn's goal: to deconstruct, debunk, and demystify pornography. Such an approach "insists that pornography is not after all special, is not a privileged order of representation; that it shares many of its modes of address, many of its codes and conventions, with representations which are not looked upon as a 'problem' in the way pornography is. This has significant consequences for any feminist politics around pornography in particular and around representation in general."[72]

In a debate that has cast women in the very oppositions defined by Sade—I am thinking again of Robin Morgan's characterization of feminists who defend pornography as "Sade's new Juliettes"[73]—it is impossible to categorize Angela Carter as a good girl or a bad girl, for she, like her protagonist, has escaped from absolutes. She rejects the argument of feminists who defend the right to engage in sadomasochistic practices on the grounds of essentialism or psychological determinism. She also finds the claim that "feminists should not desire or be aroused by physical manifestations of dominance or submission" naive because "it too ignores the social and political realities in which our sexuality is constructed."[74] Carter insists that the young woman understand why she finds her objectification erotic. A recent critic of "The Bloody Chamber" complains, "We are asked to place ourselves imaginatively as masochistic victims in a pornographic

---

[70]Kappeler (n. 5 above), p. 146.

[71]Catharine A. MacKinnon, "Sexuality, Pornography, and Method: 'Pleasure under Patriarchy,'" *Ethics* 99 (1989): 342.

[72]Annette Kuhn, *The Power of the Image: Essays on Representation and Sexuality* (London, 1985), p. 22.

[73]Morgan, *Anatomy of Freedom* (n. 8 above), p. 116.

[74]Karen Rian, "Sadomasochism and the Social Construction of Desire," in *Against Sadomasochism: A Radical Feminist Analysis,* ed. Robin Ruth Linden et al. (East Palo Alto, CA, 1982), p. 46.

scenario and to sympathise in some way with the ambivalent feelings this produces."[75] This is precisely Carter's point. We cannot achieve freedom, according to Angela Carter, until we understand our own historically determined involvement in sadomasochism. And if we are to move beyond the oppositions of male/female, dominant/submissive, sadist/masochist, then a reconceptualization of the mother's role might be the place to begin.

[75]Lewallen (n. 31 above), p. 151.

Discourses on and of AIDS in West Germany, 1986–90

JAMES W. JONES

Department of Foreign Languages, Literatures, and Cultures
Central Michigan University

AIDS IN WEST GERMANY brings together discourses about gays, women, drug addicts, prostitutes, blacks, and hemophiliacs. All are outsiders, each group with its own specific and yet intertwined discourse shaped by history. AIDS is not the first time these groups have been brought together; the history of homosexuality, of conceptions of the female, of the black in Germany, and of the sick or insane extend into the medieval period.[1] Yet AIDS, a "new" disease, has shaped the images, the stereotypes, of the Other at this period in West German history in a new way. How this occurs within the borders of one influential segment of the West German media is the focus of the first section of this article. The ways in which members of one "risk group"—gay men—respond to those conceptions of AIDS and its signification of stereotype form the discussion in the second section.[2]

It is not my intent in this article to provide an overview of the wide vari-

An earlier and much abbreviated version of this essay was published as "Conceiving AIDS in West Germany: Some Public Discourses," copyright by the author, in the *Cornell Western Societies Papers* (1990).

[1]The Jew, the black, the female, and the homosexual are all figures with a history of stereotyping within the Western discourse of the Other as sexually perverse and pathological. Sander Gilman's pathbreaking work in this area has been decisive in helping to shape my reading of the West German AIDS discourses (see his *Disease and Pathology* [Ithaca, NY, 1985], and *Disease and Representation* [Ithaca, NY, 1988]).

[2]The following have also significantly contributed to my reading of AIDS discourses: John Borneman, "AIDS in the Two Berlins," in *AIDS: Cultural Analysis, Cultural Activism*, ed. Douglas Crimp (Cambridge, MA, 1988), pp. 223–36; Susan Sontag, *AIDS and Its Metaphors* (New York, 1989); Paula Treichler, "AIDS, Homophobia, and Biomedical Discourse: An Epidemic of Signification," in Crimp, ed., pp. 31–70; and Simon Watney, *Policing Desire: Pornography, AIDS, and the Media* (Minneapolis, 1987).

This essay originally appeared in the *Journal of the History of Sexuality* 1992, vol. 2, no. 3.

ety of discourses competing to define AIDS. The focus here is on two mass-circulation newsmagazines, *Der Spiegel* and *Stern,* as creators of a kind of "official" discourse within the public realm. Both magazines (but especially *Spiegel,* which bills itself as "the German newsmagazine") reflect the discourses on AIDS in West Germany from the federal and state governments and from various aspects of the medical establishment ("AIDS experts," researchers, and physicians directly involved in treating people with AIDS). Of course their reporting on that "official" discourse is filtered through their own biases, creating the second discourse on AIDS to be analyzed here. The choices made as to the subjects and objects of AIDS, as well as their modes of presentation, form the way in which this "disease" (for AIDS itself is not a disease but a name for a variety of illnesses) is created.

These two magazines are problematic choices. Their readership is made up largely of fairly well educated, middle- to upper middle-class individuals. Both magazines are perceived as and see themselves as taking a liberal political stance. Yet this latter point is precisely what makes them valid sources by which to demonstrate the development of a public discourse on AIDS in West Germany. *Spiegel* strikes a polemic tone in many of its pieces, no matter what the subject, but it does serve as the newsmagazine of record for West German politics and culture, and it was the first West German magazine to publish an article on AIDS. Further, *Spiegel* has been regarded as an important source of the West German discourse on AIDS by large parts of the West German gay male community. Several articles by gay men have been published criticizing *Spiegel*'s reporting on gays and AIDS from 1983 to 1986.[3] *Siegessäule,* a monthly West Berlin magazine for gay men, refers to *Spiegel* as a "leading organ" of the German press.[4] For these reasons, I have focused more attention on *Spiegel. Stern* provides further proof that *Spiegel* is not alone in the development of West German discourses on AIDS during this time period.

The reading of the construction of AIDS in the reports of these magazines aims at revealing how the governmental discourse and the journalistic discourse combine to create definitions of AIDS and people with AIDS that are ultimately extremely political in intent and effect. The chief questions I shall focus on here are: What are the cultural values attached to AIDS and people with AIDS in West Germany? How do two mass-circulation newsmagazines interpret and shape these values?

[3]See, for example, Eberhard Hübner, "Inszenierung einer Krankheit," in *AIDS als Risiko,* ed. Volkmar Sigusch (Hamburg, 1987), pp. 218–33; and Kuno Kruse, "AIDS in den Medien," in *Leben mit AIDS—mit AIDS leben,* ed. Johannes Korporal and Hubert Malouschek (Hamburg, 1987), pp. 304–18.

[4]Andreas Salmen, "Kommentar: Wir sind im Krieg!" *Siegessäule* 5 (January 1988): 9. Unless otherwise noted, all translations of material quoted from German sources in this essay are my own.

I

Let me begin with a brief recounting of the important dates in the social history of AIDS in West Germany. *Spiegel* published its first article in May 1982, entitled "Terror from Abroad." Although in the United States the term "AIDS" replaced the initially proposed "GRID" (gay-related immune deficiency), the syndrome remained linked to gay males, especially American gay males, for several years. The human immunodeficiency virus (HIV) was discovered in 1983 in France and in 1984 in the United States. In September 1983, the first "AIDS-Hilfe" (AIDS support network) was formed in West Berlin, a city that still has one of the largest populations of persons infected with the virus. Tests to indicate the presence of antibodies to this virus, intended for testing donated blood, were devised in 1984 and were applied to blood used in West Germany in 1985. By this time, however, HIV had already affected a large percentage of West German hemophiliacs. A "Safer Sex" campaign, chiefly directed at gays, was begun by women and gay men in 1984, and in 1985 the ministry of health mailed an informational brochure on AIDS to all 27.5 million West German households.

By January 1987, however, it had become clear that AIDS was affecting large numbers of addicts and prostitutes, and it was feared that these two groups, whose borders are fluid, represented the path by which AIDS would "spread" to the "general population." Bavarian officials, in particular Secretary of State (Staatssekretär) Peter Gauweiler, attempted to convince the federal government to introduce measures that would force members of "risk groups" to be tested and would create lists of those infected. Unsuccessful, the Bavarian cabinet introduced its own health measures in February 1987. As of this writing, thirteen people who are HIV-positive have been arrested and convicted of "attempted dangerous bodily harm" in West Germany, twelve of them in Bavaria. Anonymous testing is offered at all West German departments of public health, even in Bavaria. Prisoners and people entering hospitals for treatment often are tested without their consent, which is illegal (except in Bavaria), or by forcing their consent (for example, by threatening to deny or prolong medical treatment should the patient refuse the test).

Since January 1987, *Spiegel* has published more than a hundred stories on AIDS: sixty-two stories in 1987, forty in 1988, eight in 1989, and thirteen in 1990. This includes four cover stories in 1987 and two in 1988, along with five essays on the topic and three separate series, one on the effect of AIDS upon sexual expression, another in which those with AIDS recount their experiences, and the last consisting of excerpts from the German translation of Randy Shilts's 1987 book, *And the Band Played On: People, Politics, and the AIDS Epidemic.*

The concern for identification of the sick shapes every aspect of the West

German AIDS discourses from the federal and state governments, the courts, *Stern,* and *Spiegel.* At the beginning of 1987, two strategies in the "battle against this disease" compete for primacy. The "hardliner" battle plan (promoted by Gauweiler) focuses on strictly separating the infected from the healthy. The "liberal" plan (advocated by Rita Süssmuth, federal minister of health) concentrates on education of the public as to the modes of transmission and the steps for prevention of infection and seeks compassion from the healthy for the infected.

What is "AIDS" within the public discourse represented in these magazines? It receives many names: "Epidemic," "Virus," "Death," "Killer," and "Plague" are the most often mentioned. Images depicting AIDS as a metaphor for horror or guilt are even more revealing. AIDS becomes a "threatening apocalypse,"[5] or its actions are compared to those of the devil: "the way the snake in the Garden of Eden abuses the human urge to love in order to plunge them into misery."[6] The term is written as "Aids," a typographic decision shared by some (but by no means all) other publications until 1988.[7] More important, I think, is the refusal of these journalists to differentiate between HIV infection and AIDS. They write of "Aids-sick," "Aids-infected," "Aids-diseased," and "Aids-positives," but clearly the people to whom they refer are not all people with AIDS. This conflation of the two categories continues throughout this period and signals a crucial aspect of these magazines' concept of that infected Other. Here, HIV infection leads inevitably to AIDS, which leads inevitably to death; thus, if one is HIV-positive, then one has AIDS and is consigned to the realm of the threatening and the dying.

Death may be the end, but in this conception it is only the beginning. "Aids" represents a threat, not only to the health of individuals—which is of relatively minor concern since they exist within the limits of (governmentally/medically) defined "risk groups"—but also to the health of the "Normalbevölkerung" (that "general population" so often evoked), which is the cause of the explosion of "Aids-Talk" in the media during this period. Fueling the fear of infection from the diseased body of the Other is the belief that AIDS represents unregulated lust. Gays, prostitutes, and addicts are not in control of their desires or do not allow their desires to be

---

[5]Hans Halter, "Das Virus muß nur noch fliegen lernen," *Der Spiegel* 41 (November 16, 1987): 241.

[6]Wilhelm Bittorf, "Die Lust ist da, aber ich verkneif's mir," *Der Spiegel* 41 (March 9, 1987): 238.

[7]Since 1988, however, even the majority of gay publications write the term as "Aids." The change within the gay press would seem to indicate that by this point it had become accepted orthography to write the term as a German noun. This decision to transform the term from an acronym of English words into a German noun has reasons that are open to interpretation and deserve a more thorough investigation than space permits here.

controlled, and this makes them perverse and threatening agents of pathology. They stand for an entire era of liberalism (the 1960s and 1970s), which is refuted by the evidence of AIDS upon their bodies. They are, thus, reaping the just punishment for years of living outside the (marriage) law. Of course, neither magazine openly supports this view; indeed, in early 1987, both ridicule those who do. Even Peter Gauweiler does not go so far as to state his attitude in such blunt terms; only the Catholic church and the Republican party do that.[8] An analysis of depictions of the four "risk groups" and of Third World countries or American blacks reveals, however, the ways in which this conception of "Aids" as the product of perversity and also its just reward do indeed manifest themselves and, in turn, shape the political program supported by *Spiegel* and, to a less obvious but equal degree, *Stern*.

Although gay men made up the majority of AIDS cases in early 1987 (as they still do today, although their percentage is decreasing), they are curiously missing from the "risk groups" Gauweiler mentions in his debate with Martin Dannecker in the January 12, 1987, issue of *Spiegel*. The groups to which he wants to apply a "duty to report" are prostitutes (especially females) and addicts. Gays are also absent from the proposed list of those to be subjected to "forced tests" in Bavaria (hemophiliacs, addicts, prostitutes, prisoners) mentioned in February 9 and February 16, 1987, reports on the proposed Bavarian "catalog of measures." Since gays do not represent a path for the infection to spread to heterosexuals, they would only divert attention from the aim of containing the disease within already recognized bounds by means of these proposed measures.[9] Gays may not be named—yet—but their presence is everywhere.

In his conversation with the openly gay social scientist Dannecker, Gauweiler conjures up images of diseased gays spreading the illness through their "fun in their perversions."[10] That they are not confining their "perversions" to themselves becomes clear in reports on gays—always American gays—carrying their disease to other countries such as Brazil, Japan, Haiti, and Thailand. AIDS in Haiti is explained by the accepted be-

[8]*Stern* takes an even stronger stance on the side of the liberal line than does *Spiegel* in several editorials attacking Gauweiler's proposals, the AIDS phobia whipped up by the sensationalistic *Bild-Zeitung*, and the refusal of the Catholic church to support the government's safer sex campaign. See, for example, Michael Jürgs, "Keuschheit statt Kondome?" *Stern* 7 (February 5–11, 1987): 3; Jürgen Kestling, "Die Rechnung der Moralisten," *Stern* 9 (February 18–25, 1987): 220.

[9]Later the risk groups would again be rearranged. In "Aids: 'Warum sich also testen lassen?'" (*Der Spiegel* 42 [April 25, 1988]: 238), there are only two worthy of mention—gays and addicts.

[10]"*Spiegel*-Streitgespräch: Aids: Sex-Verbot für Zehntausende? Staatssekretär Gauweiler und Sexualwissenschaftler Dannecker über Meldepflicht und Seuchenbekämpfung," *Der Spiegel* 41 (January 12, 1987): 165.

lief that "Our Men Had to Sell Themselves" to New York City gays.[11] The story on Brazil, under the headline "Jumbos Full of Gays," begins with New York gays invading Rio de Janiero to infect the local population, as the accompanying photo of two men kissing demonstrates ("Infection at Carneval").[12] Such images of gays serve as the foundation for a discourse on AIDS as foreign and therefore threatening. Indeed, despite the title, the report mostly concerns the transmission of HIV among heterosexuals, who become infected from the "famous Brazilian transvestites." Transvestites, gays, the female prostitute who closes the article—there is no difference among them, for they all represent the same pathology.

Gays—American gays—are the source of AIDS, and gays—all gays—are a threat. Thus it is not surprising to read this statement from the Bavarian minister of education: "It cannot be a matter of creating yet more understanding for marginal groups, but rather of thinning them out. . . . This marginal group must be thinned out because it is contrary to nature."[13] How to justify "thinning out" this "marginal group"? By categorizing gays as insane. Gaetan Dugas (Shilts's infamous "Patient Zero" to whom forty infections are traced) is "love crazy," according to Spiegel.[14] Gauweiler refers to innate defects.[15] They cannot control themselves; therefore, the state must control them.

This marginal group is divided into good gays and bad gays. Good gays "allow themselves to be enlightened to a superior degree," according to Dr. Wolfgang Stille, one of Spiegel's most often cited "experts" on AIDS in West Germany and a constant voice, along with his fellow physician Dr. Eilke Helm, in support of the view that the legal rights of the majority must take precedence over those of the minority.[16] A Swedish doctor says that cooperative gays make excellent bloodhounds because they eventually tell the names of everyone with whom they have had sex.[17] Good gays get tested, cooperate with their physicians and with government officials, and stop having sex of any kind. Bad gays promiscuously practice perverse sex, which Spiegel delights in describing. They are "promiscuously living homo-

11 Peter Schille, "'Unsere Männer mußten sich verkaufen': Spiegel-Reporter Peter Schille über Aids und Armut auf Haiti," Der Spiegel 41 (September 7, 1987): 172–79.

12"Brasilien: Jumbos voller Gays," Der Spiegel 41 (February 23, 1987): 173.

13Heinz Höfl, "'Wir lassen niemand ungeschoren': Spiegel-Redakteur Heinz Höfl über Aids-Politiker Peter Gauweiler," Der Spiegel 41 (March 2, 1987): 30.

14"Aids: Hürde zu den Heteros übersprungen," Der Spiegel 42 (February 22, 1988): 139.

15"The [homosexuals] should all be tested for the virus, but they will not allow themselves to be examined out of—in my opinion—sometimes unfortunately also defects in their character" ("Spiegel-Streitgespräch: Aids: Sex-Verbot für Zehntausende?" p. 161).

16"Aids: Harte Hand," Der Spiegel 41 (May 4, 1987): 132.

17"Aids: 'Wir haben Angst vor der Angst': Spiegel-Report über den Kampf gegen die Seuche in Europa," Der Spiegel 41 (February 16, 1987): 146.

sexuals,"[18] an interesting choice of terms in which "living" evokes its opposite—dying—because of its context as a marker of AIDS. Bad gays are Americans from New York or San Francisco, and, increasingly, bad gays are from West Berlin, an outpost of "foreigners" (gays, Turks, emancipated women, asylum seekers) politically attached to West Germany.

Such stereotyping began with the first article in *Spiegel* in 1982, increased in size and fervor between 1984 and 1986, and was well established by 1987. These images permeate not only the texts of *Spiegel* reports and the language of the politicians and physicians whom they quote but also the photos chosen to illustrate these texts. The AIDS patients who are pictured are almost exclusively American males, whom one assumes to be gay because that is why they are there. Many photos of men, who are specifically identified as gay, focus on particular body parts, especially on the buttocks, or on specifically homoerotic or gay acts such as kissing or having one's arm around a friend's waist. Through such depictions, gays become their lust, which becomes their disease. Even when the articles are not chiefly about gays but instead concern the topic of the illness, photos of gay men accompany the text, as in one of *Stern*'s excerpts from the 1988 book by Masters, Johnson, and Kolodny entitled *Crisis: Heterosexual Behavior in the Age of AIDS*, which places photographs of gay men at a gay pride march alongside a text about heterosexual transmission of HIV. Gays are thus the sign that always speaks "AIDS."

Although "promiscuously living homosexuals" remain a focus of the journalistic AIDS discourse, their previously central position is taken by prostitutes and addicts beginning in 1987. Usually the concern is for female prostitutes and addicts, as they are held to be the path of infection for the heterosexual population. The borders between the two categories are not fixed because addicts, according to the magazines and their quoted experts, have given up control of their bodies to the will of their addiction. In order to get money to buy drugs, they sell themselves. But their blood has already been polluted through active membership in the community of addicts. The male customer of the prostitute can never be sure whether the person he has hired is healthy. The German term for "john," *Freier*, takes on an additional meaning within this context, for it can also connote the assumption that the male customer is free of infection. The prostitute-addict must infect him. The "chain of infection" links the bordello to the marriage bed when he sleeps with his healthy wife, and the chain continues when she, unknowingly diseased, gives birth to a sick baby. These fears motivate and shape not only the official (governmental, medical) discourse on

[18]"Aids: 'Ich bin positiv': Wie Infizierte leben und leiden," *Der Spiegel* 41 (August 17, 1987): 58.

AIDS reflected in the magazines' reports but also their textual and pictorial images of prostitutes and addicts.

Prostitutes need to be tested in order to make sex safe for men who want to *fremdgehen* (literally, "go foreign," an entirely appropriate word in view of its inclusion of the "foreign" within this context). Like gays, prostitutes themselves rarely speak. In photos, these women become their function, that is, they exist as those body parts which men desire to buy. Thus, photos focus upon breasts, buttocks, genitals.

Male customers are innocent victims and witnesses to the crime. The male victim is best illustrated in a photograph that concludes the only *Spiegel* essay on AIDS by a female editor, Ariane Barth, entitled "An Infection of the Collective Fantasy." The photo shows a woman in disheveled clothes, her hair streaming backward, her breasts slightly exposed, and her eyes—like those of the prostitutes pictured elsewhere—barred with black. She is writing the message "Welcome to the AIDS Club." Reprinted from the magazine *Wiener*, the image derives from American folklore, as Gary Fine has shown.[19] This message concludes a story that has sprung from the collective fear and fantasy of young heterosexual males. Told throughout the United States—and now Europe—the story presents an innocent young man who meets an attractive (that is, apparently healthy), sensuous young woman and takes her to his home. They enjoy a night of sexual pleasure. In the morning, he awakes to find her gone. When he goes into the bathroom, he sees the message written in red lipstick on the mirror: "Welcome to the AIDS Club." (In some variants, she simply looks him in the eyes and tells him her news.) The trusting and healthy male falls prey to the act of a plotting, vengeful female. Innocence and guilt are clearly defined; control and separation are needed for protection. This image—frightening in all its implications for intimate relations today—lies behind the way people with HIV infection are represented and discussed by the official discourse in West Germany.[20]

The same is true of addicts. They rarely speak except to support what the

---

[19] Gary Alan Fine, "Welcome to the World of AIDS: Fantasies of Female Revenge," *Western Folklore* 46 (July 1987): 92–97. See also Jan Brunvand, *Curses, Broiled Again* (New York, 1989), p. 196.

[20] Even more frightening images become attached via the caption to this image, which reads "ein modernes Menetekel" (in Ariane Barth, "Eine Infektion der kollektiven Phantasie: *Spiegel*-Redakteurin Ariane Barth über das Ende der sexuellen Revolution durch Angst vor Aids," *Der Spiegel* 41 [April 6, 1987]: 123). The use of this Old Testament word conjures up a history—sublimated as well as conscious—of the Jew as defiler of non-Jewish blood and destroyer of non-Jewish races. "Menetekel" were the first two words the fiery hand wrote upon the wall of King Belshazzar's royal chamber. The Hebrew prophet Daniel interpreted the words as meaning "God hath numbered thy Kingdom, and finished it" and "Thou art weighed in the balances, and art found wanting" (Dan. 5:25–27). *Menetekel* as a German noun has come to signify a (perhaps secret) sign of imminent danger.

magazines see as necessary. They exist as objects of discourse, always referred to as "Fixer" and not the more "polite" term, drug addict. The image of the addict as a dark, pathological threat runs again and again through recountings of accidents involving innocent children and dirty needles discarded in public parks. A four-year-old boy is such a victim: "A dirty 'Fixer'-needle had fallen into his hands in between the swing and the slide at a playground near a day-care center in Berlin."[21] Here even the needle, an extension of the Berlin addict, takes on a power of its own to infect: *it* fell into the boy's hands.

Addicts are difficult patients: their addiction is a sign of illness ("For me, all drug addicts are sick," stated the minister of health for Nordrhein-Westfalen),[22] but they do not let themselves be educated as to AIDS preventive measures. In photographs, they are reduced to their function: a woman sticking a needle into her foot, an arm dripping blood with the needle freshly withdrawn, corpses splayed upon the floor in public restrooms—the consequence of their illness.

Hemophiliacs are similarly pictured, most often attached by a needle in the arm to a unit of Factor VIII. But they are innocent victims. The guilty are American blacks who sold their blood, infected through prostitution and addiction, and German medical science, which relied on high dosages of (American) blood products to treat their patients. "Innocent victims," but more than just the discourse of AIDS is at work here. Also affecting the presentation and self-concept of hemophiliacs is a West German cultural perception of disease in general as a failure of the individual, whereby the individual becomes a kind of damaged goods, no longer fit to remain within society as an equal partner.[23] This cultural response becomes clear as well in the refusal of insurance companies to pay compensation for personal suffering ("Just exactly where is the suffering?" asked one insurance company executive) and in their eventual agreement to pay compensation according to the value that the company placed upon the life that was lost. (In the insurers' judgment, a pupil with good grades was worth several thousand marks more than a pupil of the same age but with only average grades.)[24]

A fifth category of the "Aids-infected" who threaten not only West German but European health are blacks. Africa is a "Death House" or simply a land of AIDS, as in the illustration of an African businessman who

---

[21]"Drogen: Neue Pumpe," *Der Spiegel* 42 (May 30, 1988): 55.

[22]"*Spiegel*-Streitgespräch: 'Das bringt euch alle in den Knast': (NRW) Gesundheitsminister Heinemann und Sozialsenator Scherf über AIDS, Prostituierte und die Staatsdroge Methadon," *Der Spiegel* 42 (February 1, 1988): 87.

[23]Carol Poore discusses this in her article, "Disability as Disobedience? An Essay on Children with Disabilities," *New German Critique* 27 (Fall 1982): 161–95.

[24]"Aids: Skandal schlechthin," *Der Spiegel* 43 (January 2, 1989): 57.

infected Belgian women, captioned "Traveler in Aids."[25] He is represented as a dark shadow standing upon Africa, a lighter shadow. Europe is in white, as are the seven women with whom he had sex but whom he did not infect. The ten Belgian women whom he did infect are black stick figures. Central Africa is identified as the source of AIDS and thus carries the guilt for this disease.[26]

According to *Spiegel*'s version of history, American gays (especially from New York City) were driven out of Havana ("gay bordello of the USA") by Fidel Castro. These "expelled tourists" turned nearby Port-au-Prince into their next "center of homosexual vacation lust." American gays are described as "conquerors," "hunters," "the rich men from overseas" who brought AIDS. They destroyed the health of the men and then their country destroyed the Haitian economy by declaring Haiti "the cradle of AIDS." The images obviously speak to the fears of diseased gays ultimately infecting newborns and provide a body metaphor for the disease, but these are *Spiegel*'s words, not those of the United States. After being infected by Americans, "these muscular occasional whores, hardly one of whom is homosexual," spread the disease to their women through their non-European sexual customs: "Bourgeois faithfulness is white decadence, a cover for weakness in love." The article concludes by speaking for the tattered community: "The population [*das Volk*] considers its life to be a curse and a condemnation. . . . Things cannot get any worse than this."[27] Thus, gays began a process that blacks are finishing. Both are foreign, both guilty, in the verdict of *das Volk*—as expressed through *Spiegel*.

Several articles provide key examples of the discourse on AIDS within *Spiegel*. In a five-part series entitled "'Why Did It Have to Be Me?' HIV-Positives Portray Their Fate" (August 17–September 14, 1987), those directly affected do speak, separated according to "risk group."

The liberal position is already crumbling, marching nearer that of the repressive measures desired by hardliners. The preface gives currency to an entirely fictitious story of a woman intentionally giving AIDS to men and sets the story in New York City. This is "Welcome to the AIDS Club" again, set within its "real" (foreign, specifically American) milieu. Addicts, as well as prostitutes, have infected themselves: "drug addicts, who have infected themselves with contaminated needles"; "male and female prostitutes who have infected themselves through sexual intercourse or through shooting up heroin."[28] The choices made as to the order of the series and the editing of these "reports" within the series also reveal this shift.

[25]"Aids: Groteske Täuschung," *Der Spiegel* 41 (January 26, 1987): 177.
[26]"Aids: Hürde zu den Heteros übersprungen" (n. 14 above), p. 139.
[27]Schille (n. 11 above), pp. 176–79.
[28]"Aids: 'Ich bin positiv'" (n. 18 above), p. 58.

In general, these "Reports on Experience and Suffering" are confessions of having broken the taboos set by the majority society. Mary confesses that she led an impudent adolescence and left all morals behind at the age of sixteen. Ingo tells how he "infected himself"—he did not wear underwear, cut his penis on the zipper of his jeans, and then had sex with an English woman he had just met. Hannes (the first of four "homosexuals" interviewed, three of whom are given names beginning with *H*) gives up his promiscuous life-style after receiving his test result. For each confession the penalty is the same: AIDS. The threat of infection to the majority society comes from heterosexuals who have transgressed, often with a foreigner (part 1 of the series), and from addicts and prostitutes (parts 4 and 5). The infected are not like most people: they are disturbed, they are promiscuous, and they do not have names (hemophiliacs are described only as "A Mother," "A Married Couple," "A Wife"). Heterosexual Christine describes the Lebanese man who she believes infected her as "totally schizophrenic to some extent." Gay Rudi narrates a vampire-like story of one man drinking another's blood so as to infect himself and die a kind of "love death."

Control is needed, which may be the self-control of the heterosexuals or their partners who use condoms, the control of marriage, the control of prison (three of the four addicts, all males, are in prison), or the control of safer sex education among gays and prostitutes. Yet that control is not complete, not secure. Not everyone insists on condoms. Not everyone tells her or his sexual partners of her or his HIV status. Even the testing system cannot always be trusted. False positives and negatives mark their lives. The series on one level aims at sympathy and a superficial understanding of what it is like to be HIV-positive, but on another level it disturbs that possibly sympathetic stance through the uncertainty it creates. Education and safer sex may not be enough. Possibly Gauweiler is right.

Similarly, an article in *Stern* (February 18–25, 1987) about people with HIV carries the title, "We Infected Ourselves." It begins with brief first-person narratives of ten representatives of the various risk groups detailing how they acquired the virus and how they have changed their lives since learning of their HIV status. The article seeks to adhere to the liberal line: "The fear of Aids is becoming a hysteria. How can one confront that if not through frankness? Whoever keeps silent abandons adolescents, who are supposed just to be finding their way toward their sexuality. Abandons those people who do not live according to conventional norms. Abandons the level-headed health politicians who want to avoid the worst by means of an education without taboos. Abandons not only the sick, but also tens of thousands of 'positives' with their troubles and fears."[29] It concludes,

[29]Marlies Prigge, "'Wir haben uns angesteckt': Die Angst vor Aids," *Stern* 9 (February 18–25, 1987): 26.

however, with the unsettling results of a recent poll revealing that 74 percent of the West German public favored forced testing for not only those defined as "at risk," but also for the general population.

Spiegel's support for the liberal position changes radically in an essay by Hans Halter in which he poses the question, "Is Aids throwing humanity back into the Stone Age?" (November 16, 1987). Its answer can be read in its attack on the very measures *Spiegel* had so long supported: "The worldwide epidemic is taking on apocalyptic dimensions. . . . The government in Bonn has offered only 'education' and condoms until now; both bring too little." This is only a description in the issue's table of contents of Halter's essay, entitled "The Virus Just Has to Learn How to Fly." The essay begins by quoting from Revelations 6:8 about a vision of death on a horse with hell following behind. Who could death be? It is "that tall blond," Gaetan Dugas, Shilts's infamous "Patient Zero," that "mobile bachelor." The virus did learn to fly via the Air Canada steward, whose blurry photo at the bottom of the first page is captioned "Aids-spreader."[30]

The scourge is spreading, Halter believes, and he accuses Süssmuth (and therefore the federal government) of hiding facts and dispensing mistruths. Michael Koch, chief advisor to Gauweiler and author of an extensive report in the January 11, 1989, issue on how AIDS was spread by young people using drugs in a small Swedish city, does have the correct answers. The "total infection" (*Durchseuchung*) Halter describes as the bringer of the apocalypse is illustrated in a table headed "Unbroken Trend," which indicates the cumulative number of AIDS cases by quarter from 1981 to June 1987. The last two columns cannot even be contained within the table; they invade the text itself, a visual metaphor for the disease he describes. Halter concocts a fictional male prostitute (Detlef) who will "murder" dozens of gays in order to make a living. This image obviously is intended to play upon fears of sexual Others and the fluid borders between sexual identity and sexual acts. To secure the borders, Halter calls for mandatory testing (which *Spiegel* had long opposed), while he also proposes a variety of means "which would put a few stops to the epidemic": gay marriages, prostitutes on the public payroll, and needle exchanges.[31]

But these pseudosuggestions from the liberal closet are not all. Education, he claims, has not proven effective even among gays, and condoms are unreliable. He quotes Cardinal Ratzinger: "One need not speak of a

[30]Halter, "Das Virus muß nur noch fliegen lernen" (n. 5 above), p. 241. Halter was the object of much criticism from West German gays and AIDS activists for earlier essays on gays and AIDS in which he described the "homosexual life-style" solely as consisting of promiscuous, usually anonymous, sex, and in which he seemed to be looking for a scapegoat for AIDS. See the responses described in Hübner (n. 3 above); and Kruse (n. 3 above), as well as the letters to the editor published in *Der Spiegel* 41 (November 30, 1987): 7–9.

[31]Halter, "Das Virus muß nur noch fliegen lernen," pp. 248, 250.

punishment of God. It is nature which is defending herself." Although the virus, as he describes it, changes shape rapidly, Halter warns: "The death virus is still chiefly transmitted through blood and body fluids. Things do not have to stay this way."[32] The window of opportunity represented by the word "still" must be used while it is available. What is to be done has already been made clear: the duty to report names of the infected, forced testing of all who are suspected of being HIV-positive, forbidding HIV-positive prostitutes to practice their profession. These are precisely the measures that Bavaria had instigated in February and that *Spiegel* at that time decried as ridiculous and repressive.[33]

Stern is less openly polemic in its questioning of the efficacy of education and condoms because it has no equivalent of Hans Halter on its staff; nonetheless, it shows the same movement away from support of the liberal position. Supportive editorials disappear, replaced by interviews with Michael Koch, articles on the refusal of heterosexual "swingers" (whose number *Stern* inflates from several hundred in 1987 to several thousand in 1988) to take any precautions, and excerpts from Masters, Johnson, and Kolodny's *Crisis: Heterosexual Behavior in the Age of AIDS*.[34]

Stern's reporting stresses the need for people with HIV to identify themselves (as opposed to having the state identify them) and seems to rely upon their good will to tell prospective sexual partners of their HIV status. However, articles about irresponsible people with HIV demonstrate that such trust is misplaced. One horrifying account tells of a French journalist who wrote a book about how she purposely set out to infect men with HIV (a story we have seen before) after she was diagnosed with the virus. (*Spiegel* never carried an article on this book.)[35] The clear implication is that the state must step in to identify the diseased and to protect the healthy.

The excerpts from Masters, Johnson, and Kolodny's "study" underline the need for state measures. The first of three excerpts includes a series of quotations from heterosexuals explaining why they are not monogamous (implicitly, monogamy = health). The authors describe these people, a certain percentage of whom they claim must be infected, as "carriers of the virus, . . . oblivious to the possibility of being infected, . . . a major vector

[32] Ibid., p. 253.

[33] For responses to this essay, see the letters to the editor in *Der Spiegel* 49 (November 30, 1987): 7–10. The letters attacked its apocalyptic tone and its twisting of the facts. Some did praise him for expressing views that they shared, but most criticized him.

[34] William H. Masters, Virginia E. Johnson, and Robert C. Kolodny, *Crisis: Heterosexual Behavior in the Age of AIDS* (New York, 1988). The book's title was translated by *Stern* as *Das verdrängte Risiko: Aids und Heterosexualität*. I quote from the original English edition in the text but provide the German translation in the notes, with a citation to *Stern*.

[35] See Katharina Zimmer, "'Ich war die ideale Beute für das Virus,'" review of *Pourquoi moi?* by Juliette [pseud.], *Stern* 8 (February 18–24, 1988): 259.

in the continuing spread of the epidemic. . . . Irresponsibly clinging to their own personal excuses for not being tested, silently [they] spread slow death to those with whom they couple in erotic abandon."[36]

In the second excerpt, we find a boxed section carrying the headline, "'Rather Dead than Celibate': Why Many Homosexuals Do Not Change Their Behavior." Here gay men describe why they will not stop having sex. "Here is one of the clear problems of the AIDS epidemic. Many gay men who know they are infected with the AIDS virus are continuing to have sex with other men. In fact, even some men who have been diagnosed as having full-blown AIDS have continued to have sex with numerous partners."[37] Neither the book's authors nor the witnesses they call to testify, however, say whether that sex is "safe" or not; instead the authors simply term any homosexual sex "irresponsible behavior." Such language intentionally raises in the reader the fear of gay men as creatures driven solely by lust, disregarding even the certainty of an ugly, painful death and possibly infecting nongays.

A brief look at one last article reveals the change in *Spiegel*'s discourse from support of the liberal to support of the hardliner stance. The most recent cover story on AIDS, from April 25, 1988, concerns the issue of HIV testing. The cover headline asks, "How Certain Is the Aids-Test?" As always the distinction between the test's reaction to the presence of HIV antibodies and a diagnosis of AIDS evaporates. The images in the cover photograph are even more revealing. The six people standing inside test tubes are all naked. We view, from left to right, a middle-aged man facing a woman in her twenties or thirties, another man, perhaps in his forties or fifties, looking down (the only one not looking at the viewer), another woman similar in age to the first and facing the next man, and two men in their twenties, facing frontward. Who are these people? They represent the "risk groups" who ought to be tested: the john and the female prostitute in the first four people, gays signified by the two men on the right. Missing

---

[36]Masters, Johnson, and Kolodny, pp. 112–13; "Virusträger, . . . blind gegen die Möglichkeit, infiziert zu sein, . . . einen bedeutenden Übertragungsfaktor bei der Ausbreitung der Epidemie. . . . Verantwortungslos [klammern] sie an ihre persönlichen Vorwände gegen einen HIV-Antikörper-Test und still und heimlich [können] sie den Menschen, mit denen sie sich paaren, einen langsamen Tod bereiten" ("Das verdrängte Risiko: Aids und Heterosexualität," *Stern* 11 [March 10–16, 1988]: 161).

[37]Masters, Johnson, and Kolodny, p. 129; "Das Hauptproblem: Viele Homosexuelle, die wissen, daß sie mit dem HIV-Virus [sic] infiziert sind, betätigen sich weiterhin sexuell mit vielen Partnern" ("'Lieber tot als keusch': Weshalb viele Homosexuelle ihr Verhalten nicht ändern," *Stern* 12 [March 17–23, 1988]: 117). I translate this as: "Many homosexuals who know that they are infected with the HIV-virus continue to be sexually active with many partners." Notice how the German version has left out and edited what in the original was a bit more carefully phrased. The German version is even more sweeping in its indictment than was the original.

from this line-up is the addict, but the hidden arms of the first woman might well conceal the mark of her disease. The category appears early in the story when the risk groups are reduced to two: "homosexuals" and "Fixer." The story refutes the recent claim made by members of the Bavarian AIDS commission that one in three tests (which *Spiegel* had earlier termed "a kind of bourgeois death on the installment plan")[38] gives a false result. Any opinions to the contrary are discounted because "at present, the HIV test, which 'tracks down' antibodies to the Aids-virus in the blood of the tested person, is the only weapon that medical personnel have in the battle against the spread of Aids."[39] The other weapons—education and condoms—have proven themselves, according to *Spiegel,* ineffective. The threat has only grown.

The effects of this kind of discourse, not only in *Spiegel* but also within West German governmental and medical circles, are wide-ranging and carry frightening implications. The discourse medicalizes and technologizes the persons who are its objects. In many instances, they become identical with the disease—for instance, adolescent hemophiliacs are "pint-size virus-carriers."[40] They lose their voices, their names, even their faces disappear behind black boxes. Ultimately, any authentic expression from those directly affected is erased. An HIV-positive woman is quoted as saying that she and her friends who are positive do have safe sex and behave responsibly. But *Spiegel* immediately denies the validity of her statement by claiming that she represents only a small number of such positives who exist within a social network and lead "a relatively normal life."[41] Physicians and medical researchers are turned into saviors and saints who sacrifice their personal lives, even their own health, in order to help these people.

The exclusion of people with AIDS and HIV-positives as operative subjects has led to a shift within the discourse from concerns with medical-scientific issues to concerns with protecting the legal rights of the uninfected. All the answers in the former arena seem to have been found: the virus is identified, tests are available and reliable, some drug therapies have arrived, and we all know that a vaccine will not be created within the near future. According to this discourse, we do have ways to identify the infected, and there are some laws—new laws in Bavaria, older laws intended for other purposes in other states—that can be enforced to contain their threat (a prostitute who offers to engage in unsafe sex is imprisoned; a retired American army sergeant is convicted for engaging in

[38]"Recht: Gestochen und geritzt," *Der Spiegel* 41 (August 24, 1987): 63.

[39]"*Spiegel*-Titel: Aids: 'Warum sich also testen lassen?'" *Der Spiegel* 42 (April 25, 1988): 244.

[40]Ariane Barth, "*Spiegel*-Titel: 'Wenn er fröhlich singt, kommen mir Tränen': *Spiegel*-Redakteurin Ariane Barth über HIV-infizierte Kinder," *Der Spiegel* 41 (July 20, 1987): 60.

[41]"Aids: Wie ein Dolchstoß," *Der Spiegel* 42 (June 27, 1988): 51.

unsafe sex). Further, the infected are viewed as mentally disturbed. The American sergeant is diagnosed as having "an egocentric, narcissistic personality that does not orient its action toward responsibility for others."[42] A Frenchman convicted of attempted murder by means of unsafe sex is said to suffer from schizophrenia.

Accompanying this move from the medical to the legal realm, *Spiegel* openly supports stricter control measures. Sweden's use of state force is cited as a model. "State force, which Swedish authorities have been accused of applying all too quickly in dealing with Aids, is only used as an ultima ratio."[43] Ratio is the key. The four persons to whom such reasonable force has been applied are all addicts. The state placed them in hospitals, far removed from cities (the sites of their "disease"), and "cured" them by replacing heroin with methadone. One unfortunate remains hospitalized but the other three are being reintegrated into society. Control thus proves effective and nondisruptive of the social fabric; in other words, as an advertisement for a video security system appearing alongside a story on AIDS in Brazil ("Stopping Vampires") in the previous issue put it, "Trust is good, control is better."[44]

The best control is to be found in Cuba. By means of forced testing of large numbers of its population, *Spiegel* notes, Cuba remains the only country where the infection rate is diminishing. The approval lurking behind this repetition of Cuba's unquestioned claim to success signals *Spiegel*'s own support for introducing equivalent measures in West Germany. Hans Halter's attitude has not changed appreciably. Although he now terms Cuba's measures "a barbaric practice" in a recent essay, "Menetekel at the Wall" (December 4, 1989),[45] he continues to praise East German steps (forced testing, lists of those with HIV, deportation of foreigners who test positive) as exemplary. The opening of the wall can only signify a tragic future for the once relatively "Aids-free" German Democratic Republic.

Further proof of the continued strength of *Spiegel*'s attitude that those with HIV represent a threat in need of control can be found in the controversial gay activist Rosa von Praunheim's recent essay on AIDS among gays in West Berlin, "Screwing under the Safer Sex Poster" (May 14, 1990).[46] Here Praunheim fully supports exactly the picture that Halter has

---

[42]"Aids: Kurz vorher Handzeichen," *Der Spiegel* 42 (November 7, 1988): 31. The quote in the original describes him as "'eine egozentrische, narzistische Persönlichkeit, die ihr Handeln nicht an der Verantwortung für andere' ausrichte." Note the feminization of him in this description.

[43]Renate Nimtz-Köster, "'Es ist nicht Liebe, was du mitbringst': *Spiegel*-Redakteurin Renate Nimtz-Köster über Aids-Bekämpfung in Schweden," *Der Spiegel* 42 (June 13, 1988): 206.

[44]"Brasilien: Vampire stoppen," *Der Spiegel* 42 (June 6, 1988): 164.

[45]Hans Halter, "Menetekel an der Mauer," *Der Spiegel* 49 (December 4, 1989): 262.

[46]Rosa von Praunheim, "Bumsen unterm Safer-Sex Plakat," *Der Spiegel* 20 (May 14, 1990): 244–47.

sought to create of gays as refusing all reason while immersing themselves in lust and endangering others (that is, nongays) with their unsafe practices. While his reasons for doing so arise from quite different desires—he believes West German gays must be saved from themselves—his article only provides even more support for such attitudes as Halter's. In so doing, Praunheim has taken a step away from the effort at demystifying West German AIDS discourses that he pursued in his film *Ein Virus kennt keine Moral* (A virus knows no morals), which will be discussed in Section 2.

A stereotype of the person who has been infected with HIV as foreign, perverse, and outside the borders of the normal and acceptable makes possible the acceptance of repressive measures arising from the fear of infection. The state cannot allow the majority's blood to be tainted by the impure. The specter of concentration camps, which arises in various articles in these magazines as well as in narratives by persons with HIV,[47] steps further and further onto the stage of the discourse on AIDS that lives inside, but more important, outside the pages of *Stern* and *Spiegel*.

II

The analysis cannot, must not, stop here. This discourse is not the only one competing to define West German conceptions of AIDS and of people with HIV infection. In the space of this article I cannot examine the wide variety of counterdiscourses that have arisen in response to those expressed in *Spiegel* and *Stern*. I would like, however, to point to the necessity of looking at how other newsmagazines and newspapers have reacted to "Aids," how other media conceptualize and present it (in particular television, which I believe has provided people with AIDS and HIV-positives a qualitatively and quantitatively richer opportunity to engage in their own discourses), and how the various AIDS institutions have responded.[48]

Here I wish to examine how gays have reacted to that discourse on AIDS described in Section 1 and how they have created alternative discourses, ones I term "discourses *of* AIDS," since in them a group of those directly affected does speak. The reaction to a discourse on AIDS by a gay-motivated discourse of AIDS began years earlier than 1987, just as *Spiegel*'s own discourse began in 1982 and focused, until 1987, chiefly upon gay men. In order to see the ways in which West German gay men have reacted to safer sex campaigns, to fear of infection, and to the deaths of their friends, we must look back to 1986. Obviously, such reaction did not begin

[47]See, for example, Marlies Prigge, "Aids-Kranke ins Getto?" *Stern* 12 (March 12–18, 1987): 20–33, in which the author raises the specter only to attempt to prove that it is inappropriate for the present historical moment.

[48]Of particular interest would be the art exhibit "Vollbild AIDS," which presented works by a variety of gay and nongay artists reacting to the health crisis (see Frank Wagner, *Vollbild AIDS: Eine Ausstellung über Leben und Sterben* [Berlin, 1988]).

then, but the discourse I am analyzing really began in earnest at that point. Certainly, gay men did respond (and continue to do so) quite vehemently to representations of them in the mass media, in particular in *Spiegel*. Authors of several articles in *Siegessäule, Leben mit AIDS—mit AIDS leben* (1987), and *AIDS als Risiko* (1987) attack *Spiegel* for its outright falsification of statistics and quotes, as well as its negative stereotyping of homosexuals.[49] In issues following essays by Hans Halter or Rosa von Praunheim, the column that publishes letters to the editor is filled with responses from gay men to what they perceive as portrayals of them as mindless creatures of lust who endanger all whom they touch.

Spiegel is a sign of the times, for gays, and these gays know how to decipher it. Yet they do not merely react to such a discourse on AIDS as *Spiegel* presents; they are, of course, also influenced by it in their own conceptions of what AIDS means for them. *Spiegel* and *Stern* are conduits for and creators of a discourse about AIDS that, as I have tried to show, operates to separate those with HIV from the general population, figuratively and literally, so as to be able to control the threat to the body politic which they are made to represent. It is not my intent to trace a series of rebuttals within the gay press. Rather, I want to elaborate how several crucial issues from the representation of gays within that discourse on AIDS described in Section 1 become center points for a discourse of AIDS by one group of those greatly affected by it. I then will describe the implications of their discourse for concepts of gay identity and gay community.

Many of these issues and implications can be found in a debate between two leading figures in the West German gay movement, Rosa von Praunheim and Martin Dannecker. Their conversation, moderated by Ingrid Klein, was first published in *Sexualität Konkret* (1986) and then included in the republication of that issue, with some additions and revisions, in 1987. The two men had worked together on Praunheim's first important film, *Nicht der Homosexuelle ist pervers, sondern die Situation, in der er lebt* (Not the homosexual is perverse, but the situation in which he lives)

---

[49]Several articles discuss the stereotypic and homophobic images that *Spiegel* presents. See Andreas Salmen, "Wir sind im Krieg!" *Siegessäule* 5 (January 1988): 9; the following articles in Sigusch, ed. (n. 3 above): Gunther Schmidt, "Moral und Volksgesundheit," pp. 24–38; Ulrich Clement, "Höhenrausch," pp. 210–17; and Hübner, pp. 218–33; and Kruse (n. 3 above), pp. 304–18. Especially good on the period before 1987 is Frank Rühmann's *AIDS: Eine Krankheit und ihre Folgen*, 2d ed. (Frankfurt am Main, 1985). Helmut Zander responds to the *Spiegel* series "Warum ausgerechnet ich?" in his *Der Regenbogen: Tagebuch eines Aidskranken* (Munich, 1988), pp. 221–22. To cite only the most recent example, Andreas Salmen, in an article entitled "Aidspolitik der DDR wird scharf attackiert" in *Die Tageszeitung* (January 10, 1990), writing about the restrictive AIDS policies of the German Democratic Republic, states: "This AIDS policy was applauded chiefly by Western hardliners. *Spiegel*, known for apocalyptic scenarios in which sex-obsessed gays bring AIDS to all humanity, is the most loyal fan of the GDR policy" (reprinted in *die schwule presseschau* 9 [February 1990]: 22).

(1971). As Praunheim says, what they portrayed "relatively harmlessly" came to be practiced in the ensuing years "much more eccentrically" and grew into an ideal of "homosexual behavior": drugs, backrooms, leather, sex without emotions.[50] Praunheim sees a chain of causes and effects: homosexuality became promiscuity, which caused AIDS, which always causes death. To break the chain, gays must stop having promiscuous sex and must adopt safer sex practices. He accuses Dannecker of betraying the community by not advocating safer sex vigorously enough and, indeed, for misleading the community by downplaying the numbers of those infected in the early years of the epidemic.

Dannecker answers that their film also criticized society for its oppression of gays and affirmed precisely that gay culture which society negated. Dannecker sees a need to alter the social conditions of sexuality before sexuality can be changed, which in turn would make possible a transformation in sex practices. Safer sex campaigns stand at the end of a long process of change. Thus, to propose masturbation at the present time as the safest erotic practice (as Praunheim does) is not only "ersatz satisfaction" but "autistic sexuality" and "immature behavior." He further criticizes Praunheim for his moralistic tone, expressed, Dannecker feels, most clearly in the *Spiegel* article (1984) where Praunheim claimed to speak for gays: "When you state in *Spiegel* that we are acting just like we always have, and that is accidental homicide, then you are playing with a metaphor in order to exert a moral pressure."[51]

But Dannecker himself is by no means free of moral views about gay sexuality. This "sexual scientist" states that all clinical experience shows that gays "themselves devalue their sexual practices" and therefore "a very strange, addicted behavior arises." Indeed, in 15 percent of gays, he claims, promiscuity is "compulsive."[52] Thus, a significant percentage of gays cannot rationally control their desires. The campaign for safer sex must fail if it focuses on practices, not on desires. It assumes that rational forces can control sexual expression, and this assumption, especially for gays, is not true. It will fail, Dannecker believes, not only because it aims at the wrong place on the body, but also because it is a largely foreign (American) element that is being introduced into Germany.

The lines seem drawn: morality–science, fear–reason, erotic acts–sexuality as identity, West Germany–United States, the present–the future, death–life. The tension within these pairs fuels the AIDS discourse among gay men. In some ways, Praunheim does indeed represent an outsider point of view with his "American" emphasis on practical steps to stop the tide of

[50]Rosa von Praunheim and Martin Dannecker, "'Das ist rein kriminell': Ein Streit-gespräch, moderiert von Ingrid Klein," in Sigusch, ed., p. 82.

[51]Ibid., pp. 90, 84.

[52]Ibid., pp. 88, 96.

dying, steps that often correspond to those of the government and of *Spiegel,* in which he serves as a spokesperson for gays. The AIDS discourse of West German gays is qualitatively different from that in the United States, although the two share many similarities. The majority of West German gays, if I may judge by the variety of publications I have read, are united in their resistance to the picture that *Spiegel* portrays of them as sex maniacs. Yet, both Praunheim and Dannecker share a view closer to that of *Spiegel.* Praunheim's call for a new morality and Dannecker's for reshaping the sexual drive reveal an attitude toward gay sexuality that is ambivalent at best.

Other writers have seen the link between gay promiscuous sexuality and AIDS as reinforcing the largely unconscious fear on the part of gays that maybe heterosexuals are right, after all—maybe homosexuality really is sick and unnatural. But they cannot allow that fear to surface, for it would call into question the basis of their gay identity. In addition, West German gays view government measures as an attempt to control gay sexuality. They understand the discourse of AIDS as the discourse of discrimination and a clear threat of harsher measures to come if obedience is not evident.

These fears, unconscious and conscious, lead on the one hand to attempts to remove "morality" from a discourse of AIDS while maintaining "pleasure in sex" and on the other hand to a promulgation of monogamy and "correct" sex practices as the agenda for "health." The gay discourse of AIDS centers then on the issues of what gay sexuality is and who defines it. The safer sex advertising campaign of the Deutsche Aids-Hilfe (DAH—German AIDS support group network) signifies the attempt to preserve the identity of gay sexuality within the parameters of risk-free erotic practices. Picture ads are most successful at this. Naked men photographed from the front are always in couples or in groups. Sex between them is erotic, fun, even promiscuous and perhaps anonymous. The brief texts reinforce that focus: "Without a lot of words. Everything that's hot and safe—safer sex"; and "Sweat. Cum. Safer sex." ("Schwitzen. Spritzen. Safer Sex.")[53]

These ads are quite different from the original one that showed only two naked male torsos in an embrace with the tops of jeans covering the bit of waist exposed. These safely sexy men had no faces and their nonpresent genitals would not be allowed to come into contact with each other. The DAH ads are also very different from the single ad of the national campaign, sponsored by the Ministry of Health, that might be seen as referring to a gay man. It pictures a solitary man sitting on a beach and turned away from the viewer. The title reads: "Don't leave me alone." But that "official"

---

[53]Advertisement on the back cover of *Siegessäule* 5 (October 1988); advertisement from *Siegessäule* 6 (January 1989): 33.

discourse makes itself heard in other ads from the DAH. A photo of one man whispering into the ear of another at a café bears the text, "Anyone can be positive. Without knowing it. That means everyone has to protect himself and others. In other words, just live positively."[54] The entreaty to speak and the image of the unknown but always menacing health status derive from that "Aids-Talk" so abundant in *Spiegel* and elsewhere. Not all gays have greeted this campaign with open arms. Many, like Dannecker, feel it does not address the deep-seated anxieties that a condom tries to cover. One reporter in *Siegessäule* describes the difference: "The more rigid safer sex definition of the Americans has become the norm almost all over the world. Generally *any* unprotected anal intercourse, regardless who the partners are, is considered unsafe, and quite often even oral intercourse without a condom is declared unsafe," whereas the West German view proposes a "more differentiated safer sex line that puts more stress on each person's critical autonomy and ways of dealing with the situation which each particular individual may find."[55]

There are no answers to the question of what gay sexuality is. That is the problem. AIDS has made uncertain the already unstable boundaries that existed prior to the epidemic between the wide variety of sexual identities and erotic practices that gay men might embrace simultaneously, not sequentially. The campaign for safer sex seeks to maintain the variety of possibilities while not, according to many West German gay critics, addressing the issue of the instability and even untenability of those possibilities. For many, the condom represents a "foreign body" in the ritual of sex and (in anal sex) within the body itself; thus, it becomes an icon of AIDS when it is meant to ward it off.[56]

The safer sex campaign was thus seen both as a means of control and as an avenue toward redefining gay sexuality. These issues are not resolved, but the discussion moves more and more toward seeing the solution as lying solely within the gay community. Through the link with gay sexuality, AIDS becomes a vehicle for emancipation. In an essay by Till Streu on "The Fear of Death," the fear induced in gays by AIDS is seen as a fear of death, a fear that the medical establishment nurses more often than it battles. "Buddies" (gay men who volunteer to help a gay person with AIDS deal with the disease, including those fears) serve in Streu's essay as exemplary helpers who overcome the taboo of death and disease. Their success derives from their own acceptance and proclamation of their gay identity. Those who need a buddy most, according to Streu, are closeted

[54]Advertisement on the back cover of *Siegessäule* 5 (August 1988).

[55]Michael Bochow, "Eine politische Tagung: 5. Internationale Aids-Konferenz in Montreal," *Siegessäule* 6 (August 1989): 7.

[56]Hans-Georg Wiedemann, "Liebe—Sexualität und die Krankheit AIDS," in Korporal and Malouschek, eds. (n. 3 above), p. 213.

gay men, but unfortunately the process of self-acceptance, for many, cannot be completed because they begin too late. This essay puts forth a unique emancipatory philosophy. It is better, Streu believes, for men who are homosexual but have not assumed a gay identity to contract AIDS and die, a process that would force them to come out, than it is to continue living a closeted life, which entails the shackles of loneliness and sexual promiscuity. Death becomes a sign of liberation, life the totem of an oppression to be cast aside.[57]

While this particular strategy is not pursued by any other author, the effort to channel a general AIDS phobia into gay emancipation has become a dominant theme since 1988. Andreas Salmen, who (along with Robert Kohler) has been the chief writer on AIDS for *Siegessäule*, began in April 1988 to map out the strategy that has found the most resonance. In a commentary entitled "The Elimination of the Homosexual," Salmen demonstrates how the discourse on AIDS in West Germany is part of a discourse on homosexuality. By turning AIDS into a heterosexual disease, which is the aim of the safer sex discourse, Salmen writes, gays and the deaths of gays do not exist. Thus, gays—made visible and threatening by AIDS—will be rendered invisible and their threat can safely, silently be defused. The implication is that such invisibility will then allow the government to apply whatever measures it desires to gays. Salmen thus pleads for keeping AIDS as a gay disease: "Only we ourselves will be able to break the silence about us."[58] Such a position is clearly problematic. Just as the portrayal of AIDS as affecting everyone aims at defusing stereotyping and scapegoating but can also lead to precisely that, so too does the depiction of AIDS as a disease singularly affecting gays carry the possibility for both increased emancipation and oppression.

By January 1989, the attempt to turn AIDS into a vehicle of gay emancipation seems to have found a focus. A variety of self-help groups had formed in many West German cities, where those directly affected by AIDS could find a voice and with it ways to deal personally and publicly with the disease. The step of "coming out" as a person with HIV infection began to be institutionalized. Within the "Aids-support groups," the liberal-Left political parties (Social Democrats, Greens, Alternative List) and gay political groups (for example, the newly formed Committee on AIDS and Human Rights) used AIDS as a starting point from which to fight societal homophobia. The focus for such an emancipation cannot be the role of a victim. In an interview, Sophinette Becker, a Heidelberg psychologist who treats many gay men with HIV infection, poses the problem of a gay identity defined solely by AIDS: "If the whole thing that makes up

---

[57]Till Streu, "Die Angst vor dem Tod," *Siegessäule* 5 (February 1988): 14–15.
[58]Andreas Salmen, "Die Ausgrenzung des Homosexuellen," *Siegessäule* 5 (April 1988): 11.

gay life is practically always solely defined by AIDS, then I ask myself, just what kind of a life it is that's to be defended against this virus. I think there must also be a gay life without AIDS. If gay life only consists of AIDS now, then I ask myself where the resources are supposed to come from to defend that life against AIDS."[59] Because at present gay identity is largely subsumed within an AIDS identity, the danger of losing oneself into a conformity to that discourse of "AIDS = gay" is stronger than ever. One of the DAH safer sex ads, entitled "Living Gay," also stresses this in its text, "Our life cannot be separated from AIDS any more. And yet: living gay is more," which accompanies a picture of seven gay men touching, laughing, sitting together.[60]

The discussions of using AIDS as a gay disease and of refusing the victim role led to concrete political action. The magazines *Rosa Flieder* and *Siegessäule* strongly urged support for local and national protests of the Bavarian catalog of measures in April and October 1987. *Rosa Flieder*, always a bit more radical than *Siegessäule*, set the tone: "Gays, Defend Yourselves!" Ten thousand people marched through downtown Munich and protested in front of the city hall.[61] The repressive measures put into effect in Bavaria seem to have ignited both a genuine fear of such measures on a national level and a sense that a purely reactive position to the AIDS crisis was allowing that fear to become a reality. In addition to political focus, the reporting within these journals also represents an avenue by which gays have sought to counteract the public discourse on AIDS and, more important, to create their own discourse of AIDS. The images of Sweden and Cuba as models for dealing with HIV infection are strongly attacked in stories describing Swedish gays who refuse to cooperate with authorities and the reality of internment camps in Cuba. Andreas Salmen proposes concrete steps toward creating a new politicized gay identity: a reorganization of the AIDS support groups to concentrate on prevention and on providing care, the development of more groups run by and for HIV-positives, the establishment of ACT UP groups, and the creation of a

[59]Robert Kohler, "Den Widerspruch auszuhalten: Interview: Sophinette Becker," *Siegessäule* 6 (January 1989): 12.

[60]Advertisement on the back cover of *Siegessäule* 5 (June 1988).

[61]Headline in *Rosa Flieder* 52 (April–May 1987): 12. The magazines seemed somewhat surprised at this large response. They had expected a continuation of the apathy that had existed among the gay body politic. Ralf König, a popular gay cartoonist, satirized the priorities of that silent gay majority before the smaller response to the national protest in October. In the cartoon, the deejay of a gay bar interrupts the music to read to the patrons the news of a West German television network's decision to cancel "Dynasty." This ignites the crowd's anger, and they plan a mass demonstration and petitions; they see Gauweiler behind it and realize that a unified response is the only way to achieve their goal. All these steps are precisely what the gay press urged its readers to take in order to protest the Bavarian measures (in *Rosa Flieder* 55 [October–November 1987]: 40–41).

means to run drug experiments, and finding a way to grieve for the dead. Thus, the issues of defining and controlling gay identity are placed squarely within the gay community.

The most significant step in gays taking power over the definition and control of a gay identity and a gay discourse of AIDS has been the formation of self-help groups by and for people with AIDS and HIV. The Rainbow Project in Hamburg is a well-known example, due in part to the description of its founding in Helmut Zander's diary, which I shall discuss later. Cologne groups have formed a "Stop AIDS Project" in which gays invite small groups of friends to their homes to explore their feelings, anxieties, and desires about safer sex. West Berlin's SchwuZ (Schwules Zentrum) recently sponsored a very successful safer sex night as an erotic alternative to the baths. The gay press has been influential in this process by reporting on these efforts and by providing interviews with people with AIDS. In contrast to those in *Spiegel,* these interviews allow the men to express a wide variety of feelings, not only those that correspond to the tenor of the publication. Indeed, the men interviewed often criticize the gay community's response.[62] As mentioned earlier, Rosa von Praunheim ignited a controversy with his *Spiegel* essay, "Screwing under the Safer Sex Poster" (May 14, 1990). In response many leaders of the gay movement and of AIDS organizations have broken off their involvement in screenings of his *Aids-Trilogie* and have declared him persona non grata in the movement.

But the tensions cited earlier remain unresolved. Americans supply leadership for the West German response to AIDS. Not a German but an American, Scott Barry, was awarded the Federal Service medal for cofounding the AIDS support group in Düsseldorf. San Francisco's Stop AIDS, Shanti, and Names Projects serve as models for ways to deal with the crisis.

The need for a Stop AIDS Project and the response to the safer sex night reveal another unresolved tension, between the fear of lust and the use of lust to overcome "repressed" fear. There is also a tension between medical (drug, technological) and nonmedical (homeopathic, "natural") methods of dealing with AIDS. Only recently (in 1989) have articles in

---

[62]For two very different perspectives on living with AIDS, see "Gespräch mit einem AIDS-Kranken," *Rosa Flieder* 52 (April–May 1987): 17–19; and Andreas Salmen, "'Es gibt keinen Automatismus hin zum Tod': Gespräch mit Herbert, 34 Jahre, aids-krank," *Siegessäule* 5 (September 1988): 14–15. In the former, Peter Siglar, a German who lived in San Francisco and who made two videos about his life with AIDS ("Noch lebe ich ja" [1987], and "Im Grunde sind wir Kämpfer" [1988]), talks about his integration into a gay community that enables him to create a positive life out of being HIV-positive. In the latter, Herbert describes his exile from that community and how he believes that he has remained alive by refusing to join a community of HIV-positives.

Siegessäule and its successor, *magnus,* treated alternative therapies favorably. At the same time, the role of the physician is understood in various degrees ranging from the doctor as advisor or facilitator, with patients having an equal voice in their "treatment," to the doctor as an all-knowing source of orders to be followed.[63] In addition, a new tension between gays and non-gays within the various AIDS counseling agencies has arisen. As the response to the syndrome has broadened from small groups of gay men, along with some nongay friends, to encompass increasingly large bureau-cracies and offices within nongay agencies (such as the Catholic church), a distinctively gay voice has sometimes been lost. The bureaucratization of AIDS often means the heterosexualization of AIDS, and gays have begun to discuss the need for forming new groups in order to meet their specific needs.[64]

These tensions inhabit two major responses by gay men to AIDS in West Germany: the first book-length testimony of a gay man with AIDS, Helmut Zander's 1988 *Der Regenbogen: Tagebuch eines Aidskranken* (Rainbow: The diary of a man with AIDS)[65] and Rosa von Praunheim's 1986 film *Ein Virus kennt keine Moral,* which exposes the will to power of these competing discourses of AIDS.

I want to look at Zander's text with two questions in mind: How does he respond to the discourses on AIDS available at the time? And in what way does he create his own discourse of AIDS in the process? I see Zander's text as an example of the search for alternatives to the prevailing conceptions of people with AIDS as victims and as infectious threats to others (gay and nongay). This search is composed of unresolved tensions, remains problematic, and has by no means come to a conclusion.

Zander is a gay man infected with HIV, a devout Protestant, and a trained social worker. These identities and the prevailing discourses on AIDS provide him with possible scripts to enact as someone with HIV and, later, a person with AIDS. According to the prevailing "knowledge" of the time in West Germany, HIV infection led inexorably to death: "Positive, that means in my case something completely different. For most

[63]See "Lernen mit der Infektion zu leben," *Siegessäule* 5 (November 1988): 17–19, and Bernhard Bieniek, "Zwischen Moden und Realismus," *Siegessäule* 6 (May 1989): 20–21.

[64]See, for example, the following survey of such counseling centers: Ejo Eckerle, "Aids-Beratung im Test: Der Trend: weiblich, routiniert und hetero," *magnus* 2 (February 1990): 14–19.

[65]Two other first-person narratives have since appeared: Helmut Reinhold Zielinski, ed., *Ist dir überhaupt klar, dass ich AIDS habe?* (Mainz, 1989), a collection of letters from a young gay man with HIV to the editor, a priest who works with the "Aids-Hilfe" in Düsseldorf; and Marc Philippe Mystre, *Andere Inseln deiner Sehnsucht,* ed. Liliane Studer (Zurich, 1990), the diary of a gay man with AIDS, begun shortly after his lover died of AIDS and ending before his own suicide. One book about a gay man with AIDS appeared prior to Zander's diary: Josef Gabriel, *Verblühender Mohn* (Frankfurt am Main, 1987).

people it means certain death." Thus, he initially sees no chance to resist the course that AIDS must take. At first he experiences the "identity" of being HIV-positive as an identity defined by others: "'That's just like in a novel,' shot through my head. . . . I know the course of this disease from stories all too well."[66] The daily press, television reports, his own experiences with friends who have died, and gay films such as Arthur Bressan, Jr.'s *Buddies* (1985) script his fantasies.

As he tells his friends of his diagnosis, he seems to take on the role of victim. He constantly expects and, thus, finds rejection because he feels he has become identified as a "leper." When his lover, Pascale, subtly indicates he is indeed still interested in a sexual relationship, Zander chooses to ignore that offer and speedily renounces any erotic expression ("the latter I can forgo"). The script will not allow for an HIV-positive to have sex, unprotected or not, with an HIV-negative. He does, however, have sexual relationships. One occurs during a moment of weakness when he is seduced by Jimmy, a British rock singer: "Jimmy, you seduced me into something which I did not consciously intend."[67] Another experience reawakens Zander's sexual identity because he shares it with a man, Peter, who is HIV-positive.

Through becoming part of a larger group of gay men with AIDS or HIV, Zander is able to reject the scripts written for him and begins to write his own. By fall 1986, Zander is moving beyond the subjective limits of his own illness and toward the realization that his illness is controlled by himself and by the society in which he lives. He criticizes a support group for people with AIDS/HIV because its members accept the role of victim, which denies them any power. "No fighting spirit, especially no political one. It was a gay group through and through, and here it became clear to me once again just how many homosexuals are simply defensive. Just don't stick out. Just don't grab anyone. Just don't question any political structures." In contrast, because of his experiences as a political activist for human rights, Zander sees the need to change the social definition of people with AIDS/HIV: "I will have to come to grips with dying of AIDS myself. But I will not look on without doing anything as society systematically makes life difficult for those who are infected with HIV by its reactions to them. I still have great things ahead of me and do not want to view this disease individualistically."[68]

The diary chronicles Zander's journey from "I" to "we." His arrival in the company of others with HIV/AIDS is not simple nor is his vision of "we" unproblematic. The healthy are automatically excluded, and his gay

---

[66] Zander (n. 49 above), pp. 8, 9, 29.
[67] Ibid., pp. 34, 194.
[68] Ibid., pp. 81, 67.

friends who are sick do not want to join. Most problematic is the new script that Zander writes for himself as a kind of savior/Christ-figure in the support group he cofounds, called the "Rainbow Project: Initiative Health Center for Persons with AIDS, Cancer, and Other Diseases." In describing the planning for the first meetings, he writes: "We also carry a responsibility for the many others who will come after us." Before he met Jimmy, Zander had resolved to renounce sex for the greater calling of the group. In his description, he becomes Christ, Jimmy the devil: "You are the man for me who the devil must have been for Jesus in the desert." He explains his view using the famous phrase from Luther: "Here I stand, I can do no other."[69]

Although Zander's personal vision of himself as savior, or at least Good Samaritan, renders this community of "we" somewhat problematic, the creation of such a community represents a marked step forward within the gay discourses of AIDS, for it allows gay people with AIDS/HIV to speak to each other and to the uninfected. In the community, identities can be created that resist the pressure to conform to simple categories. As a document of the change within gay discourses of AIDS that developed during 1986 and 1987, Zander's diary reveals the power that can be gained by daring to act instead of merely reacting. Clearly, he does not understand all aspects of the mechanisms of the social construction of disease, and neither does he face all his own motivations and repressions. But by creating a space, he does make it possible for people with AIDS/HIV to begin to take control of their lives.

An alternative method of empowerment is proposed by Rosa von Praunheim in his satirical film *Ein Virus kennt keine Moral*. He foresees concentration camps for people with AIDS and proposes armed resistance by gay revolutionaries as a solution. But the contrast between Zander's diary and Praunheim's film is revealing. Zander describes the social construction of AIDS and focuses on finding a way for people with AIDS to devise their own discourse of AIDS in opposition to it. His solution (in 1986–87) lies in a community of people with AIDS, in large part because of the urgent need he feels *as a person with AIDS* to achieve this goal. Praunheim, who is HIV-negative, creates a film (in 1985–86) in which are represented all the discourses of AIDS in West Germany at that time. He deconstructs those discourses by satirizing and parodying them. Because he is not infected, he does not need to create a space in which people with AIDS can survive.

[69]Ibid., pp. 130, 195, 196. Luther's words from the well-known "A Mighty Fortress" ("Ein' feste Burg") are parodied in the AIDS discourse: "And if the world were full of devils that threaten to devour us, we trust in our immune system. That's how we'll empower us!" ("Und wenn die Welt voll Teufel wär' und wollt' uns gar verschlingen, wir bauen auf Immunabwehr. So sollt' es uns gelingen," quoted from Günter Amendt, "Jetzt ist alles Gras aufgefressen," in Sigusch, ed. [n. 3 above], p. 71, my own rather free translation).

Instead, he can focus on dissecting the stereotypes within the dominant discourse about people with AIDS, gay men, medical researchers, the family and lovers of gay men with AIDS, gay social institutions, therapists, and so on.

The film follows several characters through the early period of the AIDS epidemic in West Berlin, each representing a certain social institution or a way of talking about AIDS. The boulevard journalist hunts down stories and photos of AIDS "victims," later spitting out sensationalistic headlines into three telephones at once. A gay man who owns a gay bathhouse becomes ill with AIDS and seeks solace in vain from his lover, who also becomes ill; from his mother, who confesses she has always hated men; and from his female therapist, who wants him to bring all his repressed emotions to the surface via childish role-playing situations. A female (heterosexual) medical researcher views gay men as guinea pigs. She becomes infected by the bite of a green monkey while on a research expedition to Africa (where a black man representing the European stereotype of an African—face streaked with colored designs, enormous genitalia flapping as he dances—rapes her from behind). A kind of Greek chorus of men in drag sings a commentary upon the action depicted. They conclude the film with a punning reprise of "He's Got the Whole World in His Hands," singing the lyric as "You have your fate in your hands." Clearly, Praunheim's intent is to demonstrate how our concept of AIDS lives within a discourse of stereotypes—about gays, women, blacks, disease, people with AIDS. Once we understand that any view of a group has been socially constructed, we can change that view by changing that construction. That aim was carried out in the way the film was presented in West German cinemas. Immediately following its screening, a public discussion of the stereotypes and topics presented in the film ensued in the movie theater.[70] Although Praunheim has moved away from the demystifying aim of his first (and only feature) film on AIDS, that does not negate the significance of the film itself. Indeed, the contrast between the reception accorded to *Ein Virus kennt keine Moral* and to his recent *Aids-Trilogie* is revealing. Whereas the first film

[70]Praunheim continues to chronicle the effects of AIDS upon gays in his 1990 *Aids-Trilogie: Schweigen = Tod* (Silence = Death), *Positiv* (Positive), and *Feuer unterm Arsch* (Fire under our ass). The three documentary films depict the ways gay men confront AIDS and, in particular, the manner in which governments as well as individuals continue to fail to deal with the health crisis. The first two films focus on gays with AIDS in New York City, the last on gays in West Berlin. The films function as an indictment of the broader society (in the United States) and of the gay community (in West Berlin) and are intended as propaganda pieces in the spirit of ACT UP, the radical AIDS-activist organization. As mentioned earlier, West Berliners and West Germans involved in AIDS organizations and gay groups have reacted strongly against Praunheim's blanket indictment of all West German gays for refusing, in his opinion, to face the "facts" about AIDS, give up their promiscuity, make public their HIV status (if they are positive), and band together to demand their rights.

was welcomed for the most part as a much needed attack upon the growing AIDS hysteria, his trilogy of documentaries has been roundly denounced as a capitulation to homophobic definitions of gays and gay life.

Together, Praunheim's film and Zander's diary elucidate the spectrum of discourses of AIDS that gay men in West Germany have created over the past several years. The film directs its attention outward at the official, public discourse on AIDS and inward at the discourses of AIDS within the West German gay community in its attempt to demystify the ways in which AIDS is imagined and lived. The diary concentrates most of its attention upon the empowerment of people with AIDS/HIV, giving rise to the fear that this could lead solely to the formation of support groups and become divorced from political action. But events and actions within the gay community since September 1987, when the diary ends, have shown that gay discourses of AIDS continue to develop in both directions—toward creating ways for all people to live with AIDS and toward making it possible to do so by changing the social construction of AIDS.

In the end, then, the issues involved in the discourses of AIDS center on speech, the control of speaking, and the act of identification through speech. An official, public discourse carries an appeal to speak addressed to those people within what it terms "risk groups." They must be made to identify themselves so that their health status can be ascertained. They must attest in order for society to test. The ability to speak within this discourse is granted largely to voices that will utter agreement with these goals.[71]

Within gay discourses of AIDS, too, the plea to speak exists, but here its goal is altogether different. These discourses create possibilities for speech that counter the prevailing discourses of the majority and empower the "infected," who have been denied a voice. People with AIDS/HIV must

[71]In only a few years, this discourse has become well established. Its power shapes aspects of experience beyond that related solely to "Aids," as can be seen in an article entitled "Otto Graf Vieh" (Orthographie) in the June 1, 1987, issue of *Spiegel* (pp. 99–104). A professor in Bavaria bemoans the "infection" of the Bavarian dialect by "the Prussian speech bacillus" (*den preußischen Sprachbazillus,* p. 99). Prussia (the antithesis of Bavaria) becomes a metaphor for West Berlin. As we have seen, that city signifies "Aids" within the West German official discourse. The embodiment of this viral infection he finds in the only professor for Bavarian literature—a Berliner. A citation in the "Hohlspiegel" column, which prints ironic uses and misuses of language, at the end of the previous issue (May 25, 1987, p. 278), shows that this discourse had not, however, reached all areas of the public sphere. The *Landshuter Zeitung* (a Bavarian newspaper) is quoted from its report on an informational evening about AIDS, sponsored by the Christian Socialist party: "It is not, however, as is widely suspected, for the most part homosexuals who are in danger, but likewise hydrosexuals [*sic*]. Further, AIDS can also be spread through hedrosexual [*sic*] contact." ("Es seien aber nicht wie landläufig vermutet werde, in erster Linie nur Homosexuelle, sondern gleichermaßen Hydrosexuelle, gefährdet. Darüberhinaus breite sich Aids auch bei hedrosexuellen Kontakten aus.")

speak if these possibilities are to be exercised. The range of speakers is broadened and the question of what can or will be said thereby also finds new answers.

The interplay between the discourses analyzed here (of government, medicine, and an important voice in journalism and within the gay community) reveals dynamics of action and reaction that continue to shape the reality for everyone in West Germany, not just for those directly affected. Understanding how those dynamics are shaped and the means by which they become concrete reality (for example, legal measures, medical treatments, journalistic depictions) represents the first step toward changing them. AIDS, the signifier of terror and pestilence, will be infused with new meanings. The questions are, Who will give it those meanings, and how can we understand and control those meanings?

Notes on Contributors

BRUCE THOMAS BOEHRER is associate professor of Renaissance English literature at Florida State University. He is the author of *Monarchy and Incest in Renaissance England: Literature, Culture, Kinship, and Kingship* (forthcoming, 1992). He has also published articles in *PMLA, ELH, SEL, Milton Studies, Renaissance Drama, South Atlantic Review,* and other journals.

ROBYN COOPER is senior lecturer in the department of fine arts, University of Sydney. She has recently completed a second article on Alexander Walker, "Alexander Walker on Woman, Science, and Beauty," forthcoming in *Gender and History.* She is currently working on Victorian women and beauty.

JOHN C. FOUT is professor of history at Bard College. He is the editor of two books on European women's history. Currently completing an anthology on "Male Homosexuals, Lesbians, and Homosexuality in Germany, 1871–1945," he is also writing a book-length study entitled "The Moral Purity Movement in Wilhelmine Germany: The Male Gender Crisis and the Concern about the Regulation of Masculinity." He is the founding editor of the *Journal of the History of Sexuality* and general editor of the Chicago Series on Sexuality, History, and Society.

LESLEY A. HALL is senior assistant archivist, Contemporary Medical Archives Centre, Wellcome Institute for the History of Medicine, London. She is a professionally qualified archivist as well as holding a doctorate in the history of medicine. Her book, *Hidden Anxieties: Male Sexuality 1900–1950,* was published in 1991.

GERT HEKMA is assistant professor for gay studies at the Sociological Institute of the University of Amsterdam. He has published many articles in a variety of journals and is coeditor of several collections on the history and sociology of homosexuality, including *The Pursuit of Sodomy: Male Homosexuality in Renaissance and Enlightenment Europe* with Kent Gerard. His current research is on homosexuality and violence.

JAMES W. JONES is associate professor of German at Central Michigan University. He has written on AIDS and American literature and has recently published a study of gay and lesbian literature from the 1880s to 1918, entitled *"We of the Third Sex": Literary Representations of Homosexuality in Wilhelmine Germany.*

RENÉ LEBOUTTE is assistant professor in the department of history and civilization at the European University Institute in Florence. A specialist in historical demography, he was for a number of years assistant curator at the Musée de la Vie Wallonne in Liège and the State Archives in Namur and Brussels. He has published many articles and books on the economic and social history of the eighteenth and nineteenth centuries.

JONAS LILIEQUIST is a historian at the department of history, Umeå University, Sweden. He is completing his doctoral thesis on sexuality and taboos in early modern Sweden, preliminarily entitled "'Den onda andans ingivelse': En historisk-antroplogisk studie av tidelagsbrottet i 1600 och 1700-talets Sverige" (At the devil's instigation: The historical anthropology of bestiality in seventeenth- and eighteenth-century Sweden).

JOHN MACNICOL is reader in social policy at Royal Holloway and Bedford New College, University of London. He has published extensively on the history of British social policy and is currently researching the history of the idea of an "underclass" in Britain and the United States over the past century.

THEO VAN DER MEER is currently a fellow of the Netherlands Organization for Scientific Research at the Institute for Criminology and Sociology of Law at the Free University of Amsterdam. His publications include *De wesentlijke sonde van sodomie en andere vuyligheeden,* a study of persecutions of sodomites, and a number of articles in Dutch, English, and German. He is preparing a dissertation on the sodomite subcultures in seventeenth- and eighteenth-century Holland.

JEFFREY MERRICK is associate professor of history at the University of Wisconsin—Milwaukee. He has published articles on the gender politics of the beehive in early modern Europe and patriarchalism and absolutism in eighteenth-century French politics. He is currently working on a book about the uses of family models in French political culture from the Renaissance to the Revolution.

P O L L Y   M O R R I S is associate lecturer in history at the University of Wisconsin—Milwaukee. She has published "Sodomy and Male Honor: The Case of Somerset, 1740–1850" (*Journal of Homosexuality,* vol. 16 [1988]) and is working on a book on sex and reputation in the eighteenth and nineteenth centuries.

R U T H   P E R R Y is the author of *Women, Letters, and the Novel* (1981) and *The Celebrated Mary Astell* (1986), editor of George Ballard's 1752 *Memoirs of Several Ladies of Great Britain* (1985), and coeditor and theorist of a volume of essays on nurturing creativity, *Mothering the Mind* (1984). She was the founding director of the women's studies program at MIT, where she is currently professor of literature and women's studies. The working title of her current project is "Novel Relations: The History of the Novel and the Family in English Society, 1750–1810."

R O B I N   A N N   S H E E T S is associate professor of English at the University of Cincinnati, where she teaches Victorian literature and women's studies. She is coauthor of a three-volume series, *The Woman Question: Society and Literature in Britain and America, 1837–1883.* She has also published several articles on nineteenth- and twentieth-century literature in a variety of journals, including *ELH, Nineteenth-Century Literature,* and *College English;* "Pornography and Art: The Case of 'Jenny'" appeared in *Critical Inquiry,* vol. 14 (1988).

R A N D O L P H   T R U M B A C H is professor of history, Baruch College, City University of New York. He is the author of *The Rise of the Egalitarian Family: Aristocratic Kinship and Domestic Relations in Eighteenth-Century England* (1978). He has recently published a series of articles on the history of sodomy as preliminaries to a more general two-volume work tentatively entitled *The Sexual Life of Eighteenth-Century London* (forthcoming).

Index